KARL E. MEYER, a Princeton Ph.D., was London bureau chief for the *Washington Post* before working on the editorial board of the *New York Times* from 1979 to 1998.

SHAREEN BLAIR BRYSAC was a prize-winning producer of prime-time documentaries for CBS Reports. The recipient of several Emmy awards, she is a contributing editor to *Archaeology* magazine. The couple live in New York and Connecticut.

Further praise for TOURNAMENT OF SHADOWS

'I did enjoy *Tournament of Shadows*. Meyer and Brysac have unravelled an exciting piece of chicanery, war and high adventure, retold it with the appropriate pace and panache and brought it up to date with a bizarre Nazi expedition to Tibet. At the same time, they understand the historical context and repercussions of the events they describe' Lawrence James, author of *The Golden Warrior* and *Raj*

'In *Tournament of Shadows*, not only do the literary and historical styles come into an excellent novelistic concert but the events themselves are borne back to us from the past and into the light of our common and contemporary day. Chechnya, Daghestan, Serbia, Palestine, Cyprus, Tibet, Afghanistan, Kashmir: I felt I had a better grasp of all of them when I finished this enthralling book' Christopher Hitchens, author of *The Trial of Henry Kissinger*

'In their well-written and fair-minded book, Meyer and Brysac tell the story of the Game, leaving readers with a powerful sense of what it was like to be a participant. The sheer sweep of the contest, its imperial scale and its exhilaration are admirably conveyed' David Gilmour, *New York Review of Books*

'An impressive feat of historical synthesis that draws on sources ranging from published biographies to secret memos buried in the archives of the East India Company, this rousing history is written with some of the élan exhibited by the most stylish participants in the Great Game itself' *Publishers Weekly*

'Engrossing'
Scotland On Sunday

'A gripping, timely, and perceptive yar
Kirkus Reviews

Also by Karl E. Meyer

Pundits, Poets and Wits
The Plundered Past
Fulbright of Arkansas

TOURNAMENT
of SHADOWS

*The Great Game and the Race
for Empire in Asia*

KARL E. MEYER
&
SHAREEN BLAIR BRYSAC

An *Abacus* Book

First published in the United States of America in 1999
by Counterpoint, a member of the Perseus Books Group
First published in Great Britain in 2001 by Little, Brown and Company
This edition published by Abacus in 2001

Portions of this book originally appeared in slightly different form in
Archaeology Magazine, *The World Policy Journal* and
The Quarterly Journal of Military History.

A CIP catalogue record for this book
is available from the British Library.

ISBN 0 349 11366 1

Printed and bound in Great Britain
by Clays Ltd, St Ives plc

Abacus
A division of
Little, Brown and Company (UK)
Brettenham House
Lancaster Place
London WC2E 7EN

www.littlebrown.co.uk

To
Margaret and Fred Blair
and to all the Meyers, past,
present and future.

∴

CONTENTS

∴

LIST OF MAPS

∴

AUTHORS' NOTE

..

THERE ARE NINE-AND-SIXTY WAYS OF CONSTRUCTING TRIBAL LAYS, instructs the poet, and every one is right. We have applied the same agnostic principle to the insoluble matter of spelling proper and place names. At sacrifice of consistency, we have adopted the most familiar and accessible usages, save in quotations, where the author's text is respected. Thus it is *Bokhara*, not *Bocara*, *Boghar* or *Bukhara*, and we refer to *Genghis Khan*, not to the scholarly *Chingiz*, the widely used *Jenghiz*, or Voltaire's *Gengis* or Gibbon's *Zingis*, not to mention a dozen other variants. Romanizing Chinese has been especially troublesome. Pinyin is the system officially approved by the People's Republic of China, and most of us realize that Peking is now Beijing. But how many of us recognize that Chiang Kai-shek, as he is rendered in the old Wade-Giles method, has become Jiang Jieshi? So we have mostly stuck to Wade-Giles in the pre-1950 period (Ch'ing Dynasty and not Qing), while preserving Chiang in his long-familiar form throughout. Place names change for political reasons, too. The careful reader will notice that Chinese Turkestan becomes Sinkiang Province (or Xinjiang in the pinyin system); the sharp-eyed will also note that the endpaper overview of Asia uses current Chinese spellings (Xining, not Sining), and pinpoints elusive ancient sites (Khara Khoto).

Wherever possible we turn to Henry Yule's indispensable *Hobson-Jobson*, as an authoritative glossary of colloquial Anglo-Indian words and phrases. For a non-British view of things past, we have relied on Parshotam Mehra's *A Dictionary of Indian History, 1707–1947,* as well as a large and growing body of Indian and Pakistani scholarship.

Our goal has been to describe familiar events in a fresh way, drawing on recent scholarship and newly opened archives, and to throw a sharp beam on neglected or unknown figures and incidents. Our approach is broadly chronological and thematic, which necessarily requires repetition of information in earlier chapters, in the belief that readers may skip around, or ahead. Thus the ox-bows in our narrative are not the result of carelessness or amnesia, but are intentional.

At every point we have benefited from the help of librarians and archivists in four capitals and at a dozen universities. Scholars, journalists, soldiers, and survivors of every nationality have given generously of their time; their names are listed in the Acknowledgments. We have tried, within the text, to identify sources of important quoted matter, with fuller references in the chapter-by-chapter bibliography, annotated candidly, the better to encourage every reader to excavate further in this rich seam of pertinent history.

Two matters resisted ready resolution, the first being currency values. Broadly speaking, from 1820 to 1870, one Indian rupee was worth two British shillings or twenty-four pence, so ten rupees were worth roughly one British pound. After 1870, the rupee's value fluctuated, falling to nearly one shilling in 1894–95, then rising to sixteen pence in 1898–99. A Victorian pound was worth more or less five American dollars, but since there were no equivalents then of television sets or automobiles, the current dollar equivalent is a matter of spirited conjecture.

An additional problem regards the use in Russia of the Julian or old-style calendar before 1918. This has been especially puzzling when drawing on Russian sources for the years 1860–1900, when the Julian dates were twelve days behind the Gregorian calendar in use in Europe, and the years 1900–1918, when they were thirteen days behind. It is not always possible to determine which calendar an author is using, or whether the dates have been corrected, so some inconsistencies are unavoidable.

SELECTIVE CHRONOLOGY

.·.

1910	Chinese occupy Lhasa; Dalai Lama flees to India
1911–12	Manchu (Qing) Dynasty falls; Chinese Republic proclaimed; civil war breaks out
1912	Dalai Lama returns to Lhasa and asserts Tibetan independence (1913)
1913–16	Stein explores northern Silk Road
1914	Simla Conference fails to win Chinese agreement on Tibetan borders and status
1914–18	World War I
1915	Gandhi arrives in India
1917	Bolsheviks seize power in Petrograd
1919	Third Anglo-Afghan War sees bombing of Kabul
1920	Bell's mission to Lhasa; wins backing for reforms
1923	Panchen Lama flees Tibet and begins exile
1923	McGovern, in disguise, is first American to reach Lhasa
1924	Bailey's mission to Lhasa; British-backed reformers deposed
1925	Roosevelts and Cutting explore Tibetan borderlands
1925–28	Roerich Central Asian expedition
1927	Chiang Kai-shek moves Chinese government to Nanking
1927–33	Hedin leads Sino-Swedish Expedition in Central Asia
1930	India's Congress Party begins civil disobedience campaign
1930–31	Stein's fourth and failed (Harvard) expedition
1931–32	First Dolan-Schäfer expedition to eastern Tibet
1931	Japan occupies Manchuria
1932	Franklin Roosevelt elected President
1933	Death of Thirteenth Dalai Lama
1934–35	Roerich leads U.S. Department of Agriculture expedition into Asia
1934–35	Dolan and Schäfer return to eastern Tibet
1935	Cutting is first American invited to Lhasa
1935	Fourteenth Dalai Lama born in Amdo
1937	Ninth Panchen Lama dies at Jyekundo
1937	Japan invades China
1938–39	Schäfer leads SS expedition to Lhasa
1939–45	World War II
1940	Burma road closed
1942–43	Tolstoy-Dolan OSS mission to Lhasa

The View from the Khyber

THIS BOOK HAD ITS INCEPTION ON A SUNNY DECEMBER MORNING IN 1990 when my wife Shareen and I found ourselves on the far side of the Khyber Pass gazing down at Afghanistan. We were accompanied by a wizened Pathan soldier, armed with what looked like a nineteenth-century musket, and by a somewhat bored official chaperon assigned to us by the Foreign Ministry of Pakistan. We were not bored. Our car had threaded through a great outdoor museum of empire and conquest. Stamped in abutting cliffs were the emblems and memorials of long-departed British regiments, scores of them. We came upon a concrete guardhouse, with vertical gunslits, only yards from a tablet stating that we were at the doorway to the Indian subcontinent. At intervals, we glimpsed the Khyber Railway, with its ninety-two bridges and thirty-four tunnels over a twenty-five-mile route. This engineering marvel, completed by the British in the 1920's, was prompted by security fears stemming from incessant uprisings on India's North-West Frontier. The rails flanked a far more ancient highway through the Khyber, completed in the sixteenth century by Mughal engineers, and later a principal link in the Grand Trunk Road from Kabul to Delhi. Mughal workmen doubtless came upon Greek coins dating from the conquests of Alexander, examples of which are still to be found in the bazaars of Landi Kotal, the last town on the Pakistan side of the frontier and still garrisoned, as it was a century ago, by the Khyber Rifles.

From a promontory near Landi Kotal, Shareen and I could make out trucks and cars inching toward Jalalabad, the nearest big city in Afghanistan. We were looking here not at a museum display but at a country whose sorrows belied the peaceful morning mist below us. By 1990, the last Soviet soldier had already returned home, ending a nine-year invasion and occupation that claimed a million lives and displaced a third of the population. But the Soviet withdrawal did not end the devastation. Instead, the conflict deepened as a dozen factions, each aided and armed by outside patrons, tore each other and their country apart. Incongruously, some of the most anti-American fighters had been assisted covertly by Washington, on the apparent belief that Muslim militants were the most reliable anti-Communists. It was a belief encouraged by Pakistan's military intelligence, which had its own designs on Afghanistan and its Islamic neighbors, soon to be independent once again, across the Oxus in former Soviet Central Asia.

In a word, an ongoing conflict known as the Great Game, or in Count Nesselrode's graphic phrase, the Tournament of Shadows, is about to enter a new millennium. Why and how this came to be is the subject of this book, which we decided to write that December morning at the Khyber Pass.

From the moment I first learned of it some decades ago, I have been fascinated by the original Great Game, the clandestine struggle between Russia and Britain for mastery of Central Asia. Not only did its episodes teem with improbable drama, but the Game itself was a Victorian prologue to the Cold War. It was fought in the press as well as in Himalayan passes, it pitted aggressive hawks against cautious doves, it witnessed the rise of spy services and proxy wars and inspired the grandiose theory that control of the Eurasian "Heartland" would assure mastery of the world.

It didn't happen. Russia's seemingly inexorable expansion into Central Asia did not save the Tsar or his Communist heirs, nor did it undermine British rule in India. Nor, despite dire warnings by soldiers and propagandists, did the two empires ever come into direct conflict in Central Asia. What did happen, however, was dramatic enough. Persistent British suspicions of Russian motives brought about two Afghan wars, the invasion of Tibet, and a full-scale mobilization during a frontier dispute in 1885. These fears also led to the subjugation of Egypt and the partition of Persia into spheres of influence (which occurred, needless to add, without the consultation of Egyptians or Persians).

What could have energized so much far-flung movement? A familiar explanation was put forth by the Victorian scholar J. R. Seeley in *The Expansion of England,* which sold a phenomenal 80,000 copies soon after its publication in 1883. Great Britain was then the world's preeminent power: it ruled the seas and commanded the biggest overseas empire known to history. Yet, as Seeley observed, British eyes were continually and anxiously focused on the remotest corners of the backward East: "Every movement in Turkey, every new symptom in Egypt, any stirrings in Persia or Transoxiana or Burmah or Afghanistan, we are obliged to watch with vigilance. The reason is that we have possession of India, and a leading interest in the affairs of all those countries which lie upon the route to India. This and only this involves us in that permanent rivalry with Russia, which is for England of the nineteenth century what the competition with France for the New World was to her in the eighteenth century."

Seeley spoke for his age. That Britain had the right, indeed the duty, to rule an Empire and to intervene anywhere to defend it was a commonplace shared by most Britons during the nineteenth century. Thus Benjamin Disraeli, at once astute realist and imperial romantic, delighted his Queen and much of her country in 1876 by proclaiming Victoria an Empress. The new title would underscore, her Prime Minister took care to add, "that the Parliament of England have resolved to uphold the Empire of India."

The message was plainly directed at Russia, whose continuous southward advance into Central Asia lay at the core of British fears. In 1800, the frontier bases of the two empires were 2,000 miles apart; by 1876, that distance had been halved, and by century's end the gap between the Tsar's domain and British India was only a few hundred miles—indeed as little as twenty miles separated outposts in the lofty Pamirs. Russian expansion seemed limitless and threatening. In 1914, the explorer

Fridtjof Nansen reckoned that over four centuries the Tsarist realm had expanded at an astonishing rate of fifty-five square miles a day, or about 20,000 square miles a year. To alarmists, it seemed likely that the Russians were carrying out a master plan whose eventual object was the direct invasion of India or its subversion by inciting Indian Muslims against the Raj. It made no difference that Russian Foreign Ministers denied any such purposes, since assurances that there would be no further conquests were invariably followed by fresh annexations.

Still, as Russians heatedly rejoined, their Emperor was only doing in Asia what the British claimed as their mission in India: bestowing the benefits of a Christian civilization and economic progress on less fortunate peoples. Moreover, Russians could justly point to their own security concerns in Central Asia, whose open grasslands historically served as highways of conquest for Mongol invaders. All this was argued in innumerable speeches, memoranda, pamphlets, articles, and books, the latter commonly buttressed by maps and learned appendices. As the debate ebbed and flowed, both empires deployed a clandestine legion of agents to map and meddle, bully and bribe, across an immense arc spanning from Iran to the deserts of Mongolia. Backing up these covert operations was an almost continuous series of Asian frontier wars and punitive expeditions, beginning in the 1830's and culminating with Britain's forcible opening of Tibet in 1904.

So runs the accepted account of the Great Game, whose main incidents have been described in a number of admirable books, most recently by the British author Peter Hopkirk. But a fresh subtext caught our attention as we pressed our own researches in archives and memoirs, and in our travels through Central Asia: a parallel theme that resonates for Americans in this century. We were repeatedly impressed by the courage and brilliance of the Game's young principals, British or Russian, and by the feckless irresponsibility of their older superiors, civilian and military, who for the most part escaped serious accounting for their misjudgments.

The true heroes of this book are the soldiers and explorers, Russian and British, who in serving two empires also served knowledge. Their legacy is found in journals, charts, maps, diaries, letters, sketches, and photographs—the authentic jewels in the imperial crown. In his history of the Royal Geographical Society, Ian Cameron reminds us that for decades after its founding in 1830, every issue of the Society's *Journal* contained a treasure trove "in which some remote corner of the earth is spotlighted and for the first time examined in the beam of scientific appraisal." We forget how little was known in the mid-nineteenth century about Asia as well as Africa, about the Himalaya no less than the Nile. This is especially true of Central Asia, which has no profiled coastline or famous ports, and whose geography is seldom studied in schools.

Picture an immense saucer of land, comprising 1.5 million square miles, or half the area of the continental United States. Imagine a vast grassy steppe and salt marshes, swept by bitter winds. Then add dozens of oasis cities, joined by Islamic faith and ancient caravan trails, inhabited by peoples who can be fierce or friendly, hospitable or treacherous. Finally, frame the huge inner core with an outer circle consisting of the world's highest mountains and its deadliest deserts, and by roaring rivers whose shifting courses served to confound cartographers and treaty makers. West of this core lies Persia and the Caucasus, to the north is Russia, to the east China, and immediately to the southeast Nepal and Tibet, and just below Afghanistan to the south lie present-day Pakistan, Kashmir, and the Indian subcontinent. This was the region where three empires met—the British, Russian, and Chinese—or rather collided, since frontiers were not precise and much of the map was blank.

Filling in those blank spaces required feats of endurance by a procession of great explorers. In the course of a century, they solved all the major riddles of Asia's physical and cultural geography. They found the sources of India's great rivers, made known to the world the holiest of mountains and lakes, measured with amazing accuracy the heights of passes and the loftiest Himalayan peaks, including Everest, all this being accomplished with the indispensable help of Muslim spies and Hindus posing as pilgrims and using prayer wheels to record their calculations. They determined the truth about mysteriously roaming lakes in the Taklamakan Desert and recorded the shifting path of the river Oxus. They rediscovered the Silk Road, its lost cities, sacred caves, and libraries.

Yet those carrying out these feats are for the most part forgotten today. An example is the greatest of Russian explorers, Nikolai Przhevalsky, who dreamed of going to Lhasa and exploring Tibet. He endured parched deserts, blinding dust storms, plagues of insects, and chronic intestinal disorders that hastened his death at forty-nine.

Buried in a cold, distant grave crowned with a bronze eagle overlooking the lake of Issyk-Kul, beneath the Tian Shan or Heavenly Mountains, Przhevalsky left his name attached to scores of flora and fauna, including the ancestor of the modern horse. In his steps came other adventurers, most of them outsiders: the Nazi-loving Swede Sven Hedin, the Hungarian-born British explorer Sir Aurel Stein, and the mystic Russian painter Nicholas Roerich, who became a curious footnote in the history of Roosevelt's New Deal. But if figures like these are mostly in limbo, the large, essential supporting cast of Cossack escorts, Hindu pilgrims and Muslim *munshis* (or secretaries), Buriat lamas, Persian interpreters, and Afghan guides have with few exceptions passed into oblivion.

These explorations were cultural as well. They involved encounters of a memorable kind with ancient Asian civilizations. "The sacredness of India haunts me like a passion," declared England's greatest propagandist of empire and patron of Indian archaeology, George Nathaniel Curzon. "To me the message is carved in granite, hewn in the rock of doom: that our work is righteous and that it shall endure." If Curzon was blind to the inherent paradox of extolling the glory of the Indian past while resisting self-rule for Indians present, he was scarcely alone in the imperial age. But the deeds described in this book could not have been carried out by ambivalent doubters given to irony and intricate analysis. The players in the Great Game were men of action, not reflection.

The young were driven by both ambition and belief in the rightness of their cause; their elders were often possessed by half-examined ideas and a determination not to appear weak: a fateful chemistry that in different times helped plunge the United States into Vietnam and the Soviet Union into Afghanistan.

It is a common political error to underestimate the power of surges of public opinion that drive events. Lord Palmerston, an exuberant activist in foreign affairs, was among the first to assess accurately the changes wrought by the French and American Revolutions, the rise of democracy and the penny press. "Opinions," he maintained, "are stronger than armies. Opinions, if they are founded on truth and justice, will in the end prevail against the bayonets of infantry, the fire of artillery and the charges of cavalry." But there is an essential corollary: even when not founded on truth or justice, an opinion clothed in an appealing slogan can create war scares overnight, propel armies and navies across the globe, sow enmity between nations, and build or demolish empires.

In Palmerston's time, many Britons thought the worst of Russian ambitions, and believed it essential to oppose Russian advances everywhere. Their fears were persuasive to a young British officer, Captain Arthur Conolly. While serving in Afghanistan, Conolly came to believe it was his personal mission to frustrate Russian schemes of conquest in Central Asia and convince its independent Muslim rulers to band together and seek British protection. His determination hardened in 1841 when he learned of the imprisonment and torture of a fellow officer, Colonel Charles Stoddart, at the hands of the Emir of Bokhara. Conolly pleaded successfully for a chance to save Stoddart, befriend and reform the Emir, and foil the Russians. In short, he wished to play a leading part in "a great game, a *noble* game" in Central Asia, as he wrote to a friend.

Conolly's letters subsequently passed to the military historian Sir John Kaye, who in quoting from them, introduced the term "Great Game." The phrase was later taken up and given universal currency in *Kim* (1901), Rudyard Kipling's novel about Kimball O'Hara, the orphaned son of an Irish soldier, who frustrates a Russian plot in British India. In real life, however, the Game yielded few winners. Most of the young Russian or British officers who contended with brigands and capricious emirs, who braved the wildest of terrains and the perils of disease or accident, came to violent ends for negligible gains. Their fate anticipated on a small scale the massive blood sacrifice of World War I, a hemorrhage from which Britain never fully recovered and which brought on the Bolshevik Revolution in Russia.

Now it threatens to happen all over again. In the few months between August and December 1991, centuries of Russian rule ended in Central Asia. Six new republics, predominantly Islamic but vibrantly distinct, are grouped around the Caspian Sea, the current landlords of untapped oil and natural gas reserves that rival those in the Persian Gulf. Pipelines, tanker routes, petroleum consortiums, and contracts are the prizes of the new Great Game. India and China, each with exponentially growing energy needs, are vying for access, along with Russians, Europeans, and Americans. Turkey, Iran, and Pakistan have their own political, economic, and cultural interests in the former Soviet Republics, where slumbering rivalries have abruptly awakened among Azeris, Armenians, Tajiks, Uzbeks, Turkmens, and other long-subject peoples. As before, Afghanistan forms the problematic heart of a problematic region, and its roads, following the path of old caravan routes, are contested and vital arteries of commerce. But it is a bloody muddle, made worse as before by outsiders.

Americans took part in all this first as bit players, then as partners, and finally as successors to the British, just as the Soviet Union carried on the imperial policies of the Tsars. What might be called the Cold War handover from Britain to the United States went beyond conventional diplomacy. If few Americans approved of the British Empire or mourned its demise, many nevertheless believed that Washington had a special mission to promote liberty elsewhere and spread the benefits of free markets and technology, and had the right of intervention to defend vital interests. But the handover also extended to intelligence services. During World War II, Americans came as rapt disciples of the British secret services, whose Oxbridge graduates excelled at deception and decipherment. Malcolm Muggeridge, a wartime intelligence professional, recalls the neophytes' first steps: "From those Elysian days I remember so well in London when the first American arrivals came among us straight from their innocent nests in Princeton or Yale or Harvard, in Wall Street or Madison Avenue or Washington, D.C. How short a time the honeymoon period lasted! How soon our British setup was overtaken in personnel, zest and scale of operations, above all in expendable cash!"

Among the arrivals was Allen Dulles, soon to serve as OSS resident in Switzerland, and later as Director of Central Intelligence in the Eisenhower and Kennedy Administrations. In 1914, as a new alumnus of Princeton, Dulles sailed for India to teach for a year at a missionary college. On board, Dulles read Kipling's *Kim* for the first time. Its imprint was so indelible, according to his biographer, Peter Grose, that the novel was at Dulles's bedside when he died in 1969. Recruiting agents from the best schools, Dulles sought to imbue them with the same élan.

Dulles was to learn that this British faith in schoolboy esprit had its shortcomings, when his friend H. A. R. Philby, British Intelligence's liaison in Washington, turned out to be a KGB mole. Philby was known to all the secret world as Kim, a nickname deriving from his own affinity for Kipling's boy-spy. Indeed Philby was born in 1912 in India, and at six was given his nickname by his father, St. John Philby, then a civil servant of the Raj, later a celebrated Arabist and convert to Islam who married a Saudi slave girl. Curiously, or perhaps not so curiously, the Soviets erroneously believed that St. John Philby was really a British secret service agent—hence their eagerness to recruit the son. Thus in every sense the Great Game assumed a second life during the Cold War.

It remains only to be said that this volume is a memorial to all the adventurers, European or Asian, whose bravery is worthy of a less ambiguous purpose.

Karl E. Meyer

PART I

CHAPTER ONE

The Horse Doctor

IT RAINED, RAINED, RAINED, AND THEN RAINED AND RAINED some more. The drops hammered the leaking roof of the verandah, creeping like capillaries into the cracks in the plaster opened by a recent earthquake, forming rivulets in the rafters that had been tunneled by tireless armies of white ants. Pacing on the verandah, figuratively if not literally pulling his hair, was a middle-aged Englishman who in 1808 had left a wife and friends in London, abandoned a lucrative veterinary practice, and sailed halfway around the world—and for what? To suffer the seemingly endless Indian monsoon? To dwell in a half-rotted house whose sinking floors trembled with each step? To live in the dreadful remoteness of Pusa, a riverside village 300 inland miles from Calcutta?

The nearest big city was Patna, which nowadays is the capital of Bihar, India's most backward and violent state, notorious for its incorrigible corruption and its bandits known as *dacoits*. Even Bihar's mitigating blessing—the exceptional fertility of its soil—has also been a curse, entrenching a class of oppressive feudal landlords, called *zamindars*. Add to this extremes of heat and cold and a history of famines, recurrent floods, and frequent earthquakes. "Welcome to hell," was how a newspaper editor in Patna greeted an English visitor in the 1980's.

Pusa may not have been hell for William Moorcroft, the new Superintendent of the Stud at Pusa, but in the first months after his arrival it seemed a back-country purgatory. There he was, responsible for improving the blood stock of the East India Company's cavalry mounts, which he was supposed to do overnight. But the fine breeding stock he had been promised proved to be utterly unfit nags, many weakened by disease, in part because their forage consisted of decomposing weeds grown in shallow, pestilential marshes. At every point, it seemed, he collided with incompetence, corruption, and outright thievery. The best stallions were stolen for sale at fairs—all of which was the harder to remedy given his ignorance of the customs and language of a watchful staff of 1,200 souls on the Pusa estate.

Small wonder he restlessly weighed possibilities of a furlough. Yet his employment had been noted in this obscure entry dated March 8, 1807, in the London personnel files of the East India Company. It specified that in consideration of the "excellent proof of his preeminent talents," Moorcroft had been employed at the munificent salary of 30,000 rupees per annum on the understanding that "his whole attention is to be devoted to the line of service to which we have assigned him."

Seldom in the Company's history was such an undertaking so splendidly and imaginatively flouted.

A horse doctor by training, known for his enthusiasm and quickness of wit, William Moorcroft sprang from England's common grass. He was forty-one years old when he arrived in India to restart his life in 1808 as the Superintendent of the Stud responsible for breeding faster and sturdier cavalry mounts. In his own person, however, Moorcroft had no use for saddles and bridles. On the slimmest authority, he wound up leading a miniature army into Central Asia, parleying with princes and kings, opening the way for a new breed of self-made explorers, and becoming one of the first recruits in a covert army burrowing in the interstices of three empires. That his achievements are finally known owes much to his diligent biographer, Garry Alder, whose *Beyond Bokhara* (1985) is the essential quarry for all who write about Moorcroft.

In making his way upward through pluck and determination, Moorcroft mirrored an age of democratic upheaval. He was born in 1767 in the market town of Ormskirk in Lancashire, the natural son of Ann Moorcroft, the daughter of a local farmer. His family had sufficient means to secure his apprenticeship with a Liverpool surgeon, under whose tutelage he acquired skills that were to give him the aura of a demigod in Asia. Young William's career took a fresh turn when an unknown disease decimated cattle herds in Lancashire, and he was recruited to treat stricken animals. So impressed were county landowners by his proficiency that they offered to underwrite his education if he abandoned surgery to attend a veterinary college in Lyons at a time when no such schools existed in Britain. He arrived in France early in the revolutionary year of 1789, excelled in his courses, and became the first Englishman to qualify professionally as a veterinarian. Resettling in London, he established a "Hospital for Horses" on Oxford Street, built a flourishing practice, helped found the first British veterinary college, proposed new surgical methods for curing lameness in horses, and acquired four patents on machines to manufacture horseshoes. His affinity for horses was such that Moorcroft remembered every one he encountered as if the creature were a person, or so his friends said.

In 1803, Moorcroft's skills came to military notice when a citizen army was mobilized to defend Britain against a threatened Napoleonic invasion. He joined the Westminster Volunteer Cavalry and took part in frequent parades, donning a dazzling dress uniform: a dark-blue greatcoat with scarlet edgings over a blue jacket trimmed with gold, white leather breeches, black boots, white gloves, all crowned with a dragoon's helmet and bearskin crest. Certified as a master horseman and named to the regimental general committee, Moorcroft helped plan brigade exercises and state funerals, including Lord Nelson's in January 1806. He was thus initiated into the bonding rites of the regimental mess, where plebeians informally mingled with patricians. Among his new friends was Edward Parry, a director of the East India Company, who persuaded his colleagues that he had found the long-sought paragon to manage the Company stud in up-country Bengal. To ensure his acceptance, Moorcroft was offered a tax-free salary of 30,000 rupees, then equivalent to £3,000 a year, a compensation exceeded in India only by the Governor-General, the Commander-in-Chief, and a handful of others. Alas for Moorcroft, this became too well known among his envious, and ultimately vengeful, bureaucratic superiors.

It took six months to sail around Africa and through the Bay of Bengal to Calcutta, the seat of British rule. The city itself was already among the marvels of Asia: a shimmering facsimile of Europe rising above a forest of sailing masts on the banks of the river Hooghly. Known as the City of Palaces, Calcutta reflected the tastes and wealth of nabobs homesick for the London of Wren and Hawksmoor. A Town Hall with doric columns was being built on the Strand Road, near a Church of St. John's, inspired by St. Martin's-in-the-Field on Trafalgar Square. Government House was a copy in brick of Kedleston Hall in Derbyshire, a compliment that Lord Curzon of Kedleston was pleased to recall when he occupied its premises a century later. Less attractive to arriving Europeans were the drenching monsoon rains, the oppressive heat, the stench of sewage, and the peril of disease. But these discomforts hardly mattered to the excited newcomers, known locally as "griffins," who disembarked at the clamorous Calcutta docks, infused with visions of gain and glory. William Moorcroft, like his fellow passengers, knew for sure he was not in Ormskirk anymore when he was borne from the docks in a palanquin, a boxed chair rushed through the clogged streets of Calcutta by four shouting bearers.

THE INDIA THAT MOORCROFT KNEW WAS ODDER THAN WE IMAGine; indeed no theme park could capture its peculiarities. What had been a British trading settlement only a century earlier had ballooned by 1808 into a colony whose size and population were already several times greater than Great Britain's. Growth came through conquest and cunning under a procession of audacious commanders, of whom Robert Clive and Richard Wellesley, the Duke of Wellington's older brother, are distantly remembered today. Yet all this happened under the authority of a mercantile enterprise, the Honorable East India Company, known familiarly as John Company, or simply "the Company."

Chartered by Queen Elizabeth I in 1600, the Company was authorized by successive British Governments to make wars, administer justice, issue currency, and exercise—through its Governors in Calcutta, and its Court of Directors in London—virtual sovereignty over India. By chance rather than design, it evolved into a grandiose experiment in privatization. As the Company's powers grew, so did uncertainty about its primary mission. Its directors were obliged to promote British commerce and the interests of its shareholders.

Yet what did the Company owe to its millions of Indian subjects, or to its princely vassals, whose numerous realms formed an exotic quilt on the map? As difficult to calibrate was the Company's external obligation to British strategic interests during a century of global conflict with France. Eventually, to assure greater accountability, Parliament in 1793 established a Board of Control with the authority to endorse or to dictate the orders issued by the Company. Thereafter it became the practice for the Crown to approve a Governor-General, who invariably was a home-grown aristocrat rather than a Company man. Thus, over the decades, the Company evolved into a baffling hybrid, something less than an independent entity, but far more puissant than any government ministry. The arrangement was, Lord Macaulay famously remarked, "the strangest of all governments, designed for the strangest of all empires."

On one matter, Company and Government were of a single mind. Immobility impeded security. All-weather roads were virtually unknown in India in 1807. Until the ancient Grand Trunk Road was improved and metaled in the 1850's, the river Ganges was the main artery joining the Company's isolated outposts. It took three months on horseback to get from Calcutta to the frontier. Hence the need for cavalry brigades capable of rapid deployment. Cavalry officers, always European, recruited high-caste Indians to regiments known for their splendid dress uniforms, their mystique, and celebrated names, like

Skinner's Horse, the senior regiment, which disported in canary-yellow *kirtas,* or jackets, the only unit permitted that color. Cohesion and pride of blood set cavalry officers and *sowars,* the native horsemen, apart, not always to the liking of the infantry officers, and *sepoys,* the native foot soldiers. Byron Farwell, a chronicler of colonial wars, relates that a fusilier subaltern named his cat "Indian Cavalry," since the creature did little but eat, sleep, play games, and fornicate.

Even so, by the early 1800's, the Company concluded that it needed far more than eight cavalry regiments, that its mounts were insufficiently sturdy, and that the Army major in charge of its stud was overaged and underqualified. Such were the circumstances that led to Moorcroft's passage eastward.

ONCE SETTLED IN PUSA, THE NEW SUPERINTENDENT FOUND HIM-self the nominal overlord of a lushly fertile 5,000-acre estate. He also discovered that his predecessor, the Indian Army major, had gullibly relied on local landowners, the *zamindars,* to provide him with their best horses. Too often, undersized mares were bred with *zamindari* stallions, the best colts kept back, and studbooks falsified. Everywhere he looked, he found depressing signs of laxness, neglect, and ignorance.

Nevertheless, his gloom dispelled and his characteristic optimism restored, Moorcroft instituted necessary reforms, took brisk charge of his staff, and weeded out manifestly deficient horses. Most productive were his experiments with the oat seed he had brought from England. Ignoring the conventional belief that the crop would not grow in tropical soil, Moorcroft became the first to cultivate oats on a large scale in India, and he set aside 3,000 acres at Pusa for the health-giving crop. Yet each reform required streams of letters and reports, as well as extended discussions with suspicious inspectors from Calcutta, always impatient at the slowness and cost of progress. But nobody doubted Moorcroft's dedication and knowledge of horses, so that when he proposed a tour of horse fairs and outstanding Indian studs, his managing board in Calcutta promptly granted approval.

Moorcroft's first journey, covering 1,500 miles in eight months, began in January 1811 and took him to the limits of the territories under control of the East India Company. But Calcutta's writ still extended unevenly through the northern plains encompassing Benares, Lucknow, and Delhi. This was formerly the heartland of the Mughal Empire, whose disintegration in the eighteenth century opened the way to British dominion. It is worth pausing to consider this interesting empire, whose methods of control anticipated and influenced the British Raj.

Like the English, the Mughals were foreign invaders, formidable in battle and skilled as administrators. They carried their culture and Islamic faith into India from Central Asia by way of Persia and Afghanistan. Babur, who conquered Delhi in 1526, claimed direct descent from Tamurlane and Genghis Khan. For nearly two centuries, their descendants, known as the Timurids, kept the peace in central and northern India. The Mughals promoted an imperial lingua franca, Urdu—Hindustani in grammar, Persian in script—which served as the medium of the educated, much like Latin in medieval Europe. Mughal public works—palaces, forts, mosques, gardens, and mausoleums like the Taj Mahal—remain unrivaled. But most of the laborers and craftsmen who did the work, like most of the empire's subjects, were Hindu. Rather than convert by the sword, successive rulers evolved a pragmatic modus vivendi. Hindu princes could keep their thrones and titles, and enjoy limited independence, if they collected taxes and raised armies for their Muslim overlords. The earlier emperors named Hindus to great offices of state and did not molest their temples and festivals, though the Mughals expressly favored Islam and forbade construction of new temples. This compromise was unsettled in the eighteenth century, initially by onerous tax increases and then by the zealous Emperor Aurangzeb, a centralizer who strove to affirm the Islamic character of the state. Waves of princely revolts followed against his heirs, bringing the chaotic disorder that gave the arriving British their opening.

In swift and expeditious strokes, the British harassed and evicted their European rivals, recruited and trained native armies, bribed and corrupted vacillating princes, allied themselves with, or made war against, shifting coalitions of the Maratha Confederacy, whose rulers were Hindus. They simultaneously placated or subdued the emerging Sikh kingdom in the Punjab, the warlike Gurkhas in Hindu Nepal, and the Muslim nawabs in the remnants of the Mughal Empire. The British absorbed not only Mughal territory but Mughal practices. They promoted the use of English, and recruited Indians into the lower and middle administrative ranks. For the most part and with important exceptions, the British did not interfere with India's various religions. Things being equal, the British were content to work through existing rulers of conquered states, permitting a circumscribed autonomy so long as there was no doubt who was really in charge. To ensure compliance, a British official with the title of Resident was posted at each princely court. Until 1857, the British even maintained a Mughal emperor on a stage-set throne in Delhi, the former Mughal capital. So useful was the so-called subsidiary alliance system that in 1947, the year of independence, some 600 so-called native states accounted for half the territory and a fourth of the people in British India.

The system had its British critics from the beginning, and their dissent, together with the rise of a dedicated civil service, helped mitigate its evils. The evils were succinctly noted by a British observer in the 1850's:

> The native Prince, being guaranteed in the possession of his dominions but deprived of so many of the essential attributes of sovereignty, sinks in his own esteem, and loses that stimulus to good government which is supplied by the fear of rebellion and deposition. He becomes a *roi fainéant,* a sensualist, an extortionist miser or a careless and lax ruler... Thus, in spite of the Resident's counsels and attempts to secure good government, the back of the State, so to speak, is broken; the spirit of indigenous political life has departed: the native community tends to dissolution; and annexation is eventually the inevitable remedy.

This passage, by the Oxford scholar Sidney Owen, exactly described Oudh, to whose capital, Lucknow, Moorcroft was proceeding.

OUDH WAS REPUTEDLY THE FLESHPOT OF INDIA, AND OPULENT Lucknow a byword for extravagance, foppery, and corruption. Yet Oudh, which properly rhymes with proud rather than rude, was also something better and brighter. In a final flowering of Mughal culture, Oudh became deservedly famous in India for the dress and sophistication of its people, who excelled at Urdu poetry, the culinary arts, kite- and pigeon-flying, music, theater, and calligraphy. Lucknow's builders inimitably mingled Western and Mughal styles, spawning turban-domed structures that are the unacknowledged models for the bijoued picture palaces on a thousand American Main Streets.

We have a later pen-portrait of Lucknow by a young British woman, Honoria Lawrence, who was struck by the city's resemblance to Moscow or Constantinople: "Gilded domes, surmounted by the crescent—tall, slender pillars, lofty colonnades, half-grecian looking houses of several stories high with pillars, verandas and windows, iron railings and balustrades" all mixed up with "cages of wild beasts and brilliant birds, gardens, fountains and cypress trees." Honoria, whose husband Sir Henry Lawrence was to be the hero-martyr of the siege of Lucknow in the Great Mutiny, found it a "bewildering mixture of Europe and Asia" that altogether "comes nearer to anything I have seen to realise my early ideas of the Arabian Nights."

One can imagine Moorcroft's own wonderment as he headed on horseback into this city of gilded spires and minarets, preceded by his sepoy escort and followed by carts laden with telescopes, watches, and other trading goods, to the Muslim Nawab's palace. He was greeted by the Nawab, Sadat Ali Khan, whom the British had installed on the throne in 1798 to replace an unstable and profligate predecessor. Sadat Ali was to be the last of Oudh's rulers with any sense and independence. An exile in Calcutta while the predecessor chosen by his brother reigned, he acquired Western ways and fluency in English. With eloquent dignity, he protested bullying humiliations by successive Governor-Generals, who stripped his kingdom of half its territory. He kept his treasury solvent, curbed the rapacity of landowners, and if faulted by some as penurious, this was only by comparison with his predecessors. The Nawab's army of courtiers, even in hard times, was borne seasonally from palace to palace by 700 elephants, 1,500 horses, and a procession of gilded carriages two stories high. Now near the end of his reign, graying and overweight, Sadat Ali continued to favor European dress, including an admiral's braids, scarlet hunting finery, and wigs of every shape.

Moorcroft, on being introduced by the British Resident, was guest of honor at a state banquet almost certainly followed by the customary elephant battles, fireworks, and dancing girls. These went prudently unmentioned in Moorcroft's reports to Calcutta, which dealt instead with the good bones and blood of Sadat Ali's horses, and the intelligent enthusiasm on the part of the Nawab himself for such notions as importing a giant steam pump from England to irrigate and cool Lucknow's parks. Yet the Superintendent's first foray anticipated what was to come. Moorcroft somehow failed to acquire the ideal breeding horses that he sought in Lucknow or in a dozen other cities on the same tour. But he was introduced to the courtly life of India, the etiquette of princes, and the distractions awaiting the foreign traveler in India. The obvious need was to look elsewhere for horses.

BACK IN CALCUTTA, MOORCROFT GAVE A FULLER ACCOUNTING of his journey and his conversations with horse dealers, native chieftains, and various British Residents. It was their consensus, he reported, that the desired steeds were to be found in more distant breeding grounds of the Punjab and Rajputana, or possibly in the fabled city known as Bokhara the Noble. Even before his Company superiors gave their approval, Moorcroft was proposing a second journey. He would need an armed escort, a convoy of pack animals (but this time no cumbersome carts), cash, trading goods, and companions. The Company was guardedly agreeable.

In January 1812, Moorcroft was in nearby Hajipur to select stallions for the Governor-General's bodyguard. Then restlessly he made his way to Benares, probing across the frontiers of British India into what was still Maratha territory. Near Gwalior he met the British Resident, Richard Strachey, an astute "political" who had recently crossed India's great northern desert to Peshawar, where he had served as secretary to the Company's first mission to Afghanistan. Strachey, whose family would serve the Raj for more than a century, observed almost nonchalantly that there was "nothing particularly formidable" about going to Bokhara along old caravan trails. Moving on to Delhi, Moorcroft heard in the bazaar that Bokhara was the place to find "the greatest horse market in the world," and his mind was made up. Through the Delhi Resident, Charles Metcalfe, Moorcroft recruited a Persian named Mir Izzat-Allah to make a covert scouting trip to Bokhara and describe the route, which remarkably, with the help of an allowance from Moorcroft, the Mir did. His journal was eventually published, providing Europeans with one of the earliest firsthand accounts of Central Asia.

While in Delhi, Moorcroft took full advantage of the slow Indian mails. He informed Calcutta of the mission he had given Mir Izzat-Allah and hoped his superiors would not object, assuredly aware that by the time his letter arrived, the Persian would have departed. His Board's reply, when it finally came, expressed doubts about the whole Bokhara project, adding sharply: "It is of course understood that Mr. Moorcroft will not enter on the journey without a previous communication with Government." The Superintendent of the Stud did not read the message, since he was already a hundred miles away in Hardwar, where he was fascinated to hear that fine breeding horses might also be found in Tibet. While mulling this over, Moorcroft propitiously met another born wanderer, Captain Hyder Young Hearsey.

Hearsey was typical of the buccaneers turning up in the far corners of the subcontinent. His father was a British officer, his mother an Indian, a "Jat lady," and like Moorcroft, he was illegitimate. Schooled in England at Woolwich but deprived of the usual means of ascent afforded his legitimate siblings, he signed on at sixteen as a soldier with the Nawab of Oudh and within a year was in deputy command at Agra Fort under a French mercenary. He next served an Irish adventurer, and then after forming his own cavalry regiment,

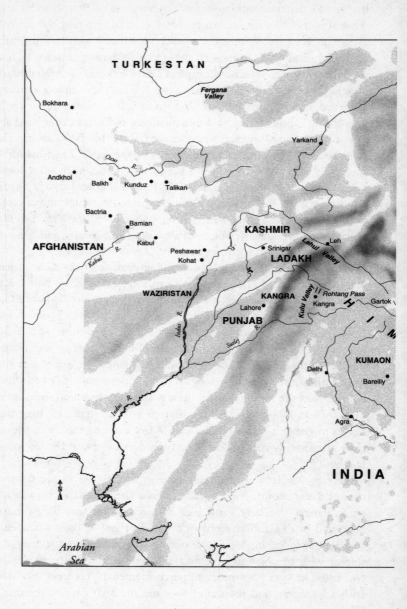

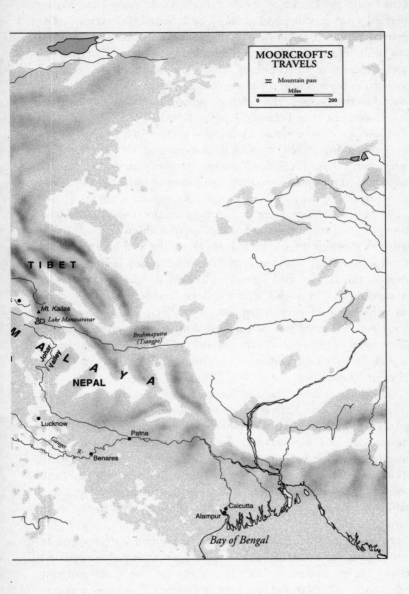

**MOORCROFT'S
TRAVELS**

⇌ Mountain pass

Miles

0 ————— 200

TIBET

Mt. Kailas

Lake Manasarovar

Brahmaputra
(Tsangpo)

Johar
Valley

NEPAL

H I M A L A Y A

Lucknow

Ganges

Patna

R.

Benares

Calcutta

Alampur

Bay of Bengal

joined with the British in the Maratha wars. At thirty-nine, having married a native princess of Cambay, he acquired as dowry an estate near Bareilly, on the frontiers of British India. His land controlled a pass to the Himalayan foothills then ruled by Nepalese Gurkhas. For pocket money, he levied tolls on traders, and for adventure, he joined two British officers in an 1808 expedition surreptitiously seeking the source of the Ganges. His behavior provoked remonstrations from British authorities and clashes with the Gurkhas.

Moorcroft at once sensed a congenial partner. What better choice for "prosecuting difficult geographical enquiries," he informed Calcutta, than Hearsey, with his "courage, spirit of enterprise, acquaintance with the language, manners and habits of the Hindoostan and its borders." For his part, Hearsey must have been as agreeably impressed by Moorcroft. Here was an Englishman new to India who now proposed to go disguised as a pilgrim, without anybody's permission, through an uncharted gorge to the forbidden Tibetan plateau. Moorcroft was then forty-five, and Hearsey, having climbed some of this terrain, well knew the hazards ahead. Nevertheless he promptly threw in his lot with the horse doctor, a measure of the confidence that Moorcroft inspired. (And affection: after their journey, Hearsey named one of his sons William Moorcroft Hearsey.) They were joined by two other recruits: Ghulam Hyder Khan, an Afghan orderly of exceptional toughness and loyalty, and an old Brahmin, Pundit Harbalam.

The pundit, a title meaning "learned Hindu," said he had visited Tibet as a youth and knew where to find the precious shawl-wool goat, a creature coveted by the British. On his advice, Moorcroft and Hearsey disguised themselves as *gosains*, Hindu trading pilgrims, donning white robes, red turbans, beads, and sashes. "Mr. Moorcroft," Hearsey wrote in his journal, "casts a most ludicrous appearance, a large patch of lamp black around each eye and his face and neck first stained with the juice of walnuts, then smeared with the ashes of burnt cow dung."

On April 15, 1812, Moorcroft formally notified Calcutta that he was heading for Tibet, and three weeks later his expedition was on its way. He led a caravan of fifty-four, counting porters and hangers-on, its pack animals trailed by a herd of livestock. Trusted bearers carried money belts in which were hidden 2,000 gold rupees. Stuffed in saddlebags were glass beads and other ornaments, choice spices, European broadcloth, cutlery, shotguns, and "spying-glasses," all valuable trading goods. Since they were purportedly Hindu pilgrims, Moorcroft and Hearsey had to keep their logs surreptitiously. Walking beside them was Pundit Harbalam's nephew, Harkh Dev, who carefully counted his twenty-four-inch paces. At intervals, the youth reported his totals to Hearsey, who at trip's end prepared a surprisingly accurate map, thereby pioneering a clandestine technique later adopted with spectacular results by British surveyors.

For his part, Moorcroft filled specimen bags with flora and fauna and kept a careful log of his discoveries. His motive, however, was not love of knowledge for its own sake, nor did he ever betray a mystical affinity for natural grandeur. He belonged to the practical world of Adam Smith, and the Empire he envisioned was bound by commerce. It was up to the East India Company to determine, as he put it, whether Central Asians would be clothed "with the broadcloth of Russia or of England," and whether they would buy their implements of iron and steel from St. Petersburg or Birmingham. In Moorcroft's view, "at present there is little doubt to which the prize will be awarded, for enterprise and vigour mark the measures of Russia towards the nations of Central Asia, whilst ours are characterized by misplaced squeamishness and unnecessary timidity." Under British tutelage, the region could form a rampart of defense for British India.

Immediately, however, as the caravan crept through the Himalayan foothills, and as the party switched from horses to yaks, messengers from Tibet met the "pilgrims" at the mountain village of Niti, at 12,000 feet. They had strict orders to repel the foreigners.

Short of stature, unthreatening, and with an ingratiating smile, Moorcroft proved a virtuoso at building footbridges across cultural divides. At Niti, he and Hearsey were the first Britons to encounter a remarkable people with a special history, the Rawats of the Johar Valley; by befriending them and winning their services as guides to Tibet, they initiated a partnership that literally remade the maps of Asia. The Rawats believed their ancestors were Hindu migrants who came from faraway Rajputana to the borderlands of Tibet in the twelfth century. Over the centuries Rawats intermarried with neighbors called Bhotias, a Hindu people of Tibetan origin. Though the Bhotian Rawats had Hindu names, they were not deemed orthodox by Hindus in the plains and were able in Tibet to pass readily as Buddhists. It was this clan, so adept at mediating, that provided "the pundits" for the surreptitious British surveys of India's borderlands through the entire Victorian era.

With his charm, the promise of gain, and proficient use of his medical kit (he successfully treated a village boy for dropsy), Moorcroft gained the friendship of two influential Rawats, Deb Singh and his brother Bir Singh. The orders from Tibet were ignored. Bir Singh's son Amer was given permission to serve as a guide for the putative pilgrims through the treacherous Niti pass and over snowfields swept by icy winds to the Tibetan plateau, their ostensible purpose being to visit two sacred lakes and the holiest of mountains, Kailas.

This was more than a physical test. In the 1790's, Tibet was closed to foreigners at the insistence of China, a policy that endured for more than a century, and which also served the interests of Buddhist rulers in Lhasa. The Dalai Lama, Tibet's secular and spiritual leader, was chosen as an infant by divination as the reincarnation of the deceased incumbent. This resulted in long periods of rule by regents, breeding intrigues complicated by rivalry with the second most important Tibetan leader, the Panchen or Tashi Lama, who headed the great monastery of Tashilhunpo some 250 miles southwest of Lhasa. In 1774, before borders were sealed, the redoubtable Sixth Panchen Lama requested a visit by a British emissary to discuss a treaty of amity and commerce. Governor-General Warren Hastings entrusted the mission to a twenty-eight-year-old Scot, George Bogle, known for his "good breeding and great kindliness of disposition," in the words of a celebrated future emissary, Francis Younghusband. Bogle was instructed to describe in detail Tibetan customs, to sound out prospects for trade, to decipher Lhasa's relations with the Chinese Empire, to bring back various Tibetan goods and curiosities, and—this became a leitmotif in European interest in Tibet—to determine whether Tibet, as rumored, possessed lavish lodes of gold and silver. (Among the gifts Bogle carried back to Calcutta were strips of gilded Russian leather stamped with the Tsar's double-headed eagle, small ingots of gold and silver, and purses of gold dust.)

Barred by the regent from entering Lhasa, Bogle compensated by befriending the Panchen Lama. In this first encounter between a Tibetan and a British officer, conducted in Hindustani, the Lama received Bogle courteously. Bogle lingered, took a Tibetan wife who bore him two daughters, and returned to Calcutta believing a treaty of amity was possible. But his second trip to Tibet was postponed when the Panchen Lama died of smallpox in 1780 while visiting China, and a year later Bogle himself died in Calcutta before undertaking a planned mission to Peking. An invaluable volume of his journals was presented to the East India Company for publication, but his records simply vanished in the vaults. After Bogle's death, Hastings sent another emissary, Samuel Turner, to Tashilhunpo in 1783–84, but hopes for trade with the reclusive kingdom faded when Nepalese Gurkhas made war on Tibet in the 1790's. Rebuffed in its appeals for British help, and with a strong nudge from China, Tibet sealed its borders to all Europeans. The sole Briton to reach Lhasa in that time was a cantankerous loner, Thomas Manning, who somehow breached the wall in 1811–12, mostly to satisfy his own curiosity.

Such was the background as the two British "pilgrims" turned up without permission at the Tibetan frontier outpost at Daba. The climb had taken a week. In July 1812, having staggered into Daba, Moorcroft and Hearsey presented their ceremonial gifts to local authorities. When the Tibetans seemed at a loss how to respond, Amer Singh proved his value as an intermediary. He offered to stand surety for the pair until a decision on their presence was taken in Gartok, the provincial capital, high on the Tibetan plateau (13,000 feet).

At this point, while Moorcroft was visiting Daba's crowded administrative center, a pug and a terrier bounded into the room. In his report to Calcutta, Moorcroft recounted his surprise as the dogs, both Western breeds, "suddenly rushed towards me, fondled, caressed me, frisked, jumped, barked and appeared as much rejoiced at seeing me as if they had recognized in me an old and favoured acquaintance." But then the dogs performed a trick that gave the

Englishman pause: "They appeared desirous of showing their acomplishments by sitting up on their haunches and pushing forwards their forelegs...as is sometimes taught to those animals in imitation of presenting firearms." Clearly they had been taught this military drill by foreigners. "They were said to have been brought by *Ooroos*," Moorcroft wrote.

Ooroos meant Russians. If Russians had indeed reached this remote corner of Tibet, Moorcroft observed to his friend Charles Metcalfe in Delhi, "I have little doubt that Buonaparte has received important information respecting the condition of countries never pressed by the foot of an Englishman though within thirty-four days journey of the Company's Provinces." This was July 1812. Although Moorcroft did not know it, France and Russia were no longer allied, and indeed Napoleon's Grand Army, 600,000 strong, had recently crossed the river Niemen to invade Russian territory. But Moorcroft was invariably ahead of his time, and the singular incident of the dogs in Tibet foreshadowed a century of British obsession with Russia's eastward advance.

FROM DABA, IT WAS FIFTY MILES TO GARTOK, SEAT OF THE GARPON, or Governor, of western Tibet. Gartok's bustling summer market was an ideal place to inquire about horses and, in particular, about shawl wool. Called *pashmina* (from the Persian *pashm,* meaning wool), this fleece was found in Tibet and its sister Buddhist state, Ladakh, where it was collected from mountain shrubs and rocks on which a species of Asian goat, *Capra hircus,* rubbed itself. Tibet and Ladakh exported shawl wool to Kashmir, which jealously protected its monopoly on its finished "cashmere" shawls. So lively was the demand for these woven garments that the Company years before had instructed George Bogle to bring back a pair or two of the shawl-wool goats, which he was prevented from doing.

The Garpon was used to meeting Hindu and Buddhist pilgrims on their way to nearby Mount Kailas, and he greeted the odd couple civilly. He listened attentively to their plans to visit sacred sites and, after carefully examining their trading goods, acquired a bolt of green and red broadcloth. When Moorcroft tried casually to bring up the *Ooroos,* the Garpon exhibited "an air of reserve and circumspection." The Englishmen later heard from others that the Russians were regular visitors to Tibet, the markets of Kashmir, and the great oasis cities in Chinese Turkestan.

The Garpon agreed to sell shawl wool and horses and talked earnestly about future trade. The two "pilgrims" could visit the sacred lakes of Manasarovar and Rakas Tal, yet on one point he was adamant: they could not venture further into Tibet, and they had to return as they came, through the Niti pass. Exasperated and frustrated, Moorcroft and Hearsey privately discussed ignoring the order when they heard sobering news from a Kashmiri merchant. The shawl-wool monopoly was enforced by the death penalty and the Garpon was already at mortal risk for selling wool to outsiders. Concern for their own lives, and those of their Niti guarantors, persuaded the travelers to honor their promises. It was a prudent decision. The Garpon was subsequently imprisoned for three years for his excessive liberality to the *gosains.*

As a consolation, Moorcroft and Hearsey became the first Englishmen to see and describe the sacred lakes and mountain that are central to the cosmology of two world religions. Glinting like a gem in Tibet's western plateau at more than 14,950 feet, Lake Manasarovar is revered by Buddhists as the Turquoise Sea. The great Tibetan saint Milarepa lived on its shores as a hermit in the twelfth century, composing lyrics in praise of its austere beauty. Eight Buddhist monasteries surround its fifty-four-mile shoreline, each providing shelter to pilgrims, for whom a circumambulation is equal to a single symbolic turn of the eternal Wheel. The lake is as sacred to Hindus, who believe it emanated from the mind of Brahma the Creator and that a great *lingam* or phallus once arose from its waters. A portion of Gandhi's ashes were scattered in the lake and the dying Nehru lamented that he never visited it. So venerated is Manasarovar (Tibetan for the Undefeated) that it is blasphemy to hunt its aquatic birds or catch the fish that thrive in its 200-square-mile area. Nevertheless pilgrims were then easy game for the *dacoits,* or robbers, lurking on its shores.

Mirrored in Manasarovar's waters is Mount Kailas, 22,028 feet high. This is the lofty abode where the great god Shiva sits in perpetual meditation. Some say Buddha dwelled in its heights with 500 followers who deferred their own Nirvana to work for the salvation of others. To the devout through the ages, Kailas is revered as the source of four great Asian rivers—the Ganges, the Indus, the Sutlej, and the Brahmaputra—all flowing through Lake Manasarovar. But the empirical Moorcroft, aided by two servants, combed Manasarovar's shores and could find no outlet, even though his caravan companion, the Hindu pundit, recalled years before seeing a channel that connected it to Rakshas Tal, its smaller sister to the west. When Moorcroft and Hearsey's account was published in a geographical journal, a recondite argument ensued over Tibetan hydrography that persisted until its apparent resolution in 1907 by the Swedish explorer Sven Hedin. The old pundit was right, Hedin concluded, because the effluent was periodic, depending on the monsoon, a possibility suggested in an unpublished note by Moorcroft. Unchallenged was Moorcroft's other finding, that Rakshas Tal, Manosaravar's smaller sibling, covering 140 square miles, was the source of the main branch of one of India's major rivers, the Sutlej.

As the caravan began its descent from the plateau, Hearsey recorded the occasion with a watercolor showing his partner astride his yak, his head capped by a flowing turban—the only certain likeness of Moorcroft that survives. It was a moment worth noting. Central Asia was then mainly a blank in Western atlases. Few guessed the incredible size and complexity of the Himalaya, a belt of crumpled peaks 600 miles long and 300 miles wide. Six mountain systems, each with a network of spurs and parallel ranges, comprise the chain. The Vale of Kashmir and the Tibetan plateau are the only sizable level areas within this vertical jumble. It fell to Moorcroft and Hearsey to become the first Europeans to explore all these regions. This was before the founding of the Royal Geographical Society and its counterpart in St. Petersburg, the Imperial Russian Geographical Society. It was decades before the cult of personality had developed around the quintessential Victorian hero, the topeed sahib. Moorcroft's timing was poor, and obscurity his penalty.

ON THEIR RETURN TO THE SUTLEJ VALLEY FROM THE TIBETAN plateau, Moorcroft and Hearsey were aware of a final hurdle before reaching the safety of British India. The caravan had to pass rapidly and without permission through the intervening Nepalese hill-states of Kumaon and Garhwal, thinly policed by tough Gurkha watchdogs. These warriors would not be fooled by turbans or walnut-stained skin. They knew Hearsey from previous frontier skirmishes and were aware that Moorcroft was a ranking official in the Company's Military Department. The "pilgrims" were now passing from Tibet through Nepalese territory that the British were known to covet. Their progress was scarcely secret since the caravan now included eight yaks and, far more important, a noisy flock of shawl-wool goats that Moorcroft had acquired from villagers in Niti in return for trading goods.

Moorcroft and his companions tried to pretend nothing was amiss as they moved forward with guns loaded, warily alert both to Gurkha patrols and the notorious tigers of Kumaon. In October 1812, after several anxious weeks on the road, the caravan was halted at Pali by the local Nepalese Governor. Cheerful bluff and injured innocence did not persuade, and in due course Gurkhas overwhelmed the entire party and bound its members hand and foot. For a terrifying instant, Hearsey saw Moorcroft's prone body, then the flash of a *kukri*, the stubby curved Gurkha knife, and assumed his companion was dead and that he was to follow. Instead they were dragged off as prisoners, their arms lashed behind them. To Hearsey, writing in his journal about that day, the Gurkhas were a "cussed deceitful race" and "cowardly shitten rascals."

In the days that followed, Moorcroft and Hearsey were released and permitted the run of the camp, though their servants continued to be shackled and abused. But day by day conditions improved. It appeared the Nepalese wished to make a point without provoking a casus belli. Moorcroft used the time, as was his custom, to treat the afflictions of local people and to smuggle letters to British authorities regarding his party's captivity.

Detention gave Moorcroft and Hearsey ample opportunity to learn more about the Gurkhas, Goorkas, or Ghorkas, among a dozen spellings for these hardy mountaineers. Mongolian by origin, Hindu by faith, and originating in villages northwest of Katmandu, the Gurkhas were the gendarmes of the Nepalese rajah. In frontier regions adjoining British India, they had by 1812 become oppressive warrior gangs. In a recurrent cycle, the proximity of Europeans stirred the unrest that the Gurkhas tried forcibly to suppress; which in turn provoked anger in Calcutta about frontier turbulence, which then engendered schemes of territorial aggrandizement. Hearsey's comments in his journal illustrate the cycle. He blames the Gurkhas for the "horrible state of slavery" in these Himalayan foothills, yet his indignation was mixed with practical and strategic calculations: "To India, this country is a wall, which if in the possession of a European enemy would ensure to them the conquest of the whole flat land." Not only was the cooler climate salubrious but British rule would give the region's inhabitants the benefits of law and Christianity. As for the Gurkhas, he presciently added, "They are hardy, endure privations, and are very obedient, have not much of the distinction of caste, and are a neutral kind of Hindoo, eating in messes almost everything they meet with, except beef. Under our government they would make excellent soldiers."

As they did. Two years later, responding to an appeal by aggrieved local headmen, the British declared war on Nepal, expecting a swift and easy victory. Instead, three of four British expeditionary forces were unexpectedly repulsed. Charles Metcalfe, the British Resident in Delhi, observed in a memorandum to the Governor-General: "In this war, dreadful to say, we have had numbers on our side, and skill and bravery on the side of our enemy."

Eventually, Colonel Sir David Ochterlony, commanding 40,000 regular troops, confronted the best Gurkha General, Amar Singh Thapa, with an artillery barrage that blew apart Gurkha stockades. Assisting Ochterlony were irregular forces whose commanders included Captain Hearsey. Demoralized Gurkhas began deserting to the British, who promptly formed them into new battalions, becoming the first Gurkha recruits in the Company army. His army in full retreat, the Rajah of Nepal sued for peace and ceded the provinces of Kumaon and Garhwal to the Company, which thereby gained the Himalayan foothills and the site of Simla, the future summer capital of the Raj. An unusual clause in the 1816 treaty gave the victorious British the right to recruit Gurkhas, who thereafter fought with distinction for Crown and Country, most recently in the Falklands War.

MOORCROFT'S CAPTIVITY ENDED AMICABLY. HIS SMUGGLED LETters reached Calcutta, the British Governor-General sent an appeal to the Rajah of Nepal, and the Nepalese Governor at Almora ordered his release. His detention was something less than an ordeal. He and his companions got back their firearms and were provided with bearers to carry their baggage to the frontier, which they crossed in November 1812. Moorcroft's real punishment came later, in Calcutta. His board was interested not in Tibetan lakes or shawl wool but in the horses the Superintendent of the Stud failed to find in a self-authorized jaunt. These complaints were gently seconded by the Governor-General, Lord Minto, who in a letter of reproof said he would not have authorized Moorcroft's Tibetan expedition, owing to its dangers, its deviation from his official duties, and the "strong political objection to a measure so likely to give umbrage and excite suspicion as the passage of an English gentleman high in the service and confidence of this Govt., without permission, but especially clandestinely and in disguise through the Nepaul country." None of this smoothed his dealings with the Board of Managers of the Company Stud. In 1816, Moorcroft was embroiled in a protracted feud over breeding operations, sharpened by his sarcastic responses to criticism. When he broached the idea of a new horse-buying expedition to Bokhara, a searing reply warned Moorcroft to keep "steady" at his stud duties and not "waste his time" on "wild and romantick excursions to the banks of the Amoo [Amur] and the plains of Chinese Tartary." The ink was barely dry when Moorcroft began preparing an even more ambitious quest for "the finest horse markets in the world."

Moorcroft's passion to see and acquire Central Asian horses was more than an excuse for travel. What Moorcroft coveted most were the Turkmen horses, distinguished by their pale golden coats, narrow chest, long necks, and sturdy legs. These were the "Heavenly Horses" of Fergana, whose ancestors sprang from the skies. The stamina of these steeds was a matter of fact not of legend. The "good Turcoman horses" that Marco Polo saw could travel upwards of a hundred miles a day for weeks on end. Their descendants, the long-necked Akhal-Teke, are bred to this day in the Republic of Turkmenistan.

Such were the creatures that Moorcroft hoped to find in Central Asia. He pleaded, cajoled, and persisted, and his seven-year campaign was rewarded in May 1819 with a letter from his friend Charles Metcalfe. Now head of the Political and Secret Department, Metcalfe granted him "leave to proceed towards the North Western parts of Asia," in order to procure horses "to improve the breed within the British Provinces or for military use." In fact, the horse doctor was to be an intelligence scout in an epic journey that took him across Afghanistan to Bokhara the Noble.

CHAPTER TWO

.:.

A River Too Far

P HRASED AT ITS GENTLEST, THE TRAVELER'S LOT IN BRITISH
India in the 1820's was not easy.

This was before the advent of railroads, before the old Grand Trunk
Road was improved and new roads built, before a network of hill stations, cantonments, and frontier settlements sprang up along the way.
For Europeans, nature was omnipresent and hostile. The heavy rains
brought no respite from winged pests, a particularly nasty specimen
being the blister-fly, which wriggled into one's clothing, and when
crushed left a spiteful stain and blister. Poisonous reptiles might turn up
anywhere. Lady Falkland, wife of the Governor of Bombay, wrote that,
in her residence, despite its army of servants, she was accustomed "to
the sound of a snake coming to an untimely end, and have sometimes
been awakened in the morning by the servants killing one on the verandah." On the road, travelers were liable to hear baying jackals, troops
of chattering monkeys, and tigers growling in the forests of the night.
Nor was sleep enhanced by the prevalence of Thugs, the thousand or
more devotees of the Hindu goddess Kali who believed they had divine license to rob and strangle strangers. No campaign by the British

Raj was more popular among Indians than its eight-year campaign to eliminate the Thugs, which pretty much succeeded by 1837, the year Victoria's reign began.

All methods of travel were onerous. Passage by river was slow and tiresome, and in the absence of coaches, going overland meant riding horseback or being carried three to four miles a day in a palanquin. The latter usually involved buying a litter, hiring bearers, packing provisions into wicker baskets, and making arrangements with the postal service, or *dak,* which delivered people as well as mail on well-traveled routes with dak bungalows spaced every fifteen to fifty miles. The normal team consisted of eight *palkee-burdars,* or palanquin-bearers, and two *bhangy-burdars,* or luggage porters. Just how it felt within a palanquin was graphically described by Captain Richard Francis Burton, not yet the celebrated explorer but a serving Indian Army officer in the 1840's: "Between your head and the glowing sun, there is scarcely half an inch of plank, covered with a thin mat, which ought to be, but never is, watered. After a day or two, you will hesitate which to hate most, your bearers' monotonous, melancholy grunting, groaning chaunt, when fresh, or their jolting, jerking, shambling, staggering gait, when tired. In a perpetual state of low fever you cannot eat, drink, or sleep; your mouth burns, your head throbs, your back aches, and your temper borders on the ferocious." To escape the sweltering summer heat it was necessary to travel at night, which meant hiring *mussalchees,* or torchbearers, as well. The total cost was about a shilling a mile, then a considerable sum, yet even so, as Burton dourly complained, "we cannot promise you much pleasure in the enjoyment of this celebrated Oriental luxury."

With all that in mind, one begins to grasp the audacity of William Moorcroft's great journey to the Punjab, Ladakh, Kashmir, Afghanistan, and Bokhara, all beyond the comparative security of British India, a five-year trip that reached remote lands no Englishman had seen since the reign of Queen Elizabeth I. His journey started in May 1819, when Moorcroft was fifty-two, then a grandfatherly age to lead a small army over mountains and deserts, without diplomatic credentials. Of his affronts to his superiors, perhaps none was more insufferable than how near Moorcroft came to triumphant success.

MOORCROFT'S PREPARATIONS TOOK NEARLY A YEAR AND IN-
volved the logistical headache of assembling eight tons of supplies,
including chintz hangings, mosquito nets, and "portable necessary-
houses." It also required a careful selection of a military escort, or-
derlies, cooks, carpenters, and grooms, plus transport—horses, mules,
and camels. Moorcroft's previous journeys gave him a valuable roster
of recruits. Joining the expedition was the Persian interpreter, Mir
Izzat-Allah, the "native gentleman of talent and industry" whom
Moorcroft had sent on alone to Bokhara in 1812. Another tested
companion was an Afghan, Ghulam Hyder Khan, the "stout soldier
and faithful servant" on his Tibetan trip. But Moorcroft's riskiest
choice proved his wisest. He invited nineteen-year-old George Trebeck, a recent arrival in Calcutta, to be second in command, charged
with choosing routes and keeping geographical logs.

Trebeck was also a lawyer and advised Moorcroft on writing a will
to provide for his wife, Mary, whom he had left behind in London,
and his common-law Indian wife, Purree Khanum, the mother of his
children, Anne and Richard. Both spouses were provided with capital trusts, the balance passing on their deaths to the children. One
yearns to know more. In his voluminous journals and letters, Moorcroft was conspicuously reticent about his personal affairs, which was
not unusual in British India. Until British memsahibs arrived in
greater numbers, what Europeans called amours with native spouses
produced offspring known variously as Eurasians, East Indians, Indo-
Britains, half-castes, and (in this century) Anglo-Indians. Victorian
historians generally drew a curtain around these households, and in
biographies of notable Company officers, Indian spouses tended to
become invisible.

The prevailing practice was described by Burton, who during his
seven years in India acknowledged three amours:

> The *Bibi* (white woman) was at the time rare in India; the
> result was the triumph of the *Bubu* (colored sister). I found

every officer in the corps more or less provided with one of these helpmates. We boys naturally followed suit...[The *Bubu*] is all but indispensable to the student, and she teaches him not only Hindostani grammar, but the syntaxes of native Life. She keeps house for him, never allowing him to save money, or, if possible, to waste it. She keeps the servants in order. She has the infallible recipe to prevent maternity, especially if her tenure of office depends on such compact. She looks after him in sickness, and is one of the best of nurses, and, as it is not good for a man to live alone, she makes him a manner of home.

That Moorcroft's eye roved as much as his feet was evident in his admiring remarks on the attractiveness of Asian women. He was even described as a voluptuary by Victor Jacquemont, a French traveler who followed in his steps a decade later. "I live like a hermit," Jacquemont wrote home from Kashmir, "and my virtue is the subject of universal admiration. Mr. Moorcroft did not set a like example of European continence here. His principal occupation was making love, and if his friends are surprised that his travels were so unproductive, they may ascribe it to this cause." However, others testified that Jacquemont was no hermit, suggesting that travelers in India were not under oath in writing home.

Indeed, in delving through the archives of the Raj—sorted, indexed, and freely accessible at the British Library—one is continually aware how much was unwritten, or implied. The stated purpose of Moorcroft's mission, for example, was solely to acquire horses for the Military Department, which continued to pay his full salary. Yet his reports went straight to the Political and Secret Department. He was provided with documents bearing the Company's seal stating in English, Persian, Russian, and Chinese that he was an employee searching for horses. But when Moorcroft asked the Governor-General to provide a letter of introduction to the Emir of Bokhara, the request was rejected. As Charles Metcalfe explained, "it was never intended to accredit you or vest you with a public character," since in the event of trouble, the British Government would itself be committed, "unpleasantly and contrary to its design." In what was to become a general practice, the Company was entirely supportive of Moorcroft's expedition, so long as it could disown him the instant he left British India.

THAT MOMENT ARRIVED ON MARCH 6, 1820, ALONG THE BANKS of the river Sutlej, whose winding course marked the boundary between British territory and the western Himalayas. In the absence of boats, the party crossed on inflated buffalo skins expertly paddled by ferrymen, causing Moorcroft to reflect that an entire army could become truly amphibious by carrying with it these portable skins. The passage took less than two hours for what resembled a small expeditionary force: 300 persons, including a trimly uniformed escort of twelve Gurkhas, sixteen horses and mules, £4,000 worth of trading goods from Messrs. Palmer & Co. and Mackillop & Co. of Calcutta, and enough medical equipment to stock a field hospital.

The field hospital was Moorcroft's universal passport. His caravan was invariably greeted by a queue of the afflicted, especially villagers half-blinded by cataracts. Before he reached the Sutlej, his medical reputation had flown before him. Once he entered territory controlled by the Sikhs, still mostly unmapped, he needed the permission of their ruler, Ranjit Singh, to proceed. Moorcroft headed directly and separately for the Sikh capital, Lahore, leaving Trebeck and most of the party behind. While waiting for permission to enter Lahore, the doctor opened his clinic and with his needle addressed forty cataract cases, treated a woman with a cancer on her tongue and a man with hydrocephalus. "I was by no means dissatisfied with the general results," he remarks in his notebook, to which he appended clinical notes on the merits of operating in open air.

Ranjit Singh was then known to all as the Lion of Lahore. Illiterate and unlettered, this remarkable soldier-diplomat was only seventeen when he began welding Sikh clans into an Indian kingdom whose might was rivaled only by the British Raj. European visitors were impressed by his one-eyed ugliness, his plain dress, his dislike of bloodshed, and his resilient use of mercenaries. In 1809, with equal resilience, the East India Company sent an able negotiator, Charles Metcalfe, to secure Ranjit Singh's promise of aid in the event that Napoleon, as widely rumored, attempted an invasion of India. The Company also wanted the Maharajah to acknowledge British sovereignty over territories south of the Sutlej River. Ranjit Singh proved willing so long as the British for their part gave him a free hand north of the Sutlej, a bargain sealed at Amritsar in a treaty that Metcalfe brought triumphantly back to Calcutta. This was all known to Moorcroft, who doubtless was briefed as well about Ranjit Singh's delight in women, boys, and strong liquor; his interest in horses and guns; and his habit of detaining guests for weeks or even months. As Moorcroft was about to discover, Ranjit Singh at forty also feared his sexual powers were ebbing.

This medical aspect was divulged gradually, after Ranjit Singh, seated on his golden throne, greeted his visitor and expressed warm appreciation for Moorcroft's gifts, notably a brace of pistols and an elegant miniature cannon. When talk turned to horses, the Sikh ruler clapped his hands to summon his mounts, and a marveling Moorcroft noted their rich saddles and bridles, and the variety of breeds— "Dhani and Ghep, the Lakhi Jangal, Rohtas, Atak, Kabul and Bokhara." The following day brought an equestrian display in which fifty horses, splendidly caparisoned but different from those he had already seen, executed complex movements in unison, yet, Moorcroft noted, "Not a single horse neighed, or was restive or vicious in the slightest degree, or was uneasy at mounting, or diverged from the path."

In successive audiences, the two discussed trade and Moorcroft's belief that the Punjab, with its fine soil, climate, and water resources, was destined to prosper. But it became apparent that Ranjit Singh was preoccupied by real or imagined ailments, and finally permission for a complete physical examination was given to Moorcroft, who could detect no organic faults. Prudently, the Englishman prescribed a placebo, dietary abstention, and avoidance of worry.

In mid–May 1820, after sixteen days as the Sikh ruler's guest, Moorcroft obtained the documents necessary to travel by way of the Kulu Valley to Ladakh and Yarkand, and from there to Bokhara. That he made a favorable impression in Lahore is evident in the pavilion

in which he resided, facing the Shalimar gardens. A wall plaque, still
visible to today's visitors, recalls the residence there of
WILLIAM MOORCROFT, TRAVELLER.

MOORCROFT WAS STILL SEPARATED FROM THE REST OF HIS CAR-
avan as he proceeded during drenching rains in June through a
patchwork of once independent hill-states, each with its own Hindu
Rajah, and all unwilling vassals to Ranjit Singh. His first call was at
the court of Rajah Sansar Chand in the Rajput kingdom of Kangra.
The Rajah, then in his summer palace at Alampur, was known for his
lavish hospitality. Here Moorcroft learned that Trebeck and the rest
of his party were still unwillingly detained by Sikhs in the Punjab,
requiring an appeal to Ranjit Singh, which meant a not-unwelcome
six-week delay at Kangra.

Rajah Sansar Chand was close to Moorcroft's age and a friendship
developed. They talked at length about schemes for economic improvement, a Moorcroft theme wherever he traveled. They examined
the Rajah's choice collection of colored drawings and played chess,
while Moorcroft took time to record local alphabets for Calcutta's
Asiatic Society. These diversions ceased abruptly when the Rajah's
younger brother, Fateh Chand, was stricken by piles and symptoms
of cholera. Moorcroft's radical but painful surgery proved effective,
and the grateful Hindu ruler, in an act of symbolic adoption, exchanged headgear and addressed the English plebeian as "brother,"
the equivalent of adopting him into a royal house older (as Moorcroft proudly reported to a friend) than that of the Bourbons.

Small wonder that Moorcroft, being treated as a friend of kings,
began to behave as if he were an envoy plenipotentiary. His hosts
could never quite believe he was only authorized to buy horses, and
assumed he possessed supernumerary powers, an impression that
Moorcroft, it would appear, did not discourage. With enthusiasm and
sympathy, he took up the causes of his hosts in his reports to Calcutta. Weeks of hearing how the Sikhs used their treaty-protected
mastery north of the Sutlej to extort produce and taxes reinforced

his distaste for Ranjit Singh's tyranny over non-Sikhs. As he headed toward the Himalayas, far from the Company's scrutiny, Moorcroft by insensible degrees saw himself as a potential shaper as well as a chronicler of history.

These *folies de grandeur* were surely encouraged by the matchless scenery unwinding before him. After braving monsoon rains over the Dulchi Pass in August 1820, Moorcroft descended into the Kulu Valley, with its lush forests, streams, and terraced farms. "The bottom of the valleys glitter with ribands of water," Moorcroft remarks in a rare effusive passage. "Vast slopes of grass declined from the summits of the mountain in a uniform direction separated by clumps of cedar, cypress and fir. The surface of the ground was literally enamalled with small asters, anemones and wild strawberries." Arriving at Sultanpur, capital of the Kulu region, Moorcroft rejoiced to find "Mr. Trebeck in good health and spirits and the rest of my party as well."

Moorcroft recruited more than a hundred additional bearers for the trek through Kulanthapitha, the valley's traditional name, meaning "the end of the habitable world." The terminus itself was Rohtang Pass, whose 13,300-foot height was first accurately calculated by Trebeck. The pass separated green hill country from Himalayan crags. Climbing zigzag past the gorges of the River of the Moon, the party reached a lofty saddle that opened out upon an enormous crescent of snow-peaked mountains. The caravan inched downward into the Lahul Valley and the Buddhist kingdom of Ladakh, where Moorcroft tried boldly to make history.

ON THE FAR SIDE OF THE ROHTANG PASS, THE PEOPLE WERE Buddhist, their culture Tibetan, the spareness of their landscape relieved by temples with tinkling bells, red-robed monks, prayer flags, and horizontal hillside dwellings. Moorcroft and Trebeck were among the first Europeans to reach the Lahul Valley, an old Asian trading route, and their reception was friendly. Local headmen provided porters, mules, and supplies, and as in Moorcroft's earlier trip through the Himalaya, two Indian pundits counted their paces to measure distances as they proceeded. Trebeck, by now an accomplished geographer, took compass bearings and, using a barometer and thermometer, calculated the altitude of passes.

News of the advancing caravan soon reached Ladakh, whose rulers had no prior contacts with the British but were well aware of the East India Company's unbroken sequence of conquests. A Muslim emissary was sent to appraise the newcomers, and it developed that Moorcroft's Persian interpreter, Mir Izzat Allah, had known the emissary's master, a *pirzada,* or holy man. This opened the way for Moorcroft's successful audience with a Ladakhi official, who provided the *laissez-passer* enabling him to become the first English official to enter a remote and reclusive country.

Despite its Tibetan character, Ladakh had no political ties with the Dalai Lamas ruling in Lhasa since the fifteenth century. To sustain their precarious autonomy, Ladakhis learned to tread softly in a difficult neighborhood. To the east lay China, whose nearest outpost was Yarkand, a thriving commercial center in inner Asia. To the west lay Kashmir, an Afghan province only recently conquered by the Sikhs. Ranjit Singh now demanded from Ladakh the tribute money it had paid to the Afghans. Far to the north lay the Russian Empire, whose agent, a certain Aga Mehdi, was said to be making his way over the mountains to Ladakh to establish commercial relations.

Such was the situation in September 1820 as Moorcroft and Trebeck arrived in Leh, the capital of Ladakh. Wary but curious, the Rajah of Ladakh and his chief minister, or Khalun, prepared for a winter of parleying as the snows began sealing in their cloistered kingdom.

With its flat-topped houses, its cluster of *gompas,* or lamaseries, and an eight-story palace hugging the hillside, Leh was a smaller version of Lhasa. Moorcroft's party was quartered in a high-walled compound with solid gates that shielded it from the curious crowd without. Settling in, Moorcroft remarked on the bliss of resting comfortably "without hearing the rush of torrents or the crash of avalanches." During his extended stay, he compiled a veritable encyclopedia about Ladakh, describing its annual dance dramas, its abundance of "necessary houses" for the hygienic removal of night soil, and its medicinal but delicious crops, notably rhubarb. He also described a sarsinh tree with fragrant yellow flower and an agreeable olive-like fruit, thereafter known scientifically as *Eleagnus moorcroftii*. These and a hundred other topics filled his discursive letters, prompting Sir Alexander Cunningham, the author of a scholarly history of Ladakh, to observe a generation later that Moorcroft's accounts were "marked by great shrewdness of observation, and by the most scrupulous accuracy."

As before, Moorcroft's field clinic attracted a procession of patients, including the high officials of Leh, the head lama of an important monastery, the imam of the local mosque, the master of horses at the palace, and Kashmiri merchants. He tried without success to promote use of chimneys and to introduce smallpox vaccinations (the vaccine he so laboriously imported proved inert). His good works, his obvious respect for the Ladakhis, and his disarming manner added to the personal capital he now invested in a diplomatic gamble.

It was not a small or hesitant gamble. He envisioned Ladakh as the trading crossroads of Central Asia and as a backdoor route to China—an ideal springboard, in a phrase, for British mercantile and political interests. Such a development had roots in history and law, he maintained, since Ladakh had once acknowledged the authority of Mughal emperors and paid tribute to Delhi, where a Mughal still nominally reigned. Thus Ladakh was British by inheritance. Hence it made sense for the Ladakh Rajah to refuse tribute to the Sikhs and to seek British protection. This was agreeable to the Rajah, who in May 1821, signed an "engagement" to establish ties with British merchants and permit their passage through Ladakh to China and Central Asia. This was joined to a formal request for British protection. As Moorcroft explained: "On the one hand I averted from an amiable and harmless people the oppressive weight of Sikh exaction and insolence, and on the other I secured for my country an influence over a state, which, lying on the British frontier, offered a central mart for the extension of her commerce to Turkestan and China, and a strong outwork against an enemy from the north, should such a foe ever occur in the autocrat of the Russians."

Brashly, Moorcroft sent his "engagement" to the British Resident in Delhi, along with a letter to the Governor-General from the

Rajah of Ladakh offering formal allegiance. He enclosed a copy of a personal letter to Ranjit Singh censuring Sikh oppressions, asserting that Ladakh was part of Delhi's patrimony, and warning him not to meddle with Ladakh until he heard from the British Government "regarding the state of its intentions and affairs." This was bundled together with a lengthy report to Charles Metcalfe and dispatched in August 1821. But his friend Metcalfe was no longer head of the Political and Secret Service, he was now Resident in Hyderabad, and Ranjit Singh forwarded without comment Moorcroft's injudicious letter to an amazed Resident in Delhi, Sir David Ochterlony.

Moorcroft's enthusiasm clouded his judgment. The Company placed a high value on its alliance with Ranjit Singh, who had punctiliously honored the 1809 treaty yielding up territories west of the Sutlej in return for a free hand to the east. So it was with "surprise and displeasure" that the Governor-General learned of Moorcroft's "height of indiscretion" in suggesting to Ranjit Singh that Britain could interfere in the affairs of Ladakh. Planted like a grenade in the letter Moorcroft received in March 1822 was the word "reprehensible." His "engagement" was repudiated, his salary suspended, and his bright hopes for Central Asian trade dismissed without a mention.

EVERYTHING ELSE SEEMED TO GO BADLY. THE CHINESE IN YARKAND would not give Moorcroft's caravan permission to proceed, despite the emollient efforts of his go-between, Mir Izzat-Allah. The winter of 1821–22 was exceptionally cold in Ladakh, hampering an exploratory trip he and Trebeck undertook northward toward the Indus River. He lost a porter through an accident, and failed to catch the Tibetan wild ass, the kiang, which he coveted. His bank drafts were not honored back home. There were even clumsy attempts on Moorcroft's life—a nighttime shot fired into his room and poison inserted in his food—which he attributed to would-be assassins serving Ranjit Singh.

But Moorcroft's optimism budded with improved weather and a chance encounter with another European on a side trip to Dras.

This village on an upland plateau is said to be the coldest permanently inhabited place in the world outside Siberia. Here, in balmier
July, Moorcroft's party came upon a lone Hungarian traveler with
the memorable name of Alexander Csoma de Körös. Armed only
with a walking stick and an indestructible constitution, Csoma was
certain he would find in Tibet the hidden Asian roots of the enigmatic Hungarian language. Moorcroft shared his own working Tibetan dictionary with the traveler, for whom he gained access to
important monastic libraries in Ladakh. Csoma failed to prove his
thesis, but he did compile the first systematic Tibetan grammar and
dictionary, and so popularized Central Asian travel in Budapest that
the peregrinating Hungarian was thereafter a fixture in the region.

There was a sequel. Back in Leh, Moorcroft showed Csoma a letter that had been carried across Asia by Aga Mehdi, known in
Ladakh as a merchant from Yarkand, but in reality a Russian scout.
His true name seems to have been Mekhti Rafailov, and he was apparently a native of Kashmir who served the Russians in a manner
resembling Moorcroft's for the Company. In 1808, Aga Mehdi made
the difficult passage over the mountains to Ladakh, where he acquired shawls and presented the Rajah with a letter from the Tsar.
While Moorcroft's party wintered in Leh, news came that the Russian agent was en route and the Briton eagerly hoped to meet his
counterpart. But when Aga Mehdi's richly laden caravan arrived in
April 1821, it was without its leader, who had died on a freezing
pass. It developed that the Russian agent was probably responsible
for the Chinese refusal in Yarkand to admit Moorcroft. In Aga
Mehdi's last mission, he was carrying a message in Russian addressed
to Ranjit Singh. Moorcroft surreptitiously copied the letter, a preliminary bow between competitors in the tournament to come.

With Csoma's help, the message was translated, and evidently it
was nothing but a letter of introduction. This did not prevent Moorcroft from citing Aga Mehdi's travels as evidence of a treacherous
Russian campaign to dominate Central Asia and threaten British
India. Why else should Tsarist agents seek trading links more than
2,000 miles from the Russian frontier? Using ancient caravan routes,
Moorcroft believed, Russian forces could advance directly by way of
Ladakh toward the Indian lowlands. Since Chinese rule was tenuous

in eastern Turkestan, the Russians could bring off a *coup de théâtre,* playing on Muslim disaffection and subduing all China, thus destroying Britain's lucrative tea trade. Such was the Tsar's "monstrous plan of aggrandizement" hidden by innocent garments of trade, the work of an "ambition most gigantic." Since Russia had recently fought alongside Britain against Napoleon, and was still considered an ally, these reflections, set forth at length in reports to Calcutta, added to the belief that Moorcroft was prone to fantasy. Yet within a generation, his arguments were a commonplace in every regimental mess in British India.

In September 1822, having spent two years in Ladakh, Moorcroft's caravan finally prepared to depart for Bokhara by way of Kashmir rather than Yarkand. There were long rounds of farewells with Ladakhi officials and with the patients whom Moorcroft had treated. Reassuring news arrived from Calcutta. The dispatches he had addressed to Charles Metcalfe had chased that officer across India and had not been ignored but were forwarded from Hyderabad in July 1822 to the Political Department in Calcutta. Moorcroft might yet get his due from his superiors, or so he hoped as his caravan headed for Kashmir.

BY CHANCE, KASHMIR WAS VERY MUCH IN VOGUE. KASHMIRI shawls were the haute couture rage in France, where the former Empress Josephine was said to possess hundreds. In Britain, the surprise best-seller of 1817 was *Lalla Rookh* by Thomas Moore, a verse romance about a daughter of the Mughal Emperor Aurangzeb and her adventurous passage from Delhi to Kashmir to become the bride of the King of Bucharia. Moore had never seen Kashmir, his heroine was imaginary, the story a concoction, but his poem swept Europe. Grand Duke Nicholas, the future Russian Tsar, was so enamored that when he and the Grand Duchess visited Berlin in 1822, they cast themselves in the poem's leading roles in a sumptuous royal entertainment featuring a series of tableaux vivants. For as Moore's poem said,

Who has not heard of the vale of Cashmere,
With its roses the brightest that earth ever gave,
Its temples, and grottos, and fountains as clear
As the love-lighted eyes that hang over their wave?

Moore's Kashmir was an Orientalist fantasy, a harbinger of Shangri-La. The real Kashmir had been off-limits to Europeans until Ranjit Singh defeated its Afghan rulers in 1819. When Moorcroft and Trebeck settled in a timber garden-house in Srinagar in 1822, they were the first Western visitors in more than forty years. They were escorted by a Sikh cavalry officer and welcomed by the Sikh Governor, a calculated show of hospitality by Ranjit Singh. But Kashmir's inhabitants were hungry and miserable, their wretchedness underscored by the Vale's natural beauty. Moorcroft's clinic was busier than ever. He set aside Fridays for examinations, Saturdays for surgery, and sometimes treated 300 patients a day. Other days he explored Kashmir's lakes, ruined palaces, and mosques, and studied the ornamental deodar tree. The Vale resembled Scotland, he noted, but the land was defaced by abandoned orchards and farms, and by irrigation canals choked with weeds. "Everywhere the people are in the most abject condition," he wrote, "exorbitantly taxed by the Sikh government, and subjected to every kind of extortion and oppression by its officers." Kashmir's desperation, he argued at length, made it especially vulnerable to a Russian invasion, the more tempting because its mountain walls made it a natural fortress.

In what stretched into a year's stay, Moorcroft took time to study the manufacture of shawls. He examined the pasturage of shawl goats, questioned designers, and directly employed hundreds of artists and embroiderers. All this yielded pages of foolscap notes sent to Calcutta to augment the "public capital" of knowledge. To stimulate the British shawl industry, he commissioned thirty-four paintings, now in New York's Metropolitan Museum of Art, depicting in brilliant colors the characteristic teardrop patterns. More than anybody, Moorcroft was responsible for the improved quality in Europe of the shawl, and for popularizing the Paisley pattern, named after a town in Scotland but originating in the Vale of Kashmir.

There were more urgent reasons for tarrying. A credible militia was essential for the northward trek through the Punjab into the anarchic Pathan hills beyond the Indus, the next goal. Weeks were needed to train and equip local recruits to augment the caravan's by now diminished Gurkha escort. Trebeck supervised the making of lances, swords, and copies of British guns, and drilled a score of Muslim volunteers. In an important coup, he purchased a pair of miniature brass cannons. Other difficulties were harder to address: the rumors about Moorcroft's recall or dismissal, and the fever that felled him, delaying their departure from Srinagar. In September 1823, his health recovered and rumors ignored, Moorcroft took his leave of the comparative safety and comfort of Kashmir.

Once beyond the Vale, the caravan paused at a tiny Punjab kingdom, Rajaori, where Moorcroft found time to answer a letter from John Palmer, a friend in Calcutta. He pleaded with Moorcroft to return to Calcutta where he would be greeted as a hero, before his rumored dismissal became fact. But to do that, Moorcroft responded with spirit, would constitute "a base cowardly and scandalous forfeiture of my own honour and consistency, a breach of my covenanted faith in the Honourable Company, and a dereliction, almost traitorous, of my bounden duty to my country." He pressed on.

MOORCROFT'S CARAVAN BYPASSED LAHORE AND HEADED WITH-out incident over the great Punjab plains to the Pir Panjal pass and the river Indus, beyond which lay the fractious tribes of Afghanistan. As men and animals ferried the Indus, Moorcroft studied an old and celebrated fort on the hills ahead, and in a characteristic minute argued that mobile gunboats would be a better defense against invaders. Once past the river, the party was on its own, in territory controlled by the fierce, unruly Pathans.

Letters had already gone ahead to Peshawar, whose Afghan governors, or *sirdars*, responded with what seemed a warm invitation to proceed. Fears that this was a ruse appeared to materialize as they approached the walled caravanserai of Akora. They were greeted on the banks of the river Kabul by armed horsemen and an envoy from Abbas Khan, the plundering chief of the local Khattuck clan. The messenger spoke politely of paying the necessary tolls and suggested they remain in place until his Khan came for a visit. With equal politeness, Moorcroft rejected the suggestion of paying fees, and the next morning his party, backed against the river, was surrounded by a shouting throng of armed horsemen. On hand as well were messengers from Peshawar, who said they had vainly pleaded Moorcroft's case, but that the Khattucks believed his saddlebags were packed with gold and jewels. As the force prepared to attack, Trebeck withdrew half his militia to the edge of a ravine, brought one cannon forward, and called out orders to fire if the horsemen did not instantly retire. "The tone of Mr. Trebeck's short but emphatic address, the steady countenance of our men and the lighted match of the gunner," in Moorcroft's words, caused the horsemen to waver, then retreat. This victory in an initial test of nerves helped ensure a civil welcome in Peshawar, where the caravan arrived in December 1823.

Afghanistan at the moment and not unusually was embroiled in a ferocious power struggle, one that involved Moorcroft's hosts, Peshawar's two *sirdars,* who were also brothers. They were planning a rising in Kabul to support the claims to the throne of their younger half-brother, Dost Mohammed Khan, against their archrival, Shah Shuja. Moorcroft's unexpected arrival might prove useful, or so they thought. Peshawar had not seen an English visitor since 1809, when the great Company administrator Mountstuart Elphinstone, then Governor of Bombay, came to solicit Afghan aid in the event of a French invasion. That Moorcroft was simply looking for horses seemed hardly possible to the Afghans. If his trip had a diplomatic purpose, the more reason to cultivate his goodwill. Besides, his medical prowess had already given him the aura of a magus; it was whispered in the bazaars that he could turn lead into gold, and that he was a century and a half old.

Moorcroft turned this friendly reception to account by searching for horses. His hosts in Peshawar told him that the Waziri steeds were the finest but warned that Waziristan was wild and dangerous. Such warnings were a goad to Moorcroft. Having successfully treated an ailing Waziri holy man, who volunteered to serve as guide, Moorcroft departed with a small party. At the fortified city of Kohat on the way to Waziristan, he was overtaken in March 1824 by an excited George Trebeck. So impressed were Peshawar's chiefs by the young Englishman, that they had offered him military command. It was Moorcroft's turn to urge caution and reject a risky course, but on his return to Peshawar, he set a very different example.

The long-rumored message from Calcutta finally arrived in April 1824. Its tone was starchily bureaucratic. "Little prospect remains, either of accomplishing the original and authorized ends of your journey or of your even penetrating into the desired quarter," said Calcutta. "Your public spirit and the information you have obtained is greatly valued but you can no longer be spared from your important duties at the stud." He was instructed to return as practicable, but if he had already reached "Caubul or the vicinity of that place," he would have the discretion to continue to Bokhara. Moorcroft found the loophole he sought by making a distinction between the "kingdom" of Kabul or being at the gates of the "city" itself, several hundred miles northward. Since he was now near the "kingdom," he replied, he would proceed first to the "city," then to Bokhara, returning by way of Khokand, Yarkand, and Ladakh.

Moorcroft's habits of command were now reflexive. Here he was, the captain of an expedition, leading a caravan and its military escort into unknown lands whose people viewed him as a sorcerer and whose rulers courted him as a potentate. In British India, he was acted upon; here he was the actor. He enjoyed the prerogatives of rulership with few of its tedious duties. So far, he had been fortunate. Though he had suffered accidents and sometimes painful diseases, he had escaped serious injury. He had led his caravan almost unscathed over lofty passes and broad rivers, acquiring precious information on uncharted terrain. Why should he turn back? Besides, travel was addictive. Balkan peasants believe that if you are smitten by incurable wanderlust, you were born under a lilac-bleeding star. It was surely so at Moorcroft's birth.

In any case, the Waziri horses proved a disappointment once again. Bokhara was still the place to find superb mounts. No sooner did the Peshawar chiefs offer an escort to see his caravan through the Khyber Pass than Moorcroft was on his way.

THE KHYBER PASS IS THE FUNNEL THROUGH WHICH THE RICHES and armies of Asia have immemorially flowed. It bestrides the main trade routes from Persia, China, and Central Asia, and bisects the Grand Trunk Road from Peshawar to Kabul. As recently as 1953, according to Murray's *Handbook for Travellers* (16th edition), caravans two miles long, consisting of heavily loaded, double-humped Bactrian camels, bullocks, and asses, passed through it Tuesdays and Fridays in winter, Fridays only in summer. This was no doubt an established practice going back to the sixteenth century, when the Khyber first became the preserve and pride of the Afridis, a Pathan clan renowned for its love of war and its skill at smuggling. To this day, the Afridis remain lords of the Khyber, the omniscient monitors who provide the irregular police, or *khassadars,* escorting tribal dignitaries or convoys of lorries.

So it was in 1824 when Moorcroft and Trebeck became the first Englishmen to see and describe Asia's most celebrated pass. On the bluffs flanking the long corridor were hundreds of squatting Afridis, who ruminatively studied the caravan. Protected by their own escort from Peshawar, the party endured the stares, the stifling heat, the stinging wind, and the loss through heatstroke of Moorcroft's devoted spaniel, Missy. Once through the great pass, Moorcroft's caravan made its way safely to Jalalabad. There his Peshawar friends met with their rivals' emissaries in a failed peace attempt, and while the deliberations dragged on, Moorcroft searched for Hellenistic coins in the fruit orchards around Jalalabad. The caravan then proceeded to Kabul, a seventy-mile journey through a dozen defiles whose heights offered an ideal perch for Afghan sharpshooters, as proved the case during British and Russian invasions in years to come.

In June 1824, shortly after his 57th birthday, Moorcroft's party entered Kabul, where his caravan found shelter within a walled palace below the Bala Hissar, the great fort adjacent to the city. Moorcroft filled his notebooks with descriptions of Kabul's labyrinthine bazaar, its eighty mosques and elaborate funerary monuments, including the tomb of Babar, founder of the Mughal Empire. But baffled by the shifting intrigues among tribes, clans, and families, Moorcroft proved no wiser than later visitors.

He and Trebeck chanced to be present when the iron-willed Dost Mohammed Khan emerged as ruler after deposing his nephew. Seeking to befriend the Dost, Moorcroft presented him with a double-barreled shotgun, and was informed that henceforth he and his party all would be deemed "nephews" by Dost Mohammed. This new relationship scarcely signified friendship, Moorcroft wrote, "when the circumstances of D. M. Khan cannonading his nephew have been duly weighed." In his grossest misjudgment, Moorcroft went on to urge British support for Dost Mohammed's chief rival, the more accommodating Shah Shuja, adding that "a single British regiment would suffice" to change rulers. He proposed such a "forward policy," using a term that would later resonate, to thwart Russian machinations. Moorcroft's sympathetic and meticulous biographer, Garry Alder, generously remarks that he was half right: "In this July letter, the Russians in general are the bogey men. They are active and hostile in Lahore, in Kabul, everywhere. Yet even in this alarmist nonsense, Moorcroft was anticipating the future. He was a full-fledged, classic Russophobe before almost any of his countrymen had even discerned the possibility of a Russian threat to British interests in Asia, let alone thought about how to respond to it."

Moorcroft kept his views to himself as civil violence brushed close to his encampment. In August 1824, during a lull in the fighting, his caravan quitted Kabul and followed an old trade route through the Hindu Kush to the fertile watershed between the Oxus and the Indus rivers. This was the Bamian Valley, and there Moorcroft paused to investigate reports that two enormous Buddhas were carved in a cliff. These reports proved correct. Standing in niches were two colossi, each originally covered with gold leaf, the bigger 175 feet high, the smaller 125 feet, among the largest human likenesses ever carved. The figures were seen and described by the Chinese pilgrim Hsüan-tsang, in A.D. 632, the year Mohammed died, when 5,000 monks lived in caves around Bamian, then a thriving meeting place of traders and pilgrims from China, Persia, India, and Hellenistic Central Asia, and a stopover on the ancient road from Bactria to Taxila. High on the cliff above the larger Buddha, Moorcroft wrote his name in charcoal, a violation of his rule against graffiti, which nevertheless confirmed his priority as Bamian's Western rediscoverer. The inscription was still legible in the 1960's, but its fate, like that of the giant Buddhas, is uncertain given the unremitting carnage in Afghanistan.

Thus far, Moorcroft's expedition had progressed without serious loss of property and little loss of life. The caravan's saddlebags were stuffed with trading goods and morale was high. "If we arrive safely beyond the Afghan frontier," Trebeck wrote, "we shall have overcome the difficulties most to be apprehended." But having crossed the Hindu Kush into the deserts of Turkestan, they entered a chaotic borderland ruled by petty warlords. It was their misfortune to fall into the hands of the most predatory, Murad Beg, the Khan of Kunduz, whose 15,000 Uzbek horsemen roamed between Afghanistan and Bokhara.

Not many affluent *feringhees,* or foreigners, passed this way, and Murad Beg was unimpressed with the letters of welcome produced by Moorcroft that were signed by various princes, including Murad Beg himself. The Khan professed to believe that Moorcroft was a spy, that his saddlebags were stuffed with riches. He demanded an impossible sum for release of the caravan, detained its members in squalid quarters, and seemed prepared at any moment to plunder and kill. A despairing Trebeck wondered what reliance anybody could place "upon a wretch who murdered his uncle and brother, prostituted to a robber his sister and daughter, and sells into slavery women he has kept for a very considerable time in his seraglio."

Mir Izzat-Allah, the invaluable interpreter, ailing and demoralized, left the party for Delhi, only to die in Peshawar a year later. Others deserted. Outside the encampment, Uzbeks watched in ominous silence. More worrisome were Murad Beg's repeated declarations that he was considering murdering them all, interspersed with fresh ransom demands and mirthless laughter. Yet Moorcroft summoned his energy for an improbable feat. A newcomer who had joined the caravan in Kabul, Mir Wazir Ahmad, told him "that if I had the strength of body and mind sufficient to undertake and perform at one stretch in the disguise of an Oozbuck a journey of about one hundred and forty miles without being discovered, I might reach the residence of

Kasim Jan Khoja in Talikan and through personal application possibly succeed in interesting this individual in my favor."

Kasim Jan Khoja was a *pirzada,* or holy man, united by double marriage to Murad Beg, giving him clan authority over the robberking. To reach him, Moorcroft had to escape Uzbek horsemen keeping watch on prisoners, which he did by dressing himself "in the habiliments of an Oozbuck" and affecting a waddling gait. By prior arrangement, he met with two guides who provided a horse. Riding for two nights without rest, passing numerous Uzbeks without arousing suspicion, Moorcroft and his companions reached the pirzada. There he related all that had befallen his party, and the exorbitant ransom demanded by Murad Beg. Having come into this land by invitation, and having committed no offense, Moorcroft said he relied on Khoja's respect for the traditional decencies shown to strangers "to relieve me from a treatment without precedent and wholly undeserved."

Moorcroft touched the essential chord. The pirzada interceded successfully on behalf of the captive infidels, who after the payment to Murad Beg of 2,000 rupees were finally able to proceed across the Oxus to Bokhara.

IN FEBRUARY 1825, SURROUNDED BY A NOISILY CURIOUS CROWD, their number halved by desertion and their supplies depleted, Moorcroft and his companions stood before the gates of Bokhara. "After a long and laborious pilgrimage of more than five years," Trebeck wrote, with a trace of sectarian animus, "we had a right to hail the domes and minarets of Bokhara with as much pleasure, as had the wearied remnant of the first Crusaders the sight of the Christian banners waving triumphantly on the walls of the Holy City." This was not Christian Jerusalem: they were allowed to pass through Bokhara's thick earthen walls but as infidels could move only on foot past the thousand-year-old citadel, known as the Ark.

An ancient center of learning, famous for its many *medresses,* or seminaries, and boasting a library second only to that in Shiraz,

Bokhara was renowned for its canals, its gardens, its fine carpets and silks. Genghis Khan, self-described as the Scourge of God, destroyed its mosques and torched its libraries in 1219. A Bokhariot historian who witnessed the city's destruction summarized the Mongol assault in a sentence: "They came, they uprooted, they burned, they slew, they despoiled, they departed." Nevertheless the city rapidly recovered its position as trading center of Transoxiana, and less happily, as the region's principal slave market. Marco Polo's father Niccolò and his uncle Maffeo reputedly visited Bokhara in the mid-thirteenth century, and judged it "the noblest city" in the Persian kingdom. Its fame, enhanced by its inaccessibility, spread through Europe.

"Master Anthonie Jenkinson, from the City of London," a Tudor merchant, was the first Briton to give an account of Bokhara. Young and personable, Jenkinson befriended Ivan the Terrible in Moscow, then traveled eastward by ship and caravan, survived attacks by brigands, gained the goodwill of emirs and khans, and finally reached Bokhara in 1558. He hoped to secure a market for British goods, especially wool, but his charm and his courage notwithstanding, he found few takers in the Bokhara bazaar, whose merchants insisted they could buy woolens more cheaply in Persia.

A similar fate awaited William Moorcroft, whose caravan was laden with broadcloth and other English goods, laboriously trundled over mountains and deserts for sale in Bokhara. The profits were meant to purchase the sturdy horses of Central Asia. Early in his four-month stay, Moorcroft obtained a summons to meet Emir Khan Haydar at the palace. The ruler was seated in a small throne room, dressed drably, wore a loosely folded white turban, and frequently consulted a large book that lay open before him.

Moorcroft described the Emir as about forty-eight, with an olive complexion and an expression in which benevolence was mixed with distrust and hauteur: "He enquired after the health of the visitors, their names, ages, country and occupations; and from the long intervals between questions, it was suspected that a Secretary, concealed behind, was occupied in committing the dialogue to writing. He asked the name of the King of England, and was curious to know why he was called George the Fourth." The Emir remarked that reports had exaggerated the wealth of the Moorcroft caravan, to which the Briton replied that his journey was "merely an experimental one," and that he hoped larger-scale commercial intercourse would follow. Moorcroft presented his gifts, the prize being his two miniature brass cannons, and agreed to pay ten percent duty on all goods sold locally. But like Jenkinson, he was disappointed by the response in local bazaars, whose merchants, many of them Indians, claimed to prefer cheaper Russian imports. In fact Russian faces were by then so familiar in Bokhara that from the day of his arrival, urchins flocked around Moorcroft shouting "*Ooroos, Ooroos,*" the cry he first heard in Tibet thirteen years before.

Believing his fears of Russian infiltration vindicated, Moorcroft recruited a clandestine network, and instructed his "news-writers," each with a coded symbol, to monitor Russian moves. Yet Moorcroft bore no animus toward individual Russians, and at Bokhara's slave markets he purchased and freed three Russian captives, only to be ordered by the emir to sell them back. In other respects, Moorcroft and Trebeck were in official favor, as evidenced in their being allowed to ride on horseback within the city walls. The doctor again opened his surgery. His practice enabled him to write a detailed treatise on the intestinal worm prevalent in Bokhara, for which he correctly blamed the foul sewage system. Moorcroft crammed his journal with notes on everything from the cultivation of cannabis and the fine Bokharan cotton to methods of making the local white bread.

Nonetheless his failure to acquire the desired horses was troubling and frustrating. Moorcroft had turned fifty-eight in Bokhara, and talked wistfully of retiring, preferably to Ladakh, where he had been promised an estate. Still, to redeem his reputation he felt he had to return to India with outstanding breeding stock. "Before I leave Turkestan," he wrote to a friend, "I mean to penetrate the tract that contains perhaps the finest horses in the world, but with which all intercourse has been suspended during the last five years. The expedition is full of hazard, but *le jeu vaut bien la chandelle.*" He hoped to find "moderately good horses" across the Oxus in a region controlled by his erstwhile tormentor, the Uzbek warlord Murad Beg.

He was well aware that in retracing his way through a nest of robbers, "I may almost be said to tread on gunpowder."

In July 1825, Moorcroft and Trebeck headed south from Bokhara, leading a caravan of sixty horses, as many men, and a train of camels. To escape desert heat, the caravan moved forward at night and by early August, crossed the Oxus. On the river bank itself, he wrote warmly about the improvements possible in the region once it was rid of the tyranny of Murad Beg: "A body of European emigrants would speedily have allies in the natives of the neighboring districts tired of the confusion, oppression and tyranny under which they have long labored…"

It was his final entry. He was interrupted and put down his pen. In the succeeding days he tried negotiating a safe conduct with Murad Beg's representatives at Balkh. Erroneously called "the oldest city in the world," said to have been founded by Cain and Abel, Balkh has been identified as ancient Bactria, the Hellenic city where Alexander the Great took the Princess Roxanne as his wife. It flourished under Islam until its destruction by Genghis Khan. The ancient walls survived, but Balkh was little more than an inhabited ruin when Moorcroft arrived in search of horses. When none were found, he embarked on a three-week side trip to another walled town, Andkhoi, a hundred miles to the west, where there were said to be horse markets. He was accompanied by Mir Wazir Ahmad, who had helped him escape Murad Beg.

At Andkhoi, Moorcroft apparently fell ill and died on August 27, 1825, but the precise circumstances of his death were never determined. Some believe he was poisoned, and for years afterwards the legend persisted that he feigned death and secretly made his way to Ladakh or Tibet. What is certain is that at Andkhoi his horses and property were impounded, including the thirty volumes in his portable library. Mir Wazir Ahmad managed to take his body to Balkh, where he was buried in an unmarked grave outside the city walls. While arranging the burial and sending a letter reporting Moorcroft's death, the faithful Trebeck was stricken by fever, cause also uncertain. He died a few months later in the nearby town of Mazar, whose chief seized the caravan's remaining horses and goods, and sold into slavery all surviving members of the party. Ghulam

Hyder Khan, the tough old Afghan, escaped and turned up two years later in Bareilly, the sole survivor of Moorcroft's two great Asian expeditions.

In 1826, *The Asiatic Journal* published a note on "Mr. Moorcroft's Death" based on extracts of a letter in Persian from one Aga Hussein to Mullah Shakoor, dated November 4, 1825. It was the only significant memorial to be published. Apparently Moorcroft's superiors in Calcutta made no serious effort to determine the circumstances of his death and did little or nothing for the families of others in his expedition who died. Nor did the Company take any steps to secure the prompt publication of the voluminous journals Moorcroft had bequeathed, in order that "a plain record may be given for what I have done for the benefit of the public." It was doubtless the revenge of the nameless pen-scratchers in Calcutta. In 1830, the Royal Geographical Society acquired some of Moorcroft's papers, and published excerpts in the first issue of its new journal. An indifferently edited version of Moorcroft's and Trebeck's journals, omitting all the entries about Kabul and Bokhara, was eventually published in London in 1841, and to this day it remains their sole literary legacy.

A century later, in 1934, the gifted and idiosyncratic travel writer Robert Byron visited the Kunduz marshes where Moorcroft had died of a fever. In *The Road to Oxiana,* Byron said he was warned that his visit was tantamount to suicide. He tried to sleep in a walled mulberry grove next to a stagnant pool filled with fatal mosquitoes, only to find a wasps' nest and scuttling scorpions in the wall. "When I suggested removing to a neighboring garden, [local people] said that it was full of snakes." But like Moorcroft, Byron did not complain, and was entranced, as he made his way along the Kunduz River by the sprays of wildflowers, the steeply sloping saddles and escarpments of waving grass leading upwards to the main Hindu Kush, all of which, he wrote, "made us long to be on horses." Moorcroft would have understood. *Le jeu vaut bien la chandelle.*

CHAPTER THREE

The Road to Kabul

THE RAW AND RUGGED LANDSCAPE OF AFGHANISTAN LOOMS
in the background. The earth, the hills, and the city walls of Jalalabad are dun-colored, reminding us that *khaki* derives from the Persian
and Hindustani words for dust. Pull focus to the foreground, and we
see a panting horse bearing a wounded rider. He leans backwards, gripping his saddle. His head is turned, his eyes gaze sightlessly. His whole
being expresses exhaustion, shock, defeat. The painting, titled *The Remnants of the Army*, depicts Dr. William Brydon, said to be the sole British
survivor of the Kabul garrison after its catastrophic retreat from Kabul
in 1842. From the Battle of Hastings to Dunkirk, the British have taken
a certain gritty satisfaction in recalling military disasters, and no disaster
was more complete, more astonishing, and, one may fairly add, more
warranted, than the British defeat in the First Afghan War.

Remnants was among the famous paintings of its time, as familiar to
Victorians as *Custer's Last Fight* was to generations of Americans. It
was the work of Lady Butler, née Elizabeth Thompson, the painter
laureate of imperial warfare. Soldiers prized Lady Butler's accuracy in
depicting uniforms and horses, and Queen Victoria herself bought

The Roll Call, which was the sensation at the Royal Academy Summer Exhibition in 1874. The very titles of Lady Butler's military canvases express (in Jan Morris's phrase) the British mystique of splendor in misfortune: *Steady the Drums and Fifes, The Defence of Rorke's Drift,* and *Floreat Etona,* the last celebrating the front-line gallantry of a young subaltern. Yet like the Victorian era itself, Lady Butler's life was scarcely as one-dimensional as its imagery. Her husband was Lieutenant General Sir William Francis Butler, an Anglo-Irish Catholic whose career was the stuff of "Boy's Own" fiction. He was posted first in Burma, Madras, and the Channel Islands, where he befriended the exiled Victor Hugo; then in Canada, where he took part in campaigns against Red River rebels and Irish Fenian revolutionaries, earning decorations; he served next in the Ashanti Wars in West Africa and the Zulu Wars in South Africa, gaining a knighthood; then in the vain and desperate expedition to save General Gordon in the Sudan. Yet early on Butler came to sympathize with those he fought. He questioned the need and rightness of imperial wars, and wound up a strong supporter of Irish Home Rule. The relief expedition in 1884 to save Gordon, he once wrote, was "the very first war during the Victorian era in which the object was entirely noble and worthy."

Only in poetry did soldiers refrain from asking the reason why. In life, those in the field were often baffled and angry at decisions taken by distant political superiors. So it was with the First Afghan War, a conflict, moreover, whose outcome was foreseen by an intuitive double of General Butler's, Sir Charles Theophilus Metcalfe. We have met him before, as the political agent who championed Moorcroft.

If Lady Butler had painted a group portrait of the splendid sahibs who founded the Indian Empire, Charles Metcalfe would stick out as the least soldierly. He was chubby, ungainly, bookish, a poor horseman and indifferent hunter. He was a melancholic, for whom being "a good fellow" was a task to be mastered. But in that he succeeded. One of his chiefs, Lord Minto, fondly described him as "the ugliest and most agreeable clever person" in all Europe or Asia. Unlike other founders of British India—Malcolm, Munro, and Mountstuart Elphinstone, who were Scots—he was English, the son of a major in the Bengal Army and later a director of the East India Company. In

1835, the younger Metcalfe was named provisional Governor-General, and his friends in Calcutta hoped that, for once, an able and popular Company alumnus would be rewarded with the supreme post.

It was not to be. What weighed against Metcalfe was the British Cabinet's belief that the highest office in India should go to an English lord. How better to bring fresh ideas and a home-country perspective to Calcutta? Besides, as the President of the India Board of Control asserted with enthusiasm on the occasion of appointing just such a paragon (Lord Cornwallis, known to Americans for surrendering at Yorktown): "Here there was no broken fortune to be mended! here there was no avarice to be gratified! here there was no beggarly mushroom kindred to be provided for! no crew of hungry followers gaping to be gorged!"

In Metcalfe's case, there was something else: his incorrigible independence. This trait became evident soon after his arrival in India on January 1, 1801, fresh from his classical education in England at Eton. He was the first student admitted to the Company's new College at Fort William in Calcutta. There its servants were trained in the languages of India and the habits of command, both of which Metcalfe precociously acquired. But this did not impress General Gerard Lake, to whom he was initially posted as Political Assistant during the Third Maratha War. Lake was famous for his advice "Damn your writing; mind your fighting," which he followed in battling the Marathas, a confederacy of Hindu princes challenging the British for succession to Mughal supremacy. When the Maratha chieftain Holkar occupied Digh, a fortress west of Muttra, Lake's army stormed the citadel on Christmas Eve, 1804, and after its fall, Holkar sued for peace.

The plump and bookish Metcalfe volunteered to join the storming at Digh, and even better was mentioned in dispatches as "one of the first in the breach." A delighted Lake dubbed him his "little stormer," and thereafter no toast or tribute to Metcalfe was complete without resurrecting the phrase.

At the time of the assault on Digh, the East India Company was among a cluster of powers vying for mastery of the subcontinent. When Metcalfe left India thirty years later, the Company was unquestionably paramount. South of the Indus, its only independent rival of consequence was Ranjit Singh's Sikh kingdom. British merchant adventurers were now civil servants, and the Company was a Government despite its name. As the Company's role changed, so did its attitude toward its native subjects. As carefully phrased by Sir Penderel Moon in *The British Conquest and Dominion of India* (1990), "There developed a greater sense of responsibility towards the millions of Indians over whom the Company now ruled, but also a greater sense of superiority to them."

This air of superiority, tinged with disdain, was not shared by Metcalfe. He relished the sophistication of India's high cultures. He had two sons (acknowledged) by an Indian mistress and lamented the lack of social intercourse between rulers and the ruled. He believed in minimal interference with Indian customs and beliefs, though he used his powers as Resident in Delhi to abolish slavery, capital punishment, and suttee, the ritual in which widows cast themselves on their deceased husband's pyre. But he did this out of respect for reason and universal human rights, and not with the evangelical zeal of a missionary. "Our dominion of India is by conquest," he was at pains to point out. "It is naturally disgusting to the inhabitants and can only be maintained by military force. It is our positive duty to render them justice, to respect and protect their rights, and to study their happiness. By the performance of this duty, we may allay and keep dormant their innate disaffection."

Metcalfe also evidenced a talent for intrigue. As an envoy to Ranjit Singh's court, he outwitted adversaries by recruiting a spy network that reached from stables to the harem. During the Gurkha wars, he put together (with the aid of Moorcroft, among others) a cross-border undercover team whose work cleared the way for a British offensive, but as the years passed, he changed his mind about covert operations. In 1831, as senior adviser to the Governor-General, Metcalfe opposed sending one of his own protégés, Alexander Burnes, to lead a spying mission along the Indus on the pretext of bringing five gift horses and a gilded state carriage to Ranjit Singh in Lahore. This flimsy subterfuge, Metcalfe protested, was "unworthy of our Government." If British agents were caught, they might meet with insult, provoking a war. The Company would not dream of attempting such a fraud on an equal European power, he said, and its double standard in dealing with native states was "the greatest blot in the character of our Indian policy." The British talked piously of noninterference, but when British interests were at stake, Metcalfe admonished, "we become impatient and overbearing . . . Submission or war is the alternative which the other party has to choose."

His protests were overruled, and Burnes's spying mission went forward. It is difficult to believe his dissent was welcome. Fittingly if unfairly, his hopes for the Governor-Generalship finally dissolved in an argument over free speech.

OF BRITISH TRADITIONS THE COMPANY IMPLANTED IN INDIA, none proved more fruitful than the principles of free speech and the free press. Yet as with much else blown eastward, this outcome was adventitious. The first seed took root in the 1770's at a Calcutta jail, where a tempestuous Irish adventurer named James Augustus Hicky was imprisoned as a debtor. During his confinement, he read a treatise on printing, and so instructed, whittled a font of type good enough to print handbills. Hicky then managed to retain a lawyer, the almost identically named but unrelated Irish rake and author William Hickey, who applied to a Calcutta court for a writ of habeas corpus. While his case was being argued, Hicky paid the necessary rupees to import proper printing equipment from England, since, as his lawyer said, "it occurred to Hicky that great benefit might arise from setting on foot a public newspaper, nothing of that kind having appeared." Once freed by the court, Hicky in 1780 founded *The Bengal Gazette*. It was a novelty, "every person read it" (writes William Hickey in his memoirs), and its popularity grew since its editor had a "low wit" and "a happy knack at applying appropriate nicknames and relating satirical anecdotes." Hicky, alas, overdid it, and the *Gazette* became "the channel of personal invective and the most scurrilous abuse of individuals of all ranks, high and low, rich and poor." His victims brought suit, and won crushing libel judgments against the editor, whose two-year-old paper was then suppressed by the Governor-General, Warren Hastings.

Nonetheless, the seed was planted, and Calcutta soon abounded in journals of all sorts, the majority vociferously critical of the Government. Nearly all were English-language journals, but as early as the 1820's, several appeared in Bengali. So vexed were officials by newspaper heckling that in 1823 two regulations were issued to gag the press, the severest penalty being deportation. Leading the fight against the gag orders were five eminent Bengalis (including Dwarkanath Tagore, an ancestor of the Nobel laureate) who could not be deported, and their arguments were robustly taken up by English-language newspapers. The clamor reached a crescendo during Metcalfe's term as provisional Governor-General, and in January 1835, in response to a petition protesting the press regulations, he voided "the truculent law." As Metcalfe saw it, "If India could only be preserved as part of the British Empire by keeping its inhabitants in a state of ignorance, our domination would be a curse...and ought to cease."

In this, Metcalfe had the eloquent and influential support of the historian Thomas Babington Macaulay, who lived and worked as a civil servant in India from 1834 to 1838. In a landmark minute submitted to the Company in May 1835, Macaulay called India "perhaps the only country in the world where the press is free while the Government is despotic." In other despotic states, the historian contended, writers were afraid to criticize public measures with severity: "If the emperor of Russia puts forth an ukase, no Russian writes about it except to defend it." In India, where the Company also ruled by ukase, there was no Parliament to serve as a check, and so it was the more imperative to expose its decisions to unfettered criticism.

Metcalfe and Macaulay carried the day, and freedom was restored at first to the English-language press and soon thereafter to the proliferating vernacular papers. Except for infrequent and bitterly contested emergency regulations, the liberation was permanent. Still, the agitated arguments in London over Metcalfe's order did not help his candidacy for a full term as Governor-General. He had become too "controversial." But if Metcalfe were eliminated, who was to be

"given India"? An abrupt spin of the British political wheel produced an interesting answer.

FOR A BRIEF SEASON, IN 1834–35, SIR ROBERT PEEL'S TORIES
formed a Government, and it persuaded the Company's Court of
Directors to approve an experienced diplomat, recently *en poste* in St.
Petersburg, as Governor-General. Lord Heytesbury was feted at a
farewell dinner and was almost shipboard when the Tory Ministry
fell, returning the Whigs to power under Lord Melbourne. After re-
scinding the appointment in September 1835, Melbourne prevailed
on the nettled directors to accept a fresh nominee: George Eden, the
second Baron Auckland, a Whig who had already done well as President of the Board of Trade and as First Lord of the Admiralty. Still a
bachelor at fifty, with two unmarried sisters, Emily and Fanny, Lord
Auckland was affable, handsome as a Roman bust, and innocent of
any knowledge of India.

The catalytic agent was probably Emily, known for her caustic wit
and chiseled features, still a beauty at thirty-five. For several years she
was involved in a flirtatious pas de deux with the widowed Melbourne. By all accounts it was only a flirtation, and Miss Emily
claimed, implausibly, that Lord M. "frightens me, and bewilders me,
and he swears too much." She now decided to accompany Auckland
to India, and asked the Prime Minister for a book from his library as
a parting gift. Embarking on the *Jupiter* that September with her
brother, younger sister Fanny, nephew William Osborne, and their
pet dog Chance, Emily had in hand an inscribed copy of Milton,
whose *Paradise Lost* in its opening stanza laments "the loss of *Eden*."
For Emily, too, India was to be a form of banishment from the demi-
paradise of great country houses and cultivated repartee to a distant
country devoid of Society and altogether too HOT ("I do not know
how to spell it large enough," she complained). Her comments on
the longueurs and delights of British India were set forth in a hundred lapidary letters home later to be repolished and collected in a
minor Victorian classic, *Up the Country* (1866). Fanny, too, wrote vo-

luminously about their six years in the East, and like Emily, illustrated her journals with vivid sketches of scenery and people. We thus have two intimate views from the heights of the dramatic events that ensued in India.

The first auguries were promising. In Calcutta, Metcalfe swallowed his disappointment and in February 1836 convivially welcomed the new Governor-General, with whom he had attended Eton. Faithful to his instructions from the Court of Directors, Auckland said his first concern was to promote education and improve the administration of justice. As regards foreign policy, he assured an anxious Metcalfe that nothing would be more foolish than to interfere in Sikh or Afghan affairs.

Among the rulers writing to congratulate the Governor-General was Afghanistan's Dost Mohammed. He took the occasion to appeal to Auckland for help in recovering Peshawar, an Afghan possession that had recently fallen to Ranjit Singh. Assailing "the reckless and misguided Sikhs and their breach of treaty," the Emir requested British advice on what to do. Lord Auckland loftily replied, "My friend, you are aware that it is not the practice of the British Government to interfere with the affairs of other independent states."

No doubt the sentiment was sincere. Auckland was genuinely shocked when a European jury acquitted a man named Hughes who hoisted on a gibbet several workmen he believed were robbing him and set fire to bales of straw below, killing one Indian. "I wonder how we are allowed to keep this country a week," the Governor-General expostulated. Exuding goodwill and compassion, Auckland was likewise upset when his triumphal and leisurely progress through the Upper Provinces, commencing at Calcutta in October 1837 and involving an Imperial cavalcade of 12,000 soldiers and servants, wives and children, 850 camels, 140 elephants, and hundreds of horses and bullocks, in all costing 70,000 rupees a month, inconveniently coincided with a terrible famine that claimed an estimated 800,000 lives. "You cannot conceive the horrible sights we see," Emily Eden wrote, "particularly children; perfect skeletons in many cases, their bones through their skin, without a rag of clothing, and utterly unlike human beings. Our camp luckily does more good than harm…We began yesterday giving food away in the evening."

India's recurrent famines were related to two distinct monsoons, one sweeping through the Bay of Bengal and across Calcutta, the other drenching the southwest coast, which normally cross paths in northern India. If they fail to meet, farms are blighted until the following year; if the monsoon fails twice, the result is famine. No Briton has described the monsoon better than Mounstuart Elphinstone, once the Governor of Bombay: "Its approach is announced by vast masses of clouds that rise from the Indian Ocean, and advance toward the north-east, gathering and thickening as they approach the land." The monsoon generally begins with "violent blasts of rain which are succeeded by floods of rain. For some hours lightning is seen almost without intermission," sometimes illuminating the whole sky, at other times distant hills, and during all this time the thunder never ceases to roll. Before the storm, fields are parched, the atmosphere charged with dust, the winds a hot furnace. When the storm is over "the whole earth is covered with a sudden but luxuriant verdure; the rivers are full and tranquil; and the sky is varied and embellished with clouds."

For centuries all India was hostage to this awesome phenomenon. Only with the advent of railroads in the mid-nineteenth century, which made it possible to rush grains to stricken areas, were the effects of famine ameliorated.

THE EDENS ALWAYS DID THE DECENT MINIMUM, BUT IT WOULD stretch the record to say they did more. Lord Auckland was not truly interested in things Indian. Writing home in 1837, Emily was blunter: "As to India, looking at it dispassionately and without exaggerating its grievances for fun, I really think I hate it more now than at first." Still, her sharpest words were directed at the shallow and obsequious Europeans, especially the women whose looks evaporated in a country "where everybody looks more than fifty." She sensed and deplored the memsahibs' isolation from everyday realities of Indian life, notably in Simla, the Himalayan hill town that, thanks to its salubrious climate, was just becoming the summer capital of the

British Raj. "Like meat we keep better here," as Emily pithily put it. There in 1838, the accession of Victoria as the new Sovereign was celebrated in a Queen's Ball at which 105 Europeans dined on salmon from Scotland and sardines from the Mediterranean, while a band played airs from *I Puritani*. Surrounding the guests were 3,000 native mountaineers wrapped in hill blankets, who prostrated themselves whenever a European was nearby. "I sometimes wonder," marveled Miss Eden, "they do not cut all our heads off and say nothing about it."

Writing of this very period, the noted military historian Sir John Kaye described Simla as "that pleasant hill Sanatorium" where Governors-General, "surrounded by irresponsible advisers, settle the destinies of empires without the aid of their legitimate fellow-counselors." Simla, Kaye acidly remarked, had been the cradle of more political insanity "than any place within the limits of Hindustan."

Appropriately, it was at Simla that Auckland formalized the great initiative with which his name is indissolubly joined. As Governor-General, he had to walk a narrow line on administrative and domestic matters, but foreign policy was something else. In that realm, he could be a potentate treating with other potentates; he could make and break nations, as did his predecessors. Since it took five months for dispatches to arrive from London, Auckland had considerable scope for his initiatives—the more so since he had different masters, with conflicting priorities. The Company's Court of Directors was concerned with commerce and stability, and shunned foreign adventures. But plenary authority was exercised by the Cabinet's Board of Control on Indian Affairs, and by the Foreign Office, whose senior ministers viewed India as a capital chess piece in the game of nations.

During the 1830's, British diplomats and strategists began to perceive a new global adversary, the Russian Empire, whose armies and agents seemed almost as threatening as those of the Tsar's former ally, Napoleon. After conquering the Caucasus, Russian armies were pushing eastward and Russian operatives were probing the desert grasslands from Oxiana to Chinese Tartary. Russia's eventual goal was believed to be India, which could be invaded through Afghanistan or Persia. Nobody took the Russian menace more seriously than Melbourne's Foreign Secretary, Lord Palmerston, who relished crusades and was prone to patriotic hyperbole. Afghanistan and Persia were, in Palmerston's eyes, the defensive bulwarks of India. He feared that a weak, corrupt Persia was already half in the Tsar's pocket. Hence his concern in 1837 when Persian armies attempted to conquer Herat, an Afghan city routinely described in press accounts as the "gateway to India." For his part, Lord Auckland began to refer to Herat as "the western frontier of India" although Herat was a thousand miles from the Indus River.

Melbourne was skeptical about Palmerston's combative diplomacy but did not interfere with a Foreign Secretary who chanced to be his brother-in-law, having recently married the Prime Minister's widowed sister. In the Cabinet, Palmerston found an important ally in John Cam Hobhouse, once Lord Byron's chum and now President of the India Board of Control, who in urgent terms conveyed to Calcutta the fears in London about Russian intrigues in Asia. So alerted, the normally cautious Auckland abandoned his earlier views and prepared to take action. In this he was swayed by an inner circle of advisers in Simla, the most influential being Sir John Macnaghten, Secretary of the Political and Secret Department and a master of Asian languages. Emily Eden wearied of the Secretary's lectures, slyly observing that he "speaks Persian rather more fluently than English; Arabic better than Persian; but, for familiar conversation, rather prefers Sanscrit."

Macnaghten had small experience with the give-and-take of diplomacy and politics. He had lived too long in a world of agents' reports and confidential dossiers. These convinced him that Herat was about to fall as a result of Russian intervention in behalf of Persia, and that Tsarist agents were wooing the susceptible Afghan ruler, Dost Mohammed. Armed with names, dates, and dire details, Macnaghten then persuaded a worried Lord Auckland that a dramatic countermove was imperative. Specifically, in alliance with Ranjit Singh's Sikhs, Britain could at little risk and cost unseat Dost Mohammed and reinstate his deposed predecessor, Shah Shuja, who for thirty years had been living in British territories as a Company pensioner.

This extraordinary project was announced to the world in the sonorous cadences of the Simla Manifesto, dated October 1, 1838. It accused Dost Mohammed of "schemes of aggrandizement" (that is, trying to recapture formerly Afghan Peshawar from the Sikhs, who had just conquered it) and of giving "undisguised support to the Persian designs in Afghanistan." Although not mentioned by name in the Manifesto, Russia was condemned indirectly in its reference to Persia's assault on Herat. But the Simla Manifesto was not meant to persuade. It was a call to arms by a Governor-General who believed that an unprovoked invasion of Afghanistan would somehow impart luster to the reign of Britannia's new Queen and foil the knavish designs of the Russian Tsar. In any event, Auckland had at last made a big decision, and once dear "G." was set on a course, as his sister put it, it was impossible "to get out of his Lordship's head what had been put into it." We are permitted to imagine him at Simla, indulging an after-dinner cigar on the verandah of Auckland House, gazing meditatively at the deodar-decked Himalayas, persuading himself he was walking with Destiny. In reality, he had sentenced tens of thousands to death in a pointless and dishonorable war.

ONLY A WILLING SUSPENSION OF DISBELIEF CAN EXPLAIN WHAT came to be called the First Afghan War. As originally envisioned, the operation was based on four assumptions: that Ranjit Singh's Sikhs would do most of the fighting; that Afghan Herat was about to fall to Persia; that Dost Mohammed was little more than a Russian vassal; and finally, that Afghans would tolerate, indeed even welcome, a British puppet in his place. Before a single British soldier crossed the frontier, it was apparent that these assumptions were all mistaken or misguided. Nevertheless, the whole cumbersome enterprise lurched forward, and like an overloaded cart careering downhill.

That Ranjit Singh would be a troublesome ally became evident in June 1838, months before the Simla Manifesto, when John Macnaghten left his bureaucratic warren to negotiate a treaty with the Sikh ruler. The British wanted the Sikhs to furnish the manpower needed to restore the deposed Shah Shuja to the Afghan throne. In return, Shah Shuja was to renounce all claims to Afghan territories, especially Peshawar, that had been seized by the Sikhs. As a further bonus, the British offered to pay the costs of the expeditionary force and to provide officers. But the "Lion of Lahore" knew this was an offer he could safely refuse. He insisted on a guarantee that the British Indian Army would accompany his soldiers, and that Shah Shuja, once enthroned, would pay a generous annual subsidy to the Sikh kingdom. Macnaghten yielded on all points, and only then informed Shah Shuja of the Tripartite Treaty he was expected to sign. The former Afghan king was angry and humiliated. He resented paying any tribute to the Sikhs, whom the Afghans despised; he demanded offsetting payments from independent emirs in the Sind; and he insisted—this was most important—on leading his own army into Kabul so as not to appear a groveling puppet. Macnaghten agreed to the offsetting payments and promised to provide officers for Shah Shuja's own army—only to encounter fresh objections from General Sir Henry Fane, Commander-in-Chief of the British Indian Army. If Britain was to be directly involved, the general contended, it should not be a piecemeal but a full-dress operation worthy of the task.

Such was the genesis of what was grandly called the Army of the Indus, comprising 9,500 men from the Bengal and Bombay armies, about 6,000 mostly Hindu troops under Shah Shuja, some 38,000 camp followers, plus 30,000 camels and enough sheep and cattle for ten weeks' meals. Each regiment had 600 stretcher-bearers, along with cooks, tailors, cobblers, water-carriers, fiddlers, nautch dancers, and fortune-tellers to cater to the troops, who also brought along their wives, parents, children, aunts, and uncles. General Fane in fact had asked for an even bigger force, and when rebuffed, presciently bowed out, transferring overall command to General Sir John Keane, Commander-in-Chief of the Bombay Army. The skirling bagpipes and brass bands could be heard for miles, and a cloud of dust darkened the skies as this human tide inched toward Afghanistan.

The meeting near Ferozepore between Ranjit Singh and Auckland—complete with fireworks and balls, suppers and dancing girls, presents and counter-presents—"began to assume some of the glory of Henry VIII and Francis I on the Field of the Cloth of Gold," wrote a later historian. The cagey Sikh was pleased to salute the expeditionary army at a grand ceremonial on the Sutlej River, the boundary between his state and British India. But the Maharajah was not disposed to let this thundering herd march through his own territories. To oblige him, a detour was devised. The Bengal Army would march circuitously to Afghanistan from Sind through Baluchistan to the Bolan Pass, where it would join the Bombay Army and become the Army of the Indus, while Ranjit Singh's smaller force took the direct route from Peshawar and the Khyber Pass to Kabul. Given these concessions, it is hardly to be wondered that Ranjit Singh was elated and did not seem to mind even when his elephants collided with Lord Auckland's, pitching the Sikh monarch unceremoniously to the ground. Still, it must have somehow occurred to Auckland that this might be an omen, that he had surrendered too much to an aging monarch whose power was rapidly seeping away.

Emily Eden's account of the December 1838 visit was vivid and prophetic. "He is exactly like an old mouse," she said of her first glimpse of the Maharajah, "with grey whiskers and one eye." Ranjit Singh was dressed in plain red silks, and seated next to him was Heera Singh, "a very handsome boy," who as Ranjit's favorite, "was loaded with emeralds and pearls." During the ensuing parades, military salutes, banquets, inspection of troops and treasures (including the "Mountain of Light," or Koh-i-noor, diamond), and potlatching of gifts, Miss Eden also noted Ranjit Singh's fragility and profligate habits; she noted too the careless frivolity of the old ruler's son and presumed heir, Kurruck Singh. When Ranjit Singh died, she foresaw, "this great kingdom, which he has raked together, will probably fall to pieces again." On Christmas Eve, he was left speechless by a stroke; six months later, he was dead. A turbulent scramble for power followed, and the principal rock on which Lord Auckland's Afghan strategy rested was to crumble.

However profligate and autocratic, Ranjit Singh had imposed a rough unity on diverse peoples and cultures. Afghanistan by contrast was less a nation than a congeries of tribes and clans rooted in city-states with fluid boundaries and loyalties, whose rulers were figuratively and literally at each others' throats. It was like England during the War of the Roses, a realm where kings reigned by sufferance and where alliances were determined by dynastic marriages or fiercely eloquent diatribes by rival nobles. There were added complications. Afghan polygamy meant large ruling families, so the usual struggles for supremacy were literally fratricidal (Dost Mohammed, the incumbent ruler, had seventy-two brothers or half-brothers). Besides, Afghans spoke different, mutually unintelligible languages, and though nearly all were Muslims, a Persian-speaking Shiite minority lived uneasily alongside a Pushtun-speaking Sunni majority.

The pervading mushiness was illustrated by the ongoing struggle for Herat. Ancient, populous, and prosperous, Herat had been devastated by Mongols and Turkmens before becoming a seat of Afghan government in the eighteenth century. It was sometimes subordinate to Kabul, sometimes independent. Herat was famed for its great earthen walls with their burnt-brick ramparts, which sheltered 100,000 people, and for its great mosque adorned with gleaming tiles and elegant minarets.

Although nominally Afghan, Herat was coveted by Persia because its inhabitants for the most part were (and are) Persian-speaking Shiites. A new Persian ruler, Mohammed Shah, ascended the Peacock Throne in 1834, and he was notably more friendly to the Russians than the British, and with reason. His long-reigning predecessor had signed a mutual defense treaty with the British, who promised to help Persia with troops or money against any European aggressor if the Shah undertook to prevent European armies from entering Persia. These terms were spelled out in a definitive 1814 agreement in which Britain sought to protect India from French and/or Russian attack. Yet in 1826, when Russian armies grabbed Persian territory in the Caucasus, the British, short of funds, ignored their earlier promise, claiming the treaty language was ambiguous. Stung by Persia's defeats, and amid considerable muttering about *Albion Perfide,* the new Shah decided to attempt some grabbing himself. In 1837, he turned to none other than the Russians for help in annexing Herat to make up for losses in the Caucasus to the same Russians.

Hence the consternation in London when Russian officers and French engineers turned up in Tehran to help as "advisers." A high-level British diplomat rushed to Persia to protest this assistance, but it was Persia's turn to cite ambiguous treaty language. In the Shah's view, the Russians and the French were not foreign interlopers but invited guests. In St. Petersburg, the Tsar's Foreign Minister, Count Nesselrode, on alternate weeks either denied or minimized the Russian presence. Unappeased, the British feared that a Russian-aided Persian Army would bring the Bear (by now a cartoon cliché) to the very "threshold" of India. Such was the context as the Shah mustered his army at Sharud and advanced through Khorasan to the walls of Herat. In November 1837, tens of thousands of Persian troops, aided by Russian officers, commenced their siege.

Enter at this point an American, a British intelligence officer posing as a native horse dealer, and a *faux* American with great gifts as a spy and antiquarian scholar.

THE AMERICAN WAS JOSIAH HARLAN, A SOLDIER OF FORTUNE notwithstanding his Quaker origins in Pennsylvania. He was born in 1799 in Newlin Township, Chester County. He sailed east in quest of adventure in 1823, entered the Company's service, and though lacking medical training, signed on as an assistant surgeon with the Bengal Artillery, then bound for a punitive war in Burma. In 1826, when the fighting was over, Josiah Harlan resigned his commission and moved on to Ludhiana in northern India. It was here that Shah Shuja, the deposed Afghan monarch, maintained his court in exile. After joining the royal circle, the young Pennsylvanian disguised himself as a dervish, so his memoirs relate, and undertook a spying mission to Kabul. He returned to report that Dost Mohammed was momentarily too well entrenched to be overthrown, and Shah Shuja, grateful for his efforts, bestowed on Harlan the titles of "King's Nearest Friend" and "Companion of the Imperial Stirrup." Harlan then proceeded to Lahore and the court of Ranjit Singh, whom he served as a mercenary and bagman, using Sikh gold to speed the conquest of Peshawar in 1834. The American for obscure reasons quarreled and broke with Ranjit Singh, and turned up in Kabul a year later as aide-de-camp to the Sikh monarch's archrival, Dost Mohammed Khan.

Harlan offers us this graphic sketch of the Afghan Emir, who was then forty-nine and in vigorous health:

> When he stands erect his height is six feet, but there is a slight stoop in the neck arising from a rounded contour of the shoulders…The outline of his face is Roman. Having a curved jaw, a low retreating forehead, hair of the head shaven, and the turban worn far back, gives an appearance of elevation to the frontal region…The nose is aquiline, high, and rather long, and finished with beautiful delicacy; the brow open, arched, and penciled; his eyes are hazel-gray, not large, and of elephantine expression; the mouth large and vulgar, and full of bad teeth…The shape of the face is oval, rather broad across the cheeks, and the chin covered with a full, strong beard, originally black, now mixed with gray hairs. This appendage is dyed once a week, that is on Thursday morning in process of general ablution in *hummaun* or warm bath…

Most striking to Harlan was his chief's extreme modesty and politeness, a quality known as *shirrun i huzzoor,* which mixed incongruously with a sometimes boisterous manner, his rapacity for gold, and his vanity concerning his oratorical talents. He had "perfect knowledge" of the people he led, and doubted every motive except self-interest. He was, according to Harlan, an "exquisite dissembler" capable of "the most revolting cruelty" and was until the age of thirty addicted to drunkenness. Surrounded by revelers and maddened "by the maniac draught of the frantic bowl," the younger Dost and his companions caroused and drank with prostitutes, singers, and fiddlers, becoming "promiscuous actors in the wild, voluptuous, licentious scene of shameless bacchanals." (One senses here a certain prim Quaker teetotalism in Harlan's reminiscences.)

Dost Mohammed was sufficiently impressed by Harlan to make him second in command of a punitive expedition in 1838 against Murad Beg, the same prince of Kunduz who sadistically tormented William Moorcroft's party some years before. Harlan's army, consisting of 1,400 cavalry, 1,100 infantry, 2,000 horses, and 400 camels, crossed the Hindu Kush and followed the path of Alexander through the province of Balkh. On the highest pass, that of Khazar, some 12,500 feet above sea level, Harlan unfurled the American flag, and his troops fired a twenty-six-gun salute. He leaves us a memorable snapshot of the moment when "the star spangled banner gracefully waved amid the icy peaks and soilless rugged rocks of a sterile region, seemingly sacred to the solitude of an undisturbed eternity." The army then descended past "glaciers and silent dells, and frowning rocks blackened by age," defying the pelting of snow and rain as "these phenomena alternately and capriciously coquetted with our ever changing climate."

Having attended to the punishment of Murad Beg, the expedition returned to Kabul in 1839 to learn that the Government of India was sending an army to restore Shah Shuja to the Afghan throne. Dost Mohammed named Harlan as defending commander-in-chief. The task proved hopeless when the Dost's subjects heard reports of the huge size of the advancing army and deserted their leader en masse because "a fallen prince has not even a faithful slave." Harlan made his way back to Philadelphia in 1841, where a year later he published *A Memoir of India and Avghanistaun* [sic], *with Observations on the Present Exciting Prospects of Those Countries.* Dost Mohammed's former commander-in-chief was suitably lionized and styled himself General; he married, acquired a farm, and tried to promote the use of camels by the U.S. Army. When the Civil War broke out, he raised a regiment known as Harlan's Light Cavalry, and a few years later urged Congress to provide $10,000 for a Central Asian expedition, which he proposed to lead, to acquire fruits and wine grapes. When that plan failed, he migrated to San Francisco, where he apparently practiced medicine until his death in 1871. He is today almost wholly forgotten in the country whose flag he so proudly unfurled in the Hindu Kush.

SIR HENRY LAWRENCE, HIMSELF EXCEPTIONALLY COOL AND brave, once wrote of Major Eldred Pottinger that no British man-at-arms in India had shown greater and earlier promise. "Yet, hero as he was, you might have sat for weeks beside him and not have discovered that he had seen a shot fired." Reticence was Pottinger's hallmark, and it enabled him to move with tactful stealth in the most dangerous settings. Born in 1811 of Ulster Irish parents, young Eldred was trained as a cadet in England and gazetted as a second lieutenant in the Bombay Artillery on his arrival in India in 1827. India abounded in Pottingers, and Eldred's uncle Henry was a well-connected political officer in the Province of Cutch, and very soon the nephew—who proved adept at languages—became a "political" too (the term for an officer seconded to the Political Department).

In 1837, by now fluent in Persian and Pushtu and all of twenty-six, Eldred Pottinger, disguised as a horse dealer, took the road for an intelligence foray to Kabul by way of Shikapur and Peshawar. His camouflage succeeded in Kabul, but on returning he fell into the hands of the Uzbek robber-king Murad Beg. His captors were suspicious of his pale skin, his lapses in Muslim usage, and the papers and books in his bags. In his best colloquial Persian, Pottinger explained he was a recent convert from "the land of many mountains" south of Hindustan where people were fair. The Uzbeks debated his fate, and apparently baffled, let him go. It was a useful, if frightening, initiation.

In August 1837, Pottinger on his own initiative and still posing as a horse dealer, turned up in Herat as it braced for the Persian attack. After settling in a discreet abode and mindful of his recent ordeal, he decided to make his identity known to Herat's cold-eyed vizier, Yar Mohammed Khan. The vizier asked Pottinger to sit beside him and listened intently as the officer asserted that he had no official authority but was willing to help if asked by the Heratis. The audience went well, and knowing that gifts were obligatory, Pottinger (as he noted in his journal) "presented my detonating pistols, which were the only thing I had worth giving." A few days later, the young officer was summoned to a friendly meeting with Herat's ruler, Shah Kamrun, and Pottinger was therafter able to go everywhere boldly.

By November, Herat was encircled by a Persian force, 30,000 strong. Food supplies sank perilously as the besiegers burned orchards and farms, and blockaded the city's five gates. The din of artillery was continuous. Rocket batteries fired wildly. Mortars lobbed shells of rock or chunks of marble taken from tombs. As the defenders recovered their nerve, they turned to Pottinger for technical and tactical advice. He supervised the repair of the city walls and the sowing of mines; most important, he trained cavalry for surprise sorties— though he was sickened by the reciprocal mutilation of bodies, especially the grisly custom of flaunting enemy heads as trophies.

Pottinger's standing was such that in January 1838, he was asked by Shah Kamran to serve as a Herat's envoy to the Persian camp. When the astonished Persians discovered he was British, they crowded around Pottinger shouting, *"Afreen! Afreen! Khoosh Amudyd; Anglish humiseh Dostani Shah-in-Shah."* (Bravo! Bravo! Welcome. The English were always friends of the King of Kings.) Greeted by the Russian general commanding that sector, Pottinger was civilly invited to partake of tea and *kallyans* (pipes), before being taken to the Persian vizier. Herat's envoy explained that he was an English traveler, that he was bearing a message from Shah Kamran to Mohammed Shah, and that he also had letters from the Government of India for Colonel Charles Stoddart, whom Pottinger understood was a military observer accompanying the besiegers: "I further said I wished to see Colonel Stoddart immediately as I believed the letters were of some importance." Impressed and thrown off guard, the Persians did as he asked.

Colonel Charles Stoddart was in his tent pulling on his jacket, preparing to meet an unidentified visiting dignitary, when Pottinger appeared and introduced himself. Reticence was thrown aside, and the two Britons exuberantly joked and gossiped in a glow of spontaneous complicity. But their encounter was the only fruit of the otherwise futile mission. His presence now known to the besiegers, Pottinger became their bête noire. After the fighting resumed, a Persian officer rode to Herat's gate to urge its defenders to purge themselves of infidel *feringhees*. The Heratis shouted back that if the Persians authorized their own *feringhee,* Stoddart, to serve as the Persian envoy, the city would accept any agreement the two *feringhees* might reach. This exchange was barely over when James McNeill, the British envoy to Persia, arrived hurriedly at camp to present a letter from Queen Victoria to her royal cousin, Mohammed Shah, only to be followed by the Russian envoy, Count Simnovich, with an offer of more money and advisers from the Russian Tsar, tipping the balance against Victoria's appeal to the goodwill of a regal relative.

In June 1838, as Herat's food supplies had dwindled alarmingly, a Russian contingent led a six-day assault on the city's five gates. By most accounts (excluding his own), it was Pottinger who rallied the wavering garrison, notably the Vizier, Yar Mohammed, when the attackers succeeded in smashing through the two lower gates. Witnesses said that Pottinger's shouts all but shamed the calculating Vizier into a decisive display of courage, in which Yar Mohammed used his staff to smash the besiegers on the slopes of the massive city walls. (The military historian Sir John Kaye, after perusing Pottinger's manuscripts, determined that the modest officer had erased all references to himself.)

Finally, that August, a year after the siege had commenced, a show of British naval force effectively relieved Herat. It was Colonel Stoddart who went to the royal tent and politely informed the King of Kings that two British gunboats filled with Royal Marines were already in the Persian Gulf, and that if his forces took Herat, or any piece of Afghanistan, it would be deemed an act of hostility against Britain. "The fact is that if I don't leave Herat, there will be war, is not that it?" "It is war," responded Stoddart. "All depends on your Majesty's answer—God preserve Your Majesty!" The dejected Mohammed Shah capitulated, and after his retreat blamed British treachery for Persia's difficulties. For generations thereafter "the Herat question" and Britain's gunboat diplomacy clouded Anglo-Persian relations.

Thus ended the siege that Lord Auckland continued to cite after its collapse as Britain's principal justification for invading Afghanistan.

WATCHING THESE EVENTS FROM KABUL WERE TWO OF THE sharpest European eyes in Central Asia. Charles Masson used his keen vision to spot ancient coins, and gathered more than 80,000 specimens, a cache that provided the first chronology of the ruling dynasties in Afghan lands during the blank centuries following the death of Alexander the Great. He was a proficient draughtsman; he executed first-rate renderings of the Giant Buddhas at Bamian and doubtless drew accurate sketches of Afghan fortifications during his years as a "newswriter," or undercover agent, in Kabul.

Masson's other special talent was mystification. So thoroughly did he conceal his own tracks that in 1910, sixty years after his death, he was described as an American by Sir Thomas Holdich in *The Gates of India*. Holdich, the great surveyor of British India, had the highest opinion of Masson as an intelligence operative, scholar, and explorer who for twelve years roamed, usually penniless, through unknown lands, leaving behind a published record "which is unsurpassed on the Indian frontier for the width of its scope of inquiry into matters political, social, economic, and scientific, and the general accuracy of his conclusions."

The belief that Masson was an American goes back to 1830, when he informed a British Resident in Persia that he was from Kentucky and en route through a leisurely tour of the Orient. Subsequently, in Lahore, a French mercenary guessed he was Italian because he spoke fluent French with a slight accent. Others assumed he was as French as his name, and he duly became an entry in a nineteenth-century edition of *Biographie Nationale*.

In reality, he was born James Lewis in Aldermanbury, Middlesex, in 1800, the son of George Lewis, an oilman and member of the Needle Makers Company. Just where he acquired his fine manners and learned Greek, Latin, and French has been the focus of learned debate. New material keeps coming up. A London rare book dealer recently sold a first edition of Masson's *Narrative of Various Journeys* in which a letter was pasted, written around 1845 and signed by W. J. Eastwick, a British official closely involved with the early phases of Anglo-Afghan relations. Eastwick identifies Masson by his real name and asserts he was educated at Walthamstow, and then worked as a clerk at Durant & Co. (names not mentioned before) until a dispute with his father caused him to enlist as a private in the Bengal Artillery and ship for India in 1821.

After six years, following his participation in an especially nasty siege and four futile, costly assaults at Bharatpur in the Maratha Wars, he vanished without leave and was judged a deserter (a sympathetic biographer in mitigation notes that military service with the Company was then a lifetime engagement, almost penal servitude). Next Lewis turned up in Central Asia with an exotic new identity, or "legend" in current intelligence parlance, and set out for Kabul with a vagabond Pathan, their combined possessions being a handful of chupatties, a cotton wrap, a knife, and an earthen vessel, the false bottom of which concealed their net fortune of thirty *pice* or farthings. As a mendicant foreigner with gracious manners, Masson was never molested, and came to know Afghanistan literally from the ground up.

From 1833 onward, Masson assembled his impressive collection of ancient Hellenic coins, which, together with a trove of antique rings and brooches, he sent to Calcutta along with a scholarly manuscript of some merit. By this time, Masson and his skills were known to Colonel Claude Martine Wade, the British Agent in Ludhiana, whose charge was Shah Shuja, the pretender to the Kabul throne. As Wade put it to Calcutta, Masson's long residence in Afghanistan gave him complete knowledge of the country, as if he were "a native of it, on terms of intimacy and familiarity with its inhabitants." Indeed, his contact with indigent peasants gave him insights not to be expected from those "confined to beaten paths." So why not offer Masson the job of being a "newswriter" in Kabul, the term being a euphemism for a recognized spy?

Of course there was the matter of Masson's desertion, which Wade skated carefully around, calling it "a crime viewed by our government with a degree of rigour which scarcely admits of pardon." If the severity of the offense was too great to admit of a pardon, Wade hoped nonetheless that he could correspond with Masson and be indemnified for "any small sums" he advanced to him. In any case, the putative newswriter had a superior education and fine manners, and would not disgrace his employers. Calcutta concurred, and Wade was authorized to pay Masson 250 rupees a month with the promise of a King's pardon should he prove satisfactory.

It is rare to have such precise documentation on so interesting a transaction, which in its modest way opened a new path in which archaeologists, antiquarians, ethnologists, and journalists could use their respective callings as a cover for espionage.

ONCE BACK IN KABUL, CHARLES MASSON WAS ALL HIS EMPLOYERS could have wished as an enterprising and knowledgeable "newswriter." But inconveniently, the more he knew and learned, the less he felt able to support Lord Auckland's grand scheme of invading Afghanistan to re-enthrone Shah Shuja. Perhaps because he also was at heart a nomadic freebooter, and in equal part because he learned to speak the local languages, Masson liked Kabul and its inhabitants. "There are few places where a stranger so soon feels himself at home, and becomes familiar with all classes, as at Kabul," he tells us in his travel account. "There can be none where all classes so much respect the claims to civility, and so much exert themselves to promote his satisfaction and amusement."

Masson was struck as well by the religious tolerance in Kabul. Whereas in much of the Islamic world, the devout would not so much as eat with a Christian, "Here none of these difficulties or feelings exist." Christian Armenians by his account were more than tolerated; they intermarried with Muslims and attended each others' weddings and funerals. But the same tolerance was not to be found in other Afghan cities, especially Kandahar, which was rife with fanaticism.

The "newswriter" ascribed much of the credit for Kabul's amenities to its ruler, Dost Mohammed, who had given his kingdom the calm it required after a long period of commotion: "He is beloved by all classes of his subjects, and the Hindu fearlessly approaches him in his rides, and addresses him with the certainty of being attended to. He administers justice with impartiality, and has proved that the lawless habits of the Afghan are to be controlled." Masson took account of Dost Mohammed's riotous youth, his plain white linen raiment, and reticent manner ("he would be scarcely noticed in durbar save for his seat") but warned the stranger to be cautious in judging his character from appearances, since he "has proved himself an able commander, yet he is equally skilled with stratagem and polity, and only employs the sword when other means fail."

Unfortunately for the British, Masson's assessments were filtered through his "control" in Ludhiana, Colonel Wade, who was wholly committed to replacing Dost Mohammed with Shah Shuja, who had three times tried, and three times failed, to regain his throne. Just as regrettably, Masson's influence was also undercut by his rivalry with, presumed jealousy of, and antipathy to the young and handsome Alexander Burnes, who was to be the central figure in the Afghan tragedy, and whom we have yet properly to meet.

∴

CHAPTER FOUR

"Here Comes the Messenger"

PRESUMABLY THE DISMAL CALEDONIAN WEATHER PLAYED A part, along with the disparity between ambition and opportunity in a small country. For whatever reason, from the time Scotland and England united under a single parliament in 1709, few people emigrated more eagerly than the Scots, a source of persistent English raillery, most of it good-natured. ("Sir," said Dr. Johnson, "the noblest prospect which a Scotchman ever sees is the high road that leads him to England.") Certainly no people did more to extend and defend the British Empire—note that it was never called the English Empire, signifying that overseas at least, the Scots were partners, not subordinates. And beginning with Warren Hastings, who as Governor-General in the 1770's surrounded himself with North Britons, the Scots made British India their own. They built roads and bridges, trained soldiers and civil servants, staffed hospitals, and healed the afflicted, while others tirelessly labored to save the souls of Britain's heathen subjects.

Alexander Burnes personified the Scottish connection. Born in Montrose in County Angus, on the rocky east coast of Scotland, Alexander was a kinsman of Robert Burns (who spelled his name differently). Like the poet, this Burnes spoke and wrote fluently, made friends easily, liked a dram, and was hardy as a thistle. He was a questing romantic, never happier than when on the road, doomed, as he wrote a friend, "to live a vagabond forever." Early on, Burnes caught the attention of a townsman named Joseph Hume, who had gone to India poor, returned rich, and was elected to Parliament to represent Montrose. A Radical reformer himself, Hume saw his own spirit in young Alexander, whom he summoned to London at sixteen to meet a director of the East India Company, which resulted in an offer of a cadetship in the Bombay Infantry. After two months studying Indian languages, Burnes embarked in 1821 for the long voyage out.

He was accompanied by an older brother, James, a surgeon, who had just won a post in the Medical Department of Bombay. The brothers enjoyed two advantages, the first being blood. An Edinburgh man was then Governor of Bombay, and a Glasgow man was Governor of the Madras Presidency. Within weeks Alexander Burnes, the protégé of a Montrose man, was attending the Governor's grand ball in Bombay to bid farewell to an Eskdale man, the noted soldier and diplomat John Malcolm. The ball was, Burnes wrote home, "the most splendid fête I had ever beheld." Still, these tribal links, however useful, mattered less than the head start given Scots by an exceptional school system. At the time Scotland boasted four ancient universities (Aberdeen, Edinburgh, St. Andrews, and Glasgow) to England's two (Oxford and Cambridge). For its size, no country in Europe had more or better schools than Scotland, where the commitment to learning was reinforced by kirk, family, and competitive necessity. So it was that Scotland in the century after 1750 graduated 10,000 medical doctors, to England's meager 500, as related by Linda Colley in *Britons* (1992). Perhaps only Prussia produced better soldiers, and it was reckoned in Georgian Britain that one of four regimental officers was a Scot. "I was born a Scotsman, and a bare one," wrote Sir Walter Scott. "Therefore I was born to fight my way in the world."

Once in India, Alexander Burnes showed himself an incisive writer and outstanding linguist, so proficient that he was soon an interpreter in Hindustani for the Third Regiment Bombay Native Infantry. Promotions followed rapidly, and Lieutenant Burnes, barely eighteen, took part in a field force in the province of Cutch. He next acquired fluent Persian, and was praised by superiors for his exceptional tact. In 1829, Burnes, tipped as a rising man, was transferred to the prestigious Political Branch.

His first important task was to accompany by way of Sind and the Indus five English dray horses, a stallion and four mares, together with a state carriage that the Company in 1830 wished to present to the horse-loving Ranjit Singh. (This was the mission to which Metcalfe had objected as an unworthy ruse.) No European had fully explored Sind and Lower Indus since Alexander of Macedon, and humanly enough, Alexander of Montrose relished the distinction. Still, the princes and peasants in the Sind were not in the least fooled about the real purpose of Burnes's scouting mission. As his party made its way upstream on the Indus, an aged holy man burst out, "Alas! Sind is now gone, since the English have seen the river, which is the road to its conquest." So it proved when General Sir Charles Napier conquered and annexed Sind fourteen years later (sending a single, punning word to his superiors, so legend has it, "Peccavi," or "I have sinned").

Once in Lahore, the young subaltern's linguistic skills charmed Ranjit Singh, who initiated him into courtly pleasures. One evening he and the Maharajah were diverted by dancing girls dressed as boys, who brandished tiny bows and arrows. "This is one of my regiments," said Ranjit Singh, presumably winking his one good eye, "but they tell me it is one I cannot discipline." Burnes was sober enough to notice that his host's limbs were withered and his chest was contracted and that he was dependent on a nightly dose of spirits stronger than the strongest brandy, and so Burnes found it probable that "the career of this chief is nearly at an end."

He cast the same clinical eye on Shah Shuja and his opulent court in exile at Ludhiana. Burnes judged the Afghan pretender corpulent and melancholy, though at times affable and talkative, adding, "From what I learn, I do not believe the shah possesses sufficient energy to seat himself on the throne of Cabool; and that if he did regain it, he has not the tact to discharge the duties of so difficult a situation." After surveying the fortifications and the strategic passes of the Lower Indus, Burnes made his way to Delhi, where he received a written commendation for his work from the Governor-General. Even more welcome, a letter followed from Calcutta approving Burnes's proposal to lead a hazardous intelligence mission, this time to Afghanistan and across the Oxus River to Bokhara. This of course was the fatal route taken by William Moorcroft seven years before.

In 1832, Burnes crossed into Afghan territory. He was accompanied by a young medical officer, Dr. James Gilbert Gerard, and both wore turbans and flowing native dress. "You would disown your son if you saw him," Burnes wrote to his parents:

> My dress is purely Asiatic, and since I came into Cabool has been changed to the lowest order of the people. My head is shaved of its brown locks, and my beard, dyed black, grieves—as the Persian poets have it—for the departed beauty of my youth. I now eat my meals with my hands, and greasy digits they are…I frequently sleep under a tree, but if a villager will take compassion on me I enter his house. I never conceal that I am a European, and have as yet found the character advantageous to my comfort. I might assume all the habits and the religion of the Mahomedans, since I can now speak Persian as my own language, but I should have less liberty and less enjoyment in an assumed garb. The people know me by the name of a Sekunder, which is Persian for Alexander, and a magnanimous name it is.

In Kabul, Sekunder was asked, in his first meeting with Dost Mohammed Khan, why he wore Asian dress. He explained to the Afghan chief that he wanted to travel without being pointed at, and that he had no wish whatever to conceal from anyone "that I was an Englishman." (In common usage, the Scots abroad referred to themselves, though never the Empire, as English.) Impressed by Burnes's soldierly élan, the Dost in due course offered him command of the Afghan Army, with its 12,000 horses and twenty cannons, so that he might destroy the "insolent Sikh." Burnes politely declined, but the favorable impression he made in Kabul was tantamount to a passport as he headed across the Hindu Kush. ("Dost" is an honorific meaning "friend," and in Kabul, it needs saying, nearly every male seemed to possess the regal "Khan" in his name.)

At Balkh, identified as the site of ancient Bactria, Alexander's city, Burnes paused to locate the grave of William Moorcroft. The "Mother of Cities" was the same dusty village Moorcroft had seen, its old importance intimated only by its ruins and the many coins in its sandy soil. Balkh's Afghan inhabitants grudgingly agreed to lead Burnes to the grave site. It was a bright moonlit night, and with difficulty they located the grave near a mud wall because "the bigoted people of Balkh" had refused permission for Moorcroft to be interred in the main burial ground. Burnes, the irrepressible romantic, was moved to add, "It was impossible to view such a scene at the dead of night without many melancholy reflections."

Like Moorcroft, though with less difficulty, Burnes and Gerard, posing now as Armenians, ran the gauntlet of ransom-hungry Uzbek chieftains in their final sprint to Bokhara. In June 1832, six months after leaving Delhi, they passed through Bokhara's great main gate, and prudently dismounted, since only the faithful were permitted to ride within the city walls. Burnes exchanged his turban for the Uzbek sheepskin hat, found modest quarters, and tried to fade into the city's alleys. He assured Bokhara's inquisitive vizier that he and Gerard were Europeans who liked to travel, and wanted only to inform the world of the city's wonders. His prudence enabled him to exit safely and publish the first description of Bokhara by a Briton since Tudor times. He took careful notes about its bazaars, well-stocked with Russian goods, its 300-odd seminaries, and its slave markets. He confirmed that it was common practice for Uzbek man-hunters to capture Russians for sale in Bokhara's markets. Burnes conversed at length with a representative victim, Gregory Pulakoff, the son of a soldier who had been kidnapped twenty years before while asleep at a Russian outpost. "The Mahomedans are not sensible of any offense in enslaving the Russians," he wrote, "since they state that Russia herself exhibits the example of a whole country of slaves, especially in the despotic government of their soldiery."

Burnes's three-volume *Travels into Bokhara* was an overnight sensation on its publication with expeditious speed in 1834 by John Murray, whose colophon was itself a stamp of approval. Like Byron, another Murray author, Burnes savored the delight of awakening to find himself famous. Upon his arrival in Britain from Bombay, he was dubbed "Bokhara Burnes," fêted in Montrose, invited to a tête-à-tête with King William IV at Brighton, and lionized as a gold medalist by the recently formed Royal Geographical Society.

HIS FURLOUGH OVER, AND THE LAST DANCE A MEMORY, THE restive lion found himself back in India at his old post as Assistant to the Resident in the province of Cutch. However, in 1836 Lord Auckland, newly arrived as Governor-General, seeking somebody who knew something about Afghanistan, turned to Bokhara Burnes to return to Kabul with the stated purpose of opening Central Asia to British commerce. Auckland's real aim was to serve an ultimatum on Dost Mohammed that would effectively turn his country into a British protectorate. But that was not spelled out to Captain Burnes on beginning what would be a two-year journey, accompanied by Lieutenants Robert Leech of the Bombay Engineers and John Wood of the Indian Navy.

Proceeding from Peshawar through the Khyber Pass to Kabul, the Britons were met outside the main gate by a cavalry escort led by Akbar Khan, Dost Mohammed's favorite son. Akbar seated Burnes on an elephant for a triumphal entry, since his father regarded the Scot as a friend and assumed he was now an emissary with negotiating power. In reality, Burnes had no authority, and no instructions beyond urging Dost Mohammed to abandon his claims to Peshawar and keep all other European powers out of Afghanistan. It was Burnes's hope that through reason and eloquence he might somehow keep the peace between the Afghan Emir and the British Government.

On hand in Kabul with orders to help Burnes was Charles Masson, the "newswriter" who reported to Captain Wade in Ludhiana. Masson thought the entire operation ludicrous. Open Central Asia to British commerce? An absurdity and a fallacy, since no treaties were needed because by long tradition trade was already free. Why send an envoy without negotiating instructions? The likely result would be to incur the host's contempt. In any case, Masson thought

Burnes was too deferential to Dost Mohammed, too willing to fill his house with black-eyed damsels, and (we may safely assume) too famous and too young. Still, for all his envy and spite, Masson quickly grasped the hard truth: that the mission was a sham and a British assault on Afghanistan all but preordained. Some months later Masson received a letter from Burnes after the latter's return to British India, confirming the hurtful reality: "I have had the satisfaction of being told that I was sent to do *impossible things* at Cabool, so all my labour that did not succeed was not expected to succeed! Politics are a queer science."

Before he learned this, Burnes spent a year trying in his dispatches to press the case for working with and not against Dost Mohammed. "He is a man of undoubted ability," he wrote to Macnaghten, "and has at heart a high opinion of the British nation." How much wiser for Britain "to make Cabool in itself as strong as we can, and not weaken it by divided powers" because a strong king could bind the nation together. Fragmentation would only tempt Russia and Persia to "step in and destroy the chieftains in detail." As to Peshawar, Britain obviously could not betray its ally, Ranjit Singh, but the Sikh ruler was old and frail, and upon his death his kingdom would collapse. Why not strengthen Afghanistan as a solid buffer state, and as part of an overall bargain promise the Dost restitution of Peshawar after Ranjit Singh's passing?

It didn't help that all these dispatches went first to Ludhiana, where Captain Wade worked over their contents. At one point Wade notified Burnes that he had the "prerogative" to comment on all dispatches before passing them along. With some heat, Burnes retorted that a "prerogative" was only enjoyed by kings, to which Wade answered that he was wrong, and sent him the definition from Johnson's Dictionary. In any case, Wade, a staunch advocate of ousting Dost Mohammed, always had the last word as he remarked upon, compressed, and sometimes tampered with Burnes's reports.

Burnes's weekly dispatches took on new urgency in December 1837. For the first time as a certainty, a flesh-and-blood Russian officer turned up at the gates of Kabul. It was manna from Mars for the war party in Simla.

Captain Ivan Viktorovich Vitkevich was aide-de-camp to the Governor of Orenburg, a Russian frontier garrison, and also reported to the Political Department of the Foreign Ministry in St. Petersburg. He arrived in Kabul shortly before Christmas, prompting a dinner invitation from Captain Burnes. "He was a gentlemanly and agreeable man, of about thirty years of age, spoke French, Turkish, and Persian fluently, and wore the uniform of an officer of Cossacks," wrote Burnes. He had been three times in Bokhara, and so there was "a common subject to converse upon, without touching on politics." Burnes found him "intelligent and well informed on the subject of Northern Asia. He very frankly said that it was not the custom of Russia to publish to the world the result of its researches in foreign countries, as was the case with France and England." They never met again. Burnes regretted that it was "impossible to follow the dictates of my personal feeling of friendship towards him, as the public service required the strictest watch, lest the relative positions of our nations should be misunderstood in this part of Asia."

For his part, Vitkevich had reason for reticence. His life history was Dostoyevskian. A Lithuanian by birth, he belonged as a student to the Black Brothers, a revolutionary sect of Poles and Lithuanians seeking independence from Russia. He was arrested, tried, and sentenced to death, but because of his youth, his sentence was commuted to military duty. Banished to Orenburg, north of the Caspian Sea, Vitkevich studied the Kazak and Persian languages, proved proficient, served as a capable negotiator with rebellious Kazaks, and was sent on an intelligence mission to Bokhara, to find out whether it would remain neutral if Russia attacked nearby Khiva. He was first spotted by the British in eastern Persia in 1837, while riding to the Shah's encampment during the siege of Herat. Major Henry Rawlinson tried to question the young officer, but Vitkevich feigned ignorance of any common languages. Later, at the Persian expeditionary headquarters, the two met again, conversed easily in French and Persian, and Rawlinson was startled to learn that Vitkevich was in fact on a mission to Kabul.

In Kabul, the Afghans did not know what to make of the Russian, who described himself as a messenger, or bearer of letters. Vitkevich was greeted coolly but civilly by Dost Mohammed, whose aides skeptically noticed that the crested letter, dusted with gold leaf, said to be from the Tsar himself, bore no signature. The missive was shown immediately to Burnes, who made a copy and asked Masson to examine the original. "Captain Burnes pointed out to me the large exterior seal on the envelope," Masson recalled. "I sent for a loaf of Russian sugar from the bazaar, at the bottom of which we found precisely the same seal." The newswriter was sure the letter was faked, that Vitkevitch had no negotiating authority, but was simply bluffing. Burnes should have laughed off the soi-disant messenger, Masson complained, and would have done so had he any sense of humor. In any case, Dost Mohammed gave little encouragement to Vitkevich, since the Emir's preference was to reach an arrangement with the British.

In January 1838, Auckland formally responded to Dost Mohammed's overtures with a message sternly advising him to give up hope of regaining Peshawar and instead to "appease the feelings of the powerful sovereign" (Ranjit Singh) whom he had offended. This was followed in March by a virtual ultimatum: "You must desist from all correspondence with Persia and Russia; you must never receive agents from [them] or have aught to do with [them] without our sanction; you must dismiss Captain Vitkevich with courtesy; you must surrender all claims to Peshawar . . . In return for this, I promise to recommend to the Government that it use its good offices with its ancient ally, Maharaja Runjeet Singh, to remove present and future differences between the Sikhs and Afghans at Peshawar." Protesting that Auckland asked everything and gave nothing, Dost Mohammed then began to receive Vitkevich, playing to British suspicions. In April 1838, an empty-handed Captain Burnes left Kabul.

As he wound back to India, Burnes reconsidered his course. He knew by then that an invasion army was being mobilized, and that Auckland was intent on restoring Shah Shuja to the Afghan throne. Who was he to put himself above the Governor-General? Possibly Auckland was right, and in any case oughtn't he help assure the success of an important enterprise in which he might play a major role?

Bokhara

CHINA

TURKESTAN

Oxus R.

AFGHANISTAN

KASHMIR

To Simla

To Herat

Kohistan

Bamian   Charikar   Jagdalak
          Kabul   Jalalabad
                    Gundamuk   Kabul R.
          Jagdalak   Peshawar
          Pass   Khyber
                            Pass
Ghazni

Indus R.

Maiwand

Kandahar   Lahore

                            INDIA

Quetta

Bolan
Pass

Shikarpur

N

SIND   Indus R.

FIRST AFGHAN WAR
1839–42

——— British Advance to
       Kabul, 1839
•••• British Retreat from
       Kabul, 1842
≡≡   Mountain pass

0   Miles   200

He ventilated his doubts in letters to friends, and began to temporize in official dispatches. In a feckless sentence written in June 1838 he remarked that the British Government had but to send Shah Shuja to Peshawar "with an agent or two of its own regiments, as an honorary escort, and an avowal that we have taken up his cause, to ensure his being fixed for ever on his Throne." (The historian Kaye found that Burnes had struck out his original line in the same space, saying that of Shah Shuja personally, he had "no very high opinion.") Burnes nonetheless concluded with a resounding appeal for the Dost, saying "if half you must do for others were done for him, and offers made [that] conduced his interests, he would abandon Persia and Russia tomorrow."

By the time he reached Simla in July, Burnes dreamed of being the principal political officer of the Army of the Indus. But Auckland had already chosen Macnaghten to be the Envoy and Minister of the Government of India. Burnes was asked to precede the advancing expeditionary force to assure a peaceful reception from the emirs of Sind and Baluchistan. The Governor-General tried to soften the blow by asking Burnes to look carefully at the superscription of the letter. It was addressed to "Lieutenant-Colonel Sir Alexander Burnes, Knight." He had but recently celebrated his thirty-third birthday, and was very pleased.

INITIALLY, IT SEEMED THAT AUCKLAND AND MACNAGHTEN WERE right. As the martial cavalcade lumbered across Sind toward Baluchistan in the spring of 1839, Burnes cowed, bullied, and bludgeoned the local rulers into permitting its progress and agreeing to pay tribute to Shah Shuja. Yet compliance was wrested through force majeure as these resentful princes became vassals, and their discontent dogged the Army of the Indus as it proceeded through parched deserts, continually harassed by cattle rustlers. Still, even if parboiled in their red uniforms and weakened by subsistence rations, the troops did arrive, with few losses, at the Bolan Pass.

Bolan is a natural wonder and a strategic nightmare: a fifty-mile defile that rises from 450 feet above sea level to 5,600 feet. It proved wilder and more daunting than the Khyber Pass. The perpendicular cliffs, the winding gorge, the precipitous ascent—all the melodramatic features later depicted in Victorian lithographs—caused the awed soldiers to gape. At its summit, the Bolan Pass was crowned by Quetta, in 1838 still only a wretched collage of mud houses around an oasis on the edge of the Iranian plateau. Over the years, after its conquest by the British, Quetta became the defensive linchpin of a contested frontier, and its cantonment boasted 12,000 troops, the largest garrison in British India.

Getting the Army of the Indus, with its herds of cattle and camels, up through the vertiginous pass was a Herculean labor, especially since hostile snipers kept aiming at stragglers. Here Macnaghten deployed what he believed was the all-purpose lubricant: bribes, more politely called subsidies. Huge payments were made to the Baluchi prince, Mehrab Khan of Kelat, master of the Bolan Pass, who protested that his lands were despoiled by British foragers and warned that the Afghans would never accept Shah Shuja: "You may keep him by main force for a time on the throne, but as soon as you leave the kingdom, your Shah Shuja will be driven beyond the frontier."

The first obstacle overcome, another generous bribe assured the passivity of the tribal keepers of the treacherous Kojak Pass as the army advanced toward its first big Afghan objective, Kandahar. Outside its walls, the regiments from Bombay and the Punjab, which had proceeded separately, merged into a single force with some 10,000 camp followers. Kandahar offered no resistance. Shah Shuja, who led the way through its gates, was greeted, so Macnaghten reported, "with feelings nearly mounting to adoration." Others noticed that the huzzahs died when the city's devout inhabitants saw the multitude of infidels outside their walls. Fewer than a hundred Afghans turned out for Shah Shuja's ceremonial installation as their new Emir.

At the next objective, the fortress at Ghazni, the Army of the Indus faced its first serious hostile challenge. Here the British employed a technique that was to be used successfully against other Afghan forts: blowing a gate open with gunpowder, and then storming the breach, a tactic requiring the bravura and discipline for which the thin red lines were renowned. At Ghazni, an Afghan deserter provided crucial help by informing the besiegers that one of its three gates was not walled up and hence vulnerable to sappers. Diverted by a feint bombardment at their rear, the defenders were caught by surprise when the Kabul Gate was daringly mined by Lieutenant Henry Durand of the Bengal Engineers, and a storming column led by Brigadier "Fighting Bob" Sale and Colonel William Henry Dennie rushed in the breach. By the victors' count, the storming had cost seventeen British and Indian lives, as against 1,200 of the defenders.

The fall of supposedly impregnable Ghazni reverberated to Kabul. Dost Mohammed, suddenly abandoned on all sides, took flight to the Hindu Kush and across the Oxus, eventually finding sanctuary in Bokhara. So it came to pass, as the British hoped, that the Afghan capital fell without a battle. Shah Shuja, mounted on a white charger, "dazzling," one observer wrote, "in a coronet, jeweled girdle and bracelet," led the way to the throne he had lost thirty years before. He could now laugh at his nickname: the Luckless Prince, or Shah-e-Kam-Naseeb, as even his own troops called him. Macnaghten and Burnes, in full diplomatic regalia, were followed by the officer corps, by Shah Shuja's mostly Hindu troops, and finally by the Bengal and the Bombay divisions. Yet the people of Kabul were noticeably muted in greeting an exile who had failed in three previous attempts to regain his crown, and who now returned on the backs of unbelievers.

Macnaghten could not care less. The expeditious conquest was to him sweet vindication, an augury that the British could as readily annex Herat, advance to the Oxus, and subdue the Punjab. "We have a beautiful game on our hands," he confided to a friend, "if we have the means and inclination to play it." The driveling in Calcutta, he added, was "beneath contempt...Oh! for a Wellesley or a Hastings at this juncture!" Macnaghten's mood was infectious. "I suspect this will prove the biggest step that English authority has ever taken at one stride in this quarter of the globe," a young lieutenant wrote to his family. "...Just look at Caboul on the map. Look at Herat. I expect very soon to see Chinese Tartary and Siberia amongst Her Majesty's dominions."

Moving swiftly, the British consolidated their gains. Garrisons were established in Ghazni, Jalalabad, Kandahar, and Kabul. To secure communications, British troops occupied Quetta and Ali Masjid in the Khyber Pass. Smaller units were sent to Bamian to guard the northern passes, and messengers raced south with the fabulous tidings. So complete did the victory seem that the greater part of the Army of the Indus returned to India in the final months of 1839. Left behind were a division at Kandahar and two brigades at Kabul. All Simla rejoiced. Emily Eden wrote that events sustained "G.'s" judgment, adding that the hill station's formerly forlorn war wives saw "with their minds' eye their husbands eating apricots and drinking acid sherbet" and were "satisfied." When the news reached London, doubters were silenced by jubilation over the first splendid victory in the new Queen's reign. Auckland was elevated to an earldom, and Macnaghten was given a baronetcy. "I can indeed see," Miss Eden wrote on the eve of the great victory, "how despotic power without the bother of Parliament, and immense patronage, may be rather pleasant."

It was a moment when to be English was very heaven. This was the first time that the British for a sustained period physically occupied the entire North-West Frontier of their Indian Empire. Yet, as remarked by Sir Kerr Fraser-Tytler, the British Minister in Kabul a century later, it also proved the last.

THERE WERE, TO BE SURE, LESSER VEXATIONS, AND ONE BIG, troublesome puzzle. Shah Shuja had brought from the Punjab his large household of three or four hundred—wives, concubines, children, servants, eunuchs, entertainers, and so forth. He wished to quarter his harem, or *zenana,* in the Bala Hissar, the great citadel on a hill facing the city. Macnaghten gave way, overruling officers and engineers who had strongly recommended garrisoning a brigade within the citadel. This was unacceptable to Shah Shuja, because foreigners might peep down below into his *zenana.*

Instead, the victors built a cantonment on a flat plain a mile north of Kabul, where it was vulnerable to shelling from hills rising above it. The entire garrison, a force of 10,000, was quartered within its rectangular mud walls, which in places were only waist high. The commissariat was located in a small fort outside the cantonment—"a disgrace to our military skill and judgment," was the diary comment of the commissary of ordnance, Lieutenant Vincent Eyre. The garrison settled in for what looked to be a long and agreeable tour. Wives and children arrived from India. A cricket pitch sprang up. There was boating, shooting, ice skating, horse races, and inescapably, amateur theatricals. There was cockfighting, wrestling, fox hunting, and polo, the last two ceasing when the Queen's 16th Lancers decamped for India, taking their foxhounds and polo ponies with them. And there were formal dinners, lots of them.

Sir Alexander Burnes now held the title of British Resident, and was also a Knight of the Order of the Douranee Empire, an honor conferred by a grateful Shah Shuja. Burnes presided in his courtyard mansion at dinner parties featuring "champagne, hock, madeira, sherry, port, claret, sauterne, not forgetting a glass of curaçoa and maraschino, and the hermetically sealed salmon and hotchpotch [a thick Scottish soup] all the way frae' Aberdeen, for deuced good it is, the peas as big as if they had been soaked for *bristling*."

Still, as he confided to his brother, "I am now a highly paid idler, having no less than 3,500 rupees a month as Resident at Cabool, and being, as the lawyers call it, only counsel, and that, too, a dumb one—by which I mean that I give paper opinions, but do not work them out." He disapproved of Shah Shuja's grossly corrupt ministers, but when Burnes demurred, Macnaghten brusquely cited the Simla proclamation pledging noninterference in Afghan affairs.

Nor was Burnes pleased when he perused an official Blue Book published by the British Government to defend its Afghan policies. The Blue Book contained what purported to be Burnes's correspondence, but as he wrote to his brother-in-law, the documents were "pure trickery, and I have said so in every company since I read them . . . All my implorations to Government to act with promptitude and decision had reference to doing something when Dost Mohammed was King, and all this they have made to appear in support of Shah Shoojah being set up!" In short, he was depicted as the author of precisely the course he had vainly opposed.

Small wonder he reputedly consoled himself with dark-eyed damsels, including the wives of Afghan chiefs. Trysts were facilitated by the *burkhas,* or tentlike cocoons, that cloaked women from head to toe, with a grille covering even the eyes: perfect camouflage for clandestine visits to officers' quarters. In rare cases, fraternization ended in nuptials, an example being Captain Robert Warburton of the Bengal Artillery, who married a niece of Dost Mohammed in a ceremony witnessed by Macnaghten and Burnes. But boredom and licentiousness are the incurable social disorders of occupation armies. As the months stretched on, Kabul's men of fighting age looked with ever keener resentment at the profligate *feringhees* who seduced their women.

All of this flowed from the festering problem that preoccupied and frustrated Sir William Hay Macnaghten. Getting into Afghanistan was one thing, getting out quite another. Calcutta and London insistently pressed for a complete withdrawal, and the East India Company repeatedly protested the high cost of protracted occupation. But should the British pull out, what might happen to Shah Shuja and his *zenana?* For his part, the returning monarch was wretchedly aware he was despised by his own people because his authority derived from foreigners, yet he knew if the British withdrew, his reign was in peril. Disquieting news came in bunches, all arguing for a prolonged stay. Ranjit Singh had died in Lahore, precipitating a confused scramble for succession. In Herat, the wily Yar Mohammed had deposed his Emir and was courting Persia. A Russian army had mobilized in Orenburg and in winter 1839 was advancing on Khiva. And Captain Stoddart, whom we last met in Persia, had been sent to Bokhara to court its capricious Emir, who summarily flung him into a rat-infested pit to compel his conversion. This so upset Macnaghten's cousin, Captain Arthur Conolly, that in Kabul he clamored for permission to go to Bokhara, which was eventually given.

In August 1840, a fresh drama developed. Dost Mohammed, having sought asylum in Bokhara, was put under arrest, then eluded his captors and returned to Afghanistan, enlisting support on the way. In an initial clash at Bamian, the British easily bested the Dost's newly mobilized force, but the deposed Emir held his ground successfully in a second battle at Kohistan. Having saved face, and unwilling to plunge his country into civil war, he rode to Kabul with a single companion and threw himself at the mercy of the British. "I am like a wooden spoon," he said, "you may throw me hither and thither, but I shall not be hurt." Astonished, Macnaghten received Dost Mohammed with full honors, and creditably granted him asylum in India, because, as the Envoy wrote Auckland, "we ejected the Dost, who never offended us, in support of our policy, of which he was the victim," a candid admission that contradicted the very raison d'être of the British invasion.

Still, these events were tremors, not an earthquake. Macnaghten was concerned but not alarmed. He despised "croakers," the pessimists he had repeatedly proved wrong. He grasped at each sign suggesting that Afghanistan's fractious clans were reconciled to their new king, that their country (as the Soviets would say a century hence) was at last "normalized." In April 1841, twenty months after the army's triumphal entry into Kabul, things appeared "normal" as a new army commander arrived. The new chief was Major-General William Elphinstone, first cousin of the redoubtable Mountstuart Elphinstone. The courtly and affable General had last seen action at Waterloo in 1814, and was not enthusiastic about his new post. He suffered from gout and dysentery, and his shuffling gait made him seem much older than his fifty-nine years.

The General was a family friend of Lord Auckland, whose sister Emily dubbed him "Elphie Bey." In offering him command, the Governor-General fatuously suggested that the "bracing hills of Cabul" might prove more salubrious than "the hot plains of India." Most historians have followed Kaye in blaming Auckland for choosing Elphinstone. But John Waller, a retired Inspector General of the Central Intelligence Agency, burrowed through the files and came up with an additional culprit. The original initiative, Waller writes in his 1990 history of the war, came from the Horse Guards, Army Headquarters Command in London, the arbiter of senior appointments. Elphinstone was nominated by another Waterloo veteran, Fitzroy Somerset, the future Lord Raglan, the Commander-in-Chief in the Crimean War who gave the ambiguous order that precipitated the fatal charge of the Light Brigade.

Watching all this incredulously in London was Elphinstone's cousin Mountstuart, the first Briton to lead a mission to Afghanistan.

It was all very well, he wrote to a friend, to take Afghan cities and put Shah Shuja on the throne, "but for maintaining him in a poor, cold, strong and remote country among a turbulent people like the Afghans, I own it seems to me hopeless."

THE FIRST PORTENTS MATERIALIZED IN SUMMER 1841. RESPOND-ing to persistent and anxious pressure from Auckland to cut costs, Macnaghten slashed by half the agreed subsidy to the chiefs of the eastern Ghilzai. The most famous and strongest of Afghan tribes, the Ghilzai controlled the passes and gorges on the route from Kabul to Jalalabad, and until then had scrupulously abstained from attacks on British couriers and detachments. Furious at what they saw as an im-perious breach of faith, the Ghilzai blocked the passes. Macnaghten, in his lofty proconsular tone, retorted that they were "kicking up a row" over petty matters, promising that "the rascals will be well trounced for their pains."

The affray was most inconvenient for Macnaghten, who had just been named Governor of Bombay, the second highest post in India, an office he planned to assume in November. A senior offi-cer, Brigadier Sir Robert Sale, 13th Light Infantry, was also prepar-ing to depart. Why shouldn't "Fighting Bob" lead the way, and in doing so clear the passes? In any case, the Envoy saw little to worry about and in September assured the Governor-General that progress was "perfectly wonderful" and the entire country "as quiet as one of our Indian chiefships, and more so." Sale headed with his brigade toward Jalalabad, the plan being that once the Ghilzais were punished and the passes cleared, the others would follow, in-cluding the Macnaghtens and the brigadier's formidable wife, Lady Florentia Sale.

As Macnaghten prepared to leave, he hinted that Sir Alexander Burnes might be his successor, despite the Envoy's belief that the Resident was too much of a "croaker." This was his all-purpose epi-thet for aides who brought ill-tidings, the most persistent croakers being Major Henry Rawlinson at Kandahar and Major Eldred Pottinger, erstwhile hero of Herat, now a political officer at Kohistan. Burnes's own feelings shifted from day to day, even from hour to hour, but he had a network of agents whose outlook contrasted sharply with the sunny dispatches Macnaghten kept sending south.

Burnes's most trusted source was Mohan Lal, his *munshi,* or secretary, whose personal history was unusual. Mohan Lal's father, a high-caste Kashmiri Brahmin, had taken part in Mountstuart Elphinstone's 1808 mission to Peshawar. The son was spotted twenty years later by Charles Trevelyan, the ablest of Metcalfe's protégés, who had just founded the Delhi English College. Mohan Lal graduated first in his class and was the first Kashmiri to speak fluent English. (In 1940, Jawaharlal Nehru remarked with asperity, "In a free India, a man like Mohan Lal would have risen to the topmost rungs of the political ladder. Under early British rule, whatever he might be or whatever he might do, he could not rise higher than the position of a *Mir Munshi* or at most a Deputy Collector.") Mohan Lal so impressed Alexander Burnes that he invited him in 1831 to serve as his secretary on his great journey. In *Travels to Bokhara,* the *munshi* appears condescendingly as the "Hindu lad" who helped Burnes with his Persian correspondence.

Mohan Lal was a great deal more than that. In Kabul, he was the Resident's ears and eyes, his silent partner and agile fixer, capable of becoming a fly on the wall, or a figure in the carpet. It was Mohan Lal who recruited the Afghan defector at Ghazni who told the British about the vulnerable gate. Now, in autumn 1841, Mohan Lal was everywhere, scooping up gossip and rumors. The talk at the Kabul bazaar was about the appearance at Bamian of Akbar Khan, Dost Mohammed's oldest and ablest son. Impulsive and handsome, with a bold gaze and charismatic swagger, he was worth two divisions to the Afghan rebels. This was followed by reports of a confederacy of Afghan chiefs plotting an uprising to evict the British. Then Mohan Lal heard very explicit and alarming news: that a clan chief, Abdullah Khan, had vowed to slay Burnes to avenge the seduction of a mistress or (so others said) to provide a signal for a general rising. But the Resident, his mind buzzing with other matters, rejected the *munshi's* plea to seek safer quarters. On October 31, Burnes wrote in his journal, "What will this day bring forth? It will make or mar me,

I suppose. Before the sun sets I shall know whether I go to Europe or succeed Macnaghten."

Two mornings later, a crowd thickened around his mansion, unfazed by the Resident's sepoy guards. Hearing shouts of "Sekunder, Sekunder!" Burnes faced what was now a mob from a gallery above the garden court. Suddenly there was the burst of gunfire and a bullet killed his military secretary, Lieutenant William Broadfoot. Burnes and his visiting younger brother Charles now stood alone on the gallery. When the frantic Resident tried to speak, he was shouted down and a cry went up, "Come into the garden! Come into the garden!" According to Kaye, who wove together differing accounts, a mysterious Kashmiri appeared on the balcony and offered to lead the brothers to safety in native disguise. No sooner had the pair put on their robes and stepped outside than the Kashmiri cried out, "This is Sekunder Burnes!" The brothers were hacked to pieces by the rioters, and Broadfoot's body (so Kaye writes) was devoured by dogs. The stables were now ablaze, the paymaster's treasury plundered, and looters grabbed what they could in the mansion. All guards and the entire household staff were killed.

Mohan Lal witnessed the riot from a nearby rooftop and after the melee crept into the Residency to rescue Burnes's journal. "Sometimes sanguine," says Kaye of Burnes, drawing on that journal, "sometimes desponding, sometimes confident; sometimes credulous—he gave to fleeting impressions all the importance and seeming permanency of settled convictions." Yet Kaye is quick to add that these were the traits of youth (Burnes was thirty-six when he died) and his very openness, charm, spontaneity, and candor made him the perfect scapegoat for his superiors, who did not possess and in truth distrusted just those qualities.

THE RIOTING WAS WATCHED WITH CONSTERNATION BY SHAH Shuja and his retinue from the citadel. A regiment of the Emir's own troops, led by William Campbell, a Eurasian mercenary, took to the streets to quell the rioters but could not fire field pieces in crowded quarters and fell back. No other measures were taken that day, no soldiers poured into the city, and no British officer charged at the head of his battalion. Instead, Kaye crisply notes, General Elphinstone "talked of action tomorrow when he should have talked of action today." The astonished Afghans feared their rising would be strangled at the outset, and took heart when all that seemed to happen was that Envoy Macnaghten and his family vacated their Residency, packing their glass chandeliers and other valuables, and moved to safer quarters in the cantonment.

Once there, Macnaghten sent urgent messages to Brigadier Sale, as well as to the Kandahar garrison, 300 miles distant, to rush reinforcements to Kabul. As the Envoy examined his new quarters, the sight cannot have been comforting. He was in a sprawling rectangular esplanade, measuring 3,000 by 1,800 feet, on a swamp-ridden plateau beneath hills to the north and south. The British had failed to occupy the higher Bemaru hill from which one could easily fire into the compound. A dozen stone forts encircled the cantonment, but the British had only commandeered the fort in which the commissariat was located. A shallow ditch, a low wall, and four corner bastions were all that protected hundreds of bungalows housing 5,000 troops, their families, and upwards of 10,000 camp followers. Even worse, as the ordnance officer Vincent Eyre noted in his journal, "The unwelcome truth was soon forced upon us, that in the whole Afghan nation we could not reckon on a single friend."

On November 3, the emboldened rebels, already in possession of a fort between cantonment and commissariat, blocked the lane connecting the two. When a cavalry unit charged forth to clear the way, it came under such galling fire from concealed marksmen that it was forced to retreat. Thus the cantonment was cut off from the commissariat, with its grain, hospital stores, and other supplies. A day later, the commissariat was abandoned, a move (writes Kaye) that "not only threatened the British with instant starvation, but made such a lamentable exposure of our imbecility, that all [Afghans] who had before held aloof...now gathered heart and openly declared themselves against us."

Other realities were by now evident. General Elphinstone was rattled and irresolute. His personal courage was never in doubt, but his body was so feeble he could not walk unassisted. He was bewildered by warfare very different from Waterloo, still seemed to believe that Afghans were allies, and confused his officers by expressing conflicting views in a single sentence. Yet under command arrangements, nobody had the authority to replace the courtly but befuddled general.

A second reality was that the rebels were superb shots and wore dun-colored outfits that melded into the hills from which they fired their *jezails*, muskets that had a longer reach than British rifles. The British weapon had not changed since Waterloo: it was the Brown Bess, a muzzle-loader effective to about 150 yards. The Afghan jezail, long and ungainly, could be effective at 800 yards. Having lost the commissariat, reduced to foraging among a hostile populace, and facing a more numerous and ever more aggressive adversary, the demoralized defenders seemed unable to do what once came easily. Each day's struggle became a depressing litany of squandered opportunities, failed charges, blundering retreats, and abandoned weapons, culminating in the Battle of Bemaru Heights on November 23.

Of onlookers in the cantonment, one was especially informed and articulate: Lady Florentia Wynch Sale, the daughter and granddaughter of Company servants. Born in Madras in 1787, she married Captain Robert Sale in 1808, and bore twelve children, four of whom died in infancy, while a fifth, the eldest son, perished at ten. Unflappable and outspoken, she was inured to domestic hardship while her husband fought in wars across Asia. She cherished her reckless husband, writing that nothing could induce him to behave as a senior officer should: "Despite his staff's protests, he used to ride about two miles ahead of his troops, and in action would fight like a private."

On the fateful November 23, Lady Sale wrote in her journal that at daybreak,

> I had taken up my post of observation, as usual, on the top of the house, whence I had a fine view of the field of action, and where, by keeping behind the chimneys, I escaped the bullets that continually whizzed by me. Brigadier [John] Shelton having brought forward skirmishers to the brow of the hill, formed the infantry into two squares, the one about

2,000 yards from the other, the intervening space being crammed with our cavalry...The fight continued till about 10 o'clock, by which time our killed and wounded became very numerous. In spite of our shrapnel, the fire of the enemy told considerably more than ours did, from the superiority of their juzails and jingals over our muskets. They fought also from behind sungahs and hillocks, whilst our men were perfectly exposed; our troops also labouring under the disadvantage of being drawn up in a square, from an apprehension of an attack by Afghan cavalry.

She recorded the critical blunder: the sole British field gun became too hot to fire, and contrary to standing orders, there was no second gun to replace it. The gun silenced, the enemy regrouped and captured it. Then "a party of Ghazeeas [warriors] ascended the brow of the hill, by the gorge, where they planted three standards close to each other, a red, a yellow and a green one." But the British lost heart and would not fight: "It was very like the scenes depicted in the battles of the Crusaders. The enemy rushed on: drove our men before them very like a flock of sheep with a wolf at their heels."

The men retreated until they reached a second square that had not broken, and there, remarkably, they rallied, turned about, gave a shout, retook the now-cooled gun, and fired it with deadly effect on now-panicky Afghans, who fled the hill.

All appearing to be over, I hastened home... everyone supposing the enemy were routed, and that Brig. Shelton was coming back with the troops. At this time I was standing on the ramparts, and heard the Envoy, in my presence, ask the General to pursue the flying troops into the city, which he refused, saying it was a wild scheme. Had Shelton returned to cantonments, or thrown his force into Bemaru, all would had gone well, and we had remained masters of the field... At about half-past twelve, just as we had finished our breakfast, the enemy gradually came up the hill, and their fire was so severe that our men could scarcely fill up the gaps as their comrades fell, and our whole force, both horse and foot, were driven down the hill, and our gun captured—a regular case of *sauve qui peut*.

"All have heard of the British squares at Waterloo, which defied the repeated desperate onsets of Napoleon's choicest *cavalry,*" Lieutenant Eyre lamented in his journal. "At Beymaroo we formed squares to resist the *distant fire of infantry,* thus presenting a solid mass against the aim of perhaps the best marksmen in the world."

HOPES FOR AN IMMINENT RELIEF COLUMN HAD NOW FADED, since Brigadier Sale, having been told by Elphinstone to proceed to Jalalabad if necessary to save those wounded in the fights to clear the passes. Sale did just that. Another course, vainly pressed by Eyre and others, was to abandon the cantonment for securer quarters in the Shah Shuja's citadel, the Bela Hissar. Macnaghten, still convinced he could outwit the Afghans, tried his best to bribe and divide. At one point Burnes's *munshi,* Mohan Lal, was offering, on the authority of Macnaghten's aide, Lieutenant John Conolly, "10,000 rupees for the head of each of the principal rebel chiefs." Two chiefs, including Burnes's nemesis, Abdullah Khan, were killed, but since the assassins did not produce their heads, no blood-money was paid. Yet Macnaghten realized that bribes alone would not work, and that the defenders had to discuss terms with the insurgents, especially since a potential partner, Dost Mohammed's son, Akbar, had now arrived in Kabul at the head of an Uzbek rebel band.

Macnaghten arranged for a rendezvous with Akbar at the Kabul River, where he requested a guarantee of safe conduct for the Kabul garrison if it withdrew at once, with or without Shah Shuja. For the Envoy, these were hard and humiliating concessions, and the suspicious Afghan prince seemed to assent, but then, a few days later, Macnaghten learned of a purported new overture from a British cavalry officer who had been in Akbar's camp. Why shouldn't Akbar and Macnaghten secretly join forces? Why not keep Shah Shuja on the throne? Why not let Akbar become vizier? Could this not be accomplished with British fees and pensions, and a British promise to withdraw within six months? Macnaghten embraced the double-deal, and signed a document stipulating its terms.

Two days before Christmas, the Envoy, in his customary silk hat, frock coat, and spotless linen, rode out again to the Kabul River, accompanied by three officers, Colin Mackenzie, George Lawrence, and Robert Trevor. As always, Macnaghten wore an emerald ring, said to have belonged to Mohammed, with the words "Mustafa, the last of the race," inscribed in square Arabic characters. When the party approached the river, a carpet was laid on snow-covered ground. After the exchange of salaams, Akbar asked Macnaghten if he was ready to carry out the secret compact. When the Envoy said yes, so say British sources, Akbar shouted "*Begeer!*" (Seize!), and the three officers were surrounded as the Envoy was dragged away. Macnaghten cried out in Persian, "*Az barae Khooda!*" (For God's sake!) with an expression of "consternation and horror," according to Lawrence, as he was killed, probably with the pistol he had given to Akbar. As the British officers struggled to escape, Trevor stumbled, and was killed by a Ghazi assailant. Mackenzie was saved by Akbar, who shouted as he did so, "*You'll* seize my country, will you?" Along with a very shaken Lawrence, Mackenzie was taken prisoner in an Afghan fort. There, drawn by cries, the pair peered from the window of their cell to see a ringless human hand, almost surely Macnaghten's, bobbing up and down on a pole.

THE HORRIFYING DETAILS OF THE ENVOY'S FATE SPREAD through the cantonment, where Lady Sale had the task of informing Lady Macnaghten. "Over such scenes I draw a veil," she wrote in her journal, and one doubts she told the widow that her husband's body was dismembered, his head borne like a trophy through the streets of Kabul, and what was left of his corpse impaled on a meathook, alongside Trevor's remains, in the bazaar. (The scene was repeated in 1997, when Taliban militants seized and executed Najibullah, the

Soviet-installed Communist leader, and hoisted his body in the Kabul bazaar.) The last sparks of Elphinstone's fighting spirit died with the Envoy, whose place as senior political officer was now taken by Major Eldred Pottinger, who had arrived badly wounded from his post in Kohistan. "I was hauled out of my sick room," Pottinger bitterly protested, "and obligated to negotiate for the safety of a parcel of fools who were doing all they could to assure their destruction."

On Christmas Eve, the general put the revised Afghan terms to his council. The army could withdraw, with Akbar as its escort to the frontier, if the British handed over their treasury, surrendered all but six of their field guns, leaving married officers and their families behind as hostages. Pottinger alone argued for rejection, and urged moving the whole host to the Bala Hissar to wait for a relief force. Mohan Lal conveyed fresh ill-tidings: Akbar was faithless and his offer a trick to get the British to leave, and he wanted hostages solely to assure the safety of his father in India.

Pottinger was overruled, Mohan Lal ignored, Shah Shuja told to fend for himself, and the terms accepted. The British handed over their treasury and 130 hostages, while medical officers drew lots to see who would remain with the sick and wounded. January 5 was fixed for the departure of some 4,500 troops, wives, and families, including Ladies Macnaghten and Sale, and a terrified miscellany of 10,000 camp followers, to head for passes whose names rang with menace: Gundamuk, Neemla, Jagdalak. "We are to depart without a guard, without money, without provisions, without wood," recorded Lady Sale, who while packing came upon these lines by Thomas Campbell in a book of poems:

> Few, few shall part where many meet,
> The snow shall be their winding sheet;
> And every turf beneath their feet
> Shall be a soldier's sepulchre.

When the promised Afghan escort failed to arrive, Pottinger made a final plea for a surprise march to the Bala Hissar. On January 6, still with no sign of the promised escort, the garrison began its withdrawal from Kabul. Looters swarmed the cantonment as the soldiers, their scarlet jackets buttoned to the throat, trudged toward crags buried in snow. As Eyre noted in his log, "the camp followers with the public and private baggage, once out of cantonments, could not be prevented from mixing themselves up with the troops, to the confusion of the whole column." As night fell, the sky glowed with the flames of the cantonment, presenting, wrote Eyre, a spectacle of fearful sublimity.

On succeeding days, the Afghan winter gnawed at the dispirited army. Clods of hardened snow adhered so firmly to the hoofs of horses that it took a chisel to dislodge them. "The very air we breathed froze in its passage out of the mouth and nostrils," Eyre noted, "forming a coating of small icicles on our mustaches and beards." Limbs were so chilled that only a few hundred serviceable fighting men remained. Eyre wrote in dismay that "the idea of threading the stupendous pass before us" in the face of armed tribes in such an irregular multitude was "frightful."

Akbar's escort finally turned up, and preceded the British through a narrow canyon whose heights were commanded by Ghilzai warriors. The firing commenced on day three, unchecked by the evidently sincere appeals of the escort. "A universal panic speedily prevailed," Eyre wrote, "and thousands, seeking refuge, hurried forward to the front, abandoning baggage, arms, ammunition, women, and children, regardless for the moment of everything but their own lives." Corpses were stripped of weapons and picked clean by scavenging birds.

On January 9, messengers turned up with a proposal from Akbar Khan. All families and widowed women "should at once be made over to his protection, to preserve them from further hardships." The offer was prompted by calculation as well as humanity, since Akbar's father was under British power. General Elphinstone again acquiesced; Eyre, his wife, and infant son were among the families surrendered. By now the fighting force had shrunk to 150 cavalry troopers, fifty horse artillerymen with one howitzer, and a miscellany of survivors. The five-day toll of European officers, native troops, their families, and camp followers, lost in battle or to the weather, was now 12,000. When a staff officer, Captain James Skinner, remonstrated with Akbar that a treaty had been entered into, and the garrison's safety guaranteed, he expressed regret but claimed it was impossible to restrain the Ghilzai.

On January 11, passing from Kutter-Sung to Jagdalak, the garrison's remaining troops came under withering fire, leaving the road lined with bodies. Survivors were greeted with a new message from Akbar. The Prince now demanded that General Elphinstone, Brigadier Shelton, and Captain Johnson be turned over to him as hostages for the evacuation of Jalalabad. The general again saw no alternative. He made over temporary command to Brigadier Thomas Anquetil, and departed with the two officers to join Akbar Khan.

Their general gone, their morale drained, those alive threaded through Jagdalak, a two-mile long defile. From precipitous heights, sharpshooters brought down most of the survivors. Those still alive on January 13 were picked off one by one as they approached Gundamuk Pass, where six Britons unwisely tarried to accept food from local farmers. Two were killed, and the rest fled only to be overtaken just four miles from Jalalabad. Three were slain, but with desperate exertion, the fourth escaped. He was Dr. William Brydon, the only Briton to complete the retreat.

On January 13, 1842, sentries at Jalalabad fort scanned the valley for signs of the army. Colonel William Dennie, one of the stormers of Ghazni, was in charge. "You will see: not a soul will reach here from Kabul except one man, who will come to tell us the rest are destroyed," Dennie had predicted at the outset of the British expedition. When the same officer saw the assistant army surgeon Dr. Brydon, half alive on a limping horse as he headed toward the fort, he spoke for the ages: "Did I not say so? Here comes the messenger."

THE AFTERSHOCKS OF AFGHANISTAN SPREAD WIDE AND FAR. "NO failure so totally overwhelming as this is recorded in the pages of history," wrote Sir William Kaye, in his *History of the War in Afghanistan* (1851). "No lesson so grand and impressive is to be found in all the annals of the world." After an unbroken sequence of victories, the British in India were humbled by allegedly backward Asians, a fact as worrying to the rulers as it was exhilarating to the ruled. A generation of British officers was scarred by the retreat from Kabul, whose epilogue was nearly as dramatic as the disaster itself. Here briefly is what happened to those whose story we have followed:

Sir Charles Theophilius Metcalfe, the interim Governor-General who opposed the war and who liberated the press, was passed over for appointment as Governor of Madras. He returned to England to vindicate himself, and was named Governor of Jamaica (1839–42), then Governor-General of Canada (1843–45). Raised to the peerage, and laden with honors, he died in 1846.

His successor, Lord Auckland, returned to England in 1842 after the Melbourne Ministry fell from power. Until his death by a stroke seven years later, he blamed everyone else for his Afghan debacle, which he called "a partial reverse." He was denied the usual vote of thanks for his services by the House of Lords, but when Whigs returned to office, he was again given his former post as First Lord of the Admiralty.

Emily Eden never married, and once back home published her lithographs of *The Princes and People of India,* and two successful novels, *The Semi-Detached House* and *The Semi-Detached Couple*; her letters from India appeared in *Up the Country*, three years before her death in 1869.

The Afghan War was brought to a conclusion by Lord Ellenborough, the new Governor-General. To relieve the Jalalabad garrison, a column under Major General George Pollock forced the Khyber Pass in April 1842. This was accomplished by "crowning the heights," that is sending flanking units or pickets to command the heights and protect the troops from sniper fire. Pollock's army advanced to Kabul, where it was joined by an equally aggressive force from Kandahar under Major General William Nott. This was the "Army of Retribution" that retook Kabul, executed so-called rebels, and blew up the bazaar in which Macnaghten's body had been hung.

Shah Shuja was spared the customary punishment for Afghan losers (being blinded), and after hibernating in his citadel for months, he emerged in April to review his troops and was mortally shot by his godson. This made possible the restoration of Dost Mohammed with the support of the same British Government that had deposed him. He reigned until his death in 1863 but was predeceased by his favorite son, Akbar Khan. "I cannot understand," the

Dost once marveled to a British visitor, "why the rulers of so great an empire should have gone across the Indus to deprive me of my poor and barren country." His name lingers in an Afghan saying, "Is Dost Mohammed dead that there is no justice in the land?"

When Captain Ivan Vitkevich returned to St. Petersburg in April 1839, he was repudiated (so Kaye relates) by the Foreign Minister, Count Nesselrode, who said he "knew of no Captain Vitkevich, except an adventurer of that name, who, it was reported, had been lately engaged in some unorthodox intrigues in Caubul and Caundihar." Overwhelmed by despair, it was said, he returned to his hotel and shot himself. A different if unverifiable account is that Vitkevich was visited at his hotel by a former comrade from his years in the Black Brothers underground in Poland, who denounced him as a turncoat for serving the imperial monster he vowed to destroy. A guilt-ridden Vitkevich destroyed all his papers, according to this version, then himself.

The "newswriter" and British operative Charles Masson returned to England in 1842 after twenty years in India. He published a three-volume account of his travels and died penniless at fifty-three in 1853. The East India Company's Court of Directors paid his children £100 for his papers, drawings, and coins of ancient Afghanistan; the latter are among the numismatic treasures of the British Museum, the former are today among the prized manuscripts at the India Office Library in London.

Mohan Lal survived the Afghan disaster, returned to India to write a valuable if circumspect account of the British intervention, and subsequently sailed to Britain, where he was presented to Queen Victoria. He then presented the journals of Alexander Burnes to that officer's family in Scotland. The *munshi* returned to India, lived in obscurity in Delhi, where he died in 1877.

The outspoken Eldred Pottinger received perfunctory recognition for his services, and died after a brief illness while in Hong Kong visiting his uncle, Sir Henry Pottinger, the colony's first British Governor. After being liberated in September 1842, along with some sixty or so British prisoner-hostages and their families, Vincent Eyre resumed his army career, played an important role in the Great Mutiny, returned knighted and bemedaled to England in 1863, and while visiting France during the 1867 war with Prussia, organized an ambulance service for the English Red Cross. Eyre died in France in 1881. General Elphinstone, ailing and pathetic, perished while a prisoner-hostage in April 1842 at Kabul; his body was returned to the British garrison at Jalalabad, where he was buried with full honors.

Lady Florentia Sale survived imprisonment, berated and awed her jailers, earned the nickname of the "Petticoat Grenadier," helped four of the hostage wives successfully through childbirth, lost her son-in-law but became a grandmother, kept her lip as stiff as possible in forced marches from place to place, and was in the vicinity of Bamian when liberated by her beloved spouse, Brigadier Sir Robert Henry Sale, in September 1842. Sale was bedecked with honors, named Quartermaster-General of the East Indies, and in 1845 was once again wounded, this time fatally, at Mudki during the Sikh wars. Lady Florentia published her hostage journals, lived on her widow's pension, and in 1853 traveled for her health to South Africa, where she died the same year. Her fine epitaph in the Church of England cemetery in Cape Town reads: "Underneath this stone reposes all that could die of Lady Sale."

Giving a new amplitude to the word, Dr. William Brydon was a survivor at the siege of Jalalabad, had a close call at Tezeen when he was hit by a six-pound shot, and during the Indian Mutiny survived the epic siege of Lucknow. Retiring a year later in 1859 as Surgeon William Brydon, Commander of the Bath, he returned to his native Scotland where he died in bed in 1873. Still, his shade has not been left wholly in peace. In the 1960's, the American historian Louis Dupree intensively restudied the First Afghan War. He collected folktales on the retreat route, and found that memories of specific episodes had passed orally from parents to offspring, evoking scenes that complemented the printed record. He rummaged through old records and in 1964, at the India Office Library, unearthed a signed copy of Dr. Brydon's lost report on the death-march. It was in the surgeon's handwriting, tucked in Sale's Brigade Book. Brydon graphically described the massacre at Jagdalak on January 12, when the Afghans assailed the British army's rear column: "The confusion became terrible, all discipline was at an end, and the shouts of Halt, Halt, Keep Back the Cavalry were incessant. Just after getting clear of the Pass—I with great difficulty made my way to the front, where I came upon a large body of Men and officers, who finding it was perfectly useless to remain with the Troops in such a state, [had] gone ahead to form a kind of advance Guard."

Dupree maintains that Brydon and his fellow officers were deserters. He notes that Brydon was not the sole survivor since the captive officers, their families, and scores of "other ranks" also survived, plus some 2,000 sepoys and camp followers who turned up as beggars in Kabul. Nevertheless, as Dupree acknowledges, Dr. Brydon was the sole European to survive the entire march. In the horrifying and chaotic circumstances of the final retreat, furthermore, it seems harsh and unwarranted to accuse anybody of deserting.

FINALLY, THERE WAS SIR ALEXANDER BURNES, THE CONVENIENTLY deceased scapegoat for the authors of the war. The injustice done to him in official documents became generally known when Colonel Sir John William Kaye published his *History of the War in Afghanistan* in 1851. Kaye was a serving officer in the Bengal Artillery until 1841, when he started a double life as prolific author and civil servant. He succeeded John Stuart Mill as secretary of the Political and Secret Department of the India Office in London, and his descendants served the Raj well into the twentieth century.

Kaye knew the actors in the Afghan tragedy, and had access to their secret reports, diaries, and correspondence. He demonstrated that the Government ignored Burnes's advice from Kabul, and then doctored his dispatches in parliamentary papers issued by Lord Palmerston as Foreign Secretary and Sir John Cam Hobhouse as President of the India Board of Control. Kaye's revelations posed two questions. Who ultimately was responsible for the Afghan debacle, and was an apology owed Alexander Burnes?

Palmerston and Hobhouse at first saw no reason to apologize for anything. Where were the critics, they demanded, when it seemed the Afghan operation was a success? Opposition wisdom was after the event; as to doctoring documents, Hobhouse admitted that pas-

sages were left out, and that Burnes had a preference for Dost Mohammed, but "To have published all that Sir A. Burnes said, would
have answered no good purpose." By 1842, better news from Asia
took the bite from the debate. British honor had been avenged in
Afghanistan and the hostages saved; China was "opened" after the
two-year First Opium War ended in victory for Britain, yielding
Hong Kong as bagatelle.

Still, once the British withdrew from Afghanistan, the question remained: What was the *point* of the war? To hear Palmerston and
Hobhouse, it was to defend India, to keep Russia from devouring
Herat, and to assure the stability of Afghanistan. But Hobhouse knew
nothing of India before assuming his post, and Palmerston thought
so little of India that he three times refused the post of Governor-
General. If the Russian menace were so serious, why send a novice
like Auckland with vague instructions? Why keep the East India
Company in the dark? At one point, in 1851, Hobhouse informed
the House of Commons, "The Afghan war was done by myself; entirely without the privity of the Board of Directors," meaning it resulted from a Government decision without even consulting the
Company's knowledgeable directors. Another time, in 1842, Hobhouse sought to blame Auckland, claiming the decision to invade
was contained in a dispatch from Calcutta that passed the ship bearing his own, presumably different, instructions.

It seems fair to say that what tipped the scales was British prestige
and domestic politics. Palmerston and Hobhouse inflated the Russian menace, undervalued the fighting abilities of Asian peoples, and
claimed for Britain the unilateral right of intervention. Auckland too
eagerly embraced these views, and too willingly followed London's
lead in giving General Elphinstone the command in Kabul. But he
was the agent, and not the author. In 1840, Lord Palmerston as Foreign Secretary articulated the grand strategy that sent the army to
Kabul: "It seems pretty clear that sooner or later the Cossack and the
Sepoy, the man from the Baltic and he from the British islands, will
meet at the centre of Asia. It should be our business to take care that
the meeting should be as far off from our Indian possessions as may
be convenient and advantageous to us. But the meeting will not be
avoided by our staying at home to receive the visit." To Palmerston's

most persistent critic, John Bright, this was imperial swagger. In 1861, when Palmerston was Prime Minister, his opponents brought up the matter of Burnes to embarrass him. Bright joined in calling for a Committee of Inquiry to establish who was responsible for the papers on Afghanistan published in 1839. Palmerston insisted that Burnes, however good a public servant, misjudged the situation in Afghanistan, and it made no sense to publish those portions of his dispatches that did not affect the Government's decisions. Decrying an "odious offense" against the truth, Bright demanded to know why, if Burnes's views were worthless, they were falsified and by whom. The war cost 20,000 lives, and yet, despite that terrible toll, Bright continued, a Minister of the Crown laid upon the table "documents which are not true—which slander our public servants, and which slander them most basely when they are dead and are not here to answer." Was there, or is there, Bright asked rhetorically, someone in high position "who had so low a sense of honour and right that he could offer this House mutilated, false, forged opinions of a public servant who lost his life in the public service?"

Bright dented Palmerston's composure, but the motion failed, and the Prime Minister never really had to answer for his role in the Afghan disaster. Indeed Palmerston resented having to discuss the matter. As he wrote to John Cam Hobhouse about the Commons debate, "It was really too bad to put us on our defence about a Transaction which happened upwards of twenty years ago." Good Old Pam was to have better hours and brighter causes. But regarding the Kabul disaster, his attitude was, as the British military are wont to say, Never apologize, never explain.

.:.

CHAPTER FIVE

The Russians Are Coming

I F ONE WERE TO ATTEMPT A GRAND NARRATIVE OF THE nineteenth century, a likely title in today's vernacular would be "Go for It." The age saw an unparalleled movement of peoples over land and sea, made possible by steam and rail. Earlier explorers and pioneers had pried open the gates of Asia, Africa, and the Americas. Now millions followed their lead, searching for land, work, and riches, for political and religious freedom, or simply for adventure. What emigrants did as individuals, nations did as aggregates. By 1900, most of the world's people and territory were under the dominion of less than a dozen countries, including the United States—a latecomer to the scramble for overseas spoils, having just acquired Hawaii, the Philippines, and Puerto Rico. Never before had so few ruled so many.

A mixture of impulses—pride, the claims of national interest, the lure of profits, missionary zeal, the wish to relocate prisoners or ambitious soldiers—propelled this planting of flags across the globe. Whatever their motives, those in charge believed that expansion was a good thing, that it served some providential purpose, and that ordinary settlers as well as colonial governors were bearers of a superior civilization, thereby benefiting less fortunate natives. These sentiments were celebrated in music halls and pulpits, in genre paintings and popular fiction, and in verse, as in Walt Whitman's "Starting from Paumonok" (the poet's birthplace on Long Island):

> *See, vast trackless spaces,*
> *As in a dream they change, they swiftly fill,*
> *Countless masses debouch upon them.*
> *They are now cover'd with the foremost people, arts, institutions,*
> *known…*
> *Americanos! conquerors! marches humanitarian!*

So pervasive was the imprint of the frontier that a young University of Wisconsin scholar made his reputation almost overnight with a paper contending that America's westward surge explained the country's special character. Appositely, Frederick Jackson Turner addressed an audience of historians in 1893 at Chicago's Columbian Exposition, celebrating the European discovery of the Americas. He called attention to a census finding that the United States in 1890 no longer had an identifiable frontier of settlement. He wondered what this augured, since it was to the "imperious summons of the frontier" that Americans owed that "coarseness of strength combined with acuteness and inquisitiveness; that practical, inventive turn of mind, quick to find expedients; that masterful grip of material things, lacking in the artistic but powerful to effect great ends; that restless nervous energy, that dominant individualism, working for good and for evil, and withal that buoyancy and exuberance which comes with freedom."

Turner's thesis, in the words of a latter-day Wisconsin historian, William Appleman Williams, "rolled through the universities and into popular literature as a tidal wave." Few academic papers have been so heatedly debated, generating a literature whose very magnitude attests to the idea's importance. Doubtless the Turner thesis was too simple and vaguely expressed; assuredly he failed to deal adequately with the role of women or the matter of slavery, much less resolve his own ambivalence about what the closing of the frontier signified. Yet the frontier and its mythology continue to define what is distinctive to American character, whether one considers the arguments over gun control, the persistence of clandestine militias, the popular support for NASA's space program, or that surprisingly vital legacy of President Kennedy's New Frontier, the Peace Corps.

Less commonly appreciated is the fact that American frontiersmen found their match and, in terms of hardihood, their superior, in their Russian counterparts.

RUSSIA EXPANDED EASTWARD AND SOUTHWARD IN SUCCESSIVE waves, waves so powerful that in the course of four centuries the Tsarist empire grew at the remarkable average of fifty-five square miles a day. The first great conquest was Siberia, a territory covering 5.3 million square miles, almost 2 million square miles bigger than the continental United States. As W. Bruce Lincoln reminds us in *The Conquest of a Continent* (1994), a single Siberian province, Iakutsk, is larger than India. Not only vast but rich, Siberia also possesses (in Lincoln's reckoning) a sixth of the world's gold and silver, a quarter of its timber, a third of its iron, a fifth of its platinum, as well as major deposits of oil and gas, and navigable rivers long enough to circle the Equator.

Yet Muscovy mastered this immense realm in less than seventy years, starting in the 1580's, the final phase of Ivan the Terrible's reign. The engines of conquest were the Stroganovs, mercantile barons and commercial agents to the Tsar, and the Cossacks, the word stemming from *kazak*, a Turkic term meaning vagabond, adventurer, or a person expelled from his tribe. Superb horsemen, renowned for their loyalty and ruthlessness, the Cossacks fought in the pay of the Stroganovs, and in the name of the Tsar. Some eight hundred Cossacks, armed with matchlock muskets and pikes, led by a former river pirate named Ermak, advanced into Siberia and decimated its warriors in much the way Cortés defeated the Aztecs with six hundred Spaniards. Soon Ivan added "Tsar of Siberia" to his titles, and river forts, blockhouses, and trading posts sprang up to protect a lucrative trade in fur pelts. As in America's Great West, Siberia's nomadic peoples—the Yakuts, Kirghiz, Oroks, Chukchi, and scores of others, most notably the Buriats near Lake Baikal—became the subjects of a remote Great White Father.

At first, Siberia's new masters did not know how far their territory extended. In 1648, a daring Cossack explorer, Semën Dezhnëv, sailed around Siberia's northeastern tip and through the Bering Strait, 6,000 miles east of Moscow. Using primitive navigational aids on crude boats, braving the ice floes and bitter storms that claimed most of his fleet, Dezhnëv confirmed that Asia and North America were separate continents. A provincial governor suppressed his report (a chronic Russian failing), so that his feats went unheralded for almost a century. In 1724, Peter the Great turned to a sturdy Danish-born captain, Vitus Bering, to clear up navigational puzzles and locate the rumored lands beyond Siberia's tip. Four years later, Bering sailed through the fifty-three-mile strait into the sea that would also carry his name, but failed to reach North America.

Bering came closer on his second voyage, embarking in 1741 from Kamchatka, itself a place of wonder: a volcanic peninsula in eastern Siberia with thirty-three smoldering cones. Proceeding with two vessels, Bering reached the Aleutians and sighted Alaska when, along with many shipmates, he succumbed to scurvy and died on what is now Bering Island. His charts showed the way to thousands of trappers and traders who streamed down the Alaskan coast. In 1799, a Russian-American Company was chartered to explore and colonize North America, and to propagate Christianity. Under the aegis of a dynamic resident director, Alexander Baranov, the Company kept moving south, eventually securing a foothold in California, on the Russian River, a hundred miles north of San Francisco.

There, in the resonant year 1812, the Slavic newcomers raised the Company's flag over Rossiya (Russia), a fort whose cannons guarded fifty-nine buildings, including the first Russian Orthodox church in North America outside Alaska. It was a colony too far. The Spaniards, on regaining their independence from Napoleon, no longer welcomed Russians in what was still Spanish California. Moreover, the young American Republic bridled at the Russian advance. Avowedly to deter smuggling, a Tsarist edict in 1821 barred foreign vessels from the Northwest coast down to the fifty-first parallel, reaching deep into what Americans claimed was Oregon Territory. In Washington, John Quincy Adams, then Secretary of State, informed the Tsar's envoy he would contest the edict on "the principle that the American continents are no longer subjects for *any* new European colonial establishments." This was the kernel of the famous Doctrine that President Monroe was to proclaim only four months later. Prudently, the Russians stepped back. In St. Petersburg, Count Nesselrode, the Foreign Minister, accepted the noncolonization principle. He found that the fifty-first parallel did not actually partition Oregon, and determined that California was not really part of Russia's "North West Coast," all of which was set forth in an 1824 convention.

In 1841, the Russian-American Company sold its California holdings—land, buildings, livestock, and a twenty-ton schooner—for $30,000 to a Swiss pioneer, John Sutter, the founder of Sacramento. Rossiya was renamed Fort Ross, and in time metamorphosed into a historical site worthy of two Michelin stars—as is another Sutter property, the mill in El Dorado County where gold was discovered in 1847. Thus the two frontiers touched for a brief moment, ending in a golden handshake that anticipated Russia's sale of Alaska in 1867 for $7,200,000, or two cents an acre. Russia's expansionary interests lay elsewhere, in Europe and Asia.

AFTER THE GRAND ARMY'S RETREAT FROM MOSCOW IN 1812, Russia under Alexander I emerged as a European power of the first rank. Still, Russia marched to a different drummer; even its calendar lagged twelve days behind the Gregorian system adopted in the West. The difference grew out of its geography. Russia had no natural boundaries save for the polar ice and the distant peaks of Asia and the Caucasus, leaving it permanently vulnerable to invasion. This vulnerability served as a pretext for absolutism as Russians fought off Asian and European invaders. In Hugh Seton-Watson's phrase, Muscovy evolved into a barracks-state. Absolutism also distinguished its social system. Under feudalism elsewhere in Europe, nobles, merchants, and landowners possessed rights that kings were bound to respect. In Russia, princes and peasants alike were creatures of the crown. Five-sixths of the Russian population consisted of illiterate peasants, half of whom were serfs who could be sold as chattel, beaten with impunity, or conscripted to serve a lifetime in the army. Serfdom was firmly established in Russia only in the fifteenth century, and by the eighteenth century turned into virtual slavery, whereas elsewhere in Europe serfdom all but vanished after the Black Death of 1348–49.

To many Europeans, the Westernizing reforms of Peter the Great were a stage-set façade, like the Potemkin villages hastily assembled to impress Catherine the Great. A French visitor, the Marquis de Custine, expressed a common judgment. He had gone to Russia in 1839 to confirm his belief in aristocratic rule, and was disturbed by what he encountered. "The more I see of Russia," he reported, "the more I approve the conduct of the Emperor in forbidding his subjects to travel…The political system of Russia could not stand twenty years' free communication with the West of Europe." Custine was struck by the gloomy stillness in public places: "only the horses have permission to make a noise." Here secrecy shrouded everything, "administrative secrecy, political, social secrecy; discretion useful, discretion useless. A silence that is superfluous assures the silence that is necessary. Here, discretion is the order of the day, just as imprudence is in Paris. Every traveler is in himself an indiscretion …"

European apprehension was deepened by Russia's seemingly insatiable appetite for territory at every imperial frontier. In 1721, Russia seized Estonia, northern Latvia, and the Finnish lands on which St. Petersburg would rise. A year later, Peter the Great's armies thrust into Daghestan, opening the Caucasus to Russian dominion. In 1734, with an important victory over Kazak warriors, the Russians began their advance into Central Asia. Crimea was annexed from Turkey in 1783. Poland was partitioned in 1772, twice more in 1793–95, and its eastern half was incorporated into Russia in 1832, bringing with it Lithuania, southern Latvia, Belorussia, and the Ukraine east of Galicia. Russia's annexation of Georgia provoked wars with Persia (1804–13) and Turkey (1806–12), and by winning them, the Tsar planted the double-eagle in Baku and Bessarabia. Armenia passed by treaty from Persia to Russia in 1828, and its frontiers expanded after the Turko-Russian War of 1828–29. In Northern Europe, meanwhile, Alexander's victories over Sweden (1808–09) gained Russia the whole of Finland and assured its mastery of the Baltic.

A legend spread that Peter the Great had concocted a secret plan for global dominion that his successors were sworn to carry out. Others, less fancifully, claimed that Russia and America were destined to be the world's dominant superpowers, a notion put forward as early as 1790 by Catherine the Great's agent in Paris, Baron Grimm. He confided to the empress that two nations would eventually divide all the powers of art, arms, and industry, "Russia from the Eastern side, and America, having freed itself in our time from the Western side." Other astute observers advanced the same notion, soon to be given its most celebrated formulation by Alexis de Tocqueville in *Democracy in America* (1835). "There are at the present time two great nations in the world which started from different points, but seem to tend to the same end," he asserted in his book's famous final paragraph. "I allude to the Russians and the Americans. Both of them have grown up unnoticed; and while the attention of mankind was directed elsewhere, they have suddenly placed themselves in the front rank among the nations...Their starting-point is different and their courses are not the same; yet each of them seems marked out by the will of Heaven to sway the destinies of half the globe."

Still, *pace* Tocqueville, the British were unwilling to concede anything to Russia, much less to their pushy American cousins. Among the first to sound the alarm was Sir Robert Wilson (1777–1849), a soldier of distinction who witnessed the burning of Moscow while an official military observer. He had seen the brutality as well as the bravery of the Cossacks, and reported watching in horror as their prisoners were buried alive or clubbed to death. In his *Sketch of the Military and Political Power of Russia* (1817), Wilson contended that Alexander I, having added 200,000 square miles to his realm, now planned to seize Constantinople and then invade India by way of Persia. As Peter Hopkirk remarks in *The Great Game* (1990), Wilson sowed the seeds of Russophobia in Britain, and thus "gave birth to a debate on Russia's every move which would continue for a hundred

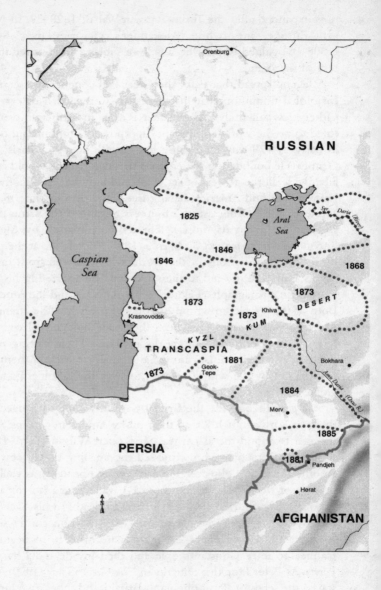

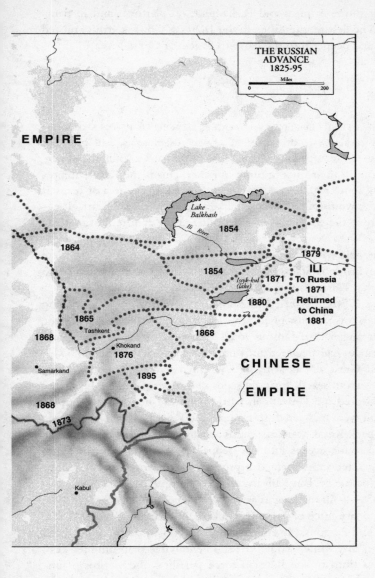

THE RUSSIAN
ADVANCE
1825-95

Miles

0   200

EMPIRE

*Lake
Balkhash*

Ili River

1854

1864

1854

1879

1871

ILI
To Russia
1871
Returned
to China
1881

*Issyk-kul
(lake)*

1880

1865

1868

Tashkent

1868

1868

Khokand

1876

1868

Samarkand

1895

CHINESE

EMPIRE

1873

Kabul

years or more, in press and Parliament, on platform and in pamphlet." The debate intensified in the 1830's as Cossack armies moved deeper and deeper into the barren vastness of Central Asia.

IMAGINE A TERRAIN FLAT AS A SAUCER, DEVOID OF PEAKS AND WITH scarcely any trees, consisting of grasslands, deserts, and brackish marshes—an unappealing terrain, except perhaps to millions of gerbils secure in their underground burrows. This is the Kazak Steppe, covering some 750,000 square miles, three times the area of Texas. It lies, in the words of one traveler, "like a caesura in Asia's heart." It extends from the former Russian frontier post at Orenburg, at the mouth of the river Or, due south to the Aral Sea. The Kazaks, a nomadic people whose ancestors once fought for Genghis Khan, were the principal inhabitants of this flatland, which one must traverse to reach what Tsarist cartographers called western Turkestan.

In the 1700's, western Turkestan had ceased to be a flourishing crossroads for caravans plying the silk routes between Asia and the Mediterranean. Its famous oasis cities—Bokhara, Khiva, and Samarkand—had declined into provincial backwaters. Yet in 1717, Peter the Great sent an army of 3,500 men across the steppe to subdue Khiva and search for gold sands said to exist nearby. The Russians defeated the Khivans in battle but were lured into a trap in which all were massacred (so claimed the Russians). In 1735, having beaten back Kazak warriors, the Russians established Orenburg as a secure base for sweeps into the steppe. By 1800, forty-six forts and ninety-six redoubts formed a protective web for Russian settlers seeking pasturage. But Khiva was still unconquered.

In 1839–40, in the biggest assault yet, General V. A. Perovsky led an expeditionary force of 5,000 Cossacks, 2,000 Kirghiz porters, 10,000 camels, and 22 guns. He embarked in autumn, in the misguided expectation that winter would be less unendurable than summer heat. All but a third of the Russian force perished, the victims of unremitting blizzards or Khivan guerrillas. Having made his point, the

Khan of Khiva sought to placate the Russians with promises of friendlier relations. St. Petersburg responded by sending embassies to Khiva, ostensibly to negotiate but actually to prepare maps for a fresh offensive.

One reads of these events, incredulously. What could have impelled this prodigious projection of power over an interminable solitude? Was it the threatening memory of Genghis Khan and his Golden Horde? A wish to square accounts for centuries of Mongol domination? So ran a prevalent hypothesis, but there were more tangible reasons. For an empire lacking natural boundaries, space itself formed a wall. The Yale scholar Firuz Kazemzadeh has pointed to Russia's abiding *horror vacui,* the fear that a hostile power might populate the empty steppe. Nor can one ignore the Russian ambition to secure an overland passage to India, for purposes of commerce and possible conquest—the abiding British nightmare. Other analysts, judging these explanations inadequate, claimed the key lay in the recesses of the Slavic soul. "Russia was as much compelled to go forward," Lord Curzon maintained, "as the earth is to go around the sun."

However, this imperial progress was not unique to Russia. Seemingly everywhere, Europeans or their offspring hurled themselves against their inferiors in technology or resistance to disease. The frontier itself—the fluctuating terrain in which peoples with different beliefs and levels of skill were thrown together—generated its own transforming energy. This was the essence of Turner's frontier thesis, and his approach was applied to Inner Asia by Owen Lattimore, an American with firsthand experience in Mongolia. For Lattimore, a frontier was not a line but a fluid zone in which border populations learned from, fought against, and illegally traded with one another, evolving a canny opportunism as power ebbed and flowed. Within this zone one glimpses a universally recognizable figure, the soldier on horseback. Eager for ribbons and promotion, quick to take offense at any slight to national honor, prone to exaggerate the threats posed by a rival power, he was always able to fan the spark of grievance into armed conflagration. And in western Turkestan, the Russians suffered an unendurable injury, the enslavement of compatriots.

SLAVERY WAS A COMMERCE, A SPORT, AND A WAY OF LIFE IN KHIVA and Bokhara, where the trade had flourished for centuries. It was said that Persian women fetched the highest prices for the harem, and that Russians made good workers, but the raiding itself—the *ala-man*—was an exciting incentive for traders. European visitors were unanimous in their condemnation of what Anthony Jenkinson, an Elizabethan traveler, called "this odious traffic." The most savage Turkmens, according to Arminius Vámbéry, the Hungarian traveler and no apologist for Russia, "would not hesitate to sell into slavery the Prophet himself, did he fall into their hands."

The diplomat Eugene Schuyler, the first American known to visit Bokhara, left us this description of what he saw in 1872:

> Entering into a large *sarai*, we went upstairs into a gallery, and found several rooms, some of which were locked, and a number of slaves—two little girls of about four years old, two or three boys of different ages, and a number of old men—all Persians...The slaves were shown to me by an old Turkoman, who acted as a broker, and who told me that the market was rather dull just then, but that a large caravan would probably arrive in the course of a few days...I asked the price of one of the boys, a lively looking lad of fifteen, who had been stolen only five months before from near As-trabad...The first price asked was more than 1,000 *tengas* (£30), which I gradually reduced to 850 *tengas* (£25); the seller constantly dilating on the good points of the boy, what an excellent *jigit* [a skilled horseman] he would make, and so on, the bystanders joining in on one side or the other.

Schuyler asked the broker how he dared sell a Muslim as a slave when as a mullah he knew this was forbidden under Islamic law. "He is not a Mussulman, he is only a Persian, a Kaffir," the Bokharan indignantly protested. "All Persians are Kaffirs [i.e. Shiites] and unbelievers." Haunted by the encounter, and despite attempts by officials, scenting trouble, to block the sale, Schuyler purchased and liberated the boy. Hussein returned with him to St. Petersburg, where he learned to read and write, and was eventually apprenticed to a Muslim clockmaker.

Doubtless a good deal of cant tainted Russian outrage over slavery. Edward Allworth, the doyen of American authorities on Central Asia, has dryly observed that Russian slave markets had long existed in Kiev, Kazan, Astrakhan, and other cities, and that slavery was quietly tolerated in Siberia as late as 1825. What most provoked Russian anger was less the practice of slavery than the abduction and forced conversion of Christians by Muslims. Moreover, as unimpressed foreigners were quick to point out, bonded servitude continued to exist on a grand scale in Russia until 1861, when Alexander II formally emancipated the serfs.

Even so, Russian anger was widely understood, especially by the British, who were in the forefront of the campaign against the slave trade. In 1838, to deprive Russians of a pretext for advancing southward, the British dispatched an emissary to persuade Turkestan's khans and emirs to abandon a repugnant commerce. The officer chosen was Lieutenant Colonel Charles Stoddart, whom we have already encountered at the siege of Herat. As a Royal Staff Corps officer posted to the British Ambassador, Stoddart had shown boldness and initiative, but tended to high-handedness in dealing with Asians of whatever rank. A friend remarked that Stoddart had no more self-control than a child, adding: "To attack or defend a fortress, no better man than Stoddart could be found; but for a diplomatic mission, requiring coolness and self-command, a man less adapted to the purpose could not readily have been met with."

The officer so characterized arrived at Bokhara in December 1838 with instructions to gain the freedom of Russian slaves and to offer British aid if Bokhara were attacked. He was also to assure the Emir he had nothing to fear from a growing British presence in Afghanistan. His first encounters at Bokhara were not auspicious. Stoddart insisted, over protests, on riding in full military regalia to the main square, then refused to dismount, as protocol dictated, when Emir Nasrullah Khan appeared to greet him. Nor did it help when the Emir found that Queen Victoria had not signed the formal message her emissary carried with him. More damaging yet was a letter handed to the Emir by one of Stoddart's servants, written by Yar Mohammed, formerly the Vizier and now Emir of Herat. It denounced Stoddart as a spy deserving execution.

Within days, Stoddart was seized, shackled, and lowered into Bokhara's infamous bug-pit. Said to be inhabited by insects and rodents bred to prey upon terrified humans, the *Siyah Chah* was a filthy hole twenty-one feet deep, littered with bones and rotting flesh. What presumably spared Stoddart's life was news of British military successes in Afghanistan. Stoddart was at intervals freed from the pit and as abruptly flung back again, an ordeal he described in letters smuggled from Bokhara to his family in Norwich, England. "Here I am," he wrote in August 1839, "nominally free but in fact a prisoner at large. The news of the probable fall of Cabool has been widely spread here and has caused great alarm. My release will probably not take place till our forces have approached very near to Bokhara. This Ameer is mad."

Cruel, capricious, a fervent believer, Nasrullah Khan may have seemed mad to his captive. Yet his erratic behavior was not entirely irrational. Along with the khans of Khiva and Khokand, he closely tracked the progress of Russian and British arms in Asia. Like his fellow rulers, he was intent on discovering how to placate and outwit both imperial powers. Since diplomatic communication was spasmodic, emissaries not to be trusted, and khanates continually brawling with each other, it was difficult to know how to respond. The new and ominous portents were the British invasion of Afghanistan in 1838, and the Russian assault on Khiva, purportedly to end the slave trade, in 1839–40. Before the disastrous outcome of the Khivan campaign was known, the British sent Captain James Abbott, and a few months later, Lieutenant Richmond Shakespear, to Central Asia. Once in Khiva in 1840, the Britons tried to secure the release of Russian captives to remove the pretext for the Tsarist offensive. Shakespear did win the confidence of the Khan of Khiva and brought about the liberation of 418 prisoners whom the Briton escorted to the Russian authorities at Orenburg. His feat won him a knighthood, and stirred concern in St. Petersburg over British influ-

ence in western Turkestan. In 1841, a Russian envoy, a Captain Nikiforov, made his way to Khiva and engaged in long discussions with
Allah Quli, the Khan. Their exchange, as preserved in Tsarist
archives, attests to the perennial plight of weaker states trapped between clashing giants:

KHAN. The rumor is that the English are prepared to occupy
Balkh [in Afghanistan].
NIKIFOROV. I have not heard, but if they intend to do this, they
will do it.
KHAN. You advise me to be at peace with them, but my friends
Abbott and Shakespear told me not to make peace with the Rus-
sians.
NIKIFOROV. I repeat to you once more that both friendship and
enmity with the Englishmen are dangerous to you. These people
seek to collect countries. In the last seventy years they have sub-
dued up to 50,000,000 people in India. They took possession of
Kabul and have come within almost five hundred miles of Herat.
These people are dangerous to Khiva.
KHAN. But I shall defend Balkh.
NIKIFOROV. You will not succeed, but had better defend yourself
and your people from English power by concluding a firm alliance with Russia.
KHAN. Will the Tsar send troops to defend me?
NIKIFOROV. One word is sufficient for this, and in the message of
his High Highness the fact that you are an ally of Russia will be
declared.

A close reading of the final exchange indicates that Nikiforov did
not really answer the most critical question put to him. If Colonel
Stoddart was tossed like a shuttlecock in this wider contest for mastery, so were the khanates, those surviving relics of glories past. Yet
states are an abstraction, and people are not. It was Stoddart's plight
that excited sympathy and indignation among British soldiers, especially when news came that the colonel, facing an open grave, had
allegedly converted to Islam. One of Stoddart's servants, who had

managed to escape from Bokhara, carried these tidings to Kabul in 1840. The report, and the *frisson* it elicited, proved an irresistible challenge to Captain Arthur Conolly, among the boldest spirits in what he was the first to call the Great Game.

THE LONG VOYAGE FROM ENGLAND TO INDIA WAS FAMOUS FOR nurturing friendships, but for some passengers it was also a spiritual pilgrimage. In 1823, Arthur Conolly, a sixteen-year-old cadet aboard the *Grenville,* sat daily at the feet of the Right Reverend Reginald Heber, the newly appointed Bishop of Calcutta. A pious and tireless evangelist, the author of "From Greenland's Icy Mountains" and other Anglican hymns, Bishop Heber found an eager acolyte in the young officer. Thereafter Conolly sought while on intelligence missions in Asia to win over Muslims to a kindlier view of Christians, the first step in his view to propagating the Gospels. He first demonstrated his intrepidity when returning from home leave in 1829–30 overland through Russia and the Caucasus to Persia, managing in a daredevil detour to get halfway to Khiva disguised as a native merchant. On this and subsequent travels, his trail was marked by the many friends he made. While in Cawnpore in 1833, he struck up an acquaintance with a prominent missionary, Joseph Wolff, who in his diary noted, "HERE I MET WITH LIEUTENANT CONOLLY," the words carefully inscribed in capital letters.

Conolly's travels convinced him that Britain could contain Russia and serve humanity by forming an Anti-Slavery Confederation that would bring together in beneficent accord the khanates of Khiva, Bokhara, and Khokand. In historian Sir John Kaye's words, he contemplated "a band of Christian heroes entering the remote regions of Central Asia as Champions of Humanity and Pioneers of Civilization," an idea he elaborated in an enthusiastic memorandum in 1838. In one stroke, he maintained, the English could suppress slavery, check Russian influence, spread Christianity, and promote navigation on the Oxus, thus opening Central Asia to British commerce.

Melbourne's Government, then anxious about the Russian advance, responded favorably, even offering Conolly £500 in expenses, and in 1839 so informed Lord Auckland, the Governor-General of India. Auckland at once sent Captain Conolly (as he now was) to join the victorious British forces in Kabul. There he lingered for months, and there he heard that Stoddart, on peril of death, had renounced his religion. Conolly pressed ardently for permission to seek his fellow officer's freedom as part of his ambitious mission. The British Envoy in Kabul, Sir William Macnaghten, happened to be Conolly's cousin and warmly approved his kinsman's plan. A very different view was taken by the British Resident and past traveler to Bokhara, Sir Alexander Burnes. "He is flighty, though a very nice fellow," Burnes remarked of Conolly. "He is to regenerate Toorkistan, dismiss all the slaves, and looks upon our advent as a design of providence to spread Christianity. 'Khiva is subdued by Russia,' said I. 'Bokhara is her ally, and Kokan not inimical, if not friendly. How, then is the league to be formed, and how are you to get two hundred thousand Kuzzilbash slaves given up for nothing?' 'It must be done.' [Said he] 'Yes, with the wand of a Prospero!!!'[Said I]"

Later, when the failure of Russia's 1839–40 assault on Khiva became known, Burnes's objections were ignored, and Calcutta informed Conolly he could depart. "Hip, hip, hurrah!" he wrote home, "I do believe that I am fairly going now." In a letter to Sir Henry Rawlinson, Conolly summed up his hopes: "If the British Government would only play the grand game—help Russia cordially to all that she has a right to expect—shake hands with Persia—get her all possible amends from Oosbegs—force the Bokhara Amir to be just to us, the Afghans, and the other Oosbeg states, and his own kingdom—but why go on; you know my, at any rate in *one* sense, *enlarged* views. *Inshallah!* The expediency, nay the necessity of them will be seen, and we shall play the noble part that the first Christian nation of the world ought to fill."

Captain Conolly set out from Kabul in September 1840 with eighty servants and a well-stocked caravan, like a character in Bunyan's *Pilgrim's Progress* seeking the path through the Valley of Despond to the Celestial City, and the salvation of Captain Stoddart.

CONOLLY REACHED KHIVA IN EARLY 1841, AND ITS KHAN GAVE him a friendly hearing, but little more. In his view, Khiva had already freed Russian captives at the urgings of Captain Shakespear, and his Khivan fighters had now readily repelled a Russian invasion. That being so, the Khan saw no reason to abandon the slave trade, much less form an alliance with his neighbors in Khokand, whom he viewed as incorrigible. As for Bokhara, the Khan warned Conolly at all costs to stay away. Undismayed, Conolly proceeded to his next stop, Khokand, where he arrived just as his hosts had gone to war with Bokhara. More encouraging was his receipt at Khokand of a packet of letters from Captain Stoddart, one of them saying, "The favor of the Ameer is increased in these days towards me. I believe you will be well treated here."

Ignoring other warnings, the officer-pilgrim gallantly moved on to Bokhara, appearing before its main gate in November 1841. An overjoyed Stoddart, free for the moment, greeted his fellow Briton and recounted his ordeal. Both were provided with quarters in the home of Bokhara's military commander. In his first meetings with Conolly, Emir Nasrullah was polite but to the point. Why were so many Englishmen wandering around Turkestan? He suspected the worst—that they were spies, bent on sowing enmity among the khanates—and repeatedly asked why Queen Victoria failed to respond to his own message dispatched the year before. His mood did not improve when a messenger brought a sack of letters to Stoddart, one of which proved to be from Lord Palmerston. The Foreign Secretary acknowledged receiving the Emir's letter to the Queen. It had been transmitted to the Governor-General of India, "in order that His Excellency may reply on behalf of Great Britain as may appear to His Excellency most conducive to the general interests of the British Government."

To Nasrullah, this was tantamount to an insult. Since the British were toying with him, he would toy with their agents. He was further emboldened by tidings from Afghanistan, whose rebellious warriors had slain the British Envoy, deposed a puppet ruler, and massacred an entire British army. Not long thereafter, Conolly and Stoddart were transferred to a fresh purgatory: an unheated cell, crawling with vermin. From time to time the Emir's ministers would pass by and chat with the prisoners, thereby feeding false hopes of liberation. Nevertheless, the captives somehow managed to smuggle messages abroad. "From our Prison in Bokhara Citadel," ran the superscript on a March 1842 letter from Conolly to his brother John beginning, "This will probably be my last note hence, so I dedicate it to you, who now alas! stand next to me," and ending, "Stoddart and I will comfort each other in every way till we die." Despite this gloomy prognosis, the messages continued for a few more months. Conolly reported in April that the Emir had declared war on Khokand, and had marched from his palace to the sound of drums and trumpets, "leaving us in the filthy clothes which we had worn for one hundred and fifteen days and nights." The Emir, having won the war and murdered the Khan of Khokand, was due to return soon to Bokhara—so wrote Conolly on May 28, the last message from either prisoner to reach England.

As the silence lengthened, and as an unconfirmed report claimed the two men had been executed, the British Government in March 1843 pronounced them dead. By then the Whigs were out, and the new Tory Ministry showed no enthusiasm for Asian crusades, and only the mildest curiosity about the fate of its servants in Bokhara. There matters might have rested save for a letter to *The Morning Herald* in Richmond, England, dated July 2, 1843, from the Reverend Wolff, who signed himself "Late Curate of High Hoyland, Yorkshire, formerly Missionary in Persia, Bokhara and Afghanistan." Dr. Wolff, having been to Central Asia and knowing its ways, offered to go forth again to determine whether the two Britons were dead or alive, in return for travel expenses. And lo, a public meeting was called, a committee formed, and the needed funds subscribed, with Lord Melbourne, the former Prime Minister, contributing £20.

Dr. Joseph Wolff was a splendid and quixotic Victorian original, unprepossessing, small of stature, with a flat homely face. "His grey eyes roll and start," *Punch* said of him, "and fix themselves, at times most fearfully; they have a cast in them, which renders their expression still wilder."Yet he possessed a magnetism few could resist. Born in 1795, Dr. Wolff was the son of a rabbi and during his youth in Bavaria searched restlessly for the truths of religion. After questioning the tenets of Judaism, he turned to the Lutherans, then to Catholicism, and finally to the Church of England. He studied theology at Cambridge and after his ordination strove to bring the light of the Gospels to Jews and other unbelievers in the Middle East, Crimea, and the Caucasus, making friends if not converts wherever he ventured. Not even his subsequent marriage to Lady Georgiana Walpole, the daughter of an earl, diminished his thirst for travel. He took her eastward with him, and after a son was born in Alexandria, set off with her permission to Bokhara and Balkh, where he said, "I think I shall there find the Ten Tribes." It was on this trip that he memorably encountered a fellow pilgrim, Arthur Conolly, in India, before returning to England with Lady Georgiana—via the United States, where he addressed the United States Congress and received an honorary D.D. at Annapolis.

Now Dr. Wolff was off again, his luggage stuffed with Bibles in various tongues, two or three dozen silver watches, three dozen copies of *Robinson Crusoe* translated into Arabic, and his canonical gown, hood, cassock, and shovel hat. His devoted Georgiana and his patrons were at the dockside for his departure on October 14, 1843, on the *Iberia* bound for Constantinople. The mood was almost festive, so great was confidence in the estimable Doctor's powers.

IN TURKEY, DR. WOLFF HEARD ENCOURAGING NEWS. SIR HENRY Layard, the British Ambassador and noted excavator of Nineveh, had received travelers' accounts indicating that Conolly and Stoddart were still alive. This, however, was disputed by others in Constantinople, and the intrepid missionary pressed anxiously forward to Trebizond and Erzerum, then around Mount Ararat into Persia, where he met with the Shah. All along the way he was informed that the two captives were almost surely dead. Dr. Wolff was unfazed, writing to his sponsors: "To Bokhara! To Bokhara! was my firm resolve; and even if the Ameer should tell me that they were dead, I was determined to demand their bodies, and put them in camphor and carry them with me to Constantinople, and thence to London."

His final lap, through the lawless Turkmen lands he had visited years before, was the most trying. The closer he came to Bokhara, the more earnestly he was entreated to proceed no further. In Merv, the ancient home of the Tekke Turkmen, reputedly the fiercest man-hunters, a Muslim holy man pleaded with him, "Do not go to Bokhara." Ignoring warnings, persisting as his servants robbed and deserted him, Dr. Wolff made his way to Bokhara, approaching its main gate garbed in full canonicals, a Bible in his hand. The gates opened, and a clamorous throng led him to the royal palace, shouting "*Salaam aleikum*" (Peace be with you).

Dr. Wolff was struck again by the human pageant around him. Half the family of man seemed present in the main square—Bokharan grandees and merchants, Tartars and Cossacks from Russia, travelers from India, Kashmir, and Afghanistan—but nowhere did he see the faces he most diligently sought. In the days that followed, he heard the following account from court officials: the presence of a Russian mission in Bokhara had for months saved the lives of Conolly and Stoddart. When the Russians departed in April 1842, the two Britons were promptly committed to the nefarious bug-pit, and were executed two months later. The pretext for the sentence was Nasrullah's discovery that his prisoners had communicated with the outside world. They were brought to the main square, and there embraced each other. Stoddart reputedly cried out, "Tell the Amir that I die a disbeliever in Muhammed, but a believer in Jesus; that I am a Christian and a Christian I die." Conolly said, "Stoddart, we shall see each other in Paradise, near Jesus." Both were beheaded, the probable date being June 17, 1842.

As Dr. Wolff absorbed this distressing news, the extent of his own peril began soberly sinking in. At the outset, the Emir had treated him affably, plying him with questions. He wished to know the names of Britain's grand Viziers and little Viziers, and whether Queen Victoria was married ("What kind of husband is he that is under the government of his wife?" Nasrullah marveled). At this time Dr. Wolff was able to meet with Bokharans and to compile an account of the city's ancient Jewish community. But the Emir's mood darkened. The missionary was arrested, accused of being a spy, and threatened with death if he did not renounce his religion. The same executioner who dispatched Stoddart and Conolly came to his cell and drew his fingers across Dr. Wolff's throat. The despairing prisoner wrote this message in his Bible to his wife and son: "I have loved you both unto death. J. Wolff. Bokhara, 1844."

What evidently saved him was a timely letter to the Emir from the Shah of Persia. Its contents can be surmised from Nasrullah's words to its Persian bearer: "Well, I will make you a present of Joseph Wolff. He may go with you." In August 1844, the missionary left Bokhara and after the predictable tribulations, returned to England. Safely in Richmond, he thought long and carefully about Emir Nasrullah. Yes, he was cruel and tyrannical, "but at the same time we must not forget his good points," added the empathetic missionary—the Emir despised money, hated bribery, protected the poor, hence was detested by the nobles, and his desire for information was unbounded. "He expressed no contempt for England, but was exceedingly anxious to become reconciled to it; but the continual suspicions infused into his mind, made him hesitate dismissing me—suspicions engrafted there by those who well knew this weak point of his nature…" Dr. Wolff thought it a great mistake for Britain not to have allowed a visit by a Bokharan ambassador prepared to offer the Emir's apology for his undoubted offenses.

Another question seems worthy of meditation. "How extraordinary!" Nasrullah exclaimed apropos the doctor's arrival in Bokhara. "I have two hundred thousand Persian slaves here—nobody cares for them; and on account of two Englishmen a person comes from England and single-handed demands their release." Sir Fitzroy Maclean, a soldier-adventurer and diplomat as well as successful author, struck on this splendid sentence for the title of *A Person from England* (1958), a vivid retelling of the foregoing story. Yet Maclean did not address the more mystifying paradox. Neither her Foreign Secretary nor her Prime Minister appears to have asked Queen Victoria to write the letter to Nasrullah that might have spared the lives of his prisoners. Just such a letter to the Emir from the Shah of Persia did save Dr. Wolff. As puzzling was the British Government's lassitude in responding to the reported execution of its servants. It was left to a middle-aged clergyman using private funds to voyage 5,500 miles to determine their fate.

The explanation surely lies in that clammy phrase, *raison d'état*. To spare a government embarrassment or inconvenience, otherwise honorable people may behave dishonorably. Embarrassed by the fate of Captain Conolly, the Government of India falsely claimed his mission to Bokhara was not authorized, adding that no pay was therefore owed to the servants who accompanied him. One may reasonably surmise that similar callousness explained the British Government's lack of curiosity about its two agents, and the reluctance of its ministers to ask their Queen to set her pen upon crested notepaper.

THE FATE OF POLITICAL AGENTS MAY BE HIDDEN OR IGNORED, BUT neither democracies nor autocracies can conceal humiliation in the field of battle. For Russia and Britain in the mid-nineteenth century, the traumatic debacles were the Crimean War and the Indian Mutiny.

The Crimean War (1853–56) claimed a half million lives, exposed gross military incompetence, forged incongruous alliances, and yet by its very excesses helped keep the peace in Europe until August 1914. The conflict ostensibly arose from a dispute in Jerusalem as to whether Roman or Orthodox Catholics had more rights at Holy Places under Ottoman Turkish protection. Nicholas I championed the Orthodox, and Napoleon III, who had installed himself as Emperor of France, supported the Roman Church. When a ruling by the Turks in 1853 favored the French, Russian troops swarmed into Ottoman provinces in the Balkans, purportedly to protect Orthodox Christians. A general war soon followed.

The conflict's deeper source lay in the character and ambitions of Tsar Nicholas I, "the gendarme of Europe," the nemesis of revolutionaries in Poland and Hungary, an opponent of every liberation movement save those on behalf of Slavs under Turkish rule. In 1852, the Tsar startled the British envoy in St. Petersburg with these words on the Ottoman Empire: "We have on our hands a sick man—a very sick man. It will be, I tell you frankly, a great misfortune if, one of these days, he should slip away from us, especially before all necessary arrangements were made." The Tsar wished to make the "necessary arrangements," such as ceding Ottoman Egypt and Crete to Britain in return for the "temporary" occupation of Constantinople and his freeing Balkan Christians from the Turkish yoke.

Britain's response was a polite but worried no. Nobody was sure what Nicholas intended. He had constructed a great naval base at Sevastopol on the Black Sea, which together with his overtures to Britain suggested he planned to seize the Dardanelles and send his warships into the Mediterranean. That could threaten the main pillars of British foreign policy—maintaining the European balance of power, ensuring British supremacy at sea, and protecting the routes to India. Hence the alarm in London when, in November 1853, a Russian flotilla at Sevastopol crossed the Black Sea and in a surprise attack destroyed an entire Turkish fleet, twelve ships in all, at Sinope. For his part, Napoleon III saw an opportunity in a war for a religious cause that might bind church and army to his own throne. In March 1854, Britain and France, having ordered their navies to protect Turkish shipping, jointly declared war on Russia.

At first the war was popular, despite the anomalous alliance of a Protestant Queen, a Catholic Bonaparte, and a Muslim Sultan against an Orthodox Tsar. Only graybeards remembered Waterloo, the generals were eager for glory, and British bored with what Tennyson called "the long, long canker of peace." Across the Channel, as the poet Lamartine said, "*La France s'ennuie.*" An allied expeditionary force sailed to the Black Sea, landed on the Crimean Peninsula, and in October 1854 commenced the Siege of Sevastopol. Dreams of quick victory faded as the siege dragged on, and the war is chiefly remembered for the charge of the Light Brigade at Balaklava, when a third of 673 cavalry officers perished in charging a Russian field battery, a debacle immortalized by Tennyson and reported for *The Times* by the great war correspondent William Howard Russell.

The besiegers at Sevastopol coped for 349 days with freezing weather, short rations, primeval hospitals, quarreling commanders, and an outbreak of cholera. In September 1855, an allied force led by the French overwhelmed the Russian redoubt, the Malakhov

Kurgan, with casualties exceeding 10,000 for the allies, 13,000 for the Russians. By then Nicholas I had died, and a new emperor, Alexander II, having little choice, began seeking peace. Under the Treaty of Paris in 1856, Turkish independence and territorial integrity were guaranteed. The Black Sea was neutralized, with all arsenals banned from its coasts and its ports permanently "interdicted to the flag of war."

Russia's defeat steadied the balance of power, and the war's sheer awfulness helped inoculate Europeans for two generations against boredom with peace. The conflict's aftershocks struck deepest in Russia, where defeat exposed an incompetent military bureaucracy and underscored the urgent need of railways to speed food and supplies to the front. A keen-eyed young officer, Leo Tolstoy, who commanded a battery in Crimea, saw for himself what was wrong. In his *Tales from Sevastopol,* which first brought him literary celebrity, Tolstoy extolled the heroism of ordinary soldiers. His more impassioned prose flowed into a memorandum entitled "The Negative Aspects of the Russian Soldier and Officer." Our soldiers are brave, he wrote, because death for them is a blessing. Privates are beaten if they smoke, seek to marry, or dare to notice when a superior pockets their pay. "The majority of officers have one aim—to steal their fortunes out of the service...We have not an army," he concluded, "but a crowd of oppressed, disciplined slaves, confessed plunderers and hirelings." Tolstoy at first intended to send his indictment to a Grand Duke, but on second thought, he more cautiously decided to channel his passion into fiction.

Tolstoy's dismay was shared by another officer, a combat veteran in the Caucasus, Count Dmitrii A. Miliutin. When Alexander II, new to the throne, initially considered prolonging the war, it was Miliutin who drafted the persuasive minute arguing the contrary submitted by the Minister of War. In 1860, the Tsar named Miliutin, by now a general, to the same post, and there he served for twenty-one years until an assassin's bomb claimed Alexander II.

Miliutin had few equals in Russia for coolness of analysis, dedication, and integrity. He quickly followed up on the lessons of Crimea. In 1861, he won approval for a "ten-year plan" to build at least 3,500 miles of railroads. That target was exceeded three times over. Along

with his brother Nikolai—ardent reformer, civil servant, teacher—
Dmitrii was a founder of the Imperial Russian Geographical Society, and was among the first to teach geography at the Nicholas
Academy of the General Staff. As War Minister, he put geography
high in the curriculum of overhauled cadet schools, whose doors he
opened for the first time on the basis of merit. More daring was the
advocacy by both Miliutins, with less success, of what in the 1860's
they called *glasnost,* meaning freer discussion of public policy.

Dmitrii Miliutin's most radical views concerned serfdom. Until
Crimea, Russia's huge, ponderous standing army relied mainly on
serfs conscripted for twenty-five years, commonly lethargic and
sullen, since few lived long enough to gain the freedom promised on
their discharge. Miliutin diagnosed the system's crippling defects in a
memorandum in 1856 that proposed a smaller citizen-army, shorter
terms of service, and a backup of readily mobilized reserves. In short,
in the words of Alfred J. Rieber in *The Politics of Autocracy,* Miliutin
"drew the logical conclusion that Russia could not create a trained
reserve which was the backbone of a modern European army without abolishing serfdom." The Minister of War joined with his brother
in pressing successfully for Alexander II's emancipation edict in 1861,
and followed with reforms that transformed the Russian army. He
ended corporal punishment and an archaic court-martial system, and
instituted universal conscription for six- and then four-year terms,
with obligatory reserve service until the age of forty-four.

Humanly, this dedicated public servant was anxious to test his reforms in battle. Miliutin's attention turned eastward, to Central Asia
and the borderlands of China. He sent his ablest officers to the frontier, indulged their forward-school forays, and quarreled continu-
ously with the Tsar's Foreign Minister, Prince Alexander M.
Gorchakov. The War Minister saw nothing wrong with baiting the
British. As Miliutin at one point protested to the Foreign Ministry,
"it is not necessary to apologize to the English Minister for our advance. They do not stand on ceremonies with us, conquering whole
Kingdoms, occupying alien cities and islands; and we do not ask
them why they do it." Besides, why should Russians pay heed to the
preachments of the British, who in the wake of the Crimean War,
were nearly ousted from India by their own native troops?

CHAPTER SIX

The Raj Imperiled

I T IS THE VICTOR'S PREROGATIVE TO NAME THE WAR, AND THE British called the uprising of 1857–58 "the Indian Mutiny," as if it were a barracks riot by disgruntled natives. Sir John Kaye, its earliest authoritative historian, more accurately entitled his narrative *The Sepoy War.* To Karl Marx, writing from London for *The New York Tribune,* it was "the Revolt in India," and on the subcontinent it is remembered as "the Rebellion of 1857" or "the First War of Independence." In truth, it was all of the above, and none of the above. It was assuredly far more than a barracks uprising, or it would not have spread so far so quickly, and lasted for nearly two years. Yet the outnumbered British could not have prevailed without the active support of so many loyal Indians. For their part the rebels could agree on little besides loathing alien rule and a wish to restore precolonial practices. Finally, savage atrocities, which for generations haunted victors and vanquished, mocked the moral pretensions of both sides.

To the Victorians, the Mutiny was more than a colonial war, it was an allegory that affirmed Britain's civilizing mission; for the historian Sir Charles Crostwaithe, it was "the epic of the Race." Every British householder knew its mythic heroes—John and Henry Lawrence, Colin Campbell, John Nicholson, and Henry Havelock—names scarcely remembered today. Its defining episodes—the Massacre at Cawnpore, the Relief of Lucknow, and the Siege of Delhi—were staples of popular folklore, sagas in which intrepid Europeans faced Asian hordes. Many Britons, Queen Victoria creditably among them, were dismayed by the excesses perpetrated by the victors, especially the grisly summary executions (a preferred method being to strap the accused to a cannon's mouth and "blow" him apart). Still, the standard British version tended to be selective and self-flattering. Ignored or played down in contemporary accounts (Kaye's being an exception) was the prevailing indifference verging on contempt for Indian traditions, before and after the Great Mutiny.

That contempt was epitomized in the story of the Rani of Jhansi, little known outside India, where her memory continues to live in ballad and bronze. As Antonia Fraser writes in *The Warrior Queens* (1989), the Rani has her parallel in Queen Boadicea, the early-day Briton who with a spear in her fist vainly led an army against the Roman invaders who had wronged her family and people. For doing precisely that, the Rani was called "the Jezebel of India" by British contemporaries. A century later, she was still accused of slaughtering "every European that fell into her hands" by the Oxford *History of British India* (1958 edition).

Known to history as Lakshmi Bai, she was possibly only twelve in 1842 when she married the aging and infirm Rajah of Jhansi, the ruler of a small Maratha principality in the northern hill country near Gwalior. The union produced no surviving children. Princely adoption was an immemorial Hindu custom, and lacking an heir the Rajah adopted a five-year-old boy belonging to his own royal family. When the Rajah died in 1853, his will asked the British to recognize the child as his successor, his widow as Regent. The British Political Agent at Jhansi warmly seconded the request, describing the Rani as "a lady bearing a high character, and much respected by everyone."

However, the succession required the approval of Lord Dalhousie, a Governor-General of exemplary energy and determination. Dalhousie took the view, as Penderel Moon tells us, that "the more of the map of India that could be coloured red, the better it would be for everyone." In eight years, Dalhousie annexed some 260,000 square miles, much of it seized by applying his new "Doctrine of Lapse," whereby the British could annex any princely state whose ruler left no direct heir. In the case of Jhansi, the Governor-General glanced cursorily at the merits, ignored its long history of loyalty to the Raj, and in 1854 refused to confirm the succession. It was perhaps the worst of all his annexations. The widowed Rani then did the unthinkable—she challenged his ruling, retained a British attorney, and in well-reasoned petitions appealed her case to London. When her petitions were rejected, British Indian authorities punished her presumption with extraordinary meanness. They confiscated the state jewels the Rajah had left her, and deducted his unpaid debts from her monthly pension, both calculated affronts to tradition. This was consistent with Dalhousie's view of India, as confided in a letter to a friend: "I don't deny that I detest the country and many of the people in it. I don't proclaim it; but I don't doubt that my face does not conceal it from those I have to do with."

All told, seven princely states "lapsed" to the Raj during the Dalhousie years. Adopted princes were even deposed from no longer existing thrones, as happened to one of the Rani's childhood friends, Nana Sahib. He was deprived in 1851 of his pension as Peshwa, the title of the chief of the Marathas, an extinct Hindu dynasty. He was given instead the empty courtesy title of Maharajah of Bithur, a dusty statelet near Cawnpore. In the rich and fertile kingdom of Oudh, a different principle was put forward in 1856 to justify annexation: the claim that its Muslim ruler was dissolute, which was true. Yet his puzzled subjects could not understand (writes Penderel Moon) "why their weak, harmless prince, who had done the British no injury, but like his ancestors, had ever been faithful to them, should be thrust aside." Along with this massive political surgery, and the displacement of old ruling elites, ever more missionaries were arriving to teach at new English schools, feeding anxiety among orthodox Hindus and Muslims that their faiths were endangered. Dalhousie himself was conscious of a new unease. Before leaving India in 1856, he worried about the paucity of European officers in what was still the East India Company army—about 40,000 Euro-

peans in a total force of 275,000 troops—and urged prompt reme-
dial steps. He was right to worry.

"THERE IS A MOST MYSTERIOUS AFFAIR GOING ON THROUGH THE
whole of India at present," a medical officer wrote his family in
March 1857. "No one seems to know the meaning of it...It is called
'the chupatty movement.'" Little bundles of chupatties, or unleavened
cakes, were carried by runners from village to village, and no European knew why. There were other omens. Lotus flowers and bits of
goat flesh were passed from hand to hand, a cryptic phrase was whispered in bazaars ("Everything has become red"), strange symbols
were scrawled on walls. Some recalled a prophecy that East India
Company rule would end a century after Clive's triumph at Plassey
in 1757, which paved the way for British dominion over Northeast
India. The chupatty mystery was never solved, nor was it ever proved
that a political conspiracy lay behind the other strange happenings.

More tangible was a rumor swirling among sepoys, or native
troops, that the cartridges for newly issued Enfield rifles were coated
in grease taken from cows, sacred to Hindus, or from pigs, anathema
to Muslims. Worse, the bullets had to be bitten. On hearing these
murmurs, the British issued an order in January 1857 instructing sepoys to mix their own grease from vegetable oils and beeswax. The
devout saw this as another ruse to demean their faiths. In March, a
Bengali trooper at Barrackpur named Mangel Pandy defied and
wounded an officer, for which he was tried and executed (*Pandy*
thereafter became British military slang for mutineer).

Within weeks defiance spread to Meerut, forty miles north of
Delhi, where eighty-five troopers who shunned the new cartridges
were stripped of their uniforms, then sentenced to ten years. In an
eruption of rage the following morning, three regiments mutinied.
They invaded and torched the Meerut cantonment, killing men,
women, and children. Shouting "On to Delhi!" the rebels, most of
them Muslims, marched to the old Mughal capital and proclaimed
themselves followers of the last Mughal ruler, Bahadur Shah, an

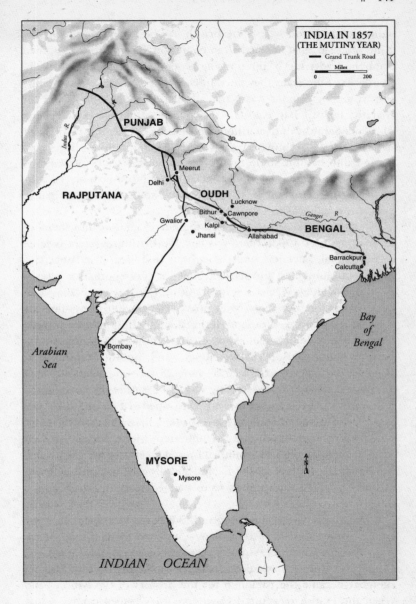

**INDIA IN 1857
(THE MUTINY YEAR)**

━━━ Grand Trunk Road

Miles

0 ———————— 200

Indus R.

PUNJAB

RAJPUTANA

Meerut

Delhi

OUDH

Lucknow

Bithur · Cawnpore

Gwalior

Kalpi

Jhansi

Allahabad

Ganges R.

BENGAL

Barrackpur

Calcutta

Bombay

*Arabian
Sea*

*Bay
of
Bengal*

MYSORE

· Mysore

N

INDIAN OCEAN

aging pensioner on whom the British had bestowed the titular title King of Delhi. Half in fear, half in confusion, Bahadur Shah assumed symbolic leadership of the uprising as sepoys fanned through Delhi murdering Europeans they encountered. The King of Delhi's counterpart among Hindus was Nana Sahib, the adopted son of the last Maratha Peshwa, Baji Rao II. A deputation of mutineers descended on Nana Sahib's court at Bithur and pleaded with him to be their new Peshwa. An equivocating sybarite of about thirty-five years, Nana Sahib had for some time been on cordial terms with Europeans in the nearby garrison at Cawnpore. Now, possibly by pre-arrangement, he switched to the rebels and soon emerged in British eyes as the arch-villain of the Mutiny.

By late spring, the British sensed the tide moving against them. In recently annexed Oudh there was but one British regiment billeted in the capital, Lucknow, and throughout India sepoys of uncertain loyalty outnumbered European troops. At Cawnpore, the veteran General Sir Hugh Wheeler was caught off guard when Nana Sahib declared for the mutineers. Most of Wheeler's 3,500 sepoys fled the garrison, leaving a thousand Britons, including three hundred women and children, in an exposed entrenchment. His charges were beset by gunfire, arson, disease, hunger, and mouth-parching heat. Wheeler in desperation agreed on June 25 to Nana Sahib's offer of safe boat passage for those willing to leave for Allahabad, a hundred miles down the Ganges. Precisely who opened fire, and why, was never determined, but on the riverbank a massacre took place in which most adult males were slaughtered. More than a hundred women and children were rounded up and taken to a dwelling called the Bibighar, or House of the Ladies, built by a British officer for his mistresses. There the captives were stabbed to death, their bodies flung into a well.

When the news reached England, the prevailing belief that the women were raped seemed to many a nightmare fouler than death. According to Cawnpore's most recent historian, Andrew Ward, the allegations of rape were exaggerated and probably unfounded. Yet Bibighar became the paradigm for the horrors of the Mutiny, and when the British recaptured Cawnpore, they forced captive mutineers to lick the dried blood from its floors before being hanged.

Tellingly, as Ward observes in *Our Bones Are Scattered* (1996), actual or imagined rape recurs as an obsessive undercurrent in British fiction set in India, notably E. M. Forster's *A Passage to India,* John Master's *Bhowani Junction,* and Paul Scott's *The Jewel in the Crown* (which begins with the rape of Miss Manners in "Bibighar Gardens").

Whatever happened at Bibighar, the slaughter of civilians by mutineers was itself deeply shaming. It served to draw the British together, and to drive Indians apart. And on the heels of Cawnpore came the report that the Rani of Jhansi had also tricked captives with the false promise of safe passage. In June 1857, rebels had overwhelmed the garrison at Jhansi, killing all British officers except a Lieutenant Taylor, who escaped to the City Fort, built on a huge granite rock, its walls twenty feet thick. The fort became sanctuary for some sixty threatened Britons and Eurasians, half of them women and children. Now the British turned to the Rani, and beseeched her to defend the very regime that had annexed her kingdom. Yet by this time Lakshmi Bai was no longer a free agent. She was subject to the wishes of desperate mutineers, to whom she gave money and elephants. Wholly unproved was the allegation, stated as fact in a British report in November 1858, that the Rani "instigated" the killing of sixty captives who were promised safe conduct. This charge, based on hearsay, thereafter stuck like pitch to her name. The massacre, in Sir John Kaye's contemporary view, "seems to have been mainly the work of our old followers." And in the more recent judgment of Penderel Moon, "There is no reliable evidence that she instigated the sepoys at Jhansi to mutiny, or had any hand in their atrocities."

Indeed, in two letters to the local British Commissioner in June 1857, the Rani condemned the "faithlessness, cruelty and violence" shown to Europeans by the rebels, who she said had threatened to destroy her palace, and to whom she acknowledged giving money to decamp. In the absence of British officials, she assumed governing authority herself—a development which, at that chaotic moment, the British welcomed. Thus for a bright and brief time, the Rani was actual ruler of Jhansi. Now about thirty (writes Antonia Fraser), "she adopted a costume which symbolically combined the elements of a warrior with those of a queen: jodhpurs, a silk blouse with a low-cut bodice, a red silk cap with a loose turban (or puggree) round it. She wore diamond bangles and large diamond rings on her small hands: but a short bejeweled sword and two silver pistols were stuck into her cummerbund."

A dozen accounts attest to the Rani's dignified presence at court, her responsible stewardship, and her skills with horse, rifle, and pistol. Yet in 1858, after the tide turned against the mutineers, it was clear the British would not tolerate her continuing as Regent. Blamed for the slaughter of the captives, she was also condemned for her association with the detested Nana Sahib. When the Rani received no answer to her letters to British officials asking their help, she concluded that she had no choice but to fight to the last.

In April 1858, a British force under Major-General Sir Hugh Rose, freshly arrived from the Crimean campaign, made a final, successful assault on the walled city of Jhansi. As her people cheered, the Rani fought in battle dress, and as the city fell, she managed to escape to nearby Kalpi. British troopers then swept through Jhansi for a day of a slaughter and looting. In his meticulously researched *The Great Mutiny* (1978), Christopher Hibbert asserts that five thousand were slain. A diary kept by an assistant surgeon, J. H. Sylvester, noted that hundreds of corpses were thrown in heaps and set afire: "Now every square blazed with burning bodies and the city looked like one vast burning ground . . . It became difficult to breathe as the air stank with the odour of burning human flesh and the stench of rotting animals in the streets." In the vindictive words of a less horrified medical officer, Dr. Thomas Lowe, "such was the retribution meted out to this Jezebel Ranee and her people."

General Rose and his troopers pressed on to the rebel base at Kalpi, where the British again prevailed, decisively, or so they assumed. In fact, the Rani had joined forces at Kalpi with Rao Sahib, Nana's nephew, and Tantia Topi, the ablest of the rebel commanders. In a daring ruse, they and their troops eluded the British and virtually without a shot captured Gwalior, the strongest fortress in India, with its ample military stores. There the rebels paused, unwisely, for the coronation of Rao Sahib as deputy Peshwa, after which he presented the Rani with a superb pearl necklace found in the Treasury of Gwalior. They were unprepared for Rose's swift attack, in which the Rani was killed, wearing her pearls and her fighting gear, on the battle's second day, in June 1858. Her jewelry vanished, and her body was cremated. In his own report, Sir Hugh Rose confirmed that she was buried "with great ceremony under a tamarind tree under the Rock of Gwalior, where I saw her bones and ashes." His report went on, "The Ranee was remarkable for her bravery, cleverness and perseverance; her generosity to her Subordinates was unbounded. These qualities, combined with her rank, rendered her the most dangerous of the rebel leaders." She is memorialized by Indians in equestrian bronze at Jhansi and Gwalior, and patriotic songs, among them this:

> *How valiantly like a man fought she,*
> *The Rani of Jhansi*
> *On every parapet a gun she set*
> *Raining fire of hell,*
> *How well like a man fought the Rani of Jhansi*
> *How valiantly and well!*

TRUE TO ITS MUDDLED AND PECULIAR CHARACTER, THE OUTCOME of the Great Mutiny was most probably determined by what didn't happen. The uprising failed to take hold in the Punjab, India's pivotal northern province, even though what had been the largest remaining independent state had been recently annexed following two Anglo-Sikh Wars. Now the Sikhs fought alongside their erstwhile foes, and the Punjab served as the secure base from which flying columns charged down the Grand Trunk Road to the Siege of Delhi. More than anything, this was the work of the Punjab's Chief Commissioner, John Lawrence. Irascible, cross-grained, and independent-minded, he was the Victorian Raj's outstanding "civilian," the term for its nonmilitary civil servants. So masterful was his performance that "Plain John" Lawrence became the first and only Indian civil servant to serve as Viceroy. In that position he put forward a far-sighted and original strategy for defending India, within and without.

Lawrence's strengths were his firsthand knowledge of India, augmented by a fluency in colloquial Hindustani and Persian, and a profound yet tolerant piety that leashed a notorious temper. He is among the outsize public servants celebrated by a latter-day "civilian," Philip Mason, in *The Men Who Ruled India* (1954). Along with his older brother Henry, his colleague on the Punjab Board of Administration, Lawrence inspired affection, fear, and respect, winning assent (writes Mason) through "a kind manner, a fundamental goodwill and a controlled ferocity." His exacting piety is evident in the phrasing of his official report submitted after the Mutiny failed, proposing a general amnesty for all not guilty of murder who had fought against the British: "There is a judge over both them and us. Inasmuch as we have been preserved from impending destruction by His mercy alone, we should be merciful to others, reflecting that if He were to mark what we have done and still do amiss, we should forfeit that protection from on High which alone maintains us in India."

When news of the Mutiny first reached the Punjab, there was no time for reflection. Lawrence had trained his juniors to show a bold front, take the initiative instantly, and assume their seniors would back them up, thus ruling more by bluff than force. His "Punjab Men" began immediately to disarm the 35,000 Hindustani troops whose loyalties were doubtful. Any who fled were hunted down, and forty troopers were "blown" in a grisly demonstration at a Punishment Parade. Lawrence now put his trust in Sikh and Muslim troops with whom he had bonded. Drawing on irregular cavalry and infantry from the tough frontier unit, the Corps of Guides, he formed the Punjab Movable Column that clattered down to Delhi, led by Brigadier General John Nicholson, a six-foot-two frontiersman renowned for his combative dark-gray eyes. ("I have never seen anyone like him," remembered Lord Roberts, later India's Commander-in-Chief, "he was the beau-ideal of a soldier and a gentleman.")

This was the force that in September retook Delhi, with Nicholson leading the storming party at the Kashmir Gate. A bullet mortally struck the commander, and the victors ran amok in an orgy of killing and looting. An intelligence officer, William Hodson, tracked down and arrested a quaking Shah Bahadur, and three of his sons.

The old Moghul was later tried for complicity in murder, found guilty, and exiled with his wives to Rangoon, where he died in 1862. His three sons were summarily executed by Hodson, who stripped rings and swords from the "rascally princes," thinking it would be "quite something thereafter to wear a sword taken from the last of the House of Timur." As to killing the sons, Hodson confided in a letter, "The whole nation will rejoice."

Lawrence did not rejoice. He was among the few voices condemning the retributive murders and the systematic spoliation of Delhi. He wrote to the new Governor-General, Lord Canning, urging an end to martial law and the looting that he feared would "render more wide and lasting the breach which has taken place between them and us." When the sack of Delhi continued, Lawrence appealed to the city's military commander "to interfere in this matter." Lawrence found it "incredible" that British officers murdered natives in cold blood: "You may depend upon it we cannot allow such acts to pass unnoticed. If we have no higher motives, the common dictates of policy should make us refrain from such outrages...Unless we endeavour to distinguish friend from foe, we shall unite all classes against us."

On such fundamentals, John was in agreement with his older brother, Sir Henry Lawrence, the hero of Lucknow. The fourth and sixth sons respectively of an Indian Army colonel and a clergyman's daughter, the brothers were reared in the common mode of their caste—childhood in Asia, boarding school in England, special training at the East India Company's school, Haileybury (in John's case), and at its military counterpart, Addiscombe (in Henry's case); then back to India where both studied languages at the Company's college at Fort William. John was the more practical, Henry the more emotional. Henry's courtship and marriage to his cousin, Honoria Marshall, a fine writer, was among the Raj's romantic idylls. The older brother served militarily in the First Afghan War, in the Anglo-Sikh wars, then for years worked (and quarreled) with John in the Punjab. Henry was joint creator with Harry Lumsden of the Queen Victoria's Own Corps of Guides, the irregular frontier unit that John Lawrence was to deploy so effectively. Throughout, Henry wrote thoughtfully on military issues, his pen sharpened by Honoria, who in sixteen years of her married life was continually on the move, and often ill, the typical perambulatory fate of the Raj's memsahibs. On January 1854, at the age of forty-five, having made her last move, to Rajputana, Honoria died.

TWO YEARS LATER, SIR HENRY LAWRENCE'S LIFE WAS CHANGED when Lord Dalhousie brought off a final spectacular annexation, offering the pleasure-loving King of Oudh the choice of deposing himself by signed treaty, or being forced out. In the Governor-General's own idiom, "We shall offer him a treaty; and if he refuses—swallow him!" With pathetic dignity, Wajid Ali Shah declined to sign. Protesting British faithlessness, he placed his royal turban in the hands of the Resident, General Sir James Outram. When the king departed for Calcutta, he left behind hundreds of dispossessed courtiers, jobless servants, and insolvent tradesmen. Only one of four in the State Army of 15,000 was to stay on under Oudh's new masters. A pall settled over Lucknow, a city of some 700,000 souls, with its fairy-tale palaces and verdant parks, and rumors flew that the British were bent on wholesale conversion.

Such were the circumstances when Lord Canning, the new Governor-General, asked Henry Lawrence to serve as Chief Commissioner of Oudh. In ill health and still in deep mourning, he was about to return with his daughter to England when the offer came. He could not refuse. On March 20, 1857, Lawrence arrived in Lucknow, and immediately sensed the perilous isolation of an unwelcome British community. The tinder of revolt was everywhere, some of it wantonly piled on by his predecessor as Chief Commissioner, Coverley Jackson, whose first act was to take over the royal palace. On learning in May of the outbreak at Meerut, Lawrence quickly moved to redeploy troops ("as bad as can be—all scattered over several miles") and to fortify the Residency, a thirty-seven-acre compound in the heart of the city. He was in the saddle from dawn to dusk supervising, prodding, encouraging, as provisions were stockpiled, heavy guns set in earthen walls, windows blocked up, trenches dug, and great iron spikes planted to hinder storming parties. This was done openly. Sir Henry affected friendly unconcern when Indian visitors came to the Residency. "Time is everything just now," Lawrence wrote. "Time, firmness, promptness, conciliation and prudence…A firm and cheerful aspect must be maintained. There must be no bustle, no appearance of alarm, still less of panic. But at the same time there must be utmost watchfulness and promptness. Everywhere the first germ of insurrection must be put down instantly."

Everything that could be done was done when the expected eruption took place, beginning with a police mutiny and turning into a full-scale siege on June 30. Nine hundred Europeans in Lucknow found refuge in the Residency, along with a garrison of 768 sepoys of known loyalty. The mutineers tried vainly to storm the compound and on being driven back trained their muskets and artillery on the defenders. In a lucky shot on the first day, an eight-inch shell fatally wounded Lawrence, denting the silver locket he always wore containing Honoria's portrait. On his deathbed, Sir Henry dictated fourteen final orders, among them these: "Carefully register ammunition for guns and small arms in store." "Organise working parties for night labour." "Entrench—entrench—entrench—erect traverses, cut off enemy's fire." "Take an immediate inventory of all supplies and food, etc." "Sir Henry Lawrence's servants to receive one year's pay." "Put on my tomb only this—'Here Lies Henry Lawrence who tried to do his duty. May God have mercy on him.'"

He lingered until July 4, 1857, and was buried in the Residency churchyard. Lucknow by then was securely in rebel control. The compound itself was on a tilted plateau bounded by a river, a royal palace, and the narrow streets of the old city, with some 7,000 sepoys encamped around it. Crammed into twelve buildings, subject to stifling heat and buzzing swarms of insects, the defenders strove to keep spirits up as rations shortened and medical supplies dwindled. When rebels tried to tunnel beneath earthen walls, the British countermined, engaging in surreal underground battles, using shovels and fists. Ninety days on, a relief column a thousand strong, commanded jointly by Sir Henry Havelock and Sir James Outram, burst through the besieging rebels into the Residency. This gallant but futile feat was insufficient to break the siege. Now with a thousand more to feed, the defenders waited anxiously for a second relieving force under Sir Colin Campbell. He was among the few senior British officers to emerge from Crimea with his name brightened. At the Battle of Alma, his Highland Brigade broke the Russian flank, and with the same panache, his troopers in India swept into Lucknow and wrested control of the city. The Residency siege ended on November 18. Among the haggard survivors emerging from its shell-pocked buildings was Dr. William Brydon, the sole British officer to complete the retreat from Kabul in the First Afghan War.

Reporting all this for British readers was William Howard Russell of *The Times*, who had also arrived from Crimea. Russell did not join in the chorus of imperial self-congratulation. He was dismayed by the degrading racism of so many Englishmen, who deemed it a patriotic duty to refer loudly to Indians as "niggers." He could not help thinking "how harsh the reins of our rule must feel to the soft skin of the natives. The smallest English official treats their prejudices with contempt, and thinks he has the right to visit them just as he would call on a gamekeeper in his cottage." That force was the basis of British rule he had no doubt, "for I see nothing else but force employed in our relations with the governed." Granted, the Raj had put down widow burning, "but I have travelled hundreds of miles through a country peopled with beggars and covered with wigwam villages." Russell generously praised the gallantry of British troopers, the civility of many commanders, but was careful to stress the Mutiny's complexity. Here we had not only a servile war but also, he tells us, "a war of religion, a war of race, and a war of revenge, of hope, of some national promptings to shake off the yoke of a stranger." He then judged the rebels as sternly as his own people. Whatever the causes of the revolt, he wrote, "it is clear enough that, one of the modes by which the leaders, as if by common instinct, determined to effect their end was the destruction of every white man, woman or child who fell into their hands—a design which the kindliness of the people, or motives of policy, frustrated on many remarkable occasions."

Thanks in part to Russell's dispatches, more Victoria Crosses—twenty-four—were bestowed for the second relief of Lucknow than for any single engagement in any British war. The VC, Britain's most coveted decoration, was established in 1854 during the Crimean war, and is cast from a bronze cannon captured at Sevastopol. Yet until 1912, no Indian in the Indian Army was eligible for the Cross. When the color bar was finally eliminated, forty Indians were so honored, from 1912 to 1947, compared with twelve white comrades. It needs finally to be added that in Lucknow today, the Residency is laudably preserved with all its markers and graves, its gaunt ruins floodlit at night, a melancholy memorial to all who fought there.

WHAT CRIMEA WAS TO RUSSIA, THE GREAT MUTINY WAS TO British India: an analogous blow to a complacent *ancien régime*. As prophets foretold, the hundredth year after Plassey brought an end to East India Company rule. The British Parliament in August 1858 ended the Company's responsibility for governing India, transferring to the Crown its possessions and its civil and military services. The Company's Board of Control and Court of Directors gave way to a fifteen-member Council that would advise the Secretary of State of India, to whom the Governor-General, now endowed with the grander title of Viceroy, would report.

Under Lord Canning, who became the first Viceroy, the wave of annexations ceased, the frontiers of 500 princely states were permanently fixed, and native rulers were accorded more formal respect. An Indian Order of Knighthood, the Star of India, was proclaimed by the Queen (the order's motto, "Heaven's Light Our Guide," was suggested by Prince Albert). Canning approved a general amnesty for all except those who killed Europeans, while the hunt went on for rebel leaders (Nana Sahib vanished, his fate never determined).

A new model Indian Army emerged: more Europeans, more advancement by merit, and a more rigorous intelligence service. By 1863, the overall numbers were 125,000 Indian and 62,000 British troops, a sharp revision of the pre-Mutiny ratio. All artillery gunners henceforth were Europeans, though there could be Indian drivers to clean the guns. Even so, and understandably, the Great Mutiny heightened British fears of rebellion, conspiracies, holy wars, and possible foreign provocation. Among likely foreign culprits in the 1860's there was but a single important suspect, the Empire of Russia. Each week seemed to bring fresh tidings of Russian intrigues, geographical expeditions, and suspicious military movements in Asia.

When the expansion-minded Dmitrii Miliutin took over as Minister of War in 1861, he acquired an invaluable ally in Count Nikolai Pavlovich Ignatiev, the new director of the Foreign Ministry's Asiatic Department. While a military attaché in London, Ignatiev impressed Lord Clarendon, the Foreign Secretary, as "a very clever wily fellow." A well-born alumnus of the Tsar's *corps de pages*, Ignatiev reported so cogently on the Indian Mutiny that St. Petersburg promoted him to major-general at the age of twenty-seven, and in 1858, sent him on a full-dress mission to Central Asia to show the imperial flag. At Orenburg, Miliutin found another ally in General A. P. Bezak, the new Governor-General, who eagerly promoted plans to fill "gaps" in the frontier by seizing territory from neighboring Khokand. When St. Petersburg withheld approval, Bezak's bold chief of staff, Colonel Mikhail G. Cherniaev, went forward anyway and captured a key fortress. The Minister of War defended the unauthorized action as necessary to "unify" the frontier and frustrate the British, arguments that were finally accepted by a reluctant Prince Gorchakov, the Foreign Minister. St. Petersburg authorized a further, calibrated advance, and Cherniaev once again exceeded orders with a daring but failed attempt in 1864 to seize Tashkent, the leading city and commercial center of Khokand.

As alarm grew in Britain, Prince Gorchakov tried to make the best possible case for Russia's forward policy. "The position of Russia in Central Asia," he declared in a November 1864 circular to his embassies, "is that of all civilized States which are brought into contact with half-savage, nomad populations, possessing no fixed organization." Border security and trade relations impel the civilized state to exert a certain authority, notably over Asiatics who only respect "visible and palpable force." The requirements of order, he went on, led to the establishment of fortified posts deeper and deeper in nomad territory. It was the same in North America as settlers pressed westward, or in British India, or in French North Africa, or in Holland's overseas territories—in every case "less by ambition than imperious necessity." Yet even as it punished native provocations, Gorchakov promised, Russia would act with moderation, and respect the independence of its neighbors.

Given the prevailing imperial Zeitgeist, it was an astute statement, and in the judgment of Seymour Becker and other academic authorities, not hypocritical. True, the Prince made no reference to an important economic incentive for expansion: the need for cotton. Until the Civil War, the American South was the main supplier of Russia's cotton, and when the Union blockaded Confederate ports, Russia sought alternative sources in the steppe. Becker found that in 1860 Central Asia accounted for only 6 percent of Russia's cotton. By 1862 the figure reached a record 40 percent as the price per bale tripled, a rise that was followed by a threefold increase in Russia's annual imports from Central Asia between 1863 and 1867.

Gorchakov's more awkward silence concerned headstrong commanders like Cherniaev, who kept expanding the empire with or without authority, taking advantage of Russia's peculiar, hydra-headed government. As described by Eugene Schuyler, a young American diplomat posted to St. Petersburg in the 1870's, there was no Russian Cabinet, properly speaking, and no united policy. Each senior minister was an independent overlord, accountable only to the Tsar. Even when a special commission of ministers reached a decision, Schuyler wrote, "each minister has the right of a personal audience with the Emperor, when he can explain in detail all his arguments," so that a commission decision could be voided almost as soon as it is was made—as recurrently happened, the American noted, when the Minister of War differed with the Foreign and Finance Ministers about Central Asia.

Thus the principle of autocracy, which successive Tsars, conservatives and reformers alike, viewed as sacrosanct, made it very difficult to determine who spoke for a Government that was secretive, repressive, and subject to the will of an absolute autocrat. What, then, was the prudent defensive course for British India?

TWO SCHOOLS EMERGED IN THE 1860'S, EACH ASSOCIATED WITH A distinguished member of the newly formed Indian Council. Speaking for the Forward School was Sir Henry Rawlinson, soldier, diplomat, and "the Father of Assyriology." His most formidable adversary was Sir John Lawrence, the savior of the Punjab, a proponent of Close Borders, or as his critics taunted, "Masterly Inactivity."

Rawlinson was a paragon of versatility: a cavalry officer renowned for his speed and endurance who fought with distinction in the First Afghan War, an emissary to the royal courts of Asia, and a scholar adventurer. While posted in Persia, Rawlinson climbed the vertiginous cliff at Behistun in Persia and over several life-threatening seasons (1835–37) copied the trilingual text that Darius the Great had his workmen inscribe in the fifth century B.C. In his sedentary interludes as consul-general in Baghdad, Rawlinson deciphered the cuneiform script, discovering that the same sign can be read in different ways—polyphonically—depending on context. For this feat, he was showered with honors on his return to England in 1856: a baronetcy, the presidencies of the Royal Geographical and the Asiatic Societies, a seat in Parliament (Conservative for Reigate), and a lifetime seat on the new five-member India Council.

For thirty years, in speeches, articles, and memoranda, Rawlinson preached the same essential doctrine. Russia was hostile, Russia was expansionist, Russia had designs on India, judgments for which he provided ample evidence. He warned that Russia would devour Khokand, Bokhara, and Khiva (as Russia did), that Russia's core strategy was to use Persia and Afghanistan as springboards, and that Herat was the crucial gateway to India that had to be defended at all costs.

For Rawlinson, the Mutiny was a somber warning of the Raj's vulnerability. Should the Tsar's officers acquire a foothold in Kabul, he predicted in a key 1868 memorandum, "the disquieting effect will be prodigious." Every native ruler throughout Northern India "who either has, or fancies he has, a grievance, or is even cramped or incommoded by our orderly Government" will begin intriguing with the Russians. Worse, Afghanistan possesses "a machinery of agitation" singularly well adapted for acting on the "seething, fermenting, festering mass" of Muslim hostility in India. It was therefore essential, he contended, for the Government of India to keep a mission in Kabul, annex the Afghan city of Kandahar, hold Herat, garrison troops at Quetta at the far end of the Bolan Pass, and lay rail and telegraph lines to the North-West Frontier. And do it quickly, he pleaded: "In the interests, then, of peace; in the interests of commerce; in the interests of moral and material improvement, it may be asserted that interference in Afghanistan has now become a duty, and that any moderate outlay or responsibility we may incur in restoring order in Cabul will prove in the sequel to be true economy."

TO ALL THIS, SIR JOHN LAWRENCE, HIS COLLEAGUE ON THE INDIA Council, was in fundamental disagreement. By now he too was a baronet. Feted and flattered, he was to be named Viceroy in 1863, later becoming Lord Lawrence. Perhaps because he served closer to the ground in India, his was the view from the ranks, not from the saddle. In his judgment, India's security lay in the quality of British rule and the contentment of the Raj's subjects, not in acquiring more territory, or in stationing envoys in Afghanistan only to be killed, thereby obliging the British to send a costly and futile punitive force. That was a lesson taught by the First Afghan War—a conflict he felt unjust and unnecessary—a lesson borne home by his years working with tribal peoples on the Punjab frontier.

Lawrence spoke his mind in innumerable messages and letters, and most cogently in a Minute written in 1867, when as Viceroy he was being pressed to choose among Afghan claimants to the throne. This he declined to do. He sought instead to convince the Afghans that the British did not covet a foot of their rugged hills. Nor would he attempt to force a British Resident upon them or to interfere, except by advice or example, in their blood feuds. He believed in recognizing the rulers chosen by the Afghans, and offering them presents or assistance from time to time, as one friend might give to another, but not in helping any claimant secure or recover the throne. And by firmly resolving not to interfere, Britain claimed the right to forbid other powers—above all, Russia—from doing the same. If Russia did interfere, and if Afghans appealed for aid, then Britain could expeditiously come to their support as allies.

Lawrence based his opinions on what he knew of Afghanistan—a country too poor to support a large occupying army, too fractious to be controlled by a smaller force. "We have men, and we have rocks in plenty," he remembered Dost Mohammed once telling him, "but we have nothing else." To attempt domination of such a people, Lawrence felt, was to court misfortune and calamity: "The Affghan will bear poverty, insecurity of life; but he will not tolerate foreign rule. The moment he has a chance, he will rebel." Nor would it make any difference if the British attempted to enter Afghanistan as friends: "The Affghans do not want us; they dread our appearance in the country. The circumstances connected with the last Affghan War have created in their hearts a deadly hatred to us as a people."

As for the Russians, he did not know what their policy was in Central Asia, but suppose, he asked, they did occupy Afghanistan to attack India. "In that case let them undergo the long and tiresome marches which lie between the Oxus and the Indus; let them wend their way through poor and difficult countries, among a fanatic and courageous population, where, in many places, every mile can be converted into a defensible position; then they will come to the conflict on which the fate of India will depend, toil-worn, with an exhausted infantry, a broken-down cavalry, and a defective artillery." Fresh British troops could then confront them with formidable advantages at frontier mountains and passes.

Or suppose, Lawrence continued, that Russia sought to occupy neighboring countries to stir up hatred against the British. In that event, "will she be able to do us more harm than we can inflict on her in such a struggle? The further she extends her power, the greater the area she must occupy; the more vulnerable points she must expose; the greater the danger she must incur of insurrection; the larger must be her expenditure." Moreover, he noted, so intractable are tribal peoples on Afghan borderlands that they have no desire to be ruled from Kabul. "There is perhaps not one of these tribes who would not seek our aid against any invader . . . Which party would be best able, under such circumstances, to win them to its side; we, or the Russians?"

Lawrence's Minute concluded with this thought: "I am firmly of opinion that our proper course is not to advance our troops beyond our present border, not to send English Officers into the different states of Central Asia; but to put our own house in order, by giving the people of India the best government in our power, by conciliating, as far as practicable, all classes, and by consolidating our resources." During the 1870's, his advice was ignored or forgotten, and Lawrence's own voice—he then sat in the House of Lords—was drowned out by cries of alarm over Russia's drive, ever deeper, into Central Asia.

WHEN PRINCE GORCHAKOV WROTE HIS FAMOUS CIRCULAR IN 1864, he apparently believed that Russia's great eastward spurt had subsided, and that expansion in Central Asia would be limited (as he had been assured) to linking up lines of forts, thus filling in "gaps." This apprehension was certainly not shared by Major-General Cherniaev, newly promoted and the recipient of three medals following his recent unauthorized forays. In May 1865, once again without official sanction, Cherniaev led a Russian army into the Khan of Khokand's realm with the aim of subjugating Tashkent, a rich trading metropolis of perhaps 100,000 people. With a force of only 1,900 men and 12 field guns, he took the walled city in a bold surprise attack, then made himself immediately popular by granting its citizens a one-year tax holiday. On learning of his dazzling feat, doubtless from Miliutin, and of its low cost and negligible casualties, Alexander II called it "a glorious affair." Cherniaev became "the Lion of Tashkent," with a Sword of Honor in his scabbard. It was left to the Foreign Ministry to explain to other powers that the occupation of Tashkent was "temporary" and that the Khan of Khokand still ruled the southern part of his domain.

Still, with his astute sense of timing and limits, Miliutin saw to it that the overbold lion was recalled. He was replaced in 1865 as Military Governor of Turkestan by Major-General D. I. Romanovsky, his spacious instructions being "while steadfastly striving not to extend our direct possessions in Central Asia, not to reject, however, for the sake of that goal, such actions and orders as may be necessary for us, and in general to keep in mind, above all, Russia's true interests." Romanovsky was reminded as well that since Asians only respect force, "the slightest vacillation and indecisiveness" would be taken as a sign of weakness. Unsurprisingly, soon after arriving in Tashkent, the new Military Governor mounted a successful offensive against Bokharan raiders.

THE FINAL CONQUEST OF THE KHANATES OCCURRED UNDER THE next Military Governor, Konstantin Petrovich Kaufmann, who assumed the post in 1867 and held it until his death in 1882. He was a soldier after Miliutin's heart: a meritocrat trained as an engineer (Dostoyevsky was among his classmates); he fought in the Caucasus campaigns and at the siege of Kars, becoming director-general of engineers at the War Ministry, where he helped restructure the military. Kaufmann was not just a general; he went to Turkestan as a proconsul. At a meeting of a special council called by the Tsar, Alexander II turned to him and said, "Konstantin Petrovich, take Khiva for me!"

Kaufmann took Samarkand first, in May 1868, in a nearly bloodless victory of deep symbolic import, since this was the city from which Tamerlane's warriors set forth to conquer Muscovy five centuries before. Samarkand's Bokharan defenders took flight, with Kaufmann's Cossacks in full pursuit. Within months, once-proud "Bokhara the Noble" had become a Russian protectorate, its army defeated, its Emir a vassal, its slave markets formally closed, its tariffs slashed on Russian wares that soon flowed into its great bazaar. Of the surviving khanates, there remained the southern part of Khokand, the bothersome lesser states of Merv and Geok-Tepe, and most challenging of all, Khiva, the remote kingdom that since Peter the Great's reign had resisted six Russian expeditionary forces. On December 1, 1869, the British envoy to Russia cabled his Foreign Office, "I have spoken to Prince Gorchakov of the alleged intention of the Russian Government to dispatch a military expedition to Khiva, and he denied positively the existence of any such intention."

Gorchakov was literally correct. Kaufmann had not yet come up with a final battle plan. The biggest difficulty was reaching Khiva, a walled oasis city surrounded by an unforgiving desert, the Kyzl Kum. Khiva was 600 miles from Tashkent, 930 miles from Orenburg, and 500 miles from Krasnovodsk on the Caspian, the three nearest possible staging bases. With an engineer's precision, Kaufmann prepared for a multiple assault, acquiring 14,000 camels to carry provisions for some 13,000 men and to haul fifty field guns. In December 1872, the final plan was presented to the Imperial Council, with the Emperor presiding, and was reportedly approved 35–9, with Prince Gorchakov in the minority.

As General Kaufmann began to move forward, two U.S. citizens obtained permission in St. Petersburg to travel to western Turkestan, becoming the first Americans to do so. One was a war correspondent native to New Lexington, Ohio, the other a scholar-diplomat from Ithaca, New York, and both were to play a catalytic role in the deepening Anglo-Russian rivalry.

JANUARIUS MACGAHAN WAS ONLY TWENTY-NINE WHEN HE arrived in Russia in 1873 as a correspondent for *The New York Herald,* but he had already made his mark reporting the Franco-Prussian War and the Paris Commune. James Gordon Bennett, the *Herald's* owner, had sent MacGahan to Russia to cover the siege of Khiva with the same insouciance he sent another staff reporter, Henry Morton Stanley, to find Livingstone in Africa. The young Ohioan had the advantage of a Russian bride, Varvara Elaguine, whom he had met on an earlier visit to Yalta, but otherwise was on his own as he arrived at St. Petersburg in February 1873, accompanied by his now-pregnant wife.

MacGahan did get the essential *laissez-passer*, thanks to the timely assistance of Eugene Schuyler, the thirty-three-year-old Secretary of the American Legation. Better yet, Schuyler proposed joining the correspondent on the first stage of his trip. The pair left St. Petersburg in March, and arrived in Orenburg by tarantass, an ungainly four-wheeled carriage mounted without springs on wooden bars. As Schuyler wrote home, he turned up with a "lobster face," his skin peeled off by wind and sun, in a country that "reminds me a good deal of the plains of Colorado, but I suppose it is still more like Arizona." At Fort Number One, just beyond Orenburg, the two parted. MacGahan headed across the desert toward Khiva, and Schuyler made his way to Tashkent, Bokhara, and Khokand, a trip that yielded a solid two-volume work, *Turkistan* (1877), a landmark in Central Asian studies.

MacGahan, riding on alone, knowing nothing of the roads or local languages, crossed the forbidding Kyzl Kum desert with the help of Kirghiz nomads, who provided him with food and *koumiss,* or fermented mare's milk. When he finally reached the camp of General Kaufmann, a Russian officer shouted, "*Vy kto?*" (Who are you?), to which MacGahan responded, "*Americanetz.*" With a wide grin, the Russian said, "You are the man who crossed the Kyzl Kum alone, are you? All right, come along and I will present you to the General." As the American reported: "I found him sitting in an open tent, wrapped up in a Bokharan *khalat*, or gown, taking tea and smoking a cigarette. A man between forty-five and fifty, bald and rather small of stature for a Russian, blue eyes, moustache, no beard, and a pleasant, kindly countenance."

In fact, the general was fifty-five, and Schuyler's dispatches to the State Department portrayed a very different Kaufmann, a vain peacock so obsessed with the rituals of rank as to invite ridicule: "He came to Central Asia with no knowledge of the country, and, by holding himself in a very lofty position, has acquired very little knowledge of it during his stay." Schuyler went on to detail instances of flagrant corruption and misrule, such as Russian refusal to pay for camels lost on the Khivan campaign (nearly all 14,000 perished), under the aegis of a haughty proconsul who "never rides through the street without a bodyguard of one hundred Cossacks."

For a journalist, access to the powerful tends to mute criticism. In articles written upon his return, the young American was at pains to describe the Cossacks as being very unlike the undisciplined brutes of hostile caricature, adding somewhat guilelessly that they were kind and gentle, "when not enraged." He wrote glowingly of Kaufmann's subsequent victory at Khiva, and though MacGahan conceded that Russia was disposed to seize as much of Central Asia as it could, he doubted it "had any immediate designs on India." By degrees he became an early version of John Reed, as smitten by Russia and its soldiers as Reed was by Lenin's Bolsheviks and the Red Army.

During the Khivan campaign, MacGahan came to admire to the point of adulation a spirited cavalry officer, Mikhail Dimitrievich Skobelev, known to Russians as "the White General" and to the Turkmen as *Göz Kanli,* or "Bloody Eyes." A fearless and resourceful soldier, Skobelev at one point disguised himself as a Turkman to scout the route to Khiva. When the Khan of Khiva, his armies badly beaten in preliminary skirmishes, surrendered his city in June 1873 with scarcely a fight, he was among the first through the walls. Two years later, Skobelev completed the subjugation of what remained of Khokand. In one engagement, he outfought and outwitted a greatly superior force and captured fifty-eight guns; in another, he routed the enemy by leading a handful of cavalry in a hazardous night attack. These feats earned him the rank of major-general, the Order of St. George, and the military governorship of Fergana, as Khokand was renamed. Skobelev's signature was the spotless white uniform and the ivory stallion with which he rode into battle, his hair curled and scented as if, one observer ventured, he were a bridegroom on his wedding night.

On his return to St. Petersburg, MacGahan, now "the Cossack Correspondent," became the first foreigner to report at length on the Khivan campaign, in articles that he reshaped into a lively, well-received book, *Campaigning on the Oxus and the Fall of Khiva* (1874). The Ohioan's career seemed fairly launched. He next covered the Carlist rising in Spain and, in a typical Bennett stunt, joined a polar expedition that attempted to find the elusive Northwest Passage. Events in Bulgaria then brought him together again with Skobelev, in a Russo-Turkish War that MacGahan's own pen did much to precipitate.

IN POLITICS AS IN PHYSICS, THE DETONATION OF A PARTICLE IN places unknown can set off a chain reaction felt in half the world. Before 1876, nobody had heard of Batak, a mountain village in Bulgaria, a country whose aggrieved Orthodox Christians had since 1396 been under Ottoman rule. In the 1870's, Bulgarian discontent swelled into rebellion. Turkish reprisals were swift and ferocious. To augment the regular army, the Turks hired tough mercenaries known as *bashi-bazouks,* and these irregulars—butchers and brigands in the eyes of Bulgars—fell murderously upon Batak and scores of other villages. Reports of massacres drifted to the chanceries of Europe, a cause of embarrassed concern to Britain's Conservative Prime Minister, Benjamin Disraeli. It had been Disraeli's policy to shore up the declining Ottomans as a counterweight to an aggressively expanding Russian Empire. With premature nonchalance, he dismissed the Bulgarian reports as "coffee-house babble."

To determine the truth, the London *Daily News,* the organ of the opposition Liberal Party, commissioned MacGahan to go to Bulgaria. There he joined his friend Eugene Schuyler, now the U.S. consul-general in Constantinople. Schuyler had also arrived on a mission of inquiry, prompted by alarming reports from American missionaries. Hearing, and confirming, one terrible story after another about the slaughter of Christians in some sixty villages, the two Americans came upon Batak. In its charred ruins they encountered a stench of rotting cadavers that almost knocked them from their horses. "Since my letter of yesterday I have supped full of horrors," began MacGahan's report to *The Daily News* on Batak. In a typical passage, he described finding the bodies of two hundred women, victims of a mass rape, who "were taken, in the broad light of day, beneath the smiling canopy of heaven, coolly beheaded, then thrown in a heap, and left to rot."

Among his readers was William Ewart Gladstone, the Grand Old Man of Liberalism, who drew heavily on MacGahan's reports, and Schuyler's corroborative accounts, in writing *The Bulgarian Horrors and the Question of the East.* His volcanic pamphlet ended with a thunderclap: "Let the Turks now carry away their abuses in the only possible manner, namely by carrying off themselves. Their Zaptiehs and their Mudirs, their Bimbashis and their Yuzbachis, their Kaimakans and their Pashas, one and all, bag and baggage, shall, I hope, clear out from the province they have desolated and profaned. This thorough riddance, this most blessed deliverance, is the only reparation we can make to the memory of those heaps on heaps of dead; to the violated purity alike of matron, of maiden, and of child; to the civilisation which has been affronted and shamed; to the laws of God, or if you like, Allah; to the moral sense of mankind at large."

With this pamphlet, which sold a phenomenal 200,000 copies in one month, Gladstone ended a short-lived withdrawal from politics to renew combat with Disraeli. New evidence of Ottoman atrocities accumulated. A report by a British diplomat, Walter Baring, estimated the number of Christian victims at 12,000 and asserted that at Batak a thousand were burned alive in a church ("the stench was so overpowering one could hardly force one's way into the church-yard"). The news flowed instantly to Russia. It provoked furious protests on behalf of brother Slavs and persecuted Christians, agitation abetted by Count Ignatiev, now the Russian Minister in Constantinople and a fervent Pan-Slavist. The Tsar could not ignore the clamor. Unable to obtain through diplomacy the guarantees he now demanded from the Turks, Alexander II chose war. In contrast with the Crimean War, most of Europe was either noncommittal or sympathetic to Russia. British opinion was divided, even within Disraeli's Cabinet. Invoking the cause of oppressed Christians, the Tsar declared war on Turkey in April 1877.

ONCE MORE, MACGAHAN WAS OFF TO BATTLE, JOINING THE RUS-sians in June as they crossed the Danube to enter Romania, still nominally a Turkish satrap but with its own king and substantially autonomous. He was the only American among eighty or so correspondents and artists. A rough-and-ready brigade still striving to define a new calling, these practitioners, so Kipling remarked, needed a horse trader's eye, the skills of a cook, the constitution of a bullock, and the digestion of an ostrich. In MacGahan's case, he started out with a fractured ankle in a cast, yet had to keep moving on horseback. He was representing both *The Daily News* and *The New York Herald*, teaming up with the *News's* senior correspondent, Archibald Forbes, in evading censorship and rushing copy to well-rewarded telegraph operators in Romania.

The prevailing belief was that Russia's progress would be a triumphal waltz to Constantinople. Thanks to Miliutin (though he did not favor the war), Russia was rapidly able to put into the field well over 200,000 men of all arms, compared with an ill-trained and widely scattered Turkish army of 135,000 men. Yet despite Miliutin's reforms, the old Tsarist practice of nepotism persisted. The Commander-in-Chief of the Danube Army was Grand Duke Nicholas, Alexander II's brother; his counterpart in the Caucasus was another brother, Grand Duke Michael, while the young Tsarevich Alexander was given a secondary command in Romania. When Miliutin proposed as Chief of Staff his highly competent director of the scientific-military committee, Grand Duke Nicholas rejected him, claiming the director, General Obruchev, held radical political views. A safer, mediocre figure was chosen instead.

The waltz ended in July, when the Russians, after traversing Romania, approached Plevna, a fortified town set in undulating hills on the Bulgarian frontier. Turkey's ablest and bravest soldier, Osman Pasha, having been rushed to the fort, immediately ordered the digging of extensive trenches and the placement of newly acquired Krupp cannons on strategic perches. Three times, from July through September, the Russians attacked; three times the Turks drove them back. The third attack, "The Great Assault," took place on Alexander's name-day, September 11. A new ally, Prince Carol of Romania, having committed his own troops, successfully pressed for the privilege of commanding the massive joint offensive. A special platform was constructed from which the Tsar and his commanders could watch the battle, with refreshments available nearby on a table covered in white damask. What they witnessed was a slaughter, in which the attackers senselessly charged into the withering fire of Winchester breach-loaders and Krupp cannons. In three days, "The Great Assault" claimed as many as 25,000 allied lives.

Still, for the Russians there was a redeeming hero, Skobelev, whom the Turks now called *Ak Pasha* (White Pasha). In every engagement during the five months' siege of Plevna, Skobelev and his ivory charger seemed always at the forefront, scornful of the shellfire that scarcely grazed him. In "The Great Assault," Skobelev's force burst through Turkish trenches and seized a redoubt southwest of Plevna, a victory owed to savage hand-to-hand fighting. Yet through a failure to send sufficient reinforcements, Skobelev was forced to retreat; of his 18,000 troops, he lost 8,000 men, including 160 officers. MacGahan described how he took the redoubt:

> He picked up stragglers; he reached the wavering, fluctuating mass, and gave it the inspiration of his own courage…The whole redoubt was a mass of flame and smoke, from which screams, shouts, and cries of agony and defiance arose, with the deep-mouthed bellowing of the cannon, and above all the steady, awful crash of that deadly rifle fire. Skobelev's sword was cut in two in the middle. Then, a moment later, when just on the point of leaping the ditch, horse and man rolled together on the ground, the horse dead or wounded, the rider untouched. Skobelev sprang to his feet with a shout, then with a formidable, savage yell the whole mass of men streamed over the ditch, over the scarp and counterscarp, over the parapet, and swept into the redoubt like a hurricane.

Unable to take Plevna by direct attack, the Russians invested the fort under the direction of their best engineer, General Edward Totleben, and by December starved its defenders into submission. When Osman Pasha surrendered, having derailed the entire Russian battle plan and beaten Russia's finest armies in three pitched battles, he was honored for his valor. "I compliment you on your defense of Plevna," said Grand Duke Nicholas. "It is one of the most splendid military feats in history." Osman Pasha, so MacGahan informs us, wore a red fez and a blue cloak with no badge of rank; he was strongly built, with a dark beard and a determined face, "yet a tired, wan face also, with lines on it that were hardly graven so deep, I fancy, five months ago." Russian officers shouted "Bravo! Bravo!" The Tsar gallantly declined to take his sword, and Skobelev declared, "Osman the Victorious he will remain, in spite of his surrender."

For the correspondents, there were other rewards. MacGahan and Forbes, who first met during the Franco-Prussian War, formed a comradely triumvirate with Skobelev, as literate and witty as he was reckless in battle. Dale Walker, in his 1988 biography of MacGahan, describes one such evening at the Brofft, Bucharest's best hotel: "[T]he three men drank icy flagons of pilsner, and sang songs to Skobelev's accompaniment on the pianoforte—songs in French, German, Russian, Kirghiz, Italian, and English, winding up the evening with 'Auld Lang Syne,' which Forbes sang in 'impeccable burr,' Skobelev and MacGahan in impeccable English."

With the surrender of Plevna, the Russians could finally undertake a broad offensive, capturing Sofia, investing the great fortress of Kars, and seizing Adrianople, third in importance among the cities of European Turkey. The way to Constantinople was open, and in Britain alarm over Russian control of the Straits rang out in music halls, adding "jingoism" to the language:

> We don't want to fight:
> But by jingo, if we do,
> We've got the men, we've got the ships,
> And we've got the money too!

Grand Duke Nicholas did not move against the Ottoman capital, but halted in January 1878 at the village of San Stefano on the shores of the Sea of Marmara, ten miles from the walls of Constantinople. There Russian negotiators, led by Count Ignatiev, imposed a treaty giving so much to Russia (and so little to the Romanians), that at the initiative of Britain and Austria, with Bismarck's support, the Congress of Berlin was summoned in June to revise it.

Reporting these developments was Januarius MacGahan, now in residence with his wife Varvara at a cottage in San Stefano, where the couple's circle again included Eugene Schuyler as well as General Skobelev. Five wars had left their scars on MacGahan. His fractured ankle was rebroken at Plevna, his hair had thinned, and he gulped quinine by the spoonful to treat what he called "gastric fever." He had contracted typhus, probably while visiting a Russian military hospital. On June 8, 1878, still only thirty-three, MacGahan succumbed, expiring at the same age and from the same affliction as his celebrated successor, John Reed, who died in Moscow in 1920. Among MacGahan's pallbearers at the small Catholic cemetery in Pera were Skobelev and Schuyler. In 1884, at the initiative of the Ohio legislature, MacGahan's remains were returned with military honors to the United States for reburial in New Lexington. Just a century later, his larger-than-life likeness, pen and notebook in hand, was unveiled on the town's Main Street facing the county courthouse, hewn from rough stone by the Bulgarian-American sculptor Lubomir Daltchev. Inscribed below MacGahan's name are the words

CHAMPION OF BULGARIAN FREEDOM

IT IS WITH WONDER AND FAMILIARITY THAT ONE LOOKS BACK today at the Great Mutiny, the conquest of Turkestan, and the Russo-Turkish War. Inextricably mixed with instances of generous gallantry that looked back to the age of chivalry were acts of barbarism that looked forward to our own time. Alongside imperial massacres one may also discern the early stirrings of today's human rights movement, with its weapons of shame and censure. More particularly, within a wider canvas, one sees evidence of the special affinity Americans and Russians have felt for each other, notwithstanding radically different political systems.

Januarius MacGahan and Eugene Schuyler were drawn to the warmth, spontaneity, and frontier bravado of their Russian friends, who like Americans were susceptible to grandiose projects and the projection of power, whether by cavalry or rails. There was as well a shared pride in a vigorous and original national culture, and a shared resentment of patronizing Europeans. If Russians sinned against human rights and acquisitively bullied their neighbors, Americans were scarcely innocent of the same imperious offenses in the Mexican War, the many Indian Wars, the Spanish-American War, and the persistence until the Civil War of an institution more abhorrent than serfdom.

Schuyler went on to write a two-volume biography of Peter the Great. He translated Turgeniev's *Fathers and Sons* and Tolstoy's *The Cossacks,* and promoted Russian studies at Yale, his alma mater, initiating a link between New Haven and Washington that was to grow deep clandestine roots. Fittingly, he was the first American diplomat accredited to Romania, and served as Minister and Consul General in Greece and Serbia. He had just arrived to assume a new consular post in Cairo when he was taken ill and died, in 1890.

MacGahan died before he had a fair chance to appraise the darker shadows in the Russian landscape. He began to do so after the incompetence he witnessed at Plevna. In a long essay following the siege, he wrote derisively of the Russian Army's overaged generals, who never read a book or newspaper and whose sole passion was card playing. "Called from their card-tables by the trumpet of war," he wrote, "they rise, rub their eyes, look around them completely bewildered, and are as thoroughly out of the current of modern war as if they had been asleep for forty years. Not even Rip Van Winkle, with his rusty gun dropping after his long sleep, was more bewildered and lost than the majority of these poor old generals, suddenly thrown into the campaign at the heads of their brigades, divisions and corps."

This was a new note for MacGahan, and one wonders how he might have responded to the later exploits of Mikhail Skobelev. In 1880, "The White General" returned to Central Asia under instructions to settle accounts with the Tekke Turkmen, a fierce, slave-taking people whose base was the walled citadel of Geok-Tepe. The Emperor's orders were explicit. Under no circumstances was Skobelev to take a single step backwards, "for this would be for Europe and Asia a sign of our weakness, would inspire still greater boldness on the part of our adversaries." In due course, in 1881, his expeditionary army surrounded Geok-Tepe and his sappers dug under its massive walls, planting a ton of explosives. The walls breached, a storming party swept into the fortress, and Cossacks massacred by the thousands. Details of the slaughter were gathered and reported by a British correspondent in the MacGahan mode, who had made his way in disguise to Turkestan. Edmund O'Donovan's dispatches for the London *Daily News* set off an uproar. Sklobelev was unapologetic and subsequently remarked, "I hold it as a principle that the duration of peace is in direct proportion to the slaughter you inflict on the enemy."

The same Russians who had seized on MacGahan's reports from Bulgaria in the same newspaper now angrily denounced the British as meddlers and hypocrites. Among the most vehement was Fyodor Dostoyevsky, who shortly before his death in 1881 spoke out in his final diary essay for a St. Petersburg journal, *The Citizen*. He touched the familiar imperial chords—not only did Russia need markets and land, but she would bring science and railroads to backward peoples. Asia was to Russia what undiscovered America was to Europe. "In Europe we were hangers-on and slaves, whereas we shall go to Asia as masters," he went on. "In Europe we were Asiatics, whereas in Asia we, too, are Europeans. Our civilizing mission in Asia will bribe our spirit and drive us thither. It is only necessary that the movement should start. Build only two railroads: begin with one to Siberia, and then—to Central Asia—and at once you will see the consequences."

And what of the alarm in England over Russian aspirations? "If one fears England," Dostoyevsky thundered, "one should sit at home and move nowhere! Therefore let me exclaim once more:'Long live the Geok-Tepe victory! Long live Skobelev and his good soldiers! Eternal memory to those valiant knights who were eliminated from the rolls! We shall record them on our rolls.'" They were among his last published words. The potential for protracted Anglo-Russian conflict was plain, especially over the least stable of buffer states, Afghanistan.

PART II

∴

CHAPTER SEVEN

Bloomsbury's War

To paraphrase Lytton Strachey's celebrated aperçu about the Victorian age, the history of Bloomsbury cannot be written: we know too much about it. In *Eminent Victorians*, Strachey bemoaned the great glut of information, the endless twin tomes with which the British then commemorated their dead ("who does not know them, with their ill-digested masses of material, their slipshod style, their tone of tedious panegyric, their lamentable lack of selection, of detachment, of design?"). By the same token, Bloomsbury is all but buried in a landfill of diaries, letters, memoirs, and journals; in single- and double-volume biographies, in essays, novels, and plays by and about Lytton Strachey and Dora Carrington, Virginia and Leonard Woolf, Maynard Keynes and Lydia Lopokova, Clive and Vanessa Bell, together with their kinfolk, friends, and lovers. Yet in this midden of words, India is the Great Unmentioned.

Just three times in 3,000 published pages does Virginia Woolf refer to India, and then only in passing. In the twelve volumes of her journals and letters, spanning from 1888 to 1941, Kipling prompts a single diary mention (January 19, 1936), when his death "has set all the old war horses of the press padding round their stalls." Of Curzon, Gandhi, or the Amritsar Massacre: not a sentence. Nor will the common reader find a word about the troubled Viceroyalty of Lord Lytton, the murder in Kabul of Cavagnari, or the Second Afghan War, events in which Bloomsbury's own ancestors played a direct part.

This reticence, whatever its cause, might have interested Lytton Strachey, or even more his younger brother James, the translator of Freud. Bloomsbury could hardly have been more closely interwoven with the British Empire. Leonard Woolf spent nearly seven years as a civil servant in Ceylon before his marriage in 1912 to Virginia, and he *did* write about colonialism, often and critically. As for Virginia Woolf, her family for generations helped build and reform the Empire. Her great-grandfather James Stephen, having observed slavery first hand in the West Indies, entered Parliament as an abolitionist ally of Wilberforce, whose sister he married; he was a pillar of the Clapham Sect, evangelical idealists devoted to imperial reform. Grandfather James was a permanent official at the Colonial Office, nicknamed "Mr. Over-Secretary Stephen" for his determined advocacy of the rights of the ruled, black, brown, or (in the case of Canada) white. Her uncle, James Fitzjames Stephen, was a brilliant jurist and theorist of British rule, who during his service on the Legislative Council in Calcutta reshaped the Indian penal code. He believed that England's "belligerent civilisation" kept the peace among India's contentious peoples, a paternalist thesis he elaborated in *Liberty, Equality, Fraternity* (1874). His essay was dedicated to Sir John Strachey, "one of the most distinguished Indian civilians," who served as Lieutenant-Governor of the North-Western Provinces and as Finance Minister to three Viceroys. Sir John's older brother, Sir Richard (knighted in the Jubilee year), was an ornament of the Raj. The founder of the Indian Government's forest service, the creator of its meteorological department, he was the public works director who vigorously developed Indian railways and canals. On his return to England, he served on the Indian Council, chaired the East India Railway Company, and became president of the Royal Geographical Society.

Lytton Strachey was the eleventh of Sir Richard's thirteen children. He was the godson and namesake of the first Earl of Lytton,

India's Viceroy from 1875 to 1880. Both Richard and John Strachey were devoted to Lord Lytton, "probably the most cultured of all the Viceroys," according to Mark Bence-Jones, the collective biographer of the genus. Poet, dreamer, Bohemian, devotee of pageantry, Lord Lytton was also the aggressive proconsul who plunged Britain into the Second Afghan War—a paradox that might have intrigued Lytton Strachey as a dissector of Victorian reputations. Yet save for a Cambridge thesis on Warren Hastings, Strachey steered clear of India even in his biography of Queen Victoria. It was easier, perhaps, to mock Florence Nightingale or General Gordon than to examine what happened when a Prime Minister with literary gifts and a Viceroy renowned for his cleverness together wielded imperial power.

HAD HE NOT EXISTED, EDWARD ROBERT BULWER LYTTON (1831–91), the first Earl of Lytton, was the kind of quirky Victorian his godchild would have relished inventing. He was a diplomat of some ability, beginning in Washington as an unpaid attaché to his uncle Sir Henry Bulwer, the British envoy there in the 1850's. His subsequent postings were like a splendid Grand Tour—Florence (where he befriended the Brownings), Paris, Athens, Madrid, Vienna, The Hague, Copenhagen, and Lisbon. While on home leave, he wooed and won Edith Villiers, a willowy pre-Raphaelite beauty, after an earlier suitor had unwisely read her "Lucille," a long poem by a certain Owen Meredith. She preferred the poetry to the suitor.

"Owen Meredith" was Lord Lytton's other self, the pen-name he adopted to avoid confusion with his father, Edward Bulwer-Lytton, author of *The Last Days of Pompeii* and a dozen or so dirk-and-doublet romances, one of them actually beginning "It was a dark and stormy night . . ." Bulwer-Lytton used his royalties to refashion Knebworth, the Lytton family seat in Hertfordshire since 1490, adding turrets, gargoyles, stained glass, and other 'Gothick' oddments. A dandy in the Brummel mode, a radical-feudal Member of Parliament, a friend of Disraeli and Dickens, Bulwer-Lytton set an exacting standard for his one acknowledged son—who also sought fame as a writer, whose sartorial taste ran to velvet jackets, bell-bottoms, silk cravats, and jeweled rings, and whose bolder verse touched the limits of Victorian propriety.

Such was the unusual diplomat, at that point British Minister in Lisbon, to whom Benjamin Disraeli in November 1875 offered the Viceroyalty of India. "The critical state of affairs in Central Asia demands a statesman," wrote Disraeli, whose Conservatives had defeated Gladstone the year before. Eager to replace a Liberal Viceroy and not averse to the deeper organ chords, the Prime Minister went on to say, "I believe, if you will accept this high post, you will have an opportunity not only of serving your country, but of obtaining an enduring fame."

The offer dismayed Lytton. "No man was ever so greatly honored," his reply began, but his ignorance of India was "absolute," he had a "*total want* of experience in every kind of *administrative* business" and suffered from "a painful and distressing complaint" that would be aggravated by the Indian climate. (The medical reference was to piles, which rendered prolonged sitting painful and caused him to slouch on the Viceregal throne, later the subject of malicious comment.) Moreover, his father having died the previous year, Lytton planned to settle at Knebworth and devote himself to literature. Disraeli would have none of it. He invoked the Queen's firm support, and later added in confidence that he planned to augment Her Majesty's title, so that one of Lytton's happier tasks would be to proclaim her Empress of India. To a connoisseur of spectacle, possibly this beguiling prospect tipped the balance. Lytton chose India. Yet as he wrote to his Liberal friend John Morley, "I have not courted or willingly accepted the crushing gift of such a white elephant."

White elephant or not, Lytton prepared himself assiduously. From no one did he receive more useful advice (according to his daughter, Lady Betty Balfour) than from James Fitzjames Stephen. At Lytton's request, the jurist prepared an elaborate memorandum on the Indian administrative system. It was a "policeman's bull's-eye," Lytton said. Thereafter, from Lytton's departure until his return, Stephen wrote to him by every mail. When his Viceroyalty came under attack during the Second Afghan War, Fitzjames Stephen fired off letters to *The Times*, defending his friend with a mastiff's tenacity. "They had in common, despite the widest differences, a certain rather rare and sturdy manliness, and an enthusiastic patriotism" which (writes Lady Balfour) evoked in Lytton "a responsive tenderness and affection which perhaps was all the deeper for having so rarely found an outlet."

Few subjects consumed as much time as Afghanistan. The long, stable emirate of Dost Mohammed had ended with his death in 1863. After a civil war lasting five chaotic years, his heir designate, Sher Ali, emerged as victor. During the interregnum, Russian forces continued their steady advance across the Central Asian steppes. Storming Tashkent in 1865, they then overwhelmed Bokhara, which along with fabled Samarkand now became a "subsidiary ally" of Russia in the new province of Turkestan. To senior British officers in India and their Conservative allies in London, the Russian juggernaut confirmed the futility of the nonexpansionist "close border" strategy approved by Gladstone's Liberals. It appeared that Afghanistan's new Emir was tilting to Russia, with grave security implications for British India.

This was the hour of the Forward School, its views ably articulated by a veteran Indian hand, Sir Bartle Frere, a hero of the Great Mutiny, a frontiersman who kept the peace in Sind and most recently was an outstanding Governor of Bombay. In an influential 1874 memorandum, Frere faulted British policy as stationary, defensive, negative. "This peculiarity in our policy will at once explain to anyone who knows Orientals, or, in fact, to anyone who knows mankind in general, [the policy's] inherent weakness...Orientals generally misunderstand our present inaction. They suspect some deep design, some secret understanding with Russia. If it is once understood that nothing will move us until the Russians appear on our frontier we shall certainly hasten that event by a great many years."

Frere's prescription was firm and explicit: post a frontier army at Quetta, assuring access to southern Afghanistan, extend railways to the foot of the Khyber Pass, and (most crucially) station British agents in the Afghan cities of Kabul, Herat, and Kandahar. In 1876, at the request of Lord Salisbury, the Secretary of State for India, Frere prepared a new memorandum for Lytton's consideration. It urged an ultimatum to Sher Ali: shun the Russians or face the consequences. Sir Bartle's memorandum did not arrive before Lytton's departure, but while stopping at Suez en route to India the new Viceroy met the man himself returning from India. Lytton found it "positively startling" that Frere's opinions coincided almost exactly with those "I put on paper confidentially for examination by Lord Salisbury and Mr. Disraeli, who entirely concurred with them."

Disraeli was pleased with his protégé. "We wanted," he informed Salisbury, "a man of ambition, imagination, some vanity and much will—and we have got him." For his part, Salisbury was more guarded. He was a Hertfordshire neighbor of the Lyttons, knew the family well, and was a little wary of "imagination." As the months proceeded, and as alarmist messages from India engulfed his desk, Lord Salisbury proffered this advice to Lytton: "I think you listen too much to the soldiers. No lesson seems to be so deeply inculcated by the experience of life as that you should never trust experts. If you believe the doctors, nothing is wholesome: if you believe the theologian, nothing is innocent: if you believe the soldiers, nothing is safe. They all require to have their strong wine diluted by a very large admixture of insipid common sense."

LORD LYTTON'S FIRST DAYS IN INDIA MINGLED SHOCK AND fascination. Even though forewarned, the Viceroy's new subjects were taken aback by his cheerful impulsiveness, his tweaking of bourgeois modalities, his negligee air. On his way to Calcutta, he stopped at Allahabad to break the railway trip and meet with Sir John Strachey, the Lieutenant-Governor of the North-Western Provinces. On the spot he asked Strachey to give up his job to become Finance Minister, a lesser post he had already held. "With your help," the Viceroy said, half in command, "I shall be afraid of nothing. You and I together shall find the means to carry out everything we desire." Strachey complied, becoming Lytton's formidable ally on the Council, enabling the Viceroy to overrule the other members, "the six second-rate men," as he privately called them.

Neither precedent nor seniority fazed Lytton. He made a speech at his own swearing-in and invited Indians to a state ball, both things that were Not Done. He reported almost proudly to Lord Salisbury that he "shocked all the proprieties of Calcutta by writing private notes to Members of Council, calling on their wives, holding levees by night instead of day." He very much wanted to shake up what he described as "a despotism of office-boxes tempered by the occasional loss of keys." Still, and surprisingly, though never previously an administrator, the new poet-prince proved better than average. He responded with energy and compassion to a calamitous crop failure in southern and western India during 1876–77. He rushed emergency stocks and appointed a commission under Sir Richard Strachey to recommend future safeguards. An important result was a new system of famine insurance that future administrations wisely replenished— one of several enduring innovations of his Viceroyalty.

With equal vigor and imagination, Lytton applied himself to the congenial challenge of proclaiming the Queen's new title, now formally approved by the British Parliament. "I have personally called it an 'Imperial Assemblage' instead of a Durbar," the Viceroy wrote to the Prince of Wales, "because it will materially and essentially differ from all previous Durbars, besides being on a much vaster scale." Even Disraeli's eyes widened at the Viceroy's grander proposals—the creation of an Indian Privy Council of Great Chiefs, in the style of King Arthur's Round Table, and an Indian Peerage, complete with a College of Heralds—all of which London vetoed. Otherwise, Lytton got his way. In late December 1876, Delhi became an Oriental Camelot. Princely tents blossomed around the old Mughal capital (white for the British, blue and scarlet for the Indians); banners unfurled from lamps with standards designed by Lockwood Kipling, Rudyard's father. On Proclamation Day, sixty-three Ruling Chiefs paid homage to the absent Empress and her Viceroy at the Throne Pavilion. All this took place against a vivid firmament of uniforms— plumes, tunics, lances, glistening boots, and sable headgear variously worn by the 11th Hussars ("Lord Cardigan's Bloodhounds"), the Bengal Lancers, the Bombay Cavalry, and all the Ruling Chiefs' troops. After the required salvos were fired and the Proclamation read, the assembled bands played the National Anthem (Britain's) and the March from *Tannhäuser*. It was, *The Times* reported, "perhaps the most splendid pageant ever witnessed in the East."

Unhappily, the lavish Assemblage coincided with the famine, prompting biting criticism in the Indian vernacular press. The Viceroy was not prejudiced against Indian peasants or Indian princes, and took meaningful steps to provide administrative berths to deserving Indian subjects. He was prejudiced against the educated middle classes. He despised the "Baboos whom we have educated to write semi-seditious articles in the native Press, and who really represent nothing but the social anomaly of their own position." His response was a harsh gag law, the Vernacular Press Act (1878), that imposed a system of censorship so bitterly resented, and so widely protested, that Lytton's successor, Lord Ripon, repealed the act only three years later.

If Lytton had a congenital fault, it was that he overdid everything. His flirting was relentless, much to the distress of his wife Edith. His chain-smoking at state dinners or from the Viceregal throne provoked scandalized comment. In 1887, when a young George Nathaniel Curzon visited Knebworth, seeking advice on how to become a Viceroy, he reported in amazement: "I can believe that Lord Lytton smokes in bed. I am sure that he says his prayers—if he says them at all—with a cigarette in his mouth." Lord Lytton proved a Viceroy with much charm, used to having his way, often insensible to the effect he produced, and with a crippling flaw—an undeveloped sense of limits. These traits were evident in his approach to Sher Ali, the Emir of Afghanistan.

WITH HIS CASCADING SABLE BEARD, GLOWERING BROW, AND strong Roman nose, Sher Ali outwardly seemed a stereotypical Afghan warlord. He was something more than that. In *The Emergence of Modern Afghanistan* (1969), Vartan Gregorian credits him with founding the first public schools in Kabul (including English lessons taught by Indians), with introducing mails and postage stamps, and with vital military reforms, such as making regular cash payments to his troops. He instituted cabinet government and tried, with limited success, to unify Afghanistan's discordant amalgam of feudal duchies and incendiary tribes.

Nor was his foreign policy unaccommodating. Despite galling memories of the British invasion and occupation of 1838–42, Sher Ali sought a détente with his powerful southern neighbor. In 1869, the Viceroy, Lord Mayo, received the Emir with royal honors at a Durbar in India. The sports-loving and magnetic Mayo, a former Chief Secretary for Ireland and Master of the Kildare Hunt, hit it off with Sher Ali ("I now begin to feel myself a King!" his guest exulted). This affinity mitigated the Emir's failure to get what he wanted—a formal treaty pledging aid in the event of an external attack, a fixed annual subsidy, and the recognition of his younger son Abdullah Jan as his heir instead of his oldest son, Yakub Khan. What the Emir did get was a jeweled presentation sword, a regal gift of cash, a mule train of weaponry, and a vague promise of future support—yet what mattered more, he liked the Viceroy. Mayo at the same time astutely initiated direct talks with Russia concerning Afghanistan. With the backing of his home Government, he sent an emissary to St. Petersburg who reached an agreement on respecting the territorial integrity of Afghanistan and defining its northern frontiers—the essential prelude to a broader settlement. Then midway in his five-year term, Mayo was fatally stabbed by a convict while visiting a penal colony in the Andaman Islands. His assailant was an Afghan Pathan whose motives were never firmly established.

So Sher Ali had to start over in 1872 with a new Viceroy, Lord Northbrook, a member of the Baring banking dynasty. He was "very civil and kind" with a great capacity for work, yet too cautious and unimaginative, in the judgment of his Home Secretary, Sir Alfred Lyall, who complained of the parliamentary expressions that infected his writing, Northbrook "being always glad to get hold of a colourless or indifferent phrase." Even so, the Viceroy was willing to take real risks for Sher Ali. Khiva had recently fallen to General Kaufmann, and all that separated Afghanistan from the Russian Empire was the oasis city of Merv. When the Emir sent an envoy to Simla to discuss what could be done, Northbrook proposed telling him "if he unreservedly accepts our advice on all external relations, we will help him with money, arms and troops" to repel an unprovoked invasion. Sher Ali was willing, but the British Government, then led by Gladstone, rejected this language as too interventionist. A deal with the British remained the Emir's preference, but thus rebuffed, he played the Russian card by entering into a correspondence begun by General Kaufmann, passing copies to the British, asking how he should respond.

In 1874, Gladstone's Liberals were out and Disraeli formed a new Conservative Ministry. It was now the turn of the Forward School, and Northbook was pressed to take a more belligerent line with Sher Ali. On this and other matters, the Viceroy disagreed, and he honorably resigned. Such was the situation as Lytton assumed the Viceroyalty in 1876. He promptly let it be known that Britain was willing to grant Sher Ali all he had asked—a treaty guarantee, subsidy, recognition of his heir—provided he would allow British officers to reside in Afghanistan. Lytton's phrases were not affable or parliamentary, but blunt and graphic. The Emir's agent was informed that the Afghan position between Russia and Britain was like that "of an earthen pipkin between two iron pots" and that if the Emir turned to Russia, Britain "could break him as a reed." As words like these flew toward Kabul, Calcutta won permission from the Khan of Kalat to station a frontier garrison at Quetta, at the crest of the Bolan Pass, the gateway to southern Afghanistan—the better to pressure the pipkin.

Early in 1877, Lytton dispatched an emissary to Peshawar to meet with the Emir's chief minister. Failure was preordained—the chief minister was ill and nettlesome, Lytton's envoy insistent on the one condition that was nonnegotiable: the posting of British missions inside Afghanistan. Were Sher Ali to accept, the British were told, then he would be pressed by Russia for comparable rights, and risk their enmity if he refused. Worse, such a concession was so offensive to Afghans that the Emir feared harm would befall British officers, bitterly estranging the two countries. All this was set forth in voluminous letters and minutes that were carefully studied many decades later by W. K. Fraser-Tytler. A long-serving Indian Army officer on the Afghan frontier, Fraser-Tytler was British Minister at Kabul in the 1940's. The documents revealed, in his view, a certain impatience on Lytton's part, "a perhaps rather rigid determination to achieve a well-defined objective, an objective, moreover, on which he had resolved before ever he left Britain."

That objective was the "ultimate expression of the forward policy, to be carried out with little or no regard for Afghan wishes, but with an unswerving determination to place the Indian defensive frontier where it had been in the days of the great Empires, in Asoka's day and in Akbar's day—on the northern ridges of the Hindu Kush and the Oxus Valley beyond." To attain this, Lytton was prepared to replace Sher Ali with a more obliging Emir, or failing that, to conquer and carve up Afghanistan. It was, concludes Fraser-Tytler, "the high-water mark of the British forward policy, the process of imperial expansion carried to its logical conclusion." To build an empire like Asoka and Akbar! What a tantalizing vision for a poet-prince who only recently presided at Delhi from the golden Mughal throne.

THE YEAR 1878 WAS DISRAELI'S *ANNUS MIRABILIS*. HE HAD ALREADY confirmed his dexterity on the highwire by purchasing Egyptian Khedive's shares in the Suez Canal Company, a coup that secured British control of "the imperial lifeline." Yet doubts about Disraeli's diplomatic stewardship surfaced anew as war broke out in 1877 between Russia and Turkey. The Tsar's armies, having advanced toward the frontiers of Afghanistan, now threatened to occupy Constantinople and seize the Dardanelles, a prospect intolerable to Britain. For months aging British warships lay anchored in the Straits almost within gunshot of Russian forces. War seemed imminent as Russia imposed a Draconian peace creating a "big Bulgaria" that unsettled the Balkan equilibrium. But through bluff and legerdemain Disraeli averted conflict. He secretly deployed 7,000 Indian troops to Malta in a show of force in April 1878 that complemented the agile efforts of Lord Salisbury, now the Foreign Secretary, to impel Russia to moderate its harsh treaty. The legerdemain worked, and the Tsar backed down. Less onerous terms were ratified at the Congress of Berlin summoned that summer by Salisbury, where (in Henry Kissinger's admiring judgment)

Disraeli emerged as the only statesman to outwit Bismarck—a short-term triumph overall (in the more critical view of A. J. P. Taylor) since it persuaded the British they could play a great role without allies, expense, or exertion. In any case, Lord Beaconsfield (as he now was) came home acclaimed as a peacemaker, pleased as well to announce a new British possession (Cyprus), acquired as a pendant from a grateful Ottoman Sultan.

In the weeks before the Congress of Berlin, as a reprisal against British moves in the Straits and Malta, the Russians dispatched a military mission to Afghanistan. It was led by Major-General Nikolai Stolietov, a senior aide to General Kaufmann, the pugnacious Governor-General of Turkestan. Together with six officers and a score or more Cossacks, Stolietov left Tashkent in June, heading for the Oxus. Sher Ali, sensing serious trouble, sent messages appealing to the Russians not to come, saying he could not assure their safety and would not receive them if they persisted. To no avail: Stolietov kept moving. He sent ahead assurances that Russia had mobilized an army in Turkestan to protect Afghanistan from the British, and was prepared to recognize Abdullah Jan as the Emir's heir—a vital addendum, since Sher Ali's nephew and rival, Abdur Rahman, had long been living in Russian territory. The Emir, half in hope, half in desperation, trying to wrest advantage from necessity, worried about Abdur Rahman, welcomed the Russians with a Durbar. Yet hardly had Stolietov arrived in Kabul on or around July 22 when he was recalled. He was informed that Russia had now settled its differences with Britain, and wished to avoid involvement with Afghanistan. It would appear Stolietov creatively stretched his instructions. He did leave Kabul in August, but his aides stayed on for months, and he and they evidently kept hinting to Sher Ali that Russia might again change its mind.

For Lytton, the electrifying news that Russians were in Kabul provided his yearned-for opening. Now he described Sher Ali "not only as a savage, but a savage with a touch of insanity." His telegrams to London all but scorched the newly laid cables. "We were told that our warnings were witless," ran one such message, "our anxieties nightmares; our calculation, the crude excursions of an untutored fancy; our conclusions airy fabrics" and more to that effect, concluding, "Now the Russian officers and troops have been received with honour at Kabul within 150 miles of our frontier" and more of the same. If Sher Ali did not *now* receive a British envoy, Lytton proposed an invasion and reordering of the vexatious kingdom. A British mission to Kabul was instantly assembled, headed by General Sir Neville Chamberlain (no relation to his better-known namesake), a veteran of the First Afghan War, a wounded hero of the Great Mutiny, and Commander-in-Chief of the Madras Army.

These preparations moved forward in September, when Parliament was in recess and Ministers of State were at country houses oiling their guns in preparation for the pheasant season. Disraeli was exhausted by his exertions at Berlin, and Lytton had come under the less skeptical, more permissive supervision of Lord Cranbrook, Salisbury's successor as Secretary of State for India. Nonetheless, despite these distractions, Lytton was instructed to delay any action until the Russians responded to a British inquiry about Stolietov. For reasons that still seem unclear—telegrams that crossed, clashing mobilization plans, or plain insubordination—the Viceroy went ahead, having already announced his Afghan mission, provoking this angry note to the India Office from Disraeli:

> I have read with some alarm the V-Roy's telegram. It appears that Lord Lytton cd not have been kept au fait to the communications that have taken place and are taking place betw. HM's Government and that of Russia on the subject of Afghanistan...As far as they have proceeded and as far as I can judge the explanations of the Russian Govt. are satisfactory, and the whole matter would have quietly disappeared, the Russian projects having been intended for a contemplated war with this country, wh., I trust, is now out of the question. What injurious effect Lytton's policy, ostentatiously, indiscreetly, but evidently officially announced in the Calcutta correspondence of *The Times* of yesterday may produce, I cannot presume to say. [The spelling is Disraeli's.]

Still, Disraeli was of two minds about Lytton. A few days later, on receiving papers from the India Office in which the Viceroy fluently defended his course, the Prime Minister leaned the other way. Owing to public opinion, firmness and decision *were* required on the

Afghan question, Disraeli now ventured. So long as the British public thought there was "Peace with Honor," he wrote to Cranbrook, "the Government was popular, but if they find there is no peace, they will soon conclude there is no honor." Disraeli again changed his mind as Lytton disobeyed what the Prime Minister thought was a clear order to avoid forcing the Khyber Pass.

"Nothing would have induced me to consent to such a step," Disraeli complained to Cranbrook. "He was told to send the Mission by Candahar. He has sent it by the Khyber, and received a snub, wh. it may cost us much to wipe away. When V-Roys and Comms.-in-chief disobey orders, *they ought to be sure of success in their mutiny*" (italics added). His candor let a small cat out of a large bag. From Downing Street to Government House in Calcutta, from Whitehall to the Hindu Kush, the game's unspoken rule was that the alchemy of success could always turn mutiny into initiative.

LORD LYTTON WAS SURE OF SUCCESS. THE MOMENT HE LEARNED that Chamberlain's mission had been firmly if civilly barred at the Pass, the Viceroy urged a declaration of war. This was an escalation steeper than Disraeli's colleagues were willing to countenance. On October 25, the Cabinet gathered for "one of the most remarkable meetings" that Disraeli could recall, as he wrote to the Queen. Was there a casus belli? Minister after minister confessed they could see none. The Lord Chancellor, the Government's highest judicial authority, (as Disraeli related) "analyzed the papers before the Cabinet, and showed that the Ameer had acted towards the Russians with the same reluctance to receive them as he had exhibited to the envoy of the Viceroy... The Marquis of Salisbury said that the Viceroy was 'forcing the hand of the Government'... He spoke with great bitterness of the conduct of the Viceroy, and said, that unless curbed, he would bring about some terrible disaster."

On the other side was Lord Cranbrook, who was for war "immediate and complete," the casus belli being "an aggregate of hostile acts on the part of the Amir." Disraeli was closer to Cranbrook than

Salisbury, and the Cabinet followed the Prime Minister's lead. It authorized giving Sher Ali until sundown November 20 to accept a permanent mission in Afghanistan and to apologize for repulsing Chamberlain. Failing that, the Emir would be a declared enemy. In Kabul, the Russians advised Sher Ali to stall the British until they consulted with their own Government on providing assistance. By melancholy coincidence, as this was happening, the Emir's favorite son died, a profoundly unsettling loss that also threw open the question of succession.

Sher Ali could all but feel the ground give way beneath him. A message from General Kaufmann in Tashkent arrived. It lamely explained that weather precluded Russian aid and advised the Emir to come to terms with the British. He tried to do so. In a tardy letter dated November 19, Sher Ali finally agreed to accept a British mission, but he failed to apologize, and in any case his message arrived ten days late. The invasion had already begun, on November 21 at 3 a.m., when Lytton telegraphed Lord Cranbrook, "*Jacta est alea*" (The die is cast). Three armies, totaling 30,000 men, advanced into the same harsh terrain, and against the same tribal adversaries that had humbled Britain in 1838–42. This time the force was garbed in discreet khaki, communicated by telegraph and heliograph, and was armed with the breech-loading Martini-Henry rifle, considered the best of its era. To the east, forcing the Khyber, were 15,000 men under Lieutenant General Sir Sam Browne, the designer of the famous belt, who had lost an arm and earned a Victoria Cross in the Great Mutiny. The center column, comprising 6,500 men and led by Major General Frederick Roberts, also VC, had as its objective the Kurram Valley. In the west, Major General Sir Donald Stewart's 12,000 men were to move through the Bolan Pass, reinforce the British garrison at Quetta, and occupy Kandahar.

As in 1838, the British expeditiously overcame Afghan resistance, seizing the lofty rock fortress of Ali Masjid in the Khyber, occupying the mud-walled citadel of Kandahar (within which the victors found "trees, spectators, beggars and ruins"), while General Roberts prevailed in heavy fighting at Peiwar Kotal, the pass at the northern end of the Kurram Valley. Seeing no way out, Sher Ali determined to plead his case directly to the Tsar, but when he fled from Kabul,

Russian frontier units barred his way. On February 21, 1879, ill and desolate, Sher Ali died wretchedly at Balkh, the half-ruined Mother of Cities, once host to Alexander the Great.

Sir Alfred Lyall, Lytton's Foreign Secretary, a friend of Tennyson's and himself a minor poet, memorialized Sher Ali in lines of uncharacteristic meanness:

> *And yet when I think of Shir Ali, as he lies in his sepulchre low,*
> *How he died betrayed, heartbroken, 'twixt infidel friend and foe,*
> *Driven from his throne by the English, and scorned by the*
>   *Russian, his guest,*
> *I am well content with the vengeance, and I see God works for*
>   *the best.*

On the contrary: it is difficult not to sympathize with Sher Ali. On three occasions in ten years, he sought British friendship and help, balking at a form of vassalage he correctly insisted his people would never endure. He was blamed for what his bullying neighbors did, defamed as a villain and a lunatic for the sin of defending his country's right to be left alone.

WITH SHER ALI GONE, LYTTON PRESSED INSTANTLY FOR CARVING the kingdom into three. The home Government balked, believing that three Afghanistans would be more trouble than one, and in any case the Conservatives were anxious for a quick end to an unpopular war. In Kabul, the throne passed to Yakub Khan, the "undutiful son, that ill-starred wretch," as Sher Ali once described him to Lytton. For want of a better alternative, the British in March 1879 began negotiations with the new Emir, who under duress gave way on everything. He agreed to allow a British Resident, acquiesced in British control of Afghanistan's foreign relations, and reluctantly handed over control of the Khyber Pass and the border districts of Kurram, Pishin, and Sibi, in return for an annual subsidy of £60,000. These arrangements were set forth in the Treaty of Gundamak, signed in the same hills from which Afghan snipers picked off the survivors of the Kabul garrison in 1841.

In Calcutta, news of the treaty prompted rejoicing, and in Britain, applause from the Government and its supporters, if with an undertone of apprehension. Lord Salisbury, Lytton's leading critic within the Cabinet, graciously congratulated the Viceroy. Five soldiers were knighted, and other honors lavishly bestowed. Yet memories of the First Afghan War haunted the festivities. Though speaking of his own political troubles, Disraeli inadvertently injected a note of fatalism in his glowing words to Lytton, "…whatever happens, it will always be to me a source of real satisfaction that I had the opportunity of placing you on the throne of the Gt. Mogul." The depth of the Cabinet's division over Afghanistan became fully known only in 1921, with the publication of Monypenny and Buckle's monumental biography of Disraeli. At the time in Parliament, the Government united behind Lytton, dismissing attacks by Gladstone's Liberals, and the forebodings of two former Viceroys, Northbrook and Lawrence. When Lawrence learned that a British mission would soon depart for Kabul, the most formidable critic of the Forward School groaned, "They will all be murdered, every one of them!"

Major Sir Pierre Louis Napoleon Cavagnari, now knighted for successfully negotiating the Treaty of Gundamak, was to head the mission. Sir Louis (his preferred first name) was Lytton's enthusiastic first choice as Envoy. Born in France, the son of an Irish mother and a Napoleonic officer, raised in Britain, and trained as a cadet by the East India Company, "Cavi" was renowned for his debonair fearlessness. He was a decorated veteran of the Great Mutiny and led or took part in seven punitive missions on the North-West Frontier. Informed of Lord Lawrence's gloomy prediction, the new Envoy shrugged, "If my death sets the red line on the Hindu Kush, I don't mind."

Still, as Brian Robson mildly remarks in a recent careful recounting of the Second Afghan War, "It may be doubted whether Cavagnari was the ideal choice of envoy." To Sir Robert Warburton, Warden of the Khyber, he was the "beau-ideal of a chief," who after chasing Pathan raiders would sit down "to write his report of ten, fifteen, twenty pages of foolscap, all in the best English, in a most beautiful clear hand, without a single blot or erasure." Yet Sir Neville Chamberlain, with whom he served as Political Officer on the aborted mission to Kabul, was far cooler, appraising Cavi as "more the man for facing an emergency than one to entrust with a position requiring delicacy and very calm judgement...If he were left at Cabul as our agent I should fear his not keeping us out of difficulties."

Yet he was just the man Lytton wanted, an officer with dash and brio, his name itself almost a battle flag. When the Viceroy met with Cavagnari at Simla before his departure, there was a holiday mood. On hand as a visitor was the Viceroy's close friend, Wilfred Scawen Blunt, with whom Lytton had once vied in bachelor days for the favors of "Skittles," later mistress to the Prince of Wales. High-spirited as the Arabian steeds he introduced to England, Blunt was a poet and amorist in the Byronic mode, and in fact was married to Byron's granddaughter, Lady Anne King-Noel. In the calm of his study, Lytton confided his grandest ambitions to his chum. In those critical weeks, Blunt informs us, "I may truly say the whole machinery of the Indian government was laid bare to me." And the Viceroy fired the poet's imagination. There, among Simla's potted plants and deodars, with the Himalayas rising toward cerulean skies, Blunt glimpsed, or thought he glimpsed, the grandeur of the New Imperialism.

On June 20, Cavagnari was at the Viceregal lodge, "full of decision and courage," in the words of Edith Lytton, preparing his departure for Kabul "in perfect confidence all will be right." By mid-July, the Envoy and his party, accompanied by General Roberts, crossed the frontier at Shutargadan Pass, where an Afghan escort welcomed them. Carpets were spread at the Afghan camp, and the Britons were treated to an agreeable repast—British curds, lamb kebabs, sherbet, Russian tea, and coffee laced with opium. Outwardly, Cavagnari was calm and cheerful, but on their way to the camp, so Roberts remembered, "We came across a solitary magpie, which I should not have noticed had not Cavagnari pointed it out, and begged me not to mention the fact of his having seen it to his wife, as she would be sure to consider it an unlucky omen." Folk wisdom taught that a lone magpie signified trouble, indeed disaster.

ONCE IN KABUL, CAVAGNARI ESTABLISHED HIS MISSION IN A walled courtyard adjoining the great fortress of Bala Hissar, not far from the Emir's own residence. At his own suggestion, the party was small as possible: numbering eighty-one, it consisted of himself, his political assistant, William Jenkyns; a medical officer, Dr. A. H. Kelly; and Second Lieutenant Walter Hamilton, in charge of a Corps of Guides detachment of twenty-five sowars (cavalry) and fifty-two sepoys (infantry). They were welcomed with full honors—a seventeen-gun salute, a band attempting "God Save the Queen," and an elephant ride to the Bala Hissar, the Britons swaying aloft in gold-and-silver howdahs.

A telegraph line connected Kabul to Peshawar, and Cavagnari's daily dispatches radiated optimism, despite the curses and spittle his appearance provoked as he rode around on his daily constitutional. He and his colleagues were the first Britons seen in Kabul for almost four decades, and older Afghans well remembered the last visitation, when British invaders razed the city's bazaar in reprisal for the murder of the sole previous British Envoy, Sir William Macnaghten. As Dr. Kelly wrote to his father, the British were "treated with every consideration by the Amir," but the people were "rather fanatical, not yet accustomed to our presence, so we always go with a troop of cavalry on our rides."

Everywhere there were reminders of calamities past. Young Lieutenant Hamilton, whose heroism while fighting in the Khyber under Sam Browne earned a Victoria Cross, rode out to Beymaru, site of one of the first British disasters in 1841. This time, he believed, God was on Britannia's side, reflections he put into a poem that included these lines:

> Though all is changed, yet remnants of the past
> Point to the scenes of bloodshed, and alas!
> Of Murder foul; and ruined houses cast
> Their mournful shadows o'er the graves of grass

The chill deepened with the arrival in Kabul of six regiments from Herat, near-mutinous soldiers who had not been paid for months. As they marched from their camp outside the city to the Bala Hissar to demand their arrears, a Pathan Guide reported to Cavagnari on the violent threats he heard. "Never fear," the Envoy reputedly remarked. "Keep up your heart. Dogs that bark do not bite." "Sahib," rejoined the Pathan, "these dogs *do* bite." Some suspected that Yakub Khan covertly promoted the unrest to get back at the despised foreigners, but subsequent inquiries uncovered no evidence of complicity. Cavagnari did not lose confidence in the Emir. "I have been quite bewildered sometimes," he telegraphed Lytton on August 30, "with stories that have been brought to me hinting that no trust should be placed in Yakub Khan, and that he is only temporizing with us. Although he is not to be thoroughly trusted, any more than any other Oriental, still, if he has any game in hand, I must confess to having not the slightest conception as to what it can be...I personally believe Yakub Khan will turn out to be a very good ally, and that we shall be able to keep him to his engagements."

Whatever the truth about Yakub Khan, one is baffled by Cavagnari's unwillingness to pay the aggrieved Heratis, which he had the authority to do. He refused throughout, explaining that he preferred to force the Emir to stand on his own feet. His course fatally overestimated Yakub Khan's judgment and courage, and gratuitously put his entire mission at risk. Conceivably he preferred martyrdom. In one dispatch from Kabul he wrote, "They can kill the three or four of us [*sic*] here, and our deaths will be well avenged." At other times his insouciance implies a total ignorance or indifference to the storm building around Kabul. Three days before his death, he complained that *The Times* took no notice of his arrival: "I am afraid there is no denying the fact the British public require a blunder and a huge disaster to excite their interest." On September 2, Cavagnari informed Peshawar, "All well in the Cabul Embassy." It was his final telegram.

The following dawn, the mutinous Heratis massed before the Emir's palace, and they were not appeased by a promise of one month's back pay. Reportedly someone then shouted, "There's gold at the house of the foreigners." When the rioters marched to the

Residency compound, its gates as always open, Cavagnari was at breakfast. His escort was caught off guard, but all quickly armed to repel the invaders. They retreated, but only to regroup and rearm. The British now barred the gates, threw up improvised barricades, but were easy targets for rifle fire from nearby buildings. The mission's best hope was immediate intervention by Yakub Khan, who reportedly ripped his beard and wept when he heard what happened. Three times during the day he sent emissaries, including his young son, who appealed vainly with the rioters to disperse.

Within hours after their retreat, the Heratis, now some 2,000 strong, renewed their assault, smashed open the gates, and from nearby buildings aimed barrage after barrage at the Residency. Cavagnari was among the first casualties. A ricocheting bullet grazed his forehead. Even though half-blinded, he was said to have led a bayonet charge before his death. Young Hamilton was now in command, and from the Residency roof his Guides fired away at the Heratis on their scaling ladders, driving the attackers back through smoke and fire ignited by oil-soaked rag bombs. Soon the attackers rolled up two field guns and at close range began shelling the Residency. Hamilton then led a handful of Guides in a direct charge through a hailstorm of musketry, and actually seized the guns. Within moments, overwhelmed in hand-to-hand fighting, Hamilton was dead. The surviving Guides at the Residency all died in action in a battle that lasted eight hours. Herati fatalities were estimated at six hundred.

Hamilton's poem reached his parents after his death. Double pensions were awarded to the families of the fallen Guides. In a telegram to General Roberts, Yakub Khan grasped what the massacre implied for him. "I have lost my friend the Envoy, and also my kingdom."

NEWS FROM KABUL REACHED SIMLA ON SEPTEMBER 5, WHEN Roberts was awakened about 2 a.m. by a messenger from his army's Kurram outpost. An aide rushed the message to Peterhof, where Roberts soon arrived to find the Viceroy already meeting with his

Council. Edith Colley described the mood to her absent husband, Colonel George Colley, Lytton's private secretary: "This is a terrible day; it all seems one terrible time since yesterday afternoon when Lady L. told me the dreadful rumours that the Residency at Kabul had been attacked...Then just at the end of dinner (which was half an hour early for the theatre), in came Z. [Sir Alfred Lyall] talking in gallant style, but with a look about his eyes which to me made it ghastly...Cavagnari's face haunts me, and all our last talks and the poor little wife at home."

Within hours, Lytton authorized an offensive against Afghanistan, turning to General Roberts, whose field force in Kurram had not yet been disbanded. The Viceroy was well aware that his reputation, present and future, was in peril. "The web of policy so carefully and patiently woven has been rudely shattered," he acknowledged in his first message to Disraeli. "We now have to weave a fresh web and, I fear, a wider one from undoubtedly weaker materials." It was nevertheless against Lytton's nature to admit error, much less apologize. On September 14, he informed Cranbrook that he expected condemnation for sending Cavagnari with so small an escort, "But there was practically no choice between sending him with a small escort or sending him with an army...I maintain that the danger of what actually *did* happen could not have been reasonably anticipated by any human being." Besides, he went on, "Who could have foreseen the fatuity of admitting mutinous regiments *into* the Bala Hisar?"

Still, it was Lytton himself who picked an Envoy notorious for his swagger to enforce a punitive treaty viewed as unendurable by a people spoiling for a fight. The disaster only hardened the Viceroy's determination to subjugate and dismember Afghanistan. Asked by General Roberts what line he should take with Afghans, the Viceroy replied: "You can tell them we shall never again withdraw altogether from Afghanistan and that those who help you will be befriended and protected by the British Government." Events, and the Afghans, finally forced a change in course. Luckily for Lytton, the damage to his Viceroyalty was mitigated by the emergence of General Roberts as an imperial hero, and by the fortuitous arrival—from Russia—of a pragmatic new Emir, Abdur Rahman.

Major-General Sir Frederick Roberts was that godsend to politicians, a likable warlord. Diminutive even in the saddle, with gnarled
face and walrus mustache, "Bobs" was so admired by war's end that
even his gray Arab, Volonel, received a campaign medal (with four
clasps) at the insistence of the Queen. Born in Cawnpore, the son of
an Indian Army general, Roberts earned his VC in the Mutiny and,
unusually, sprang to notice after long years in the quartermaster
corps. He had never held a field command until the outbreak of the
Afghan War, when his bold victories in the Kurram Valley caught
public attention. Roberts early on grasped the new influence of the
press in the age of telegraphy and the camera, and took care to cultivate war correspondents. Kipling's "Bobs" captures the image of
cheerful competence Roberts sought to convey:

> There's a little red-faced man,
> Which is Bobs,
> Rides the tallest 'orse 'e can—
> Our Bobs,
> If it bucks or kicks or rears,
> 'E can sit for twenty years
> With a smile round both 'is ears—
> Can't yer, Bobs?

However, on the principle that no nabob is a hero to his footman,
Bobs's severest critic was his own chief-of-staff, Major Sir Charles
MacGregor, who kept a diary so sulfurous that only in 1985 was it
published in full. MacGregor claimed descent from the Scottish rebel
Rob Roy, and cherished two ambitions, neither realized—to win
the Victoria Cross and rule as a king in Afghanistan. Roberts long
ago had won his Cross, and after his Kabul Field Force fought its way
into the capital in October 1879, he was to all practical purposes the
Emir of Kabul. Yakub Khan abdicated on the arrival of the British,
saying (according to Roberts) "he would rather be a grass-cutter in
the English camp than Ruler of Afghanistan." In the Emir's Audience
Hall, with suitable pomp, the general himself read the proclamation.
He announced that the British, being merciful, would not destroy
Kabul completely but would impose a heavy indemnity, that posses-

sion of a gun was a capital offense, and that all who took part in the attack on the Residency would get what they deserved. He promised informers from 50 to 120 rupees for naming the guilty, the price rising with the rank of those betrayed.

Roberts was thus faithful to Lytton's directive: "Every soldier in the Herat regiment is *ipso facto* guilty; and so is every civilian, be he Priest or layman, Mullah or peasant, who joined in the mob of assassins...For remember, it is not *justice* in the ordinary sense, but *retribution* you have to administer on reaching Kabul...Your objects should be to strike terror, and to strike it swiftly and deeply, but to avoid a *'Reign of Terror.'*" Just how many died remained in dispute. Roberts's own report put total hangings at eighty-seven. Yet Mac-Gregor, who despised Afghans and worried that "We are thoroughly hated and not enough feared," drew back at what he witnessed. "I think Bobs is the most blood thirsty little beast I know," he confided on October 19, adding a day later: "Found that men were being simply murdered under the name of justice." With full allowance for MacGregor's bile and envy, Roberts's justice was summary enough to prompt a justifiable outcry from what Roberts called "the Radical Papers" and their allies in Parliament. In India, too, there were questions. The Bombay *Review* wondered, "Is it according to the usages of war to treat as felons men who resist invasion?"

Though scarcely comparable in magnitude or duration with the Vietnam War, the Afghan conflict had a divisive effect that will seem familiar to Americans who lived through the Johnson and Nixon years. By chance, the Afghan War overlapped with the Zulu War in South Africa, precipitated when Sir Bartle Frere, formerly of India and more recently the British Commissioner in the Cape, proposed to station a Resident in Zululand. Many Britons failed to see what overriding interest justified the loss of British lives and the bloody reprisals that followed.

William Ewart Gladstone expressed these misgivings with moralizing eloquence. The Liberal leader's attacks on Disraeli's foreign policy were the centerpiece of his celebrated Midlothian campaign, named after the Scottish constituency in which the Grand Old Man chose to stand. He spoke of 10,000 Zulus slaughtered "for no other offence than their attempt to defend against your artillery with their naked bodies, their hearths and home, their wives and families." He asked his audiences to recall that "the sanctity of life in the hill villages of Afghanistan, among the winter snows, is as inviolable in the eyes of Almighty God as can be your own." The Conservatives scoffed, the Queen was appalled, but Gladstone struck a chord among middle-class Britons, turning the general election of April 1880 into a kind of plebiscite on imperial wars.

Gladstone won hands down, gaining a House of Commons majority of about one hundred. So irritated was the Queen that she wrote to her private secretary, "She will sooner *abdicate* than send for or have any *communication* with *that half-mad firebrand* who wd soon ruin everything & be a *Dictator.* Others but herself *may submit* to his democratic rule but *not the Queen."* Within days, Victoria had cooler second thoughts. Soon Gladstone, with his Biblical pieties, "half-crazy, half-silly" according to the Queen, had settled in Downing Street and was writing letters that commenced "Madam and Most Beloved Sovereign."

Supremely political, Roberts sensed the shifting tide months before the election. In November he issued an amnesty proclamation based on a new doctrine. Many Afghans, it appeared, mistakenly thought that their Emir was a prisoner in the Residency. Therefore they were not rebelling against their own monarch—the theory used to justify the hangings—and thus the British extended a general amnesty to all who took no direct part in the massacre. This did not mollify the Afghans. In December, some 10,000 tribal warriors fell so furiously on the British cantonment outside Kabul that Roberts telegraphed for reinforcements, and Lytton and his advisers feared a general uprising reminiscent of the First Afghan War.

Such was the setting in January 1880 when a new claimant for the throne at Kabul crossed the Afghan frontier. He was Abdur Rahman, "the Slave of the Merciful," a grandson of Dost Mohammed and a survivor of fratricidal wars. For eleven years he had lived on a Russian pension, being kept in reserve, so to speak, as a possibly useful spare part. On his entering Afghanistan with Russian good wishes, a bagful of money, and several hundred rifles, Abdur Rahman was immediately contacted by a British political officer, with favorable results. A telegram from Lytton to London followed: "Necessary to find without delay some Native authority to which we can restore northern Afghanistan without risk of immediate anarchy on our evacuation of Kabul…No prospect of finding in the country any man strong enough for this purpose. I therefore advocate early public recognition of Abdur Rahman."

By any reckoning, it was a remarkable denouement, a last fling of the dice. Lytton's proposal was quickly adopted, a decision reaffirmed by the new Liberal Government. "In other words," writes a latter-day chronicler, Pierce Fredericks, "a war started to forestall Russian influence at Kabul was now to be settled by the installation of a Russian pensioner in the same location." On July 22, the Viceroy and Her Most Gracious Majesty the Queen Empress formally "recognized" (not proclaimed) Abdur Rahman as Emir. It was the fruit of compromise. The Emir accepted the loss of territory, including the Khyber Pass, but there would be no British Resident in Kabul.

General Roberts became the war's anointed British hero by avenging a terrible defeat at Maiwand, where Afghan *ghazis,* or irregulars, overwhelmed a field force of 2,500, killing nearly a thousand. Maiwand was fought on July 27, 1880, months after the British assumed the war was nearly over. Abdur Rahman was now Emir, Disraeli was out, Lytton had resigned as Viceroy, and his Liberal successor, Lord Ripon, had already arrived. But the war was not over for Ayub Khan, the ruler of Herat and a claimant to the throne lost by his brother Yakub Khan. Ayub and a clamorous army of 20,000 or more *ghazis* were marching southward to seize Kandahar when they outfought—and outthought—an intercepting British force at the village of Maiwand. The *ghazis* then wheeled toward their nearby target, Kandahar, and its British garrison, 3,000 strong. To rescue the trapped Britons, Roberts led a relief force from Kabul to Kandahar, covering 313 treacherous miles in twenty-two days, and there decisively defeated Ayub Khan's *ghazis,* avenging Maiwand and relieving Kandahar. Roberts later served as Commander-in-Chief in India, and lived to fight successfully in the Boer War. He died in 1914, as Lord Roberts of Kandahar, remembered throughout Britain for his dramatic march, "Kabul to Kandahar."

THE SECOND AFGHAN WAR SCARRED MOST OF ITS PRINCIPAL actors, and changed minds as much as it altered the map. General Roberts, true enough, emerged a figuratively bigger man, but he was the exception. Writing from Kabul during 1880, he supplied a fitting epitaph for the war: "It may not be very flattering to our *amour propre,* but I feel sure I am right when I say that the less the Afghans see of us, the less they will dislike us. Should Russia, in future years, attempt to conquer Afghanistan, or invade India through it, we should have a better chance of attaching the Afghans to our interests if we avoid all interference with them in the meantime...The longer and more difficult the line of communication is, the greater the obstacles which Russia would have to overcome."

For Wilfred Scawen Blunt, who saw the war from Simla and then traveled widely through India, the experience was jolting. He no longer believed in the confident expertise of braided officers, and after seeing rural India concluded that even the Empire's good public works were a "swindle." As he wrote to a friend in Britain, "The 'natives', as they call them are a race of slaves, frightened, unhappy, and terribly thin. Though a good conservative and a member of the Carlton Club, I own to be shocked...and my faith in British institutions and the blessings of British rule have received a severe blow." Blunt expressed his new opinions forcefully in *Ideas About India* (1885) and thereafter was the Empire's unswerving patrician critic until his death in 1922.

The war deeply affected, if in a different way, Sir Alfred Lyall, the great British Indian administrator, scholar, and occasional poet. After serving as Foreign Secretary to both Lytton and Ripon, he concluded it was futile for the British to become embroiled in Afghan politics. The wiser course was to engage Russia in a definite treaty, a policy he outlined in a prescient Minute in 1881, an approach that ultimately prevailed in 1907. After six years as Lieutenant Governor of the North-West Provinces, Lyall returned to England in 1887 to write on Indian history and Asian religions while providing tactful moderating advice to successive Governments. He died in 1911.

Emir Abdur Rahman managed bit by bit to reabsorb the slices of Afghanistan that Lord Lytton wished to make into separate states, taking over Kandahar in 1881, and Herat seven years later. But the British held on to the Kurram Valley and the Khyber Pass as well other disputed frontier areas. Abdur Rahman was known, not affectionately, as The Iron Emir. He crushed two major rebellions, killed as many as 100,000 political opponents, yet pushed his country at least part of the way into the twentieth (Christian) century before his death in 1901.

William Ewart Gladstone tasted to the full the miseries of victory. He was trapped, as it were, in the paradoxes of his own making: he wished to devour Imperialism and have it too. Though he opposed the Afghan War, he was loath to yield up all its fruits and so the Khyber and Kurram remained under British rule. And having insisted Russia posed little threat to India, his Cabinet moved to the brink of war in 1885 when the Russian forces threatened to slice off part of Afghanistan. The crisis occurred not long after General Gordon died at Khartoum when a British relief column arrived one fatal day late. Russia pulled back from Pandjeh, the disputed territory, and war was averted, but the whole flareup had a staged air, in the once-scorned Disraeli manner. As for India, it was Gladstone's doctrine that British rule could be justified if it truly benefited—and was seen to benefit—the ruled. But when the Raj's chief legal officer, Courtney Ilbert, an idealist schooled by the classical scholar Benjamin Jowett at Oxford, put forward in 1883 a modest reform whereby some Europeans might be tried for some offenses by Indian magistrates, a "White Mutiny" erupted and Gladstone's Liberals ignobly backed off.

As for Lord Lytton, he returned to Britain discredited but scarcely chastened—even though it transpired that his Military Accounts Department had grievously underestimated the cost of the Afghan War, which it reckoned at £6 million, when the actual sum eventually totaled £12 million more. The blunder occurred under the otherwise watchful eyes of the Viceroy's friend, Sir John Strachey. In 1887, Lytton was named Ambassador to France and acquitted himself with his former carefree éclat; he died in Paris four years later. Still, though

Lytton failed to gain the vindication he felt he deserved, he did win a posthumous triumph. In 1911, George V proclaimed Delhi as the future seat of British India, and did so at the third and final Royal Durbar in the former Mughal capital—the first being in Lytton's in 1877, and the second Curzon's in 1903. Thus the imperial spirit was transmitted in the form of great radial avenues, immense traffic circles, spacious gardens, somewhat overblown public buildings, along a central axis, Kingsway, two miles long and twice the width of the Champs Elysées. At the new city's heart was an imposing Viceroy's House, with a Durbar Room. The future capital of independent India thus grew out of Old Delhi, with its Red Fort and ghosts of the Great Mutiny. Appositely, the architect selected as co-designer of New Delhi was Sir Edwin Luytens. His wife was Lytton's daughter Emily, and she, in a touch one could scarcely have invented, was an adherent of Theosophy and a supporter of Indian freedom. In a further curious turn, Lytton's daughter Judith (Bibi) married, and later divorced, Wilfred Scawen Blunt. What a theme for Lytton Strachey had he chosen to write about India and the pitfalls of cleverness rather than Cardinal Manning, or Dr. Arnold of Rugby.

∴

CHAPTER EIGHT

Her Majesty's
Indian Secret Service

Aᶠᵗᵉʳ GLANCING CASUALLY AT JOHN H. WATSON IN THEIR FIRST encounter, Sherlock Holmes remarked, "You have been in Afghanistan, I perceive." Dr. Watson had indeed served as an Assistant Surgeon on the North-West Frontier and was wounded at Maiwand in the Second Afghan War. For Holmes, it was an obvious inference: Here was a tanned physician of military bearing who had undergone hardship: where else in 1881 but Afghanistan? For the reader today, it wonderfully illustrates the great triad of themes—knowledge, power, and Empire—that pervaded popular writing in the late Victorian years.

As Watson was returning on the troopship *Orontes* to London, "that great cesspool into which all the loungers and idlers of the Empire are irresistibly drained," the young Rudyard Kipling was sailing the other way. Kipling was born in Bombay in 1865, and after attending boarding school in England, returned to India to work on the staff of *The Civil and Military Gazette*. No sooner was he in Lahore, whose bazaars and back alleys he knew as a Hindustani-speaking child, than he was entranced by native life. "I'm in love with the Country," he wrote a friend. "...I find heat and smells and oils and spices, and puffs of temple incense, and sweat and darkness, and dirt and lust and cruelty, and above all, things wonderful fascinating innumerable." Out of this love came Kipling's masterpiece, *Kim*, a book about knowledge and power that is something more than imperial propaganda.

Certainly few books have an odder, more diverse fan club. To Nirad C. Chaudhuri, the doyen of Bengal letters, *Kim* is "the finest novel in the English language with an Indian theme, but also one of the greatest of English novels in spite of the theme." T. S. Eliot read it aloud to his wife, and Mark Twain reread it regularly ("Write for and about boys" was Twain's advice to his friend Kipling). *Kim* was at Allen Dulles's deathbed, and Tariq Ali, the expatriate Pakistani revolutionary, declared it the book he loved most as a boy in Lahore. It has been praised, dissected, and deconstructed by Edmund Wilson, Edward Said, and Peter Hopkirk, among others, as a parable of imperialism, in which Kimball O'Hara, a young Catholic orphan raised as a native, has to decide if he is a Sahib and how to weigh the claims of the state against those of the spirit, as embodied in his friend the Tibetan Lama.

Published in 1901, *Kim* was the book that gave universal currency to the phrase Great Game and that endowed the Raj's intelligence service and its mapmakers with an enduring aura of glamour. In the end, Kim will choose to serve the Sahibs, in the form of Colonel Creighton:

> So far as Kim could gather, he was to be diligent and enter the Survey of India as a chain-man… "Yes, and thou must learn how to make pictures of roads and mountains and rivers—to carry these pictures in thine eye till a suitable time comes to set them upon paper. Perhaps some day, when thou art a chain-man, I may say to thee when we are working together: 'Go across those hills and see what lies beyond.'"

So Colonel Creighton exhorted the protégé he had sent to an imperial boarding school for spies to learn how to "pace all his distances by a bead rosary." For many of his characters, Kipling drew on real-life models, notably the "pundits" or native explorers—pundit means learned man in Sanskrit. They achieved a glory in fiction that was less often their lot in life.

ALL MAPS ARE POLITICAL, AND, IT MAY BE VENTURED, ALL MAP-makers are politicians. "Imperialism and mapmaking intersect in the most basic manner," the American scholar Matthew Edney asserts in *Mapping the Empire* (1997). "Both are fundamentally concerned with territory and knowledge." To govern or even comprehend a territory, one must map it, and as Edney writes, it took the British a century and a "massive intellectual campaign to transform a land of incomprehensible spectacle into an empire of knowledge."

The mapping of India was the province of the Survey of India. Credit for founding the Survey belongs to a young naval officer, James Rennell (1742–1830), who went out to India in 1760 and mastered marine surveying only to discover he had no chance for promotion. Rennell, aged twenty-one, resigned his commission and with the help of a messmate, was appointed Surveyor-General of Bengal. Obsessed with mapmaking (Rennell called blanks on the map "eyesores"), he traveled with a detachment of sepoys through Bengal for seven years fixing latitudes, identifying fertile land, and filling journals with detailed accounts of valleys, rivers, and towns. Exhausted by jungle fever, poisonous snakes, leopards, tigers, and brigands—not least, by near-fatal wounds inflicted by Sanashi fakirs—Rennell returned at thirty-five to England, and with a pension from the East India Company, devoted himself to geography. When he published his *Bengal Atlas* in 1779, Rennell was proclaimed "the father of Indian geography," and when he died in 1830, he was interred among the great savants and soldiers in the nave of Westminster Abbey.

The early surveys were of two kinds: route surveys, using a perambulator and compass, which charted India's principal arteries, and topographical surveys, which filled in the missing detail. Surveyors were intelligence gatherers taught to "observe everything on the

Road, or that is visible from it, which can be considered as of any importance, but particularly...Forts, Hill Forts, remarkable peaks, mountains or Hills, Ghats or Passes, Towns...villages, etc.; Rivers or Nullahs, with their names, and noticing the way the stream runs, whether right or left, at the crossing place; their breadths and directions as far as visible, up and down the stream...The bearings of the Road shall be observed as frequently... as possible."

In 1799, the East India Company, having defeated Tippu Sultan of Mysore, opened the way to India's southern peninsula, and the era of exuberant surveying dawned. William Lambton (1756–1823), a six-foot, fair-haired, blue-eyed Yorkshireman and infantry officer with a keen sense of humor, who had fought in the Mysore campaign, persuaded the Madras Government that it needed "a mathematical and topographical survey of the greatest accuracy" stretching across the Indian peninsula and continuing "to an almost unlimited extent in every other direction." Doing that required triangulation, based on the geometry principle familiar to every high school student: if you know two angles and the triangle's baseline, you can determine the other properties of a triangle. Once the baseline is measured, a suitable elevation can be selected, and using a theodolite,* a telescope with horizontal and vertical scales, the two angles at the ends of the baseline and the lines to the elevation can be measured. With a plane table—a drawing board mounted on a tripod with a metal sight rule—and a theodolite, it was now possible to plot the height of a mountain and establish the distance between points. Triangulation would provide the frame; route and topographical surveys the picture, the details such as were "immediately wanted for military purposes."

In 1817 Calcutta assumed responsibility for triangulation and re-named it the Great Trigonometrical Survey, or GTS. After Lambton's death in 1823, Colonel Sir George Everest (1790–1866) succeeded to the post of Superintendent. Unlike Lambton, who was in his assis-

---

*Lambdon's theodolite had an interesting history. The enormous instrument weighed a ton and one-half and had to be specially ordered in England. It was dispatched in 1802, only to fall victim to Napoleon's Navy, which captured it and took it to Mauritius. However, with a sportsmanlike gesture, the French forwarded it to Madras with a polite note to the Government.

tant's words "a tranquil and exceedingly good-humoured person, very fond of his joke, a great admirer of the fair sex, partial to singing glees and duets, and everything, in short, that promoted harmony and tended to make life pass easily," Everest was ill-humored, in fact, downright cantankerous, with a personality darkened by continual fevers and dysentery. But nothing was to interfere with the steady progress of the Survey that was to unify the Indian Empire in "a mesh of exactly measured triangles." Under Everest, as John Keay reckons in *When Men and Mountains Meet* (1977), the line of triangles, stretching from Cape Comorin to the mountains, "was the longest arc of the meridian ever measured, and of immense geodetic importance for calculating the curvature of the earth." Nonetheless by 1834, the Survey's small army, burdened with extremely delicate and cumbersome equipment, arrived within sight of the Himalayas, and by 1850 reached the foothills. Now roads, railways, telegraphs, canals—and military campaigns—could be planned and constructed throughout the Indian Empire. It was a stupendous achievement.*

"FRONTIERS ARE THE RAZOR'S EDGE ON WHICH HANG SUSPENDED the issue of war or peace and the life of nations," declared Lord Curzon, his era's foremost authority on Asian frontiers. He went on to remark in his 1907 Romanes Lecture at Oxford: "Frontiers are the

---

*What became of the information collected in such difficult circumstances after it left the survey is recounted by Clements Markham (1830–1916), when he took charge of the records at the India Office at Whitehall in 1868: "The old correspondence books were destroyed; the Survey Reports were unnoticed; there was no arrangement of any kind for utilizing the work of the Surveys; and the valuable collection of maps and geographical documents was carted in a heap into a corner of a passage. Many of the maps were like much-used coffee-house table-clothes; they were folded in unequal sections, the margins frayed, and the edges broken and worn away. Many were lost, while whole editions had never been distributed or even unpacked. The map mounter, Mr. Jones, afterwards said that in an experience of 14 years he had never come across anything so bad as the condition of the geographical records of the India Office."

chief anxiety of nearly every Foreign Office in the civilized world, and are the subject of four out of every five political treaties or conventions that are concluded." In Asia, the frontier question, whether it be in the jungles of Assam or the Vale of Kashmir, that so troubled empire builders would continue to disturb and embitter their successor states.

Exploring frontiers, acquiring information, marking boundaries, and making maps—viewed by indigenous rulers as a form of military surveillance—was particularly difficult for the Government of India on its Afghan and Tibetan borders. Successive Afghan Emirs did not welcome intrusions, and China was the suzerain power in Tibet. In 1792, the Chinese sealed the Tibetan frontier, but by then Tibet was not entirely *terra incognita*. Jesuit and Capuchin missionaries were there in the seventeenth century, and although not allowed to map Tibet, Jesuit cartographers in Peking trained native disciples who supplied them with information as to the physical configuration of the country. However, the British had found these maps frustratingly vague: the exact location of "mysterious Lhasa" was unknown even though the Tibetan capital was but 300 miles from Calcutta.

Mapping the Himalayas and gathering intelligence about the Russians became the concern of the "forward school" to the point of obsession. By 1864, when the Russian Foreign Minister, Prince Gorchakov, declared in his famous circular that Russia was obliged to subdue the "half savage, nomad populations of Central Asia in the interests of the security of its frontier and its commercial relations," Russia had become Britain's antagonist. In 1800 the frontier between British India and the Russian Empire was 2,000 miles apart; by 1876, that distance had been halved.

In theory, the mountains were India's protective rampart, but the same peaks were also perfect camouflage for Russian infiltrators. Tibet was a particular problem. Beginning in the 1780's, the British sent two emissaries—George Bogle and Samuel Turner—to the Land of the Snows. Both reached Shigatse, but neither was allowed to continue on to Lhasa. After Tibet sealed its borders at China's insistence in 1792, the sole Briton to reach Lhasa was an eccentric freelancer, Thomas Manning (1770–1840). A Cambridge dropout, he studied Chinese, made his way to Canton, proceeded to Calcutta and then Bhutan, thence to Phari and the Chumbi Valley in Tibet, without sanction of a disapproving East India Company.

"Fools, fools, fools, to neglect an opportunity they may never have again!" lamented Manning's future editor, Sir Clements Markham, head of the Geographical Department at the India Office and later President of the Royal Geographical Society. Manning's description of the first British encounter with Lhasa included a litany of complaints, one of which held a particular resonance for future travelers: "Dirt, dirt, grease, smoke. Misery, but good mutton."

Manning did reach Lhasa in 1811, and presented the five-year-old Ninth Dalai Lama with broadcloth, four Chinese ewers, a pair of good brass candlesticks, thirty new bright dollars, and a bottle of Smith's Lavender Water. The child was "beautiful and interesting," but Manning was unimpressed by Lhasa. The Potala, the capital's most famous landmark, offered "nothing striking, nothing pleasing" in its appearance. Of the town he said, "The avenues are full of dogs, some growling and gnawing bits of hide which lie about in profusion and emit a charnel-house smell; others limping and looking livid; others ulcerated; others starved and dying and pecked at by ravens; some dead and preyed upon. In short, everything seemed mean and gloomy…"

Manning was not the only adventurer to cross India's frontiers. Although the British Army officially forbade forays north of the Himalayas, various errant officers—with a wink from their superiors—died in the attempt. As Anita Loos was to remark appositely in a very different context, "fate just kept on happening" to the Empire's explorers. So it was that Captain Thomas George Montgomerie (1830–78), Bengal Engineers, the First Assistant at the GTS, hit upon the idea of training native surveyors who could penetrate the porous borders of the Himalayas in disguise.

Arriving in India in 1851, having studied spherical trigonometry, differential and integral calculus, and astronomy, Montgomerie found his vocation at the Survey. He made his name by supervising the survey of Jammu and Kashmir, including the frontier regions of Ladakh and Baltistan, an area of nearly 7,700 square miles, some of it ascending 20,000 feet above sea level. He also succeeded in the sensitive job of gathering intelligence in frontier areas while maintaining good relations with the Maharajah, Gulap Singh, and his successor. His diary describes typical difficulties in the field:

> The ascent of Ahertatopa [a peak in Kashmir] was easy, but I had to make up a portable lightning conductor to protect the theodolite; no iron being available, I spliced together the mining tools, crowbars etc., and pitched the conductor in the snow close to the observatory tent...We had hardly got the tent up than a severe storm came on, first a strong wind threatening to blow us down the ridge, then a fall of heavy hailstones. About 4 p.m. snow began to fall, and at 5 p.m. the lightning and thunder seemed to be centered on the peak itself. The iron stove in my tent began to crackle, the hair of my dog crackled too, and in the dark sparks were clearly visible. Our tent was in sloping snow and connected to the observation platform by only a very narrow ridge, giving just enough foothold; on either side was a precipice; communication therefore was not easy, especially at night when the snow was frozen and slippery.

During the Indian Mutiny, John Lawrence as Governor of the Punjab, anxious to demonstrate that the outcome was not in doubt, continued to supply Montgomerie with men and money, and the Survey was completed without a fatality in 1864. The only casualty was Montgomerie's health; he was invalided to England, where the Royal Geographical Society rewarded him with its Founder's Medal. On May 14, 1866, Montgomerie uttered memorable words to that august body. "When I was in Ladakh," he told the audience filled with explorers, "I noticed that natives of India passed freely backwards and forwards between Ladakh and Yarkand, in Chinese Turkestan, and it consequently occurred to me that it might be possible to make the exploration by that means. If a sharp enough man could be found, he would have no difficulty in carrying a few small instruments amongst his merchandise, and with their aid good service might be rendered to geography."

Montgomerie was not the first to train Indian surveyors: Moorcroft, it will be recalled, directed his headman to pace off distances, while another native surveyor accompanied Alexander Burnes to Bokhara in 1832. The Survey, too, had trained Indian assistants: by mid-century, while Europeans were still trying to scale the Alps, the GTS was training *Khalassies* to climb Himalayan peaks far higher than 20,000 feet to establish observation points. Nevertheless, Montgomerie's name is forever entwined with the "pundits," those Indians trained expressly to pass independently through Himalayan borders in disguise.

Nor did Montgomerie create the pundits, although Peter Hopkirk and others identify him as the model for *Kim*'s Colonel Creighton. It was Major Edmund Smyth, the Education Inspector of Kumaon, who first recruited them. Smyth was the model for "Crab Jones" in Thomas Hughes's fictionalized account of his Rugby years, *Tom Brown's Schooldays*. Described by Hughes as "the queerest, coolest fish at Rugby," Smyth was drawn to the Himalayas by his passion for *shikar,* or big-game hunting. Despite Lhasa's travel ban, Smyth penetrated Western Tibet and even swam surreptitiously in the holy lake, Manasarovar. His companion on his clandestine forays was another Indian Army Officer, Lt. John Hanning Speke, later to become Richard Burton's successful rival in the race to discover the source of the Nile.

Smyth's recruits were Rawats, a clan from the Johar Valley of Kumaon on the Indo-Tibetan border. The Rawats claimed their ancestors were Hindu Rajputs who had migrated to the valley and intermarried with the Bhotias, a semi-nomadic people of mixed Indo-Tibetan stock. Even though these pundits were mostly named Singh, they were not, according to Alastair Lamb, "hairy Sikhs" but "smooth Tibetans." The suitability of the Rawats for cross-border forays into Tibet was immediately apparent to Smyth, as he wrote to Montgomerie, "both on account of their sound knowledge of the Tibetan language and also because they had the entrée into the country."

The Rawats acquired their entrée because an ancestor, Hiru Dham Singh, led a pilgrimage in 1680 to Mt. Kailas and Lake Manasarovar. While in Tibet, he helped drive out Chinese invaders. As a reward, the Tibetans granted the Rawats a virtual monopoly over cross-border trade between Gartok and Western Tibet, and two of Hiru's descendants, Deb and Bir Singh, accompanied Moorcroft and Hearsey on their 1812 expedition to the sacred lake and mountain.

Smyth's initial candidates—Nain and his cousin Mani Singh Rawat (the nephew and son of Deb Singh)—were taken to Dehra Dun in northern India, headquarters of the Survey, in 1863. For two years they were instructed in basic techniques: determining latitude by sextant, direction by pocket compass, and altitude by boiling water. Montgomerie personally supervised the special program whereby they were drilled in pacing—Nain Singh's stride was measured at 31 inches, approximately two thousand steps per mile. They learned to maintain these exact strides even while scrambling up mountains. Disguised as Buddhist pilgrims, they marked the distance with special prayer beads, resembling those carried by Hindus and Buddhists except that they were eight beads short of the pilgrim's normal rosary of 108 beads. The small beads were made of imitation coral, and every tenth bead, made from the seeds of the udras plant, was larger. Every one hundredth pace, the pundit slipped a bead; every large bead represented a thousand paces, or approximately half a mile.

As they marched, the pundits chanted *Om mani padme hum*—"Oh Jewel in the Lotus"—while they turned their prayer wheels, which held, instead of prayers, specially coded notes. Their staffs concealed thermometers, their prayer wheels also held compasses, and a strong-box concealed the agents' sextants. Because of the cumbersome sextants, "observations of latitude were difficult." For this demanding and hazardous assignment, the Singhs were paid a starting salary of a miserly sixteen rupees a month.

Before he left for England, Montgomerie had dispatched the two cousins through Kumaon, but they were recognized and failed to cross the Tibetan frontier. They then approached Tibet from Nepal. Although Mani was unsuccessful, the more tenacious Nain Singh did succeed in reaching Lhasa in 1866, and finally put it on British maps. Nain Singh's report to the Survey records Tibetan crops, imports, and exports, and describes religious festivals and the composition of the Tibetan Army. Altogether Nain Singh traveled 1,200 miles and brought back invaluable details for a map of Tibet's southern trade-route. He also managed to chart the Tsangpo's course for 600 miles. For this the Royal Geographical Society awarded him a gold medal in 1877. Over the years Nain Singh passed on his skills to other pundits, as cousins succeeded cousins. (Their story is capably told by the Vanderbilt scholar Derek Waller in *The Pundits* [1990].)

Meanwhile, Muslim explorers, among them Montgomerie's first pundit, Abdul Hamid, who reached Yarkand in 1863, conducted their surveys for the most part on the North-West Frontier where they could pass as natives. They were known by code names such as "the Mullah" (Ata Muhammed, who explored the wild gorges of the Indus and succeeded in mapping Swat); "the Mirza" (Mirza Shuja, who mapped northern Afghanistan and the Pamirs); and "the Munshi" (Abdul Hamid).

THE MOST FAMOUS PUNDIT, THANKS TO KIPLING, WAS A BENGALI, Sarat Chandra Das (1849–1917), the inspiration for Hurree Chunder Mookerjee, alias "the Babu" or R17 in *Kim*. Das combined unusual scholarship, language skills, and an aptitude for intelligence activities so that he might be called the first true secret agent—perhaps, as some have alleged, a double one. Like Kipling's Babu, instead of employing disguises and lurking in the shadows, Das would openly charm his subjects and with his wit confound those who suspected him.

Das was born in 1849 to a Vaidya (medical) caste family in Chittagong in East Bengal. He acquired surveying skills as an engineering student in Calcutta and became an adept photographer. Recruited in 1874 to head the Bhutia Boarding School in Sikkim, he learned Tibetan there under the tutelage of Lama Ugyen Gyatso. John (later Sir John) Edgar, Deputy Commissioner for Darjeeling, gave the headmaster a copy of the recently published *Narratives* (1876) of the missions of George Bogle and Thomas Manning to Tibet. An enchanted Das read the accounts "over and over," and they kindled in his mind "a burning desire for visiting Tibet and exploring its unknown tracts." Edgar then disclosed to Das that one of the objects of the Government in establishing the school was "to train up some intelligent Bhutia lads in surveying so that they might be sent to explore the Trans-Himalayan regions and it was for that particular purpose that I had been brought from the Engineering College."

Das yearned to visit Tibet. Citing a concession obtained by the British in an 1876 convention in which the Chinese (but not the Tibetans) agreed to allow a British mission to proceed to Tibet, he nominated himself, saying he was the only European or Indian at the time who knew Tibetan. A plan was prepared in which Ugyen Gyatso, on the pretext of bringing tributes from his monastery, would test the waters in Tashilhunpo and Lhasa and see if he could obtain permission for Das to visit Tibet.

Ugyen Gyatso met no encouragement from Lhasa but did obtain an invitation for the "Indian Pandit" to visit Tashilhunpo, the monastery outside Shigatse, where he would enroll as a student. So Das entered Tibet in 1879, in the guise of a pilgrim seeking enlightenment. His trip was a personal triumph, but with a disastrous epilogue that was described frankly by Das's pupil, a Japanese Buddhist monk, Ekai Kawaguchi, who visited Lhasa in 1900.

Das was granted a leave from his teaching duties, but was irritated by the refusal of the Government of India to contribute to his and his companion Ugyen Gyatso's travel expenses. Eventually Tibetan friends would lend the pair money. The passport with the seal of the Panchen Lama cited in Das's *Autobiography* tells the story. It required the local headmen and residents of the districts through which they were to pass (the southern province of Tsang) to furnish the pilgrims with "a relay of three riding ponies and ten beasts of burden and also cooking necessaries, fuel &c., at halting stages, free of charge…"

Although not working directly for the Survey, Das and the lama detoured to Calcutta to brush up their surveying skills under the pundit Nain Singh, who instructed them in using the sextant, boiling-point thermometer, and prismatic compass. Equipped in Dehra Dun with essential presents, plus a camera, a manual of photography, 150 rupees, guns, and two umbrellas ("Please keep your eye on the umbrella," were the Babu's final words to Kim as they set out. "I shall be just four or five miles ahead."), S.C.D. and U.G., as they were known in official records, their two Sikkimese porters, and a Bhutia guide set out for Sikkim, thence to the Nepalese border.

Despite the summer weather, during the twenty-one days it took to travel to Tashilhunpo, the out-of-shape scholars suffered from cold and altitude sickness. Das even had to be carried on the back of their guide over the final pass into Tibet. When they arrived at Tashilhunpo, described by Das as "like a dazzling hill of polished gold," the Panchen Lama was away but they were invited to become guests of Losang Palden, the Sengchen Lama, the Panchen's Chief Minister. Das captures the moment:

> The room was spread with Tartar carpets; the walls were hung with rich satin and dragon-figures; representations of deities and Bodhisattvas, fringed with embroidered silk and kincobs [brocaded satin], were hung on all sides. Gilt images of deities of various sizes in sitting posture were kept in niches, which were illuminated with lamps, and a number of paper prayer-wheels were kept rotating by the action of their smoke. The room was canopied with rich China satin. The Minister was seated on a high chair of yellow China wood, resting his hands on a handsome table, richly painted with Chinese domestic scenes and natural scenery.

After salutations in the Tibetan fashion, the visitors were served biscuits, cakes, and cheese along with hot butter tea. The Chief Minister remarked that he "admired their pluck in attempting the Himalayas in search of Buddhistic knowledge." At a later meeting, to their amazement, their host, who had picked up a smattering of Hindustani from visiting Kashmiri and Nepalese merchants, expressed an interest in Das's Hindustani, Sanskrit, and English books and requested that Das tutor him. Enchanted by their camera, the Chief Minister for a week neglected everything else while he learned to take pictures. His enthusiasm carried into science and mathematics, and subsequently he asked that a lithographic press be brought from India. Others who befriended "the Babu" and "the Lama" included one Kusho-Di-chung, a noble in the Panchen

Lama's entourage, who supplied them "with information respecting the Russian advances towards the confines of Tibet and Bhutan."

Here were pundits, no longer cowering in caravanserai but treated as honored guests. The Chief Minster's apartment in which they stayed, under Das's appraising eye, is described with the lapidary precision of a Sotheby's catalog:

> ... The north and east walls of my room were concealed by pigeon-holed shelves, containing about three hundred volumes of Tibetan manuscripts. In the centre of each frame of shelves there was a shrine, enclosed in beautifully carved planks, containing engraved dragon figures. . . . The largest of the shrines was six feet by four, and was three feet deep. They contained a collection of images from various countries of High Asia, made of sandal-wood, copper, brass, bell-metal, and clay. There was a collection of fossils, such as of roots and leaves of trees, shells, and small fragments of bones. These are also called *rinpo-che*—i.e., precious curiosities. On my left hand there stood in a line four wooden trunks with painted sides which contained the minister's robes and religious dresses. On the pillars at the entrance were hung a brass mirror, a Tartar buckler, and two satin flags with an iron trident tied to one of them. These are meant to be the martial equipment of the demi-god said to be in charge of the house, to guard the Lama's property. The wall was painted with figures from the Buddhist pantheon, festoons of the fabulous *Thi-shing* or Kalpa-lata (wishing-tree) and various forms of the six-footed dragon. A number of bells, brass oblation vessels, lamp-burners, writing desks, and a few low dining tables completed the furniture of my room. The hearth was richly ornamented with irregular pieces of turquoise and cornelian and drops set on silver rings, all placed at a safe distance from the fire.

When they met the twenty-five-year-old Fifth Panchen Lama, they decided that despite an appearance suggesting high intelligence, he was not as engaging, sympathetic, or dignified as his Chief Minister. Older monks informed Das that the Great Lama was "more feared than liked on account of his cold and independent bearing."

For his part, Das impressed the Panchen Lama, who was pleased to admit him as a pupil of the monastery. He wished the pundit to take the vows of celibacy (Das had a wife in Darjeeling) and to accept the allowance made to the monks. In exchange for this singular honor he wanted to know all about India, the home of the Buddha; moreover he wanted the Bengali to tutor him in Sanskrit.

Soon, however, the Panchen Lama, encouraged by his gossiping servants, began to suspect the pundit was a British spy and engaged his own spies to watch him. When they visited Das, the pundit parried their questions with his own "difficult and abstruse questions on Buddhism." They reported back in favorable terms to their master.

In September, the travelers prepared their return to India. By then, a close friendship had developed between the Chief Minister and the "Babu," and there was an affectionate parting. The lama presented Das with paintings and statues, church utensils and musical instruments, and a Tibetan coin, sufficient to cover their expenses. As a final gift he bestowed the gilt amulet he had received from his own guru. For his part, Das promised to return to Tashilhunpo with the lithographic press, smallpox vaccine, and other items to further instruct the Chief Minister in "the wonders of the west." Das also brought back a yak-load of manuscripts in Sanskrit and Tibetan, some of which he later published. The trip was an intelligence coup, and Major General J. T. Walker, the Surveyor General, commended Das's efforts in his report: "His journey has been fruitful of information; the observations of bearings and distances have been carefully taken and recorded, and are of much value for the requirements of mapping."

THE DELIGHTED SURVEY NOW CONTRACTED A SECOND EXPEDITION although Das was discouraged from geographical surveying that was "likely to create suspicion." Instead he was to cultivate influential persons, keep a diary with regard to place and people, and pursue his investigations into the religion, literature, and history of Tibet. If he should find himself visiting a distant monastery or town, he should "take the observations necessary for a route survey, but he should make no maps of the country." This time a sum of 5,000 rupees *was* advanced to defray expenses.

Das and Ugyen Gyatso set out for their second trip in November 1881. This time it was winter, and the trip from Nepal to Tibet required harrowing ascents through passes barricaded by snow. When they reached Tashilhunpo, their friend the Chief Minister was away at his home monastery at Dongtse, but his servants offered the pair lodging until his return. A few weeks later, the Minister invited the pundits for a visit. At Dongtse, when the Chief Minister inquired about the lithographic press and the smallpox vaccine, he was told they had been dispatched separately in the care of another pundit, the brother-in-law of Ugyen Gyatso who had been detained at the frontier on orders of a Tibetan official. After dinner, the Chief Minister showed Das a book he was writing on history, rhetoric, astrology, and photography.

While they were meeting, the Chief Minister's page reported the arrival of the Tibetan lama's nephew, the Dapon Phala, the general who was governor of Gyantse. The Dapon was greeted by monks in full canonicals and with a musical salute blown from long copper horns. Das was invited to the ceremonial dinner, and no objections were offered to their visiting Gyantse. Ugyen Gyatso returned the Dapon's hospitality by surveying the town and its monastery, pundit style, with prayer beads and invoking the chant "*Om mani padme hum.*" He reported that Gyantse's fortifications consisted of a two-and-a-half-mile stone wall girdling the town. He plied an army officer with *chang* (fermented barley liquor) and questioned him about military arrangements. The officer told him there were ordinarily 500 Tibetan soldiers stationed in Gyantse, plus fifty Chinese soldiers serving under a Chinese officer—information that proved useful in 1904, when a British expeditionary force attacked the fortress.

Meanwhile, the modern-minded Chief Minister asked the pundits to teach him land surveying. Ugyen Gyatso obliged by showing the Tibetan his instruments and explaining their use. Regrettably, according to their host, only five persons in his province took an interest in science. "There are," he added, "many other learned men at Tashilhunpo and in various other monasteries in Tsang, but they only interest themselves in sacred literature; they do not care to know of the science and civilization of other great countries such as that of the *Phyling* (foreigners) and India." The Chief Minister spoke wistfully about obtaining "a sextant, various mathematical instruments, a chest of medicines, and an illustrated work on astronomy." U.G. offered to go to Calcutta to purchase them, but said he could not abandon Das, with his hope of seeing Lhasa unfulfilled. The Chief Minister replied, "That is easily provided for. I will look after the Pundit." He then arranged for Das to accompany the wife of his nephew, the Dapon Phala, who bore the title of Lhacham, to Lhasa. While awaiting their departure, news arrived of a smallpox epidemic in Central Tibet. Not only did Tibetans lack any treatment, Das reported, but "death from small pox is the most dreaded, since the victim is believed to be immediately sent to hell." (Dread of smallpox was one of the reasons the Tibetans refused to trade with India.)

Das at last set out for Lhasa on May 1, 1882. In a parting gesture, the Chief Minister touched the pundit's head with his palms and in solemn tones said: "Sarat Chandra, Lhasa is not a good place. The people there are not like those you meet here. The Lhasa people are suspicious and insincere...Stay not long in the vicinity of the Dabung [Drepung] or Sera monasteries. If you intend to make a long stay at Lhasa, choose your residence in a garden or village in the suburbs. You have chosen a very bad time for your pilgrimage, as small pox is raging all over Central Tibet; but you will return safely, though the journey will be trying and fraught with immense difficulties."

The Lhacham, a woman of about thirty dressed in a Mongol robe, who was to accompany Das, waited in the courtyard with her white pony, caparisoned with embroidered cloth and a Tartar saddle. "With her pearl-studded headdress, her gold and ruby charm-boxes, her necklaces of coral and amber, and her clothes of satin and *kinkob*," Das observed, "she looked like a heroine of romance or a goddess."

When Das grew ill on the way, and contracted a raging fever, the Lhacham, fearing he had smallpox, arranged for him to stay at the Samding monastery, the home of her stepsister, the female incarnation, the Dorje Phagmo or Thunderbolt Sow. When the monastery doctors failed to cure him, the Dorje Phagmo tried magical rites. She even gave the pundit a sacred pill containing a particle of the Kashyapa Buddha's relics, but Das's condition did not improve. In a final act of Buddhist piety, 500 recently caught fish were purchased from fishermen and released into a sacred lake. At last, Das's health improved. Her Holiness, in her last meeting with Das, sprinkled saffron water on the pundit, using the end of a peacock feather, and gave him more sacred pills. Thus blessed, he continued on to Lhasa.

Dressed in his lama robes and wearing a turban—a red pagri—which made him "look like a Ladakhi," Das, dropping with fatigue, arrived in Lhasa on May 30. The Lhacham helped him find lodgings in quarters belonging to the Panchen Lama. After all his efforts, his stay lasted only a fortnight, which he spent visiting its most important temples and shrines. He was granted a ceremonial audience, arranged by the Lhacham, with the six-year-old Thirteenth Dalai Lama. "The Grand Lama is a child of eight [sic] with a bright and fair complexion and rosy cheeks," wrote Das. "His eyes are large and penetrating, the shape of his face remarkably Aryan, though somewhat marred by the obliquity of his eyes. The thinness of his person was probably due to the fatigue of the Court ceremonies and to the religious duties and ascetic observance of his estate."

The rumors about smallpox proved to be true. "In every dwelling in the neighbourhood some one was ill," Das reported, and a caravan from Gyantse brought the distressing news that the Chief Minister had succumbed. The frightened Lhacham urged the pundit to leave Lhasa before he caught the disease—her two sons were stricken—and since the Chief Minister wished to see him again, Das arranged to return to Dongtse. His friend recovered and Das spent several months exploring Central Tibet before returning home to Darjeeling. The details of this trip—aside from brief reports in two journals—were kept confidential until 1890. As a serious student of Buddhism who knew their language, Das had better access to Tibetans and their culture than any predecessors, and his reports remain primary records of a now-vanished world.

After his second foray, Das took part in planning an aborted mission by Colman Macauley to Tibet, even accompanying Macauley, the Finance Secretary of the Bengal Government, to Peking in 1885 to obtain necessary permits from the Chinese. The mission failed when the Tibetans refused it entrée, and Das himself was by now too well known to visit Tibet again. However, in Peking, Das befriended the American Minister to China, William Rockhill, a Tibetan scholar who was eventually chosen by the Royal Geographical Society to edit the "Babu's" reports under the title of *Narrative of a Journey to Lhasa and Central Tibet*.

Inevitably, Das's success provoked malicious rumors among British India's senior officials. Some claimed he was a Russian double-agent, and others said he was a fraud. His chief ill-wisher was Lieutenant-Colonel L. Austine Waddell of the Indian Medical Service, who deemed himself the leading British authority on Tibet. In 1892, Waddell brashly sought to sneak into Lhasa by posing as a Buddhist pilgrim, and was easily detected at the frontier. In 1902, Das confided to Rockhill that Waddell "has done all in his power to insinuate that I had written the narratives of my journeys as books of fiction" and was thus "an arch impostor." It would appear that these charges resulted in Das's being assigned by the Government of Bengal to a remote outpost "to serve as a subordinate inspecting officer of schools under an officer who was junior to me in every respect."

Nevertheless, despite Waddell, the "Babu" was created a Companion of the Order of the Indian Empire and awarded the title Rai Bahadur for his services to the Government. The RGS awarded him a medal, and in 1905, the Imperial Archaeological Society of St. Petersburg elected him a corresponding member. He spent his final years at home in "Lhasa Villa" compiling a Tibetan-English dictionary. The "Babu" died in Japan on a visit to his pupil, Ekai Kawaguchi, in 1917.

THE ERA OF PUNDITRY ENDED IN 1893, WHEN THE LAST KNOWN pundits, Hari Ram and his son, were dispatched to Nepal and Tibet. For thirty years (1863–93), the apogee of the Great Game, the pundits explored a million square miles of unmapped territory, determined the source of India's Brahmaputra River, linking it with the Tsangpo in Tibet, and traced the course of the upper Oxus River, which was to form the boundary between Russia and Afghanistan. Although never attaining the top positions in the Empire's mapping hierarchy, a privilege reserved for the British officers who supervised the GTS, the pundits were employed in an independent field capacity and thus gained a degree of public recognition.

Were the pundits, then, a secret spy system? In the Government of India files, they were described as clandestine agents, but since Montgomerie published the pundits' reports, complete with maps and their methods of operation, on a regular basis in the *Journal* of the Royal Geographical Society, they were hardly secret. Indeed they were read with enthusiasm in London, Paris, Berlin, and St. Petersburg. (Das's report, published in the *Journal* in 1902, appeared in a Russian translation two years later.) In the pages of the *Journal,* code names are employed, but these are simply initials or numbers—for example, Nain Singh was known as "the Chief Pundit" or "No. 1," Mani Singh as "the Patwar" or "GM," Kalian Singh was the "Third Pundit" or "GK," and Kishen Singh became "Krishna" or "AK." (Kipling borrowed the idea of code-names—C25, R17, E23—from the *Journal* accounts.) Most of the information obtained for the Survey of India was topographical, but the reports were well seasoned with political observations, and in later years, government officials suppressed the intelligence portions of the pundits' reports. Readers of the *Journal* would not know "the Mirza" reported that the Mir of Badakhshan had "small eyes and a scanty beard" and was "given to drinking," allowing "his petty officials to do very much as they like: he is consequently unpopular."

Because the pundits entered Tibet disguised as pilgrims and gathered information secretly, in Tibetan eyes they were certainly viewed as spies—with cruel penalties for those who helped them. Sir Charles Bell was to write some years later, "The persistence of foreigners in exploring their country, so long excluded, had made [Tibetans] suspicious. In particular, the secret explorations of the Bengali, Sarat Chandra Das, carried out under the auspices of the Indian Government, filled them with distrust of the power that ruled India. In a conversation which took place in 1910, the late Prime Minister of Tibet informed me that Sarat's clandestine entry and his surreptitious inquiries constituted—together with the expedition to Sikkim in 1888—the chief causes which led Tibetans to suspect British intentions with regard to their country."

When rumors reached Lhasa that Das was a British agent, the Tibetans dispatched their own spies to Darjeeling and determined that this was so. Those officials who had failed to bar Das's entry into Tibet were severely punished and their property was confiscated. On a rainy June day in 1887, a visitor to Lhasa would have witnessed a horrifying sight. The Sengchen Lama of Shigatse, the Chief Minister who had helped and befriended the pundit and arranged for his illicit trip to Lhasa, was denounced as a traitor, stripped of his property, and flogged in the marketplace. As he prepared to die, he gave his executioners this order: "When, in a little while, I have finished reading the holy Text, I will shake this my finger three times thus, and that will be the signal for you to sink me in the river." But when he had shaken his finger the third time, "the lamentation became loud and universal," and no executioner dared come forward—"they were in tears themselves." The Chief Minister said: "My time is come: what are ye doing? Speed me under the water." He was then sewn alive into a yak-hide sack, and lowered into the Tsangpo. Adding to the shame, when the lama's reputed reincarnation appeared in the guise of a small boy, the Dalai Lama ordered the child abandoned. The Chief Minister's unfortunate nephew, the Governor of Gyantse province, the Phala Dapon and his wife the Lhacham, who had been Das's patrons in Lhasa, were thrown into prison, where they died. However, their servants were punished most severely for consorting with foreigners: their hands and feet were cut off, their eyes gouged out, and, thus mutilated, they were left to die in agony. As Ekai Kawaguchi, wrote, "The story of the Tibetans who smuggled a foreigner into Tibet and were killed, and those who concealed the fact from the Government and forfeited their property, are tales that Tibetan parents everywhere tell to their children."

CHAPTER NINE

"A Carbine in One Hand, a Whip in the Other"

No HEROES STOOD TALLER IN THE VICTORIAN PANTHEON than explorers. They were the astronauts, the film stars of the imperial era. Tinting unknown lands on a nation's map—red for Great Britain, orange for Russia, green for France—became the embodiment of cultural virility. Plants, animals, falls, rivers, even entire mountain ranges were named for these peerless travelers. Museums and galleries vied to display their collections. At the Victoria Gallery on London's Regent Street, a "Stanley and Africa Exhibition" featured "a native hut, an African primeval forest and village scene," and two slave boys. Visitors were invited to stroll through the main hall into "the heart of savage Africa." The talk of Moscow in 1867 was Russia's first Ethnographic Exhibition. Displays included 300 life-size models of the peoples of Central Asia, the Caucasus, and Siberia, 600 photographs, and an equal number of human skulls.

The growth of the penny press, illustrated weeklies, and cheaply produced books made the apotheosis of the explorer possible. No denouement of a serialized Dickens or Trollope novel held the public as spellbound as the real-life race to find the source of the Nile or

Stanley's search for Dr. Livingstone. The readers never seemed to have enough as books, often filling two volumes, followed newspaper accounts. The 1860's began with Richard Burton's *Lake Regions of Central Africa,* followed three years later by his rival John Hemming Speke's *Journal of the Discovery of the Source of the Nile.* A Prime Minister, Lord Palmerston, suggested the title for James Grant's *A Walk Across Africa* (1864)—"You have had a long walk, Captain Grant." Yet without fanfare, the most popular work in the genre was Dr. Livingstone's "simple account of a mission," *A Narrative of an Expedition to the Zambesi* (1866), a staple in every middle-class bookshelf. By the end of the century, not only fame but fortune crowned the exploits of the era's gallant adventurers as lucrative lecture fees, newspaper exclusives, and best-sellers followed the hailstorm of gold medals.

NO ONE FOLLOWED THE ACCOUNTS OF AFRICAN EXPLORATION more eagerly than a twenty-one-year-old subaltern at the prestigious General Staff Academy in St. Petersburg, Nikolai Mikhailovich Przhevalsky. He was once a hero to every Russian schoolchild, though he is forgotten or unknown outside of Russia. Backstage, Przhevalsky was a formidable influence on Russia's Asian strategy, as confirmed by the archival research contained in *Ex Oriente Lux* (1997), a revealing Yale doctoral dissertation by the Canadian scholar David Schimmelpenninck van der Oye.

While Przhevalsky was alive, his exploits filled the popular press just beginning to flourish in Moscow and St. Petersburg. Soon after his death in 1888, the Imperial Russian Geographical Society sought contributions for what was supposed to be a life-size bust near its headquarters. Rubles arrived from every corner of Russia in an outpouring matched only by the subscription for the Pushkin memorial ten years before. The modest bust sprouted into a mammoth sculpted monument, fifteen feet high, in Alexandrovsky garden, where it joined statues of Gogol, Lermontov, and Glinka. In an adulatory obituary, Chekhov declared that Russia needed the explorer "as it needs the sun," and claimed that "one Przhevalsky or one Stanley is worth ten institutes or a hundred good books." In his novel *The Gift (Dar)*, Vladimir Nabokov modeled the father of the hero on Przhevalsky. Yet, despite the plethora of books about him in Russian, and one by Donald Rayfield in English (1976), Przhevalsky remains something of an enigma.

He was, in Rayfield's words, "a man of ruthless determination and of shy tenderness, an apostle of European superiority who loathed European society, an explorer of China who despised the Chinese, a big-game hunter on an epic scale who mourned the death of his dogs, a major-general who disliked the army, a materialist and a Byronic romantic." He was probably homosexual and, more improbably, so it was later alleged, based on his facial resemblance and his proximity at the right time, the biological father of Joseph Stalin. Still, these are familiar inconsistencies in the history of hero-worship. The very qualities of self-punishing ruthlessness and Odyssean cunning found in the explorer are not the qualities one prizes in a friend. Most giants of discovery drew strength from interior wounds and were likable only at a distance. The greatest of African explorers, Henry Morton Stanley, the bastard son of a village drunk, was a dissembler who fought on both sides of the American Civil War, a hired gun who founded the cruelest of European colonies, the Belgian Congo. Not for nothing was Stanley known as Bula Mutari, the Smasher of Rocks.

Przhevalsky was Russia's Smasher of Rocks. No Asian explorer traversed more territory than he did on four major expeditions. He led the way and set the standard for other travelers—British, French, German, Swedish, Japanese, and American—in the race to Lhasa. Like his great rivals, Sven Hedin and Sir Aurel Stein, he readily exchanged the comforts of European society for the torments of mountain and desert. All three were outsiders with flexible loyalties—Przhevalsky was a Russophile Pole; Hedin was a Swede who initially courted the English and the Russians, then befriended Hitler; and Stein was a Hungarian Jew who died a knighted Anglican. All were lifelong bachelors with an aversion to marriage.

Yet Przhevalsky stood apart in his contempt for Asian peoples. When Chekhov wrote his effusive obituary (as Rayfield notes), he had not read Przhevalsky's last book, in which he proposed starting a war with China, exterminating the inhabitants of Tibet and Mongolia, and replacing them with Cossacks.

PRZHEVALSKY CLAIMED DESCENT FROM A ZAPOROZHYE COSSACK who served the King of Poland and whose heirs married into Polish nobility. When Russia conquered the province of Smolensk, where he was born in 1839, the family name changed from Przewalski to the Russianized Przhevalsky. The oldest son of a retired army officer and an ambitious strong-willed mother, young Nikolai grew up in a petty noble's estate that was modest by Russian standards: 3,000 acres with 160 male serfs. He shone at the local gymnasium. Aided by a photographic memory, he finished at the top of his class. Yet he longed to escape Smolensk, and during the Crimean War, having turned sixteen, he enlisted to join in the defense of Sevastopol. But when the eager recruit reached the front, the war was all but over, as a Russian Army, riddled by nepotism and incompetence, was bested by British, French, and Turkish besiegers. He was further disheartened by the mediocrity of his fellow trainee-officers, complaining to his mother, "There are about sixty of us, but most of them are good-for-nothings, drunks, gamblers. When I see myself with such comrades, I can't help remembering the words 'I'll be a diamond but in a pile of dung.'" He sought solace in hunting, which soon became his passion, inspiring his first published article, "Memoirs of a Sportsman."

Przhevalsky, by now a lance corporal, managed to escape regimental tedium in 1860 by passing the entrance examination for the General Staff Academy in St. Petersburg. There he devoured textbooks on geography and zoology, dreamed of exploring Africa, and wrote a dissertation proposing a survey of the vast Amur region that had been wrested by force majeure in the 1850's from China. His paper impressed his instructors, eager to improve Russia's military intelligence after the Crimean debacle. It likewise impressed the officers of the Imperial Geographical Society, especially its vice-president, Petr Semenov (1827–94), also the son of a retired officer from a remote backwater. Semenov was soon to be ennobled as Tian-Shansky in recognition for his pioneering and hazardous survey of the Tian Shan Mountains, the massive chain extending from Siberia to Chinese Turkestan.

The Society was itself a mirror of the age. Founded in 1845 in the reign of Nicholas I, it put a young science at the service of empire. It funded expeditions, published maps, collected statistics. Among its fellows were military geographers whose chief mission was mapping the Asian hinterlands, dueling with their British counterparts in a tournament traversing thousands of miles. All European geographical societies accepted as a given their role as servants of expansion. In the words of the president of France's Société de Géographie in 1877: "A country has no lasting value except by its force of expansion and… the study of the geographical sciences is one of the most active elements of this expansion." With the influential encouragement of the Geographical Society, Przhevalsky was plucked from the ranks and given the task of surveying the vast Amur River valley. It was a choice assignment.

The Amur was then called "the Mississippi of the East," in the hope that it would be an open highway to the untapped riches of Siberia. About 300 miles south of its mouth, the Russians founded Vladivostok ("Ruler of the East"), a naval port, assuring Russian status as a Great Power in the Northern Pacific. Acquiring the Amur was the "forward school" project of General Nikolai Muraviev, Governor-General of Eastern Siberia. He planned a chain of self-supporting settlements on the banks of the Amur and its scarcely less impressive 2,500-mile southern tributary, the Ussuri—a plan resisted as fantasy by the less Asia-minded Foreign Minister, Count Nesselrode. The arguments only added to the excitement about the still-unmapped Amur, so much so that a young Prince Peter Kropotkin, fresh from the Corps of Pages at the Tsar's court, grabbed at the chance of exploring the Amur as an aide to Muraviev. ("Are you not afraid to go so far?" Alexander II asked him. "No, I want to work. There must be so much to do in Siberia to apply the great reforms that are to be made." With a pensive sigh, the Emperor replied, "Well, go; one can be useful everywhere.")

Everything about the Amur valley intrigued the future revolutionary—its semi-tropical flora and fauna, its seasonal typhoons, its Cossack settlements—but Przhevalsky's interest had a more precise focus. With two assistants, one being the first of his youthful protégés, Nikolai Yagunov, Przhevalsky expeditiously mapped an area larger than Great Britain, providing the General Staff with its first hard data about Russia's new frontier with China. For this he was promoted to captain, a reward approved by the Minister of War, Dmitrii Miliutin, the ablest of the Tsar's ministers and a military reformer who was to become Przhevalsky's foremost champion.

Working closely with the Imperial Geographical Society, Miliutin secured the rubles for the military's intelligence-gathering expeditions. Przhevalsky profited from this synergy: although he was a serving officer attached to military intelligence, the Imperial Geographical Society readily sponsored his expeditions after he had been awarded its Silver Medal for the Amur mission. The explorer's travel accounts presented as contributions to geography also served (in the words of Schimmelpenninck) "as reconnaissance reports for a possible campaign into China's borderlands." Or in the explorer's own typically candid assurance to his superiors, "[My] scientific research will camouflage the political goals of the expedition and should discourage any interference by our adversaries."

PRZHEVALSKY'S FIRST EXPEDITION (1870–73), TO MAP THE ORDOS plateau and explore Southern Mongolia, was funded by the War Department, the Geographical Society, and the Botanical Gardens, with an extra thousand rubles derived from the explorer's skills at the card table. Inspired perhaps by press excitement over the "search for the Nile," he also hoped to locate the source of the Yellow River and even reach Lhasa.

Starting from Kiakhta, a Siberian outpost, the party passed through Mongolia and on to Peking in order to obtain Chinese passports for "the remoter regions of the Chinese Empire." They returned westward to Koko Nor, the "Blue Lake," the wild frontier where China, Mongolia, and Tibet converge, but when they reached the headwaters of the Yangtze, their tottering animals—they had lost fifty-five camels and twenty-four horses—and their depleted stores and funds forced them to turn back before reaching Lhasa. "We have absolutely no supplies left," Przhevalsky wrote in his diary, "the privation is terrible."

Nonetheless, on a trip that lasted nearly three years, the party of four—which included two Cossacks and the second of Przhevalsky's favorites, Mikhail Pyltsov, as well as the leader's setter, Faust—managed to travel 7,000 miles, survey 7,000 miles of routes, and collect 5,000 plant specimens, 1,000 birds, 130 skins of large and small mammals, 70 specimens of reptiles, and in excess of 3,000 insects, including new species. All were deposited, following Przhevalsky's triumphant return, with the Academy of Sciences at St. Petersburg.

Golos, the liberal newspaper, greeted the hero with a four-column panegyric calling his journey "one of the most daring of our time." His lecture before the Geographical Society evoked "thunderous applause" from an overflow audience, according to a press report that stressed his courage in contending with hostile natives and a threatening environment. Awarded the Society's Constantine Medal and newly promoted to lieutenant colonel, Przhevalsky was now appointed to the General Staff and received the Order of St. Vladimir, Fourth Class.

From the army's perspective, the trip was a success. It provided the General Staff with important information on a Muslim uprising under Yakub Beg in western China. From the standpoint of Przhevalsky's personal goals, it was also a success since at Koko Nor he met Tibet's representative to Peking, who invited him to Lhasa. As the explorer reported in his promptly published account, *Mongolia, the Tangut Country and the Solitudes of Northern Tibet,* using language calculated to provoke a *frisson* in London and Calcutta, the Dalai Lama "would be very glad to receive Russians."

In his preface, addressing a wider Western audience, Przhevalsky correctly called Inner Asia's central plateau "*terra incognita:* of its geology, climate, flora and fauna, we are almost totally ignorant." Yet as his critics would complain, for all his prodigies as a collector, his expeditions were too vast to be systematic and yielded little in the way of ethnological or historical information. Przhevalsky's weakness, which he never overcame, was his ignorance of local languages, which impelled him to rely on incompetent or indifferent interpreters, thereby compounding his condescension.

He especially despised the Chinese. "Unimaginable filth, people squatting and relieving themselves right and left in the street," he spewed forth in a letter from Peking to his mother. "The Chinaman here is a Jew plus a Muscovite pickpocket, both squared. But the lamentable thing is to see Europeans being polite to this rabble." Relying on a Russian Buriat interpreter who had trouble understanding local Mongolian dialects, and lacking any knowledge of Buddhism himself, Przhevalsky initially judged the Mongolians unclean, gluttonous, slothful, cowardly, passive, obtuse, excessively curious, apathetic, and lifeless—surely a racist caricature of a people who for centuries ruled and terrorized Muscovy. Buddhism, the explorer felt, was a pretext for "idleness, a religion that sapped vitality and hindered progress"—an imperial sentiment that prefigures Mao Zedong's informing the Fourteenth Dalai Lama that religion was "poison."

Mongolia's inhabitants repaid Przhevalsky's scorn with interest. His party was frequently attacked, and the sight of him eating a wild duck caused one of his local guides to run off and vomit. Yet it didn't matter that much, he reported to St. Petersburg, "we are all very well armed, and [rifle] fire . . . has a spellbinding effect on the half-savage natives." Przhevalsky disdained disguises, but so hostile and suspicious were the peoples he encountered that he felt it prudent to take his bearings at night—as unobtrusively as possible.

His first expedition convinced Przhevalsky that Asians were ripe for forcible absorption, at little risk or cost. Thus he became an energetic advocate of what Schimmelpenninck terms "conquistador imperialism." Displaying a mingling of fascination and condescension, an ambivalence about the Far East summarized in the Russian word *Aziatchina,* he believed Russia's future lay in Asia. His toughness was not uniquely Russian, as many of his contemporaries, when confronting "savages," believed in the European or American *mission civilisatrice.* Typically, Przhevalsky stated in an 1877 report, "Our military conquests in Asia bring glory not only to Russia; they are also victories for the good of mankind. Carbine bullets and rifled cannon bear those elements of civilization which would otherwise be very long in coming to the petrified realms of the Inner Asian khans." As for the British, he warned that if given a chance, they "will destroy our influence in all lands and countries inhabited by the Chinese and the Mongols."

THE WAR MINISTRY, EVER ATTENTIVE TO THE WEAKENING CHINESE grip on the Celestial Empire's western provinces, assigned Przhevalsky (now a lieutenant colonel) a delicate political mission on his second expedition (1876–78). He was to meet, befriend, and parley with Yakub Beg, the Emir of Kashgaria and leader of a Muslim rebellion in Chinese Turkestan. To this was added another task. As the Geographical Society explained, Przhevalsky was "to teach the Chinese authorities and population to have relations with foreigners and thus open up the path for trade and industrial venture."

The erosion of Manchu dominion in Chinese Turkestan was confirmed in the 1860's when Chinese-speaking Muslims in the neighboring province of Kansu rebelled, thereby severing connections between Peking and Urumchi, the provincial capital, and Kashgar, the westernmost of Chinese-ruled cities. In 1865, a Tajik military adventurer and erstwhile dancing-boy, Yakub Beg, led a small force over the Pamirs from his native Khokand and enthroned himself in Kashgar. He then extended his rule southward to Yarkand and Khotan and northward to Aksu and Kucha. By 1872, he had seized Urumchi, a thousand miles to the east. Both the Russians and British were alarmed, and the Beg, a wily brigand, sensing bargaining leverage, dispatched his nephew as an emissary to St. Petersburg, Constantinople, Calcutta, and London. A succession of British and Russian missions explored possible links with the adventurer, without much success. One contemporary traveler, the Hungarian Arminius Vámbéry, characterized the Beg's strategy, writing: "All that the Sovereign of the Six Cities understood by diplomatic relations with England was, in the first place, money and arms; in the second place, money and arms; and in the third place, money and arms. Beyond these his mind never reached." Still, the British were not too proud to stoop. In 1874, in return for arms and recognition as lawful Emir, a title bestowed by the Turkish Sultan, Yakub Beg granted Britain trade rights and permitted a diplomatic mission in Urumchi.

The Russians were more cautious. Prince Gorchakov, the Foreign Minister, remarked in private that he considered the area controlled by Yakub Beg "to belong to China and could only be dealt with by Russia through the Chinese." In 1874, the Beg retaliated. When Russia sent a trade mission to Kashgar, it was denied equal status with the British. Twenty thousand soldiers were dispatched to change Yakub Beg's mind, but they were diverted by a rebellion in Khokand, thus voiding the operation. Two years later, Colonel Aleksei Kuropotkin was detailed to negotiate with the Emir.

With the strong support of Dmitrii Miliutin and the geographer Semenov, Przhevalsky commanded in 1876 a much grander expedition than its predecessor. He set out over the Tian Shan range with ten men, twenty-four camels, four horses, three tons of baggage, two dogs, and a budget of 25,000 rubles provided by the War Ministry. Pyltsov, the explorer's earlier favorite, had settled down to married life as Przhevalsky's brother-in-law at the family's Smolensk estate. When his successor, Yagunov, drowned, he was replaced in the explorer's entourage by the eighteen-year-old Fyodor Eklon. Przhevalsky had already taken him to the family seat, Otradnoye, to teach him how to shoot, ride, and skin specimens, before sending him off with a rifle, new suit, traveling rug, and a twenty-ruble monthly allowance for military training at Brest. Another clean-limbed cadet, Yevgraf Povalo-Shyykovsky, was chosen as second assistant and sent off to learn photography in St. Petersburg. "I know you'll be great friends, *but then you will be thrashed together,*" he wrote Eklon. "Of course that won't happen often, but all the same it will occur—nobody's perfect."

Przhevalsky re-entered Asia with "a carbine in one hand and a whip in the other." His guns—frequently demonstrated—were accurate; he practiced herbal medicine; his aneroid barometer allowed him to predict rain; and some believed he could summon up a hundred warriors at will—all of which gave rise to the belief among the

locals that he was a saint. Although he located the "Wandering Lake,"
Lop Nor, which was to figure prominently in the adventures of Sven
Hedin and Sir Aurel Stein, a more miserable trip can hardly be imagined. Bedeviled by bad luck—an unseasonably hot spring, incompetent servants who had to be dismissed, Kirghiz camels that proved
less hardy than the Khalka camels on the first expedition—the party
endured diarrhea, headaches, fever, and a skin disease of the steppe
which caused persistent itching of the testicles. Even the dogs, Bai
and Oscar, proved unworthy, and were given away.

Above all, his encounter with Yakub Beg left the lieutenant
colonel unimpressed. "Nothing more than a political impostor," he
said of the Emir in a scathing report. As for his subjects, they "constantly cursed their government and expressed the desire to become
Russian subjects…The savage Asiatic clearly understands Russian
power is the guarantee for prosperity." A letter to his brother was
earthily derisive: "Yakub Beg is the same shit as all feckless Asiatics.
The Kashgarian Empire isn't worth a kopek." Yet even as Przhevalsky predicted the Emir's imminent downfall and urged the army to
seize more territory, the Russians held back. However, this time the
explorer proved clairvoyant. Renowned for his tantrums, Yakub Beg
died in 1877—from apoplexy, poison, or perhaps as a suicide—after
beating his secretary to death and thrashing his treasurer. After a
chaotic succession struggle, his kingdom was retaken by China. To
forestall a Russian advance, the Celestial Empire incorporated it into
a new province called Sinkiang, or New Dominion, with its seat in
Urumchi.

In September 1877, Przhevalsky's caravan set off for Lhasa, refur-
bished with more efficient servants, better horses and camels,
firearms, 7,200 rounds of ammunition, twenty-five bottles of brandy,
a hundredweight of tea, and (for the commander's insatiable sweet
tooth) seventy pounds of Turkish Delight, monpansier, and mar-
malade. Yet again, after a time, his supplies were exhausted, the leader
himself fell sick, and the caravan had to turn back before reaching its
goal.

Przhevalsky had another cause for disappointment. On his first expedition a Mongolian lama had told him about Shambhala (Przhevalsky calls it Shambaling), the proverbial Asian paradise, the place

where "at some future time the followers of this religion will migrate." Shambhala, the lama went on, "is an island lying far away in the northern sea. Gold abounds in it and corn grows to an enormous height. Poverty is unknown...." The lama wondered if Przhevalsky knew where that island might be. The Russian jokingly suggested England. "Well, that must be Shambaling!" exclaimed the lama, who begged to be shown the country on a map.

In Sanskrit, Shambhala means "the place of peace, of tranquillity." Hindus knew it as Aryavarsha, the land from which the Vedas came; to the Chinese it was the Western Paradise, to Russian Old Believers it was Belovodye, and to the Kirghiz it was Janaidar—attesting to a widespread yearning for a city sublime. According to the Tibetans, Shambhala was the source of the mystical system of the Kalachakra, the texts that were taught to the King of Shambhala by the Buddha. Catholic missionaries had returned with accounts of Shambhala in the seventeenth century. Alexander Csoma de Körös, the Hungarian traveler writing in the first half of the nineteenth century, gave Shambhala's bearings as "forty-five to fifty degrees north latitude, beyond the river Syr Darya." Przhevalsky could have read about Shambhala in the recently published (1876) journal kept a century before by the Scot George Bogle, when he visited Tibet. At Tashilhunpo, seat of the Tashi or Panchen Lama, Bogle heard about "Shambul." Madame Blavatsky, founder of Theosophy, kept the legend alive, offering a geographic variation in *The Secret Doctrine* (1888), writing that "fabled Shambhallah, the headquarters of the Mahatmas, the sacred brotherhood" was located "somewhere in the Gobi."

His curiosity spurred by the lama's prophecies, Przhevalsky set out for Lhasa again in 1879. In his mission proposal to Colonel Kuropatkin, the War Ministry's Asia specialist, he did not dwell on Shambhala, but instead proposed to gather "inasmuch as may be possible, intelligence concerning the political structure of Tibet, its relations with its neighbors, and finally, the possibility of establishing relations with the Dalai Lama." From the publications of their sister organization, the Royal Geographical Society, the Russians knew that their rivals had succeeded in sending their pundits to Lhasa, and as early as 1869, the Ministry of War proposed to attach its own agent to a Mongolian delegation heading for Tibet to search for a new incarnation of Jebdzun Damba Khutuktu, the head of the Mongolian Church, in order to gather "information about Tibet." In an 1878 report, Przhevalsky himself recommended the use of Russian pundits—two lamas were to be dispatched to Lhasa by the Russian consul in Urga, Mongolia, prior to his own visit. According to the Russian scholar Alexandre Andreyev, one lama, possibly Dorzhiev (see Chapter 11), was recruited as Przhevalsky himself advanced on Lhasa.

At forty, he was famous at home and abroad, and acclaimed as the greatest European explorer of Central Asia since Marco Polo. He was accompanied by Eklon and a new favorite, Vsevolod Roborovski, a lance corporal with a talent for drawing; an interpreter; and eight Cossacks armed with the usual arsenal of carbines, revolvers, 9,000 pounds of ammunition, and a hundredweight of lead shot. Twenty-three groaning camels carried sugar, dried fruit, crates of brandy and sherry, brick tea, tsamba (roasted barley), and 1,500 sheets of blotting paper for drying specimens. For good measure, a flock of sheep trailed behind, to be consumed en route. Great care was taken in choosing presents to impress the Tibetans, among them tinted photographs of St. Petersburg's leading actresses, which proved to be unexpectedly popular, and wild strawberry jam prepared by Przhevalsky himself for the Dalai Lama. If necessary, so the explorer assured his companions, he would bribe or shoot his way to Lhasa. As the party's rapid-fire demonstrations never failed to impress their hosts, three weeks at firearms drill, according to Przhevalsky, was their "guarantee of safety in the depths of the Asian deserts, the best of all Chinese passports."

Passing through the Chinese-controlled oasis of Hami in the Gobi, Przhevalsky noted its strategic position: "Once this point is occupied by an enemy, the whole Chinese army to the west will be cut off from its sources of supply, i.e. from China proper." He noted as well that the Chinese infantrymen rode lazily on horses, their guns were dirty and rusty, and many smoked opium that their officers sold them. His report encouraged Minister Miliutin to keep pressing China for rights to the Ili Valley after the collapse of Yakub Beg's kingdom.

Traveling southeast to Dunhuang, Przhevalsky was among the first Europeans to inspect "the Caves of a Thousand Buddhas," the great honeycombed art gallery in the cliffs that later visitors, notably Sir Aurel Stein, would explore. As he proceeded through the Nan Shan range, the Russian indulged the imperial explorer's prerogative, conferring European names—Marco Polo, Ritter, and Humboldt—on mountain ranges. It was during this, his greatest expedition (1879–80), that Przhevalsky came upon a wild horse in Dzungaria, the Mongolian *takhi*, subsequently known to the world, in honor of its European discoverer, as *Equus przewalskii*. Found only in the borderlands of Mongolia and the Dzungar steppe, Przhevalsky's Horse was a living link to its ancient ancestors depicted in cave paintings, and closely related to Genghis Khan's celebrated tireless mounts. Przhevalsky's Horse was but one discovery; a multitude of new and rare fauna and flora also returned skinned and dried in the Russian's saddlebags.

After the long journey to the northern borders of Tibet, a Tibetan militia at Nagchu turned the party back about 145 miles from Lhasa. A disheartened Przhevalsky nevertheless managed to engage in some mischievous Great Gamesmanship. In his unpublished travel diary, discovered by Andreyev, there is an entry for December 3, 1879, in which he confesses he "took out the maps of Tibet and the surveys" made by the pundits—and published by the RGS—so as "to incite the Tibetans a bit more against the English." Intoning the names, places, and distances between their towns in order to impress the Tibetans with the breach of their security, he declared: "Here are the maps of your country, drawn by the English spies, whereas you believe your country is unknown." Przhevalsky noted that their faces registered surprise and horror. They demanded to know when the surveys were made. "Not more than four or five years ago," he retorted.

The order to expel Przhevalsky's party came from Lhasa, where it was feared that the Russians were proselytizing missionaries. Some even suspected a plan to kidnap the Dalai Lama. The Chinese passport granted by Peking on which Przhevalsky had counted backfired. Now his party could no longer obtain supplies from a terrified populace. Threatening to tell the world of Tibetan inhospitality to foreigners, the Russian demanded to see the written order. The Tibetans eventually produced a document signed by eleven leading men of Nagchu. It is a poignant document, in light of Tibet's fate:

Tibet is a country of religion, and certain people have come here from countries outside at various times. But those who do not have an established right to come, by the unanimous decision of princes, lords and people, are refused entry and, on the pain of death, are ordered to keep out…Now at Pong Bung Chung…in the Nagchu District on the 13th of the 10th moon, intending to come to Tibet, have appeared Nikolai Przhevalsky…we have carefully explained the above circumstances and they have said that if we give them a written certificate that they may not enter they will go away; otherwise they will set off tomorrow for Lhasa. Whereupon we have asked them to go away, like anyone who does not hold an established right.

Despite failing to reach its ultimate goal, the third expedition yielded, besides the famous horse, a rich botanical harvest: the red *Rosa przewalskii,* four new rhododendrons, including the aromatic, white-flowered *Rhododendron przewalskii,* three new species of honeysuckle—*Lonicera nervosa, syringantha,* and *tangutica,* delphiniums, gentians, *Daphne tangutica, Euonymus przewalskii, Caryopteris tangutica,* a new maidenhair fern, *Adiantum roborowskii,* and a new poppy, *Meconopsis quintuplinervia.*

A disappointed Przhevalsky returned to Russia amidst universal relief. Rumors in the Western press had reached Peking and Petersburg that he had been taken captive by the Chinese or killed by bandits. A Hungarian explorer, Count Széchenyi, complained in a Russian gazette, "Search parties were sent for Livingstone, Payer, Nordenscheldt; but no one is even thinking of looking for Przhevalsky." At home in Russia, he was restless despite the outpouring of honors, speeches, and banquets. In his account of his third expedition, *Iz Zaisana cherez Khami v Tibet,* Przhevalsky summed up the appeal of Central Asian travel and described the *Sehnsucht,* the overwhelming longing that affected so many of the explorers when they returned: "A sad, yearning feeling always comes over me as soon as the first bursts of joy on returning home have passed. The further time flies amid ordinary life, the more this yearning grows, as if something unforgettable, precious had been abandoned in the wilderness of Asia which could not be found in Europe…an exceptional bliss—freedom—which may be savage but is infringed by nothing, almost absolute."

WHEN PRZHEVALSKY RETURNED IN 1881, THE TALK OF PETERSburg was of General Skobelev's storming of the Turkmen stronghold of Geok-Tepe, which completed the Russian conquest of Central Asia north of the Oxus, and of the British Major Cavagnari, whose murder had sparked the Second Afghan War. But Russian euphoria at Britain's humiliation was short-lived when Miliutin had to concede all but the west of the Ili Valley to China. Alexander II, who had liberated the serfs and was about to announce constitutional reforms, was assassinated by an anarchist bomb. Miliutin, the scourge of incompetence and apostle of expansion, was replaced by Adjutant-General Vannovsky, who had less acquisitive views. With Russia mired in a severe recession, with famine raging and a profoundly conservative new Tsar, Alexander III, as ruler, the Government was not in a forward mood. However, when the Tsarina, Maria Feodorovna, invited Przhevalsky to Gatchina to meet the thirteen-year-old heir to the throne, the future Nicholas II was much taken with the explorer. Their conversations were to sow the seed of the future Tsar's passionate and fateful interest in Central Asia. The Tsarevich presented the explorer with a lightweight aluminum telescope, and Przhevalsky would provide Nicholas with reports of his exploits in letters dispatched from his fourth and final expedition.

Preparing this expedition (1883–85), Przhevalsky recruited his ablest favorite, Pyotr Kozlov, who was to become Russia's next great Central Asian explorer. The two had met when Przhevalsky was in Smolensk inspecting an estate that he was in process of acquiring. The older man noticed a day-dreaming nineteen-year-old clerk at a nearby distillery. In a might-be-true anecdote, the older man asked the youth what he was thinking. Kozlov replied, "I was thinking how much brighter those stars must shine in Tibet."

Kozlov had the dashing good looks that Anna Karenina found in her Vronsky (also a frontier officer in the Tsar's army), and Przhevalsky all but adopted him. For his part, Kozlov was equally smitten. "When I first set eyes on Przhevalsky," he later recalled, "I recognized the powerful figure, his imperious, noble and handsome face. This dedicated explorer, this sensitive connoisseur of the world of nature, the peerless Przhevalsky, aroused in me a burning passion for the Asian world. I fell ineluctably under the spell of this pure and unaffected man." Until his mentor's death, "Kizosha" would share "Psheva's" life, and his obsession with Tibet.

On his final expedition. Przhevalsky explored the mountainous borderland between Mongolia and Tibet, identified the springs that feed the great lakes that are the source of the Yellow River, found a rare hedge sparrow, *Prunella koslowi*, which he named for his new favorite—but yet again failed to reach Lhasa. On the way home, he crossed the deadly Taklamakan Desert on a meridianal course, beginning at Khotan and moving along its westernmost edge to Aksu. (Ten years later Sven Hedin would traverse its length.) Back in St. Petersburg as adviser to the War Ministry with the rank of major general, he prepared a secret memorandum, "New Thoughts About War with China," which he later adapted as the last chapter of his final book. In it Przhevalsky urged the forcible annexation of western China, Mongolia, and Tibet, and their colonization by Cossacks. He claimed that the nomadic Asians "all yearn to become subjects of the White Tsar,* whose name, like that of the Dalai Lama, appears in the eyes of the Asiatic masses in a halo of mystic light." These masses would benefit from Russian rule and, as to legality, "international law does not apply to savages." Prudently, Alexander III and his ministers rejected the forcible annexation of western China but did not reject using other means of bringing Asian masses closer to the White Tsar.

---

*Some Lamaists believed the Russian Tsar was the reincarnation of the fourteenth-century Tibetan monk, Tsong-ka-pa, while the goddess Palden-Llamo returned as Queen Victoria, beliefs the respective empires did not discourage.

In 1888, Przhevalsky was preparing his fifth expedition. Tibet was its focus, and the War Ministry showed keener interest, since the British, having absorbed Sikkim, were making overtures to Lhasa. As the explorer promised the War Minister, "Aside from the scientific results, the trip will present a good opportunity to gather details about the activities of the English in Sikkim regarding Tibet." To friends, he complained of "old age and corpulence" and vowed he would die on the road amidst "his family." In fact he did die in 1888, far from Tibet's borderlands, near Lake Issyk-Kul in the foothills of the Tian Shan. Przhevalsky's devoted Cossacks prepared his grave on the shores of the lake, where the site was marked by a great stone plinth crowned with a bronze eagle. The town in which he was stricken was renamed Przhevalsk by imperial edict. As with other heroes, his faults were buried with him. In his obituary for *Novoye Vremya (New Times)*, Anton Chekhov compared him with Stanley as the necessary antidote to "sick times." "Their loyalty to an idea, their noble ambition," the author said of such explorers, "whose basis is the honor of country and science, their stubbornness, their urge, undaunted by any privations, dangers or temptations of personal happiness, to reach the goal they have set, their wealth of knowledge and their love of work, their acclimatization to heat, hunger and homesickness, enervating fevers, their fanatical belief in Christian civilization and science make them in the eyes of the people heroes who personify a higher moral force."

This was surely a partial truth, a dramatic truth, but not the whole truth.

∴

CHAPTER TEN

Mystical Imperialism

T HE YEAR IS 1891. A RUSSIAN FRIGATE, THE *PAMIAT AZOVA,* lies in Colombo harbor. The imperial party, composed of the twenty-two-year-old Tsarevich Nicholas and a miscellany of Grand Dukes, Princes, and Guard Officers, is stopping at Ceylon. The heir to the Throne of all the Russians is midway through a ten-month Asian Grand Tour suggested by his father Alexander III in the hope that Nicky will get to know his future Central Asian subjects and, equally important, forget his mistress, the tiny ballerina of the Maryinsky Theater, Mathilde Kschessinska. In India, Nicky has found the tiger shoots and balls irritating, complaining to his mother, the Empress Marie Feodorovna, "How intolerable it is to be once again surrounded by Englishmen in their scarlet uniforms." She has replied, urging him to be "very courteous to all the English who are taking such pains to give you the best possible reception." She warns that he must set his personal comfort aside—"you will do this, won't you, my dear Nicky?" Above all, he must "dance more and smoke less in the garden with officers just because it is more amusing." The Tsarevich must "leave a good impression with everybody everywhere."

Perhaps the most important member of the party in the context of our story is Prince Esper Esperovich Ukhtomsky (1861–1921), whom we will meet again as the sponsor of Agvan Dorzhiev at the Russian court. Ukhtomsky's father founded a steamship company to link the Baltic with India and China via the Black Sea. His son, while still a St. Petersburg student, developed a scholarly interest in Buddhism and had become Russia's most important collector of Tibetan and Mongolian art. Upon graduation, Esper Esperovich entered the ranks of the Department of Foreign Creeds in the Ministry of the Interior. He is now its chief. He is a member both of the Imperial Russian Geographical Society and the Russian Committee for the Study of Central and Eastern Asia. A staunch protector of the Buriats, the Mongol people living around Lake Baikal in Siberia, Ukhtomsky leads the Eastern lobby which also includes such influential figures as the Finance Minister, Count Sergei Witte, and the Buriat society doctor, Pyotr Badmaev. These men are advocates of an aggressive forward policy in Asia, and are known collectively as *Vostochniki,* or "Easterners," or in their most extreme mode as proponents of *Zheltorossiya,* or "Yellow Russia."

Chosen to accompany the Tsarevich on this trip, Ukhtomsky will recount their adventures in the multi-volumned *Travels in the East of Nicholas II, Emperor of Russia, when Czarevitch 1890–91,* in which he will give vent to his pan-Asiatic notions: "We are, and must be supported by the idea of an ever-possible advance of the irresistible North over the Hindu Kush." The book will be published in many editions, assuring Ukhtomsky's future position as Tsar Nicholas's consultant on eastern affairs.

The Tsarevich is hardly ignorant about the East. In l881, when the intrepid Przhevalsky became his tutor on Central Asia, Nicholas was much taken by the explorer's exploits and tales of lamas and Buddhism. Nor will the intensely religious Nicholas be immune to occult persuasions—after the birth of the hemophiliac Tsarevich Alexis, the Romanov court would become a collective for seers, monks, and mystics. As Count Witte explained: "A soft haze of mysticism refracts everything he beholds and magnifies his own functions and person."

Now his imperial highness informs the Russian Consul in Colombo that he wishes to "have the honor of meeting" Colonel

Olcott (1832–1907), a retired American officer who sports an enormous Santa Claus beard and is the champion of a worldwide Buddhist revival. It happens that Henry Steel Olcott, now resident in
Colombo (the Sinhalese are Buddhists), is also the "chum" and associate of the Tsar's compatriot Helena P. Blavatsky. Together in 1875
they founded the Theosophical Society.

The Russians have already called at Adyar, near Madras, where the
Society has established its international headquarters. Ukhtomsky is
convinced of the deep spiritual kinship between Russia and "the
East," in which he includes Islam, Brahminism, Buddhism, and Confucianism. In his book, Ukhtomsky inserts remarks assuredly designed to alienate his British hosts:

> Clearly history is preparing new and complex problems in
> the East for the colonizing states of Western Europe, which
> are not really at home in Asia (as we Russians always have
> been, and still are, without being aware of it) . . . The jour-
> ney of the Tsarevich through the civilized countries of the
> East is full of deep significance for Russia. The bonds that
> unite our part of Europe with Iran and Turan, and through
> them with India and the Celestial Empire, are so ancient and
> lasting that, as yet, we ourselves, as a nation and a state, do
> not fully comprehend their full meaning and the duties they
> entail on us, both in our home and foreign policy.

Olcott, in the fourth volume of his memoir, *Old Diary Leaves,* recalls the delightful hour-long meeting with the Tsarevich's party
aboard the frigate. He is particularly drawn to Ukhtomsky "because
of his intense interest in Buddhism, which for many years he has
made a special study among the Mongolian lamaseries." The Prince
invites Olcott to make a tour of the Buddhist monasteries of Siberia
and asks for a copy of the Theosophical Society's Fourteen Proposi-
tions so that he "might translate them and circulate them among the
Chief Priests of Buddhism throughout the Empire." Which, Olcott
notes with satisfaction, he did. As for his compatriot Mme. Blavatsky,
Ukhtomsky is enthusiastic about the "Russian lady who knew and
has seen much."

The age of mystical imperialism had dawned.

NOT JUST RUSSIA BUT ALL EUROPE WAS DRAWN TO THE ESOTERIC religions and spiritual spices of the Orient. Starting in the Georgian Age, British merchant fleets sailed homeward with mystical creeds and Sanskrit grammars mixed with more earthbound cargoes. The timing was propitious: the light from the East arrived at a moment of moral crisis and revolutionary upheaval in the West. Chance seemed to clear the path. Alexander Hamilton, an East India Company servant fluent in Sanskrit, was taken prisoner in Paris during the Napoleonic wars, and taught Sanskrit, then almost unknown in Europe, to his fellow captives. One of his pupils was the Romantic poet Schlegel, who returned to Germany in 1808 and wrote the first book there on the language and creeds of the Indies, sparking a fashion. So smitten was the philosopher Schopenhauer on reading *The Upanishads* that he called it "the solace of my life," adding hopefully, "it will be the solace of my death."

This anxiety about the afterlife became especially acute after the appearance in 1859 of Darwin's *Origin of Species*, with its unspoken challenge to Genesis. Across Europe and America, disciples flocked to new faiths of every kind, ranging from the occult arts to the science of spiritual healing. Unbelievers scoffed and cried fraud, but persons of standing in the West concerned themselves with Spiritualism, Reincarnation, Channeling, the Brotherhood of Masters, Great White Lodges, Cosmogenesis, and a host of Secret Doctrines said to spring from the timeless wisdom of the East. Still, even as they scoffed, the worldly saw a gleam of utility in the otherworldly. Thus it happened that in Russia and England the Mystical Channel developed into an interesting new medium for imperial intrigues, or in some cases anti-imperial agitation. It was, however, a medium that eluded easy manipulation, and a cloak of ambiguity shielded its avatars, so that it was often hard to say who was using whom.

This was especially true of Helena Petrovna Blavatsky (1831–91), whose precise loyalties were the focus of exasperated speculation for decades in Britain and Russia. Madame Blavatsky, the author of *The*

Secret Doctrine and other bulky occult works, has never been out of print or entirely forgotten. Self-described as "a hippopotamus of an old woman," HPB, with her hypnotic gaze, seems to spring from faded photographs. In his memoirs, Rudyard Kipling recalls that his father, Lockwood, who knew her well, spoke of Madame Blavatsky as "one of the most interesting and unscrupulous impostors he had ever met."

Soon after her arrival in 1879 at Simla, then in its heyday as summer capital of British India, everybody who counted had an opinion about HPB, as she was commonly known. She sailed to India from New York, where she first gained her reputation as a clairvoyant and where she and her devoted disciple, Colonel Olcott, had founded the Theosophical Society in 1875. "TS" Lodges rapidly multiplied, and HPB and the Colonel were anxious to propagate the new faith in India, nearer to its cradle in Tibet.

Blavatsky's fascination with Tibet and Buddhism dated from her childhood. Her maternal grandfather, Andrei Fadeyev, was administrator for the Kalmyk settlers in the Caspian seaport region of Astrakhan, and while her father was away on military duty, Blavatsky's mother—who wrote a novel about Kalmyk life—took her to live with the Fadeyevs. Distant ethnic cousins of the Buriats, the Kalmyks had migrated from Dzungaria in Central Asia to the lower Volga region in the seventeenth century but were still practitioners of Tibetan Buddhism. Helena met and was impressed by the Kalmyk leader Prince Tumen and his Tibetan lama. Somewhat later she would claim that the tenets of Theosophy had been vouchsafed to her by just such lamas, her "Himalayan Masters" during the seven years she claimed to have spent in Tibet. There she learned of a divine hierarchy of Masters, or Mahatmas, the terms being synonymous, who belonged to an invisible Brotherhood headed by the Lord of the World who inhabited Shambhala, the source of universal wisdom, located by Blavatsky beyond Tibet, somewhere in the Gobi Desert.

First in the chain of command was Buddha, then came a series of Masters, of whom the most accessible to HPB were Morya (known simply as M) and Koot Hoomi (called KH), each in the Hindu mode enjoying a variety of incarnations and tasks (KH attended the University of Leipzig and curated an underground Occult Museum). Others in the Brotherhood included Jesus, Confucius, Solomon, Lao Tze, Moses, Abraham, Plato, Mesmer, and the two Bacons, Roger and Francis. The Brotherhood was hidden from most mortals, and was sometimes persecuted by humans under the influence of the Dark Force, but it communicated with Adepts, like Madame Blavatsky, through letters written in gold ink or other psychic means. According to Peter Washington in his history of Theosophy, *Madame Blavatsky's Baboon* (1995), her cosmology was a blend drawn from Buddhism and other more improbable sources, notably the mystical novels of Edward Bulwer-Lytton.

Fascinated, baffled, and scandalized by this new High Priestess and her American consort, the powerful along with the obscure, Indians as well as Europeans, flocked to Theosophy, so that by 1885, 106 lodges had been chartered in India, Burma, and Ceylon, out of 121 lodges worldwide. An important reason for its popularity among Indians was that Theosophists took Buddhism and Hinduism seriously, not with the sneering condescension of many Europeans. In fact, it was her extravagant regard for Hindus and visible contempt for their rulers that caused HPB to be regarded as a spy and placed under British surveillance.

The movement also had its political spillover among Europeans. A notable convert was Alfred Percy Sinnett, the influential editor of *The Allahabad Pioneer*, then the leading newspaper in India, whose rising star was Rudyard Kipling. Another catch was Allan Octavian Hume, the wealthy son of the radical Scottish parliamentarian Joseph Hume. "AO" was a decorated hero of the Great Mutiny, the "pope" of Indian ornithology, and a high-ranking civil servant. Hume eventually broke with Blavatsky, and took up the national cause. In 1885, on retiring from the civil service, Hume summoned the first meeting of the Indian National Congress, in the hope of winning a greater role for Indians in administration under the British Crown. Over time, under Gandhi and Nehru, the Congress became the main propellant of independence, and in India today Hume's role as forerunner is still remembered and acknowledged. (The thirteen-year-old Nehru was, in fact, initiated into the Theosophical Society by its third leader, Annie Besant, and the "thrilled" youngster later saw "old Colonel Olcott with his fine beard.")

Theosophy's links to Indian nationalism were of special concern to British officialdom because of Blavatsky's Russian connections. Born the daughter of Baron von Hahn, into the lesser ranks of Russian-German nobility, she was the cousin of Count Sergei Witte—railway magnate, Russian Finance Minister, and (as of 1904) Prime Minister. So widespread was the belief that HPB was a Russian agent that for months she was followed everywhere by Major Philip D. Henderson, chief of the Simla police, prompting indignant protests by Colonel Olcott. In 1884, she was accused of serving "Russian interests" by a special investigator, Richard Hodgson, employed by the Society for Psychical Research, a charge amply ventilated in the press and furiously denied by Madame herself.

In fact, documents first published in 1993 suggest that British suspicions were not entirely off the mark. In a seemingly authentic letter from Odessa in December 1872 to the Director of the Third [Intelligence] Section (discovered by the American scholar Maria Carlson), HPB set forth her qualifications as an agent to "Your Excellency and my native land," with this candid explanation: "Hundreds of people believed and will undoubtedly believe in spirits. But I...must confess that three-quarters of the time the spirits spoke and answered in my words and out of my considerations, for the success of my own plans. Rarely, very rarely, did I fail by means of this little trap, to discover people's hopes, plans and secrets. I have played every role, I am able to represent myself as any person you may wish."

What the Third Section, precursor of the notorious Okhrana, made of this offer is not known. Yet there was nothing secret about HPB's association with Mikhail Katkov (1818–87), the publicist and journalist whose *Moscow Chronicle* was read by all who mattered in St. Petersburg, where its influence (in the estimate of George Kennan) nearly outweighed the rest of the press together. Once a liberal advocate of parliamentary democracy, Katkov had by the 1870's become an almost fanatical reactionary, an apostle of imperial expansion to the East and South, and an opponent of liberal reforms and of Russia's alliance with Germany, which he helped terminate. Portly, heavily bearded, and known for his percussive enthusiasms, Katkov presided at a huge dinner table, surrounded by his eleven children, two adopted nephews, and assorted hangers-on. He was not a groveler, and in a famous 1887 editorial courted Alexander III's wrath by exposing the details of a secret defensive treaty, the Dreikaiserbund, signed by the emperors of Russia, Austria, and Germany.

Madame Blavatsky was a frequent and well-paid contributor to the *Chronicle,* which serialized her book on occult India, *From the Caves and Jungles of Hindostan.* When Katkov died in 1887, she contributed an effusive panegyric, speculating that "some dark forces" might have been to blame since the "riffraff" in Berlin and Austria were rejoicing that he could no longer "crush their lying brains under his heel."

And now, HPB moved with a master's dexterity as rumors of a Sikh rebellion against British rule swirled around her. The Sikhs, fierce fighters whose support of the Raj tipped the scale during the Great Mutiny, were said to be plotting a revolt in collusion with their exiled Maharajah. His name was Duleep Singh (1838–93), and he was Queen Victoria's favorite Indian prince, a vivid, undeservedly forgotten personage. His life was the stuff of a grand opera scored by Puccini, but with a libretto by Dürrenmatt.

DULEEP SINGH WAS THE HEIR OF RANJIT SINGH, THE LION OF Lahore, under whose leadership the Sikhs became masters of the rich and fertile "Land of Five Rivers." Their rule was enforced by the Khalsa, a disciplined army second in India only to that of the East India Company. With its elephant-drawn field cannons, its European officers, and its 53,000 infantrymen, all smartly dressed in red jackets and blue turbans, the Khalsa was, in the words of then Governor-General Sir Henry Hardinge, Britain's "bravest and most warlike and most disruptive enemy in Asia." While Ranjit Singh lived, the Punjab was allied by treaty to the British, but his death in 1839 led to a chaotic struggle for succession. Ranjit Singh had forty-six wives and left four acknowledged sons, of whom Duleep Singh was the last. The boy's mother was Rani Jandin, the old Lion's youngest wife, and his true father (it was commonly gossiped) was her lover, a former *bhishti,* or palace water-carrier. No matter: Ranjit Singh acknowledged the child as his own, and the Rani, herself the daughter of a palace door-keeper, was by all accounts the cleverest of the Lion's mates.

As Ranjit Singh's various offspring and relations slew each other, Rani Jandin managed in 1843 to have her son proclaimed Maharajah on his fifth birthday, with herself as Regent. There followed a test of wills with the Khalsa, whose commanders threatened to install their own candidate on the throne at Lahore. To fend off the army, the Rani and her ministers encouraged its commanders to do battle with British forces now mobilizing on the far bank of the Sutlej. The result was the first of two Sikh Wars, both of which, after consider-able exertion, the Company's soldiers won. ("Another such victory and we are undone," murmured Hardinge after the Battle of Feroze-shah in 1845.) When the Khalsa surrendered in a solemn ceremony, a grizzled warrior cried out as he lay down his musket, "*Aj Ranjit Singh mar gaya*" (Today Ranjit Singh is dead).

Having prevailed, however, the British drew back from annexing the troublesome Sikh state, and instead turned the Punjab into a protectorate. Duleep Singh remained on the throne, under the tute-lage of an astute Resident, Sir Henry Lawrence. The arrangement was not a success. The Rani and the Resident quarreled constantly and bitterly, and the former was finally banished by the latter, who complained of "her general misconduct and habits of intrigue." A fresh uprising on her behalf led to the Second Sikh War, in which British troops ostensibly fought in the name of Duleep Singh—and having won, expeditiously removed him from his throne. A new Governor-General, Lord Dalhousie, saw no alternative to outright annexation of the Punjab, and the elimination of "a brat begotten of a *bhishti,* and no more the son of old Ranjit Singh than Queen Vic-toria." In 1849, the ten-year-old Maharajah, warned that hesitation could only make things worse, signed away for himself and his heirs "all right and title to the sovereignty of the Punjab" and all its state property, expressly including "The gem called the Koh-i-Noor," which was to be surrendered to the Queen of England.

The Koh-i-Noor, the Mountain of Light, was unearthed in the sixteenth century and originally weighed 787 carats. The diamond passed from Mughal Emperors to Afghan Emirs, then to Ranjit Singh, and eventually to Henry Lawrence's brother John, who (so the story goes) carelessly mislaid it in a waistcoat pocket until its recovery from a forgotten tin box by an aged servant who thought it nothing more than a "bit of glass." The gem, the size of a pigeon egg, was presented to the Queen with the compliments of the East India Company, and shipped westward under armed guard in 1850. It was last worn in state by the present Queen Mother at the 1937 coronation of her husband George VI.

There remained the matter of what to do with the "brat"—not a simple problem. His mother had just fled to Nepal, where she was certain to be a focus for disaffection, leaving the East India Company literally *in loco parentis*. The Governor-General approved putting the young Maharajah under the guardianship of a Scottish medical officer, Dr. John Login, who found for him a suitable young companion named Tommy Scott. The Maharajah liked Tommy, learned fluent English, absorbed such alien curiosities as *The Boys' Own Book*, and found nourishment in the Holy Scriptures. In 1850, on turning twelve, Duleep Singh announced his determination to "embrace the Christian religion," a decision that caused anxiety in Calcutta lest the Sikhs suspect coercion. After an inquiry, Lord Dalhousie found no improper influence. "This is the first Indian prince," he marveled to a colleague, "of the many who have succumbed to our power and acknowledged it, that has adopted the faith of the stranger. Who shall say to what it may lead? God prosper and multiply it!" Duleep Singh did more than embrace the religion of the stranger: he cut his hair, and "broke caste" by conspicuously making tea with his own hands.

In 1854, on Dalhousie's recommendation and with the approval of the Company's Court of Directors, Duleep Singh sailed to England. Soon after his arrival, the fifteen-year-old Maharajah was presented to Queen Victoria, who was then thirty-five. She was enchanted; it was first of many meetings and led to a close friendship and extensive correspondence. As the Queen wrote in her journal, after re-

ceiving him, "He is extremely handsome and speaks English perfectly, and has a pretty, graceful and dignified manner. He was beau-
tifully dressed and covered with diamonds...I always feel so much
for these deposed Indian princes." She reported all this to her
Viceroy, Lord Dalhousie, adding that it was "not without mixed feelings of pain and sympathy that the Queen sees this young prince,
destined to so high and powerful a position, and now reduced to so
dependent a one by our arms...it will be a pleasure to us to do all
we can to help him and to befriend and protect him."

Victoria was as good as her word. It is difficult not to be touched
and impressed by her voluminous correspondence with, and about,
Duleep Singh, as generously extracted by Michael Alexander and
Sushila Anand in *Queen Victoria's Maharajah* (1980). She stuck by
him, and forgave his worst trespasses. At her insistence, he was called
Maharajah, was granted what appeared to be princely pension of
£50,000 per annum, and was portrayed in his regal sash and aigrette
by the court artist Winterhalter. With his pension, he acquired Elveden Hall, near Thetford in Suffolk. There the "Black Prince" played
host at elaborate hunts for titled guests, including the Prince of
Wales; the Maharajah himself was reckoned the fourth best shot in
Britain, once felling a record 780 partridges with a thousand cartridges. Duleep Singh was well aware how much he owed to the
Queen. At one of their meetings, Victoria graciously placed in his
hands the Koh-i-Noor, and with deferential tact he returned it, saying "It is to me, Ma'am, the greatest pleasure to have the opportunity, as a loyal subject, of *myself* tendering to my sovereign, the
Koh-i-Noor."

The Queen approved the Maharajah's unconventional choice of a
bride, named Bamba, half German and half Ethiopian, whom he met
at the American Protestant Mission in Cairo. Victoria understood his
conflicted silence during the Indian Mutiny—after all, "his best
course was to say nothing." She loyally (if vainly) backed him up
when he protested that his pension was subject to excessive deduc-
tions and was inadequate to the style of life he was expected to
maintain. She remonstrated gently when the Maharajah went public
with his grievances in angry letters to *The Times*. ("If I might advise
you—it would be better not to write to the papers. It is beneath you

to do so.") What proved beyond Victoria's healing words was the midlife crisis (as we would call it) that followed when the Maharajah discovered he was not an English squire, but an Indian Sikh.

IN 1861, DULEEP SINGH WAS ALLOWED A VISIT TO INDIA, WHERE he was greeted with the prescribed twenty-one-gun salute, yet the authorities cautiously forbade a trip to the Punjab. He was permitted a reunion in India with his half-blind mother (still a "she-devil" in the view of the Viceroy, Lord Canning). As much to be rid of her as to accommodate him, the Government approved the son's request to allow her to sail with him to England. There the Rani died two years later. The reunion reconnected the Maharajah with a painful past. He now heard a very different view of his patrimony, and how it was taken from him. Each subsequent quarrel over money, each real or imagined snub, each refusal of his principal demand—an impartial hearing of his grievances—rubbed raw his sense of loss. To placate the Queen, Prime Minister Gladstone agreed to proffer a seat in the House of Lords, but what might have been an interesting experiment failed as the Liberals lost the next election.

Duleep Singh was by now the father of two sons and three daughters, and as his household bills grew, so did his anger and frustration. In the 1880's, he began examining his rejected religion. He listened intently when two Indian cousins, one of them the Sikh militant Thakar Singh Sandhanwalia, journeyed to Elveden with important tidings. It appeared that Nanuk, the Hindu founder of the Sikh faith, prophesied that an Eleventh Guru named Deep Singh would be stripped of his inheritance, forced into exile, and suffer great hardships before returning in triumph to the Punjab during a war between the bear and the bulldog. After that, the Eleventh Guru would purify the Sikh religion. The import seemed obvious: Duleep Singh was Deep Singh, whose descendants were destined, as the sacred books promised, to reign for three generations "over the land between Calcutta and the Indus," with the propitious advent of a war between Russia and England.

In 1885, it so happened, England and Russia were briefly at the brink of war over the occupation by the Tsar's forces of the Pandjeh, a disputed tract in eastern Afghanistan. It also happened that the Maharajah's cousin, Thakar Singh, headed a Sikh reform group, Singh Sabha, allied with the Theosophists. Not only was Thakar Singh Madame Blavatsky's prime link to the Punjabi Sikhs, whose creed she studied and greatly admired, but he was a possible author of her occult Mahatma Letters. Thakar Singh made no secret of his hostility to Christian missionaries, or his ardor for Sikh liberation. He now became the Maharajah's principal champion and intelligence source within India.

In the midst of the Pandjeh crisis, professing a wish to show his loyalty, Duleep Singh sought permission to sail to India in support of the British cause. In Calcutta, his offer was seen as a ruse by intelligence operatives—especially Colonel Henderson, who had shadowed Madame Blavatsky in Simla. Secret cables were rushed to Sir Henry Mortimer Durand, the Foreign Secretary of India, detailing a plot in which Duleep Singh would accompany a Russian army through Central Asia, and incite a rebellion by native troops, who would sabotage rail and telegraph lines, aided by a cabal of disloyal princes. The memory of the Mutiny was fresh, and the scenario seemed all too plausible.

Hence the consternation in Calcutta's Government House when the Maharajah on his own authority embarked in March 1886 on the P & O steamer *Verona*. Prior to his departure he released this open letter, addressed to "My beloved Countrymen," saying that obedient to his destiny he was returning to India "to occupy a humble sphere" and begged forgiveness for converting to Christianity when he was very young. Yet in resuming his Sikh faith, he had "no intention of conforming to the errors introduced into Sikhism by those who were not true Sikhs—such, for instance, as wretched caste observances or abstinence from meats and drinks." He was compelled to write his open letter "because I am not permitted to visit you in the Punjaub...Truly a noble reward for my unwavering loyalty to the Empress of India." He signed himself "Your own flesh and blood, Duleep Singh."

Once on the *Verona*, the Maharajah wrote a farewell note to his Empress blaming her ministers and begging her forgiveness for not personally paying "my last homage before starting for India." A second message, consisting of a single word, went by telegraph to his Sikh friends in India: "Started."

In India, anxious officials pondered Duleep Singh's proclamation and the intercepted telegram. On their desks were intelligence dossiers detailing symptoms of unrest ("The spirit of the Sikhs is not dead and they are full of national fire") and signs of incipient rebellion, fanned by the vernacular press. So what was to be done? The safest but legally dubious solution was to arrest the Maharajah in Aden, then under the authority of the Indian Government, relying on a catchall regulation adopted in 1818 permitting arrests to prevent "internal commotion." But could the measure be used against a British subject (and regal favorite)? It says much about the panic in Simla that even the leading liberal on the governing council, Sir Courtenay Ilbert, ruled out "for reasons of State" further deliberations over legality. With the approval of the Viceroy, Lord Dufferin, an arrest warrant was issued naming the Maharajah but not his children ("We must not court ridicule by serving warrants on babies"). In Aden, the British Resident boarded the *Verona* and as courteously as he could, avoiding the word "arrest," informed Duleep Singh that he could not proceed further. Passengers and crew cheered in support as the Maharajah and his brood, all prisoners of state, filed down the gangway.

They were incarcerated in the Residency, and from there Duleep Singh fired angry cables to the Viceroy protesting his use of the word "disloyal," and refusing to return to England until he was promised a full and fair hearing. Lord Dufferin was polite but unyielding. From Balmoral, the Queen did her best to plead her friend's case: "The Queen Empress thanks the Viceroy for his last kind letter of the 5th of May about the poor Maharajah Duleep Singh. He was so charming and so good for so many years that she feels deeply grieved at the bad hands he has fallen into and the way in which he has been led astray, & the Queen thinks it will have a very bad effect in India if he is ill-used & rather severely punished & especially if the Maharanee (an excellent pious woman) & their six children especially the two boys, quite Englishmen, are in poverty or discomfort." The Queen offered to speak to the Maharajah when he calmed down, and reiterated her wish that he or his son be given a British peerage with suitable emoluments.

In Aden, Duleep Singh was formally initiated into his ancestral faith, in a ceremony witnessed by the prescribed five Sikhs. The Maharajah had already sent his family back to England, and in his lonely misery he had become something of a hero to his people. "Poor Duleep Singh!" wrote the editor of the Lahore *Tribune.* "Your countrymen can only weep for you." When his appeal for an impartial inquiry was once again rejected, he cabled the Viceroy: "I return to Europe. From 1st of July next I resign the stipend paid to me under Treaty of Annexation, thus laying aside that iniquitous document." In June, he boarded a French mail steamer bound for Marseilles, and proceeded directly to Paris. Once settled there, he confided his plans to a ducal shooting-partner: "I wrote yesterday to the Russian Ambassador offering my services to the Emperor and requested a passport which as soon as I receive I shall go to St. Petersburg. If I am well received by the Emperor I shall go to the border of India. If not I shall go to Pondicherry [a French possession] and be a thorn in the side of Lord Dufferin."

The Maharajah's arrival in Paris occurred at a turbulent moment. On Bastille Day, huge and boisterous crowds shouted and sang their support for General Boulanger, the Minister of War, who many believed was destined to crush Germany and regain Alsace-Lorraine. In the event, Boulangism proved to be bombast, and within a few years the General meekly accepted banishment to Brussels, where he committed suicide on the grave of his mistress. But the movement confirmed a popular hunger for assertive militarism, and presaged the unraveling of Bismarck's intricate system of alliances binding Germany to Russia and Austria-Hungary. Out of the ferment a new alignment arose, pairing an odd couple, Republican France and Tsarist Russia, a partnership solemnized in 1894, with profound reverberations two decades later.

It was a confusing moment, and a shrewder participant than Duleep Singh could have misread shifting signals. He expected a heartfelt welcome from the Russian chargé, and instead was brushed off with a letter saying the Imperial Government "protects peace" and had no wish to provoke troubles in India. A more candid explanation can be inferred from the chargé's cable to the Russian Foreign Minister, Nikolai Karlovich Giers ("probably the most seasoned and able statesman of his time, after Bismarck," in the view of George Kennan). The chargé, Prince Ernest Kotzebue, reported that Duleep Singh had shown him a letter he had just received from Queen Victoria, asking if she should believe rumors that he was offering his services to the Russians. In questioning him, Kotzebue continued, "I have come to know that he hopes to extract a large sum of money from the English Government. Hence, it is to be feared that the offers which the oriental Prince makes us are only a means of blackmail." It was what Giers needed to know. The son of a Lutheran postmaster who had risen through merit, Giers was a firm advocate of restraint and stability. He wished to preserve Russia's alliance with Bismarck, was dismayed by the Pandjeh war scare, and strove to calm Anglo-Russian relations. He had no use for the forward-school adventures in Central Asia supported by his most nettlesome critic, the Muscovite editor Mikhail Nikiforovich Katkov.

Katkov had his own sources in France, and learned soon enough about Duleep Singh. The likely go-between was his paper's Paris correspondent, Elie de Cyon (1843–1910), a figure out of a Conrad novel: born a Russian Jew, trained as a scientist, and at the time an ardent proponent of a Franco-Russian alliance. In his memoirs, Cyon claims he tried to interest the French in giving military aid to Duleep Singh, without success. In turn, Cyon was introduced to the Maharajah through Patrick Casey, an Irish expatriate who, with his brother James, had befriended a fellow enemy of the Crown. Thus the Sikh prince, who once caroused with the Prince of Wales, now toasted the Empire's downfall with Fenian revolutionaries.

The Caseys tutored the novice rebel in conspiratorial ways and ferried through the print shop his increasingly militant proclamations. Katkov liked what he learned, and cared not a whit what the Foreign Ministry thought. He invited Duleep Singh to Moscow and volunteered *The Moscow Gazette's* backing, which then meant a good deal. Katkov's paper was described in 1886 by a British visitor, Sir Charles Dilke, as the most powerful in the world "because it is all-

powerful or nearly all-powerful in one great empire." Katkov was at his polemical prime. In one celebrated article he likened the visits of Giers to Bismarck to the supine pilgrimages of Russian princes to the Golden Horde of the Tartars: "If Germany stands so high, it is because Germany stands on Russia."

In Paris, two problems attended Duleep Singh's departure in March 1887. He had acquired an English mistress and lacked a passport (Russia was among the few countries that required a passport). The Maharajah decided to take along eighteen-year-old Ada Wetherill as his honorary wife, and to embark for Berlin under the alias "Patrick Casey." Between trains at the Berlin terminal, the putative revolutionary was victimized by a pickpocket who made off with his money and travel documents. From Moscow, Katkov came to the rescue. He contacted a crony at the Interior Ministry, who made sure the frontier officials waived the rules for the Maharajah—a fact seized upon by Giers, when informed of this wire-pulling by a complaining British Ambassador. "*C'était un acte de trahison!*" the Foreign Minister protested, and promised to do all he could to prevent further mischief-making by the Maharajah. When the Tsar learned of all this, he remarked to his Foreign Minister, "It is passing strange that the British Ambassador should have at his disposal better police than I have."

Nonetheless Duleep Singh was allowed to remain in Moscow, a tacit tit-for-tat for British hospitality to Russian revolutionaries viewed as terrorists and criminals. Unable to obtain a personal audience with the Tsar but with Katkov's coaching, in May the Maharajah laid before the Imperial Government "the humble prayer of the Princes and people of India for deliverance from their oppression." Writing directly to Alexander III, Duleep Singh boldly guaranteed the "easy conquest of India" since he was able "to raise the entire Punjab in revolt." Should an invasion of India be undertaken by Russia, he added, "an army of not less than 200,000 men and 2,000 cannons" would be required. The Maharajah promised that other Indian princes, if allowed to manage their own affairs, would pay "a large tribute annually to the Russian Treasury," possibly as much as ten million pounds.

This dramatic proposal did not have its intended effect. Tsar Alexander was cautious in deeds if not always in words. "I am glad that I have taken part in actual warfare and seen with my eyes the horrors which are inevitably connected with a military action," he once wrote. "After such an experience, not only will a ruler never desire war, but he will employ every honourable means of sparing his subjects the trials and terrors of armed conflict." Moreover, the Tsarina, Marie Feodorovna, was the sister of Alexandra, the Princess of Wales, so the Tsar was the brother-in-law to the heir to the British throne. The invasion scheme was so wild, its author so unsteady, that even a bolder Tsar would have drawn back. Still, Alexander III did pencil in marginal notes that indicated interest, and he did authorize further discussions by others with the Maharajah.

In India, HPB, possibly through Elie de Cyon or Thakar Singh, got wind of the purported Sikh plot. Either through genuine misunderstanding, or as a deliberate diversion, she claimed that France was the external *force diabolique,* and used her information to counter doubts about her loyalty to India. In great alarm, she wrote to a friend, the editor A. P. Sinnett, in February 1887, that through "some theosophists" she learned of "this horrid conspiracy" and wanted to "upset these French plans." She concluded fervently: "I am ready to become an infamous *informer* of your English Govt., WHICH I HATE, for their sake, for the sake of *my Society* and of my beloved Hindus . . . Ah! if only Master would show me the way! If he would only show me what I have to do to save India from new blood-shed, for hundreds and perhaps a thousand innocent victims being hung for the crime of the few. For I feel, however great the harm will be done, it will end with the English having the best; Master says the hour for the retirement of you English has not struck, nor will it— *till the next century.*"

HPB appealed to Sinnett to pass on her warning to the Viceroy, and to accept her gesture as proof she was no Russian spy, begging him as a gentleman and man of honor not to compromise her needlessly because "I would indeed be regarded as an infamous *mouchard,* an informing *spy,* and this shame is worse than death."

Nothing came of what Colonel Henderson called "the Dalip Singh business." Whatever hopes the Sikh prince had for Russian en-

couragement expired with the fatal stroke that claimed Mikhail
Katkov, "The Thunderer," on August 1, 1887. Though Duleep Singh
lingered in Russia, he knew he was beaten. He married his British
companion, who had borne him two daughters, settled in Paris, and
there suffered a disabling stroke in 1890. Soon thereafter he dictated
to his son Victor a letter to Queen Victoria begging her forgiveness
for all he had done "against You and Your Government." The Queen
graciously pardoned him, and saw her Maharajah for the last time in
1891 at Grasse: "He is quite bald and vy. grey...I asked him to sit
down—and almost directly he burst into a most terrible and violent
fit of crying...it was vy. sad—still I am so glad we met again and I
cld. say I forgave him." He died two years later, at fifty-five, and following a church service was buried in a stone vault at Elveden.
Among the wreaths was one "From Queen Victoria."

So matters rested until 1997, when Swiss banks, responding to a
global campaign to identify holders of accounts unclaimed since
1945, published 1,872 names. Most were Holocaust victims, along
with a miscellany of Nazis, Fascists, and collaborators. One entry was
for Princess Catherine Duleep Singh, "last heard of living in Penn,
Bucks in 1942." With this clue, Christy Campbell, an enterprising
reporter for the London *Sunday Telegraph,* checked old Bucking-
hamshire directories, found the princess's name, and located her will,
filed in 1943 after her death. She wished her ashes to be interred in
Elveden, her father's Suffolk estate, later the home of Lord Iveagh,
head of the Guinness family, but no mention was made of any Swiss
bank accounts. The princess was one of Duleep Singh's three daughters by his first marriage. Campbell's story, headlined "Nazi Gold
Fortune Awaits the Heir of the Maharaja," was picked up by papers
all over India, and she hoped a lawful claimant would come forward.
   It developed that the Maharajah's five daughters and two sons all
died childless; in the jargon of genealogy, they were fin de ligne. As
the reporter learned from a Punjabi historian, this was the result of
the curse of Gobind Singh, the great Sikh spiritual leader, who had
a golden treasure box buried with him. The guru warned that who-
ever touched it would "vanish from the light," a warning ignored by

Ranjit Singh, who dug it up, passing the curse to Duleep Singh. But other descendants of the old Lion came forth in India. Campbell flew to Amritsar to meet Ranjit Kaur, the great-great-great-granddaughter of Ranjit Singh, a descendant of Sher Singh, the Maharajah assassinated before the five-year-old Duleep was enthroned. Ranjit Kaur recalled her mother's description of meeting two of Duleep's daughters, Sophia and Bamba, during a homecoming in the 1920's at the Shalimar Gardens in Lahore: "My mother remembered exactly how the princesses looked, one in bottle-green, the other in a maroon sari in fine French georgette...My mother cried; they looked so beautiful, our cousins, come here after so many years. The princesses cried too. They could not bear it. They could speak no Punjabi; they had to speak through translators with the fine English accents they had been taught...Then the police broke up the crowd. It was too dangerous politically. My mother never saw them again." The matter of who has legal title to the unknown contents of the Zurich bank vault is still unresolved.

CHAPTER ELEVEN

Emissary to
the White Tsar

FEW FIGURES OF IMPORTANCE IN THE IMPERIAL DUELS OF
Central Asia have been so commonly misrepresented as Agvan
Dorzhiev (1854–1938), the Buddhist lama and Russian subject who
fought long and worthily for Tibetan nationhood. It was his presence
that brought British bayonets to Lhasa in 1904, an event whose magnitude required a suitable provocation. So Dorzhiev "was elevated to the
position of Evil Genius at the Court of the Dalai Lama, two parts
Rasputin to one part Macavity the Mystery Cat," in the apt phrase of
Patrick French, the biographer of Sir Francis Younghusband, leader of
the Tibetan expedition. Indeed Dorzhiev in one of his aspects was
Macavity. When he so wished, he left no tracks. It did not help his cause.

At least three times Dorzhiev passed invisibly through India, slip-
ping over frontiers and eluding police scrutiny while a guest at Buddhist monasteries, but his appearances at the Russian court were not
secret—they were announced in the press. For Lord Curzon, the
Viceroy of India, angered and humiliated by lapses of his intelligence
service, the import was plain. Tibet was supposedly closed to foreigners, and the Dalai Lama returned unopened urgent messages from

Curzon.Yet here was a presumed Russian agent commuting across the Himalaya, lending substance to reports that the Tsar had already signed a secret pact with China to allow Russian officials and mining engineers into Tibet. "I am myself," Curzon wrote in 1902 to the Foreign Secretary in London, "a firm believer in the existence of a secret understanding, if not a secret treaty, between Russia and China about Tibet; and, as I have said before, I regard it as a duty to frustrate their little game while there is still time."

Was there really a "little game"? It cannot be ruled out. The British themselves prompted its initial moves. In 1868, the Journal of the Royal Geographical Society published the first in a series about Tibet based on clandestine visits by Indian pundits posing as pilgrims. This "cunning enterprise" was noted with keen interest in St. Petersburg by the military-scientific section of the General Staff, writes the Russian scholar Alexandre Andreyev. Among the many nationalities in the Russian Empire were several groups of Mongolians—a potential *indigène cadre* for similar forays. In recently opened archives, Dr. Andreyev found that as early as 1869 the Imperial Geographical Society and the General Staff tried to recruit the Russian equivalent of pundits among Buriats and Kalmyks.

The Buriats were a Mongolian people who for centuries lived near Lake Baikal in Eastern Siberia. Revered as the "Holy Sea" or "Blue Miracle," the lake is a natural wonder nonpareil. It is the earth's deepest body of fresh water, filling an abyss fifty miles wide, 250 miles long, and more than a mile deep, with a surface area (12,162 square miles) bigger than Belgium. Near its shores the Buriats tended their livestock, pursuing a nomadic life that persisted after their conversion in the seventeenth century from shamanism to Tibeto-Mongolian Buddhism. The Kalmyks, also Mongolians by virtue of language, culture, and appearance, belong to a clan that migrated circa 1632 from Dzungaria in Central Asia to the lower Volga region. Renowned for their horsemanship, Kalmyk warriors joined Cossack cavalry regiments and fought so well against Napoleon that Alexander I awarded them a fertile domain whose revenues were to be used for schools and hospitals. Protected by royal favor, the Kalmyks adhered to Buddhism and looked to Lhasa as their Holy City—ideal potential recruits for Tsarist secret services.

Andreyev found that in 1869 a senior officer on the Imperial General Staff proposed sending a Buriat, Naidak Gomboev, as part of a religious delegation of pilgrims who eventually proceeded to Tibet in 1873. What came of this plan is unclear. Mysteriously, key pre-revolutionary files relating to Tibet are still missing in the archives of post-Soviet Russia. But it appears that Agvan Dorzhiev was among the pilgrims who made their way to Lhasa, so that a connection with the General Staff is not implausible. Even so, the core question is how Dorzhiev viewed his own role, and what his purposes were—and on this, the record seems clear. Far from being a Russian agent, Dorzhiev saw himself as Tibet's emissary to the White Tsar. His purpose was to create a Tibetan-Mongolian federation in collaboration with Russia. As events dictated, he changed his tactics. Dorzhiev continued to pursue the same goal in Bolshevik times, and did so until his death in Stalin's Gulag. A learned monk as well as statesman, a tutor to the Dalai Lama, Dorzhiev was among the first to acquaint the West with the rich traditions of Tibetan Buddhism. His influence reached the United States. He was the "root lama" to Geshe Wangyal, who in 1955 resettled in Freehold Acres, New Jersey, and there founded what was to be the first Tibetan Buddhist monastery open to Americans.

If Dorzhiev had realized his dreams for Tibet and Mongolia, he might well have won a niche beside Gandhi, Sun Yat-sen, and Thomas Masaryk in the pantheon of nation-builders and freedom-seekers. Regrettably for the people he championed, it was not to be.

GHOOM MONASTERY, NEAR DARJEELING, WAS THE UNMONITORED way station to India for monks and mystics. Here in 1885–87 Madame Blavatsky, the founder of Theosophy, met Sarat Chandra Das, the pundit who covertly explored Tibet for the British. Years later, Madame's American disciple, Colonel Olcott, stopped at Ghoom, where he was given (as he describes in *Old Diary Leaves*), a white silken scarf that the Panchen Lama presented to Das during the pundit's stay in Tashilhunpo. Das also gave the Colonel rare Ti-

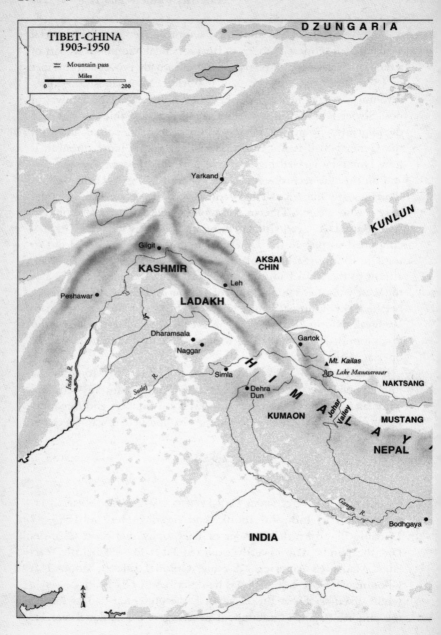

TIBET-CHINA
1903–1950

≋ Mountain pass

Miles

0   200

DZUNGARIA

KUNLUN

Yarkand

Gilgit

KASHMIR

AKSAI
CHIN

Peshawar

Leh

LADAKH

Dharamsala

Naggar

Gartok

Mt. Kailas

Lake Manasarovar

NAKTSANG

Indus R.

Sutlej R.

Simla

Dehra
Dun

KUMAON

H
I
M
A
L
A
Y

Johar
Valley

MUSTANG

NEPAL

Ganges R.

Bodhgaya

INDIA

N

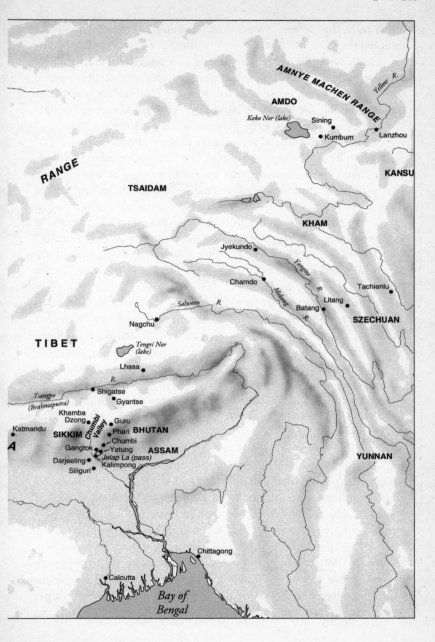

betan texts that were forwarded to Madame. Subsequently, having founded the Buddhist Text Society in Bengal, Sarat Chandra Das invited Olcott to address its first general meeting. In an intricate feat of deduction, K. Paul Johnson, a scholarly explorer of the esoteric tradition, maintains in *The Masters Revealed* (1994) that among the real-life models for Madame Blavatsky's Tibetan Masters were Das and his fellow pundit Ugyen Gyatso, along with their Tibetan patron, Losang Palden, the chief minister of the Panchen Lama.

In 1900, British police questioned Das about a mysterious Buriat and a Kalmyk who had recently visited Ghoom. The monks were guests of the Mongolian abbot, Sherab Gyatso. Like Das and Ugyen Gyatso, the abbot was a British agent, and like them received 55 rupees a month for supplying information on suspicious visitors. In their responses, all three agents were "economical with the truth." The Buriat was Agvan Dorzhiev, then one of seven teachers of the Thirteenth Dalai Lama, and the Kalmyk was his companion, Ovshe Norzunov.

Dorzhiev was not someone easily lost in a crowd; he had the manner of command and a calm but determined gaze. Born of devout parents in remote Buriatia, schooled in a local *datsan* or Buddhist monastery, Dorzhiev early on showed a facility for languages, especially Tibetan, the difficult *lingua franca* of lamaism. At fourteen he set off for Urga, the Mongolian capital, to continue his studies, and five years later traveled to Tibet with his tutor, the Great Abbot Penden Chomphel, just possibly, as Andreyev speculates, at the behest of the Russian General Staff.

In a memoir written around 1924, Dorzhiev asserts that he set off for Tibet, via Alasha, Kumbum, and Koko Nor, together with the Mongolian princes and lamas, dispatched to accompany there the eighth reincarnation of the Urga Khutuku, the Grand Lama of Mongolia. Dorzhiev wished to remain in Lhasa but was refused permission on the grounds he was a prohibited "foreign European." Unfazed and persistent, he appealed his case, and eventually was permitted, in 1880, to enroll in one of the seminaries at Drepung, the largest Tibetan monastery, where he earned the Buddhist equivalent of a doctorate of metaphysics. So completely did Dorzhiev dispel suspicion that after the enthronement of the Thirteenth Dalai Lama he joined the inner curia, initially as the Work Washing Abbot, whose duty it was to sprinkle saffron-scented water on His Holiness. So taken was the young pontiff with Dorzhiev that when the Thirteenth attained his majority in 1895, the outsider from Siberia became his chief political adviser.

Nga-Wang Lopsang Tupden (Thupten) Gyatso (1876–1933), the Great Thirteenth Dalai Lama, was the first Incarnation in more than a century who actually ruled. His four predecessors passed away before coming of age, their demise reputedly assisted by their Regents, a circumstance not unwelcome to the Ambans, the representatives of China in Lhasa, who preferred childish god-kings. The Thirteenth survived, having taken the precaution of putting his own Regent under house arrest, and his reign lasted almost four decades. He strove to end Tibet's Chinese bondage and did win de facto independence though not recognized statehood. "His courage and energy were inexhaustible," writes his friend and biographer, Sir Charles Bell. "He recoiled from nothing."

The search for the Thirteenth followed the usual practice. When a Dalai Lama "retires to the heavenly fields," the oracles at Nechung and Samye provide clues to the whereabouts of the next incarnation or *tulku*. A council of lamas carries out the search. To prevent powerful nobles from adding to their privileges, the Dalai Lama was customarily chosen from a peasant family. Besides the appropriate physical signs, like long ears and tiger skin marks on his legs, the candidate must recognize the possessions of his predecessor, such as the *dorje,* a ritual object shaped like a dumbbell, connoting the thunderbolt of the Hindu god Indra. When high lamas verified that the spirit of the Twelfth had passed into the three-year-old Thirteenth, the news was transmitted to Peking and after his confirmation by the Manchu Emperor, the young boy was ceremoniously enthroned.

During the Dalai Lama's minority, a Regent, himself a *tulku*, was chosen by a National Assembly, composed primarily of monks, and the Kashag, or cabinet, consisting of three laymen and one monk, nearly all from noble families. But real power lay with the monasteries and their puissant abbots. As much as a third of the male population joined Buddhist orders, and of these as many as fifteen percent were "fighting monks," armed and rebellious. When they descended on Lhasa and terrorized the populace, they had to be quelled by the Dalai Lama's own troops. Nor did they eschew politics. The enormous monasteries nearest Lhasa, Drepung, Sera, and Ganden, were particularly troublesome. The Chinese, realizing their power, sought monastic support by lavishing quantities of "presents." Complicating matters was the role of the Chinese Resident or Amban, who took sides in internal politics.

At the center of this labyrinth, ensconced in the immense Potala, was the Dalai Lama, plus his parents and siblings, newly ennobled and frequently meddlesome. Tibet in 1895 was an outlying province of a crumbling Chinese Empire, whose Manchu rulers had been humiliated only that year in a disastrous war with Japan. Peking was too weak, too corrupt, and too remote to defend Tibet against "the powerful elephants from the south," the British. For their part, the British were frustrated in their negotiations with Peking and Lhasa. In 1885, the British obtained Chinese permission to send a mission from India to Tibet, only to have the project vetoed by Lhasa. As compensation, Peking was obliged to recognize British annexation of Upper Burma. This followed a clash concerning the ill-defined status and frontiers of Sikkim, over which China and Tibet both claimed authority. To enforce their own claims, the British destroyed a frontier fort and routed a Tibetan force, causing the Amban to proceed to the disputed border and negotiate directly with the Indian Foreign Secretary. The resulting 1890 treaty defined a border, acknowledged British control of Sikkim, and provided for opening a British trade mart within Tibet. Yet when the Government of India tried to open that mart, Tibetans objected, insisting China had no right to negotiate in their name. Protests caromed from Lhasa to Peking, and exasperated British officials suspected that China covertly encouraged Tibetan obduracy.

Such was the setting when Dorzhiev advised the youthful Dalai Lama to seek the protection of the White Tsar.* The Buriat played

---

*The Russians carefully cultivated the belief that the Tsar was the "tsagan" or "White Khan," the heir to Ghengis Khan. What we know as the Golden Horde was actually called the White Horde by the Russians, thus the appellation "White Tsar."

skillfully on the fears of his monastic brethren, who had been warned by the Chinese that the British wished to abolish lamaism, and who feared the trade mart would open the way for missionaries. In his memoir, Dorzhiev recalls the advice he gave to Tibetan high lamas. When the question of seeking help from foreign Christians arose, he said, "because Russia is the enemy of Great Britain, she will come to the assistance of the Land of Snows to prevent her being devoured." Under the White Tsar's tolerant rule, he maintained, "the pure teachings of the Buddha flourished among the Torgut [Kalmyks] and the Buriats." He reminded them that the Tsarevich passed through Buriatia on his Asian Grand Tour, bestowing favors on its inhabitants. Dorzhiev cited the legend of Shambhala, which he located somewhere in Russia, and explained that Nicholas II was also an incarnation. "Such a Bodhisattva-tsar," he said, "could also bestow favors on Tibet." As if to confirm Dorzhiev's prescience, in 1890 a French expedition led by the Central Asian explorer Gabriel Bonvalot and the Duc de Chartres's eldest son, Prince Henry of Orléans, appeared on Tibet's borders. Stopped north of Lhasa by Tibetan officials, the Chinese Amban, and an armed escort, the Prince (according to Dorzhiev's memoir) urged Tibetans to befriend the French and Russians, "the strongest powers in the world," who had recently become allies. This coincided with the statement by the omniscient Nechung Oracle that spoke of a prince: "An emanation of a Bodhisattva [seemingly d'Orléans but possibly the Tsar] is in the North and East." The oracle also pointedly repeated a pungent proverb, "Even dog fat can be good for a wound."

It was therefore determined that Dorzhiev should go to Russia, a momentous decision since no Dalai Lama had ever appealed to foreign Christians. Even if he failed to obtain the White Tsar's help, the Lhasa authorities reasoned, Dorzhiev could call attention to Tibet's plight. In 1898, wearing the thumb-ring of the Nechung Oracle for good luck, Dorzhiev and two companions set out for St. Petersburg via India. He traveled as a Mongol claiming Chinese citizenship, using a passport provided by the Amban in Lhasa. When the party was challenged by a suspicious Tibetan border guard, a bribe and three prostrations eased its passage. When stopped by British police at the Indian frontier, Dorzhiev showed his Chinese passport, persuading them that although he was Mongolian, he was a Chinese citizen who had "decided to return to his homeland by the easier sea route." Finally, after pausing near Darjeeling, the party boarded a train bound for Calcutta.

Buddhism originated in India, and the pilgrims visited Bodhgaya in Bihar, where Buddha attained enlightenment while sitting under the Bodhi tree. From Calcutta, they continued by sea to Peking. Finally, on reaching his old home in Buriatia, Dorzhiev received the essential letter from Prince Esper Ukhtomsky (1861–1921) inviting him to St. Petersburg.

Prince Ukhtomsky was the logical intermediary. He had spent most of 1886 studying "the Lamaist question," reporting on conflicts between the proselytizing Orthodox missionaries and the Buriats. Traveling incognito, he visited the Buriats and their *datsans*, and conferred with their clergy in Urga and Peking. Unlike Przhevalsky, the apostle of the carbine and whip, Ukhtomsky did not belittle Asian cultures, and instead approached Buddhism and Islam with sympathetic curiosity. As to missionaries, the Prince ventured the skeptical notion that their conversions were often the result of bribes.

Ukhtomsky himself leaned to the mystical, and as a student of Theosophy, the occult, and esoteric Buddhism, he was increasingly drawn to the "luminous realms" of Asia "where hatreds and the fraternal quarrels among nations dissolve before the divine power." He believed fervently, as Schimmelpenninck van der Oye has documented, that the Buriats were a central element of Russian policy in the East. "Trans-Baikalia is the key to the heart of Asia, the vanguard of Russian civilization on the frontier of the 'Yellow Orient,'" he remarked. Thousands of lamaists made annual pilgrimages to Mongolia and Tibet, bringing into "this Asiatic wilderness" ideas of the White Tsar, and these non-Slavs would be drawn to the giant Russian Empire "not by cruelty but by kindness."

In 1895 Ukhtomsky found a new platform as editor of the *St. Petersburg News*, and in its columns he published his most celebrated sentence, seized upon ever since by Russophobes: "Properly speaking, in Asia we have not, nor can we have, any bounds, except the boundless sea breaking on her shores." Since Russia was on a "higher spiritual plane" than Britain, the Prince felt, there was no need to emulate its crude brand of imperialism, which was merely a cover for commercial exploitation. Russia had no reason to employ force since "it could depend mainly on benevolence to fulfill its manifest destiny." All of this was divinely ordained, and would occur through "some process of natural fusion." He criticized British India for its "exotic mushroom universities and expensive administrative reforms carried out with all the blind energy of self-sufficient ignorance," and scoffed at the irony lurking "in such cheap catchwords as 'native congresses,' 'a free native press,' 'the right of natives to be citizens of a great colonial empire.'" Russia offered the antidote to the evils of Western imperialism: the more the East was exploited, "the brighter becomes the name of the White Tsar." Largely forgotten today, his editorials were viewed in London, Berlin, and Paris as litmus words on Russia's Far Eastern policies.

WORKING WITH PRINCE UKHTOMSKY WAS AN EQUALLY INTEREST- ing figure, Zhamsaran (Pyotr Aleksandrovich) Badmaev (1851– 1919). A fashionable practitioner of Tibetan medicine and an adviser on Mongolian affairs to the Russian Foreign Ministry, he was also the most influential Buriat in St. Petersburg. When Badmaev con- verted to Orthodox Christianity, none other than Alexander III acted as his godfather at the ceremony. Yet it was his Tibetan medi- cine that won him access to the Romanov court. In his laboratory he prepared an entire pharmacopoeia of alchemic remedies, "infu- sions of asoka flowers," "Nienchen balsam," "black lotus essence," "nikrik powder," and the "Tibetan elixir of life," which he pre- scribed for Petersburg's upper classes. Eventually, he would be sum- moned to treat the hemophiliac Romanov heir, Alexis. It was also whispered that he successfully treated the Tsar for a stomach ailment with a mixture of henbane and hashish—"the effects of which were marvelous." Although some thought his presence sinister, according to James Webb, an historian of the occult, Badmaev "stood head and shoulders above the crowd of magi and holy fools who clamored around the steps of the throne."

Among those seeking his herbal pills and potions was the Finance Minister, Sergei Witte (1849–1915). The prime architect of Russia's forward policy in East Asia and godfather of the Trans-Siberian Railway, Witte wrote approvingly in his memoirs of Badmaev's plan to construct a 3,500-mile spur to the already overlong railroad. Although Alexander III was skeptical about the project, dismissing it as "all so new, strange, and fantastic," Witte's enthusiasm swayed the Government. In 1893, it advanced two million rubles to P. A. Badmaev and Co. to extend the railway from Irkutsk on Lake Baikal to the Chinese city of Lanzhou across the Gobi Desert. Ostensibly, the new line would help expand Russian trade in Central Asia.

The deeper motive was to provide a commercial cover for thousands of Buriat infiltrators who then could foment a pro-Russian revolt against the Manchu Dynasty. The resulting territorial gains would make possible a Pan-Buddhist confederacy in Central Asia under the White Tsar. Count Witte, then the dominant figure in Russian politics, supported the plan, which comported with his own grand design: "From the shores of the Pacific and the heights of the Himalayas, Russia would dominate not only the affairs of Asia but those of Europe as well." Or, as he put it in a confidential note to Nicholas II: "Given our enormous frontier with China and our exceptionally favorable situation, the absorption by Russia of a considerable part of the Chinese Empire is only a matter of time."

When Badmaev became aware of his compatriot Dorzhiev's influence in Lhasa, he was quick to sense new opportunities for employing Buriats and Kalmyks. "I am training young men in two capitals—Peking and Petersburg—for further activities," Badmaev informed the Tsar. By 1895, Tibetan reluctance to entertain foreign Buddhists had been somewhat overcome, and Badmaev's Buriat emissaries were apparently entertained in Lhasa by none other than Dorzhiev himself. The intelligence they gathered was so highly regarded that Nicholas II bestowed gold medals on two of Badmaev's Buriat agents, Ochir Jigjitov and Dugar Vanchinov. In appreciation for his hospitality, Dorzhiev received a gold watch inscribed with the imperial monogram, which he collected on his visit to Buriatia in 1898.

The most successful of Badmaev's protégés was Gombodjab Tsybikov (1873–1930), a leading member of the Buriat intelligentsia and a teacher at the Oriental Institute in Vladivostok. Tsybikov was at one level a Russian agent, but like Dorzhiev, as the historian Robert Rupen points out, in working for a Greater Mongolian State he was also a nationalist who later came into conflict with Soviet authorities. In a mission for the Imperial Geographical Society, Tsybikov succeeded in entering Tibet from Amdo traveling as a Buddhist pilgrim. In 1900–1901, he visited not only Lhasa but a number of monasteries. Using his camera surreptitiously, he returned to Russia with a portfolio of photographs, including some of the earliest of Lhasa, along with a bundle of Tibetan texts, earning him the Geographical Society's Przhevalsky Medal. He also provided notes on Tibet's government and population, the size of the standing army and the Chinese garrison, the practice of polygamy and polyandry, and the independent position of women.

As to Badmaev's ambitious railway scheme, nothing came of it save for the loss of the two million rubles advanced to his company. Nonetheless, Badmaev retained his mansion on the Vyborg road and his position at court, where he advised the Tsar not only on medical matters but on politics. Rasputin's biographer, René Fülöp-Miller, asserts that Badmaev's files combined medical and encoded political data. In any case, before his death in 1919, the obscure Buriat doctor transformed a small Tibetan pharmacy into a great sanitarium, and spawned a homeopathic dynasty whose cures are today available on the Internet.

HAVING PROMOTED BADMAEV AT COURT, UKHTOMSKY NOW BEcame Dorzhiev's principal sponsor. Through the Prince's mediation, the lama appears to have met with the Tsar at Peterhof, his palace on the Gulf of Finland. By this time, the once shy and sensitive Tsarevich was the Autocrat of All Russia. Yet after reigning four years, Nicholas still disdained politics, hated confrontation, and had difficulty asserting himself. He was bullied by his uncles and, as his Empire veered from crisis to crisis, browbeaten by his wife, the Tsarina Alexandra Feodorovna. His cousin, Grand Duke Alexander Mikailovich, recalls in his memoirs that the slightly undersized Nicholas dreaded being alone with his outsized uncles: "the instant the door of his study closed to outsiders—down on the table would go with a bang the weighty fist of Uncle Alexis…two hundred and fifty pounds…packed in the resplendent uniform of Grand Admiral of the Fleet…Uncle Serge and Uncle Vladimir developed equally efficient methods of intimidation…They all had their favorite generals and admirals…their ballerinas desirous of organizing a 'Russian season' in Paris; their wonderful preachers anxious to redeem the Emperor's soul…their clairvoyant peasants with a divine message." The Tsar's irresolution caused his War Minister, General Vannovsky, to lament that he "takes counsel from everyone: with grandparents, aunts, mummy and anyone else; he is young and accedes to the view of the last person to whom he talks." Still, it should be noted that Witte, who preferred Alexander to his son, asserts in *his* memoirs that Nicholas "has a quick mind and learns easily. In this respect he is far superior to his father."

Into these murky waters waded the emissary of the Dalai Lama. No official account of the lama's audience with the White Tsar has turned up—the Russian archives are silent on the matter so we have only Dorzhiev's own recollection: "When I talked with him [Nicholas II] about Tibet, he told me how Russia would help Tibet not to be lost to enemy hands." When the Tsar consulted with his Foreign Minister, Count Lamsdorff, his War Minister, General Kuropatkin, and his Finance Minister, Witte, they suggested through Ukhtomsky that a Russian official be sent to Lhasa. Dorzhiev replied: "Definitely do not send a European. The nobles, ministers, ordinary monks and lay people have made an oath not to allow them. For the moment, there is no way to send anyone." If the Tibetans allowed Russians in Lhasa, other Europeans would not be far behind. Dorzhiev relates that "this made him [the Tsar] a little displeased." As to Russian help in countering the British and Chinese, the Tsar asked "to receive the request officially in written form" from the Dalai Lama. On both sides, the meeting fell short of expectations, but a dialogue had opened between Lhasa and St. Petersburg.

From St. Petersburg, Dorzhiev traveled south to the lower Volga, where he sought to renew and strengthen ties between the geographically separated Kalmyk and Central Asian Buddhists. There he met Ovshe Muchkinovich Norzunov (born ca. 1874), whom we have met as the other invisible guest at Ghoom monastery. An educated Kalmyk from the province of Stavropol, Norzunov was to become Dorzhiev's steadfast lieutenant.

Dorzhiev continued his "*sondage politique*," traveling to Paris in quest of further allies. His Russian friends introduced him to the anthropologist and Buddhist scholar Joseph Deniker, and through the professor he met a number of French notables interested in Buddhism, including Georges Clemenceau and (it would appear) Alexandra David-Neel, a devotée who by sheer grit later made her way to Lhasa. At the Musée Guimet, Dorzhiev conducted a lamaist ceremony, which was translated by Buddha Rabdanov, an eminent Buriat—and recorded on wax cylinders. While in Paris, Dorzhiev purchased a phonograph and cylinders, as well as photographic equipment.

On his return to Russia, Dorzhiev was reunited with Norzunov, who, it was now agreed, would attempt a pilgrimage to Lhasa. The two traveled to Urga, Mongolia's capital, then separated as the Kalmyk headed toward Tibet. Norzunov passed as a Mongolian pilgrim until his caravan crossed the Gobi, when, after being halted by Kurluk Mongols, he was discovered to be a Russian. His accent and the European jacket beneath his fur garment gave him away. A bribe sufficed to satisfy the Kurluks, who guided him part of the way to Nagchu, where he eluded the Tibetan border guards who had earlier blocked Przhevalsky. Braving March gales, Norzunov arrived safely in Lhasa and there presented the Dalai Lama with a letter from Dorzhiev "describing in detail the greatness of the Russian people, the critical situation of China and expressing the opinion that the connection with Russia promises a great future for Tibet."

After six weeks in Lhasa, Norzunov headed home, following the favored route through Darjeeling, Calcutta, Peking, and Urga, arriving in Russia in August 1899. He bore an urgent summons to

Dorzhiev to return as soon as possible to Lhasa, where the emissary was received by the Dalai Lama "with trust and charity." At the Great Lhasa Chanting ceremony, tens of thousands witnessed Dorzhiev's presentation to the Dalai Lama of diamonds, silks, and silver ingots cast as horseshoes, some of them gifts of the White Tsar. Dorzhiev wisely took care to provide the monasteries with their portion of Russian largesse.

Even so, the Buriat's successes, and his new rank as Senior Abbot, provoked murmurs of envy and displeasure. According to Deniker, some were scandalized by a photograph of Dorzhiev with a Russian lady. He was forced to destroy the photographic equipment—considered demonic by the monks—that he had brought from Paris. In the pontiff's court, according to Dorzhiev's memoirs, dissension had become open and bitter:

> In those times, the influential people of Tibet had these things to say about politics. Some thought, "Since the kindness of the Manchu Emperor has been so great, he will not forget about us even now. Therefore, we should not divorce ourselves from China." Others said, "The Chinese government will collapse before long. Therefore, so long as we have no agreements with the enemies [the British] nearby, we will certainly be conquered. So it would be good if we had close relations with them." Still others said, "The Russians, being very rich and powerful, we would not fall into the enemy hands. Also, since they are far away, they could not devour us. But for just that same reason, it is difficult to work with them."

In St. Petersburg, meanwhile, Norzunov accepted a commission from the Imperial Geographical Society to photograph Tibet with a camera it provided him. He very probably met with the Tsar. A note from Ukhtomsky to Nicholas II asked him to receive two Kalmyks, one being Norzunov. "You know how I love Buriats," remarked the ever-hopeful Prince, "but Kalmyks are closer and more akin to us on account of their martial character and other virtues. We have not yet had the last word on the awakening of Central Asia."

In January 1900 Norzunov stopped in Paris, where at Dorzhiev's request, he took delivery of four crates of steel begging bowls that had been ordered to replace an earlier shipment lost when a coracle capsized in a Tibetan river. On his departure from Marseilles on the steamer *Dupleix*, he took aboard one of the crates; the remaining three were to follow on another ship. He arrived in Calcutta that March with a passport from General Nipi Khoraki, the Governor of Stavropol, and a letter of introduction to the French Consul. Concealing his identity, Norzunov registered at the Continental Hotel as Myanoheid Hopityant, an employee of Stavropol's Post and Telegraph Department.

His troubles began when British customs discovered he was carrying a .45 caliber sporting rifle, and confiscated it. Tipped off by a Russian-speaking Briton that he was about to be arrested, Norzunov panicked. He decamped for Darjeeling by train. In spite of his Chinese disguise, he was spotted and placed under house arrest at Ghoom monastery by the Deputy Police Commissioner for Darjeeling. Police records describe him as about 5 feet 10 inches tall, "broad and well built, head now shaved, Mongolian features, slight moustache twisted down Chinese fashion, medium complexion." His age was given as twenty-six. He at first told his interrogators he was a trader from Peking taking the less arduous route to Lhasa. Later he altered his story: he was a Khalkha Mongolian named Obishak. Under further questioning, he finally admitted he had come from Marseilles by way of Calcutta.

From Ghoom, Norzunov managed to get word of his plight to Dorzhiev, who was then about to depart for Russia. Cool as Macavity, Dorzhiev arrived in May at Ghoom as Abbot Sherab Gyatso's guest, carrying a document certifying that Norzunov was a Buddhist who had already made a pilgrimage to Lhasa. When his document failed to impress the British, Dorzhiev felt he had had no choice but to continue his own travels.

A police escort took Norzunov to Calcutta and placed him under arrest. During his detention, Thomas Cook & Son cleared up the matter of the crates of begging bowls that had been impounded, along with the rest of Norzunov's luggage. They forwarded 590 metal bowls, two phonographs, and a camera to Lhasa. Norzunov was expelled from India aboard the *Dupleix* to Odessa, "on the ground that it is undesirable that a Mongolian or quasi-Russian adventurer with several aliases should trade with Tibet through British India." In a final interrogation, Norzunov produced a letter of recommendation from Prince Ukhtomsky, on the stationery of the Imperial Russian Geographical Society, describing him as a member "undertaking a journey to Tibet on a pilgrimage and in the interests of commerce and science." Norzunov now acknowledged his travel expenses had been paid for by a rich Chinese Mongolian lama from Urga named "Akchwan Darjilicoff" who had studied in Lhasa before visiting Europe. The same rich lama had ordered the steel bowls in Paris from J. Deniker and Cie. He was merely the courier.

Two months after his expulsion, the indefatigble Norzunov was again on his way to Tibet, which he reached in winter 1901. While in Lhasa, he took the photographs commissioned by the Geographical Society. They were published along with an introduction by the American diplomat William W. Rockhill in *The Century* magazine in 1903.

"DARJILICOFF'S" NAME MEANT NOTHING TO NORZUNOV'S IN-terrogators and it would appear that neither the Abbot of Ghoom nor Das volunteered further reports on the matter. (It was their silence that earned Sherab Gyatso, Ugyen Gyatso, and Sarat Chandra Das their probably unwarranted reputation as double agents.) The real Dorzhiev, having thwarted his would-be captors, made his way by sea to China, where he witnessed the Boxer Rebellion. He recorded his impression of a Boxer massacre at the Chinese city of Aigun on the Amur River: "Those who killed everyone and burned the city down without leaving a trace may have been men, but their brutality was greater than that of tigers and leopards." Finding Peking besieged by Chinese rebels, he proceeded to Japan, then to Vladivostok, and traveled by train and steamer to St. Petersburg, only to learn that his patron, Prince Ukhtomsky, had just been dispatched to Peking. To break the tedium of waiting for a royal audience, Dorzhiev revisited Paris, and ordered more begging-bowls.

Eventually, Dorzhiev, armed with a letter from the Dalai Lama, met with Tsar Nicholas on September 30, 1900, at Livadia, the Tsar's palace at the Crimean resort of Yalta. This time the audience was reported in the columns of the *Journal de Saint-Petersbourg*. Having witnessed the Boxer massacres in China, the lama was now convinced that the intrusion of Europeans and their missionaries in Asia could have catastrophic results. As described by the Russian Foreign Ministry, the purpose of this mission was to seek "the intercession of Russia for Tibet, which is menaced...by England, mainly from Nepal." There was the ritual exchange of presents, but otherwise the White Tsar proffered little. Dorzhiev made better headway with the Minister of War, General Kuropatkin, who promised the Tibetans the "cannons of the latest make" which the Russians had captured during the Boxer Rebellion. All this Dorzhiev reported on his return to Lhasa, where he presented the Dalai Lama with the Tsar's gifts, a gold watch studded with diamonds, and a "gorgeous set of clerical vestments."

In 1901 Dorzhiev and Norzunov were again on the move, passing through Nepal en route to Petersburg. According to a British intelligence report, Dorzhiev's abrupt departure from Lhasa was prompted by the Chinese Amban, who, angered by his unauthorized diplomatic negotiations, issued a warrant for his arrest. In Katmandu, Dorzhiev visited monasteries and made offerings of powdered gold and saffron at the great Bodh–Nath stupa. In a boastful moment, he showed the chief lama the inscribed watch worth 300 rupees given him by the Russians—an episode promptly reported to the British. At the Nepalese border, British guards searched his luggage but failed to find the gifts he was carrying from the Panchen Lama, or the letters from the Dalai Lama intended for the Tsar. Nor did border officials discover Norzunov's Russian passport, which he had hidden in the sole of a boot, or the films tucked in a small box inside his trousers. In Colombo, with the assistance of the Russian consulate, the party of six embarked without incident on the Russian liner *Tambov* on June 12, 1901, bound for Odessa.

There Dorzhiev and his party were accorded a rousing welcome, complete with roses, blaring music, and crackling fireworks. The

Russian press described the group as "Extraordinary Envoys of the Dalai Lama of Tibet." The British Consul General, in a hastily cabled report, remarked that when the Grand Lama's mission disembarked, "they were met with real Russian cordiality, with bread and salt on a gold-plated tray," all of which "produced a deep and pleasant impression on the Lamas." As much pomp surrounded Dorzhiev's audience with the Tsar at Peterhof. The Dalai Lama's letter, written in Tibetan with a copy in Mongolian, was resoundingly firm: "The Buddhist faith of the Tibetan people is threatened by enemies and oppressors from abroad—the English. Be so kind as to instruct my ambassadors how they may be reassured about their pernicious and foul activities." The Tibetan pontiff made no specific requests for assistance, but rather expressed a hope for protection. A passage suggesting Dorzhiev's influence asserts: "Your Majesty does not reject people who confess different religions...and especially expresses solicitude towards the Buddhist Kalmyks and Buriats."

In a careful response, Nicholas was noncommittal. His Majesty expressed pleasure "about your wish to establish regular connections between the Russian State and Tibet" and ventured the hope that "given the friendly and fully well-disposed attitude of Russia, no danger will threaten Tibet in her fortune hereafter."

Besides meeting with the Tsar, Dorzhiev conferred with Finance Minister Witte, War Minister Kuropatkin, and Foreign Minister Lamsdorff. When asked if St. Petersburg might open diplomatic relations with Tibet, Dorzhiev responded that if the Russians allowed a consulate in Lhasa, the British would want representation as well. The Dalai Lama's emissary suggested instead that Russians could open a consulate just across the Chinese-Tibetan border, with Buddha Rabdanov as consul. With its advantageous location and a telegraph connection to Lhasa, the consulate could promptly pass news from Tibet to the Russian Foreign Ministry. Authorized the following year, the consulate was opened at Ganding in Szechuan, in autumn 1903.

As before, Dorzhiev returned to Lhasa laden with gifts and, according to his memoir, "documents written in solid gold letters stating the relations between Russia and Tibet." But this was not a treaty. The Buriat's missions had not achieved Lhasa's overriding objective, a formal alliance in which Russia would agree to protect the Tibetans. In his invaluable recollections, published in 1926, the Russian diplomat Ivan Yakobevich Korostovets provides a sense of the lama's negotiating style: "Dorzhiev spoke with marked authority and expertise, and mightily pleased the Tsar, in spite of his fantastic plans, which were not to be realized and which implied a Russian advance across the Himalayas in order to liberate the oppressed people...He behaved in a very modest way yet demanded respect, while at the same time he was mysteriously anxious to avoid attracting the attention of the English to his mission."

Aside from specialized academic works, little attention has been paid by biographers to Nicholas II's obsession with the East. Following his Asian Grand Tour in the company of Ukhtomsky, the Tsarevich consented in 1893 to serve as chairman of the Siberian Railway Committee, a major Witte project. Indeed, his support for Witte's ambitious schemes contributed to the ill-starred Russo-Japanese War of 1904–5, which in turn contributed to the Finance Minister's downfall. Many of the Tsar's advisers justifiably complained that Russia's limited resources were squandered in Asia. The War Minister, General Kuropatkin, noted with alarm in his diary entry for September 22, 1899: "The Emperor is restless on foreign policy matters. I consider one of the sovereign's more dangerous character traits to be his love for mysterious lands and individuals such as the Buriat Badmaev and Prince Ukhtomsky. They inspire him with fantasies about the Russian Tsar's greatness as ruler over all Asia. The Emperor is drawn to Tibet and similar places. This is all very worrisome, and I shudder about the harm these delusions may cause to Russia."

In March 1903, Kuropatkin communicated his fears to the Finance Minister: "I told Witte that our sovereign has grandiose plans in his head: to absorb Manchuria into Russia, to begin the annexation of Korea. He also dreams of taking Tibet under his orb. He wants to rule Persia, to seize both the Bosphorus and the Dardanelles."

Despite Witte's successes as Finance Minister—during his ten-year tenure, the revenues of the empire nearly doubled—he was brought down in 1906 after Russia's military debacle in the East, his demise hastened by the intrigues of his rivals. Witte was demoted to the purely ceremonial post of President of the Committee of Ministers. As his stock declined, so did Ukhtomsky's. Yet if Dorzhiev failed to obtain the wholehearted support for Tibet he sought from the Russians, his missions played to the worst fears of Lord Curzon, the Viceroy of India, who was rarely half-hearted about anything.

CHAPTER TWELVE

.:.

Curzon's Hour

GEORGE NATHANIEL CURZON WAS NOT YET FORTY WHEN HE was named Viceroy of India, and his lovely Vicereine, *née* Mary Leiter of Chicago, was not quite thirty when they sailed eastward on the P & O liner *Arabia*. Their arrival at Bombay on December 30, 1898, was Curzon's noontide. No Viceroy had more ardently sought the position, none was better prepared, and certainly none had seen more of what everybody then called the Orient. Not merely India and China, not just Japan, Siam, and Korea, but also Bokhara and Samarkand, the shores of the Caspian, the "singing sands" of the Sinai, the long-inaccessible Great Mosque of Kairwan in the Sahara, the throne of the Afghans in Kabul—all this Curzon had seen. His two-volume *Persia and the Persian Question* (1892), for which he had worn out horses, boots, and guides, immediately became the standard authority. When his *Pamirs and the Source of the Oxus* (1896) won a gold medal from the Royal Geographical Society, Curzon confessed the honor gave him greater pleasure "than it did to become a Minister of the Crown."

Curzon's tireless voyages were the more impressive considering his disability, a curvature of the spine that tormented him until his death in 1925. Pain was chronic, and contributed to a peevish sarcasm that so hindered his political career. The steel corset that encased his frame, writes Harold Nicolson, "gave to his figure an aspect of unbending perpendicular, affecting also the motions of his mind: there was no middle path for him between rigidity and collapse." For Curzon, everything came down to a reasoned application of a focused will. In demanding too much of himself, he too often vented scorn on the less efficient, the less driven. "Try to suffer fools more gladly," gently remonstrated his friend and putative superior, Lord George Hamilton, the Secretary of State for India in London, "they constitute the majority of mankind."

Curzon belonged to the privileged minority, and he knew it. His forebears crossed the Channel with William the Conqueror and thereafter pursued with more tenacity than distinction the family motto, "Let Curzon holde what Curzon helde." For eight centuries, the Curzons kept tenure of their estates in Derbyshire, 10,000 acres, and for generations sent a succession of Members to Parliament, most of them lackluster backbenchers. Their one indisputable achievement was construction of a Palladian masterpiece, Kedleston, whose noble exterior and majestic rooms were completed felicitously by Robert Adam. Here Curzon was born in 1859, the eldest son of the fourth Baron Scarsdale, a clergyman and, like many upper-class fathers, a nonchalant parent.

Young George, his two brothers, and six sisters were left mostly in the care of a stern governess, Miss Paraman, who succumbed to "paroxysms of ferocity" while dealing with her charges. She insisted (to quote Nicolson again) on "obedience, success and the more detailed forms of religion." The lessons of discipline stuck, but the unjust punishments he suffered bred in Curzon a combative spirit, redeemed by his quickness of mind and (when he wished) personal charm. In 1872, he entered Eton, where he won every academic prize, proved a rebellious trial to his masters, developed the curvature of his spine, suffered the loss (at sixteen) of a caring mother, and fell under the spell of the Indian Empire.

By his own account, that epiphany occurred during a spirited address to the Eton Literary Society by Sir James Fitzjames Stephen, friend and adviser to Viceroy Lytton, a despiser of liberal soppiness, and uncle of the yet-unborn Virginia Woolf. Stephen said (as Curzon recalled) "that there was in the Asian continent an empire more populous, more amazing, and more beneficent than that of Rome; that the rulers of that great dominion were drawn from the men of our own people; that some of them might perhaps in the future be taken from the ranks of boys who were listening to his words." The seeds thus planted germinated at Oxford and flowered during a visit to India in 1887, when "the fascination and, if I may say so, the sacredness of India" persuaded Curzon that there was no higher honor than serving at that altar. He had found a vocation, in much the same spirit that others turn to cloth and cowl.

WHEN CURZON WENT UP TO BALLIOL COLLEGE, OXFORD, IN 1878, he was already dubbed The Coming Man. "Everyone remarked his present eminence and predicted his future fame," recalled his near contemporary Winston Churchill. At Oxford too he seemed to waltz to the summit, becoming president of the debating society, the Oxford Union; dominating the Conservative society, the Canning Club; turning out prize-winning essays on recondite themes. Only once did his ability to cram fail him, when he gained only a Second Class rather than the all-important First in his final examination. "Now I shall devote the rest of my life to showing the examiners have made a mistake," the embarrassed paragon remarked. He compensated by winning the most coveted Oxford fellowship, to All Souls.

Still, Curzon's precocity was too amply evident. Of his speaking style, a Balliol colleague said, "He spoke copiously, even long, was more inclined to overpower than to persuade, and in repartee or sarcasm was apt to be too heavy handed." His non-admirers had their revenge in the "accursed doggerel" that followed him past the grave. In lines for a student masque, ascribed to his schoolmates J. D. Mackail and Cecil Spring Rice (later boon companion to Theodore Roosevelt), his overbearing manner was rendered thus:

My name is George Nathaniel Curzon,
I am a most superior person,
My cheek is pink, my hair is sleek,
I dine at Blenheim once a week.

Not entirely fair or accurate: the private Curzon was self-depreca-tory, relished telling jokes against himself, and sought out unconven-tional and witty friends, one being his classmate Oscar Wilde. "You are a brick," Wilde wrote Curzon after the latter had defended the former in an undergraduate contretemps. "Our sweet city with its dreaming towers must not be given entirely over to the philistines." Curzon never shied from jousts across political fences, though his lance could be sharp. On joining a club (the Crabbet) founded by the rakish anti-imperialist Wilfred Scawen Blunt, he once with a bland smile addressed his host: "My dear Wilfred, your poetry is de-lightful and your morals, though deplorable, enchanting. But why are you a traitor to your country?" (Subsequently Curzon won the club's laureate award, with a poem in praise of sin.)

Curzon's airs were superior, but not joyless. Still, on one root ques-tion he was invariably earnest. The British Empire, he believed, was "the greatest instrument for good that the world has seen." More-over, the noble work of governing India was "placed by the in-scrutable decrees of Providence upon the shoulders of the British race." At Oxford, this claim of divine stewardship was linked to clas-sical Greece and the teachings of Plato by the eminent theologian and professor of Greek, Benjamin Jowett, the Master of Balliol and one of the moral legislators of Victorian England.

Under Jowett, Balliol became Oxford's intellectual flagship, and his owlish countenance was among the monuments that important vis-itors all wished to see. He cultivated the influential, and kept a note-book listing the names of acquaintances likely to help his college or its students, his mission being "to inoculate England with Balliol." A bachelor with a grumpy distaste for small talk, "The Jowler" was eas-ier to admire than like. His cutting remarks instantly circulated, such as his tart summary of a colleague's windy sermon: "All that I could make out was that today was yesterday, and this world the same as the next." Or as he remarked to Margot Asquith, wife of the soon-to-be Prime Minister (also of Balliol): "My dear child, you must believe in God in spite of what the clergy tell you."

Jowett had a particular interest in India; his two brothers had served and died there. Like other eminent Britons before and afterwards, he tended to see the subcontinent as a blackboard on which new theories could be chalked and analyzed. He belonged to a tradition that began with Benthamites ("the greatest happiness for the greatest number"), Christian evangelicals, and reformers like Lord Macaulay and Sir Charles Trevelyan. Liberals and conservatives alike assumed that Western education was the key to raising native peoples from sloth and ignorance. To this Jowett added a practical corollary: that the Indian Civil Service could provide India with a governing elite that was disinterested and benevolent, in the fashion of the Guardians in Plato's *Republic* (which Jowett translated). These Guardians were to be generalists, their minds honed by Greek and Latin, though Jowett also saw merit in studying Sanskrit, Vernacular Indian History, Economics, Land Tenure, and Religions—all courses at the School of Oriental Studies inaugurated by the university in 1883. The best university men, some of them Indian, were to be chosen through rigorous tests, which as a member of the Committee on Examinations, Jowett helped prepare.

Jowett once confided to his longtime friend and confidante Florence Nightingale, "I should like to govern the world through my pupils." He made an impressive start. Those who passed the ICS examinations were obliged to attend a university for a probationary two years. Jowett offered a place at Balliol to each successful candidate ("poaching," his academic rivals snorted) and provided all entrants with a special tutor (Arnold Toynbee, uncle of the noted historian). Consequently more than half the probationers chose Oxford in the 1890's, compared with Cambridge's twenty percent. According to Richard Symonds's tally in *Oxford and Empire* (1986), 600 of 2,200 Balliol matriculates from 1875 to 1914 obtained imperial posts, half in the Indian services. Within Britain, Balliol accounted for more than forty seats in the House of Commons—and for seventeen years, from 1888 to 1905, three successive Viceroys of India were Jowett's pupils.

It was a heady triumph for The Jowler, Oxford, and Plato. Indeed there *was* a striking likeness between the Platonic prescription and India, where the British hierarchy replicated that in *The Republic:* Guardians at the peak, the warriors next, followed by merchants and Other Ranks at the bottom. As remarked by Philip Mason in *The Men Who Ruled India* (1954), the four basic Hindu castes—sages, warriors, traders, and menials—likewise corresponded with this pyramid. Mason, a Balliol man who served twenty years in the Indian Civil Service, notes that the British Guardians were a caste apart from those they ruled. They were forbidden to own land or engage in trade, and were governed by their elders—all this "on exactly Plato's principles." In India as in Plato's ideal state, the military was subordinate to the civil, but (as in *The Republic),* some of the ablest officers could be chosen for the Political Department and thus rise into the ranks of the Guardians.

A fine scheme, but with a palpable catch. As with Plato, Jowett's focus was on good government rather than self-government. The Raj was a paternalist autocracy imposed by an alien race, and while its admirers made much of its good works—schools, courts, hospitals, roads, irrigation—little was said about consent of the governed. Jowett himself believed qualified Indians should be represented in the highest councils. Yet progress towards bureaucratic power sharing, much less elective government, was glacial, slowed by the hostility of lower-status Europeans. As for Curzon, his inability, or rather unwillingness, to reconcile efficiency and democracy proved his undoing in what would be the last classic imperial adventure, the British invasion of Tibet. ·

"THERE IS MORE GREAT AND PERMANENT GOOD TO BE DONE IN India than in any department of administration in England," Jowett wrote to Lord Lansdowne, the first of his three pupils to accept the Viceroyalty. In that spirit, Curzon grasped the same reins. He had now completed his great voyages, gained valuable experience as parliamentary Under-Secretary for Foreign Affairs to Lord Salisbury, and secured his financial independence with an interesting match. In 1895 he married Mary Victoria Leiter, whose father founded the Chicago dry-goods emporium that became Marshall Field. "Of family, as the word is here understood," sniffed *The Times* of London some years later, "he had none; of position, none save that which he created for himself." Yet his daughter was to occupy (as her biographer Nigel Nicolson observes) the most splendid position that any American, man or woman, held in the British Empire.

Mary's face complemented her father's fortune (reckoned by Nicolson at $20 million in 1890's dollars). At five-foot-eight, with her wisp of a waist and captivating gaze, she was the belle of every ball after her debut in Washington, where the first Englishman to propose to her was Cecil Spring Rice of the British Legation, co-scribbler of the Oxford "superior person" doggerel. At a London ball in 1890, she met George Curzon. Both were smitten. There followed a protracted, on-again, off-again long-distance courtship that survived his sending texts of his speeches instead of billets-doux. He finally proposed in 1893 but insisted their engagement be kept secret for two years so he could visit Afghanistan, "my last wild cry of freedom." The wedding was in Washington, the marriage successful. Mary was self-assured and sweet-tempered, and when George accepted the Viceroyalty, she passed inspection at Windsor by the Queen Empress, who informed Curzon his wife was "wise and beautiful."

Having settled in Calcutta at Government House (whose design, auspiciously, was inspired by Kedleston), the new Viceroy made clear that he was not going to be a Great Ornamental, the phrase applied to his sedate predecessor, Lord Elgin. Curzon plunged into his work, assaying such diverse questions as creating a new North-West Frontier Province, coping with a threatened famine by a timely visit to Gujerat (the rains came along with him, confirming belief in his miraculous powers), founding a steel industry, launching a Directorate of Criminal Intelligence, stabilizing finances and currencies, and always riding herd on a bureaucracy that he faulted as dilatory. He hated the system of circulating endless minutes among departmental chiefs: "All these gentlemen state their worthless views at equal length, and the result is a sort of literary Bedlam." "Efficiency of administration," he admonished, "is a synonym for contentment of the governed."

Curzon took personal charge of the Foreign Department, whose policies were of keenest interest to him, involving as they did relations with Russia, China, Persia and the Persian Gulf, Afghanistan, and—a recent and exasperating item—Tibet. It appeared that the Tibetans had trespassed into British-ruled Sikkim, demolishing boundary pillars. They also obstructed compliance with the Anglo-Tibetan Convention of 1890 and the ancillary Trade Regulations of 1893, providing *inter alia* for the establishment of a British trading mart within Tibet. To these injuries was added insult when the boyish Thirteenth Dalai Lama returned, apparently unopened, urgent missives from the Viceroy that had been delivered by a Bhutanese landowner named Ugyen Kazi. Or so Curzon had been told. Later, he doubted whether Kazi had ever reached Lhasa or was to be trusted at all.

Adding to his perplexity was a dispatch in October 1900 from the British chargé in St. Petersburg. Enclosed was an item from a Russian newspaper reporting that Nicholas II had at his palace in Yalta received Agvan Dorzhiev, described as the "first Tsanit Hamba to the Dalai Lama of Tibet." "I have not been able, so far," the chargé added, "to procure any precise information with regard to this person or to the mission on which he is supposed to come to Russia." Curzon shrugged at first. He then learned that Dorzhiev was a Russian Buriat who passed through India under the noses of Bengal police, his presence unreported by the same native agents, Sarat Chandra Das, Lama Ugyen Gyatso, and the Abbot Sherab Gyatso, on whom Curzon relied for intelligence on Tibet. The cumulative effect was to change the Viceroy's stance on Tibet from "patient waiting" to "impatient hurry."

This sense of urgency was rooted in Curzon's long-held belief that Russia's ultimate ambition was dominion of Asia. "It is a proud and not ignoble aim, and it is worthy of the supreme and material efforts of a vigorous nation," he observed in a 1901 Minute. Yet if Russia were entitled to her aims, "still more so is Britain entitled, nay compelled, to defend that which she has won, and to resist the minor encroachments which are only part of the larger plan." Piecemeal concessions were to be shunned, he maintained, since each morsel "but whets the appetite for more, and inflames the passion for a pan-Asiatic dominion." Curzon's fears were quickened by events in China: the chaos in Peking during the Boxer Rebellion, the steady Russian penetration of Mongolia and Manchuria, and the likelihood (as speculated by George McCartney, the British watchdog in Kashgar) that Russia would next devour Chinese Turkestan, bringing Cossacks to the very borders of Tibet.

That Russia might invade India or its neighbors was scarcely far-fetched to Curzon, who was quick to recall that Napoleon and two Tsars—Paul and Alexander I—seriously discussed a joint assault. Such an operation was now more feasible because Russia was at India's doorstep and could speed troops across the steppe by rail. In 1888, Curzon had been among the first foreigners to book passage on Russia's new Trans-Caspian Railway, and saw for himself the alarming mobility made possible by steam and steel. The Russians themselves advertised these possibilities. Curzon noted in *Russia in Central Asia* (1889): "General Prjevalski, in one of his latest letters, dated from Samarkand only a month before my visit to Transcaspia, recorded his opinion of the line, over which he had just travelled, in these words: 'Altogether the railway is a bold undertaking, *of great significance, especially from the military point of view in the future*'" (Curzon's italics).

So what should be done regarding Tibet? The Viceroy advised his superiors in London to bypass China, whose claims of suzerainty over Tibet were a "farce." British dealings "must be with Tibet and Tibet alone." It was essential "that no-one else should seize it, and that it should be turned into a sort of buffer state between the Russian and the Indian Empires." Soon enough, he warned the Secretary of State for India, Lord George Hamilton, "steps" might be required "for the adequate safeguarding of British interests upon a part of the frontier where they have never hitherto been impugned." Hamilton's response—this was July 1901, when Britain was already mired in the Boer War—cautioned that consultation was essential before taking "steps." "Strong measures," however justified, "would be viewed with much disquietude and suspicion."

Curzon bided his time. In 1902–3, circumstances played into his willing hands, and his Tibetan project became inextricably associated with its chief executor, Francis Edward Younghusband (1863–1942).

SOLEMNLY GOOD-LOOKING, YOUNGHUSBAND GAZES FROM UNDER imposing brows from his page in imperial history. The *Dictionary of National Biography* describes him as "soldier, diplomatist, explorer, geographer, and mystic," much the sort of fellow who might appeal to Curzon, as he did when they first met in 1894. Fittingly, the venue was Chitral, a lofty kingdom on the far edge of India's North-West Frontier, where Captain Younghusband was Political Officer. Curzon's irritating certitude, his House of Commons debating manner, grated at first, but the young officer soon discerned other qualities: warmth, tenderness, loyalty, and political views that matched his own.

Younghusband was the frontiersman's frontiersman. Born in the Indian hill town of Murree, he was a son of an Indian Army general and a nephew of the explorer Robert Shaw, the first Briton known to cross the Himalayas to Yarkand and Kashgar. In a familiar rite of passage, young Francis returned to England for schooling at Clifton and Sandhurst, winning a Guards commission. Once back in India, he embarked on missions that took him from the Indus to the Afghan border; from Kashmir to Kulu; then in a great arc from Manchuria's Long White Mountain to Peking and across the Gobi Desert. His transit of China, and his explorations of the High Pamirs and the Karakorum, won him the Founder's Medal of the Royal Geographical Society (1890), resulted in a well-received book (*The Heart of a Continent*, 1896), and led to memorable encounters on two occasions with Tsarist officers scouting the nebulous boundaries of the British, Russian, and Chinese empires. Meeting with Colonel Grombtchevski in the High Pamirs, he posed for photographs and debated with him in French on the logistics of invading India. Then ungallantly, he misled the Russian about nearby passes, recommending a route "leading from nowhere to nowhere," without grass or fuel. When Colonel Yanov, after equally friendly libations, ordered Younghusband to leave "Russian territory," the Briton did so under protest, yielding only because he lacked an escort and faced thirty Cossacks. There were no hard feelings; Yanov pressed a gift of venison and apologized for being required to behave like a policeman. An official apology later followed from the Russian Foreign Minister for what was said to be a misunderstanding.

At Chitral on the North-West Frontier in 1893–94, under arrangements possible then, Younghusband was granted a leave of absence to report for *The Times* of London on a campaign by the legendary Guides (in which his brother George was an officer). A dynastic war was underway among Chitrali claimants to the throne; Russian meddling was suspected, and a British unit was under siege at a remote fort. Two relief columns were mobilized, one marching from Peshawar, the other from Gilgit. Against the odds both survived punishing passes, lifted the siege, and left the fort with a reinforced garrison. Younghusband recounted this for *The Times* and more fully in a book (co-authored with his brother). It was during this campaign that he met Curzon, who on returning to Britain used his firsthand authority to persuade the Government to hang on to the Chitral fortress lest the Russians take it first (which, it became known later, they planned to do).

At this time, something else important happened to Younghusband. At Chitral, he read *The Kingdom of God Is Within You* by another former frontier officer with a mystical temper, Leo Tolstoy. "It has influenced me profoundly," he wrote in his diary. ". . . I now thoroughly see the truth of Tolstoi's argument that Government, capital and private property are evils. We ought to devote ourselves to carrying out Christ's sayings, to love one another (not engage in wars and preparations for wars) and not resist evil with evil." Tolstoy did not explain how all this could be done, Younghusband added, but said a few great ones, like Columbus, must find the way: "And this is what I mean to do."

Thereafter Younghusband the spiritual explorer cohabited with Younghusband the martial imperialist, a curious joint pilgrimage with many odd detours. Certainly Tolstoy did not deter him from obtaining an extended leave to travel to southern Africa, where, as a *Times* correspondent, he again sang the praises of Pax Britannica. There he met Cecil Rhodes, visited Rhodesia, and was present in

Johannesburg at the time of the Jameson Raid, the botched attempt to stir an uprising against the Boers. Younghusband evidently knew of the raid beforehand, and seemingly approved the operation in collusion with Flora Shaw, the newspaper's Chief Colonial Correspondent. At a dramatic public inquiry on the affair in London, Miss Shaw artfully managed to protect both the newspaper and Younghusband from charges of complicity in a rash act of war.

The fuss subsided and Younghusband returned to India, where his superiors took him down several pegs by posting him as Resident in Indore, not a very challenging or visible assignment. He wrote in discouragement to Curzon in August 1901 asking whether he should resign from the Indian Political Department. "I have always had the ambition to work at the great main questions of Asiatic Policy," he said, "and it is to these that I now wish to turn my undivided attention." At around this time, the Viceroy—who advised him to stay put for the moment—knew he had found the right man to lead a mission to Tibet.

IN 1902, MIDWAY IN HIS FIVE-YEAR TERM, CURZON PERSUADED A doubtful Cabinet in London to authorize a Coronation Durbar for Edward VII. Not only was the Durbar an accepted feature of Indian life, he contended, but it would be "an act of supreme public solemnity" demonstrating the Raj's unity and strength. It was to take place in Delhi, seat of the old Mughal Empire, in January 1903, its pageantry more "Indo-Saracenic" than "Victorian Feudal," with Curzon himself as impresario. "You talked about stage management," Curzon confided to a friend in London. "That is just what I am doing for the biggest show that India will ever have had."

The Coronation Durbar reflected not only Curzon's love of pomp but his heartfelt belief that the "Oriental mind" thrived on spectacle. On a famous occasion years before, he turned up for an audience with the Emir of Afghanistan wearing medals and decorations purchased from a theatrical costume shop. As it transpired, in the event,

at what people called the "Curzonization," a million or so onlookers
had plenty that was genuine to gape at. Column upon column of
heralds and dragoons, plus veterans of the Mutiny, preceded the
Viceroy and Vicereine, borne aloft on a silver howdah. Next in the
elephant procession were the Duke and Duchess of Connaught, representing the Crown, leading fifty Indian princes, in exact order of
precedence. As *The Times* correspondent (one of a pampered brigade
of journalists) wrote, the effect was like "a succession of waves of
brilliant colour, breaking into foams of gold and silver, and the crest
of each wave flashed with diamonds, rubies and emeralds of jewelled
robes and turbans, stiff with pearls and glittering with aigrettes." At
the climactic State Ball, four thousand breaths stopped as the Viceregal couple entered, he in his white satin knee breeches, she in her instantly celebrated dress, fashioned of cloth-of-gold encrusted with
emeralds in the pattern of peacock feathers. For Curzon, it was a
gratifying success, the only serious blemish being his home Government's refusal to let him announce—in the fashion of Oriental potentates—a reduction in salt taxes (he was allowed only to hint
vaguely at "measures of financial relief").

The Durbar did not appeal to Younghusband. During its preparation, Curzon summoned him to Delhi, and the frontier officer felt
the Viceroy's idea of presiding from the old Mughal throne was "a
little too much." But when Younghusband found himself next to
Curzon at a lavish lunch the following day, the Viceroy talked "literally the whole time" about the frontier, the newly formed Central
Asian Society, and local problems at Indore. It was an audition. On
being summoned afresh to Simla in May 1903, a dumbstruck
Younghusband was offered the starring role. He was to lead a mission just within the borders of Tibet—not yet to Lhasa itself because
of delicate political considerations that, Curzon hinted, were subject
to change. All this was settled during the Simla season. "My dear Father," wrote an exhilarated Younghusband. "This is a really magnificent business that I have dropped in for."

In subsequent discussions, Curzon stressed that Younghusband was
not to do or say anything without prior approval that might bind the
Government of India or displease the Viceroy's skittish superiors in

Whitehall. Curzon had obtained a green light for sending a Tibetan Frontier Commission, comprising up to a dozen Britons and officials and an escort of 200, to Khampa Dzong, just within the Tibetan frontier. In July 1903, the Commission arrived at the Tibetan town, camped at 16,000 feet in the valley below a massive frontier fort, and there lingered for five futile months, unable to find anybody willing to address long-standing British complaints. The Chinese Amban sent an unhelpful underling, and the Tibetan delegates refused even to carry messages to Lhasa. Younghusband the soldier used his free time to write a lengthy memorandum on Russian penetration of Tibet, while Younghusband the mystic awoke at dawn to glimpse the first rays gilding the summit of Everest.

Events then played into Curzon's hand. While the Commission languished, the Tibetans arrested two Sikkimese scouts who were on intelligence missions for the British. They were reportedly tortured, possibly executed, while their distraught families pleaded for their release. The Viceroy seized on the plight of the prisoners as "conspicuous proof" of Tibet's "contemptuous disregard for the usages of civilization." Another telegram reported a Tibetan act of aggression against Nepalese yaks. These lesser grievances were subsumed within a much graver cause for concern: persistent and credible reports that Russia and China had concluded a secret agreement giving the former exclusive rights of access to Tibet.

Curzon pressed the case for advancing further into Tibet at a difficult time for his long-serving Conservative Government. The Boer War, which broke out in 1899, unexpectedly proved Britain's severest military test since Waterloo. It had taken three years and an imperial force of 500,000 men to subdue some 40,000 Boer commandos, whose leaders agreed to indulgent surrender terms in May 1902. The Prime Minister, Arthur Balfour, was also caught up in a Cabinet crisis. His Colonial Minister, Joseph Chamberlain, formidable with his pince-nez, had challenged the sacrosanct tenets of free trade by speaking out in the summer of 1903 for imperial tariff preferences. In an effort to mollify and straddle, Balfour reshaped his Cabinet in September. Chamberlain was out, but so were ardent free-traders, among them Lord George Hamilton, the Secretary of

State for India. Into the Cabinet as Chancellor came Chamberlain's son Austen, while to succeed Hamilton, Balfour turned to St. John Brodrick, once Curzon's schoolmate at Eton and Balliol.

Balfour's was a familiar dilemma. He did not wish a tired Government to seem indecisive, yet he certainly had no wish to plunge Britain into another costly colonial war. It was in this spirit that Brodrick, the new Secretary of State for India—Curzon's senior by a few years, but his junior in ability—advised that a "full estimate of expenditure" was essential before any further advance into Tibet. In any case, an advance was contingent on "a rupture of negotiations," which Brodrick failed to notice had already occurred. Curzon responded in a long, tactful cable recapitulating the Government of India's decades of frustration with an incommunicado neighbor. He estimated only a small force, costing £153,000, would be required. The matter went to the Cabinet, which approved a cautionary policy statement. Brodrick's telegram of November 6, 1903, read in full:

> In view of the recent conduct of the Tibetans, His Majesty's Government feel that it would be impossible not to take action, and they accordingly sanction the advance of the Mission to Gyantse. They are, however, clearly of the opinion that this step should not be allowed to lead to the occupation or permanent intervention in Tibetan affairs in any form. This advance should be made for the sole purpose of obtaining satisfaction, and as soon as reparation is obtained a withdrawal should be effected. While His Majesty's Government consider the proposed action to be necessary, they are not prepared to establish a permanent mission in Tibet, and the question of enforcing trade facilities in that country must be considered in the light of the decision conveyed in this telegram.

The negatives were strong yet the telegram cast but a dim light on the meaning of "obtaining satisfaction," "reparations," and "enforcing trade facilities." The haze from Whitehall proved as hazardous as the lofty terrain, averaging more than 14,000 feet above sea level, into which Younghusband now led a British expeditionary force.

IT SEEMS A LAW OF POLITICS THAT A GROWTH HORMONE IS LODGED in military estimates. Colonel Younghusband (as he now was) had a long wish list as he began discussions with Lord Kitchener, India's recently appointed Commander-in-Chief. Yes, Kitchener agreed, he could provide a lot of "white faces" to accompany native troops. He assigned to the mission a Maxim gun unit from the Norfolk Regiment, a half-company of sappers, eight companies of Sikh Pioneers, six companies of Gurkhas, and a Royal Artillery battery with two ten-pounder screw guns. Moreover, said Kitchener, "I will give orders that not a single man is to be under six feet."

Yet Brodrick's telegram posed a nice problem. Officially, the expeditionary force was an escort, authorized to accompany Younghusband as Commissioner as far as Gyantse, some 150 miles within Tibet. This meant naming a separate commander for the escort. The officer chosen—Brigadier General J.R.L. Macdonald of the Royal Engineers—brought to the operation both an abhorrence of risk and a determination to prove himself "the General Officer Commanding." The question of who was in charge so exasperated Younghusband that twice during the mission he threatened to resign.

Macdonald's caution was understandable. "No military force, before or since, has faced such vehement opposition from climate and terrain," writes Peter Fleming in *Bayonets to Lhasa* (1961), a careful reconstruction. Eager to get moving, Younghusband chose to defy the elements and head into the subzero Tibetan winter. Some 2,000 fighting men, most of them Sikhs and Gurkhas, assembled at Siliguri, the railhead of a narrow-gauge spur of the Darjeeling line. There were no base facilities. Everything had to be improvised—tents, latrines, water supplies, and hovels for the porters. Far more daunting was arranging portage. Pack animals consumed ten pounds of fodder or more daily, and those in forward columns exhausted whatever grazing could be found. The deeper into Tibet, the more strenuous the exertions to support the spearhead. In a musty report on supply arrangements, Fleming found a cumulative tally of the creatures that supported Curzon's "small force": 7,096 mules, 5,234 bullocks, 6 camels, 138 buffaloes, 185 riding ponies, 1,372 pack ponies, 2,953 Nepalese yaks, 1,513 Tibetan yaks, and 1,111 Ekka ponies. Casualties for this herd approached 9,000. A laconic final entry enumerated the human contingent in the supply chain: some 10,091 porters, of whom eighty-eight were to die of frostbite and exhaustion.

As interesting in a different vein is the "Kit List" kept by Younghusband and uncovered in the India Office Library by his biographer, Patrick French. The expedition leader's kit included sixty-seven shirts as well as nineteen coats (a full dress coat, a morning coat, an Assam silk coat, two jaeger coats, a Chesterfield coat, a poshteen long coat, a Chinese fur coat, etc.) plus a shikar hat, a khaki helmet, a white panama, a thick solar topi, and the imperial cocked hat. These habiliments, along with tents, a bath, beds, rifles, swords, and other impedimenta, were crammed into twenty-nine containers that were carried (as French reminds us) "up and down the mountain passes, through forests and icy rivers, over dry plains where your eyeballs could freeze in the sockets."

Sensing a good story, Fleet Street editors vied for the right to accompany the mission. Five correspondents joined the march, cabling their copy on the unrolling telegraph lines that linked the expedition to the world behind. Tibet did not disappoint. It was the last inhabited place of any importance to close its borders to Europeans, and in forcing its gates the Younghusband Mission wrote the epilogue to five centuries of Western exploration.

TIBETANS DID NOT KNOW WHAT TO MAKE OF THE CARAVAN THAT crawled like a huge caterpillar through Jelap La, the pass leading to the Tibetan plateau. When anything went wrong with a mule's load, which happened often on rough track with no shoulder, the mule had to be halted. This meant halting the entire caravan. "Multiply that appreciable interval by the number of mules in the rear, say five hundred, and you find that it takes perhaps a full half hour before the five-hundredth is on the move again," recalled a subaltern who under the pseudonym "Powell Millington" wrote a light-hearted account of his adventures.

It was December, and the mission encountered no resistance as it advanced into the Chumbi Valley. The conflict rather was within the expedition itself. At Macdonald's orders, the escort occupied a fort at Phari, violating a promise by Younghusband that no hostile action would be taken so long as the Tibetans held their fire. The colonel reprimanded the brigadier general, though it made military sense to garrison the well-positioned fort. Thus commenced what became a leitmotif: the differences over protecting troops versus alienating Tibetans.

The differences surfaced again during a first clash with Tibetans, at the village of Guru in March. Here the defenders threw up a barricade that could not be bypassed, behind which were a thousand matchlock rifles. Macdonald urged a surprise attack, which Younghusband overruled in favor of a parley. The Tibetan delegates adamantly insisted that the invaders had no business in their country and had to turn back. When the British force nevertheless advanced, stones and oaths flew and a Lhasa general allegedly fired the first shot at a Sikh soldier. The Norfolk gunners now directed their two Maxims, nicknamed Bubble and Squeak, at the astonished and terrified Tibetans. "I got so sick of the slaughter," the unit's commander wrote to his wife, "that I ceased fire, though the general's order was to make as big a bag as possible...I hope I shall never have to shoot men walking away again." To Younghusband, it was a "terrible and ghastly business" but somehow not a massacre since the Tibetans were armed and incited by "a fanatical Lama from Lhasa."

To the Tibetans, it was a massacre, the more disgraceful, they complained, since as a token of good faith their fighters had defused their matchlocks during the parley and were unprepared when the Maxims opened fire. The Tibetan toll was 628 killed, 222 wounded. British casualties were twelve wounded, none mortal. Macdonald reported that the escort fired 1,400 machine-gun rounds and 14,351 rifle rounds.

The action at Guru did not play well in England. There were hostile questions in Parliament and adverse press comments concerning (as *The Spectator* wrote) "an expedition which has never been popular, if only because we are obviously crushing half-armed and very brave men with the irresistible weapons of science." Nor did Younghusband's cause benefit when, having reached Gyantse, he authorized what seemed a provocative sortie, sending Bubble and Squeak and all his cavalry forty miles eastward toward Lhasa. He had no authority to go beyond Gyantse, and the rest of the escort and its commander were then billeted westward at Chumbi. When Macdonald learned of the sortie, he immediately ordered a recall. Younghusband forwarded his telegram by a slow pony and appended his own contrary message to the commanding officer: "On political grounds I would have the strongest objection to your returning, unless the enemy have so increased in strength that the result of a conflict would be doubtful."

What spared Younghusband greater trouble was an unexpected Tibetan assault on the mission compound, known as Chang Lo, in the environs of Gyantse. Since encamping in April, the British found the friendliness of the local inhabitants "almost excessive," *The Times*'s correspondent reported. A popular street song captured the mood:

> At first enemies of our faith they were,
> And then "Outsiders" we labeled them;
> But when in the land their rupees did appear,
> They became known as sahibs and gentlemen.

Thus lulled, the garrison was caught off guard on May 5 when 800 Tibetans stormed the compound at dawn. But their musket barrage caused more noise than injury and awakened the defenders, whose rapid fire killed upwards of 200 attackers. Total British casualties were two wounded. The subaltern writing as "Powell Millington" found this baptism under fire almost agreeable, given the inaccuracy of the Tibetans' jingal muskets and chunky bullets: "If what you desire on the battlefield is mild excitement with the minimum of risk, I would recommend exposing yourself to jingal-fire at, say, from six- to twelve-hundred yards."

"The Tibetans as usual have played into our hands," Younghusband all but gloated in a private message to Curzon. His official telegram made the skirmish sound like a dramatic and deadly ambush: "Attack confirms impression I had formed that Lhasa Government are irreconcilable . . . I trust that Government will take such action as will prevent the Tibetans ever again treating British representative as I have been treated." Replying from London, Brodrick agreed that "recent events make it inevitable that the Mission must advance to Lhasa unless the Tibetans consent to open negotiations at Gyantse," for which they deserved a month's grace. Yet the Secretary of State wished it "clearly understood" that the Cabinet contemplated no departure from the narrow goals set forth in his earlier telegram. That same May, in a consequential turn of events, Curzon embarked on home leave for Britain, becoming the first Viceroy to do so. The acting Viceroy in his absence was Lord Ampthill, the Governor of Madras, able and careful but without Curzon's authority or élan.

Curzon's homecoming began a long slide downhill. To be sure, he was greeted in May 1904 with the fanfare due a Viceroy who, unusually, was as famous at home as in India. He was "Imperial George," his oval face recognizable in cartoons and caricatures. But as he accepted the Freedom of the City of London, honorary degrees, and the Wardenship of Cinque Ports, he suffered "constant and almost unendurable pain" in a neuralgic right leg. Worse, Lady Curzon, who preceded him by four months, was ill throughout the summer and suffered a miscarriage in September. From unsanitary drains (at a Cinque Ports castle in England, not India) she contracted peritonitis, complicated by pneumonia and phlebitis. Newspapers in Britain and India published daily bulletins on her progress. Her recovery was slow, but sufficient for her to return to Calcutta with her cherished George in November 1904.

Nor did Curzon's public life prosper. Indian controversies dogged him. The most aggravating concerned Lord Kitchener, the Commander-in-Chief recently chosen with Curzon's full approval, who bridled at his subordination to the military member of the Viceroy's Council. Kitchener's bluff regimental heartiness concealed an aptitude for conspiracy. He hinted that he would resign unless the traditional "dual system" of providing for civilian control of the British Indian Army was scrapped, its evils being described in scary press reports that he inspired. His case impressed a susceptible Prime Minister. The Russo-Japanese War had broken out, creating fresh uncertainties in Asia. Prime Minister Balfour's Conservatives were heading into a difficult election and could ill afford an open break with Kitchener, a national hero. The essential point seemed clear enough—whether the Government of India should retain the power of giving orders to the Commander-in-Chief, or whether he "should be largely emancipated from that control," as summarized by Ampthill, writing as acting Viceroy. Curzon had on his side precedent, good sense, and the support of a flotilla of imperial grandees.

Yet to Curzon's dismay and astonishment, Kitchener was supported by the Secretary of State for India, once his closest friend, St. John Brodrick. They had known each other since 1874, when as Brodrick liked to recall, a "tall, breathless, pinkcheeked and well-groomed boy with black hair" entered his railway compartment en route to Eton. The two attended Balliol, served in Parliament together, and when they were apart Curzon for years wrote a weekly letter to "Brodder." We cannot know what turned Brodrick against Curzon—envy, an unwitting slight, or an unrequited crush—but the Viceroy set himself up for his humiliation. Rather than step down after his highly successful five-year term as Viceroy ended, he sought a second term. In a penciled note written late in life, Curzon said of Brodrick: "Burning to distinguish himself at the India Office as the real ruler of India, as distinct from the Viceroy, egged on by Councillors bitterly hostile to me, in a position to gratify a certain latent jealousy of my superior successes in public life . . . he rendered my service under him one of incessant irritation and pain, and finally drove me to resignation."

Francis Younghusband knew nothing of this as he advanced from Gyantse to the gates of Lhasa.

ON AUGUST 3, 1904, THE BRITISH MISSION HAD ITS FIRST GLIMPSE of the gilded roofs of the Potala. In the press cliché of the day, the Forbidden City was finally unveiled. Younghusband's boldness was widely applauded, even in Russia. He had led with minimal losses a major expedition over the "Roof of the World," fighting land battles at higher altitudes than any previous European force. He had done so against the recommendations of "Retiring Mac," his overcautious escort commander who had strongly opposed advancing to Lhasa and once there, proposed an immediate withdrawal. Instead, on Younghusband's orders, the British encamped for seven weeks at a compound not far from the Dalai Lama's Summer Palace on the outskirts of Lhasa.

As before, the British Commissioner's most difficult task was to locate a competent partner to conclude the agreement that was the object of his mission. The Dalai Lama was not to be found—he had fled to Mongolia days before, accompanied by Dorzhiev. It thus seemed a promising start when the Chinese Amban, Yu-t'ai, arrived in a sedan chair to pay an official call at the British compound. Ignoring Macdonald's warnings, Younghusband on the next day returned the Amban's call, riding through Lhasa armed only with a ceremonial sword, accompanied by a small escort. Nothing untoward occurred. Yu-t'ai welcomed him with fireworks, band music, tea, and cigars. The Amban said he was willing to help, but that the Tibetan authorities were still paralyzed by shock and confusion. "Everyone is in fear, not of us, but of each other," as Younghusband wrote.

Taking advantage of the hiatus, the British soldiers and their press contingent explored Lhasa, becoming the first Britons to do so since Thomas Manning's solo visit nearly a century before, in 1812. "We found the city squalid and filthy beyond description, undrained and unpaved," reported the disenthralled *Daily Mail* correspondent, Edmund Candler. "Not a single house looked clean or cared for. The streets after rain are nothing but pools of stagnant water frequented by pigs and dogs searching for refuse." Still, Candler allowed that above this squalor the Potala towered superbly, "its golden roofs, shining in the sun like tongues of fire." *The Times*'s Perceval Landon found more to admire. A pilgrimage path, he marveled, worn smooth and slippery by millions of feet, wound around the Potala to a gigantic stone, its entire surface containing a carved gallery of Buddhas of all sizes and colors, jostling each others' knees in their profusion: "at a distance in the sunlight it looks as if a vast carpet of vivid color has been thrown over the face of the rock." (Shortly thereafter, Landon raced back to London ahead of his colleagues so that his book, *The Opening of Tibet,* might be published first, but he had to settle for a photo-finish in 1905 with Candler's lively if thinner *The Unveiling of Lhasa.*)

Still, despite a diligent search, neither the press brigade nor British officers found any evidence of a significant Russian presence in Lhasa. They did come upon the two Sikkimese scouts, whose alleged torture and rumored execution had served as a casus belli. It appeared that neither had been starved or mistreated, beyond an initial beating, during nearly a year of close confinement. None of this was helpful to a British Government trying to justify the invasion. The question now became what kind of salvaging agreement could be wrested from the Tibetans.

CURZON AND YOUNGHUSBAND WERE IN ACCORD ON THE OUT-come they desired: a permanent Tibetan relationship with British India, certified by the presence of a British Agent in Lhasa. To be sure, Tibet was nominally part of China, yet so was Nepal, and a British Resident had been posted there for years. The Government of India *had* tried to do business with Lhasa through China, but in vain. A British voice was needed where it mattered, in Lhasa. The home Government did not concur, and its fears were embodied in a single name: Major Cavagnari, the British Envoy in Kabul whose murder in 1879 led to the Second Afghan War.

Whenever Tibet came up in the House of Commons, Cavagnari's fate came up too. "The association connected with the name of Cavagnari," Sir Henry Campbell-Bannerman, speaking for the Liberals, warned Parliament in May 1904, "does not seem to invite us to undertake a similar policy today." Kitchener said he was sure that a Resident serving in Lhasa would be murdered, and so advised the Government. Curzon sought to counter these arguments during his home leave. The analogy was incorrect, he maintained in a memorandum. Tibet was not an independent state with a warrior culture, as was Afghanistan, but a remote dependency of a declining China.

Why should Britain disallow herself from what Russia was doing in Mongolia, another Buddhist state that also was nominally a Chinese province?

Yet it was apparent by summer 1904 that Curzon's moment had passed. Against him were the Prime Minister, most of the Cabinet, his Commander-in-Chief, Lord Kitchener, and his old chum and nominal superior, Brodrick. The home Government's caution was understandable. Britain was now in a naval race with an ever more threatening Germany, and was leaning ever more eastward to Russia, whose ambassador was raising awkward questions about Tibet. "All that H.M.G. [His Majesty's Government] as a whole know or care about Tibet," Curzon wrote to Younghusband from England on July 13, 1904, "is that it is a nuisance and an expense; and all they want to do is to get out of it in any way that does not involve positive humiliation. This is the not unnatural attitude of an administration never strong and now tottering to its fall."

There were personal considerations. The Tibetan mission was, *au fond*, Curzon's war. The Viceroy's rigid stance and thunderbolt dispatches did not win friends in Parliament. "Let me beg you as a personal favour," Sir William Harcourt said to him when his Viceroyalty began, "not to make war on Russia in my lifetime." Or, as Arthur Balfour liked to complain, Curzon behaved as if India were an independent country, and not always a friendly one at that.

In Lhasa, meanwhile, Younghusband the soldier-mystic somehow got along with the Buddhist monks. Pressing hard against restrictions imposed by London, and on two points exceeding them, Younghusband gained Tibetan adherence to a nine-point Convention. It was signed in September 1904 with appropriate pomp—the monks in red, the Chinese in blue, and the British in imperial braids—in the Dalai Lama's audience hall in the Potala. Representatives of Tibet's National Assembly and Council, the abbots of Drepung, Ganden, and Sera monasteries; and Ganden Tri Rinpoche, the Regent in the absence of the Dalai Lama, agreed that (1) Tibet would respect the Anglo-Chinese Convention of 1890 and Sikkim's borders, as defined in the text; (2) the Government of India could establish trade marts in Gyantse, Gartok, and Yatung; (3) amendments to the 1893 Trade Agreement would be negotiated separately; (4) no duties were to be levied on goods from India beyond tariffs mutually agreed to; (5) roads leading to the trade marts were to be kept in repair by Tibetans; (6) Tibet was to pay an indemnity of 7.5 million rupees (£500,000) for the dispatch of armed troops to Lhasa, payable in seventy-five annual installments; (7) as security for the indemnity, the British were to occupy the Chumbi Valley until it had been paid and until trade marts were open; (8) all fortifications between Lhasa and the British frontier were to be demolished; and (9) Tibet was to have no dealings of any kind with any foreign power without British consent. A separate article appended to the accord gave the British Agent at Gyantse the right to visit Lhasa "to consult with high Chinese and Tibetan officials on such commercial matters of importance as he has found impossible to settle at Gyantse."

At first glance, it seemed all the British could have wanted. Moreover, the Chinese Amban helped negotiate and witnessed—though he did not sign—the first direct agreement between Tibet and Britain. Even Brodrick was initially favorable, and telegraphed his congratulations, but hardly had the wax seals cooled than the Secretary of State changed his mind. The separate article giving British agents the right of access to Lhasa was (he now thought) an attempt to achieve by stealth what the Cabinet had expressly forbidden, entangle Britain in Tibetan affairs. The £500,000 indemnity was too high and the 75-year occupation of the Chumbi Valley too long, conflicting with assurances that Britain had given Russia and exceeding Younghusband's instructions. When Brodrick consulted his Cabinet colleagues, he found they too believed Younghusband had "sold" them. Balfour concurred. From his Scottish home, the Prime Minister wrote on October 6, "Younghusband, by disobeying our orders, has placed us in a very false position," paraphrased by Brodrick as "Arthur Balfour considers the honour of the country is involved in repudiating Younghusband."

New instructions flew from Whitehall to Lord Ampthill, still the acting Viceroy. He was to amend unilaterally the Tibetan Convention by revoking the provision for visits to Lhasa, limiting the occupation of the Chumbi Valley to three years, and reducing the indemnity by two-thirds to 2.5 million rupees (which the Chinese immediately paid, thereby reaffirming their claim to control Tibet). An interesting private letter to Ampthill from Sir Arthur Godley, the Permanent Under-Secretary of State at the India Office, offered a disinterested civil servant's view. Godley hoped the official verdict would be appreciative of Younghusband's "really important achievements, and as little harsh towards his errors" as was consistent with a full statement of the case. Four or five months ago ("as I reminded Mr. Brodrick"), his note continued, it seemed that Younghusband would come back from Lhasa without a treaty and with Britain's tail between its legs. "The actual situation is very different now, and I think they ought to show some gratitude to the man to whom their escape from a very awkward position is due."

Younghusband knew he risked censure for stretching his authority. He was taken aback by its vehemence, even meanness, as he became the surrogate for the real target, Lord Curzon. A few decades earlier Younghusband's man-on-the-spot initiative would have made him a hero. Now it was "dishonourable" to get better terms for his country than his masters sought. Brodrick even tried to deprive him of the victor's customary knighthood, and failing that, saw to it that he received the lowest grade, a KCIE. The controversy effectively ended Younghusband's public career. Sir Francis subsequently headed the Royal Geographical Society, promoted Britain's first Everest expeditions, and devoted himself to the World Congress of Faiths and to spiritual treatises like *Life in the Stars* (1927) and *The Reign of God* (1930). He died peacefully in July 1942, during the Blitz, in the arms (as his surprised biographer Patrick French determined) of his married mistress, Madeline Lees.

Lord Curzon, having resigned as Viceroy in August 1905, suffered a more grievous loss a year later, the death of Lady Curzon, who had borne him three daughters. She was thirty-six. Curzon replied by hand to nearly all 1,150 letters of condolence. Her burial was at Kedleston in a tomb he designed. He composed her epitaph: "Perfect in love and loveliness / Beauty was the least of her rare gifts… She was mourned in three continents / And by her dearest will be / For ever unforgotten." For eleven years after his resignation as Viceroy, Curzon was excluded from politics. He served, not happily, as Foreign Secretary after World War I, hoped to be Prime Minister but was passed over in 1924, and died the following year. Brodrick, having done what he could to injure Curzon, tried without success to repair relations with his former friend. Macdonald wound up his military career as commander of a minuscule garrison in Mauritius.

Yet the unhappiest victims were assuredly the Tibetans. The scale of their offenses—destroying frontier pillars and incarcerating British spies—did not warrant the massacre at Guru or the invasion of their capital or the huge indemnity. They were losers in a second, profounder sense. Had Britain carried out the agreement Younghusband obtained, the long-term result would have been to enhance Tibetan claims for autonomy within the Chinese Empire. Having decided to end rather than defend Tibet's isolation, Britain could have worked to achieve for Tibet the status of a neutral buffer state, as Curzon proposed. We are left with what happened. Curzon's moment was over in 1904; the Younghusband mission was an anachronism; and nearly a century later the matter of Tibet remains unfinished business.

∴

CHAPTER THIRTEEN

The Desert Wanderer

Maps are to exploration what Scriptures are to theology: the font of authority for ascertaining truths distantly glimpsed. Maps were the sacramental bread and wine for contestants in the Great Game. Lord Curzon once grandly described this competition as an "incomparable drama," whose actors were "a few silent men, who may be found in the clubs of London, or Paris, or Berlin, when they are not engaged in tracing lines upon the unknown corners of the earth." Curzon, the most energetic and romantic of Viceroys, was writing at the turn of the century, when his attention was drawn to the vaguely defined and ill-protected North-East Frontier of British India. Hence Curzon's interest in the work of Sven Hedin, the lone Scandinavian entry in the imperial drama.

Hedin was a cartographer nonpareil. His meticulous maps more than anything established Hedin as the greatest Central Asian explorer of his time, even perhaps of the modern era. In order to fill in those "white spaces" (a favored phrase), Hedin sacrificed his human companions as well as scores of dogs, horses, yaks, and camels. It was typical of this driven competitor that he confessed to greater fond-

Photo 1   William Moorcroft (far left), disguised as a Hindu pilgrim, explores western Tibet in this 1812 watercolor by his turbaned companion Hyder Hearsey—the only certain likeness of the elusive Moorcroft.

Photo 2   Mohan Lal, the astute Kashmiri *munshi,* or secretary, who in 1842 vainly warned the British of the imminent Afghan rising at Kabul.

Photo 3   Sir Alexander Burnes, the British Resident at Kabul, murdered while serving an Afghan policy he opposed.

Photo 4   George Eden, first Earl of Auckland and Governor-General of India, the ill-starred begetter of the First Afghan War.

Photo 5   Emir Nasrullah Khan, who tormented two British officers in his notorious "bug pit" while waiting for a letter from Queen Victoria.

Photo 6   Emily Eden's portrait of Maharajah Ranjit Singh, the aging Lion of Lahore, on whose Sikh army the British excessively relied.

Photo 7   The Bolan Pass, the fifty-mile defile through which the Army of the Indus and its 30,000 camels tramped into Afghanistan in 1839.

Photo 7   Afghan irregulars, superior marksmen whose lethal jezails outdistanced the British musket, the Brown Bess.

Photo 8   Dr. William Brydon, completing the retreat from Kabul, in Lady Elizabeth Butler's celebrated *The Remnants of an Army*.

Photo 10　Januarius MacGahan, the young American correspondent whose accounts of the "Bulgarian Horrors" supplied tinder for the Russo-Turkish War of 1877-1878.

Photo 11　General Mikhail Skobelev, fearless (and ferocious) in subduing Central Asians, who rode into battle in spotless white.

Photo 12　Major Sir Louis Napoleon Cavagnari meeting with Kabul chiefs three months before his murder in Kabul in September 1879 ignited the Second Afghan War.

Photo 13   Lord Lytton, on the Viceregal throne, *circa* 1877, his slouching posture due to a physical condition that many misread as indolence.

Photo 14   Madame Blavatsky, the founder of Theosophy, an agent of mystical influence in British India during the 1880s.

Photo 15   Lord Curzon and his Chicago-born Vicereine, Mary Curzon, at a tiger hunt, *circa* 1902. The Viceroy's rigid stance was due not to pride or arrogance but a painful steel brace to support an infirm spine.

Photo 17   Sarat Chandra Das, the pundit who posed as a Buddhist pilgrim. His missions to Tibet in 1879 and 1881 benefited scholarship as well as the Raj.

Photo 16   Duleep Singh, Victoria's favorite maharajah, portrayed in the glory of his youth by the court artist Winterhalter.

Photo 18   The "Lhacham" as photographed by the "Pundit."

Photo 19 A rare photograph of Agvan Dorzhiev, the Dalai Lama's envoy to the "White Tsar," who passed invisibly through India to Russia.

Photo 20 Dorzhiev, leaving the palace at Tsarskoye Selo Palace near St. Petersburg after an audience in 1901 with Nicholas II.

Photo 21   Nikolai Przhevalsky, in martial regalia, *circa* 1885, pondering his next moves as Russia's preeminent Asian explorer.

Photo 22   Pyotr Kozlov, Prezhevalsky's dashing successor, who outlived the 1917 Revolution but like his mentor failed to reach Lhasa.

Photo 23   The Lamas (and British agents) of Ghoom Monastery. Lama Ugyen Gyatso (left) stands next to the Mongol Abbot Sherab Gyatso, seen with four other lamas in a *circa* 1895 snapshot.

Photo 24 Francis Younghusband—full beard, brooding brows and black cap—while leading a secret mission to Kashgar in 1891 with fellow Britons George Macartney (left), Henry Lennard (with dog) and Richard Beech.

Photo 25 Colonel Younghusband's army, dwarfed by the Potala, forcibly entering Lhasa in 1904, the last such feat of the imperial age.

Photo 26   Sartor Exploratus: The diplomat William Rockhill donning native garments like those he wore during his Tibetan forays for the Smithsonian Institution, in 1888–89, and 1891–92.

Photo 27   William Montgomery McGovern, disguised as a "Tibetan coolie," reached Lhasa in 1923, causing the nettled British to question his honor (undeservedly).

Photo 28   Sir Aurel Stein as he looked on the Silk Road to his human companions and his successive terriers, all named Dash.

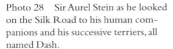

Photo 29   Pictures from an Expedition. The Roerich party in Urga (Ulan Bator) in 1927. Nicholas Roerich, white-bearded, sits alongside Pyotr Kozlov, hat in his lap; George Roerich is at far left in back row.

Photo 30   Nicholas Roerich is greeted a year later by Colonel F. M. Bailey standing on the right in the garden of the British Residence at Gangtok, the Russian unaware of Bailey's hostile backstage role. Helena Roerich is seated on the right.

Photo 31 Charles Bell, in his diplomatic uniform, with the Thirteenth Dalai Lama (seated) and the Maharaj-Kumar Sidkeong of Sikkim in 1910. During the pontiff's Indian exile, Bell as political officer in Sikkim was his British host.

Photo 32 The Panda Hunters. Suydam Cutting (center) flanked by Theodore Roosevelt, Jr. (left) and Kermit Roosevelt at Yunnan, China in 1929, in their Field Museum quest for the Giant Panda. The baffled Chinese assumed all three were sons of the "King of America."

Photo 33 "The Lhasa Ladies," as they were called by the British diplomat Frank Ludlow: Phünkang Shapé, a Tibetan noble, is flanked by his wife Kuku on the left and his sister Kay.

Photo 34 Hitler's cordial handshake with Sven Hedin followed the Swedish explorer's speech opening the Berlin Olympics in 1936. A German Olympic official looks on.

Photo 35 Ernst Schäfer, hands crossed, presides at dinner in Lhasa with other members of the SS mission to Tibet in 1939. Second from the left is Bruno Beger, later tried as a Nazi war criminal; fifth from the left is Tsarong, and second from the right is Mondo, one of the four "Rugby Boys."

Photo 36   Captain Brooke Dolan with his Lhasa Apso, "Miss Tick," as photographed by Major Ilia Tolstoy, co-leader of the secret OSS mission in 1943, Lhasa's first official contact with Washington.

Photo 37   His Holiness the Fourteenth Dalai Lama, age seven, in his first meeting with Americans at an audience at the Potala. Tolstoy presented a signed photograph of President Franklin Roosevelt.

ness for animals than people, and at expedition's end always found it "more difficult to say goodbye to the dogs than to the men." Thanks to his hard-won maps of the most inaccessible Himalayan ranges, and to his detailed charts that determined the sources in Tibet of India's most sacred and majestic rivers, Hedin, though a Swede, became Sir Sven, Honorary Knight Commander of the Indian Empire, having won the other suitable laurels that the British could bestow: degrees from Oxford and Cambridge, the coveted Founder's Medal of the Royal Geographical Society (1898), and its still more prestigious Victoria Medal (1903). Yet after 1910, he turned bitterly against the English, who for their part rescinded his knighthood and, no less hurtfully, removed his name from the roll of Honorary Corresponding Members of the RGS. In an icy farewell on his death in 1952, Sir Clarmont Skrine, a former Consul General at Kashgar and a member of the RGS Council, explained why in the Society's *Journal:* "By temperament Hedin was a Nazi, to whom exploration was a *Kampf*, a struggle not only against the forces of nature but also on paper, against rival explorers. It is not surprising that he espoused in turn the causes of Kaiser Wilhelm II and Adolf Hitler."

This was true. Hedin became an ardent admirer of the Nazis, even though his German great-grandfather was a rabbi. Hedin's support of Hitler's New Order almost from first to last is confirmed in captured German documents preserved in Washington, though these records have been neglected and their significance ignored. The Swede's enthusiasm for the Führer went well beyond fellow-traveling sympathy. His glowing oration opened the Nazi Olympics in 1936 and a few years later, when the brutality of the Third Reich was plain even to the purblind, he lent his name to an SS ethnographic "research" institute in Munich. Hedin was as well the spiritual godfather to an SS expedition to Tibet led by a Heinrich Himmler protégé, Ernst Schäfer, the details of which have been long immured in British and American archives.

Possibly career considerations influenced Sven Hedin's shift of loyalties, which occurred just as Berlin was entering the Asian competition and spawning its own schemes to unsettle the British Empire. But Hedin's enthusiasm was suspect; he overdid it. Before the First World War, Hedin showed few symptoms of political zealotry. What he displayed abundantly was arrogance and vanity, and he was especially proud of his skill as a cartographer; it was his profession, almost his religion. In 1909, Hedin's competence was challenged in the very high church of his creed, the Royal Geographical Society, and from that point he turned against Britain and to the less exacting Germanic ecclesia on the banks of the Spree.

This seems the most plausible explanation for Hedin's open embrace of Britain's enemies in two World Wars, when as a Swede he could have remained neutral in both. It is not an explanation that has been offered before, yet the clues are compelling in the strange but forgotten story of the "Desert Wanderer."

BY ITS VERY ARCHITECTURE AND INTERIOR DECORATION, THE four-storied One Saville Row building, home to the Royal Geographical Society from 1871 to 1913, embodied Victorian imperialism. The fanlight over the front door represented the hemispheres; the curved panes separated by leads represented the parallels and meridians of the globe. On entering, the visitor beheld the names of the recipients of the Society's gold medals emblazoned on dark green panels. Inside lay the glass-roofed Map Room, the "Mecca for all true geographers, the home port of every traveller," as the RGS's celebratory volume claimed. Here the men "who were to wipe out 'Unexplored' from the maps of the continents trained for their labours"; here the world's "white spaces" were colored in, here falls and rivers were named after illustrious members.

It was in the Society's Map Room that Dr. Livingstone's heartless body, wrapped in calico, placed in a bark cylinder, and carried on a two-year journey from the heart of equatorial Africa by his devoted companions Susi and Chuma, lay in state for two days on its way to its final resting place in Westminster Abbey. By the century's turn, however, the fickle public, once fascinated by Livingstone, Richard Burton, John Speke, and the Welshman-turned-American correspondent, Henry Morton Stanley, had lost interest in Africa. The Victorian tropical adventurer had been replaced in fashion's limelight by the Edwardian polar explorer—Vikings with names like Nansen, Amundsen, and Nordenskiöld and homegrown talents Shackleton and Scott. However, their chief rivals were the Himalayan explorers who continued to capture the public's imagination and a fair share of the Society's gold medals. Now, in the age of scientific discovery, the Society's meetings, once devoted to arguments about the source of the Nile, reverberated with discussions of a more arcane nature— trigonometric projections, theodolite observations, and plane-table surveying.

The average Victorian knew little of the mountains of Tibet or the deserts of Central Asia. The oft-stated mission of the Society was public education: improving the teaching of geography, inspiring the next generation of explorers. "The *[Geographical] Journal*," wrote Ian Cameron in the Society's centenary volume, "was the fountain-head, the source from which information subsequently filtered down, via word of mouth, via libraries, via other journals and societies, via books, magic lantern lectures, photographs, newspapers and finally via schools, to a public who the more information they were given the more they wanted."

Indispensable to Victorian explorers and serious off-continent tourists was the Society's famous *Hints to Travellers*. Abandoned on Antarctic ice floes, buried in shifting desert sands, this imperial flotsam was stuffed into every explorer's kit. *Hints* evolved from a thin pamphlet edited by Sir Francis Galton, the meteorologist, who was the father of eugenics and cousin to Charles Darwin. It went through various editions until the eighth (1901) grew into two volumes devoted to the practical aspects of exploration.

In 1893, a new president, geographer Sir Clements Markham (1830–1916), had taken office, and it was during Markham's reign that the Society reached the zenith of its fame, power, and influence. "There was a rich fullness of life," as Hugh Robert Mill, the Society's distinguished librarian wrote, "truly the Royal Geographical Society seemed then a goodly company; it was an honour to belong to it as a Fellow, a privilege indeed to serve as a senior member of the staff." Under Markham its annual dinners where Cabinet Ministers, great ambassadors, poets, and social lions met were the "glory of the year." Best of all the functions was the *Conversazione* where the president received the fellows and their ladies, and the Council "appeared in the awful dignity of the Orders of the Garter, Thistle and St. Patrick." There were few Council members who could not boast at least "the insignia of a modest CMG (Companion of St. Michael and St. George) or CIE (Commander Indian Empire)."

The Society raised Sir Clements from secretary to president in the hopes that the embarrassing fiasco that led to his predecessor's resignation—the battle to admit the occasional "Victorian lady traveller" to membership—would be forgotten. Although Queen Victoria was a patron of the Society, it was axiomatic that women could not be fellows. In 1892, the distinguished Council unanimously agreed to the election of women, but a group of fellows objected to the twenty-two who were proposed. Among the dissentients at a special general meeting who voted for exclusion was Lord Curzon, recently arrived from his travels on the Trans-Caspian Railway. The future Viceroy and later husband to two American wives was violently opposed to the admission of women on grounds that "Their sex and training render them equally unfitted for exploration." "The genus," proclaimed Curzon, "of professional female globe-trotters with which America has lately familiarized us is one of the horrors of the latter end of the nineteenth century." Although a compromise was reached whereby the twenty-two globe-trotters were allowed to remain, no more women would be elected until 1913, when Curzon himself was president, a compromise that prompted *Punch* to comment:

> *A lady an explorer? A traveller in skirts?*
> *The notion's just a trifle too seraphic:*
> *Let them stay and mind the babies, or hem our ragged shirts;*
> *But they mustn't, can't, and shan't be geographic.*

Markham's own proclivities were for youths—when available, well-born naval lieutenants or public school boys—but he idealized rugged heroes, a penchant shared by the public at the time. By the time he took office, the age of the professional explorer had dawned. No more military adventurers on extended leave, the new *genus explorator* received Government and Society funding. These professionals supplemented their grants with high lecture fees and royalties from best-selling books.

Markham's great protégé was Robert Falcon Scott, whom he pushed or encouraged, depending on one's point of view, in his final fatal dash to the South Pole in 1912. It was rumored among the fellows that Scott's unnecessary, albeit heroic, death contributed to Markham's. But Sir Clements's *"beau ideal,"* he once confessed at the Society's monthly meeting, was the Swedish explorer Sven Hedin. Tough as old boots and headstrong as an unbroken stallion, Hedin would come to exemplify both the best and worst qualities of the Edwardian hero. Capable of heroic sacrifice, hampered by near blindness, this Swede was willing to go to any extreme to achieve his goal—international fame.

BORN IN 1865 AS ONE OF SEVEN CHILDREN OF A SCHOLARLY AND artistic family—Hedin's father, Ludwig, was the city architect of Stockholm—Sven began his own cult of hero worship as a child. "At the early age of twelve," he wrote in the opening passage of *My Life as an Explorer,* "my goal was fairly clear. My closest friends were Fenimore Cooper and Jules Verne, Livingstone and Stanley, Franklin, Payer, and Nordenskiöld, particularly the long line of heroes and martyrs of Arctic exploration." An early memory was of the homecoming of Baron Otto Nordenskiöld who had just transversed the Northeast Passage in the *Vega.* The Arctic explorer returned to Stockholm on a cold and rainy spring day to enthusiastic cheers, which "roared like thunder from quays, streets, windows and roofs." Fifteen-year-old Sven decided at that moment: "I, too, would like to return home that way."

His heart set on Arctic exploration, he was diverted elsewhere by a chance to tutor a Swedish boy whose father was chief engineer in the Nobel oil firm at Baku. He used his free time in the Caspian city to study languages—eight per day—and his vacations to travel through Persia, Mesopotamia, and the Caucasus. On his way home, he visited the peripatetic Central Asian traveler Arminius Vámbéry in Budapest. Back in Stockholm he used his letters home as the raw material for a book, making his successful debut as author with his

account of his travels illustrated with his own sketches. He pressed
Vámbéry to contribute the first of many celebrity forewords. Hedin
immediately followed with a second book, a translation and abridg-
ment of Przhevalsky's travels for which he persuaded his hero Nordenskiöld to write a foreword. Eventually Hedin was to write nearly
fifty books based on his own best-selling recipe: to a generous helping of descriptive writing, add a spattering of derring-dos, pepper
with historical asides, baste liberally with meetings with the high and
mighty, finally, top off with one near-death experience. One example from his name-dropping autobiography suffices.

Hedin was walking down the streets of Teheran one day with his
Swedish host, the Shah's dentist, Dr. Hybennet.

> All at once, we noticed a band of running *ferrashs,* or heralds,
> garbed in red, wearing silver casques, and carrying long, sil-
> ver staffs in their hands. With these staffs they made a way
> through the crowd, for the King of Kings was out driving. A
> troop of fifty horsemen followed these heralds, and then
> came the grey carriage of the Shah, drawn by six black stal-
> lions, in gorgeous silver caparisons, each left-handed horse
> bearing a rider. The Shah wore a black cloak over his shoul-
> ders, and on his head a black cap, with a huge emerald and a
> jewelled clasp.

As the carriage rolled past, Nasr-ed-Din called out to Hybennet:
"*In ki est?*" (Who is that?) Hedin had seen the Shah, but more importantly for the reader and the author, the Shah had noticed the
twenty-year-old Hedin.

Hedin's ambition was to be not only a writing traveler but also an
explorer with scientific credentials. Realizing that this new profession
demanded something more than mere topographical observations,
Sven journeyed to Berlin to begin the systematic study of geology and
geography with Baron Ferdinand von Richtofen, the doyen of Central Asian geography and the coiner of the appellation "Silk Road."
However, Hedin interrupted his studies when King Oscar II of Sweden sent him as "dragoman" and interpreter with the formal status of
vice-consul on a mission to the Shah of Persia. Hedin prolonged his
stay with a two-year trip through Persia and Central Asia. In Askabad,

in Russian Transcaspia, he met the military governor and future commander of the Russian Army in the Russo-Japanese war of 1904–5, General Kuropatkin, who, astonishingly, as it was an extremely sensitive area, gave orders to provide the young Swede with a Cossack escort and the latest maps of the Pamirs and the Russo-Chinese border. Taking the newly opened Trans-Caspian Railroad, Hedin visited Merv, Bokhara, and Samarkand. Kuropatkin warned him against crossing the Pamirs in December, but exhibiting his life-long penchant for assaulting mountain passes in winter and deserts in summer, Hedin proceeded, despite deep snow, to cross the Terek Davan Pass.

Kuropatkin also provided the traveler with an introduction to the Russian Consul General in Kashgar, Nicholas Petrovsky, who served as Hedin's genial host. In 1860, Russia had forced the Ch'ing (Manchu) Dynasty to open its dependency, the oasis city of Kashgar, to Russian trade. Petrovsky, who arrived there in 1882 with a guard of forty-five Cossacks, thus became for twenty-one years the behind-the-scenes master of Chinese Turkestan. Feared by the Chinese, the Russian was admired by the Turkic-speaking natives who called him the "New Genghis Khan." Looking back years later, Hedin described the diplomat as he appeared in 1890: "Petrovsky was a very learned man, very knowledgeable in the history of Central Asia, in archaeology and in East Turkic languages. He was tall, usually dressed in a local green *khalat* or mantle and a likewise green *calotte* [skullcap]. His eyes flicked jovially behind his gold-rimmed spectacles. In the evening we would sit for hours making great plans."

On his first visit, Petrovsky showed his guest around the consulate (since 1956, the Hotel Seman). The Swede was impressed by his office with its books and barometers, aneroids and seismometers. Hedin paused in front of the huge ordnance map of western Asia, which showed "the whole 3000-kilometer-long road from Teheran through Khorasan, Transcaspia, Bukhara, Samarkand, Fergana and East Turkestan to Kashgar," where he had now arrived safely. The map showed that he was "not far from the foot of Kunlun and hardly two weeks' ride from secretive Tibet." "Marvelous visions and future projects" loomed before him.

It was also in Kashgar, in 1890—fourteen years before the British invaded Tibet—that the Swede met two Britons, Francis Younghus-

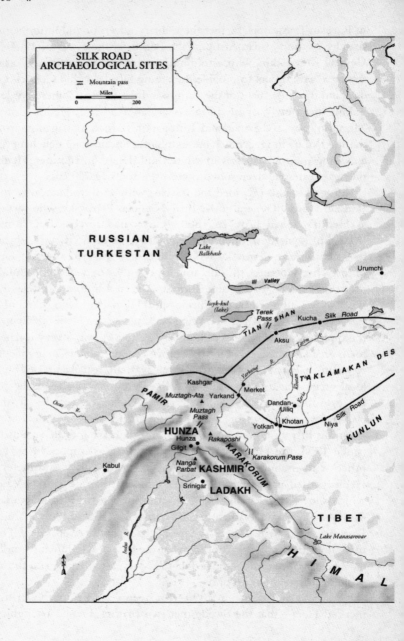

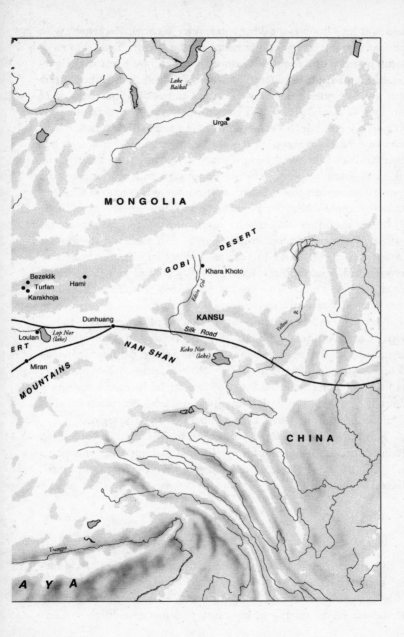

band and his Chinese-speaking interpreter George Macartney, who had just completed a reconnaissance of the Pamirs. Younghusband, Hedin noted approvingly, was camped not in a house but in the garden of Chini-bagh (Chinese Garden), in a "huge *kibitka* [a Kirghiz tent] with wooden floors, covered with carpets," whose walls were hung with "costly shawls and rugs from Kashmir." Macartney was relegated, according to Petrovsky, to living with the servants. A few years later Macartney would rebuild Chini-bagh, which was to become his home for twenty-eight years, as Britain's man in the Central Asian listening post, enduring Petrovsky's rudeness because the Russian was aware that Macartney's mother was Suchow Chinese. Petrovsky knew where the British stood on miscegenation.

There was undoubtedly talk of Younghusband's recent exploit: his death-defying crossing, before the days of crampons and all-weather gear, of the 19,000-foot Muztagh pass, which marked the boundary between India and China. Hacking his way with pickax, using knotted turbans and reins for ropes, with frozen feet, Younghusband, guided by his Ladakhi caravan leader Mohammed Isa, succeeded in what Hedin would call "the most difficult and dangerous achievement in these mountains so far." (Isa, also present in Kashgar, but at the time perhaps beneath the notice of the Swede, would lose his life accompanying Hedin on his 1905–09 expedition to Tibet.) While Hedin was staying with the Russian Consul, he formed a lifelong if competitive friendship with Younghusband, who described his rival as "physically robust, genial, even tempered, and persevering."

When the Chinese refused permission for his advance to Peking, Hedin returned to Stockholm via Russia, making a pilgrimage to the tomb of the greatest of the Russian Central Asian explorers, Nikolai Przhevalsky.

IN 1892, WITH HIS "YEARS OF APPRENTICESHIP IN ASIATIC EXPLORING" behind him, and with the financial backing of King Oscar and a few private individuals including the Nobel brothers, Carl and Emmanuel, Hedin made preparations for his first expedition to Central Asia, a three-year, 10,500-kilometer journey, which would make him famous. He was invited to speak to the Imperial Russian Geographical Society in St. Petersburg, where his presentation (in Russian) was so successful that his hosts promised him free transport for his party anywhere in their empire. This caused Hedin's American biographer, George Kish, to speculate that the Russians saw Hedin, a neutral Swede, as the ideal emissary, someone who could provide valuable information on Central Asia without arousing the suspicion of the British.

In October 1893, he left Stockholm "burning with desire once more to take the road of wild adventure" and proceeded to Orenburg in Russian Central Asia, the end of the eastern railroad line. From there he went mostly by horse or camel-drawn *tarantass* to Tashkent. Ignoring warnings about winter weather, Hedin's party set out in February to cross the Pamirs. Climbing, crawling, or sliding on the brink of abysses, narrowly escaping burial by avalanches and freezing to death in a blizzard, the party made its way across the mountain passes to Pamirsky Post, the farthest outpost of the Russian Empire. Here Hedin was "overwhelmed with hospitality and goodwill," the Russians holding him "a voluntary prisoner for twenty days."

On this as well as his other expeditions, Hedin used Kashgar as his base, where, during winters, he relished Petrovsky's "bubbling samovar" and in later years Macartney's Christmas hospitality. But lured by tales of lost cities in the sand, where "gold ingots and lumps of silver lay exposed," Hedin became the first European to attempt crossing the Taklamakan Desert in the more difficult west-east direction. (Przhevalsky had already crossed north-south, along the Tarim River.)

Reckoned by geographers as the second largest desert in the world (320,000 square kilometers), the Taklamakan remains a vast uninhabitable waste. In Turkic, Taklamakan means "Go in and you won't come out." Whipped and sculptured by unceasing winds and surrounded on three sides by mountains, it forms an ever-shifting shroud over the ruins of the Silk Road's vanished cities. Sir Clarmont Skrine, who lived next to it in Kashgar, graphically evoked its special terrors: "The yellow dunes of the Taklamakan, like the giant waves of a petrified ocean, extend in countless myriads to a far horizon...They seem to clamour silently, those dunes, for travellers to engulf, and for whole caravans to swallow up, as they have swallowed up so many in the past."

Hedin chose a route running roughly west to east, transversing the Taklamakan between the Yarkand and Khotan rivers. His crossing in the ferocious heat of summer won him his first medals from both the Imperial Russian and the Royal Geographical Societies and gained him his lifelong reputation—for ruthlessness.

Leaving Kashgar on his thirtieth birthday (February 17, 1895), Hedin proceeded to Merket, a town on the Yarkand River. As the party of five men, eight camels, two dogs, and their mobile provisions—three sheep, ten hens, and a cock—advanced to the dunes on April 10, the assembled villagers looked grave, and an old man audibly muttered, "They will never come back." Optimistically, Hedin had predicted that the crossing could be completed in two weeks, providing, of course, that the caravan averaged an impossible eighteen kilometers a day.

For two weeks everything proceeded smoothly. What water they needed they got by digging a brackish well. After resting briefly beside two beautiful small lakes on April 23, they resumed the march. Because Hedin had been told by his native guide, Yolchi, that they were no further than four days from their goal, the Khotan River, he ordered the water casks to be half-filled to reduce the strain on the camels. Three days later, they encountered their first real dunes and the whirling clouds and columns of dust of their first kara-buran, the horrific "black sandstorm" for which the desert was famed. Hedin now discovered they had only enough water for two days. However, he refused to turn back, preferring to press ahead to achieve his goal.

From then on the Taklamakan story becomes a recitation of a scorching, waterless hell: first the dogs expire, then the camels die, and three of Hedin's men are abandoned in the waste. Only the resolute leader, dressed in his best suit "for if I was to die and be buried by the sandstorms of the eternal desert, I would at least be robed in a clean white shroud," and Kasim, the last of his men, manage to crawl onward. On their fifth day sans drink, Kasim falters and is abandoned. Hedin alone manages to make his way to the Khotandaria and water. In a last heroic gesture he fills his watertight Swedish leather boots to the brim with the precious liquid, passes his spade handle through the straps, and returns to a delirious Kasim, who is thus rescued at the last moment. Later Islam Bai, Hedin's trusty Kirghiz caravan leader, left for dead in the desert, reappears leading a sole camel, which he managed to load with the explorer's money, maps, diaries, and rifles. Two men and seven camels died, Hedin's surveying instruments were lost, nothing of scientific interest was found, but in the years ahead his desert calvary, which included tales of his men driven delirious from drinking camel urine, became the centerpiece of Hedin's popular lectures.

Still determined to survey the desert between the Khotan and Keria rivers, Hedin retreated to Kashgar to await replacement instruments. He organized a new caravan and discovered extensive ruins of buried cities, which would spur the interest of subsequent archaeologists. Hedin mapped the intricate river system of the Tarim Basin and attempted to solve the riddle of Lop Nor—Przhevalsky's location of the lake did not agree with that on old Chinese maps. Subsequently, Hedin proved that because erosion caused its tributary river to shift course, the lake had "wandered" and changed shape. Next, Hedin journeyed along the northern rim of Tibet, the closed country whose penetration had already become his idée fixe. Finally, he made his way through the Ordos country to Peking, where the accommodating Russians shipped his luggage gratis to Stockholm and provided a Cossack guard for the 3,000-kilometer ride to the Russian railhead at Kansk, Siberia.

On reaching St. Petersburg, he was summoned to an audience with Nicholas II at Tsarskoe Selo. The Tsar, simply dressed in a colonel's uniform or a red peasant's blouse with no military insignia, depending upon which of Hedin's accounts is to be believed, showed a "benevolent interest" in the explorer's adventures, tracing them by means of a red crayon on a huge map of Central Asia. Nicholas asked Hedin to tell him frankly what he thought of the Anglo-Russian Boundary Commission's drawing of the agreed new line in the Pamirs, which defined the borders of Afghanistan. Hedin replied that "it would have been more natural and simple to let the border follow the main ridge of the Hindu-kush, which separates the waters, than to cut through the level tableland, where it had to be marked by artificial piles of stone, and where friction might easily arise because of the wanderings of the nomads." Knitting his brow and stamping the floor, the Tsar exclaimed emphatically: "That is just what I have pointed out all the time; but nobody has told me the plain and simple truth of the matter!" The Tsar ended the interview by assuring the young explorer of his continued interest and promising help for a future expedition.

The Imperial Geographical Society bestowed the first of the medals that showered on the explorer like Zeus's golden rain on Danae. Only one disappointment nettled. When he arrived on May 10 by steamer from Finland, there was not the triumphal procession he had dreamed of as a schoolboy, only his dockside family. Hedin had been upstaged by Fridtjof Nansen who, only two weeks before, had completed his journey across the Arctic Ocean in the *Fram*. However, Hedin's ego was stroked by the Swedish King, who took the floor at the palace reception for Nansen and toasted Hedin in front of 800 notables.

ON NOVEMBER 22, 1897, HEDIN APPEARED FOR THE FIRST TIME before the members and invited guests of the Royal Geographical Society. He illustrated his lecture not with slides but with spontaneous chalk drawings on a blackboard—a great hit with the audience, which applauded each figure. Sir Clements Markham, who was in the chair, paid tribute to the explorer, "*Geographicus nascitur et fit*," whose work had never been surpassed "in completeness and in thoroughness."

Next it was Russia's turn to bestow lavish favors on the still-young Swede as he undertook a second (1899–1902) perambulation around the Tarim Basin. The Tsar offered Hedin a private railway car for this expedition into Central Asia, and insisted on a Cossack escort, although it was reduced at Hedin's request from twenty-four to four, the explorer pleading that a Swede at the head of an armed escort would arouse suspicion among Tibetans that the team had a purpose other than "geographic and scientific."

Indeed news of the Tsar's patronage had already stirred suspicion among Hedin's new friends at the RGS. In a letter marked "Strictly private," Hedin tried to reassure John Scott Keltie, for twenty-five years the Society's Secretary and editor of its *Journal*: "I do not understand what you mean when writing, 'Of course one cannot blame you for going to Central Asia in the service of Russia.' Nobody ought to be more sure than you that I have no political intention whatsoever and that I go only in the service of geography. If the Tsar has shown me a friendship and kindness very rare indeed, it is not at all to bring me over in the Russian Service, but because—as he said the other day to the Danish Minister: '*Voilà un jeune homme qui m'a beaucoup plu. Certainement je ferais tout ce que je peux pour faciliter son voyage, mais je voudrais faire encore quelque chose pour lui.*' I do not get a single kopek from Russia and I should never have accepted a proposal in that direction. The means are given exclusively by Swedes, the King and Mr. L. Nobel give the greatest part."

Hedin then shared with Keltie his real goal: Lhasa. Tibet's holy city ranked with the North and South Poles among the supreme goals for Western explorers. Lhasa had been reached by Indian pundits acting for the British, and by Russian Buriats and Kalmyks, but was otherwise closed to Europeans. Hedin now tried to adopt the Russian approach. Of the four Cossacks in his escort, two were Kalmyks. The Swede hoped to persuade the Tibetans to welcome the Kalmyks as co-religionists in a caravan that also included thirty Muslims and a Tibetan-speaking Buriat lama—as well as thirty-nine camels, forty-five horses and mules, seventy asses, fifty sheep, and eight dogs.

Concerning the Cossacks, Hedin sought to placate Keltie with this addendum to a May 1899 letter: "Strictly private: You may be perfectly assured my political and personal sympathies are absolutely on the English side, specially after the step taken against Finland [to tighten Russian control over the country]. It is even as disagreeable for Sweden to see the proceedings of Russia in the West as it is for England to make the same observation as to India, and in this way I am sure we regard Russia with just the same eyes. If I take Kosaks with me, you may be sure I should never be such a poor diplomatist as to take them with me to the Indian frontier."

Hedin's expedition began auspiciously, with the discovery of the ruins of Loulan, once a flourishing commercial center and imposing Chinese garrison on the ancient Silk Road. But this was overshadowed by Hedin's failure to force his way into Tibet. He planned to reach Lhasa disguised as a Buriat lama, his head and mustache shaved, his skin darkened with fat, soot, and brown pigment, but his ruse did not succeed. Though scarcely tall by European standards, Hedin towered over the Central Asians, and as he rode past a Tibetan encampment near the northern frontier, he heard the ominous shout, by now familiar to all Westerners, "*peling*," meaning European.

At Tengri Nor, only a few days march from Lhasa, he was halted by a Tibetan militia bearing a proclamation from the Dalai Lama: "Let letters be sent with all speed to Namsu and Naktsang, that no Russian can have permission to travel on any of the roads of Nakchu and inwards as far as my kingdom extends. Let letters be sent to all the chieftains. Watch the frontiers of Naktsang. It is absolutely essential to guard strictly every part of the country. It is entirely unnecessary that any European shall enter into the kingdom of the holy books and spy out the land. In your provinces they have nothing whatsoever to do. If they say they have, then know they must not travel to Lhasa. And if they do travel, then shall you lose your head. See to it that they turn back by the way they came."

After a second attempt by another route, Hedin finally turned back, but by then two-thirds of his caravan was lost, "decimated and shattered." This was in 1902, only a year before a British expeditionary force led by Francis Younghusband finally ended Tibet's isolation. Still, as consolation, the authorities in Lhasa did allow Hedin to take a shortcut through Western Tibet to Ladakh. On reaching Leh, he found an invitation to Calcutta from Lord Curzon, whom the explorer had met on the occasion of his lecture at the RGS. Although this involved a horseback journey of more than 300 miles to Srinagar, and a winter crossing of the Zoji-la pass on foot, Hedin accepted. With a 3,000-rupee loan from the Durbar Fund arranged by Curzon, Hedin outfitted himself in an English-tailored suit before proceeding via Lahore, Delhi, Lucknow, and Benares to Calcutta.

Hedin spent fourteen days with the Curzons, initially at the Viceroy's weekend retreat at Barrackpore, fifteen miles upriver from

Calcutta. Even at Barrackpore, the Curzons lived in splendor, attended by a vast retinue of servants that accompanied them from Calcutta. The lodge was set in a 350-acre park amid Gothic follies, menageries, gardens, bandstands, a Corinthian temple dedicated to the war heroes of the Java campaign, and the glittering tomb of Lady Canning lit by an eternal flame, all inlaid in faultless velvet lawns. Arriving after a two-hour ride up the Hooghly in the small steam launch, Hedin was met by the Viceroy and Vicereine. During his visit, Hedin reported that whenever Curzon had the opportunity, "he invited me to come into his study and we discussed Tibet." As Hedin informed Keltie, Curzon even promised to write a letter extolling the Swede's Tibetan feats—"it should be a splendid recommendation for me, if it could be published in some way or other, and I am sure his opinion should raise the price of my next book" (*Through Asia,* which he in fact dedicated to Lord Curzon).

This encounter between two vain men had a looking-glass quality. Nietzsche's Superman observed and deplored the very traits in Balliol's Superior Person that were readily evident in Hedin himself. The Viceroy was "proud," "cold," his ambition knew no bounds, he had few if any friends, and was separated from subordinates "by an unbridgeable chasm." One may reasonably surmise that Curzon's aloofness was also heightened by suspicions about Hedin's contacts with the Russians.

Those suspicions were certainly not allayed by Hedin's return route: to Kashgar and then to St. Petersburg for another audience with the Tsar. Both before and after, Hedin sought to calm Keltie. Speculation that Russia planned to possess Tibet was "ridiculous." He did not know Russia's plans, the Swede wrote, "but I think they are more dangerous neighbors for us [than] for you, and England is strong enough to keep her Colonies. Mr. Petrovsky [the Russian Consul in Kashgar], who does not like the English, always said that although it was very easy to take Eastern Turkestan, it should never 'pay,' it should cost a lot of money. But my old Friend Keltie, don't think I am going to help Russia to take Tibet. I have a good deal of friends in Russia, but I have more in England and my political sympathies are with England."

In any case, in their meeting at Peterhof in the suburbs of St. Petersburg, Nicholas was delighted when Hedin praised his Cossacks.

Back in Sweden, King Oscar ennobled the explorer: Hedin's coat of arms, graced with a map of Asia, surmounted by three small shells, signified his pilgrimages, and the motto "*Voluntate et labore*" ("Through will and work") would hang in Stockholm's Riddarhuset. In 1903, Markham awarded him the Royal Geographical Society's Victoria Medal. In his acceptance speech, Hedin worried all too presciently that the time for "adventurous journeys will soon be gone...The part of Central Asia I have visited, I am sure will be of very great interest not only to geographers in England, but also to politicians."

THE YOUNGHUSBAND INVASION IN 1903–1904 LED TO THE FIRST open quarrel between Hedin and his British friends. "War against Tibet! Why? The Tibetans have never asked anything better than to be left alone," he protested to Keltie. "They have never broken treaties! Never! There is a convention between Russia and China, but not with Tibet. But Russia! Is there really in the whole world a single fool who believes that Russia could *ever* (even before the Japanese War) do anything against Tibet!" Let all Russians be settled in Lhasa and "I will be damned if not a few thousand Englishmen would be able to defend the passes of the Himalaya. But this is a political question. The wrong and unjust thing is to invade a friendly and silent neighbor without any cause whatsoever."

Hedin warned Keltie that he had written a "sharp" article for an influential Berlin weekly that might cost him half his English friends, and his article for *Die Woche* creditably spoke for all small nations: "The British campaign in Tibet is new evidence of the imperial ruthlessness which appears to characterize the geopolitical endeavors of our time and has doomed the position of the small state that is powerless to defend itself, regardless of whether it is Christian or not." Writing personally to Curzon, he repeated afresh how much he admired the Viceroy but assailed the "unprovoked aggression by a great power against a weak and small country." The Viceroy replied stiffly that "as the guardian of India I cannot afford to see Russian influence paramount in Lhasa and I have intervened to prevent it."

However, when Hedin was attacked in *The Times* as a spy, Curzon was apologetic: "For my own part I have never suspected you of being a Russian agent. Geography is the most cosmopolitan of sciences, and you are the most cosmopolitan of men. But you are a scientist before anything else—the man who more than any other has shown with what resources a great explorer ought to be equipped and what so equipped he ought to accomplish. I hope therefore in the interest of the world that you will perform one more big journey before you settle down. From this point of view I am almost ashamed of having destroyed the virginity of the bride to whom you aspired, viz. Lhasa."

Curzon's language was revealing. Long forbidden and inviolate, Tibet excited something like a subliminal eroticism in her Western suitors. The aptly named Younghusband expedition provoked a stream of books describing the opening, penetration, or unveiling of the country. In an editorial on "The Capture of Lhasa," *The Spectator* spoke of Asia as "the 'woman's apartment' of the world." Captain "Powell Millington," who accompanied Younghusband, described "assisting in drawing aside a purdah." The same carnal overtone was evident in the language of a Colonel Tanner on the Indian Staff Corps, who described a frontier perch where "the traveller will be rewarded with a peep at Tibet," a country likened by another Briton in 1894 to "the modern Brunhilde asleep on her mountain top," needing to be awakened by "Siegfried," *i.e.* the Viceroy of India. The bride was now ravished, and older fantasies quickly gave way to a *tristesse* that can be felt to this day.

Still, Hedin's indignation over the invasion did not diminish his efforts to draw the veil further apart, even though, as he confessed, "The longing that had possessed me to penetrate the Holy City in disguise was completely gone. The charm of the unknown had passed." Instead he prepared plans for an exploratory assault on the Tsangpo–Brahmaputra gap, the last sizable white tract marked "Unexplored." And for this, he would need British support for an expedition that would commence in India with the blessings of Lord Curzon. But the political wheel had turned, and by 1905 Curzon was out of office and out of favor, and Younghusband reprimanded for exceeding his authority while in Lhasa. Germany was now the focus of British fears, and Britons were more concerned with the Kaiser's dreadnoughts than with the Tsarist intrigues in Asia. In this changed climate, the ruling Liberals were exploring the course urged by Sir Alfred Lyall years before, and sought direct negotiations with Russia to resolve differences over Persia, Afghanistan, and Tibet, an effort culminating in the Anglo-Russian Convention of 1907.

Now the Secretary of State for India was the Liberal paladin, Lord Morley of Blackburn, the friend and biographer of Gladstone, noted (as a contemporary wrote) for his contemplative eyes and indeterminate chin. As a critic of imperialism, Morley had opposed the Tibet invasion in language very like Sven Hedin's—but in a fresh turn, the Swede was now as dismayed by British restraint as he previously had been by its absence.

Before resigning as Viceroy, Curzon had agreed to help Hedin, promising Indian surveyors trained at Dehra Dun, and even a military escort for his expedition. But Morley had no interest in further Tibetan adventures, nor would he allow foreigners to enter Tibet from Indian soil. So angry and frustrated was Lord Curzon over the change in tide that he refused to meet the new Viceroy, Lord Minto, with the usual ceremony. "When I see Curzon's immense gifts," Morley wrote Minto, "I cannot but be sorry that the gods poured some evil dose into the bowl and spoiled their whole brew."

EVEN AS THE GROUND SHIFTED UNDER HIM, SVEN HEDIN KEPT HIS footing in keeping with his Nietzchean view of exploration as "the affirmation of Superman in the form of a 'struggle against the impossible.'" When he arrived in Simla, Lord Minto was newly ensconced as Viceroy in the Raj's summer capital. In his popular account of his third expedition, *Trans-Himalaya,* Hedin describes admiringly the various entertainments. At a state dinner now held, not as in former days at Auckland House or Peterhof, but at the monumental new Viceregal Lodge, there were platoons of scarlet-liveried servants scurrying around guests, "all in full dress, in grand uniforms of various colours, and glittering with orders." After a herald announced the approach of Lord Minto, the Viceroy greeted the explorer simply with the words, "Welcome to Simla." To the strains of music, the party moved to the dining room where they were regaled with "choice French dishes," eaten from silver plate. The guests then rose to take part in the levee, where 500 gentlemen and their ladies were presented to the Viceroy, standing near his throne. The Viceroy returned each bow as Hedin counted, "Nine hundred times! When Indian princes or Afghan ambassadors pass before him, he does not bow, but lays his hand on the hilt of his guest's sword as a sign of friendship and peace."

Having played host to Hedin at the Viceregal Lodge, Minto left the unpleasant task of informing his guest that he was forbidden to enter Tibet from India to his Foreign Secretary. Later, however, swayed by the explorer's prestige and persistence, the Viceroy relented. Telegrams flew between Simla and Whitehall, but Morley was adamant: Hedin could not go to Tibet. "Here, before the ink on the Chinese settlement [the Anglo-Chinese Convention of 1906] is dry," Morley admonished his Viceroy, "before we have even seen the text of it, here is a policy from Simla, of expeditions, explorations, and all the other provocative things. Consider the row we made (very rightly) about the Buriat escort for the Dalai Lama. And now here we are, sending a whole squad of explorers in every direction, and Sven Hedin with a troop of Native Assistants, a force of Gurkhas, and a British Officer in charge. I cannot but think of this as Curzonism pure and simple." Queried in Parliament, Morley replied: "The Imperial Government has resolved to keep Tibet isolated from India."

Hedin inveighed furiously at the "fossilized politician" who obstinately thrust himself, like Kipling's "Lady of the Snows" into the role of "gatekeeper between India and Tibet."* A furious missive went off to Keltie from Simla: "You are wrong in your letter when you say I should get facilities which no British officer could obtain. *Everything* has been refused. No assistants, no escort, and: 'prevent Sven Hedin

---

*"For the Gates are mine to open
and the Gates are mine to close
and I set my house in order,
said the Lady of the Snows."

from entering Tibet from British territory.' Lord Minto has [done] all
in his power. . . . The Viceroy has sent three long telegrams to the
Secretary of State—the last telegram 200 words—but always refusal.
I have never been treated by any Asiatic tribe as by the Home Government." Hedin found it "comical" that Younghusband, described as
"my oldest and best friend and fellow traveller in Central Asia" (his
role in the Tibetan invasion evidently forgiven) was the new Resident in Kashmir and thus "shall be the very man who has to stop me
with force if I try to cross the British frontier into Tibet!" It was all
fodder for an interesting episode in his next book. Hedin erupted: "I
have brought all my baggage, 20 boxes, up here, and all my money,
50,000 Rupees. And now! I have never begun a journey under such
conditions. My real enemies are in London—the Tibetans *cannot* be
so rude."

However, the British hadn't reckoned with Hedin's pride, ambition, guile, or his obsession with the "three large white spots" still
yawning "like blank pages, north of, in the centre of, and south of
the highest and most extensive mountain-region on earth." Hedin
distinguished between his "geographical morals" and his "ordinary
morals." When it comes to geographical matters, Hedin explains,
"my moral is very, very bad." He informed the powers in Simla, as he
headed toward Kashmir, that having forsworn Tibet, his goal was
Khotan, the desert oasis in Chinese Turkestan. Younghusband, the
new Resident in Kashmir, was once again courted and won over by
the explorer he had met years before in Kashgar. The Briton now
provided his friend with crucial help: he delayed an Indian Government telegram with orders that Hedin was not to leave Leh without
a valid Chinese passport—which he lacked—until a week after his
Swedish friend had left. He also recommended his favorite Ladakhi
caravan *bashi,* Mohammed Isa, who had thirty years' experience,
much of it in Tibet, to Hedin. "Sven Hedin put his arms around my
neck when he left," wrote Younghusband to his wife, "and if I had
given him the slightest encouragement wd. have embraced me!"

At Leh, Hedin assembled his largest caravan under the Ladakhi's
direction. By then the British had guessed his true intentions, but
they could only prevent him from crossing into Tibet from Indian
territory. Once Hedin's party crossed the Tibetan border, there was

little the British could do. His failure at Simla had stiffened his defi-ance: "My life and my honor depend on showing the whole world who is stronger in Asia, Morley or myself."

In September 1906, *The Times* reported that "it appears that the mention of Khotan was intended to throw the Tibetans [and the British] off the scent, for after organizing a fresh caravan at Leh, and making a northward start, he turned sharply to the east when two marches short of the Karakoram pass, in order to continue his work in South-Western Tibet." After losing nine mules in one day—only six animals of the nearly one hundred he commissioned survived the trip—Hedin reached the provincial capital of Shigatse, where he had been invited by the Tashi (or Panchen) Lama, who viewed strangers more benignly than had the Dalai Lama. Hedin spent seven weeks at Tashilhunpo monastery and was invited to observe the New Year's festivities. The explorer was enchanted by the Ninth Incarnation: "Wonderful, never-to-be forgotten Tashi Lama! Never has any man made so deep and ineffaceable an impression on me. Not as a divin-ity in human form, but as a man, who in goodness of heart, inno-cence and purity approaches as near as possible to perfection."

Now that the Dalai Lama had fled to Mongolia to escape Colonel Younghusband's expeditionary force, Hedin, obviously dissembling, claimed to have lost interest in Lhasa. (He was to write a later ad-venturer, the Austrian mountaineer and author of *Seven Years in Tibet*, Heinrich Harrer, "You have reached the city of my dreams.") Yet he knew this was to be his grandest venture, an expedition whose dis-coveries might occupy nine oversize volumes (as it did). In fourteen months he colored in a remarkable 65,000 square miles of "white spaces" in Tibet, declaring with characteristic modesty that these were "the finest results since Stanley discovered the northern bend of the Congo." Besides mapping the "unexplored" areas of what he called the Trans-Himalayan range, Hedin believed (as he wrote in September 1907) that he was "the first white man to penetrate to the sources of the Brahmaputra *and* the Indus, the two rivers famous from time immemorial, which like a crab's claws, encircle the Hi-malayas." He claimed he was the first to identify the source of India's third great river, the Sutlej, at the base of the Ganglung glacier. These feats entailed a complete circuit of the holy Mount Kailas, from which, he wrote in a gust of emotion, "august and serene Shiva looks down from his paradise" on the innumerable humans below "who circle, like asteroids in the sun, round the foot of the mountain." In the same euphoric state, he thoroughly mapped the sacred lake, Manasarovar, "the hub of the wheel which is the symbol of life! I could have stayed there for years," tracking down as well the elusive effluent linking the lake to its smaller sister, Rakas Tal. The one shadow on his triumph was the loss, following a stroke, of his invaluable caravan *bashi,* Mohammed Isa. All this and more Hedin communicated in excited letters to his friend "my dear oncle Keltie." But as he headed home in 1908, he had already received a pointed note from Keltie warning of squalls ahead because "certain people" were inclined to be critical of Hedin's claims. In the event, it wasn't a squall but an ambush, in which his chief antagonist was Colonel Sir Thomas Hungerford Holdich.

HOLDICH WAS AN IMPOSING OFFSTAGE PRESENCE IN BRITISH INDIA from the time of his arrival in 1865 as a Royal Engineer assigned as an assistant surveyor with a Bhutan expedition. His passion for exactitude and skill as an artist (a sketch-book and battered paint box were always in his haversack) led to an immediate job at the Survey Department, and in due course he became Surveyor-General of India. For two decades until his retirement in 1897, he was posted on the North-West Frontier, where he served with distinction in the Second Afghan War and with successive field forces. No British officer had a keener sense of strategic topography than this author of *The Indian Borderland* (1901), *Tibet the Mysterious* (1906), and *The Gates of India* (1909). His survey of the Pamir Plateau, where he worked with a Russian team in defining the frontiers of Central Asia, earned him the RGS Founder's Medal in 1887, and three decades later he was the Society's President during the difficult final two years of World War I.

He was proud, prickly proud, of his Indian Survey Department, especially of its pundits who had "faced all difficulties and braved all dangers," who had been in Lhasa and "mapped it as if it were London." Through their efforts, building on the work of other British explorers, he wrote in the *Journal* in 1901, "we have learned all there is to know of the general physiography of High Asia, including that land of ancient mystery, Tibet." Hence Holdich's impressive eyebrows were predictably raised by Hedin's spacious claims, though he had on past occasions praised Hedin's great skills.

Holdich's doubts were shared and sharpened by the RGS's cadre of Himalayan authorities, notably the mountaineer Dr. Tom Longstaff, who had just ascended the 23,500-foot peak of Trisul, setting a record that lasted 23 years, and Captain Cecil G. Rawling, renowned as a crack shot, who had twice crossed Tibet's forbidden frontiers and had surveyed 38,000 square miles of unmapped territory, feats he described in *The Great Plateau* (1906). In October 1908, Rawling sent this note to Keltie: "I don't want to run Sven Hedin down in any unnecessary way but you asked me if I had any remarks to make on his journey...He has without doubt made a fine journey but if you will look at the attached maps it will be seen that more than half of it is along the very routes I have been...Ours were the pioneer discoveries, firstly Hargreaves and me, then Ryder and me. Sven Hedin has simply followed in our footsteps with the additional journey of joining up two parts. In my opinion he lays claims to things he does not deserve. We say the 'hitherto unknown chain' and Ryder and Wood fixed his peaks...But still I don't want to claim anything, if it pleases him, let him have it or someone else must put the case right. I will fight for others but not for myself. But I have fully realized now that if one does not 'brick by brick' write oneself up and claim everything, one gets nothing; the more you talk about yourself, the more people swallow. What drivel gets written and what is more wonderful, believed...Longstaff has done ten times as much."

Hedin was unprepared for what awaited him. He was coming to Britain fresh from a hero's welcome in Stockholm. There were ringing bells, hurrahs, and waving hats, and 5,000 schoolchildren turned out at the city's harbor. He had been welcomed by the King's adjutant and driven in a carriage to the palace, where Gustav V presented him with the Grand Cross of the Northern Star, one of Sweden's highest honors. Thus buoyed, he made his way to London, where all seemed to go well on February 8, 1909, when he addressed the RGS at Queen's Hall. The audience, *The Times* reported, was packed with luminaries, including three ambassadors, three ministers, a miscellany of admirals and Members of Parliament, Markham, Keltie, Colonel Holdich, Captains Scott and Younghusband, the explorer Sir Aurel Stein, Curzon, and the Secretary of State for India, now Viscount Morley of Blackburn. Hedin received a standing ovation from the packed hall. Behind the roving speaker loomed a large map of Tibet, and Hedin illustrated the lecture with eighty slides showing the people, landscape, and temples of Tibet. He made no mention of the political difficulties he had encountered at the beginning of his trip.

Today Hedin's tale of "marching with death through Northern Tibet" seems maudlin and melodramatic, but this experienced lecturer knew how to provide what his audiences expected. He was especially mindful of the English predilection for furry creatures. Lacking food in the subzero cold of Burtse, Hedin said, his regrets were mostly for his animals, a sentiment with which his listeners could sympathize: "I have had hundreds of servants, and I have forgot many of them. But I have not forgotten a single one of the dogs; they stand before my memory as clear and alive as if I had left them yesterday…and when I leave them they look after me with long wondering melancholy eyes, and I cannot possibly take them all home with me…"

In concluding, the Swede spoke about Tibet and the Russian menace to this audience of specialists: "Even light field artillery could only with the greatest difficulty be transported over Tibet, and a strategical railway would be an absurdity. In the great latitudinal valleys there is no hindrance to a railway, but I cannot see how the material could be brought there, and then—those valleys do not lead to India…I think it difficult to find another country that has got—from a strategical and defensive point of view—such a favourable geographical situation as India, and all those fears expressed by Vámbéry or General MacGregor are, to use rather a polite word, much exaggerated."

As requested by the president, a smiling Lord Morley offered a good-natured "vote of thanks" punctuated by "hear, hears," hurrahs, laughter, and applause:

...It occurred to me, while I was listening to Dr. Sven Hedin, how different is the career and how different the duties of a great explorer from those of a politician. He told us that he tried to drive a flock of sheep, and that he found he had no gift for driving sheep. If he had been in the profession of politics, he would have found that those gifts were sorely needed. I mention that because it occurs to me that Dr. Sven Hedin may think that the Secretary for India, who, after all, holds the keys of the frontier gates of India is, unlike himself, a hard-hearted, a cold-blooded, and a timorous man . . . We thought it inexpedient that he should approach Tibet from the Indian side. I will not be guilty of the intolerable bad taste of attempting for a moment to show that my decision was not over-cautious. I think a good deal of what Dr. Sven Hedin has said tonight rather shows the decision was a right one as far as it went. But I will not argue it because, after all, be the decision as wrong as you like, Dr. Sven Hedin has tonight had his revenge, for he has drawn me captive— though captive impenitent at his car, and I am very glad to find myself able to congratulate him on the great exploit he has performed in spite of it.

In reply, Hedin could not resist tweaking Morley, who had done him a great service: "During the whole time I was in Tibet he kept the frontier between India and Tibet closed to all travelers, and so I was left quite alone with the great white patch which I had decided to explore as carefully as possible. Everybody will understand what that meant for me—especially in a time when the white patches on the map of the Earth are not very numerous."

Yet this was only the first hurdle. The RGS *Journal* had already published an article by the mountaineer Tom Longstaff, questioning Hedin's claims (evoking a stung protest to Keltie from Hedin deploring these "meanest and most envious attacks" appearing in England, "the country to which I have given all my maps!"). But this was a pinprick compared to a subsequent onslaught in the *Journal* by Holdich on Hedin's surveying methods. "What shall we get from Sven Hedin?" Holdich asked. And what was "scientific map making" if not based on triangulation and topography? Anything else was "temporary makeshift awaiting better opportunities." However since "neither triangulation nor topography (in the strict sense) played any part" in the Swede's routine, Holdich warned that "the very glamour of achievement should lead younger generations of explorers (not possessing his remarkable topographical memory and artistic skill) to adopt methods which, at any rate, are not those which the Geographical School set itself earnestly and resolutely to teach." Soon other veterans of the Indian Survey joined in, objecting to Hedin's failure to credit more fully the findings of previous explorers and doubting the validity of his term, "Trans-Himalaya." To respond, Hedin was invited to deliver a second lecture on February 23 in the RGS sanctum at One Saville Row to a small but distinguished group, including his severest critics.

Once again, Hedin's platform performance was formidable, save for his gratuitous assault on the Indian pundits, whose reports he termed "useless for scientific purposes." A pundit "can easily pass a very great lake, and never tell you whether it is salt or fresh. He can cross a river, and not tell you whether it is a big or small river. He can cross a mountain without telling you whether it is solid rock or loose material. I mean it is impossible for a geographer to draw any valuable physico-geographical conclusions from a report of a Pundit, and what we get from them is the topographical idea of a country." He spoke too strenuously, and fired arguments like artillery shells when a modicum of humor and modesty might have disarmed his opponents. Even an admirer, the equally audacious Lieutenant F. M. (Hatter) Bailey, wrote his parents, "I think he did a great deal but it is a pity he did not let other people praise it instead of praising it himself."

As to his maps, he offered this angry reply, recorded in the *Journal*: "In reality the conditions were such, that I had to travel a great deal in disguise, and I cannot see how a triangulation of the country should be possible under such conditions. In another critical article [Holdich's] the same author asks why I did not take Russian topographers with me when the Indians I had asked for, and whom Lord Curzon so kindly had promised me, were refused. This question is probably only meant as a joke, so I don't reply to it at all...And I cannot understand how anybody can be so absurd as to blame me, or 'regret,' as it is called, that I did not introduce trigonometrical mapping in the blanks of the map of the Bongba country. With the same right somebody may blame me for not having started some gold-mining companies, and built some cathedrals on my way through Bongba."

Holdich did not attend the second lecture, but his former colleagues in the Survey were present in force. In the discussion period, Colonel Godwin-Austen, known for his pioneering surveys of the Karakoram, recalled the Strachey brothers, Richard and Henry, who had traced the river sources and the Manasarovar outlet in the 1840's. Sir Henry Trotter, formerly the chief controller of the pundits, emphatically defended his agents' geographic skills. Another objector, Captain Rawling, spoke of his own work in Tibet with Captain C.H.D. Ryder and Lieutenant Bailey, whose plane-table surveying in 1904 confirmed the exceptional accuracy of prior calculations by Pundit Nain Singh. As to the Indus and the Sutlej, whose source Hedin claimed to find, others beginning with Moorcroft had pointed the way, and besides, what exactly was a "source"? All these themes were woven in a concluding critique by Tom Longstaff, who said that Hedin's vaunted Trans-Himalayan range had been explored by Pundit Nain Singh in 1874, whose work formed the basis for a map published in 1889. Concerning the Brahmaputra, Longstaff went on, the priority for locating its source belonged to a party of British sportsmen in 1864, one them being Edmund Smyth, who as it happened was the first recruiter of the pundits. Longstaff with a flourish produced a letter written by the eighty-five-year-old Smyth describing his earlier discovery of the headwaters of the Brahmaputra.

If Holdich was not present, his hand could be sensed as conductor of this well-orchestrated chorus. Curzon, who also did not attend, did what he could to assuage Hedin's bruised ego, arranging for honorary degrees and (with Morley's second) an honorary Knight Commander of the British Empire. What mattered more, Curzon defended Hedin in the *Journal,* where he credited the Swede with filling in a great "white patch" in Tibet, becoming the first European to trace the main branch of the Indus to its glacial origin, and with the "determination" if not the discovery of the sources of India's other two great rivers. It did not suffice. As Charles Allen remarks in his balanced account, *A Mountain in Tibet* (1982), it was not only Hedin's claims that were on trial, but his style, his treatment of exploration as an all-or-nothing contest, his churlish refusal to make the customary bow to predecessors, "his lack of modesty in success, his crowing over others and his stress on triumph gained through suffering." Not for nothing did the British call their Central Asian contest a Great Game, in which manners and rules mattered, and Hedin quite simply had proved himself a mucker. For all his admiration of England, this was something he never could grasp. Nor did he forgive or forget his humiliation, as he headed across yet another river, the Rhine, to embrace his unconditional defender, Kaiser Wilhelm's Germany.

SVEN HEDIN'S PROGRESSIVE ESTRANGEMENT FROM THE BRITISH can be tracked, step by step, in his correspondence with Keltie. Writing from Stockholm, he initially tried to mend fences, promising to dedicate the scientific results of his expedition to the Survey of India, and reporting that he has asked German mapmakers to name various ranges after Montgomerie, Strachey, Ryder, and the Pundit Nain Singh. In August 1910, he informs Keltie that the Germans have turned all this down and want only Asiatic names, "So I am sorry to have to give it up, as it was meant as a token of admiration for British explorers."

Later that year, Hedin announced to Keltie that the first volume of his scientific work will be "a disagreeable surprise" to "certain gentlemen," amplifying: "Poor Longstaff! So far as I have proceeded [there] is very little left of him." Unabashedly, Hedin asks Keltie if he can get Lord Curzon to review the book, because "I hate to be reviewed by dilettantes, as Holdich and Broadfoot, who have really a very limited understanding of physical geography." In any case, Hedin has found "extremely important documents" about Tibet two hundred years before showing that the Chinese, Indians, and Tibetans "are in perfect agreement with me as to the *real* situation of the sources at Brahmaputra and Sutlej."

Two months later, in March 1911, he informs Keltie that his maps correct still other errors, that Loulan "was situated exactly where I found it, and not where Stein and Huntington [the American geographer] will have it." He goes on to extol his findings about other archaeological sites, ancient rivers, and geology, and ends with a grand operatic crescendo: "I do not boast, but I am going to defend my ground as long as I live. What did it matter that Sir Henry Rawlinson dared to say that it was Livingstone who found Stanley and not vice-versa! The truth will always conquer lies so what does it matter that I, on Febr 23rd 1909,…stood as a criminal before my accusers, [rather] than as a triumphantor amongst friends, although I returned from the greatest journey I had ever undertaken and brought home new knowledge about the country north of the Himalaya, which ought to be of the most burning interest to every subject of his Brit. Majesty, at any rate more interesting than a very doubtful record on the great ice, without a shadow of epoch making geographical discovery."

In 1912, the waters parted further as Hedin weighed in against Britain's evolving alliance with Sweden's historic adversary, Russia. Adventurers built Great Britain, he admonishes Keltie, and politicians will destroy it: "I have tried to find out only one high point in which British and Russian interests meet in Europe." He relates that "old Vambery" had written him to deplore the "most importunate and desperate alliance" and Hedin reports his own expulsion from the Imperial Geographic Society in St. Petersburg: "But what could you suspect from a society which, since 1869, has had only one and the same president! Old Semenoff has no doubt some merits. He is a Jew who has denied the religion of his father. He has instituted a gold medal with his own name and portrait in the decorations, which some years ago was given to me; I was the first who got it. In 1857, he made a little trip in Tian Shan, and to celebrate his 50 years' jubilee he calls himself Semenoff-Tianshansky! What should you think of me if I called myself Hedin-Transhimalayaski! You should believe I were mad."

The letters thereafter fade away. Civilities ceased completely after August 1914, when the Great War broke out. In the first critical months, Hedin volunteered his services as an ostensibly impartial neutral to judge atrocity charges directed against German forces on the Western Front. He visited occupied Belgium and France, was an honored guest at the Kaiser's imperial headquarters, met with the Emperor's supreme commanders, and returned to Sweden to publish a two-volume book acquitting Germany. Huge printings of the German edition, *Ein Volk in Waffen* (*A People in Arms*), were practically given away to German troops, prompting an even more prolix sequel about the Eastern front that ran some 900 pages, the theme being German *Kultur* versus Russian barbarism. In 1915, a notice appeared in *The Times* that the British had stripped Hedin of his knighthood, and the RGS rescinded his Fellowship. On July 15, with impenitent sarcasm, Sven Hedin penned this letter to the president of the Society:

> Sir: At my return from Lemberg yesterday I found your letter of March 23 informing me that the Council of the R.G.S. has removed my name from the list of Honorary Corresponding Members. I congratulate you on this noble and chivalrous deed and I congratulate myself thus to have gained the political liberty which I believe could be claimed even by a member of the R.G.S.! I beg you to present to the Council my hearty thanks for the 17 years during which I had the honour of belonging to the most renowned and the greatest of all Geographical Societies in the world. My name has been removed from the list of Honorary Members but the deep and warm regards I have always felt for British exploration and British geographical work will forever remain to an invisible member of the Royal Geographical Society.

Until the eve of her defeat, Hedin was certain Germany would win, and on November 11, 1918, Armistice Day, writing in a Swedish newspaper, he extolled Kaiser Wilhelm as the greatest, the last, and "the only true ruling personality of our time." All this was bitterly recalled in London as Hedin continued to send his scientific volumes for review by the RGS *Journal*. All this was noted with unsurpassable iciness by Sir Charles Bell, the former British mission chief in Lhasa, in a note to the new RGS Secretary, Arthur Hinks, dated February 3, 1925:

> I am interested to see the two letters which you send to me from Sven Hedin. They are quite characteristically impudent. Almost as soon as the war started, Hedin came out most offensively on the German side...[He] was so arrogantly anti-British that he was expelled from this Society; the only man who was expelled. The enemies were just taken off quietly. The Council felt that they must mark particularly their feeling of the gross ingratitude of Hedin after the way he had crawled to us to obtain all sorts of favours and had after long importunity been given a British order ...From time to time he has sent us books such as his *Southern Tibet*—the first volume of which was inscribed to the Society with his kind regards. By order of the Council this fly leaf of the book was removed before it was placed in our Library...That I think is all there is to say about Sven Hedin. We simply cut him, but derived some amusement at his misfortune when in 1918 he had a book in the press entitled "Germany Triumphant" just at the time Germany collapsed.

Excommunicated by the British, Sven Hedin found ever more fervent devotées in Germany. In 1925, he was invited to lead an expedition sponsored by the Swedish Government but underwritten by Lufthansa and the German aircraft industry, whose managers wanted Hedin to investigate the feasibility of a Berlin-Peking air route. The declared aim of what became known as the Lufthansa expedition was to establish weather stations across western China. But in 1927, times had changed: Chiang Kai-shek's Nationalist Government was installed in the new capital of Nanking, and much of Chinese Turkestan was in the hands of warlords. Foreigners now needed permission and protection to roam China's western steppes and deserts. After protracted negotiations, Hedin, who always preferred to be the only European on his trips, agreed to a Sino-Swedish expedition whose official leader was to be Chinese. Hedin's so-called wandering university of scientists included ten Chinese, nine Swedes, one Dane, eleven Germans, plus thirty-four servants and two hundred and ninety-two camels. With Hedin as shadow chief, the expedition left on a six-year mission to explore Inner Mongolia, western Kansu and Sinkiang provinces, with Lufthansa bearing the costs of the first year, supplemented in subsequent years by the Swedish Government, and, most significantly, by a Chicago benefactor of Swedish descent, Vincent Bendix. At mission's end, at the request of the Nanking Government, Hedin undertook a further survey of the Silk Road. The results were published as *Reports from the Scientific Expedition*, running to thirty-five volumes, which occupied the explorer until his death in 1952.

Hedin's German companions appear to have been blood-and-iron nationalists who despised the new Weimar Republic. A diary kept by Huang Wenbi, a Chinese member of the team, as edited by his son Huang Lie and published in Beijing in 1990, has this entry for July 7, 1927: "The day before yesterday there was a party for foreign members and they sang military songs. After the party they did a drill…The old party of Germany still holds to its policy of aggression and their ambition is obvious…Hedin is very close to the old party." Huang feared all too credibly that the Germans were surveying the land and weather of western China to prepare for a new war against Britain and Russia. Remarking on their arrogance, he added four days later, "Foreigners travel here as if it were no man's land. It is shameful to have a weak country!"

An American observer of all this was Owen Lattimore, who, in a letter to a colleague, remarked in 1934 that although the Chinese formally led the expedition and were supposed to get all its finds, Hedin "was actually allowed to export, permanently, enormous collections." Lattimore, then a free-lance scholar in Central Asia, had already met Hedin in Peking and was "distinctly impressed." Though the "expeditionaries" (see Chapter 15) blamed the Swede for "queering the pitch" in China, Lattimore wondered if Hedin's concessions to nationalist demands wasn't "perfectly right." In China (as Lattimore wrote to Arthur Hinks at the RGS in 1930), "it isn't the rules that matter, it's all knack. The positive thing that the Chinese secured was jobs for a number of their men."

As for the "howl" raised against Hedin for robbing the country of its treasures ("now the standard catchword"), Lattimore remarked that the Chinese on his team would have to stand with him or be accused of being traitors. The American took amused note of Hedin's feud with the British, saying the Swede "may not have shown any conspicuous flashes of the old cricketing spirit, but then the British themselves are apt to forget cricket on the Indian frontier, and they have certainly, since the war, carried their feud against Hedin to extreme lengths."

Yet not only German nationalists admired Sven Hedin; his fans included the Social Democrats who governed Berlin, where a street in the fashionable Zehlendorf district in 1927 became Sven-Hedin-Strasse. The name survived all of Berlin's upheavals, including the four decades when U.S. troops were billeted in the same neighborhood. Hedin's feats mattered more than his politics, and it was thus a coup for Adolf Hitler when the famous Swede in due course heaped praise on the Third Reich. Hitler also reciprocated where it counted: on the map. In 1937, Hedin was honored again in Berlin, this time with a Sven-Hedin-Platz, and his seduction was consummated when he accepted more sinister honors from Reichsführer Heinrich Himmler.

CHAPTER FOURTEEN

The Spoils of Serindia

Archaeology is not a science, it's a vendetta." Sir Mortimer Wheeler's oft-quoted admonition derived from extensive field experience, especially on the Indian Subcontinent. As the excavator of the Bronze Age cities of the Indus and as the Director General of Archaeology in India, attainments that established his own high standing in Britain, Wheeler knew firsthand how a digger's reputation might hinge on arcane rivalries and bureaucratic whim, on diplomatic intrigue and unpredictable bursts of nationalism. All these hidden reefs help explain why the public at large has heard relatively little about Wheeler's stellar colleague, Sir Aurel Stein.

Stein was the preeminent Western scholar, explorer, and excavator of innermost Asia from the 1890's until his death in 1943. Sir Leonard Woolley, the discoverer of the Royal Cemetery at Ur, called Stein's forays "the most daring and adventurous raid on the ancient world that any archaeologist had attempted." His four Silk Road expeditions once filled entire rooms in the British Museum and New Delhi's Museum of Central Asian Antiquities (now the National Museum). Retracing ancient caravan routes while documenting the spread of Buddhism from India to China, Stein repeatedly crossed 18,000-foot passes, settling down to work in the deserts of Chinese Turkestan. It took 182 packing cases to hold the finds of his third expedition (1913–16) to the region he preferred calling Serindia, from the Greek word for China, *Seres,* meaning silkworm. Not the least of his prizes was the world's oldest dated printed book (A.D. 868), a Chinese copy of a Buddhist text known as the Diamond Sutra. When asked to comment on Stein's remarkable achievement, Sven Hedin summed it up in one word—Excelsior!

Unlike Hedin, Stein never benefited from royal sponsors. Nor did he possess the personal wealth that enabled Heinrich Schliemann, the discoverer of Troy and Mycenae, or Sir Arthur Evans, the excavator of Knossos in Crete, to dig without earning a living. Instead, as a salaried civil servant, Stein had to wheedle sabbaticals and scrounge funding for his expeditions from the Indian Archaeological Service. In the process he became adept at manipulating "the mysterious process of officialdom," according to his friend, Sir Edward Maclagan, Governor of the Punjab. It helped that he was a master at stroking such diverse and difficult patrons as Lord Curzon, India's Viceroy, and Sir Henry Rawlinson, president of the Royal Geographical Society. Over the years, although he was an outsider, born in Budapest of Jewish ancestry, Stein won many of the empire's prizes: knighthood in 1912, medals from the RGS in 1909, the Royal Asiatic Society in 1932, and the Society of Antiquaries in 1935; and honorary degrees from Oxford, Cambridge, and St. Andrews.

Yet not until his final decade did Sir Aurel Stein believe he had outlived and outwitted those who thwarted his lifelong ambition, to follow the path of Alexander the Great into Afghanistan. Here he hoped finally to establish how a Hellenic people reached deep into Asia. To describe what happened requires opening an exploratory trench into archives and unpublished correspondence, where the truth about archaeology-as-vendetta is so often interred.

Let us eavesdrop. The year is 1922, the month is May, and two men are deep in conversation inside a tent at Mohand Marg, a lofty mountain camp, north of Srinigar in Kashmir. The younger is clearly the visitor. He is Cornelius Van H. Engert (1887–1985), a mountain-climbing American diplomat who at thirty-four has an impressive résumé. Posted to Ottoman Turkey at the start of World War I, this Harvard graduate has for the last ten years seen history being made at Constantinople, Syria, Asia Minor, and elsewhere in the Near East. Engert has just come from Kabul, on the first official mission by an American to Afghanistan, and his report on its complex politics is of intense interest to Sir Aurel Stein.

Stein has long and vainly sought an excavation permit from the Afghan Government. Following the bombing of Kabul by the Royal Air Force during the brief Third Afghan War in 1919, a wave of anti-British anger gripped the capital. Sir Aurel has been hostage to such adverse events but is exhilarated by what he hears from Engert, amplifying in a subsequent letter to Percy Allen, his close friend and soon to be president of Corpus Christi College at Oxford:

> I found him a delightful guest and a man of a most scholarly mind…He gave me a full & unbiased account of the state of things at Kabul, where he found a curious reflex of the Young Turks' spirit to prevail, with a corresponding increase in the autochthone pride & vanity. He is confident that I shall be allowed to proceed to Afghan soil, and attributes the difficulty so far experienced chiefly to the desire of "twisting the lion's tail" and enjoying as long as possible the sight of the Govt. in the position of a humble supplicant. In the end, he thinks, the request will be graciously granted. May his prediction prove true!

Stein came to rely on Engert's reports from Kabul, especially as they dealt with the machinations of Alfred Foucher, a French archaeologist. Once Stein's devoted protégé, Foucher had become, thanks to an ambitious wife, his rival. Playing on Afghan hostility to Britain, Foucher won for the French an archaeological monopoly similar to one they already enjoyed in Persia. Nettled and disappointed, Stein reported to Engert in December, "So I have to accept the sad fact of access being barred to me to a field towards which I have looked all my life and for which I had prepared myself to the best of my ability…"

Stein vowed to persist, informing his friends that he did not wish to end his days "tamely in the study or poking into areas which others have searched over & over again." Instead he hoped his end would come quickly: he wished to die as "a victim of avalanche or a Pathan knife" instead of "annihilating civilization." Indeed, escaping the stifling embrace of civilization was the central motif of his life.

MARC AUREL STEIN—HE WAS NAMED IN THE IMPERIAL MANNER after the Roman Emperor Marcus Aurelius—was born in 1862 to Jewish parents who had converted to Christianity, as did many co-religionists in the Austro-Hungarian Empire. Young Aurel received a classical education at gymnasiums in Budapest and Dresden, where, besides Greek, Latin, and German, he mastered French and English. While in the Lutheran Kreuzschule in Dresden, Stein became fascinated by Alexander the Great, prompting his studies of Persian and Sanskrit at the universities of Vienna and Leipzig before he obtained his doctorate in 1883 at Tübingen. With the help of friends of his uncle Professor Ignaz Hirschler, a distinguished eye surgeon and a member of the Hungarian Academy of Sciences, Stein received a stipend for postdoctoral studies in England.

One of Stein's first stops in England was the Oriental Institute in Woking, which was run by a fellow Budapester, William Gottfried Leitner, known for his work on an obscure Asian mountain tribe, the so-called Dards. Although Stein found the ethnographer "a rather strange man," he nevertheless took up residence at the institute, where in congenial surroundings he took Punjabi lessons to prepare himself "for a possible position in India by learning a modern Indian language." Stein also sought out Dr. Theodore Duka, a Hungarian exile who had served the British as a surgeon in India. Duka was the biographer of yet another Hungarian, Alexander Csoma de Körös, the traveler William Moorcroft met in the Himalayan foothills. Csoma died before he reached Chinese Turkestan, where he believed the Hungarian people had their roots. At Duka's house, Stein met Sir Henry Yule, a pioneer geographer of Central Asia and translator of

Marco Polo. Another guest was the dashing Sir Henry Rawlinson, the Gold Medalist and two-time president of the Royal Geographical Society. Both Yule and Rawlinson, former pillars of the Raj, took an interest in Stein's career, and the young archaeologist would reciprocate with effusive dedications in his books. As his first biographer Jeannette Mirsky expressed it, Stein had mastered "the fundamentals of how the real world works."

Returning to Hungary in 1887 for compulsory military service, Stein acquired another essential skill: at the army's Ludovika Academy, he became proficient at surveying and mapmaking. At twenty-five, he headed for India. On Rawlinson's recommendation and with Yule's endorsement, Stein had obtained the dual posts of principal of the Oriental College at Lahore and registrar of Punjab University. In Lahore "by far the most interesting" of his new friends was Rudyard Kipling's father, Lockwood, described in *Kim* as "the white-bearded Englishman," the keeper of the "Wonder House," a great repository of Gandharan Buddhist art. Unlike other European Orientalists who never ventured to the Subcontinent, Stein was able to study the Buddhist art from Gandhara (now in Pakistan), then rarely seen outside the Punjab, under Kipling's guidance and pursue his interest in the extraordinary cultural encounter that had occurred along the Silk Road, as the German geographer Ferdinand von Richthofen was the first to call it.

Although Stein's thesis that Buddhism spread from India via the Silk Road through Central Asia to China has been amended by modern scholars, his work still provides valuable insights into the early history of the region. Because India is rich in artifacts but poor in ancient historical records—manuscripts disintegrate in the pervasive humidity—the story of Asia's conversion to Buddhism was veiled in myth and surmise until Stein's researches.

From China's former capital, present-day Xian, the ancient Silk Road crossed south of the Gobi Desert to Dunhuang, where it divided to bypass the Taklamakan Desert. The southerly route proceeded westward from Miran and Khotan in Chinese Turkestan to the Afghan cities of Herat and Kabul. From Dunhuang, the northern Silk Road passed through Turfan to Kashgar and thence southward to the Levant and northward to Samarkand in what is now the Republic of Uzbekistan. For nearly a millennium until its decline in the fifteenth century, the Silk Road was the principal artery through which goods and ideas passed from Asia to Europe. Caravans brought silk, spices, rhubarb, and porcelain to Europe in exchange for gold and such Western delicacies as walnuts and figs.

Along these routes Buddhist monks created imposing monasteries, carved effigies of heroic proportions, and filled whole galleries of cave temples with paintings and sculpture. In monastic libraries they stored silk temple banners depicting scenes from the life of Buddha, along with sacred texts copied from Indian originals. Some of these remote complexes were enormous honeycombs of decorated caves, and their rediscovery before World War I caused a sensation. The quantity and quality of cave art was a revelation, but as surprising were manuscripts showing that Buddhism was not the only faith that flourished in the oasis cities along the Silk Road. Jews, Christians, Manicheans, Nestorians, and Zoroastrians also reached and settled in these far-flung outposts before succumbing to the onslaught of the Muslims in the tenth century.

REPORTS OF A GREAT BUDDHIST CIVILIZATION BURIED BENEATH the sands of the Taklamakan first surfaced in 1890 when an Indian Army intelligence officer, Captain Hamilton Bower, returned to Calcutta with fifty-one birch bark leaves he had acquired from trea-sure-hunters digging near the town of Kucha on the northern Silk Road. Written in Sanskrit in an archaic Indian script, the Bower manuscript dealt primarily with medicine and necromancy. Dating from around the fifth century A.D., it was the oldest known Indian manuscript, its leaves preserved by the arid climate of the Takla-makan Desert.

Bower's discovery in Chinese Turkestan (as it was then called) stirred a race for artifacts, mostly by Europeans but joined by the oc-casional Japanese or American scholar. In the pivotal oasis city of Kashgar, a bidding war ensued between the Russians and the British as rival diplomats, Nikolai Petrovsky and George Macartney, competed for manuscripts, books, pottery, and coins in the bazaar. These "antiquities" gleaned from the area around Khotan, a little kingdom that lay on the route from the Oxus Valley to China, were gathered from local treasure-seekers and forwarded to St. Petersburg and Calcutta. Soon, as Stein was to report, there was even an extensive industry of forged 'old books'—and scholars as well as diplomats began to carve out "spheres of influence."

Stein had been following Sven Hedin's forays into the Taklamakan in the Royal Geographical Society's *Journal,* where the Swede published the results of his 1898 expedition. During this search for "the lost cities of the Taklamakan," Hedin obtained about 500 small objects: manuscripts and coins now in Stockholm. But, as he later wrote, he willingly left scientific research to later "specialists." For Hedin, "It was sufficient to have made the important discovery and to have won in the earth of the desert a new field for archaeology." Stein generously acknowledged Hedin's priority although a friendly rivalry soon ensued between explorer and scholar.

Both men were short in stature, indifferent to hardships, and lived into their eighties. Neither married. Both shared a fondness for dogs—Stein owned a succession of seven fox terriers all named Dash. Although both contributed extensively to Central Asian research, Stein inched upward through the Indian bureaucracy while Hedin's career resembled a rocket trajectory. Hedin accomplished three important forays through Central Asia before he was forty-three. Stein was thirty-seven when he embarked in 1900 on his first expedition. Unlike Hedin, Stein never claimed "firsts." He preferred to track other footsteps: along the paths of the seventh-century Chinese pilgrim Hsüan-tsang or of Marco Polo or in the wake of Alexander the Great.

Stein began his explorations during his winter vacation of 1897–98. After obtaining a small grant and necessary permissions, he accompanied the Indian Army's "butcher and beat it" raid led by General Bindon Blood into the Buner region of the North-West Frontier. There and in the Swat Valley lay ruins of the Graeco-Buddhist kingdom of Gandhara (flourished sixth century B.C. to fifth century A.D.) for Stein's small team of Indian surveyors to explore. This was followed by a proposal for an expedition to Khotan in Chinese Turkestan, which he submitted to the Punjab Government. Adroitly playing the Russian card, he noted that the Imperial Russian Academy of Sciences had already "arranged to send three savants for the exploration of *Turfan* (Southern Chinese Turkestan) where ancient manuscripts have been found." Lest his superiors had further doubts about the competition, he added, "I am also informed that Dr. Sven Hedin's explorations . . . are likely to be resumed."

The proposal was still grinding through the bureaucratic mill when, in April 1899, the newly appointed Viceroy, Lord Curzon, visited Lahore to confer with the Government's Afghan politicals, the "Lords of the Marches" as Stein dubbed the commanding officers of the North-West Frontier. Stein went to the rail station for the "great show" as troops in dazzling white uniforms welcomed Curzon. In his pocket diary, he noted the "Viceroy's fine speech" praising the English public schools. A week later, the Punjab Government asked him to serve as "the Viceroy's *cicerone*," and Stein happily escorted Curzon around Lockwood Kipling's museum.

"The day before yesterday I had the opportunity to introduce myself personally to Lord C," Stein wrote his brother Ernst. "I had half an hour to present my explanation and found in Lord C. an expert questioner and listener." When Stein presented Curzon with reprints of his articles, he found the Viceroy was familiar with his "roving expeditions on the borderlands" as well as his Khotan project. In the end Curzon promised to help. The jubilant archaeologist wrote, "This was the most stimulating *collegium ambulatorium* I have experienced so far in India." Personally he found His Excellency "with all his dignity, very charming."

For Curzon, archaeology was almost an obsession. As a recent graduate of Oxford, he haunted the British Museum, where he became familiar with the sculpture of Egypt, Assyria, Greece, and Rome. As Viceroy, he was scandalized by the sorry dilapidation of Indian monuments, remarking that "were Germany the ruling power in India, I do not hesitate to say that she would be spending many lakhs [a lakh equaled 100,000 rupees] on a task which we have rather plumed ourselves on our generosity in devoting Rs. 61,000, raised only a little more than a year ago to 88,000." He concluded with his trademark asperity, "When I reflect on the sums of money that are gaily dispensed on the construction of impossible forts in impossible places, which are to sustain an impossible siege against an impossible foe, I do venture to hope that so mean a standard may not again be pleaded, at any rate in my time."

It was Curzon who launched the Archaeological Survey of India and who appointed himself Director of Antiquities. He increased its grants with his own—or more precisely, his American wife Mary's—personal funds. Under his stewardship the Survey managed just in time to safeguard India's architectural treasures, notably the Taj Mahal.

Now Curzon arranged for Stein's caravan to enter the politically sensitive area of Chinese Turkestan from India. Various state governments would share the costs, and British and Indian museums would divide the finds. The Survey of India would provide equipment and an experienced pundit, Ram Singh, "to carry on a continuous system of surveys by plane table, astronomical observations, and triangulation" during the whole of their travels. (Stein's maps would not be criticized at Royal Geographical Society meetings!)

FOR EACH OF HIS FIRST THREE EXPEDITIONS, STEIN PRIDED himself on plotting three different itineraries over the Karakorum Mountains. Two major routes cross the range that connects the Himalaya and the Kunlun mountains on the east with the Hindu Kush and the Pamirs on the west: the Gilgit, or western route, now runs through Pakistan; the eastern track runs from Leh in Ladakh. Starting from Srinigar, in Kashmir, Stein's first trip took him from Gilgit through Hunza, whose kingdoms had only recently come under British control, then over the mountain passes to China. Army engineers had cut a mule track to Gilgit, allowing him to minimize the danger. The trip over the Karakorum Pass, he assured his brother, was now "a tour for ladies." Kashgar was so refined that he wondered whether to take along his black tails for dining. "The world," he half-complained, "where civilization and the mail does not reach has become very small."

Stein was excessively modest. His first Karakorum crossing with its spectacular views of Nanga Parbat and Rakaposhi peaks took six weeks. He broke the trip with a brief detour to survey the Muztagh-ata massif and, after a five-day trek to the mountain, he could not re-sist climbing the 24,321-foot peak. He tested his endurance in a six-hour ascent through freshly deposited snow and succeeded in reaching the summit, a feat twice denied Hedin. The peak over-looked the entire breadth of the Pamirs, "a seemingly endless succes-sion of valleys and ranges." Proudly, Stein records, he had not succumbed to the altitude sickness—headache and nausea—that af-fected some members of his team.

When Stein reached Kashgar in late July, his party followed the short poplar-lined avenue outside the city walls to the gate of Chini-bagh, the British Residence, where he was welcomed "in the harti-est fashion."

In 1900 Kashgar differed little from the lively market town that Younghusband and Hedin had visited a decade before. Its 40,000 people lived in two distinct districts, the older, called the Mo-hammedan City, inhabited mostly by Muslim Uighurs, and the New City to the south, whose population was primarily Han Chinese. Moats and thick crenellated walls pierced by four enormous iron gates enclosed the city. Chini-bagh, pleasantly situated on a high cliff, commanded a panorama of the broad Tüman River valley, which carried the runoff from the melted snows of the Tian Shan Mountains visible to the north. On clear days from Chini-bagh's roof, Stein could see the snow-covered Muztagh-ata to the south. At night the great gongs of the Chinese guardhouses sounded the hours and at nine o'clock, when the gates of the city were closed, a gun was fired and trumpets were blown. (The gongs are now silent, and the old British residence is today a decaying relic in the shadows of a big tourist hotel misleadingly called Chini-bagh.)

What had changed, Stein discovered, was that Chini-bagh had a charming new mistress. George Macartney had returned from home leave with a bride, a twenty-one-year-old Scot, Catherine Theodora Borland. Self-described as "the most timid unenterprising girl in the world," Theodora had never traveled and had "none of the qualifica-tions" for her new life "beyond being able to make a cake." A few years earlier, Stein wrote, the British residence had been a simple walled-in orchard with a little garden house, "such as every respectable Kashgari loves to own." But with carpets, cushions, lampshades, Russian stoves, a harmonium, and a piano, Theodora had gradually transformed the "tumbledown mud-built garden house into a residence which in its cozy, well-furnished rooms now offered all the comforts of an English home."

The Macartneys had traveled overland from Scotland through Russia to Kashgar. After they crossed the Terek pass running over the ridge of the Tian Shan Mountains, a Cossack escort, thoughtfully provided by Petrovsky, met them with "a comfortable little carriage" for their journey through the desert to Kashgar. However, at the time of Stein's visit, political arguments had caused relations between Petrovsky and Macartney to deteriorate to the point where they were no longer speaking.

Alone in this far outpost of Central Asia—Kashgar lies farther from the sea than any other city in the world—with only the occasional explorer or game hunter for company, Macartney tried to stem the Russian advance but waged a losing battle. The collapse of Manchu domination of the province had begun in the 1860's when Chinese-speaking Muslims in the adjoining province of Kansu rebelled, effectively severing connections between Kashgar, the provincial capital Urumchi, and Peking. When, after the demise of Yakub Beg (see Chapter 9), St. Petersburg recognized Peking's paramountcy in Sinkiang, China permitted Petrovsky to open a consulate in Kashgar. To punish the British for their flirtation with Yakub Beg, China denied the British equal consular status for more than two decades.

These diplomatic entanglements explain why George Macartney (later Sir George), who arrived in Kashgar in 1890, had no official position until 1893, when he became Special Assistant for Chinese Affairs to the Resident in Kashmir. When he was finally designated British Consul in 1904, the Chinese refused to confirm his appointment, and it was not until 1909 that his position was regularized. Petrovsky outranked and outflanked Macartney and, as if to rub it in, retained an escort of 100 Cossacks. After Russian railroads were built, Russian goods poured in, a Russo-Chinese bank and post of-

fice opened, and the gold ruble replaced the silver Chinese tanga as
common currency. In 1900, as Stein was crossing the Karakorum, the
Boxer Rebellion had just broken out, the Russians occupied
Manchuria, and Petrovsky had become the virtual ruler of Sinkiang.

In Kashgar, the nominal Chinese administrator, the Taotai, lived in
terror of the charming but arrogant Russian. When Macartney asked
the Taotai for help on behalf of Stein—introductions to the local officials, or ambans, of Khotan and Keriya—the Taotai, after confessing
that he was "a coward and a fool," refused for fear of offending Petrovsky. Because the Russian suspected that Stein was a British spy, he
refused even to see the archaeologist, pleading illness. As a constant
reminder of his frustrations, Stein wrote he could hear snatches of
Russian airs sung in the evenings by the Cossack guard, wafting across
from the Russian Consulate. Stein was not to meet their "sahib" until
his return from Khotan, nine months later. Nonetheless, comfortably
ensconced under Chini-bagh's hospitable roof, the archaeologist bus-
ied himself with the practical tasks of the expedition.

AMONG THE TRAITS THAT SET STEIN APART FROM HEDIN WAS HIS
consideration for men and beasts. No member of his four expeditions
was buried on a mountaintop or left dying of thirst in a desert. Although frostbite cost Stein every toe on his right foot during his second expedition, it was not from rashly scaling Himalayan heights in the
dead of winter. While Hedin's expeditions moved as rapidly as possible
through the desert, Stein anticipated working in the Taklamakan for
weeks at a time. For this he required fresh drinking water for men and
camels, and he commissioned seventeen-gallon galvanized-iron water
tanks—the optimum size for a Bactrian camel to carry—in Calcutta.
When the temperature fell in wintertime, blocks of ice would supplement the tanks.

A great maker of lists and a master of the art of packing, Stein purchased in England or procured in India: a camera and 800 glass negatives, a green Willesden canvas bath, a rot-proof ground sheet for his
wool-lined tent, a Stormont–Murphy Arctic Stove that burned com-

pressed fuel cakes steeped in paraffin, a folding table, folding candle lanterns, rot-proof canvas buckets and well-drilling equipment, a fur-lined coat and semiarctic winter clothing, mule trunks and leather-covered storage baskets for his instruments, a medical kit, stores of condensed food including meat lozenges, compressed food tablets, chocolate, and jam. He had also arranged a loan from the Rawal-pindi arsenal of two carbines and two revolvers. In Kashgar, he pro-cured eight camels and twelve ponies and some additional water tanks jerry-rigged from some iron Russian kerosene tanks.

Unlike other operatives in the Great Game, Stein never traveled in disguise. In fact one picture shows him as a full-fledged country gen-tleman: in front of his tent, hands as usual in his pockets, a heavy serge overcoat covering what appears to be a dark wool suit. One wonders what the locals made of his khaki-colored spats, high collar, and cravat.

Even in subzero temperatures when the ink froze in his pen, Stein kept a journal and forwarded a meticulous monthly account to the Government *babus* in Calcutta in which he recorded every anna spent, along with prodigious notes. In addition, he wrote letters to friends, which he sent home by the *dak* runners who brought his mail. Thus notices of his progress regularly appeared in *The Times* and the RGS *Journal*. Spare moments were spent correcting galleys—two books, one scholarly, the other a popular account, recording each of his first three expeditions.

Before his arrival, Macartney's letters had provided Stein with es-sential information on the climate and necessities of transport, and over the years the Resident assumed roles beyond his normal man-date. Macartney became Stein's banker—arranging for the archaeolo-gist's salary to be paid in Chinese money—and his agent, hiring both men and animals. He badgered Peking for passports and permits, in-tervened on Stein's behalf with local Chinese authorities, and in-structed the archaeologist in the complex "form and manners which Chinese etiquette considers essential for politic intercourse." Stein was far more appreciative of his host's special talents than Younghus-band, who complained of his half-Chinese translator's tendency to approach problems from a Chinese point of view—"Macartney is a good enough fellow in his way but he is not English." Macartney was

Stein's listening post, forwarding news of plans of archaeological rivals as well as the *Weekly Times*. So it was through Macartney that Stein heard the news first of the death of Queen Victoria and then the outbreak of World War I. "Macartney's ever-watchful care protects me from afar," Stein wrote a friend in 1914. For his part, Stein's friendship, once bestowed, was "as true as steel."

Keeping three men from his original team, Stein now added two camel men and a Chinese-speaking Kashgari, Niaz Akhun. As interpreter Niaz would serve Stein "honestly," but Stein's praise was qualified by what he termed Niaz's "small personal failings such as his inordinate addiction to opium and gambling and his strong inclination to qualified looting." Finally after six weeks' preparation and a farewell dinner hosted by the Macartneys, Stein left Kashgar on September 11 to winter in the desert.

One important resource for him was the *Record of the Western Regions* by the Chinese Buddhist monk Hsüan-tsang [Xuan Zang; ca. 596–664] recounting his pilgrimage to India to collect sacred texts. Throughout his first three expeditions, Stein relied on the help, friendship, and scholarly interest of local Mandarins, his way eased by invoking the name of his "Indian Pausanias, Hsüan-tsang." Stein wrote that his appeal to the memory of the peripatetic "great monk of the Tang dynasty" never failed to secure him a sympathetic hearing with these scholars. Khotan's amban, the learned and pious Pan-Darin, became Stein's great friend without whose "ever ready assistance neither the explorations in the desert nor the survey work in the [Kunlun] mountains which preceded it could have been accomplished."

Stein planned his first excavations for the area of Khotan. This caravan city had a particular resonance for the Chinese pilgrim Hsüantsang's modern follower, for it was here that the monk recorded locals worshiping "rats as big as hedgehogs, their hair of gold and silver colour." (Khotan's citizens believed the rats appeared when the king prayed for deliverance from the Hiung-nu, or Huns, who were ravaging the border.) The city had recently acquired a different distinction: it was the center for a fraternity of looters who plundered the ancient settlements. But while he perused the coins, terra-cotta figures, and other antiquities proferred to him, Stein was able to coax valuable information about these sites.

TODAY'S TRAVELER APPROACHES THE CARAVAN CITIES OF YARKAND and Khotan by bus or van, threading past the same rows of willows, poplars, mulberry bushes, and tamarisks that cloaked the road and lined irrigation ditches in Stein's day. There is the smell of burning dung, and microscopic loess dust causes a permanent haze. Now as then there is a sameness to the smaller cities of Sinkiang Province. Army trucks and Chinese buses with Uzbek drivers bully their way through roads clogged with load-bearing yaks, the odd camel, and the occasional horse with a Kirghiz rider. Few tourists venture as far as Khotan, much less to the remoter sites of Niya or Dandan-Uiliq, and visits to local jade and silk factories tend to preempt trips to local museums. Lop Nor, in Sinkiang Province, which fascinated both Hedin and Stein, is off-limits: it is where China's nuclear arsenal is tested. No matter, one is assured. Whatever treasures were found at these long-abandoned sites were carted off to European museums, leaving little but desiccated tree trunks and eroded mud bricks to evoke the great Buddhist civilization that spawned the ruins.

Even in Stein's day much had to be imagined. Nothing like Egypt's lofty temples, obelisks, or gold-filled tombs exist; here there is nothing to match Persepolis's mighty staircase or Babylon's glazed brick lions; nor are there friezes depicting gods battling barbarians, like those the Germans uprooted at Pergamon. Even the great northern Silk Road city of Khara Khoto, still a major crossroads in Marco Polo's day, pales in comparison with Luxor or Nineveh. None of this mattered to Stein. His interests were historical: he was obsessed by literary remains. His most important finds were manuscripts, often pried from "ancient rubbish heaps," and, if they failed to stir the imagination of the general public—even now those boxes and boxes of manuscripts, silk hangings, sculpture, and coins are mostly relegated to the basement of the British Museum—it was irrelevant.

Bounded by three mountain ranges—the Pamirs to the west, the Tian Shan or Celestial Mountains to the north, and the Kunlun to the south—the Tarim Basin watershed, the area that Stein would eventually explore, is larger than Germany, France, and Britain combined. Stein often compared "tame deserts," those found in Arabia and America, which were empty but hospitable places where life-sustaining water could be found, to "true deserts"—the "dune-covered Taklamakan and the wastes of hard salt crust or wind-eroded clay of the Lop." In true deserts the absence of moisture precluded "not only human existence but also practically all animal and plant life." In the Taklamakan, Stein wrote, the traveler "first passes through a zone of desert vegetation, mostly in the shape of tamarisks, wild poplars, or reeds, surviving amidst low drift sand." Further out "there emerge from the dunes only shriveled and bleached trunks of trees, dead for ages." Finally these too disappear among totally bare accumulations of sand, in places rising 300 feet or more. Stein's biographer, Jeannette Mirsky, compares the Taklamakan to "a mummy's shroud," where to recover the lineaments of its living past, Stein would have to cut through sand wrappings—"a task as heroic as any designed for Hercules."

His adventures in the frozen desert at the four sites of Yotkan, Dandan-Uiliq (meaning "the houses with ivory"—the buried city Hedin had visited but identified only as the "ancient city Taklamakan"), Niya, and Endere are described in *Sand-buried Ruins of Khotan*, Stein's popular account of his first expedition, and they need not concern us here. It suffices that Stein's "proceeds"—including manuscripts in Kharoshti, Indian Brahmi, Khotanese, Chinese, and ancient Tibetan—filled twelve large boxes and were so intriguing, when he reported them to colleagues, as to spark a flurry of expeditions.

As for the Chinese, Stein displayed the Eurocentric condescension of his contemporaries. The scholarly interest of Amban Pan-Darin embarrassed Stein because he dwelt on the fact "of all these old records being carried away to the Far West. What could he show to the Fu-tai or Governor-General at Urumchi, who had been so inquisitive about the object of my excavations and who undoubtedly would wish to hear of the results?" He could only assuage his friend's nervousness by promising to send him photographs of the documents in duplicate.

In May, Stein again enjoyed the comforts of the "little oasis of Anglo-Indian civilization" in Kashgar. This time a friendlier Petrovsky helped obtain permission for Stein to travel on the new Trans-Caspian Railroad to Europe, and arranged transport for Stein's "proceeds," which were forwarded to England.

THE ARCHAEOLOGICAL EXCAVATION OF THE NORTHERN SILK Road began in 1898 when Dmitri Klementz, keeper of the Ethnological Museum at the Imperial Academy in St. Petersburg, accompanied by his botanist wife, reported finding near Turfan 130 cave temples full of paintings dating to the Buddhist era. On this expedition, funded by the Academy, Klementz photographed the ruins and brought back manuscripts and fragments of wall paintings. An account of a visit to Turfan in 1878 by the botanist Albert Regel—reportedly on a Russian intelligence mission to Central Asia—had guided Klementz to the·ruins. Regel had described numerous temples and "Buddhist idols" near the walled city of Karakhoja, not to be confused with the more eastern site of Khara-Khoto. On their way to Rome to the International Congress of Orientalists, the Klementzes stopped in Berlin where they met Professor Albert Grünwedel, director of the Indian Department in Berlin's Ethnological Museum. After studying Klementz's copies of the paintings, Grünwedel enthusiastically reported that "they showed types of frescoes characteristic of ancient Indian, ancient Iranian and Buddhist Chinese styles." There was no doubt, he concluded, "that we are confronted with a Central Asian sister school of Buddhist painting of ancient India." In the same report, the professor sounded the alarm that would reverberate through the next three decades: the preservation of the paintings was "greatly endangered" by the Muslim inhabitants who defaced and destroyed paintings and sculptures; some villagers had broken off pieces of the brightly colored frescoes to fertilize their fields.

Klementz suggested a joint Russo-German expedition. When this proved impossible, Grünwedel organized the first so-called Turfan Expedition. Raising funds proved difficult: official organizations were lukewarm, and the bulk of private monies came from Friedrich

Krupp, the German arms manufacturer. The endearingly collegial Stein, visiting Berlin in 1901, gave practical advice to his rivals on conditions in Chinese Turkestan. The Russians helped with travel arrangements and visas for the team that was to pass through their territory. The three-man scouting expedition, in the field from December 1902 to April 1903, returned to Berlin with forty-six chests of antiquities, each weighing eighty-odd pounds, from the area around Turfan.

Due to Grünwedel's ill health, Albert von Le Coq led the second German expedition. Of Huguenot descent and heir to a wine fortune, von Le Coq preferred scholarly pursuits. After studying Persian, Sanskrit, Arabic, and Turkish, he served as an unpaid volunteer under Grünwedel at the Ethnological Museum. Thanks to Grünwedel's success and with funding from the Kaiser, von Le Coq and his deputy Theodore Bartus (the museum's jack-of-all-trades, who had been on the first expedition) set out for Turkestan in 1904. When Grünwedel joined them some months later, he found Bartus with "his usual masterly skill" sawing away at frescoes, treasures that would fill upward of a hundred crates. Their most spectacular finds were the ninth-century frescoes, many portraying larger-than-life-size figures, from the caves in the cliff faces of the Buddhist monastery at Bezeklik (meaning the "place where there are paintings").

In 1928, shortly before his death, von Le Coq wrote a popular account of his field work, *Buried Treasures of Chinese Turkestan*. Unlike Stein, who was never one to relate the dangers of the desert, von Le Coq graphically described the horrors he encountered, including the deadly *buran*, the sandstorm feared and noted by the ancient Chinese:

> Quite suddenly the sky grows dark, the sun becomes a dark-red ball of fire seen through the fast-thickening veil of dust, a muffled howl is followed by a piercing whistle, and a moment after, the storm bursts with appalling violence upon the caravan. Enormous masses of sand, mixed with pebbles, are forcibly lifted up, whirled round, and dashed down on man and beast; the darkness increases and strange, clashing noises mingle with the roar and howl of the storm, caused by the violent contact of great stones as they are whirled up

through the air. The whole happening is like hell let loose, and the Chinese tell of the scream of the spirit eagle so confusing men, that they rush madly into the desert wilds and there meet a terrible death far from frequented paths.

To escape injury when overwhelmed by the *buran,* "men and horses must lie down and endure the rage of the hurricane." Even if one escaped, there were other natural terrors—gorges filled with wolves, mosquitoes, and sand flies that "tormented everyone who tried to rest there." Add to this scorpions "whose sting is a very serious matter" and "a kind of great spider that, in spite of a hairy body the size of a pigeon's egg, can take mighty jumps with its long, hairy legs." The cockroaches too, were repulsive, "in size quite as long as a man's thumb, with big red eyes and formidable feelers." It was enough, von Le Coq complained, "to make a man uncontrollably sick to wake in the morning with such a creature sitting on his nose, its big eyes staring down at him and its long feelers trying to attack its victim's eyes." Fortunately, omnipresent fleas were "not very obtrusive," but "the louse, on the contrary, is *the* domestic animal of all Turkestan and Tibet."

Altogether four German expeditions scoured the area around Turfan from 1902 until the outbreak of World War I in 1914. Their finds included manuscripts written in twenty-five scripts and fifteen languages, some showing that the heretical Manicheans had reached inner Asia. In 1912, the Oriental Commission of the Berlin Academy of Sciences began to coordinate research on the "Turfan collection" of 30,000 manuscript fragments that had arrived in wooden boxes, each sheaf preserved between glass plates sealed with an adhesive strip.

(During World War II most of the Turfan collection survived, although a direct hit by Allied bombers on the Ethnological Museum destroyed twenty-eight of the Bezeklik paintings that could not be removed from the gallery walls. In autumn 1943, the portable part of the collection was dispersed to various mines. After the war, in western Germany, the Allies handed over the Turfan material to the Mainz Academy of Science and Literature, while Soviet authorities gave their share to East Germany. Only after unification in 1990 was the Turfan collection reunited in Berlin's Dahlem Museum.)

Klementz's reports before the Rome Congress of Orientalists in 1899 coupled with Stein's finds had thus initiated an "international race for antiquities." Writing from Kashgar, Macartney kept his unfunded and despondent colleague abreast of all the "poaching on his archaeological preserves around Turfan" by his rivals. Privately, Stein ridiculed the Germans, who, he said, "always go hunting in packs" while he occupied himself writing up finds and making fruitless proposals.

Afghanistan was uppermost in his mind. April 1902 found Stein in Peshawar in Curzon's newly established North-West Frontier Province. There he met again with the Viceroy in hopes of interesting him in his plan to excavate ancient Bactria in northern Afghanistan, a likely storehouse of Graeco-Buddhist artifacts. During his allotted hour, Stein answered His Excellency's questions, and noted in his diary: "V. recognizes strength of my argument about this time now to secure those sites for India's or B[ritish] Museum. Seems to appreciate proposal & not to shrink from political difficulty. Doubt whether he quite realizes my reasons for starting from Russian side. Hurried off. V. looks fresh & as young as in 1899. Struck by his clear eyes and sensitive mouth which shows working of thoughts. His manner seems simpler & more easy than in public. Promise all duplicates also pottery etc. for Indian Museums."

Notwithstanding the Viceroy's support—Curzon immediately telegraphed the Secretary of State for India and followed with a letter to the Afghan Emir—the Bactrian project was rejected by its putative host. The Emir replied that he could not "in any way advise the said Doctor [Stein] to carry out his intentions . . . to secure such unobtainable and non-existing objects of research."

By this time, Curzon's attention had turned from India's North-West Frontier to the northeastern border with Tibet. Sensing an opening, Stein applied for leave from his new position as Inspector of Schools in the Punjab to accompany Colonel Younghusband's expeditionary force. Younghusband turned him down. Stein had considered his claims "to such a 'deputation' as preeminent" and was sorely disappointed when the prize went to Lawrence Austine Waddell, a medical officer whom Stein considered an amateur Orientalist.

Stein's friend and supporter, Colonel Harold Deane, now Commissioner of the North-West Frontier Province, offered his "apologies about Tibet." Lockwood Kipling commiserated as well: "It seems a thousand pities that you could not have joined the pic-nic. Results they must bring back of some kind but whether they will be of the best and most valuable remains to be seen. I notice my friend Perceval Landon sends to the *Times* charming descriptions of landscape and of plants and flowers, and general matters which after all is the kind of thing for the *publicum* but not much of historical and archaeological side. I often think you must be inclined to fret a little, even in summer camps, at not being allowed to share in the foray."

In 1906 Stein finally took to the field again. In proposing a second Central Asian expedition, he invoked "the spectre of Russo-German competition" and questioned "whether such favourable conditions [in Sinkiang] will prevail for a prolonged period and whether political changes may not arise which would close that field to researches from the British side." It was the same year that Curzon was forced to resign, and it fell to his successor, Lord Minto, to endorse Stein's proposal. Reporting on his meeting with the new Viceroy in Peshawar, Stein tried to be optimistic: "Lord Minto understood what I told of my hope for another Troy and did not seem to mind that I could not promise there a pendant to the Elgin Marbles, only perhaps the earliest products of Graeco-Buddhist art and relics of Zoroastrian antiquity." Whitehall and the Government of India acquiesced. "Rejoice" was the one-word confirmation Stein received from a friend.

.·.

CHAPTER FIFTEEN

The Last of
the "Foreign Devils"

IN PLANNING HIS EPOCHAL SECOND EXPEDITION, SIR AUREL Stein sounded more like Metternich than an archaeologist. He had just heard from his friend George Macartney that for archaeological purposes Chinese Turkestan had been "partitioned" by the Congress of Orientalists into "spheres of influence." As a result, Stein complained to the secretary of the Royal Geographical Society, John Scott Keltie, that the rich Turfan area on the northern Silk Road fell to the Germans, his "rivals and meddlers," while the British sphere on the southern Silk Road appeared to be "rather hazy." For their part, the Russians were preparing an assault on Kucha, another northern site, when, in April 1906, Stein set out once more over the Karakorum. In these circumstances, Stein informed Keltie, he was keeping his own plans as quiet as possible since his competitors commanded "far greater financial resources than I can hope to have at my disposal, and are probably less handicapped in other respects."

It was the final scramble for antiquities in the imperial twilight, before the rise of nationalism challenged the old assumption that the right to dig and take was the unlimited franchise of European overlords. Though scarcely the worst offender, Stein would face ever more suspicion and hostility in China, culminating in a disastrous fourth expedition, cosponsored by Harvard's Fogg Art Museum, an ill-fated prelude to his long-deferred dream of excavating Balkh, Alexander the Great's metropolis in Afghanistan.

This time Stein traveled via Chitral and the Wakhan corridor in eastern Afghanistan, the "short cut across the Pamirs." His friend, Colonel Harold Deane, Chief Commissioner of the North-West Frontier Province, had "diplomatically closed an eye to a certain gap between them [his dominions] and the Chinese frontier," and also obtained permission for Stein's route from Habibullah, the Afghan Emir, conveyed in an "imposing Firman of the 'God-created government.'" To Keltie, who edited Stein's material for the RGS *Journal,* while forwarding articles to *The Times,* he declared: "This concession may be a good omen in regard to future plans about Balkh, a goal for me since my boyhood..."

Stein planned to trace the route followed by 10,000 Chinese invaders in A.D. 747. Starting in Kashgar, the Chinese Army had succeeded in invading Gilgit and Yasin in spite of Afghanistan's overpowering obstacles. In *On Central Asian Tracks* (1933), his popular account of his first three expeditions, Stein wrote that it was "the only recorded instance of an organized force of comparatively large size having ever surmounted the formidable natural barrier which the Pamirs and Hindu Kush present to military operations." And, by following the initial route, in spite of his haste "to get to the ground earlier than the French expedition," he was able to gather useful intelligence about lines of communication between the Oxus Basin and China, and to identify a number of "ancient sites described by early Chinese Buddhist pilgrims."

Stein had his sights fixed on the ruins of Loulan, the ancient Chinese garrison town Hedin had discovered near Lop Nor, the "wandering lake," in 1900. But first Stein visited Khadik and Niya, where he wrote Keltie,

> the archaeological yield of the last three weeks has been far richer than I could reasonably expect. The British Museum will not be indifferent, I think, to the five pony loads of se-

lected antiques which are on their way to Kashgar...The way to Lop Nor is long, & the big French party under Pelliot, which reached Kashgar at the end of August, is also bound for that goal. I am trying to get there in time & yet do not like to leave tasks behind me undone. At sites yielding much I feel that European assistants would be useful. But where is the money for them to come from? I console myself with the thought that their absence saves additional baggage—and time on the march.

In December, after carefully preparing an advance caravan with a five-week supply of food and donkeys to carry as much ice as possible to supplement their water supply, Stein embarked on a race to Loulan. Stein's large column—local diggers had been added—struck out across the frozen Lop Desert straight into the searing fifty-mile-an-hour northeast wind. Seven days later the party reached the desolate ruin where Loulan's "rubbish dump" yielded, besides the first example of the lost language of Sogdian—the ancient language of the region of Samarkand and Bokhara—a number of official documents in Chinese and some Kharoshti tablets, suggesting that there might have been an ancient Indian Empire on the very threshold of China. Still, as Stein wrote Keltie, "Notwithstanding all antiquarian interests, one does not particularly enjoy the particles of ancient refuse settling in one's throat or freezing to one's beards."

Stein had by then perfected his own style of ambulatory archaeology, and at Miran he made further important finds of Tibetan manuscripts and frescoes. However, his most spectacular results occurred on a twenty-three-day visit (May 21 through June 13, 1907) to the Mogao caves of Dunhuang.

Stein first heard of the caves from a Hungarian geologist in 1902. More recently a Muslim trader had told him that a mass of ancient manuscripts might be there. Similar rumors had also reached the Germans but, as Macartney reported, relations between von Le Coq and Grünwedel had soured. Grünwedel had fallen ill and was unable to lead the second expedition. Upon recovering, he informed von Le Coq that he was on his way to Kashgar, where he expected to meet his colleague. Letting a toss of a gold Chinese coin decide whether he should head toward Dunhuang, a seventeen-day trip south across the Gobi, and investigate the rumor, or rendezvous with Grünwedel, a disgruntled von Le Coq returned to Kashgar. However, as their host Macartney confided from Chini Bagh in November, their jealous enmity had deepened: "Grünwedel is ill, can't go on horseback & has to be looked after like a big baby...No doubt had [von Le Coq and his associate Bartus] known that you also were on the war-path, they would have dragged Grünwedel off, ill or not, long before now." Stein momentarily had the field to himself, but the French sinologist Paul Pelliot was nipping at his heels.

THE MOGAO CAVES OR THE "CAVES OF THE THOUSAND BUDDHAS," twelve miles south-west of Dunhuang, in Kansu (Gansu) Province, contain the world's richest trove of Buddhist wall paintings, sculptures, and manuscripts. This was partly the result of geography: Dunhuang is at the junction of the northern and southern branches of the Silk Road, leading east-west, and also of the north-south road between Mongolia and Tibet. Originally inhabited by the Chinese, Dunhuang was captured by the Tibetans in the eighth century. then reclaimed by the Chinese. Next, the Uighurs, a people of Turki origin, established a kingdom only to be driven out by the ferocious Tanguts, Buddhists of Tibetan origin, who in turn were displaced by the Mongols. Finally the region fell to the Muslims. From the fourth to the fourteenth century A.D., and perhaps even later, Buddhist monks painted 45,000 murals in some 500 grottoes on cliff faces a mile long. They carved and colored about 2,000 statues within the caves—one of them a giant Buddha, 113 feet high, with toes as big as yaks—and, as Stein and Pelliot were to discover, they stowed away more than 50,000 manuscripts.

When Stein reached Dunhuang (the name means "Blazing Beacon") in March, 1907, the caves were in the custody of Wang Yuan-lu, better known as Abbot Wang. A Taoist monk, Wang had collected alms and embarked on a restoration program for the badly neglected caves. While exploring the rock-temples in 1900, he came upon a bricked-in cache of manuscripts, scrolls, and banners, the so-called Cave 17. Wang was not good at keeping his discovery secret and stories about the hoard soon reached Kashgar, Urumchi, and the provincial capital of Lanzhou. When Stein arrived, Wang was away seeking alms, and the grotto was locked. While waiting for him to return, an excited Stein explored the neighborhood, making two dramatic discoveries: the remains of the famous Jade Gate and remnants of China's Great Wall, which had extended to the province.

Stein later wrote of his first meeting with Abbot Wang: "He looked a very queer person, extremely shy and nervous, with an occasional expression of cunning which was far from encouraging. It was clear from the first that he would be a difficult person to handle." But after hours of "diplomatic wrangling," Stein's Chinese secretary, Chiang Ssu-yeh, persuaded the monk to show them the library. Stein all but gasped at what he saw: "The sight disclosed in the dim light of the priest's little oil lamp made my eyes open wide. Heaped up in layers, but without any order, there appeared a solid mass of manuscript bundles rising to a height of nearly ten feet, and filling, as a subsequent measurement showed, close on five-hundred cubic feet."

With barely enough space for two people to stand, it was impossible to examine anything inside the "black hole," but Stein was allowed to study the bundles on a newly built loggia which served as a makeshift reading room. In the lengthy negotiations that followed, the archaeologist invoked the spirit of his "patron saint," Hsüan-tsang, who once spent seventeen years collecting Buddhist sacred books in India. Stein eventually convinced Wang, also an admirer of the seventh century pilgrim, to part with twelve cases of artifacts. Stein's Dunhuang haul included paintings on silk, embroideries, sculptures, and, most importantly, more than a thousand ancient manuscripts written not only in Chinese but also in Tibetan, Tangut, Sanskrit, Turkish, and a scattering of other, obscurer languages. The crown jewel was the world's oldest known printed book, dated May 11, 868, the *Diamond Sutra*, a popular Buddhist scriptural text. All this, Stein proudly wrote to his friend P. S. Allen, cost the British taxpayer a mere £130, the sum he donated to Wang for the upkeep of the site.

Because of Wang's presence and the anticipated difficulties with local Chinese administrators, Stein was unable "to rescue the whole hoard"—which he might have done were it possible to pack and transport all the material without attracting notice. Because Stein could not read Chinese, he did not make the best possible choice—as Stein was often told by his critics. However, Stein's motive was not profit, glory, or plunder; his mitigating purpose was scholarship. He hoped to illuminate links between Dunhuang and "Buddhist learning as transplanted from the Tarim Basin" and to provide finds of direct importance to Indian and Western research. In this he succeeded. Wang's custodial reserve did not extend to the magnificent silk banners, and Stein carried off a splendid haul. Writing to Keltie, Stein urged discretion: "The whole clearing had to be done in secret, and not until I am on my way to England would it be advisable to tell the story *coram publico*...But of course, there is plenty to do left for a professed Sinologist like P[elliot]."

PAUL PELLIOT ARRIVED AT DUNHUANG IN FEBRUARY 1908. UNLIKE Stein, he traveled most of the way in the comfort of European and Russian trains, and he was accompanied by an army medical officer and a photographer. A superb linguist and "an exceptionally well-armed philologist," Pelliot achieved mastery not only as a Sinologist but also in Mongolian, Turkic, and Iranian studies. Already a professor at twenty-five at Hanoi's Ecole Française d'Extrême-Orient, Pelliot was as colorful as he was controversial—he supported his collecting habit through his skill at cards. At twenty-one, he happened to be in Peking during the Boxer Rebellion, and his bravura feats during the siege of the foreign legations won him the Légion d'honneur. (He captured an enemy banner, and during a temporary ceasefire climbed over the barricades, met with the opposing general, and returned with gifts of fresh fruit.) Controversial, because he succeeded in obtaining prime material at Dunhuang that Stein had overlooked: some 40,000 manuscripts and 230 paintings on silk, cotton, and hemp. Finally, he did not have Stein's scruples about removing sculpture; he sent fifty pieces to Paris.

Pelliot's one and only campaign lasted until 1909, and his journey, as he casually reported to a Sorbonne audience, "passed peacefully, without a single shot being fired; and we even had the almost embarrassing good fortune, as explorers, to return in perfect health." When he returned to Peking he brought with him choice samples, which he showed to Chinese scholars. As soon as the Peking authorities learned of Wang's dealings, they ordered him to desist and sent a party to remove ten thousand bundles from the abbot's custody, much of which was unfortunately lost or stolen.

In 1910, a Japanese team arrived at Dunhuang for its share of the spoils, as Macartney reported to Stein. Four years later, Sir Aurel himself returned to the area, purchasing four more cases of manuscripts from the nearby towns. A month later, Russia's great Orientalist, Sergei Oldenburg, made his way to the caves, returning with several hundred scrolls and thousands of fragments, presently in the collection of the Institute for Oriental Studies at the Russian Academy of Science in St. Petersburg.

Stein seemingly persuaded Wang that it was "a pious act" on his part to rescue "for Western scholarship all those relics of ancient Buddhist literature and art which were otherwise bound to get lost sooner or later through local indifference." Although Stein and his successors claimed the Chinese were not interested in Dunhuang's treasure, this was not so. Even before Stein's visit, Abbot Wang had forwarded sample rolls of Chinese texts to the local administrator at Lanzhou. The official decided the cost of transporting seven cartloads of manuscripts to the provincial capital was too great, and that they should remain *in situ*. A Chinese scholar, Ye Changchi, who from 1902 to 1906 was Provincial Education Commissioner for Kansu, kept a detailed record of what he knew of the library cave and its contents in his diary (*Yuandu Lu riji chao*), only recently published. Ye Changchi also obtained copies of paintings, scrolls, and a rubbing of a stele from the library cave from the Lanzhou magistrate, but the scholar was unable himself to make the journey to Dunhuang. When word reached him that Stein and Pelliott had carted off so many examples from the library, he wrote in his diary (January 23, 1910): "What was my role as imperial envoy? I am ashamed and full of remorse that I dared to blame others."

Stein's ruse at Dunhuang would come back to haunt him in 1930, when China's National Commission for the Preservation of Antiquities protested his act with dignity and eloquence:

> Sir Aurel Stein, taking advantage of the ignorance and cupidity of the priest in charge, persuaded the latter to sell to him at a pittance what he considered the pick of the collection which, needless to say, did not in any way belong to the seller. It would be the same if some Chinese traveler pretending to be merely a student of religious history went to Canterbury and bought valuable relics from the cathedral caretaker. But Sir Aurel Stein, not knowing a word of Chinese, took away what he considered the most valuable, separating many manuscripts which really belonged together, thus destroying the value of the manuscripts themselves. Soon afterwards French and Japanese travelers followed his trail with the result that the unique collection is now divided up and scattered in London, Paris, and Tokyo. In the first two cities at least, the manuscripts lie unstudied for the last twenty years, and their rightful owners, the Chinese, who are the most competent scholars for their study, are deprived of their opportunity as well as their ownership.

A harsh judgment, but with a large measure of truth. Indeed, after his own harvest at Dunhuang, Stein was dismayed by the depredations of others. Back in the field for a third foray in 1913–16, he toured sites that the Germans had explored around Turfan, and in private letters deplored their careless methods—Stein uses the German word *Raubbau*, which conveys a sense of looting. Visiting Kucha, he deplores the lack of archaeological thoroughness in his colleagues: "The ruined monasteries & temples had all suffered so badly through moisture that Japanese, Germans & Russians contented themselves with mere scrapings." But Pelliot had recently made "a thorough cleaning." One of the

ruins had yielded an important find of thousands of Sanskrit manuscripts. It pleased Stein to note that Pelliot's superior excavation techniques were "so different from the Turfan burrowings."

ARCHAEOLOGY HAS BEEN ENTWINED WITH EUROPE'S IMPERIAL
enterprise from the time Napoleon put to sea for Egypt in 1798
with 38,000 troops and a Commission of Arts consisting of some
170 savants. Once in Cairo, the scholars established the Egyptian Institute, surveyed the antiquities of the Nile Valley, and returned with
a warehouse of sketches and notes that were published, from 1808 to
1828, in nineteen massive volumes with so many plates that 400 en-
gravers were needed for the task. Napoleon himself corrected the
preface to the Commission's *Description de l'Egypte.* "The time will
come," wrote one of the scholars, Etienne Geoffroy Saint-Hillaire,
"when the work of the Commission of Arts will excuse in the eyes
of posterity the lightness with which our nation has, so to speak,
thrown itself into the Orient."

Beginning in the 1870's, when the public marveled at Schliemann's discoveries at the site of ancient Troy in Turkish Asia Minor,
governments, and their spy services, saw an ancillary benefit in archaeology. Excavators tarry in remote regions, become fluent in local
languages, take pictures, and prepare maps—the ideal "cover" for espionage. With the 1869 opening of the Suez Canal, and the British
purchase six years later of controlling shares in the canal company,
safeguarding the "lifeline to India" became a prime security concern.
This added a new dimension to scholarly and spiritual interest in the
Holy Land. The British founded the Palestine Exploration Fund to
foster scientific investigation of "the Archaeology, Geography, Geology, and Natural History of Palestine." The Fund's birth in 1865 was
warmly endorsed not only by the Church of England and the Royal
Geographical Society but also by the Foreign Secretary, Earl Russell.
The Fund worked with the Royal Engineers in mapping the Holy
Land. Kitchener's first mission as a young lieutenant in the Indian
Army was to survey western Palestine from the Jordan to the Galilee.

In 1877, the future Commander-in-Chief reported that his team had recorded every river, road, and ruin in the area. A few decades later, in 1913, two British archaeologists were employed by the Fund to carry out an equally thorough survey of the Negev and the Sinai, including Turkish forts at Aqaba. The "Wilderness of Zinn" project was led by Leonard Woolley and T. E. Lawrence, who had excavated together at the site of ancient Carchemish in Syria.

With the outbreak of World War I, Woolley and Lawrence joined military intelligence services in Egypt, and their skills were well known to the new Secretary of State for War, Lord Kitchener. By 1915, after Turkey joined forces with the Central Powers, Kitchener approved establishment in Cairo of the Arab Bureau, a covert agency headed by yet another Oxford archaeologist, David G. Hogarth, the former director of the Carchemish dig. Out of the Bureau came the Arab Revolt and its British hero, Lawrence of Arabia. Knowledge of the terrain was crucial for guerrillas attacking Ottoman roads, rails, and forts, and especially to the triumphant advance toward Jerusalem and Damascus of Field Marshal Edmund Allenby (who carried into battle with him both a Bible and George Adam Smith's *Historical Geography of the Holy Land*).

The covert uses of archaeology were readily evident to rulers of Asia and the Middle East, and along with an awakening nationalism, their credible suspicions dogged Sir Aurel Stein—the more so, since he was trained in military cartography and pioneered in using aerial photography to locate ancient sites.

Surveying was always uppermost in Stein's accounts, and he realized its importance to his sponsors. "My scientific work has always been guided by the conviction," he wrote Keltie, "that geographical and historical researches must combine where the elucidation of ancient Asia is concerned." With Ram and his successor Lal Singh seconded from the Trigonometrical Survey, Stein surveyed the section of the Pamirs close to the Muztagh-ata and Lake Karakul, the headwaters of the Khotan River in the Kunlun mountains, and connected them for the first time with the Survey of India. During his second expedition he surveyed the Nan Shan, the mountains on Tibet's northern border, and traced the Khotan River to its source. Altogether, with his two Indian surveyors, he succeeded in mapping nearly 30,000 square miles. At the end of each expedition, Stein spent time in India at Dehra Dun, helping the Survey prepare maps that are still in use.

Although Stein's maps contributed to scholarly research, their other unstated purpose was to provide the Government of India with strategic military information. Much of the mapping remained confidential. The Indian Foreign Office, for example, sent a telegraphic message to Stein, concerning his Nan Shan survey, not "to publish anything" involving northern Tibet "without previous submission."

Not to be outdone by Sven Hedin on his second expedition, Stein crossed the Taklamakan from north to south, a route considerably more difficult than following the Keriya River northward, as the Swede had done in 1896. Stein managed to locate the mouth of the river, a feat requiring navigation of the utmost precision. However, it was while mapping a glacier in the Kunlun Range, at 20,000 feet and 16 degrees below freezing, in October 1908 that "the awkward mishap occurred" on the last day of his exploratory work. Stein lost the toes of his right foot to frostbite and had to be carried by improvised litter some 300 miles to the Moravian Mission hospital at Leh.

Stein once again returned to Europe as a conquering hero and sought-after lecturer. There were gold medals from the RGS and the Royal Asiatic Society, honorary degrees from Oxford and Cambridge, with a knighthood soon to follow. "Few more wonderful discoveries have been made by any archaeologist," proclaimed the *Times Literary Supplement*; and Sir Leonard Woolley declared it "an unparalleled archaeological scoop." Yet unlike other such heroes, Stein gave full credit to the supporting cast, and saw that his non-European team received pensions, medical assistance, grants, and awards, and that their maps were published. In accepting the Founder's Medal from the RGS in 1909, Stein thanked his friends Rawlinson and Yule, Viceroys Curzon and Minto, and finally his "two excellent native surveyors," his "chief instruments for reaping the rich cartographical harvest of our expeditions." And, at the famous dinner meeting in February 1909, at which Hedin held forth on his Trans-Himalayan survey, Stein tossed him, to the amusement of the press, a tape measure the Swede had lost at Loulan. For his part, Hedin loftily announced that archaeological investigation of the Silk Road had taken a great step forward: "From several different countries, England, Germany, France, Russia, America, expeditions have been sent out, but we can hardly talk of any competition—the deserts are big enough for as many parties as Europe, India and America can afford to send out."

THE RUSSIAN ARCHAEOLOGICAL PRESENCE ALONG THE SILK ROAD reached its crest in 1908, when Colonel Pyotr Kuzmich Kozlov (1863–1935) excavated Khara-Khoto, the fabled "Black City" of the Tanguts. Kozlov is scarcely known outside Russia, and his extraordinary feats have been forgotten. He was born in 1863 to a peasant family living on the Sloboda estates at Duchovschina, a small town near Smolensk. Discovered by Przhevalsky, Kozlov received the same military training as his mentor and at twenty, accompanied him on his fourth expedition to Central Asia. He was to make a further sortie with Przhevalsky, and when the latter died in 1888, the mantle of Russia's premier explorer passed to his student, who, like his mentor, had his eyes fixed firmly on Lhasa.

Before departing on his first independent expedition to Mongolia and Tibet in 1899, Kozlov received a letter from the head of the Russian Geographical Society, the noted geographer Petr Petrovich Semenov (soon to be Tian-Shansky): "Remember, my dear Pyotr Kuzmich, that the development of our relations with Tibet is a matter of immense importance, and it is in your hands. In that citadel of Central Asia the name of Russia must be upheld not by threats, but by humility and honor…"

On this first foray, Kozlov combed the Gobi for ruins of the lost city of Khara-Khoto, but could not find them. Instead he explored the Tsaidam in Northern Tibet, found the source of the Yellow River, spent six months in the Mekong River basin, and completed a survey of 6,200 miles for the Russian Geographical Society. At Chamdo in eastern Tibet during spring 1901, an advance party sent by the Dalai Lama met up with the Russians. Kozlov sent greetings and gifts to the pontiff, but the Tibetans refused him permission to proceed to Lhasa.

Kozlov would never set on eyes on Lhasa, but he did manage two memorable encounters with the Dalai Lama. In 1905, the Russian arrived in the Mongolian capital of Urga, where the Dalai Lama had fled as Younghusband's troops advanced on Lhasa. Sent on the personal orders of the Tsar to meet with the pontiff, the explorer cultivated the Dalai Lama's associates, notably the Buriat lama and Russian subject, Agvan Dorzhiev. Through Dorzhiev, Kozlov was introduced to His Holiness. Kozlov remembered the day he gazed on the face of the Great Reincarnation as one of the happiest he spent in Asia. The Dalai Lama sat for pencil portraits by the Russian painter Kozhevnikov (Kozlov presented two portraits to Nicholas II) and gave Kozlov a "precious collection of cult articles" for his sponsors and two bronze Buddhas as a personal gift.

Four years later, the Dalai Lama invited Kozlov to the monastery at Kumbum where the pontiff was staying on his way home from Peking to Lhasa. Kozlov's several audiences resulted in an invitation to visit Lhasa: "You will report to me on your research and finds, and I will visit your collections and photographs," the Dalai Lama said. "I have the intention of having all reports on journeys of European researchers translated into Tibetan. I will have your personal reports very carefully written down by my secretaries…the first basis for historical-geographical research on central Tibet." When they parted, the Dalai Lama asked Kozlov to send a piece of the finest gold Russian cloth and copies of his photographs as soon as he reached St. Petersburg. In return, Kozlov received further gifts of Buddhist bronze figures, Tibetan textiles, birds, and animal skins as well as a rare astronomical chart from China. Alas, wars and revolutions intervened, and Tibet's great leader and Russia's great explorer did not meet again.

Kozlov did succeed in exploring Khara-Khoto, the ancient capital of the Tanguts, after being led to the ruins by a Buriat colleague, Tsokto Badmazhapov, who found them in April 1907. "During my trip to Edzin Gol, I made an extraordinarily interesting discovery or so it seems," Bazmazhapov wrote to Kozlov. In the sands between two river valleys, he had come across the ruins of Khara-Khoto. Bazmazhapov enclosed four photographs of the ruins and asked Kozlov to show them to Semenov Tian-Shansky of the Imperial Geographical Society.

An excited Kozlov readily persuaded Nicholas II to finance an expedition, and without waiting for spring weather he and three colleagues hurried to Mongolia. By following the course of the Edzin Gol, they came upon the ruins of Khara-Khoto rising from the dried riverbed. "The Black City," northeast of Dunhuang on the Mongolian border, thrived under Buddhist Tanguts for three centuries until it was sacked by Genghis Khan in 1226. The Tanguts, whose language is related to Tibetan, controlled 500 miles of the Silk Road between Tibet and China. However, it was not their camels or crops but their horses, "the best under the sky," that tempted the Mongols. Genghis Khan wanted the Tanguts to ride with his troops on his western campaigns. When they demurred, he vowed to destroy them "down to the last slaves." In this he succeeded, but in doing so the Great Khan fell ill and died. During the Mongol era, the Edzin Gol River, the source of all the wells, dried up and the city silted over.

The walls were buried so deeply in the sands of the Gobi that, according to Kozlov, it was often possible to walk up the slope and enter the fortress. The Russians set up camp and impatiently set to work. "I shall never forget the sense of delight which filled my heart when, after removing a few shovelfuls of debris in ruined building No. 1, I unearthed a small Buddhist icon, painted on canvas," Kozlov wrote. He promptly dispatched sample finds—paintings and manuscripts in Chinese, Tibetan, and Tangut—to St. Petersburg, where his discovery of the "Black City" secured his reputation.

Kozlov was haunted by Khara-Khoto. Returning to the site in May 1909, the Russians uncovered a stupa northwest of the city wall. Due to the dry climate, its contents—manuscripts, books, bronze, and wood statues—were preserved as in a time capsule. Inside the stupa, arrayed around a wooden column, were a score of life-size clay statues facing inward, "resembling lamas, conducting a religious ceremony in front of hundreds of manuscripts in Tangut script, stacked one upon the other." Since the effigies were too large to load on horses, Kozlov photographed and buried them, planning to come back to recover them. He sent back nearly 12,000 items to the Hermitage and the Institute of Oriental Studies in St. Petersburg, where scholars were able to decipher the previously unknown Tangut language.

The Great War and the Russian Revolution put a hold on Kozlov's plans, and not until 1923 did he make his way back to Ulan Bator (formerly Urga) and Khara-Khoto. This time Kozlov thumped through the Gobi in a Buick. But when he reached the ruins, despite days of searching and sifting, he could not find his twenty lamas. Two years later, the Americans Langdon Warner and Horace Jayne, on a trip for Harvard's Fogg Art Museum, visited Khara-Khoto. In *The Long Old Road in China,* Warner described the desolation of the "Black City":

> No city guard turned out to scan my credentials now, no bowman leaned from a balcony above the big gate in idle curiosity, and no inn welcomed me with tea and kindly bustle of sweeping out my room or fetching fodder for my beasts. One little grey hawk darted from her nest high in the grey wall, her set wings rigid, and sailed low over the pebbles and sparse thorn bushes of the plain. No other life seemed there, not even the motion of a cloud in the speckless heaven nor the stir of a beetle at my feet. It was high afternoon, when no ghosts walk. But, as sure as these solid walls were built up by the labor of men, just so sure was I that the little empty town had spirits in it. And the consciousness never left me by day or night while we were there.

In 1914, Stein worked the site for eight days, and unbeknownst to Kozlov had solved the riddle of the twenty missing lamas. In its hasty search for treasure, Kozlov's team failed to cover adequately the plundered stupas or to bury the effigies deeply enough. The lamas were eaten away by wind and sand. Altogether, Stein lamented to Macartney, it was "a very Vandal *modus operandi,* but as it was Kozloff's first archaeological work one could scarcely feel surprise at the destructive results."

This was midway in Stein's third expedition (1913–16), which covered nearly 11,000 miles from westernmost China across the Tarim

Basin to the Oxus and Iran, from the Hindu Kush in the south to Dzungaria and Inner Mongolia in the north. At the grottoes of Bezeklik, noting the damage done by the Germans to the surviving paintings, he decided to remove as many as possible. Still, although Stein was not ready to acknowledge it, the era of scholarly plundering in Central Asia was over. In December 1913, Macartney warned Stein that Chinese authorities were disinclined to grant permission for excavations, and were unwilling to provide porters and transport. This was followed by Macartney's translation of an order prohibiting Lal Singh from surveying strategic sites. Stein seemed oblivious to the imperial condescension of his irritable response: "It seems like the irony of Fate that while I am fighting the difficulties of nature in a region of the dead for the sake of researches, which ought to appeal to Chinese historical instinct, I should be burdened with worries about the attitude of modern successors of those, whose tracks on this wind-worn desert I am tracing." Only through determined British pressure in Peking was Stein allowed to proceed. There followed another warning from Macartney in March 1915 that an Urumchi official had issued a further directive: "What this letter means is that you have no right to excavate, though you may examine, sites; also that you have no right to take out of China what you have excavated." Stein, now worried about treasures he had already shipped, learned with relief in April that his 150 cases of antiquities had passed through Aksu en route to Kashgar. In July, Stein reported "a fresh Chinese attempt at obstruction" to Keltie and asked him to delay publication of his report until his convoy had safely crossed the Chinese frontier.

STEIN'S FOURTH EXPEDITION ENDED IN A FAILURE SO HUMILIATING that he never wrote about it and seldom referred to it. Nor was it mentioned in his obituaries. Both Stein's biographers, Jeannette Mirsky in 1977 and Annabel Walker in 1995, note but fail to explore the circumstances surrounding the venture that was to crown an illustrious career. Who sabotaged the joint Harvard/British Museum mission? And why? The answer lay in long-unexamined Harvard archives. They reveal the rivalry between British and American museums, and between the two Harvard sponsors of the expedition. But the underlying theme is the change imposed by an awakening nationalism on the old rules of archaeology, even in innermost Asia. Spurred by this nationalism, a new generation of indigenous archaeologists, many trained in America or Europe, sought an early end to the days when Westerners, as if by writ, could uproot another nation's past.

The 1920s witnessed a procession of spectacular finds. Excited accounts of the discoveries by Sir John Marshall of unknown early civilizations at Mohenjo-daro and Harappa in the Indus River Valley were followed by Sir Leonard Woolley's remarkable excavations at Ur in Mesopotamia and Howard Carter's opening of Tutankhamun's tomb. The press attention itself radically altered the archaeological climate.

In December 1929, a sellout crowd gathered at the Lowell Institute to hear Sir Aurel Stein recount his adventures along the Silk Road. These Cambridge, Massachusetts, lectures also served as an audition for the archaeologist's prospective sponsors. Paul Sachs and Langdon Warner of Harvard's Fogg Art Museum had lured Stein from retirement, enticing him to America by dangling the prospect of a fourth expedition, one in which Sachs and Warner hoped to match or overtake their European rivals.

In two expeditions a few years earlier, Warner, the Fogg's curator of Asiatic Art, accompanied by Horace Jayne, curator of Oriental Art of the Pennsylvania (now Philadelphia) Museum, had carried out their own raids along the Silk Road. With most of the Dunhuang manuscripts already gone, Warner removed twelve Tang Dynasty fresco fragments from the caves, as well as a seventh century polychrome kneeling Bodhisattva. In fairness, Warner found the Dunhuang caves in a shocking state. They had been recently vandalized by White Russian soldiers, refugees from the Bolshevik Revolution, who had been interned by the local Chinese governor. Writing to his wife, Warner noted that "everywhere eyes are gouged out or deep scores run right across the faces…Whole rows of maidens in elaborate headdresses pass you by—but you look in vain for a complete head. Elaborate compositions of the Bodhisattva enthroned among the elder Gods with a lovely nautch girl dancing on a carpet before Him contain not a single figure that is complete...across some of these lovely faces are scribbled the numbers of a Russian regiment, and from the mouth of the Buddha where he sits to deliver the Lotus Law flows some Slav obscenity." Warner attributed the Slavic graffiti to the indifference of the Chinese. As for the morals of his vandalism, he wrote a friend, "I would strip the place bare without a flicker":

> In twenty years this place won't be worth a visit. Every pil-
> grim scratches his ill-born name and flicks off a bit of trem-
> bling plaster. All the hoard of manuscripts and paintings on silk
> and paper seems long ago to have been dispersed. What Stein
> and Pelliot and Peking and the Kansu Viceroy and the Japa-
> nese failed to get has been carried off piecemeal by the mag-
> istrates who stay only a year or so in office. Each one visits the
> caves at the end of his term and carries off as many of the pre-
> cious rolls as the priest admits are remaining. These rolls avert
> fire and flood and bring luck. They make splendid gifts to
> higher officials and sell for several hundreds of taels each.

When the Fogg's second expedition reached the caves in 1925, an angry mob forced the Americans to retreat without photographs and frescoes. Warner complained to his wife of "the priest's cupidity in wanting more money and a certain backwash from Stein and Pelliot, neither of whom could ever come back and live."

Warner's funds came from the estate of the aluminum magnate Charles Martin Hall, which also endowed Harvard's newly founded Yenching Institute for Asian Studies. Hall funds went as well to Yenching University, a Christian missionary school in Peking. The university's dean of arts and sciences was the American-educated William Hung. Only in 1978 did Hung, aged 85, reveal to his biog-rapher, Susan Chan Egan, that he had been the saboteur of Warner's second expedition. A student of Hung's, who accompanied Warner as a secretary-interpreter on his first trip to Dunhuang, discovered him one night removing frescoes with glycerin and cheesecloth.

When the second expedition arrived the following year, he notified Hung, and a representative of the National University joined the expedition. Hung also asked the Chinese Vice-Minister of Education to send telegrams to every governor, district magistrate, and Police Commissioner along the route. They were to be polite but firm: no foreigner was to be allowed near an artifact.

IN THE SUMMER OF 1929, WARNER HEARD FROM STEIN'S FRIEND Carl Keller that Stein might be available. Warner knew that "either [the] Cleveland or Philadelphia would jump at the chance of an association with Aurel Stein," but Warner naturally wanted an "entirely Harvard enterprise, if possible." Keller sent Stein a cable: "Can you lead Asiatic expedition if Harvard will finance. Answer collect. Post details." Soon, Warner wrote, they were "cautiously sidling up and sniffing at each other."

In his reply, Stein warned Keller about the risks for foreigners in removing antiquities: "Information received by me from friends thoroughly acquainted with current Chinese feeling shows that while the destructive plundering of China's ancient artistic relics from tombs, etc., is carried on unchecked and almost entirely through Chinese agency, yet systematic foreign archaeological enterprise aiming at the elucidation of China's ancient cultural past and the recovery and preservation of its relics is faced with the risk of serious obstruction by 'Young China.' This risk must be taken carefully into account at present."

Stein then proposed to appease "Chinese *amour propre* by refraining from any definite claim to those 'archaeological proceeds' i.e. antiquities, which loom so large before the average person…as the apparent main object of archaeological exploration." Stein preferred to trust in the generosity and "traditional *laissez faire* of the Chinese when it came to the final disposal of 'archaeological proceeds.'"

Nonetheless it was the "proceeds" that Harvard wanted. The university, wrote Warner, had "diverse interests" in Stein's various fields—ethnology, archaeology, geography, and geology, and its Sanskritists and Sinologues would be proud to be of service when he published his finds, but the museum was "devoted to the Fine Arts" and he would not disguise the fact that "my personal ambitions are for information and for objects related to early Buddhism."

Within a month of Stein's visit to Cambridge, Sachs wired him that he had raised $100,000 (the equivalent today of $1 million), from affluent benefactors and the Harvard Yenching Institute. One budget item was $6,500 for "presents" to local officials.

Stein wanted the support of the British Museum, so that the expedition might benefit from British diplomatic expertise. The correspondence reveals that the Americans were not keen on British involvement. Jayne wrote Warner, "You are absolutely right about Stein and the British Museum. Everywhere I go (and I'm just back from a hectic western trip) I hear that in the Orient particularly Mespot[amia] the Americans have the reputation of being easy marks for money. The expeditions such as the Oxford and Field Museum digging and our own British Museum–University of Pennsylvania affair at Ur, are only known as British expeditions. It's time we undertook things wholly for ourselves."

Warner replied: "If Stein is right in thinking that British prestige will be of any use in getting permission from the Nanking gov't to export his finds, I am heartily in favor asking the British Museum to cooperate. Even if they can't do anything but supply a small part of the funds and absorb all the credit I confess it looks as if we must acquiesce…"

Stein persuaded the British Museum to provide just enough money, $5,000, to qualify as a junior partner. In return the museum "naturally hoped to receive a characteristic and representative selection" of his discoveries.

Stein would have preferred to travel with an Indian staff, supplemented by "a couple of Chinese literati." However, he was almost seventy, had lost the toes on his right foot to frostbite, and suffered from chronic dyspepsia, so the Bostonians urged him to take an American assistant. In 1923, his friend the American diplomat Cornelius Engert had suggested a joint Anglo-American team for an

Afghan expedition; now he volunteered to accompany Stein on his current foray, adding: "As a matter of fact, I would rather be your 'bearer' in Central Asia than Ambassador to the Pope." Stein was also aware, as he complained to Keltie, of his "great *lacuna*, the want of all geological training." So, instead of Engert, he selected as his assistant a Yale doctoral candidate from Texas, Milton Bramlette, whose mentor was the distinguished geographer Professor Ellsworth Huntington. Bramlette, who was then thirty-four, was later to become an outstanding geologist.

In March 1930, when Stein returned to Cambridge en route to China for a preliminary scouting visit, Warner's unsuspected nemesis, William Hung, was lecturing at Harvard and Yenching University's President, John Leighton Stuart, was also in town. Hung typified the new breed of scholars determined to modernize China while preserving its past. Educated at Ohio Wesleyan University, he returned in 1923 to find China had become fervently nationalistic. According to Hung's biographer, a meeting was arranged with Stein at the Commander Hotel [*sic*] at Stuart's urging. Hung tried to persuade Stein, who was sure to face Chinese opposition, to give up the expedition. Instead, as he reported, the "wizened old man" arrogantly lectured him: "Mr Hung, you are young [Hung was thirty-seven]; you do not know. I have been in China long before and many times. The Chinese officials—they do not care. I know how to manage them."

Harvard's files do not record this meeting at the hotel but contain two memoranda dated March 21, 1930, about an encounter between Stein, Stuart, and Hung at Shady Hill, Paul Sachs's Cambridge home. Stuart informed Stein that the trustees had approved Yenching's $50,000 grant on the "essential condition" that Sachs and Stein would consult with the newly formed National Commission for the Preservation of Antiquities in Peking. Stein said he was prepared to do that only if the U.S. and British legations considered it advisable. Hung proposed to write directly to Sir Frederick Whyte, an unpaid adviser to the Chinese Government, who could prepare the ground for Stein with the commission. Stein rejected this proposal, viewing the details of his expedition as "strictly confidential." As a compromise, Stuart furnished Stein with a letter for Whyte detailing the serious apprehensions and possible damage that Harvard might suffer through their association with Stein's plans unless prior approval for the expedition was obtained from the commission. Presciently, Stuart wrote that this was the only way "to avert Young China agitation."

Before Stein left Cambridge, the Fogg's conservators demonstrated their new technique for removing frescoes. Stapled to Stuart and Stein's memos is a report from Harvard's research laboratories detailing the amount of glycerin, vinylite, brushes, atomizers, containers, and packing materials needed to remove a 12-foot-square painting from a wall.

At Cambridge, Stein also met Bramlette, who was to make his way to Kashmir, bring a carefully packed Marconi wireless receiver, and obtain "some colloquial knowledge of Hindustani." The geologist should also obtain practical knowledge in photography, but, most importantly, "it should be distinctly desirable" for the Texan to gain practical experience at the Fogg in the "removal of wall paintings." Stein proposed to take a limited quantity of necessary chemicals which Bramlette was to acquire from the Fogg. Langdon Warner was to supply all "the needed facilities for this purpose."

In April, Stein arrived in the Chinese capital, Nanking, where he met Whyte and the British Minister Sir Miles Lampson. After seeing Stuart's letter to Whyte, Lampson informed the Foreign Office that he advised Stein "entirely to ignore" Yenching's advice to obtain the necessary permissions from the fiercely anti-foreign commission. Lampson thought that such permissions illustrated "the 'defeatist' atmosphere in certain foreign circles in Peking in connection with foreign scientific expeditions in China." The British Minister cited recent expeditions, including one to Sinkiang under Sven Hedin, which had succeeded only when Hedin "sold the pass" by accepting "impossible conditions" that required he reorganize it as a joint Swedish-Chinese venture. Stein wrote Sachs that his advisers *all* agreed that a visit to Peking to meet with the commission as Stuart advocated, "would be likely to bring about that publicity and feared 'outcry' which he had so far avoided." Stein did not go to Peking.

On May 1, 1930, Stein and Lampson met in Nanking with Dr. C. T. Wang, the Chinese Minister of Foreign Affairs. British minutes show that Stein repeated the story to Dr. Wang that had proved so successful with the naive Dunhuang Abbot, Wang, that his goal was to trace the footsteps of his "patron saint Hsüan-tsang." Stein now explained the necessity of mapping in connection with "historical research." A discussion of routes followed and Stein expressed a wish to take a Chinese topographer if possible. The disposition of "archaeological proceeds" was not mentioned.

On May 7, the Chinese handed Stein his visa, which authorized only "the investigation of historical traces including relics of art and writing." As the conditions were satisfactory, Lampson advised Stein "to refrain from pressing for more specific facilities"—such as excavation permits.

On his third expedition, Stein had benefited from the unsettled conditions in Western China. Far from the capital, with the help of the now retired Macartney, the British explorer had struck his own deals with local officials and warlords. Now he proposed to enter Sinkiang Province again, through the back door from India. He believed it would thus be possible "to avoid whatever embarrassment *soi-disant* popular nationalist agitation might perhaps cause in case of a start from the east of China." He would rely, again, on "the personal goodwill of the Mandarins of the old scholarly type."

But in 1930 conditions were even more turbulent than in 1916. The Soviet Bolsheviks, having prevailed in a bitter civil war, now had designs on China's western provinces. Chiang Kai-shek, having broken with the Communists, had concluded his campaign against the northern warlords and had moved his capital from Peking south to Nanking. However, warlords still roamed at will in Sinkiang, where Stein's proposal to map the region, with the help of foreign (Indian) surveyors, would meet with suspicion.

In June, as Stein completed final preparations at his camp in Kashmir, Hung's friends on the Peking Commission prepared to take on Stein. In late May, Lampson had received a letter from the Chinese

Foreign Office stating that Stein, on three previous visits to Sinkiang, had "carried away without permission many Chinese antiques." If his intention was "to collect antiques and remove them from the country" he should, before starting, obtain prior approval. The Chinese also complained of Stein's previous mapping of routes from Sinkiang and Kansu to Tibet.

Also that June, a special committee of scientists and scholars, some educated at Harvard, pushed through the "Law for the Preservation of Antiquities," which permitted joint excavations, providing all proceeds remained in China. Though this news reached Stein in India, he preferred to take his chances without the committee's approval and set out from Kashmir on August 11. On arriving at the Chinese frontier, he heard that the Sinkiang Governor had orders from Nanking to bar his entry. Telegrams sped among British diplomats in Nanking, New Delhi, and Kashgar. Finally, after the British reminded the Governor that he was "under distinct obligations" to them for consignments of arms and ammunition, the Chinese allowed Stein to enter, and he was met by a friendly welcome in Kashgar on October 6. However, Bramlette, who had proved "a steady and thoroughly useful helper," was forced to return to India before the passes closed for winter. The thirty-four-year-old's constitution was not up to the task: he suffered from poor circulation in freezing temperatures and a "succession of intestinal troubles." A chastened Bramlette telegraphed Sachs that it was not "easy to admit that a young man cannot stand up to conditions that one does of Sir Aurel's age."

At Kashgar, Stein was summoned to Urumchi, Sinkiang's capital, to discuss his plans with the governor. He refused, explaining that the six-week side trip would delay his work. The governor allowed Stein to proceed only when he agreed to take along a Chinese official, a Mr. Chang, whose modest salary encouraged Stein to think he might be susceptible to "supplements in kind & coin." However, Chang's loyalties lay with Urumchi, and for five months he reported on Stein. While the governor had allowed Sir Aurel "to work," he had expressly forbidden him "to dig." Stein had to content himself with surface finds and securing the spoils of what he contemptuously described as local "treasure-seeking operations."

In December, the Peking commission stepped up its campaign. Stein was said to be surveying strategic areas as well as removing antiquities. Rumors of vast sums budgeted by Stein for bribes appeared in Chinese newspapers as well as an account of the Cambridge meeting between Stein and his sponsors at which "liberal professors [President Stuart et al.] pointed out that China had changed since the Manchus and advised Stein to cooperate with Chinese cultural organizations." The professors were silenced, according to one account, by Stein, who replied, "I only know Old China and do not pay the least attention to the slogans and catch-words of Young China." With his customary acumen, Owen Lattimore, writing from China to Warner, scented the culprit responsible for Stein's travails: "...my nostrils twitch whenever they pick up the scent of Hung & Co. on the trail of Stein."

Meanwhile, a statement from the commission in Peking went to Harvard contradicting Stein's various claims and deploring his false pretense of following his "patron saint" Hsüan-tsang's steps, when in fact he was intending to remove antiquities. Protesting that Stein's previous removal of objects was not "scientific archaeology" but verged on "commercial vandalism," the commission cited Stein's own published accounts.

Testy letters and telegrams flew between Sachs at the Fogg and Yenching Institute trustees. Sachs was forced to send a telegram on January 17 to Stein: "Serious complications for Harvard-Yenching Institute are reported to have resulted from your apparent failure to consult Commission Preservation Antiquities Peiping in accordance with their original understanding. All here remain convinced Commission's approval absolutely necessary if work is to continue in China. We have cabled Commission you will communicate with them."

But when Sach's cable arrived in March, the issue was moot. Stein's travel pass had already been canceled. In May, faced with overwhelming opposition from Peking and Harvard, Stein returned to Kashgar, where he turned over to the British Consul the few ancient manuscripts and wooden tablets he had surreptitiously collected at Niya and objects he had acquired from the locals. Lists were made for Foreign Minister Wang. Although the consulate turned over the objects to the Chinese authorities, scholars, most recently Wang Jiqing of Lanzhou University, have failed to trace them. (The photographic record that Stein made of his finds, thought to be lost, was recently discovered in the British Library.)

As if to underscore Stein's failure, a report of Sven Hedin's joint Sino-Swedish excavations in Sinkiang and Manchuria reached Harvard in June 1931. By mutual agreement, all finds were delivered to Peking; duplicates were eventually given to the Swedes. Among the items were 10,000 wooden strips with written characters, Han documents on silk, wall paintings from Turfan, pottery, and bronze implements. As Owen Lattimore observed to Warner, Hedin had not interceded on behalf of Stein, since as far as the Swede was concerned there was an old quarrel between him and the British.

Stein published an exculpatory account of the expedition in *The Times,* disputing the "wholly unwarranted allegations" advanced by the Commission: "The Chinese savants and others who had signed that protest were obviously influenced far more by nationalist bias than by any knowledge of my past scholarly labours in this field." He hoped that future Chinese scholars would recognize the "unjustified agitation" against "a confrere who has done as much as any one to throw light on the great and beneficent part played by ancient China in the history of Central Asia." Regretfully, he wrote his sponsors of the "expenditure incurred without adequate profit and to me personally a loss of time which nothing can replace." When Stein suggested that the British Minister present the Chinese with his version of the events, Lampson was discouraging: "Times have changed, and in this and other respects the Chinese are nowadays masters in their own house."

Stein continued his explorations of Asia and the Middle East, in some cases with the Fogg's money, and helped develop the new science of aerial surveying, but he never returned to China. As for Balkh, three viceroys had failed to convince the Afghans that no "political motive" was behind Stein's wish to follow the tracks of Alexander the Great. Finally in 1943, Stein's friend, Cornelius Engert, now the first American envoy posted to Kabul, telegraphed him with a "wholly unexpected" official invitation to visit Afghanistan. After all his disappointments, it seemed a fitting finale. Yet Stein wanted to make it clear that what he looked for was "antiquarian exploration, not merely a rapid visit to Kabul as if I were a 'globe trotter.'" He intended to propose to the Afghans a tour of their country—an "archaeological reconnaissance."

Stein delayed his visit in order to write up the results of his 1941–42 expedition to the Swat Valley. Writing to Engert he said, "I am fully aware that the winter months are not the right time for seeing Kabul at its best or for travelling in the northern parts of the country. But I am not afraid of its cold." On Tuesday, October 19, he arrived in Kabul in the American Legation car, "apparently in good health and spirits," Engert wrote, "with the zest of a school boy." On Thursday, while touring the drafty corridors of the Kabul museum with Engert's son, Roderick, Stein caught a chill that turned into bronchitis. On Sunday morning, realizing that he might not recover, he spoke to Engert about funeral arrangements and told his American friend: "I have had a wonderful life and it could not be concluded more happily than in Afghanistan, which I had wanted to visit for sixty years." That evening he suffered a stroke and never regained consciousness. On Tuesday, October 26, a month before his eighty-first birthday, Stein died at the U.S. Legation. After the Church of England ceremony he had requested, attended by representatives of the Afghan Emir, the Prime Minister, the Ministers of Foreign and Economic Affairs, officials of the museum, and members of the diplomatic corps, the man that Owen Lattimore, his intrepid colleague, described as "the most prodigious combination of scholar, explorer, archaeologist and geographer of his generation," was laid to rest in the foreign cemetery in Kabul. His tomb bore the inscription "English Citizen."

PART III

CHAPTER SIXTEEN

First Encounters of an American Kind

A WARM MIST OF EXOTICISM HAS VEILED TIBET SINCE ITS European discovery by Capuchin friars in the eighteenth century. Endowed with spiritual as well as physical grandeur by Western pilgrims, encumbered by bromidic phrases ("Forbidden Land," "Shangri-La," "Roof of the World"), lamaist Tibet was less a country than a state of mind. The mist only thickened after five decades of Chinese repression. As seen in films like *Kundun* and *Seven Years in Tibet,* old Tibet is more than ever an implausibly peaceable kingdom, its links with China and its ambiguous liaison with British India simply ignored. Indeed, filmgoers might reasonably conclude that the first Westerner to live in Tibet was Heinrich Harrer, the Austrian mountaineer. In reality, Harrer was preceded by a hundred-odd Britons and thirty-odd Americans, a procession led by the explorer and diplomat William Woodville Rockhill (1854–1914).

Rockhill was among the great scholar-diplomats of his time. He was the original China Hand, the principal drafter and executor of Washington's Open Door policy, the envoy nicknamed "Big Chief" who, between postings in Peking, St. Petersburg, and Constantinople, translated Tibetan texts. He became the first American to befriend and advise a Dalai Lama. John Hay, Theodore Roosevelt's Secretary of State, ranked him as one of the country's two ablest diplomats. After reading Rockhill's diary of a journey through Mongolia and Tibet, Henry Adams, who was not given to gush, wrote to the author, "I feel quite a new spring of self-esteem that I should be able to treat you with familiarity. It is as though I had lived on intimate terms with Marco Polo, and had Genghis Khan for dinner."

Rockhill initiated a century of American emotional and political involvement with Tibet. Most of the Americans and Britons who knew Tibet before its absorption by Communist China in 1950 became its advocates. But whether American or British, those who traveled west through China tended to differ with those venturing east from India about Lhasa's relations with Peking, still the central and unresolved core of the vexed "Tibetan Question." India hands generally regarded Tibet as independent in all but name, as a vital buffer between British, Russian, and Chinese empires. China hands commonly believed that Tibet was an integral part of China and that its separation could only encourage further carving-up of the Middle Kingdom.

William Rockhill was in the China camp, despite his affection for Tibet. It is worth pausing to understand why. He came of age as Americans began to gaze across the Pacific with contagious euphoria. When the U.S. Congress debated the annexation of Hawaii in 1898, Representative William Sulzer of New York waxed rhapsodic: "Let me say to the business men of America, Look to the land of the setting sun, Look to the Pacific!" There lay the teeming millions who want to be fed and clothed. There beckoned the great markets that Continental rivals were already trying to dominate. "We must not be distanced in the race for the commerce of the world," Sulzer went on, more prophetically than he might have guessed, declaring that in a hundred years the greater part of America's trade "will not be eastward, but will be westward; will not be across the Atlantic but across the broad Pacific."

Many in the American elite agreed, notably Theodore Roosevelt. No sooner had the battleship *Maine* blown up in Havana harbor in 1898 than TR, as Assistant Secretary of the Navy, audaciously ordered the Asiatic Squadron to prepare for battle against Spain in the Philippines. After Admiral Dewey's triumph in Manila Bay, President William McKinley reported that during a prayerful vigil he was prompted by Providence to put the Philippine Islands "on the map of the United States." Thereafter Roosevelt soared. Elected Governor of New York, nominated as McKinley's running mate in 1900, he succeeded to the Presidency when a demented anarchist shot McKinley. At forty-three, Roosevelt became the youngest and most effervescent of America's Chief Executives.

TR was the first President to articulate a truly global role for the United States. "Our mighty republic," he informed a wildly clapping audience in San Francisco in 1903, had become a "power of the first class in the Pacific." A canal in Panama would soon give Atlantic shipping easy access to a vaster ocean that would be to the modern age what the Mediterranean was to the ancient world. "The inevitable march of events" that gave America seemingly providential control of the Philippines gave her no choice but to become a world power.

"Before I came to the Pacific Slope I was an expansionist," Roosevelt avowed amid roars of approval, "and after having been here I fail to understand how any man...can be anything but an expansionist." Expansion required seapower, and the President was thoroughly familiar with the strategic theories of Captain Alfred T. Mahan, USN, and his most recent work, *The Problem of Asia* (1900). In its pages Mahan urged working with the British Navy to win river access to the Yangtse Valley and check the overland expansion of Russia. To Mahan, America's essential purposes in China were to prevent "preponderant political control by any one external state, or group of states" and to insist on an open door in the broadest sense, not only for commerce but for Western values and the Christian religion. To all of this Theodore Roosevelt heartily assented, and during his Presidency, America intrigued with Britain, Japan, and Germany to contain Russia's advance in the Far East. His approach was signaled in his first annual message as President. "Owing to the rapid growth of our power and our interests on the Pacific," he informed Congress, "whatever happens in China must be of the keenest national concern to us." This meant "beneficial intercourse" based on "equal rights and advantages" and (a Mahanesque flourish) access to the interior waterways "with which China has been so extraordinarily favored."

Taken together, these various strands, with their admixture of power politics, commerce, and moralism, were to typify America's China policy from Hay to Kissinger and indeed to the present day. What this portended for Tibet became evident during the lifetime of William Woodville Rockhill.

FEW AMERICAN DIPLOMATS HAVE COMPILED A MORE CURIOUS curriculum vitae. Rockhill had served in France's Foreign Legion and then worked as a rancher in New Mexico, all the while applying himself to the most difficult of Asian languages. His was Theodore Roosevelt's "strenuous life" carried to extreme, and his proficiency was both impressive and unbearable. Standing six-feet-four, adorned with a musketeer's curling red mustache, he abhorred small talk. He instilled fear rather than affection among his State Department colleagues—especially younger foreign service officers whose bad luck it was to face him as a Chinese-language examiner. "We stood in holy terror of Rockhill," recalled one such candidate, Nelson Johnson, who was to succeed him as U.S. envoy in Peking. "He was always very pleasant and affable, but he never recognized us on the street as being part of his entourage…He went along in a kind of thought-world of his own."

Rockhill's unusual apprenticeship was determined in the cradle. He was ten months old when his father, a Philadelphia attorney, died in his thirties, leaving a wife and two sons with a meager annuity. Dorothea Rockhill was a Woodville from Baltimore. Accustomed to balls and picnics at Belair, the family estate near Annapolis, with its race track and 600-acre deer park, she bridled at her straitened circumstances in Philadelphia. When William was eleven, Dorothea embarked for Paris, and with frugal panache the family settled in a small apartment near the Place Pereire. Her determination, high spirits, and air of entitlement passed to her boys, both of whom excelled at elite

French schools. With the assistance of the American Minister in Paris, William won admission to St. Cyr, the French West Point, where he learned to buckle a sword, wear a monocle, and bow with a flourish of his cape. Still, even then, he was summoned to a different thought-world. At the Collège de France, he attended lectures by the noted philologist Ernest Renan, whose analytic approach to the Scriptures had gained him fame, and nearly cost him his academic post. Renan sparked the young cadet's lifelong interest in Asia. This took a particular focus when Rockhill avidly read the published *souvenirs* of a French missionary, Abbé Huc, describing his travels through China and Tibet in the 1840's. Fascinated by Huc's account of Lhasa, otherwise off-limits to foreigners, Rockhill made inquiries at the Bibliothèque Nationale and found a tutor competent in Tibetan.

In 1873, he graduated with honors from St. Cyr, accepted a commission in the Foreign Legion, served as a second lieutenant in Oran, and resigned after three years. His family circumstances had changed. His tubercular brother Thomas had died, and his mother had remarried. At twenty-two Rockhill recrossed the Atlantic to court Caroline Tyson, whom he had first met in Paris when she was twelve. He located Caroline at a spa in West Virginia, and so captivating was his manner and Gallicized English that she broke off an engagement to accept him. It proved a good but not an easy match. The once wealthy Tysons had rashly succumbed to speculation, and the new groom, now with an infant daughter to support, was taken in by tales of easy fortunes in the booming Western cattle business. In partnership with his wife's uncle, Rockhill bought a ranch in New Mexico and took his family to what Caroline later called "Poverty Flat."

Here, for four years, the two men learned to brand and herd Texas longhorns, but at trail's end, no riches materialized. There were compensations. Work was seasonal and solitary, so Rockhill had ample opportunity to apply himself to Tibetan, Chinese, and Sanskrit. When the ranch was finally sold, the couple had sufficient means to sail for Europe and resettle in Montreux, where Rockhill's mother and her Swiss husband were living. And in the Alps, skills honed in the deserts of New Mexico resulted in published translations of the *Undânvarga,* a Tibetan version of Indian moral maxims (1881), and two sacred works from Tibetan sources, the *Prâtimoksha Sutra* (1884) and *The Life of Buddha* (1884). These earned for Rockhill the approbation of a select academic brotherhood, but one can readily imagine the translator's family, crowded into a tiny cottage in Montreux, wondering how it would end.

Rockhill's able biographer, Paul Varg, tracked down a manuscript on the early life of her father by his oldest daughter, Dorothy. She recalled the paternal sieges with the Tibetan language in Montreux, when she strove to be as small, silent, and inconspicuous as possible: "Army discipline had made of him something of a drill sergeant. We seldom met, in those days, except at lunch, and communion between us was limited on his part to 'sit up,' 'take your elbows off the table,' 'stop playing with the salt.' And yet there were times when he would emerge from weeks of moodiness into a riot of gay spirits, when he was boyish, delightful and absurd."

IN 1884 CAROLINE ROCKHILL UNEXPECTEDLY CAME INTO AN INheritance of nearly $70,000, the bequest of a cousin. With this small fortune, her husband could finally afford a trip to China, the path cleared by his appointment as Second Secretary of the U.S. Legation in Peking. His salary was a modest $1,800 per annum, increasing to $2,625 when Rockhill became First Secretary a year later. So it transpired, half by accident, that this reclusive yet supremely qualified American was reborn a diplomat just as the Celestial Empire was entering its final agonies.

From 1842 to 1912, China was like a great luxury liner slowly sinking as fissures opened beneath her sagging water line. On the bridge, oblivious or indifferent to the approaching disaster, were the ruling Manchus, comprising perhaps five million in a population of 400 million. Originally warriors from Manchuria, known as superb horsemen and archers, the Manchus swept into Peking in 1644, deposed the Ming Dynasty and claimed the Mandate of Heaven for their Qing (or Ch'ing) Dynasty. Proud of their language, said to be related to Hungarian and Finnish, shunning commerce and dominating the imperial court, the Manchus remained outsiders, affecting a scorn for their peasant subjects. To keep other outsiders from disturbing their realm, the Manchus in the eighteenth century excluded all "foreign devils" from Chinese territory. British and other traders could only enter a section of the Canton waterfront known as a "factory," and that only from October to March. Britain waged the Opium War of 1839–42 to breach the wall, resulting in a treaty that permitted four more treaty ports and the right to settle the offshore island that became Hong Kong. Subsequent treaties in 1844 with France and the United States, and with Russia in 1858, opened more ports, and eventually there were eighty. Here foreigners lived in privileged cantonments, exempt from Chinese laws, amidst such alien implants as churches, clubs, and racetracks. During what the Chinese saw as a "century of humiliation," these extraterritorial rights were all the more galling since the ports had first been pried open in an ignoble war to legalize the sale of opium, the debilitating "foreign mud" imported chiefly from India. (The British led the way in this traffic, but enterprising Yankees were not far behind; among the most successful was Warren Delano, the grandfather of Franklin Roosevelt.)

China's inability to defend its coastline invited deeper encroachments on its periphery. Until the 1850's, an outer array of tributary states ringed the Middle Kingdom, reaching from Burma and Siam northward to Mongolia and Turkestan, from Nepal and Tibet eastward to Korea and the Ryukyu Islands, all of whose rulers were in varying degree vassals to the Son of Heaven. To be sure, Chinese laws and institutions were not only different but often incomprehensible to non-Chinese, which made it easier to find excuses for annexations. In 1858, Russia took over a vast tract north of Amur. Britain followed by absorbing Lower and then Upper Burma. Russia occupied Chinese Turkestan, which it handed back in 1881 for 9 million rubles and the ceding to Russia of key border areas. France in successive moves acquired the kingdoms of Annan (Vietnam), Laos, and Cambodia to form French Indochina. Soon Russia and Japan vied for control of Manchuria and Korea.

Yet even as the ship listed, the Manchus continued to believe, or pretended to believe, that foreign barbarians had nothing to teach the Middle Kingdom. This was foreshadowed in China's first diplomatic encounter with the British. In 1793, Lord George Macartney led a naval mission laden with gifts to induce Peking to enter into a commercial treaty. The mission failed, according to an oft-repeated account, when Macartney declined to kowtow before the Emperor, only kneeling instead of pressing his head to the ground nine times. In any case, as it was unthinkable for the Son of Heaven to acknowledge the King of England as an equal, no agreement was possible. Besides, as the Emperor declared in his message to George III, "We have never valued ingenious articles, nor do we have the slightest need of your country's manufactures." Macartney, an experienced diplomat who had spent years at Catherine the Great's court, reflected in his journal that the Empire was headed for the reefs and that "much rivalry and disorder" would ensue as trading nations searched "every channel, creek, and cranny of China for a market."

He could not have guessed that a concubine of the fifth rank would preside over the imperial twilight. She was Tz'u-hsi, the Empress Dowager, China's de facto ruler from 1861 until 1908. A handsome Manchu who entered the Imperial Palace as one of hundreds of concubines, Tz'u-hsi was chosen by the Chief Eunuch on an auspicious night to sleep with Hsien-feng, the seventh Ch'ing Dynasty ruler. She bore him his only son, T'ung-chih, who succeeded at six, enabling his mother to rule as coregent. When T'ung-chih died at nineteen, Tz'u-hsi contrived to have her four-year-old nephew proclaimed Emperor, and even after Kuang-hsü attained his majority, she continued to dominate. She survived rebellions, military debacles, and famines, frustrated reform and lived profligately, resplendent in her yellow dragon robe or her cape made of 3,500 perfect pearls. Still, despite her extravagance and vanity, her passing in 1908 prompted an outpouring of grief. She died the day after the Emperor, whom she possibly had poisoned. A multitude of monks, among them Tibet's Dalai Lama, all garlanded in flowers, joined in funeral rites that culminated with the burning of an entire paper army to protect her in death. The Ch'ing Dynasty survived for three years, but that bonfire truly marked its demise.

As President Roosevelt's envoy to China, Rockhill was among the dignitaries visiting the palace to view the imperial remains, which he noted in his diary were "very impressive." One imagines that others craned to stare at his erect figure, for by then he was a legend in Peking. He knew as much about the Middle Kingdom as any foreigner, and certainly knew more of its less-traveled hinterland. His explorations had won him the Founder's Gold Medal of the Royal Geographical Society, and his knowledge of Tibet enabled him to befriend the great Thirteenth Dalai Lama. Yet he achieved his successes on a pittance, with mulish determination, and against the express wishes of his superior.

Tibet was his goal from the moment he arrived in Peking in 1884 as a Legation Secretary. Hardly had he taken up his duties—handling correspondence, obtaining visas, and aiding Americans living in China—than he sought a teacher to improve his Tibetan. Rockhill found a lama from Lhasa to tutor him as he tackled both Tibetan and Chinese, a regimen he continued for four years, with two digressions. In 1886, he wintered in Seoul to give diplomatic backing to American missionaries and merchants trapped in the disorders of a decaying Korean kingdom, still a Chinese vassal but now coveted by both Russia and Japan. In Korea, he reported to Washington, "You will see diplomacy in the raw; diplomacy without gloves, perfume or phrases."

That spring he returned to Peking to discover his wife pregnant and stricken with smallpox. She was shunned by local doctors fearful of contact with "the celestial flower," the deferential euphemism for the disease. Fortunately, a less timid physician was found, and a frantic Rockhill was at Caroline's bedside through her difficult pregnancy until their daughter, Margarita, was born.

It was a cruelly commonplace medical crisis. In dynastic China, sanitation was medieval, disfiguring diseases rampant. Yet whether out of foolishness, sangfroid, or a frontiersman's self-assurance, Rockhill in December 1888 departed on his own for an extended trip through China's poorest, wildest, and remotest regions to reach Tibet; moreover he forfeited his official post for the privilege.

Rockhill had for several years pressed for a leave to explore inner Asia, a request repeatedly rebuffed by his chief, the U.S. Minister, Charles Denby, who insisted his First Secretary was neglecting his duties. While on home leave in 1888, Rockhill took his request directly to the Secretary of State, who refused to intervene, and the First Secretary forthwith resigned. Rockhill applied for a stipend to the Smithsonian Institution, whose Secretary, Samuel Langley, authorized him to explore Central Asia at a salary of $50 a month. As a bonus, the Smithsonian provided the surveying instruments that the American stowed in his bags as he set forth through Peking's western gate with a single Chinese companion. "My outfit was simple and inexpensive," Rockhill writes in *Land of the Lamas* (1891), "for dressing and living like a Chinaman, I was encumbered neither with clothes nor foreign stores, bedding, tubs, medicines, nor any of the other impedimenta which so many travelers consider absolute necessities."

This republican boast plainly alluded to his British and Russian contemporaries, who tended to travel in imperial comfort. Fortuitously, Rockhill's Chinese servant, Liu San, had accompanied Captain Francis Younghusband of the Dragoon Guards on his celebrated journey over the widest breadth of China, from Peking across the Gobi Desert and the Muztagh pass to Kashmir. "Ours was a compact little party," Younghusband wrote in *The Heart of a Continent* (1896), "the camel-man who acted as a guide, a Mongol assistant, my Chinese 'boy,' eight camels and myself." His "boy" was Liu San, who served as "interpreter, cook, table-servant, groom, and carter."

Rockhill's party was, by comparison, steerage class. His locomotion was by a high two-wheeled cart, the mule-drawn *mappa*, obtained on a thrifty arrangement whereby Rockhill could subtract a modest sum for each day exceeding the thirty-four usually needed to reach the edge of China, or add the same amount for every day gained. He needed no interpreter or table servant, and avoided contact with inquisitive officials in regions off-limits to foreigners. From Liu San he heard boastful tales of how Younghusband had gullibly paid inflated prices for carts and mules, with his "boy" pocketing the difference (published with a certain relish by the American). After passing safely through provinces infested with bandits and armed peasantry, Rockhill arrived in Sining on the frontier. Here suspicious police came to his inn and ordered him to appear before the local magistrate the next day. Having sent Liu San and *mappa* homeward, Rockhill decamped alone at dawn. He shaved his head and face and substituted the red robe worn by Mongolian lamas for his Chinese gown. His new companions were Mongols clad in sheepskin, who joined an irregular caravan of camels and horses inching toward Tibet. He was not pursued.

His goal was Lhasa, which he knew no Westerner had reached since Abbé Huc in the 1840's. The only known foreign trespassers were the Indian pundits, the native explorers employed by the British who posed as pilgrims and used prayer-wheels to reckon distances covertly. Rockhill was their ardent admirer, especially of Sarat Chandra Das, who first trekked to Lhasa in 1879, and again in 1881. If a British explorer had accomplished a third of what he and other pundits had achieved, Rockhill expostulated, "medals and decorations, lucrative offices and professional promotion, freedom of the cities, and every form of lionisation would have been his; but as for these native explorers a small pecuniary reward and obscurity are all to which they can look forward."

Having studied carefully the failed attempts on Lhasa by the Russian Nikolai Przhevalsky and others, Rockhill concluded that distrust of foreigners among the Buddhist clergy was his most formidable obstacle. So it was with trepidation that he approached the great Lamasery of Kumbum, 700 miles east of Lhasa. This was the "Monastery of a Hundred Thousand Images," the most revered in northeastern Tibet, the birthplace of Tsong-Khapa, founder of Buddhism's Yellow Church. On his death in the fifteenth century Tsong-Khapa was incarnated in another self, becoming first in a line of the divine personages who came to be known as Dalai Lamas. Tsong-Khapa's reformed creed, known as the Yellow Hats, with its codes of celibacy and abstinence from alcohol, took firm root in Mongolia and Tibet. Over time in Tibet, the Dalai Lama assumed the triple role of incarnate diety, monarch, and monk, with all-embracing authority over his (still) devout people.

Soon Kumbum's monasteries and chapels, their gold roofs glinting in the sun, loomed on the hillside, a magnet for throngs of pilgrims to the Great Prayer Festival. Held during the first month of the lunar year, the Monlam festival attracted the numbers that Rockhill hoped would assure his safety. But with his towering form and reddish hair, how could he possibly hope to pass as a pious Asian pilgrim?

A KALEIDOSCOPE OF MONGOL-TIBETAN LIFE OPENED BEFORE THE American as he strolled through streets crowded with puppet the-aters, gaming tables, snack bars, wagons laden with sweets, meats, baked goods, trinkets, pelts, souvenirs, and (despite frequent sweeps by censorious lamas flourishing whips) peep shows featuring titillat-ing pictures of European origin. Prayer flags fluttered, masked dancers performed to drums and horns, and in temples a thousand butter-lamps flickered, illuminating two great butter bas-reliefs, each rising more than twenty feet.

Fascinated, Rockhill lingered for six weeks in Kumbum, filling notebooks with voluminous descriptions of what he saw. He was not detained or expelled, and when recognized by a lama he had known in Peking, he was introduced to others as a foreigner with a serious interest in Buddhism. Yes, of course, he must go to Lhasa, and see Tibet's most sacred shrine, the Jokhang Temple, and all the other wonders. Rockhill's hopes flowered, but at some point a contrary signal came, presumably from Lhasa. Guides vanished, erstwhile friends withheld promised aid, and it was ominously whispered that even if he survived the bleak steppe-desert between Kumbum and Lhasa, he would be murdered on arrival. Nevertheless, he set forth southwest on his own, accompanied by a Tibetan mastiff, and plod-ded onward, ignoring the warnings and shaking heads that greeted him on the way. Only when his funds dwindled did he call off his journey, 400 miles short of his goal.

Rockhill returned to China through eastern Tibet, passing thirty-six lamaseries in a bleak and lofty terrain where he estimated that a fifth of 150,000 inhabitants were monks. He stopped wherever he could, and talked at length with lamas. He learned of the violent feuds among rival lamaseries, of their graded hierarchy, in which forty-eight incarnate saints at the peak were drawn from the ruling Gelong lamas, while lowly Drabas, who were free to marry and took only minor vows, hewed the wood and drew the water.

All this went into his notebooks, along with accounts of the nomadic Drupa peoples, the flora and fauna found at heights of over 14,000 feet, and sketches of Tibetan clothing, tools, and musical instruments. On his return, Rockhill promptly recounted his journey in eight articles for *The Century* magazine, in a well-received book, and in learned treatises for the Smithsonian Institution. His work was distinguished not merely for its pith and accuracy but also for its ethnographic objectivity. His tone was so neutral that in later years his advancement was opposed by Christian groups on grounds that he was too partial to Buddhism, a charge that TR and John Hay strenuously contested.

Buoyed by his successes, Rockhill immediately sought support for a second attempt at Lhasa, this time by a different route. His plan was to leave China from Kansu Province, pass through eastern Mongolia, and traverse Tibet from northeast to southwest, ending in Nepal or Sikkim. His provisions were more generous, but only just. In a pointed comment to his Smithsonian sponsors, he reported that he left Peking in December 1891 well provided with scientific apparatus but only scantily with money: "How to travel on an empty money bag (and an empty stomach, as it turned out in my case) in a strange land, is a more difficult problem than the quadrature of the circle." He could afford two carts on the first leg of his journey, and on leaving Lanzhou, heading into turbulent Koko Nor country, he initially secured the services of four frontiersmen and a cook, purchased six stout ponies, a team of pack mules, and a supply of provisions—barley, rice, flour, vermicelli, tea—sufficient for five months ("if used with economy"). As he pressed forward, he switched from ponies and mules to yaks and camels, and hired fresh relays of Mongol and Tibetan guides. Complicating his itinerary was the need to avoid, wherever possible, Tibetan authorities likely to bar his way to Lhasa.

Pause for a moment to consider the sheer breadth of his task. Tibet proper occupies a lofty highland the size of Western Europe. The only unimpeded passage to the Tibetan plateau is through Koko Nor on the east; the world's highest mountains block other approaches. Living on a plateau with an average height of 16,000 feet above sea level, Tibetans contend with tempestuous weather, lack of arable land, parched pastures, recurrent and biting hordes of flies, mosquitoes, and lice. Rockhill not only plunged ahead without maps, through deserts and swamps, over perilous passes and around glaciers, enduring snowstorms and freezing nights in May and June, but he also needed to befriend suspicious peoples of every faith, from Buddhists and Muslims to shamanists and devil-worshipers. His overriding problem was food.

Rockhill failed to take account of summer snowstorms in Tibet, and therefore lacked the proper shoes for his baggage animals, none of which survived the trip. As the larder depleted, his party of five scavenged for game and roots, avoiding camps of nomadic herdsmen who might turn them in. What food they gathered was often close to inedible. Rockhill took rueful note of the saying that a Mongol eats three pounds of wool with his food yearly, a Tibetan three pounds of gravel, and a Chinese three pounds of dirt. "Living in a Sinico-Mongolo-Tibetan style," he remarks, "I swallowed with my miserable food the dirt, the wool, and the grit, portioned by a harsh destiny to these peoples, and I verily believe that I found enough wool in my tea, my tsamba [ground and roasted barley], my meat, and my bread while in Mongolia and Tibet to stuff a pillow. The dirt and the sand could be easily swallowed, but the wool—nothing could be done with it, no amount of mastication could dispose of it."

By July, with no fuel but the droppings of wild yaks, with no grass for pack animals, which had to be kept alive with precious barley meal, supplies gave out and the party subsisted on tea alone. Rockhill had little choice but to abandon his plan of reaching Lhasa by roundabout stealth and instead appealed for help at the nearest nomadic camp. As he feared, the local headmen reported his presence. The Tibetans forced him to halt 110 miles from Lhasa, closer than any Westerner since Abbé Huc, closer than Przhevalsky with his Cossack escorts. His journal entry was stoic: "I am ten days from Shigatse and not more than twenty-five from British India and six or seven weeks from home, but it will be four or five months before I reach there now by the long route I shall have to travel. *T'ien ming,* 'it is heaven's decree.'"

Officials from Lhasa admired his pluck. They permitted Rockhill and his party to work their way home eastward instead of north-ward, so that he might return by the unexplored Chamdo trade route. While this was under discussion, they supplied him with every delicacy of the Tibetan cuisine—sour milk, clotted cream, tsamba, mutton, and buttered tea—and then presented him with valuable presents, including a good saddle pony. "I now left with an escort of ten soldiers," he marveled, "resplendent in purple gowns, high, wide-brimmed summer hats, and all their many silver-mounted arms and accoutrements."

By the time Rockhill reached Shanghai in October, the sheer im-probability of his feat began slowly to register among his peers. He was by habit reluctant to dwell on the hazards he overcame. His pub-lished journal describes only one near-death mishap, an incident during a river crossing when ice cracked beneath his horse. Both man and mount disappeared beneath the ice. Rockhill was saved when his baggy gown and trousers billowed out and enabled him to cling to the ice: "I shouted to the men to throw themselves flat on the ice and creep out to me, which they did, and after much trouble got me out, none the worse for the ducking." Whatever the dangers or hardships, he routinely determined altitudes by the temperature of boiling water, and took sextant readings. "The method I followed in my work," he explained, "was to run the traverse by prismatic com-pass and aneroid, taking the distance between consecutive points by my watch and controlling frequently the distances thus obtained by pacing them off." He somehow kept a camera in working order, made detailed sketches of people and things, and filled hampers with Tibetan clothing, jewelry, and utensils (still preserved in the Smith-sonian's Museum of Natural History).

Of his ten-month odyssey, Rockhill was able to write with a rare note of pride, "I had travelled about 8,000 miles, surveyed 3,417 [miles] during the geographically important part of the journey, crossed 69 passes, all of them rising over 14,500 feet above sea level. I had taken a series of sextant observations at 100 points, made 300 photographs, collected between 300 and 400 ethnological, botanical and geological specimens. For two months we had lived soaked by the rains and blinded by snow and hail, with little or nothing to eat, and tea as our only beverage; and yet not one of us had a moment's illness from the day we left till we reached our homes again."

RECOGNITION CAME FIRST IN LONDON, AND THEN IN WASHINGTON as the State Department tardily took account of Rockhill's unique abilities. By accident of timing, the American's attempt to cross Tibet and reach British India coincided with a parallel journey in the opposite direction by Captain Hamilton Bower of the Indian Staff College. Bower too tried and failed to reach Lhasa but did manage an exit into China. So it was that two journeys across Tibet came to the attention of the Royal Geographical Society. The ranking military authority on Indian frontiers, Sir Thomas Holdich, examined Rockhill's itinerary. His favorable judgment was almost surely the reason why the RGS bestowed its coveted medals on both Bower and Rockhill. For the American, this meant a visit to London, where he met and liked his fellow Tibetan traveler. It also gave him a direct connection with the Society's Secretary, John Scott Keltie.

Through Keltie, Rockhill took up the cause of the Indian Pundits, especially Sarat Chandra Das, with whom the American was now a regular correspondent. Das believed (rightly) that his two secret journeys to Lhasa warranted an RGS medal, an ambition he shared with Huree Chunder Mukerjee, his alter ego in *Kim*. It took years of determined correspondence, but Rockhill did obtain Keltie's support for publication in London by John Murray of Das's *Journey to Lhasa and Central Asia* (1902), in a text edited and introduced by Rockhill. "Had it not been for your kind exertions and influence on the Society the book could hardly have been published," Das wrote to Rockhill. "...You have secured for me a place in the Temple of Fame which is higher than heaven."

In Washington, the acclaim abroad for Rockhill was not unnoticed. He had the influential support of the Five of Hearts, a coterie of wellborn insiders including Henry Adams and John Hay. In 1893, Rockhill returned to the State Department as its Chief Clerk, and in three years he was Assistant Secretary of State under President Grover Cleveland. But when McKinley and the Republicans took over in 1897, Rockhill was viewed as a Democratic holdover, and wound up as U.S. Minister in Greece. Rockhill found Athens remote from his own interests. The posting soured entirely the following year when Mrs. Rockhill died of typhoid in Athens. She was forty-two. From Montreux to New Mexico to Peking, Caroline had kept his black dogs of depression at bay with uncommon good humor. "Where his intolerance antagonized, she would charm people back," their daughter Dorothy wrote. "She made friends for him; she gave him self-confidence when his modesty and shyness stood in the way; she smoothed the rough places (and there were a great many) and laughed at them with a sense of humor that, though sometimes biting, was never so where he was concerned." Athens without her was now intolerable.

The Five of Hearts came to his rescue. "Now, about Rockhill," Roosevelt confided to a friend in March 1899, when he was still Governor of New York. "I think just as you do, that he ought not to go...I have not the faintest idea what position he could get. The country ought to have him, and yet the country is so blind that it does not see the good that he could do." Within a month, Hay found him a job, as Director of the Bureau of American Affairs, with an additional portfolio as the Secretary of State's consultant on Far Eastern affairs, with a combined salary of $8,000 a year. This was to be Rockhill's perch for six productive years.

John Hay was obsessively determined to make his mark. He knew little of the Far East, and turned to Rockhill for guidance. By late summer, the new consultant brought off a diplomatic *coup de main* that assured Hay's reputation. Rockhill drafted the circular note sent by Washington to all powers with interests in China asking each to guarantee equal commercial opportunity in their respective spheres of influence. This was the famous Open Door policy, the friend of every editorialist, that Hay inserted into diplomatic parlance by bluff and legerdemain. In private, other powers were evasive or negative about the "Open Door" but were reluctant to make their reservations public, so Hay simply declared in March 1900 that the assent of all powers—Russia, Britain, Germany, France, Japan, and Italy—was "final and definitive." All sides in America acclaimed this cost-free initiative, especially farmers eager to help feed 400 million Chinese. It was, as George Kennan has pungently argued, chiefly a public relations triumph, unenforceable and unilateral, its language too universal for Chinese realities, but the American public believed that a great blow had been struck for its principle.

Rockhill was at the center of Open Door negotiations, parsing every phrase in private and public responses to the circular, but his purpose went well beyond commerce. His interest in promoting American business was at best tepid, as various investors, especially in railroads, frequently complained. Nor was he covertly promoting British interests, even though he collaborated closely with an Englishman, Alfred Hippisley, an official in the Chinese Customs Service he had known in Peking, in drafting the circular note. His purpose instead was to protect the territorial integrity and independence of China, which he saw as vital to America's long-term interests.

China's devastating defeat in the war with Japan (1894–95) exposed the feebleness of the Manchu Empire, and the powers vied to carve out fresh leaseholds and spheres of influence. The heady craze of imperialism was at its peak. A much-discussed best-seller, *The Breakup of China* (1899) by Lord Charles Beresford, plausibly contended that China was soon to be parceled out, in the fashion of Africa. Rockhill saw no advantage for Americans in this scramble for spoils, and thought Britain (so he informed Hippisley) "as great an offender in China as Russia itself." This was not a matter of sentiment, for Rockhill had no illusions about the decadence of Manchu China. It was a matter of interest: if China fragmented into disparate spheres of influence, its markets were bound to be closed to American merchants.

Suddenly an eruption in China put Secretary Hay's policies to a severe test. A secret society, the Righteous and Harmonious Fists, better known as the Boxers and claiming supernatural powers, hurled themselves at "foreign devils," killing missionaries and their Chinese converts ("secondary devils"). The rising began in 1899 in the northern province of Shantung, where Imperial Germany had just made its presence perhaps too aggressively felt. In June 1900 rioting flared in

Peking, fourteen foreign legations came under siege, and incredibly, Government troops joined with Boxers in firing away at the trapped diplomats. All communications were cut. The sole telegraphic account of the siege came from the American Minister, E. H. Conger, who said only rapid intervention would prevent a general massacre.

"Your open door is already off its hinges," Henry Adams wrote from Paris that June to his friend John Hay. "How the deuce do you get out? For a fortnight I have been utterly aghast about it. First, the unequaled horror of those wretched people cut up in Pekin [sic] to be skinned and burned...Make an arrangement with You or Me or Him to let our citizens loose, and we'll promise never to go there again...I hope you may do it, but all know you can't. What can you do then? That's where I begin to turn green. You've got literally the world on your shoulders."

In truth, Hay did better than expected. The Secretary took up the line that had been persistently pressed by Rockhill. In a new circular on July 3, Hay declared that the United States would act concurrently with other powers to end the "virtual anarchy" in Peking, rescue the besieged, and seek a solution that would preserve China's "territorial and administrative entity." What Hay had implied by the first Open Door circular he now made explicit in the second, and this became bedrock American policy for a half century. Hay avoided war with China by characterizing the Boxers as a rebel minority. He helped mobilize a multinational relief force that managed, despite clashing egos and dismal disarray, to end the siege on August 14. Finally, as the victors began discussing reparations, Hay dispatched Rockhill to China as a special agent of the United States at the upcoming negotiations. A delighted Theodore Roosevelt wrote: "I feel as if a load were off my mind when it was announced that you were to go to China."

In Peking, Rockhill suspected that Russia, Germany, and France, separately if not collectively, sought to cripple China with a ruinous indemnity. The American had a different goal, and enjoying unusual discretionary authority thanks to Hay, he emerged as pivotal arbiter at the Conference of Ministers. By cajolery and playing on rivalry among Europeans, Rockhill won agreement on a lump indemnity of $333 million, to be divided among the powers according to losses suffered. On his return to Washington, in an innovative final touch, Rockhill won approval for using half the American portion of the indemnity to provide scholarships for Chinese students in the United States. So began a tradition of Sino-American scholarly exchanges that has survived wars and revolutions, and flourishes still.

FROM OPEN DOOR TO BOXER REBELLION, ROCKHILL'S ABILITIES were amply realized, but nothing gratified him more than his role as friend and adviser of a Dalai Lama, "the most unique experience I have ever had." This was the start of America's involvement in the "Tibetan Question," and it caught the imagination of Theodore Roosevelt, who felt a special affinity for Rockhill—a spare-spoken fellow former cowboy and citizen-soldier in the Cincinnatus mode. We commonly forget that TR gave the White House its name, and introduced the title "Mr. President," tokens of his preference for direct, unstuffy address. He relished contact with scholars and doers, with whom he corresponded as a colleague. The White House thus became privy to the arcane negotiations among three empires— China, Russia, and Britain—and the "Most Excellent Self-Existent Buddha," the Thirteenth Dalai Lama.

In March 1905, as his second term began, the President appointed Rockhill as U.S. Envoy to China. It was an interesting time. Two recent convulsions had reshaped the Asian map. The British military mission led by Francis Younghusband in 1903–4 forcibly ended Tibet's isolation, causing the Dalai Lama to flee to Mongolia and the Chinese to depose him. What precipitated the invasion was the certain belief of Lord Curzon, then India's Viceroy, that Russia was plotting to infiltrate Tibet, its agent being a shadowy Buddhist monk named Dorzhiev. The Boxer disturbances provided Russia with an excuse for quartering troops throughout all Manchuria, where they collided with the rising power of Japan. In February 1904 Japan attacked the Russian fleet at Port Arthur, igniting the first war in which both sides used modern mass-killing weaponry. It ended in Russia's defeat, provoked violent dissension at home, and led to the diplomatic intervention of Theodore Roosevelt, whose peacemaking earned him a Nobel Prize.

For the moment, Japan was up, Russia down, while in Britain enthusiasm for Tibetan adventures waned entirely as the nonimperial Liberal Party took office in late 1905. At about that time in Mongolia, the Dalai Lama asked the Russian explorer Pyotr Kozlov if he knew of any Western diplomats who understood Tibetan. Learning that such a paragon existed, and was in fact U.S. Minister in Peking, the exiled Incarnate opened a correspondence that continued until Rockhill's death.

In 1905, the Thirteenth Dalai Lama was still a novice in the devious game of nations. Fearful and distrustful of the British, he had turned to Agvan Dorzhiev to appeal to St. Petersburg for protection "from the dangers that threaten his life if he returned to Lhasa, as is his intention and duty." Tsar Nicholas made no promises, but said enough to agitate the British and anger the Chinese, who informed the Dalai Lama that if he intrigued with the Russians, he would never return to Lhasa.

What should he do? Could Rockhill plead his case with the "golden ear of the Manchu Emperor"? This was the burden of the Dalai Lama's first letters to the American Minister, whose response was not encouraging. A fresh turn of the diplomatic wheel then deepened the Lama's isolation. In 1906, Britain's Liberal Government signed a new pact recognizing China's de facto authority over Tibet. This was followed in 1907 by an Anglo-Russian Convention in which the two old rivals professed friendship and agreed to deal with Lhasa only through Chinese mediation, save for certain rights won by Younghusband. In the text for the first time the British officially acknowledged Chinese "suzerainty" over Tibet. On top of all this, friction developed between His Holiness and his host, the Buddhist ruler of Mongolia. With a firm nudge from Peking, the Dalai Lama and his entourage moved first to Kumbum, then to Wu T'ai Shan, a Buddhist sanctuary in Shansi Province

When that happened, Rockhill pulled on his walking boots and in June 1908 made his way on foot to Shansi, a five-day journey. He hoped to persuade the Dalai Lama to seek peace with China and thaw relations with British India. It was the Tibetan's first encounter with a Western envoy, and it was a success. During a week at the Dalai Lama's residence, Rockhill discovered a young man of undoubted intelligence, quick understanding, and force of character. "He seemed deeply impressed with his great responsibilities as supreme Pontiff of his faith," Rockhill recalled in a monograph on Dalai Lamas written years later. "...He is quick tempered and impulsive, but cheerful and kindly. At all times I found him a most thoughtful host, an agreeable talker and extremely courteous. He speaks rapidly and smoothly, but in a very low voice."

The Dalai Lama is five-foot-six, his face pitted by smallpox, but not deeply, his eyes dark brown and eyebrows heavy, Rockhill reported. He moves quickly but tends to stoop, having spent most of his life cross-legged. He dresses in the dark red worn by all lamas, a vermilion silk shawl over his left shoulder, and wears yellow boots with blue braiding—all this hard-won detail the Minister packed into a twelve-page letter to Roosevelt. He had more to add, but Rockhill feared he had already said too much. To be seated familiarly with the Dalai Lama, he wrote, with an abbot standing behind him, "with His Holiness's fly-flapper keeping the flies off my head, and he seeing that my tea cup was filled with hot tea, asking me to open a correspondence with him: it was all too extraordinary. I could not believe my ears and eyes."

Roosevelt's reply all but bubbled: "I think that this is one of the most interesting and extraordinary experiences that any man of our generation has had. There has been nothing like it, so far as I know. Really, it is difficult to believe it occurred! I congratulate you, and I congratulate the United States upon having the one diplomatic representative in the world to whom such an incident could happen. Now how shall I acknowledge the box containing the Buddha, and the big white silk Katag? What kind of present should I send him in return? I sent the Pope a copy of my books."

Before Rockhill could reply, a second letter arrived. The President found the interview "so important from the standpoint of the British Government" that he allowed Lord Bryce, the British Envoy, to show it "to certain of the highest officials." It was the seed generating the forgive-and-forget meeting in Peking between the Dalai Lama and his erstwhile British adversaries, the first move toward eventual rapprochement. Rockhill's reports were admiringly read at the Foreign Office, but its officials were chary of TR's bursts of enthusiasm. Sir Cecil Spring-Rice, who was best man at Roosevelt's second marriage, likened him to an impetuous youngster, adding, "You must always remember the President is about six."

IN SEPTEMBER 1908, ON A CLOUDLESS SUN-SPANGLED DAY, THE Dalai Lama did arrive in Peking by special train. He had agreed to the visit with worried hesitation, Rockhill reported, and only after peremptory representations from the Chinese. Yet his welcome seemed auspicious. An Imperial guard of honor met him at the flower-bedecked railway station. Trumpeters preceded his processional column, with its six drummers beating in slow time. A throng of sunburnt monks garbed in flowing capes of yellow and red followed. Mounted infantry with drawn swords and four buglers trotted before the great yellow chair in which the Lama sat curtained from view, borne by twenty porters. "Behind the chair was carried what I can only call an enormous sunshade," ran an account in *The China Daily News,* "since it was too small to be termed a canopy, yet too splendid, surely, to be dubbed an umbrella. But, *bien entendu,* it was very magnificent, not stiff, nor plain, nor ordinary, but rich, long-skirted and majestically waving."

The pontiff resided at the Yellow Temple, built by an earlier Manchu Emperor in 1653 for the illustrious Fifth Dalai Lama, who had been greeted as a fellow sovereign. The Great Thirteenth sought the same respect. Sharing the Dalai Lama's suite was the Mongolian Buriat, Agvan Dorzhiev, who conveyed that message to all who counted in Peking's foreign colony. Rockhill found Dorzhiev "a quiet, well-mannered man, impressionable like all Mongols," but somewhat less ignorant of politics and the world in general than the Tibetans. He certainly bore little resemblance to the sinister *éminence noire* of past propaganda, as the British who now met him acknowledged. According to Dorzhiev (as Rockhill reported), the Dalai Lama feared the Chinese were determined "to curtail the temporal power he and his predecessors had wielded before the Manchus came to the throne." Rockhill responded that whatever the situation in the past, the Dalai Lama's present position was that of a vassal. Dorzhiev did not argue. He said the Dalai Lama's paramount concern was to maintain the Tibetan Yellow Church in all its honors, and to be able to submit petitions directly to the Dragon Throne rather than to subordinates who would lose track of them, pigeonholing them in their desks. The American found these conditions reasonable. He helped Tibetans draft memorials, met frequently with the Dalai Lama, and kept his aides apprised of all that was happening in Peking.

A critical issue was the kowtow. The Great Fifth had declined to prostrate himself in 1653, and his later Incarnation felt bound by precedent. Rockhill consulted the archives and determined that the Great Fifth had indeed been treated "with all the courtesy which have been accorded to any independent sovereign, and nothing can be found in Chinese works to indicate he was looked upon in any other way." A compromise was effected whereby the Thirteenth Dalai Lama would only have to kneel to the ground during separate audiences with the Emperor and Empress Dowager. But on matters of substance, their majesties were unyielding, rejecting out of hand the Lama's request for direct access.

An Imperial edict in November made plain the Dalai Lama's subordinate status. He was no longer "The Most Excellent, Self-Existent Buddha of the West" but was instead "The Sincerely Obedient, Reincarnation-helping, Most Excellent Buddha of the West." He was put on retainer and ordered to return to Lhasa and obey the Chinese Governor or Amban. He was given no chance to discuss proposed reforms and was compelled to submit a prepared memorial to the throne to which (he told Rockhill) "not a word could be added." When the Dalai Lama asked for advice, Rockhill said he saw no way out of the difficulty, that he must submit "and the only suggestion I could make was that he should not delay too long complying." Nor did the American's view change with the deaths of the Emperor and Empress Dowager within weeks of their meeting with the Dalai Lama.

The Tibetan's pride suffered terribly in Peking, Rockhill reported to Roosevelt, and he departed in December with his dislike for the

Chinese intensified. "I fear he will not cooperate with the Chinese in the difficult task they now propose to undertake governing Tibet like a Chinese province…I have probably been a witness to the overthrow of the temporal power of the head of the Yellow Church." The President shared the Envoy's letter with Lord Bryce, the historian of the Holy Roman Empire. In forwarding the enclosure to London, Bryce recalled how the twelfth-century Emperor Henry V had arrested Pope Paschal II, forcing him to accept terms he later repudiated. The learned Envoy found "a sort of tragic interest" in observing how the Chinese government "like a huge anaconda, has entrapped the Dalai Lama in its coils, tightening them upon him until complete submission [has been] extracted."

It was in every way a learning and toughening ordeal for the young pontiff. As he made his way slowly back to Lhasa he paused at Kumbum, where he saw Pyotr Kozlov, the Russian explorer who had first told him about Rockhill four years earlier in Mongolia. Kozlov found him as impressive as before, but markedly more assured. "Our meeting was not less lively," the Russian later wrote, "but this time I had the feeling of something quite new…He had come in contact with many people and had absorbed fresh impressions that had extraordinarily extended his experience of practical affairs." One senses here Rockhill's informing counsel.

On the Dalai Lama's return to Lhasa after five years' absence, his worst forebodings came to pass. He had hardly unpacked when Chinese troops invaded. An advance cavalry force burst into the capital in February 1910, with orders to put to death the Lama's ministers and to arrest the pontiff himself. Adding to the sense of impending doom was the appearance of Halley's Comet in the Himalayan skies. On the night of February 11, after narrowly escaping capture, the Dalai Lama fled into second exile, this time heading south, to India.

CHARLES BELL WAS THEN POLITICAL OFFICER IN SIKKIM, AND IT was his responsibility to care for the exiled Buddhist pontiff. Bell needed no interpreter; he spoke Tibetan of the Lhasa dialect. Before long he became the Dalai Lama's friend, adviser, and advocate. In this role he succeeded Rockhill, who after his appointment in 1909 as Ambassador to Russia continued to worry about Tibet and corresponded from St. Petersburg with its leader. Of the letters Rockhill received from the Dalai Lama, all preserved in Harvard's Houghton Library, this from Sikkim, addressed "To Rog-Hil, " serves as a gracious epilogue to an unlikely friendship:

> We are greatly pleased having learnt from your letter that you exert yourself for the sake of Tibet. The relations between our Tibet Government and [the United States] are untroubled as before. Therefore I request the excellent Minister constantly to promote the interests of the Faith. Here we long for [news of] your great and noble deeds. Do not forget, please, to send us news about the noble-minded one as before. From Darjeeling on an auspicious day, the fourteenth of the fifth month of the Iron Pig Year [1911].

As it happened, the Iron Pig Year heralded the fall of the Manchu Dynasty. A nationalist uprising broke out in Hankow and spread throughout China. On January 1, 1912, Sun Yat-sen became provisional leader of a new regime. On February 12, just two years after the Dalai Lama's flight from Lhasa, the boy-emperor Pu Yi abdicated, bringing an end to the world's oldest monarchy. In Tibet, the repercussions followed swiftly. An armed rebellion led to the surrender and expulsion of 3,000 Chinese troops in April. When the All-Knowing and Unchangeable Dalai Lama triumphantly returned to his capital in 1913, Lhasa for the first time since the eighteenth century was entirely free of Chinese soldiers and officials. De facto, Tibet was a self-governing state, and so remained until its invasion by Chinese Communists in 1950.

From his new post in Russia, Rockhill observed these events with sympathetic fascination. He had recently published a learned monograph, *The Dalai Lamas of Lhasa and Their Relations with the Manchu Emperors of China* (1910) summing up his views. He believed it was the practice and not the principle of Chinese authority that most deeply affronted Tibetans. They suffered hard exactions of every kind without reasonable means of redress. When Tibetans sought help, especially military help against the Nepalese and the British, China was unwilling or unable to advise and adequately support them. Against this background, Rockhill regretted that the British after the Younghusband Mission failed to establish a permanent presence in Lhasa, the better to check and chasten the Chinese.

Besides, he told a British diplomat in St. Petersburg, his country and Russia had just written a friendly end to their rivalry in Central Asia. So why not an Anglo-Russian scientific mission? The eminent explorer Kozlov would be its logical Russian chief, and there were plenty of eager British candidates. Were such a mission established in Lhasa for a year with an adequate following, "the world would hear little more of Chinese encroachment, while the benefits to scientific research would be enormous." His proposal made the rounds, but was opposed in London by a skittish Liberal Government and in India by the frontier Tibet cadre. After all, as Charles Bell said, the "chief advantage of our present Tibetan policy is that it keeps Russia out."

With hindsight, one is struck by how many chances were missed to bolster Tibetan autonomy when the stakes were low. A high-minded Liberal, John Morley, as Secretary of State for India opposed any British action that might jeopardize a developing entente with Russia. He was suspicious of "frontier men." For all their bravery, they wore blinkers (so he wrote the Viceroy in India) and forgot "the complex intrigues and, if you like, diabolical machinations which make up international politics for a vast sprawling empire like ours, exposing more vulnerable surface than any Empire the world ever saw." Morley closed Tibet to all foreign explorers. With his policy of complete noninterference, enshrined in the 1907 Anglo-Russian agreement, he deprived himself of the most potent means of enhancing Tibetan autonomy.

As scholar, explorer, and working diplomat, Rockhill illuminated without resolving the matter of Tibet's rightful status. His strength was in appraising with a cool eye how very different cultures see each other. While an envoy in Greece. he translated from Latin the journals of Friar William of Rubruck, a marveling visitor to the Mongol court in the thirteenth century. On leaving his post in St.

Petersburg to become U.S. Minister in Turkey in 1911, he joined with the Sinologist Friedrich Hirth in translating a rare account by a thirteenth-century Chinese customs official, *Description of Barbarous Peoples.* The six thousand volumes in Chinese, Tibetan, and Mongolian he donated to the Library of Congress formed its first important Asian collection.

One might have thought his unusual talents would have appealed to the scholar-politician Woodrow Wilson when the Democrats assumed office in 1913, but it was not to be. Rockhill was punished for serving Republicans too well; not even a sinecure was proffered. In 1913, he made a final journey to China and Mongolia under the auspices of the American Asiatic Association. On his return to America he accepted a post as adviser to the new Chinese Republic, and was on his way back to Peking in December 1914 when he suffered a heart attack and died in Honolulu at sixty-one.

Curiously and unbecomingly, Rockhill received no official recognition or honorary degrees while he lived, and not even a library, scholarship, or chair bears his name. Nothing he wrote is in print; his name is scarcely known even to foreign affairs specialists. A Chinese pine presented by the Department of Agriculture marks his grave in Litchfield, Connecticut, the home of his second wife, Edith Howell Perkins. Few first-rate Americans have left their attainments so thoroughly unadvertised.

CHAPTER SEVENTEEN

On the
Playing Fields of Lhasa

IN THE GOLDEN AFTERNOON OF THE BRITISH EMPIRE, THE SUN never set on its playing fields. Sport of every kind was the mortar that joined remote outposts with the home country. It provided rulers and the ruled with a common topic of talk and a uniting code of conduct. The Empire has long since vanished, but the games endure. Everywhere in former British colonies and dominions, regardless of previous condition of servitude, athletes compete with zest, especially against their former masters, in rugby, tennis, football (or, in American English, soccer), and most of all cricket. In India today, cricket still reigns. Matches with Pakistan can be a veritable holy war. The game engenders an incongruous sight in Calcutta, India's largest and most volatile city, where Marxism is alive and Communists govern. On weekends hundreds of cricketers, clad in faultless white flannels, can be found playing a dozen matches in the Maidan, the great swath of green in central Calcutta—barely a ball's toss from the bronze likeness of Subhas Chandra Bose, the Bengali militant who fought against the British Raj, alongside Tojo and Hitler.

Cricket first took root in Calcutta with a two-day match in 1804 in which Old Etonians defeated Calcutta, all the players being European. The game caught on among Indians, notably in Bombay, where an impassioned tournament evolved among clubs representing Parsees, Hindus, Muslims, and Europeans. But the cathartic breakthrough came with "Ranji," the first Indian to become known universally and favorably in England. Ranji was the Maharaja Sir Ranjitsinhi Vibhaji, the Jam Sahib of Nawangar, an obscure princely state. It wasn't his title but his inventive virtuosity that dazzled British devotees. "He moved as if he had no bones," an awed teammate remarked. "One would not be surprised to see brown curves burning in the grass where one of his cuts had travelled, or blue flame shimmering round his bat as he made one of his strokes." Having earned his blue at Cambridge University, he played for England against Australia in 1899, where his searing cuts compensated for the indifferent performance of others. "RANJI SAVES ENGLAND!" the newspapers trumpeted. His color proved an advantage, setting him apart in what was deemed the golden age of cricket. The Ranji Trophy, for which Indian teams have competed since 1934, commemorates his prowess.

The cult of cricket, with its devotion to exacting rules, civility, and fair play, is among the benign legacies of Pax Britannica. The themes of empire and cricket were interwoven by Sir Henry Newbolt in "Vitaï Lampada," a poem once known to every British schoolboy, and inscribed on the hallowed walls of Lord's Cricket Ground. Newbolt takes us to a hushed school close, with an hour to go, ten to make, and the match to win. The Captain exhorts his team to play up, and play the game, for honor's sake, not the selfish hope of a season's fame. Suddenly we are on a dusty battlefield on an imperial frontier, where the Captain appears again:

> *The sand of the desert is sodden red,—*
> *Red with the wreck of a square that broke;—*
> *The Gatling's jammed, and the Colonel dead,*
> *And the regiment blind with dust and smoke.*
> *The river of death has brimmed his banks,*

And England's far, and Honour a name,
But the voice of a schoolboy rallies the ranks:
"Play up! Play up! And play the game!"

Fittingly, Newbolt attended Clifton in Bristol, the boarding school from which the largest percentage of boys passed directly to Sandhurst, the British West Point. Clifton graduated more British generals in World War I (including Douglas Haig, Commander-in-Chief of the British Expeditionary Force) than any other school. Its High Victorian chapel is a mausoleum of Empire. There the visitor will find tablets evoking the gallantry of thirty-five Old Cliftonians who fought in the 1897 campaign on the North-West Frontier, along with memorials to a dozen other wars, great and less great. Among Newbolt's notable schoolmates was Francis Younghusband, leader of the 1903–4 invasion of Tibet. At a dinner honoring his Tibetan exploits, Sir Francis spoke warmly of the Cliftonians who took part in that mission: "They all have the traits so characteristic of Clifton, and which has been so finely inculcated by Henry Newbolt, of playing the game. They have nasty jobs to do, but it is the game and they will play it through."

ALAS, OURS HAS NOT BEEN AN AUSPICIOUS ERA FOR SCHOOLBOY ideals. For Britain, the initial shock was the Boer War, which began on October 11, 1899, and was meant to be over by Christmas. It lasted for nearly three years, and it took 365,693 Imperial and 82,742 colonial soldiers to prevail over 88,000 whiskered farmers, at the expense of £200 million. The conflict also featured trench warfare, barbed wire (an American invention), and the first use of concentration camps. The Boer War persuaded the German Kaiser that the British Lion was overrated and decrepit, it provoked Kipling's celebrated phrase "no end of a lesson," and prompted a prescient diary comment by the anti-imperialist poet Wilfred Scawen Blunt: "I look upon the war as perhaps the first nail driven into the coffin of the British Empire."

The South African conflict presaged the ghastly slaughter of World War I, whose toll defeated the optimism of even the heartiest Newboltian. When the Cenotaph, the Imperial war memorial, was dedicated in Whitehall in 1920, it was reckoned that if all the war dead from the Empire were to march four abreast past the monument, the cortège would require three and a half days. To be sure, the British were victors, and after 1918 the Empire attained its greatest amplitude. But its rulers lost their swagger and certainty. Even outsize figures dwindled on the postwar stage—as evidenced by Lord Curzon. Named Foreign Secretary in 1919, four years later he faded away, his high hopes (as Harold Nicolson writes) "gradually clouded by disillusion, mortification and defeat." Faced with the radical Bolshevik threat, shaken by an explosion of nationalism, resentful of upstart Americans, the governing elite seemed to veer from paralysis to impulsive use of force.

In the Indian city of Amritsar, a rattled British general massacred hundreds of civilians during the anti-colonial ferment of 1919, the same year that Royal Air Force warplanes blasted Kabul in the Third Afghan War. Having just won what H. G. Wells first called the War to End All Wars, British forces were nevertheless fighting across half the world—battling nationalists and Communists in the Caucasus, bombing Kurdish villages in Iraq, embroiled in the Greek-Turkish struggle in Smyrna, machine-gunning demonstrators in Cairo. In Ireland, British security forces—the notorious Black and Tans—helped give birth to partition, civil war, and the avenging Irish Republican Army. Retribution reached into the fashionable heart of London in 1922 when IRA gunmen killed Field Marshal Sir Henry Wilson, an Ulsterman, as he stepped from his doorway on Eaton Place.

Sir Henry, Chief of the Imperial General Staff, was a firm believer in Russian orchestration of enemies he lumped together as Sinn Feiners and Socialists ("at our own doors"), Turkish and Egyptian nationalists, and Indian seditionists. One guesses that at the dinner table his poison list extended to the American Woodrow Wilson, whose Fourteen Points, with their promise of self-determination, "struck at the roots of the British Empire," according to Sir Maurice

Hankey, secretary to the War Cabinet and former secretary to the Committee of Imperial Defense.

This sense of embattled insecurity affected not just the Empire but also its exotic outriders and dependencies, notably Tibet. From 1904 to 1947, Britain was the sole Western power represented in the Himalayan kingdom, under a curious arrangement whereby the Government of India stationed three Trade Agents, who were really political officers, in what was officially part of China. In all those years, however, the British were unable to resolve the vexatious issues of Tibet's frontiers and legal status. The overriding aim of British Tibetan policy was to keep rival powers from Lhasa, and away from India's North-East Frontier. But what to do about Tibet—a theocratic kingdom larger than Western Europe and formally part of China? If Tibet were smaller, a British Resident could have been posted in Lhasa and Tibet could have become one more imperial protectorate. Tibet was simply too big. It was too important to China, its suzerain for more than two centuries. Before then, Tibet had itself been an independent, empire-building power, and its people still inhabited large areas of western China (or eastern Tibet, as seen from Lhasa). Russia, too, had an interest in Tibet, spiritual as well as strategic, since Buriat Mongols living in Siberia revered the Dalai Lama.

So what could be done? One possibility was to cut Tibet in two and adopt the nearby half. Another was to strike a deal with Peking to form two Tibetan zones within China, but with the zone around Lhasa assured essential autonomy (in the process adding slices of Tibet to British India). A third choice was to acknowledge Tibet as part of China but to train its armed forces and introduce Western methods so that Tibetans could defend themselves.

The British tried or weighed all these strategies. All were stillborn, and the anomalies of Tibet continue to trouble the world. Yet paradoxically, the British groomed an exceptional cadre of Tibetan frontiersmen, whose learning and dedication are apparent in a score of memoirs. Its members strove against discouragement to uphold

British and Tibetan interests, the object being to make Lhasa as strong as possible. How best this might be done was a matter for intense internal debate, so private that its substance has only lately become known in a cluster of scholarly works based on newly opened archives.

It was an exclusively British debate: no Americans were in this loop. When a young American named William Montgomery McGovern turned up in Tibet in 1923, and on his return reported rumors of a possible coup d'état, Britain's Tibetan cadre questioned his honor and tarnished his reputation. To this day, McGovern's book is not listed in bibliographies, and standard histories fail to mention the first American known to reach Lhasa.

McGovern's nemesis was Frederick Marshman Bailey (1882–1967) who, along with his colleague and sometime rival Charles Bell (1870–1945), was the most powerful personal influence on two generations of frontiersmen. Bailey and Bell embody different British attitudes toward Tibet, and their careers mark a useful trail through a relevant stratum of the past.

LET US FIRST MEET BAILEY: THE FRONTIERSMAN PAR EXCELLENCE, widely admired for his skills as explorer, linguist, diplomat, naturalist, and secret agent. Known as Eric (to distinguish him from his father, also Frederick and also an officer in the Indian Army), Bailey was born in Lahore, schooled at Sandhurst, and once in India transferred from the Bengal Lancers to the 32nd Sikh Pioneers, the better to see action. On a mission to Sikkim, he began studying colloquial Tibetan; his proficiency was later certified by the Bengali undercover explorer Sarat Chandra Das.

Bailey's abilities caught the attention of Colonel Francis Younghusband, a friend of his father's, and in August 1904 the young subaltern rode into Lhasa along with the British expeditionary force. Younghusband pronounced him "a keen and adventurous officer" and "an excellent fellow" who ought to go far. This was the beginning of Bailey's long involvement with Tibet, and from the first he showed the preternatural detachment that was his hallmark, as evidenced in his Lhasa diary: "Thur. 18. Went to Drepung [Monastery] with White and Wilton. Lama ran amok. Gymkhana. Fri. 19. Hung lama. Football . . . Sat. 27. Races. Sun. 28. Auction of silks. Football. Out fishing." Bailey was the kind of officer one might want to carry out political surgery with discretion, enterprise, and deniability. Tall, strongly built, soft-spoken, he was addicted to polo, hunting, and fishing.

Bailey's intrepidity was evident in 1911–13, when he twice explored the Tibetan borderlands, coping with clotted jungles and hostile tribes to chart the course of the Tsangpo, Tibet's longest and greatest river. Besides accounting for the river's steep, seemingly impossible drop, he collected rare butterflies and found a blue poppy that became a horticultural favorite (*Meconopsis betonicfolia baileyi*), achievements that earned him a gold medal from the Royal Geographical Society. On his second trip, Captain Henry T. Morshead of the Survey of India accompanied him, using his instruments in the most trying circumstances. Bailey recalled that it was impossible to avoid leeches, but Morshead appeared indifferent to them: "He would stand there covered with leeches and with blood oozing out of his boots as oblivious as a small child whose face is smeared with jam."

In their forays, Bailey and Morshead trespassed illicitly into China to probe sensitive frontier areas. Bailey shrugged off the formal censure that resulted. His was clearly an intelligence mission, linked to British efforts at demarcating India's North-East Frontier. By 1912, having served as Trade Agent at Gyantse and then Yatung, Bailey had come to know Tibet's two spiritual leaders, the Dalai Lama and the Panchen Lama. Bailey was forthright in a disarmingly insouciant way, casually allowing he once disguised himself as a Buddhist monk, a compass tucked in his prayer-wheel, "the usual secret service agent's equipment."

Yet there was something unsettling about Bailey, as hinted by his nickname "Hatter," prompted by his unpredictable habit of pausing in menacing circumstances, say, to identify and skin a rare shrew (*Soiculus baileyi*). He traveled everywhere with his butterfly net, once adroitly using it to save his life during a sudden snowslide, and another time to net a new variety (*Lycaenopsis morsheadi*). He could be as loftily nonchalant in dealing with people, and for all his accomplishments, was never knighted. Basil Gould, a colleague who did become Sir Basil, notes in his memoirs that when Bailey talked, he liked to stand with his back to the angle made by two solid walls and kept on looking this way and that, "as if to make sure that nobody was wanting to take a shot at him."

Still, Bailey had cause. A German sniper wounded an arm on the Western Front, where he served with the Indian Expeditionary Force, and at Gallipoli he was struck in both legs. Invalided to a safer berth as an intelligence officer in Persia, Bailey undertook a secret mission in 1918 to Russian Turkestan, then mired in revolutionary turmoil. Once in Tashkent, he repeatedly changed identities and eventually was recruited by the Cheka, the Bolshevik secret police, to find and capture a British spy, namely himself. The episode became the stuff of legend after Bailey returned unscathed by underground routes to Persia in 1921.

The following year Major Bailey was named Political Officer in Sikkim, the Himalayan kingdom within British India that controlled access to Tibet. He took over the Residence in Gangtok recently vacated by Charles Alfred Bell, whose methods and outlook were notably different from Bailey's.

IF BAILEY WAS CAVALIER, BELL WAS ROUNDHEAD: SOBER, HIGH-minded, a bit of a swot. Born like Bailey in India, educated at Winchester and Oxford, Bell in 1891 passed the demanding exams for the Indian Civil Service. He too followed his father's path, in his case entering the elite political service rather than the army. After hardship postings in Bengal and Bihar, young Bell contracted malaria and was hospitalized in Darjeeling. He thrived in the Himalayan air, and there began to study Tibetan, taking lessons from a local tailor who spoke the Lhasa dialect. What began as a pretext to extend his medical leave ended as passion; in 1905 Bell published a *Manual of Colloquial Tibetan,* the first of his shelf of works on Tibet. Propitiously, in 1908 he was appointed political officer in Sikkim, and was there in early 1910 when the Thirteenth Dalai Lama fled Lhasa and sought asylum in British India.

This was the second time the Tibetan pontiff had escaped a foreign army. In 1904, rather than be humiliated by British invaders, he took flight to Mongolia, and then Peking. After four years' exile, he returned to Lhasa only to encounter a more belligerent invasion, this time by a China determined to turn Tibet into a province and keep the Dalai Lama under its thumb. When he decided to flee, it was Bailey, as Trade Agent, who was credited with the idea of disguising the Dalai Lama as a *dak wallah*, or postal runner. His Holiness was provided with a mailbag to get by Chinese frontier posts—"the only time on record when His Majesty's mails were carried by an Incarnate God," in the words of the fifth Earl of Cawdor, who related this splendid story to Jan Morris.

Upon his arrival in India, the Dalai Lama came under the official care of Charles Bell, who at forty was seven years older than His Holiness. For nearly two years, Bell called regularly at the pontiff's lodge in Darjeeling, arriving in the forenoon according to Tibetan custom. The two talked alone, sipping tea from jade cups, and discussed matters spiritual as well political. Unlike Bailey, Bell was drawn to Buddhism and came to empathize with the Dalai Lama, who for his part was direct in seeking help wherever he could. He wanted the British to march again on Lhasa, and even proposed going to London to appeal directly to King George. Yet he made no secret of also seeking Russian help through his absent friend, the Buriat monk Agvan Dorzhiev, with whom he continued to correspond. It was Bell's task to befriend and dissuade, a task the more delicate since back home Lord Morley at the India Office referred privately to His Holiness as a "pestilent animal." Morley, the biographer of Gladstone and keeper of the pure Liberal flame, opposed all forms of intervention ("Curzonism") and sought to mend relations with China and Russia.

Bell kept his footing in these rapids. He pleaded the Tibetan cause with skill and determination, so much so that some complained he had "gone native." Outwardly he was the archetypal forward-school political officer, tall and fair, "lean and keen," but he did not look on Tibet simply as a useful buffer state. He came by degrees to believe that Tibet's high ground was not merely geographic, that its form of

Buddhism endowed Tibetans with "tolerance allied to loving-kindness," and that Britain ought do what it reasonably could to promote Tibetan autonomy.

Then late in 1911, a nationalist revolution turned China upside down. In the disorders that followed, the Tibetans seized the chance to expel Chinese troops and the Chinese Amban, or Governor. In January 1913, traveling in his golden palanquin, the Dalai Lama returned triumphantly to Lhasa, which for the first time since the eighteenth century was free of Chinese soldiers and officials. Within weeks His Holiness, asserting his powers temporal and spiritual, proclaimed Tibetan independence and put into practice modernizing reforms he had often discussed with his friend Charles Bell.

Yet changes always occurred with a Tibetan spin, as in the case of the four Rugby boys. From Lhasa, the Dalai Lama wrote to Bell suggesting that "some energetic and clever sons of respectable families" in Tibet be sent to England for education. Four boys were chosen; they were accompanied to Britain by a political officer, Basil Gould; by a Sikkimese policeman, Laden La, whose son was also to attend school in England; and by a Tibetan official named Lungshar. The Dalai Lama said he hoped the youngsters, aged from eleven to seventeen, would obtain "first-class educations at Oxford College, London."

The Foreign Office decided that Rugby and not Oxford was most suitable for the experiment, which had mixed results. The youngest pupil, Ringang, remained to study electrical engineering at London and Birmingham universities. Mondo and Kyipup, once back in Lhasa, became Tom Browns without a country, too Westernized to resume their old role in the local elite. Gongkar, the fourth, died of pneumonia in 1917 after training with the Indian Army. For the British, an added problem was the boys' escort, Lungshar. Seeing himself as an envoy-at-large, he met secretly with agents of Japan and Russia, talked of missions to Russia and America, sought repeated audiences with Cabinet members and connived (in British eyes) at setting up something like a Tibetan Embassy in London. Moreover (writes Alastair Lamb), his popularity with the India Office "was not increased when his wife undertook, with considerable success, the seduction of one of the Tibetan boys."

In short, Tibet proved a trial to the punctilious British. The country was a baffling congeries of rival noble families, contentious monasteries, and quarreling regions. So powerful was the hold of religion that a fourth or more of the male population took orders; a good many youths became "fighting lamas," or warrior priests, their headgear yellow or red, connoting the two main sects. It was like stumbling into the feudal-clerical world of Chaucer and Abelard, with the added Tibetan variable of reincarnation. Not only were Tibet's two Grand Lamas incarnations, but so were the four great Abbots of Lhasa, another sixty incarnations were of especially high status, and at a fourth level down, there were more than a thousand "Living Buddhas."

As a practical matter, the Tibetan system, as Bailey complained, "makes it very difficult to get things done. No one feels capable of taking any responsibility." Important decisions in Tibet could take years. Leading nobles had to be placated, astrological readings were mandatory, and so were the prophecies, uttered in a trance by the State Oracle of Nechung. Often enough, when the Kashag reached a decision, the Dalai Lama would refer it back again—and during the new year festivities "practically no work of any kind is done for a month," Bailey noted.

Some British frontiersmen, like John Claude White, Bell's predecessor at the Sikkim Agency, openly sneered at the lamaist system. Others, like Major Frederick O'Connor, came to believe that essential changes could be accomplished by promoting the leadership of the Panchen Lama. In 1904, the Panchen Lama, usually reckoned as the Ninth, was twenty-two, a few years younger than the Thirteenth Dalai Lama. His Serenity seemed a sensible youth. Why not assist the birth of a second Tibetan state under his leadership, with its seat at Shigatse, near his Tashilhunpo Monastery? The Panchen Lama possessed an independent power base, with court, territory, and tax collectors. In the eighteenth century, Warren Hastings's East India Company treated with the Panchen Lama as if he were sovereign, as did China at various times. In partnership with the Panchen Lama, British India could establish a secure protectorate to the north, on the model of Sikkim and Bhutan, Himalayan kingdoms already under the Raj.

Major O'Connor, the advocate of this plan, knew Tibet as well as or better than any frontiersman. He had been chief interpreter for the Younghusband mission and served as the first Trade Agent at Gyantse when that post was created in 1904. He had cultivated the Panchen Lama's friendship, and escorted His Serenity on a ceremonial visit to India, where in 1906 the Tibetan met with the Prince of Wales and the new Viceroy, Lord Minto. The trip was a success. O'Connor earned the trust of the Panchen Lama and gained the support of an important ally, Sir Louis Dane, the Indian Foreign Secretary, for a plan that was wholly consistent with "forward school" thinking of the high imperial era.

But time was out of joint for O'Connor: Curzon had just left India under a cloud, and his successor as Viceroy, Lord Minto, was happiest at the racetrack. Back home, the Liberals had formed a new Government with the anti-imperial Lord Morley at the India Office. The plan was dropped. O'Connor's superior, the Tibet-hating John Claude White, delivered a spiteful final kick, calling it an "extremely mad scheme" and urged the dismissal of its author. Still, as Alex McKay writes in *Tibet and the British Raj* (1997), an account mined from long-sealed India Office archives, "In the world of imperial *Realpolitik,* it was a masterly scheme." If it had succeeded, Britain might have incurred a year's opprobrium, and a part of Tibetan territory now occupied by China might be an Indian protectorate, like Bhutan.

Bailey was O'Connor's protégé, admired the Panchen Lama, and supported the two–Tibet strategy. Bell saw things differently. He believed British interests were best served by a united Tibet under the Dalai Lama. From the time Tibetans expelled the Chinese, Bell vainly pressed his own government for permission to visit Lhasa and repeatedly urged the sale of arms to the Tibetans. But Tibet was not a recognized nation, and providing weapons and sending a British mission conflicted with recent agreements with China and Russia. Bell bided his time, became expert at bureaucratic infighting, and learned how to influence hostile superiors. He was high-minded, but not a Boy Scout. In his Tibetan grammar, under the rubric "Diplomatic Intercourse," the first sample sentence is "The British Government is not responsible . . ." Another section, on buying supplies, offers this useful morsel: "You will make a large profit, and be able to live in comfort without working."

In 1913, Bell's persistence bore fruit, and he was at the center of a radically different approach to the Tibetan question. For a year, Britain had sought to coax China's new republican regime to a conference on Tibet. Peking's new leaders were desperate for recognition, which the British threatened to delay until China agreed to meet at Simla, the Raj's summer capital, with delegates from Lhasa—a major concession, since it implied equality of status for Tibet.

Sir Henry McMahon was now the Indian Foreign Secretary. Born in Simla, McMahon was a hard-bitten frontiersman, a former Political Agent in Gilgit, Chitral, and Baluchistan, and the officer chiefly responsible for the demarcation of the Indo-Afghan boundary. He hoped to crown his career by shifting India's North-East Frontier some sixty miles northward, running it along the Himalayan rim of the Tibetan plateau rather than the Brahmaputra Valley. He and his military advisers attached high importance to occupying the heights in order to frustrate potential Chinese political or military designs on India.

The declared purpose of the Simla Conference was to resolve disputes over Tibet's frontier with India and to clarify Lhasa's political relationship with Peking. McMahon had put forward a proposal to divide Tibet into zones, Inner and Outer, along the lines of a recent agreement between Russia and China similarly dividing Mongolia. "Inner Tibet" was to include the contested eastern borderland, which Lhasa claimed, but which China was to administer. "Outer Tibet" was to be under Chinese "suzerainty," but with Lhasa promised full autonomy.

Yet soon after Sir Henry opened the conference in October 1913, his ulterior motive became apparent. So intent was McMahon on obtaining the new boundary that he negotiated surreptitiously with the Tibetans to wrest their signature on maps showing the alignment that was to bear his name. He did this so high-handedly that (in the phrase of Neville Maxwell, a leading critical authority) his dealings with the Tibetans were disavowed by the Viceroy, censured by his superiors in London, and vigorously denounced by the Chinese. Moreover, the Tibetans insisted that their signature had been conditioned on China's agreement to Lhasa's demands, and when Peking failed to give it, the new boundaries were also nullified.

Such was the origin of the famous "McMahon Line." The conference ended in July 1914, just as World War I broke out, and Sir Henry's blundering was forgotten as he moved on to become High Commissioner of Egypt. The failure of the Simla Conference was briefly mentioned in the next edition of the Government of India's official record, C. U. Aitchison's *Collection of Treaties,* published in 1929. And there the whole abortive matter might have rested except for the most peculiar events, as set forth in the Epilogue.

EVEN SO, SIMLA WAS A PERSONAL SUCCESS FOR CHARLES BELL. HE had worked closely with the Tibetan delegation, and his status as the British Government's premier Tibetan authority was ratified with a knighthood. His protégés—such as David Macdonald, an Anglo-Sikkimese liked and respected by Tibetans—now occupied key posts on the frontier. In 1914, when the Dalai Lama offered to help the Allies, the Government of India reciprocated by providing Tibet with 5,000 rifles and 500,000 rounds of ammunition. Most important to Bell, New Delhi now understood that the Dalai Lama was the only Tibetan leader acceptable to all Tibetan factions.

Yet for ten years Bell was not allowed to visit Lhasa, the obstacle being an earlier agreement with Russia barring both powers from sending envoys to the capital. Bell's health was never robust; he was eager to write about Tibet, and in 1918 took final leave before retirement. Within a year, the war was over, Russia was Bolshevik, China was sending an exploratory mission to Tibet, and Lord Curzon, the old Tibetan hawk, had become Foreign Secretary. Bell was recalled from retirement, and in November 1920 his great ambition was realized. He became the first European to enter Lhasa on the invitation of a Dalai Lama. Bell remained for a year, joined by a medical officer and in the final weeks by David Macdonald.

By this time Bell sensed that the Raj was mortal, and that a self-governing India might not wish or be able to defend Tibet. Tibet in 1930 was not a recognized country or a British protectorate but lay in a twilight zone. Alastair Lamb's detailed diplomatic studies, especially *The McMahon Line* (1966), chart the difficult course Tibet had to steer between powerful neighbors when its neutrality was protected by no international agreement. In the sympathetic judgment of the Indian archivist Amar Kaur Jasbir Singh in *Himalayan Triangle* (1988), Tibet had granted the British exclusive political influence in Lhasa, but there was no intention of establishing a protectorate. This meant the Chinese would abstain from interference only so long as they lacked the military means.

It was Bell's hope that the Tibetans themselves would take the necessary steps to ensure their autonomy. At his urging, the Government of India had sold Tibet ten mountain guns, twenty Lewis machine guns, and 10,000 Lee-Enfield rifles, on condition the arms were solely for self-defense. A staunch friend of the Dalai Lama's and a committed modernizer, Tsarong Shapé was now Commander-in-Chief of an Army whose officers the British were beginning to train. A telegraph line that linked Lhasa to Gyantse and Sikkim was completed in 1922. A hydroelectric dam, with turbines shipped from England, was under construction. The Himalayan geologist Sir Henry Hayden was surveying mineral resources. Reciprocally, the Dalai Lama had permitted British mountaineers to approach Mt. Everest from the Tibetan side, greatly gratifying Sir Francis Younghusband, chief promoter of the expedition.

As seemingly auspicious was the opening in 1924 of an English school at Gyantse, the students consisting of several dozen sons of noble families. The headmaster, Frank Ludlow of the Indian Education Department, brought along soccer balls. He designed uniforms in "Tibetan colours" (yellow and maroon), lectured his boys "on keeping their temper when playing football and generally playing the game," and arranged matches with the British Trade Agency's staff. Football stirred so much interest that the Dalai Lama, using a new telephone line, called Gyantse to learn who had won the first match. He was informed (Ludlow noted in his diary) that "the school played well but lost 2–1."

All this attested to Bell's skill as a mediator. He had his failures, notably the vetoing by New Delhi of a visit with the Panchen Lama, then at odds with the Dalai Lama over financing the new Army. Otherwise his stay in Lhasa laid the groundwork for all these developments. His mission, certainly, was a personal success. In *Daughter of Tibet* (1970), Rinchen Dolma Taring preserves a snapshot of Bell and Macdonald's arrival for dinner at Tsarong House, home of the Army commander. The household buzzed with reports that Bell had a red face, golden hair, and a nose like a kettle spout. "He was the first European we had ever seen," Mrs. Taring recalled, "and everybody peeped at him, from every direction, whispering and giggling...Mr. Macdonald's mother was Sikkimese, so he looked like a Tibetan gentleman, with his mustache sticking up at both ends. He spoke fluent Tibetan and during the party left the dining room and spent a long time playing with my sister and me. He gave us money and repeatedly said, 'You two should come to India and go to the English school at Darjeeling with my daughters.'" Mrs. Taring subsequently did just that, and later became the third wife of Tsarong Shapé, twenty-five years her senior, on the civilized understanding that "I could marry again whenever I came across a suitable younger man" (which she did, to the eldest son of the Rajah of Sikkim).

IT WAS FOR CHARLES BELL AN IDYLL, AND HE WAS HAUNTED thereafter by the realm he had glimpsed. In retirement, he wrote four books that preserve a lost Tibet, as in a sepia picture album. Yet even as Major Bailey settled in as his successor at Sikkim, there were warnings of tensions within Tibet, beginning with the flight in 1923 of the Panchen Lama to Mongolia. He blamed "evil-minded persons" advising the Dalai Lama and the impossible demand that he provide a fourth of the costs of the new Tibetan Army. Many said the Dalai Lama had distrusted his fellow Incarnation from the time of the latter's visit to India in 1906, and now suspected he was intriguing with the Chinese. After his flight, the Panchen Lama never returned to Tibet, though until his death in 1937 he talked continually of doing so.

In 1923, Bailey had been at his post for two frustrating years. He had yet to make his own mark with the Dalai Lama, who still corresponded directly with Bell, a source of persistent contention. "I hope Sir Charles Bell does not stay with you," a petulant Bailey wrote to his mother in November 1924. "He is a hopeless fraud and has got on entirely by writing himself up—he does all he can to make the work for me here difficult—as he was jealous of giving it up after 15 years." Bailey added that he learned Bell was disliked in Lhasa because "he went about in a dandy" (a hammock carried by bearers), which only the Dalai Lama was entitled to do.

Bailey had other worries. Not only were Bolsheviks intriguing around Tibet, but a pro-Chinese faction had emerged in the monasteries, feeding on anger over modernization. As vexing to Bailey was William Montgomery McGovern, an American who turned up in Gangtok in 1922 as part of a British Buddhist Mission. The India Office in London warned Bailey that these pilgrims, mostly Oxford graduates, were a "queer crowd" who "clearly show the cloven hoof." McGovern was a lecturer at the School of Oriental Studies, University of London, and was an Oxford D.Phil., Christ Church College. He was queer only in his improbable background. He was born in New York, raised on a Georgia plantation, and came of age in the Philippines and then Japan, an itinerary determined by his restless and rebellious parents. In Japan, young William graduated with a degree in divinity at the Buddhist monastery of Nishi Hongwanji in Kyoto. At twenty-five, McGovern had already written a text on colloquial Japanese, a political account of Japan, and a treatise on Mahayana Buddhism. The treatise served as his doctoral dissertation at Oxford, where he received the degree though he had never graduated from high school or college.

McGovern's ambition was to become the first American to reach Lhasa, which he did through the kind of pluck and dissimulation at which the British excelled. When the Buddhist Mission passed through Sikkim, Bailey gave its six members permission to enter Tibet as far as Gyantse, on the understanding they would go no further and would return to India, which McGovern did. Having honored his pledge, he considered himself a free agent, turned around and headed back to Tibet.

In Darjeeling, McGovern engaged four Sikkimese servants, three mules, and three ponies. He disguised himself as a lowly coolie, dyed his hair, stained his skin with iodine and walnut juice, and wore the goggles Tibetans used to protect themselves from the dazzling light. His colloquial Tibetan was by now passable, and having entered Tibet, McGovern posed as the servant of his Sikkimese headman, nicknamed Satan. The charade succeeded, but as the party neared Lhasa, the American gave himself away by urinating in the European fashion, i.e., standing up instead of squatting. As he later wrote, a Tibetan official came riding by and seeing his posture "immediately stopped and asked me who and what I was . . . Fortunately for me, at this moment Satan and Lhaten put in an appearance. Lhaten took in the situation at once and came to my assistance in a very effective way. He rushed up, struck me with his whip, and ordered me to go on immediately."

Surviving a dozen such mishaps, McGovern turned up in Lhasa just before the great Lunar New Year fête. On a gamble, he made himself known to a sympathetic Nepalese, a technician in charge of telegraph and postal services, who provided shelter and introduced him to Tsarong Shapé, the modernizing Army commander. Through Tsarong, McGovern met the Tibetan Prime Minister and very briefly with the Dalai Lama on condition that he would keep the interview secret. When his unauthorized presence became generally known, a mob of fanatical monks shouting "Death to the foreigner!" formed around his host's home. McGovern turned himself in, and was expelled. Once back in Sikkim, he again saw Major Bailey: "We had a number of things to talk over, as I was sorry to find that my little escapade had quite unintentionally caused the Indian Government a good deal of trouble; but, business matters having been settled, Major Bailey once more became the charming and cultured host, and amused the party that night by tales of his own most interesting adventures."

McGovern recounted his own escapades in news articles and *To Lhasa in Disguise* (1924). A key passage in his book gave his account of Bell and Bailey's contrasting approaches to Asian peoples:

Sir Charles Bell aimed, not at overawing the Tibetans, but at securing their close sympathy and friendship...Thus, for example, he neither fished nor shot. He abstained from tobacco as the Tibetans regard the use of tobacco with horror ...This extraordinary regard for native susceptibilities is not always successful, but in the case of Sir Charles it seems to have worked wonders, and I was later to find that many Tibetan officials have an unusual affection for him. Major Bailey has followed the more ordinary lines of British administrators, who believe it inconsistent with the maintenance of dignity to pander too much to native ideas, but certainly his policy has not decreased British prestige in this part of the world. But I believe there is no great love lost between the past and present political officers, and as Macdonald, the trade agent and nominally Major Bailey's subordinate, is a protégé of Sir Charles Bell, the relations between the political officer and the trade agent has sometimes an interesting side.

Traveling in the guise of a lowly coolie, McGovern saw Tibet from a distinctly nonelitist perspective. He describes the harsh lot of low-born Tibetans, exemplified by the oppressive *ula* system, whereby every family, no matter how poor, had to supply transport animals to any officials passing through. His political comments were provocative. He identified two main factions in Lhasa: the pro-British court party, and the pro-Chinese priestly party, the former he believed ascendant. Still, he wondered, what might happen if the Dalai Lama died? "Will Tsarong seize the reins of government and declare himself king, as it is sometimes whispered may be the case, or will he, perhaps more astutely, be instrumental in the choice of an infant Dalai-lama of a type that can be molded to his own point of view?" So he wrote in a chapter headed "The Strong Man of Tibet."

As nettling to the British were the American's remarks about their special protégé, Laden La, "the uncrowned king" of the Darjeeling district, where "every native is absolutely under his thumb" and whose predilection for "slight tokens of esteem" had netted him a "considerable fortune." Lent by the Indian Government to act as "a guide and a guard," Laden La was now a chamberlain to the Dalai Lama, the police chief of Lhasa, a person for whom favors are "mysteriously expedited."

No other visitor had ventured such passages. Cables flew between London and India expressing astonished annoyance. Laden La successfully sued McGovern for libel. The disputed references to the police chief were removed from the book's American edition, in which Tsarong ceased to be a "strong man." The Government of India announced a new rule requiring all visitors to Tibet to obtain official permission before publishing anything. New Delhi assured Tibetan authorities that the British Government in no way approved McGovern's visit. At Bailey's request, the secretary of the Royal Geographical Society arranged for the insertion in its *Journal* of a frosty note headed "Dr. McGovern's Visit to Lhasa," claiming the American's illicit journey had done "great disservice to good relations with Tibet" and that he was "self-condemned" by boasting that frontier police were punished for failing to catch him.

The moralizing was overdone, since the same *Journal* had published numerous accounts of illicit travels to Tibet by native pundits and by frontiersmen like Major Bailey, who was officially reprimanded for a trip he later described in a book titled *No Passport to Tibet*. These inconsistencies were of little comfort to Dr. McGovern, whose Tibetan feat was virtually erased from the records. He subsequently returned to the United States, taught at Harvard and Northwestern, and wrote numerous books, including the well-received *Early Empires of Central Asia*. In World War II, he was the intelligence representative to the Joint Chiefs of Staff, responsible for preparing daily highlights for President Roosevelt. As a lecturer, McGovern was so popular that Northwestern students queued to attend his courses at the campus in Evanston, Illinois, where he died in 1964 at sixty-seven. His daughter Carol McGovern Cerf is proud owner of a snuff bottle presented to her father by the Dalai Lama.

IT WOULD APPEAR THAT MCGOVERN'S POLITICAL INSIGHTS WERE not that outlandish. In 1997, the *Journal* of the Royal Asiatic Society published "Tibet 1924: A Very British Coup Attempt?" by the British scholar Alec McKay. He conjectures that Major Bailey, when he finally visited Lhasa in 1924, concluded that the Dalai Lama was unwilling or unable to follow British "advice" and decided therefore to promote an alternative leader, Tsarong Shapé, the Army commander. No incriminating documents have turned up, and the evidence is circumstantial, but to McKay, compelling.

In 1922, Bailey arranged for a visit to Lhasa by General George Pereira, formerly the military attaché at Peking, in the guise of a "private traveller." In fact, Pereira reported to Bailey on military forces throughout Tibet, offering his seasoned opinion that it was "absolutely necessary to send a military advisor to Tsarong." The day after Pereira's departure, Tibetan authorities requested the services of Laden La, then Police Inspector in Darjeeling and formerly an aide to the Dalai Lama during his Indian exile. On arriving at Lhasa in 1923, Laden La quickly formed a police force, 200 strong, and developed close ties with Tsarong Shapé. The new chief, however, erred in providing his recruits better pay and smarter uniforms than Tibetan soldiers.

In May 1924, as Bailey was preparing to depart for Lhasa, a police-army melee occurred. As reconstructed from Tibetan sources by the American scholar Melvyn Goldstein, a policeman was fatally stabbed, inebriated soldiers were accused, and Laden La urged Tsarong to punish the culprits, which his officers did, on the spot. They amputated the accused assailant's leg above the knee, and severed an ear from an alleged accomplice. Tsarong's conservative enemies seized on the incident, claiming that the amputations violated the Dalai Lama's order abolishing such punishments.

As Bailey arrived in July 1924 for his long-sought visit, rival factions were openly vying for the Dalai Lama's favor. Tsarong Shapé's enemies charged that he planned to seize power with the aid of Laden La, and that Bailey was to deliver British support. His Holiness evidently believed such a scheme existed, and said so to his trade representative at Gyantse, knowing he would inform the British. Laden La abruptly returned to Darjeeling, claiming a nervous breakdown, and Tsarong Shapé was subsequently replaced as Army commander and demoted to Dzasa. As pro-British Tibetans lost their jobs and influence, a new favorite emerged in the Potala, the unfriendly Lungshar, who with Laden La had once chaperoned the Rugby boys to England. In summer 1924, Frank Ludlow heard rumors that his school was to be closed. Two years later he was told his contract would not be renewed. In his diary, Ludlow blamed monastic opposition, the jealous enmity of the Gyantse trade agent to whom the Dalai Lama confided his fears of a plot, and to "tom foolery on the part of Laden La, Tsarong and others in Lhasa in 1924."

Few hints of tomfoolery can be gleaned from Major Bailey's discreet diary of his Lhasa mission, now in the India Office Library. Yet Bailey relates that Tsarong Shapé once asked what might happen if the Dalai Lama died and fighting broke out between monks and the new Tibetan Army. Would Britain intervene? Bailey replied that this was not possible, given Britain's policy of noninterference. The question was more interesting than the response. Bailey was too experienced to commit himself in writing, and if indeed he did encourage a coup in Lhasa, he knew well that the "man on the spot" would be supported only if a clandestine plan succeeded.

Tellingly, Laden La suffered not a bit for his tomfoolery, and with Bailey's support he became in 1930 a Commander of the British Empire. Decades later, while researching his dissertation in New Delhi, McKay discovered in the Indian National Archives a secret file headed "Indiscretion of Laden La in associating with Tibetan officers attempting to overthrow the Dalai Lama." He was not permitted to see its contents. "It is amazing to me how Laden La manages to mislead the powers that be!" Macdonald protested in a letter to Bell in 1930. "…When McGovern published his so-called libel on Laden La, if he had gone the right way about things, Laden La would not have been in power today."

After his service in Sikkim, Bailey became Political Officer in Kashmir and British Minister in Nepal, retired in 1938, served in the Home Guards during the Second World War, becoming a King's Messenger based in Miami and Washington. Before his death in 1967, Bailey wrote about his explorations in Tibet, but not about the events of 1924. Bell completed his fourth book on Tibet, *A Portrait of the Dalai Lama,* in Canada, just before his own death in 1945. Although he never regained his former influence, Tsarong continued as a power in Lhasa and a genial host to foreign visitors. He was executed by the Chinese following their invasion in 1950.

Lungshar's fate was unkindest. After the Dalai Lama's demise in 1933, he was arrested by the new Regent, accused of practicing black magic, fostering dissension between the two Grand Lamas, and plotting to create a Bolshevik regime. The punishment was the removal of an eyeball, but such a sentence had not been administered for years and nobody knew how to carry it out. The mutilation was bungled, the pain was excruciating, but Lungshar survived to recite a hundred million "*om mani*" prayers. He died in 1939 of natural causes.

Still, Tibetans were not wholly responsible for their woes. For nearly half a century, the British were Tibet's most important foreign partners. In all that time, regrettably for Tibet, the British were unable satisfactorily to resolve the matter of Tibet's status—was it a nation or a province?—or to win agreement on Tibet's eastern and western frontiers. It proved a costly failure. On the playing fields of Lhasa, the English side sorely needed Ranji's searing strokes.

CHAPTER EIGHTEEN

.:.

The "Shambhala Project"

RUSSIA IN 1906 WAS STILL REELING FROM ITS IGNOMINIOUS
defeat by the upstart Japanese a year before. What was supposed
to be a "small victorious war" ended in the Straits of Tsushima with
Russia losing the greater part of its fleet—eight battleships, seven
cruisers, and six destroyers—and worse, losing Port Arthur, the navy's
only year-round ice-free port on the Pacific Coast. At home, so
threatening was the revolutionary ferment that Tsar Nicholas II
agreed to accept the once-unthinkable—a parliament. Battered by
striking workers, plundering peasants, naval insurrections, army rebellions, mutinous students, and an ever-expanding police force,
both regular and secret, St. Petersburg was mired in a "crisis of culture and consciousness." The correspondent of *Rebus,* the Russian
Spiritualist journal edited by Madame Blavatsky's sister, reported that
the entire capital was caught up "in an unusually powerful mystical
movement" that embraced people at every social level seeking "secret knowledge to fill the aching void." Gypsy fortune-tellers vied
with table rappers, hypnotists, phrenologists, and domesticated ghosts
at séances in some of the best palaces. Mediums and clairvoyants

adorned darkened salons like those of the Montenegrin sisters Militsa and Anastasia ("Stana"), known as Grand Duchesses Nicholas and Peter, patrons of the monk Gregor Rasputin.

Theosophy became the new cult of the intelligentsia. Figures as diverse as the Silver Age writers Andrey Bely and Boris Pasternak, the poet Zinaida Gippius, the philosopher Nikolai Berdyaev, director and actor Mikhail Chekhov, composer Alexander Scriabin, painter Wasily Kandinsky, and even Lenin's colleague Maxim Gorky and the future Bolshevik cultural tsar, Anatoly Lunarcharsky, were drawn to Theosophy and occult thought. When Madame Blavatsky introduced the Indo-Tibetan sun symbol, the swastika, which adorned the cover of her book, *The Secret Doctrine,* to the West, even the Tsarina was fascinated, perhaps because her childhood nickname was "Sunny," although her swastikas sported enamel by Fabergé.

"Admirers of Theosophy," announced *Rebus* in 1906, "are uniting and are even beginning to discuss the question of building a Buddhist lamasery (a dormitory) and a Theosophic-Buddhist temple." Leading the campaign was the Buriat lama Agvan Dorzhiev. Recently returned from Peking, Dorzhiev had accompanied the Thirteenth Dalai Lama into exile after the Buriat's audiences with Nicholas II had provided the British with their pretext for invading Tibet in 1903.

Dorzhiev proposed a common prayer-house in St. Petersburg for use by Russian Buriats and Kalmyks and, because of Russia's expanding trade relations, by Asian visitors. Yet, despite the ardent lobbying of the scholar and diplomat Prince Ukhtomsky and the Tsar's backing, the Orthodox clergy opposed the temple claiming it was an "idolatrous pagoda." In a pamphlet, Archimandrite Varlaam denounced the "power of Darkness and the times of Anti-Christ" that he feared were arriving in the very capital of Holy Russia. It took a sustained campaign to persuade the Government's Department of Foreign Creeds to grant the necessary building permit. The project began in earnest in 1909, funded by contributions raised by Dorzhiev and a considerable donation from the Dalai Lama. A pleased Nicholas II remarked during an audience with Dorzhiev that "the Buddhists should feel themselves under the wing of the mighty eagle." Tellingly, the first services were held in the temple on February 21, 1913, a national holiday marking the 300th anniversary of the House of Romanov, underscoring the White Tsar's role as special protector of Buddhism.

AMONG THE PROMINENT ST. PETERSBURG INTELLECTUALS ON THE construction committee was Nicholas Konstantinovich Roerich, an adherent of HPB's, who, despite his gifts as artist, explorer, ethnographer, visionary, and adventurer, had until recently passed into footnote limbo. Roerich designed the costumes and sets for *Le Sacre du Printemps,* the sensation of the impresario Serge Diaghilev's 1913 Ballets Russes season. The ballet's composer, Igor Stravinsky, claimed Roerich looked "as though he ought to have been a mystic or spy." In fact, recently opened intelligence archives suggest that at points in his career, he was both.

Nicholas Roerich was a worthy successor to Madame Blavatsky. A Russian mystic with a devoted following, he managed like her to baffle the intelligence departments on three continents. Like her, he was a Theosophist in quest of Shambhala who eventually made his home in India. But in two respects he surpassed HPB. Roerich gave his name to an international treaty, and in America he played an offstage role in two Presidential campaigns. He also left his mark on the New York skyline. The Nicholas Roerich Museum, in its brownstone home on 107th Street and Riverside Drive, still attracts pilgrims from around the world. Nearby is a far bigger building adorned with three balls on its cornerstone, the symbol of the Roerich Peace Pact. Once home to the Master Institute, it originally housed a Tibetan library, concert hall, cafeteria, and the first Roerich Museum, but is today simply one of innumerable cooperative apartments on the Upper West Side, the Roerich name expunged from what was to have been his great American monument.

If Rudyard Kipling's stories and poems expressed the exuberant self-assurance of Victorian imperialism, the ballet and opera productions of Serge Diaghilev played a similar role in the ever-expanding Russian Empire. Under the patronage of the Tsar and various Grand Dukes, his productions were imperial in theme and purpose. Russian embassies lent their prestige to Diaghilev seasons, which, in France, attracted *tout Paris* along with everybody who was anybody in the Russian colony, making them (as one paper wrote) "a politico-cultural manifestation of the highest importance." Indeed the 1909 season at the Théâtre du Châtelet, which established Diaghilev's reputation, was described in terms of conquest. As an admiring journalist wrote, "the Russians have come not with ships and sailors to conquer our territory, but with singers, dancers and decorators to conquer our admiration."

When the curtain rose on Borodin's *Prince Igor*, featuring basso Feodor Chaliapin as the Tartar khan, the audience gasped at Nicholas Roerich's set. Painted simply on a curved canvas, without the usual bulky scenery, it showed a glowing golden sky encompassing the tents of nomadic Tartars. Although the dances of the Polovtsky warriors, choreographed by Mikhail Fokine, were not ethnographically correct—not much was known about the Tartar tribe—Roerich's costumes were based on his own research into Kirghiz and Yakut sources. A French columnist reported that when the warriors danced, sabers slashing the air to Borodin's music, the entire audience "was ready to stand up and actually rush to arms. That vibrant music, those archers, ardent, wild and fierce of gesture, all that mixing of humanity, those raised arms, restless hands, the dazzle of the multi-colored costumes, seemed for a moment to dizzy the Parisian audience, stunned by the fervor and madness of movement."

Russian composers, artists, and impresarios tried to meld East and West, though their East was textbook Orientalism. One popular ballet, *The Humpbacked Horse*, premiered in 1864 as General Mikhail Chernaiev advanced on the khanates of Central Asia. One of Diaghilev's set designers, Alexandre Benois, recalled the finale where marching past "were all the nations of the Russian Empire come to pay homage . . . There were Cossacks and Karelians, Tartars, Little-Russians and Samoyeds." Diaghilev's prewar seasons in Paris and London brimmed with golden hordes, debauched emirs, favorite slaves, enraged shahs, Hindu gods, and smoldering Samarkand princesses. *Scheherazade's* "shocking beauty" awed Arnold Bennett, who described it in words reminiscent of a Russian journalist describing the slave markets of Bokhara:

> In the surpassing fury and magnificence of the Russian ballet one saw eunuchs actually at work, scimitar in hand. There was the frantic orgy, and then there was the barbarous punishment, terrible and revolting, certainly one of the most sanguinary sights ever seen on an occidental stage. The eunuchs pursued the fragile and beautiful odalisques with frenzy; in an instant the seraglio was strewn with murdered girls in all the abandoned postures of death. And then silence, save for the hard breathing of the executioners.

If it was effulgent Orientalism, it was also excellent box office. By 1914, another Diaghilev set designer, Léon Bakst, and the couturier Paul Poiret were dressing Parisian women in turbans and harem trousers, and perfumes were launched with names like Shalimar, Prince Igor, and Maharaja.

The fusion of art and empire took many forms—musical, literary, visual—and often its unlikely midwives were nouveau riche railroad barons in Moscow. Savva Mamontov, whose family built the northern railroad from Yaroslavl to the White Sea, turned his estate at Abramtsevo into Russia's most famous art colony and commissioned operas with pan-Slavic or Eastern themes for his private theater.

Such was the stage on which Serge Diaghilev brought forth the most startling and memorable of his Ballets Russes productions, the Roerich-Stravinsky-Nijinsky collaboration, *Le Sacre du Printemps*. The work was conceived by the artist and the composer at Talashkino, Petersburger Princess Tenisheva's art colony near Smolensk, in the summer of 1911. Roerich supplied the libretto and set designs, drawing on the Princess's vast collection of old Slavic art, embroidery, and folk costumes as inspiration for the ballet, which provoked riots at its Parisian premiere in 1913, becoming in an instant the quintessence of modernism. *Sacre's* "magic hills," "enchanted rocks," and "sacred birches," which dominate the set, became motifs of the repertoire Roerich would reiterate in his vast outpouring of paintings.

Already a bearded magus and something of a cult figure, Nicholas Roerich was keenly interested in archaeology, ethnography, Buddhism, and old Russian art and architecture. Of Viking descent, but born in St. Petersburg, Roerich traced his interest in Asia to youthful summers spent outside the city at Isvara, the estate his father bought from Count Semyon Vorontsov, the Russian diplomat. Vorontsov, after traveling through India, gave the manor house its name, which means "Lord" or "divine spirit" in Sanskrit, and it was at Isvara that Roerich became fascinated by a painting of Kanchenjunga, the sacred Himalayan peak, which hung on the wall in the living room.

In St. Petersburg, the young Nicholas attended Karl von May's exclusive gymnasium, the incubator for many of Diaghilev's future collaborators. Von May himself taught the geography course where the "May bugs" traced the Russian Empire, drawing colored maps and shaping mountain ranges out of plasticene. At home, Nicholas's family entertained Orientalists and archaeologists, and while still a schoolboy, Roerich obtained permission from the Imperial Archaeological Society to conduct digs around Isvara.

After May's gymnasium, Roerich entered both the Imperial Academy of Arts, the most prestigious in Russia, and the law school of the Imperial University, but his abilities shone most at the easel, and he went on to study art in Paris. He rapidly established his emblematic style, employing strong, flat decorative colors, an iconic variant of Gauguin, seen at their best in luminous Himalayan landscapes, which secured him a niche in the gallery of world art.

In the summer of 1900, while studying and painting ancient architecture on behalf of the Archaeological Society, Roerich met Helena Ivanova Shaposhnikova (1879–1955), his future wife, who, fittingly, claimed descent from Mongol khans. By 1903, he was already director of a St. Petersburg art school and was soon one of Diaghilev's artistic collaborators, becoming a contributor to the impresario's magazine, *Mir iskusstva* (The World of Art). The same year he moved into Princess Tenisheva's orbit, designing decorative objects and furniture for the workshops of Talashkino. Propitiously, at Helena's instigation, he joined St. Petersburg's Theosophical Society, whose head was Diaghilev's aunt, Anna Pavlovna Filosofova (née Diaghileva), after its founding in 1908. Roerich also helped Dorzhiev build the one and only Buddhist temple in the Russian capital. In addition to serving on the building committee, Roerich is credited with designing the skylight decorated with the Eight Auspicious Symbols.

It was doubtless from Dorzhiev that Roerich heard of the lama's project for unifying Russian Buddhists, Mongolia, and Tibet into a "great Buddhist confederacy." This was a reformulation of a similar grandiose project prepared in the 1890's for Nicholas II by the court Buriat, Dr. Pyotr Badmaev, the practitioner of Tibetan herbal medicine. But Dorzhiev advanced a new argument: that the hidden paradise of Shambhala was located in Russian territory, north of Tibet, meaning that the Russian Emperor was the White Tsar of ancient prophecy.

Roerich became a determined seeker of Shambhala thanks to Dorzhiev. In 1901, on his way to St. Petersburg, the Buriat had visited Tashilhunpo, where he received from the Ninth Panchen Lama a copy of *The Prayer of Shambhala*, ascribed to the Third Panchen Lama. This prophecy of the dawn of Shambhala is associated particularly with the Panchen Lamas, who are believed to be the incarnations of the kings of Shambhala. Should the Panchen ever leave Tibet, it would herald, according to the prophecy, the final apocalyptic battle that would usher in the New Age. Warlike conditions will prevail until the barbarians finally attack Shambhala, when they will be destroyed by the King of Shambhala riding on a "stone horse with the power of wind."

The Third Panchen Lama compiled a guidebook, the *Shambhala Lamyig*, with instructions for reaching the kingdom. Only those persons with exalted spiritual powers would be fit for the journey; only those with heightened awareness would find the way. The search for Shambhala, which he identified with the Second Coming of Christ and the Maitreya or Buddha to Come, obsessed Roerich. His paintings and writings thereafter conjured up his vision of "a New Age of peace, brotherhood and enlightenment," and his book, *Shambhala,* published in 1930 after his return from his first Central Asian expedition, was possibly among the sources for James Hilton's *Lost Horizon,* a best-seller in 1933.

THE ROERICHS LEFT REVOLUTIONARY RUSSIA FOR FINLAND AND then made their way to London, where, in 1919, they became members of the city's Theosophy Lodge. Inevitably along with their sons, George (Yuri) and Svetoslav, they became enmeshed in émigré politics. In Petrograd, as the city was now called, Roerich's art collection had been confiscated, and in London he contributed articles to journals supporting the White Russians, with whose armies his brother Vladimir was fighting. "Vulgarity and bigotry, betrayal and promiscuity, the distortion of the sacred ideas of human kind: that is what Bolshevism is," Roerich wrote in 1919, "that is the impertinent monster that lies to humanity." He confided to his patron, Princess Tenisheva, that he found London depressing because he sensed an affinity for Bolshevism, especially among university students. He feared his sons, then studying at London University, would fall under the influence of "the impertinent monster." His fears were misplaced. George (1902–60), a student at the School of Oriental Languages, became involved instead with Indian nationalists, among them a relative of the Bengali poet Rabindranath Tagore. Roerich's younger son, Svetoslav (1904–93), would later marry Tagore's grandniece, the Indian film star Devika Rani.

In London, Roerich also befriended Vladimir Shibaev, a Latvian who later became his secretary, literally following his master to the ends of the earth. The twenty-year-old Shibaev, the son of a Russian father and Baltic German mother, is now alleged by the Russian author Oleg Shishkin to have been a Comintern agent. According to Shishkin, writing in 1994, the Comintern sent Shibaev to London with the assignment of cultivating Indian radicals and Latin American revolutionaries, and infiltrating Masonic lodges and mystical societies (read Theosophists). Since the Bolshevik regime then had no diplomatic representation in London, émigrés like Shibaev were indispensable go-betweens with British sympathizers.

According to Shibaev's memoirs, he first met Roerich on Fleet Street, where the artist was seeking a writer to transcribe his cycle of mystical poems, *The Flowers of [Master] Morya.* Immediately attracted to Roerich, Shibaev met him often to discuss philosophy and politics, and introduced him to a circle of Indian revolutionaries.

In 1920, intending to go to India, the Roerichs booked passage, but in an astute and dramatic change of plans, sailed west instead to New York. Invited by the Art Institute of Chicago to exhibit his paintings, he also designed sets for the city's opera. Roerich was an immediate success in America and the subject of a major exhibition in New York. His early and continued acclaim depended in part on his mastery of the feverish press release. The tone is conveyed by an admirer's introduction to his book, *Altai-Himalaya,* asserting that Roerich's works elude all known categories because his paintings "resemble themselves only—and one another, like some spaceless and timeless order of initiates. Such were Leonardo, Rembrandt, Dürer, Blake, and, in other fields, Beethoven and Balzac...for their work shows flashes of that daemonic and eerie beauty which is the sign whereby they may be identified as belonging to that mythical mystic brotherhood."

Coupled with his skill as a publicist was Roerich's proficiency, acquired at Diaghilev's knee, at wooing patrons. Whereas Diaghilev had obtained patents of nobility and favorable press notices for his galosh-manufacturing sponsors, "Professor Roerich," as he now described himself, promised American moguls access to the spiritual world of his Masters. He described his paintings as Theosophical visions and messages from the Mahatmas, which possessed "healing powers." Before long, Roerich found an American replacement for Princess Tenisheva: Louis P. Horch, an affluent Wall Street currency broker who, with his wife, Nettie, was an enthusiastic art patron. Horch joined other wealthy Americans—notably Charles Crane, heir to a plumbing fortune and influential supporter of Czech President Thomas Masaryk—in providing funds on a grand scale for Roerich's projects: the Master Institute of United Arts, a school for artists; Corona Mundi, an exhibition center; two libraries, one containing Roerich's Tibetan manuscripts; a Roerich Press; and a Roerich Museum, devoted solely to the master's works—all eventually lodged in a Manhattan skyscraper. The Roerichs also acquired two other important acolytes—the Russian-Jewish émigrés, pianists Morris Lichtmann and his wife Sina.

By this time, Roerich's Theosophy had taken a new turn. As Robert Williams tells us in *Russian Art and American Money* (1980), the artist now tried "to fuse the teachings of Buddha and Lenin into a single doctrine of world-wide peace and brotherhood directed against the colonial powers, especially Great Britain." U.S. Consular records show that by 1921 Roerich's political activities began to fill dossiers at the State Department.

The Roerichs' pilgrimage to India and the Himalayas begun in 1923 was amply financed by Horch. In exchange for $300,000 in money and supplies for what was alternately billed as a scientific expedition or a "Mission of the Western Buddhists," Horch—or more precisely the Master Institute and Corona Mundi—would own the paintings Roerich created along the way. Together with George Roerich, who, having graduated from Harvard, was studying Asian languages in Paris, Roerich set up the Pan Cosmos Corporation, an import-export agency dealing with Soviet Russia. The export director was Vladimir Shibaev.

It would appear that Roerich intended to patch things up with the Bolsheviks and return at least for a visit, in hopes of retrieving his confiscated art and archaeological collections. Once in India, he rented a house in Darjeeling, near the Sikkim border where the Thirteenth Dalai Lama once lived. There, if we are to believe British intelligence reports, Roerich also met with Tibetan monks who recognized him—by virtue of the seven moles on his neck that formed the astronomical design of the Great Bear—as "the reincarnation of the great Fifth Dalai Lama."

Roerich's visit coincided with the first moves in a struggle for influence in Tibet between the new Bolshevik regime and the worried British, who posted one of their ablest frontier officers, Lieutenant-Colonel F. M. Bailey, as Resident in neighboring Sikkim. In 1924, a Bolshevik mission was in Lhasa seeking a rapprochement with the Dalai Lama, just a year after the sudden flight from Tibet of the Panchen Lama. Bailey met Roerich in Darjeeling and learned of the artist's preoccupation with the Panchen Lama and his belief that the age of Shambhala was at hand, but he could not make out Roerich's politics. By his own account, Roerich now believed he was destined to proceed into the "heart of Asia," guided by symbols and messages, as a venerable lama had assured him. What is clear from a letter written to friends at home is that Roerich knew the British were wary of their visitor: "No doubt that we will be greatly watched, especially the first year, to this effect we have already some indications—here people are greatly interested in us. Thus let us be mutually careful in letters. Call us friends, parents, mother, father, but cross out the address Guru and Teacher and the signature 'circle.'"

First, however, Roerich hurried from India to New York for the more prosaic task of obtaining a visa to Russia, and having failed, moved on to Berlin, where he saw Nicolai Krestinsky, the Soviet Ambassador. It appears from the diaries of a disciple, Sina Lichtmann (later, Fosdick) that Roerich planned to "obtain concessions for mining businesses in the Altai and for agricultural development." His plan also included founding a city with a great temple rising high above it, with a meeting hall below for the workers. In his encounter with Krestinsky, the guru, in a more worldly mode, offered to share with Moscow intelligence gleaned in politically sensitive Central Asia. He also said the Mahatmas, with whom he communicated, were sympathetic to an alliance between Leninism and Buddhism. Krestinsky, who ran a full-scale espionage operation in Berlin as his sideline, wired a full report of Roerich's visit to the Commissar for Foreign Affairs, Georgi Chicherin, who years before had been the artist's university classmate.

Roerich's timing was auspicious. It happened to coincide with the Comintern's eastward shift of focus. When hopes faded for a Marxist revolution in Germany, the Bolsheviks believed China would serve as harbinger of a global upheaval. Included in Krestinsky's report was Roerich's intimation that he might help emancipate India from British rule. Still, Roerich did not get his visa—Chicherin's favorable reply arrived after he had left Berlin. Instead, in Paris, with Shibaev's help, Roerich obtained a French passport and a Chinese visa for Sinkiang.

THE GREAT WAR HAD MOCKED VISIONS OF UNIVERSAL PEACE AND shook the Theosophical Society. Annie Besant, a woman as remarkable as HPB, had become the movement's third President, succeeding Madame Blavatsky, who passed on in 1891, and Colonel Olcott, who died in 1907. Ms. Besant, who began her adult life as a Fabian Socialist and atheist, turned to Theosophy and in 1893 sailed to India, where she plunged passionately into the national cause. One of her notable recruits was the thirteen-year-old Jawaharlal Nehru, at whose initiation ceremony she presided. She designed the original banner of the Indian National Congress (a spinning wheel was added later) and founded the militant Home Rule League in 1916, employing what became a wartime catchphrase: "England's difficulty is India's opportunity." When the British authorities ordered her deportation, she resisted and was jailed without trial, assuring her place in the pantheon of Indian nationalism.

Writing to Annie Besant in 1921, Roerich offered to donate his painting *The Messenger* to the Society at their headquarters in Adyar, outside of Madras in southern India, in HPB's memory. The offer was accepted, and in 1925 Roerich, his wife, one son, and Shibaev, by now his secretary, were in Adyar to unveil the painting, which he hoped would form the nucleus of a projected Blavatsky Museum of Art. The picture, a tempera work forty-two inches high, shows a figure representing "Humanity" opening a temple door to Madame Blavatsky, bedecked in blue robes, set against a purple-blue sky streaked with golden bolts of lightning.

After visiting the half-campus, half-ashram headquarters of the Society, Roerich and his party moved on to Srinigar in Kashmir, where the artist asked permission to proceed to Ladakh "to paint panoramas and to translate original manuscripts and folk lore." Queried by the British as to his nationality, the State Department responded that Roerich was "a Russian national," while another message from Horch in New York claimed the expedition was American. Warily and reluctantly, British authorities allowed the party to proceed from Kashmir to Leh, capital of Ladakh.

Sinkiang in 1926 was a chaotic battleground. Chinese warlords vied with Bolshevik security forces and marauding survivors of White Russian armies. Entwined with the armed bands were Indian and Chinese revolutionaries responding to orders from Comintern agents like M. N. Roy and Mikhail Borodin. Across this contested terrain, in search of the Mahatmas, swept the Roerich family's caravan, flying the U.S. flag and the tanka of Shambhala, outfitted by Abercrombie and Fitch, with excess baggage containing Nicholas's paintbrushes and canvases, George's Mongolian and Tibetan grammars, and Helena's evening gowns.

Trouble started almost immediately, as documented in testy cables from agents of the British Foreign Office and the Indian Political and Secret Service. On August 8, while still in Kashmir, Roerich telegraphed the Indian Government asserting that his party had been attacked by an "organized mob" at the town of Tangmarg. Several servants had been injured, he said, and the party demanded British protection. However, the Resident in Kashmir, Sir John Wood, sent a contrary report to New Delhi stating that the "mob" consisted of drivers who objected to overloading their trucks, and that Roerich, "who was never in the slightest danger of assault or molestation, completely lost his head, and produced firearms." In September, the Roerichs were allowed to proceed to Leh although the Resident remarked that the guru's behavior was "extremely foolish," and questioned "whether so unbalanced an individual should be given facilities for visiting frontier districts."

Crossing seven passes at more than 15,000 feet, through cold and blizzards, the Roerich party made its way into China, arriving a month later at Khotan, the oasis city bordering the Taklamakan Desert. Here it appeared the artist had a new mission—"to collect objets d'art" and to "find trade openings for certain American firms." According to Major Gillian, the British Consul at Kashgar, the professor was now representing himself as an American citizen. Again there was friction, this time with Khotan authorities, who suspected

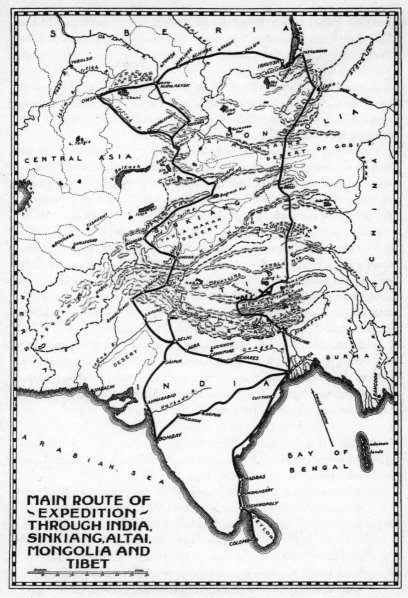

MAIN ROUTE OF
~EXPEDITION~
THROUGH INDIA,
SINKIANG, ALTAI,
MONGOLIA AND
TIBET

The Roerich expedition map, which omits their swerve west to Moscow.

Roerich might be surveying the area for military purposes. On the Taotai of Kashgar's orders, the party was disarmed and detained for four dreary months. Only after Major Gillian intervened was the expedition allowed to proceed.

In April 1926, the party turned up in Urumchi, capital of Sinkiang Province, where the curious incident occurred that fueled British and, later, American suspicions, though it was never mentioned in the father's or son's account of the trip.

Instead of proceeding east toward Peking, the Roerichs abruptly veered westward to Moscow. Informed of this, the British Consul in Kashgar cabled the British Government that it appeared remarkable that "an anti-revolutionary ex-Russian subject should be permitted, or should apply to return to Soviet Russia." When the British chargé d'affaires in Moscow was queried, he replied that he had heard nothing of the party, but that as the bearer of "a passport issued by the Provisional (1917) Government, N. Roerich would almost certainly be arrested were he to penetrate into Soviet territory." When it was confirmed that the party had indeed reached Moscow, the Roerichs and Shibaev were added to the list of citizens to whom visas for India "are not granted without reference."

Their detour to Russia was accomplished through the auspices of the Soviet Consul at Urumchi, Alexander Bystrov. During his first visit to the Consul, Roerich claimed to have gathered extensive materials during his journeys that "will be of great use to the U.S.S.R" and in his diary, Bystrov recorded:

> Today Roerich, his wife, and son have visited me. He told me much that was interesting about his travels. According to what he said, they study Buddhism and are connected to the Mahatmas and very often receive their directives regarding what must be done. By the way, they said that they have letters from the Mahatmas for Comrades Chicherin and Stalin. From what they say, the task of the Mahatmas is to unite Buddhism with Communism and to create a great Oriental federation. There is a prophecy and belief among the Indian and Tibetan Buddhists that their liberation from foreign oppression will come precisely from "the Reds" [the Northern

Red Shambhala]…According to Roerich, one may conclude that their trip through India, Tibet, and Western
China, was the fulfillment of a mission of the "Mahatmas,"
for the execution of which they were obliged to go to the
USSR and then to Mongolia, where they were to get in
touch with the Tashi [Panchen] Lama (aide to the Dalai
Lama in spiritual matters) who fled from Tibet to China, get
him out of Mongolia, and from there to set out on a spiritual journey for the liberation of Tibet from the British.

During their conversations Roerich "strongly and openly criticized
the British and highly praised the Americans" and asked Bystrov to
send a request to the Narcomindel (People's Commissariat for Foreign Affairs) requesting permission to proceed through the USSR to
America. Although Chicherin, the former school chum, agreed to
admit the Roerichs only if they acquired Soviet citizenship, Bystrov,
smitten by the Professor, ignored the cable from Moscow and issued
visas anyway. He was rewarded with the Professor's ring.

At the end of May, the party, which now included a Russian-
speaking Tibetan lama who had been a pupil of Dorzhiev, crossed
the Siberian border near Chuguchak where, despite bales of luggage,
nothing was inspected, a fact that impressed their friends in "Milton"
[the Roerichs' code-name for Moscow]. In June, the Roerichs arrived in Moscow on the Trans-Siberian Railway and were met by
their friends, the Lichtmanns, recently come from New York.
Roerich was fêted by prominent Russians, among them Lenin's
wife, Nadezhda Krupskaya, the theater director Konstantin Stani-
slavsky, Education Commissar Anatoly Lunacharsky, Commissar
Chicherin, and (very likely) Agvan Dorzhiev. With suitable ceremony, the artist presented Chicherin with a small casket containing
sacred Himalayan soil for Lenin's tomb, along with a message from
the Great Himalayan Masters for the Soviet people.

Lunacharsky, who was himself interested in Buddhist philosophy, received a series of "Maitreya" paintings, one being a portrait of a Mahatma with a face resembling Lenin's. Although Roerich was
enthusiastic about his reception, the Russians were less so. They did
not know what to make of this "half Buddhist, half Communist." For

his part, Roerich apparently sought concessions for his mining business in Siberia but was unable to obtain the essential assurances that he could come and go freely. Sina Lichtmann Fosdick's diary describes a most remarkable meeting at the GPU, forerunner of the KGB, "where the names of Maitreya and Shambhala were pronounced...Offers of cooperation were received with enthusiasm." However, after what must have been a tense meeting at the Lubyanka, the secret police headquarters, Lunacharsky advised him to leave the Soviet Union as soon as possible, advice that Roerich heeded.

According to an article in *Pravda,* the Soviets were considering a plan whereby Roerich would lead a two-year scientific expedition, equipped with Soviet passports and Browning revolvers, to Tibet. When this article was reprinted in the English-laguage newspapers, the British assumed that Roerich was now leading a Comintern expedition to Tibet.

IT WAS NOT AN OUTLANDISH NOTION. FROM THE MOMENT THEY seized power, the Bolsheviks tried to "set the East ablaze." In Tsarist times, Buriats and Kalmyks served Russia as clandestine agents in Mongolia and Tibet. And in 1919 two leading Kalmyks, Arashi Chapchaev and Anton Amur-Sanan, submitted to Lenin and forwarded to Chicherin a proposal for a Comintern mission to India's North-East Frontier. The mission was meant to supply tribes in the Nepal-Sikkim-Bhutan borderlands with arms. The memo urged using Kalmyks and Buriat Buddhist "pilgrims" to transmit "the whole idea of the Soviet Government" to their kinsmen and thereby bring Tibet "into the sphere of Soviet influence." A salient passage remarks: "It is usually believed that the key to the rich East and India is found in the Muslim countries, Persia and Afghanistan but...there is also a Mongolian-Buddhist route, which starts in the Kalmyk steppes, and leads through Altai, Mongolia, and Tibet, on to India...Tibet borders on India; this then is the way by which India could establish contact with the center of the world revolution—Russia...Agvan Dorjeev [Dorzhiev]...is ready to proceed east any time."

After fleeing with His Holiness to Mongolia after the British invasion of Tibet, Dorzhiev, as we have seen, devoted himself to the construction of the Buddhist Temple in Petersburg. Radicalized during the Russian Revolution, he joined with other Buddhists in establishing a Buriat-Kalmyk Committee in Petrograd, the first such initiative in their struggle for "national autonomy." According to the research of Alexandre Andreyev, Amur-Sanan's 1919 memorandum coincided with Dorzhiev's rail journey from his Buriat homeland to Moscow. En route, the lama was arrested by the GPU, and accused of attempting to smuggle valuable state property out of the country. Dorzhiev might have been shot but for the intervention of the Narcomindel, which now decided to employ him. Despite his ordeal, perhaps in desperation, Dorzhiev came to believe that Buddhist doctrine was largely compatible with Communist thinking. Now it was not the "White Tsar" who would be the instrument of Tibet's salvation but Lenin.

With Dorzhiev's cooperation, the Narcomindel initially planned a Tibetan expedition under the leadership of two eminent Orientalists, but the civil war intruded. In 1921, Mongolia became the first country beyond Russia's imperial frontiers to come under prolonged Communist control and Chicherin believed it could be a staging area for transmitting revolution to Tibet, China, and India. In 1922, the first Bolshevik mission, led by a Kalmyk cavalry commander, Vasily Khomutnikov, and a Buriat Lama, Dava Yampilon, turned up in Lhasa, and presented the Dalai Lama with a letter from Dorzhiev praising the Communist regime's treatment of Buddhists. The letter from his former friend and tutor had the desired effect: the Dalai Lama ordered an end to rites in which the Red Russians were anathematized. According to the Narcomindel report, the Dalai Lama told the Kalmyk that he desired better relations with Russia since "though formally there exists amity between us and England, she in fact wants to subjugate us. For this reason she has her troops stationed on our territory which is quite annoying and completely undesirable for us." Nevertheless, the Dalai Lama declined to establish diplomatic relations with Moscow, fearing it would alarm the British. He did ask for assistance in the manufacture of ammunition and for telegraphists to operate a set that the Russians presented to the Tibetans. The Narcomindel report also claimed that the British were unpopular, and that the Dalai Lama and his military commander, Tsarong Shapé, were "definitely leaning" toward Soviet Russia. The alleged pro-Russian orientation of the Dalai Lama and the "progressive" Shapé appear to have been sweeteners added to the file for the benefit of higher-ups.

A second Bolshevik mission, dispatched by Lenin himself, followed in 1924. Its leader was S. S. Borisov (Tsering Dorji), an official of the Narcomindel and an Altaic Oirot-Mongol. Borisov was instructed to "unmask English machinations" and persuade the Tibetans to "prevent English troops from penetrating Tibet." The mission remained in Lhasa for three months, but its purposes were frustrated by the coincidental arrival of Colonel Bailey. Using information supplied him by his own informant, Zambo Haldinov, a Kalmyk lama, Bailey warned the Dalai Lama about the anti-Buddhist zealotry of the "Red Russians," as the Tibetans called the Bolsheviks. In his Lhasa diary Bailey describes an encounter on July 27 in which he said he "could not understand how Dorjieff [Dorzhiev] who had always been a great friend and servant of His Holiness had turned against them, which he certainly had done if he was helping the Red Russians." The pontiff then told Bailey about the "sixteen suspicious Mongolians" who had arrived at Nagchu Pass. The Dalai Lama suspected that because the "real Red Russians" could not come to Lhasa they were "no doubt employing Mongolian agents who might be these very people."

With more "Red Russians" ready to be dispatched to Lhasa, enter the Roerichs.

ROERICH REPEATEDLY DENIED THAT HIS WAS A SOVIET EXPEDITION, yet without the tacit blessings of Moscow he could not have proceeded from Siberia through Mongolia and Tibet, nor would he have been able to procure the five cars lent by the Soviet trade mission in Outer Mongolia for "the Shambhala project." From

Roerich's remarks to Bystrov, it is apparent that the artist intended to meet with the Panchen Lama in Inner Mongolia and to accompany his return to Tibet. In *Altai-Himalaya* Roerich wrote that the spiritual leader of Tibet is not the Dalai Lama but the Tashi Lama, about whom "only good things are known." The Tibetans were even more critical of the situation in Tibet than the Roerichs were. They "await with eagerness the fulfillment of the prophecy about his return when he will be the sole head of Tibet and the true Teaching will again flourish."

Strangely, the return of the Panchen to Tibet was the one goal on which the Tibetans, Chinese, British, and Russians were agreed. The Chinese found his large entourage tiresome and expensive and wished to rid themselves of an unwanted guest; the Tibetans desired his return to Tashilhunpo but without an armed Chinese escort; and the Russians feared he might fall into the hands of the Japanese, who had used the civil war in Russia to put forward their variant of Pan-Buddhism. A month or so before Roerich's arrival in Urumchi, the Soviet Ambassador to Mongolia wrote to his counterpart in Peking that the way to frustrate Japanese schemes was to invite the Panchen to the USSR, where, with Russian help, he would be able "to return to Tibet where he is apparently eager to go and is much expected."

The British wanted the Panchen to return, but not under the aegis of the Russians, which helps explain their obsession with the Roerich expedition. Their concern was set forth in a 1929 memorandum from Miles Lampson, the British Minister in Peking. He reported that the Panchen intended to raise a Mongolian force with Soviet backing in order to attack Tibet and oust the Dalai Lama. According to Lampson, his information was based on statements purportedly made by the Panchen Lama to a Chinese general, Chang Hsueh-liang, who repeated them to the British. In 1927, the Panchen Lama did move from Peking to Mukden and was reportedly on his way to Ulan Bator. Although His Serenity never did reach Mongolia that year, he sent a large caravan to the Kumbum monastery in eastern Tibet. Although the lamaist revolution hoped for by the Narcomindel never occured, thereafter, for almost a decade, the Panchen Lama remained an enigmatic wild

card in a triangular context involving China, Britain, and the Soviet Union.

Riding eastward to Omsk on the Trans-Siberian railroad, the
Roerich party, which now included his New York friends, the Lichtmanns, made its way to the Altai mountain range in August 1926.
There the travelers paused to study rock carvings, explore archaeological sites, and collect minerals and medicinal herbs. Continuing to
the capital of Buriatia, Ulan-Ude near Lake Baikal, they then proceeded south to Mongolia. Once in Urga (now renamed Ulan
Bator, or "Red Hero"), they lingered for months to visit monasteries and to present Roerich's painting of the Rigden Jye-po, the ruler
of Shambhala, to the Mongolian people. Emulating a traditional
tanka painting, the "Great Rider" showed a red horseman bringing
freedom, symbolized by a red star. The Mongols for their part were
entranced by the "Ameri-khan" who was clearly wealthy (his fillings
led the Mongols to imagine that gold sprang from his mouth, and
that wherever he trod, gold would be found).

In May 1927, the Roerichs crossed the Gobi Desert toward Tibet.
Traveling south to Tsaidam, they lingered in the Shara Valley to erect
a stately white suburgan (stupa) dedicated to Shambhala. Within,
they placed the image of Buddha, the prophecies of Shambhala, and
ceremonial khata (scarves). When the shrine was consecrated that
August, a large black vulture appeared overhead. Beyond it, visible
through binoculars, was a huge golden spheroid body which flew
from the north, veered sharply, and then vanished behind the mountains in the direction of Tibet. In a dialogue in Roerich's *Shambhala*,
a lama explains that their sighting of what we would now call a
UFO signified that the mission had been blessed by the lords of
Shambhala. "Did you notice the direction this sphere moved?" asked
the lama. "You must follow the same direction."

It was Roerich's hope that his mission would unite all the world's
Buddhists under the Panchen Lama. Rumors that His Serenity was
on his way to nearby Kumbum monastery, together with a Chinese
military escort, caught up with the Roerichs while they were
camped in Tsaidam. According to Alexandre Andreyev, here the

Roerichs met with a Soviet agent who claimed to be a "disciple of the Panchen" and who reported that the Lama's luggage had already arrived at the monastery. Another new travel companion was a Tibetan named Chimpa, who appears to have been abandoned by a caravan of Buriat lamas sent by Agvan Dorzhiev. Chimpa, it also appears, was transporting weapons destined for Tibet. All this was recorded by Dr. Konstantin Ryabinin, a physician who joined the expedition in Mongolia and who kept a diary that is a valuable source on this extraordinary expedition.

COLONEL BAILEY, SITTING IN SIKKIM, WAS TO BE THE UNDOING OF "the Shambhala Project." On his desk at Gangtok were press accounts of the guru's progress, to which was attached a note from a Foreign Office official, Stephen Gaselee: "I think you will admit that it is not a pleasant story; that he is a worthless humbug is proved by his claim [in *The Daily Express,* May 29, 1926] that he found in a Tibetan monastery a manuscript proving that Christ left Palestine as a young man and joined a caravan bound for India, where he preached to the Sudras and Vicias, the lowest of the castes...I do hope you will point out to the [U.S.] State Department the trouble that has been caused in Central Asia by their recommendation of this Bolshevik to our good offices." When Bailey learned that the Roerich party was in Urga, he cabled Lhasa "to warn the Tibetan Government of Roerich's intention to visit Tibet and inform them of his Bolshevik tendencies."

In September 1927, the professor's party reached the first Tibetan military outpost near the Olun-nor Lakes. On October 6 they arrived on the Chang Tang plateau, where they were stopped south of the Kamrong Pass, and were told to wait until they received permission to proceed to Lhasa. No permits came. Instead they were detained for five months in one of the coldest places in Asia.

On October 17, suspecting "someone's long hand" behind Lhasa's dilatory response, Ryabinin confided to his diary what George was telling the Tibetans: "Roerich says that if the Dalai Lama refuses to accept the Mission of the Western Buddhists and if America is not given an urgent reply, then the separation of the Eastern and Western Buddhists is inevitable. Instead of gaining the friendly help of powerful America, there will be difficult consequences for Tibet."

From Lhasa, Tsarong wrote Bailey that "Americans named Mr. and Mrs. Rigden, [Rigden was Roerich's name in Tibetan] and a military officer, a doctor and a secretary have reached near Nagchukala. I do not know for certain if the party will be allowed to come to Lhasa." When Tsarong expressed concern that by denying entry to the expedition, Tibet would offend the U.S. Government, Bailey responded that even if the professor had resided in the United States for a few years, he was not an American citizen; he was a "red Russian."

Urgent letters from Roerich to the Nagchu governors, the Dalai Lama, and to Bailey followed. By November it became clear that the party was not only detained but under arrest, since having abandoned hope of reaching Lhasa, they were refused permission to proceed to Sikkim. Corpses of dead horses, mules, and camels surrounded the camp as did the wild dogs and circling ravens feeding on them. On November 10, George Roerich sent a further desperate message to Bailey: "The Mission is detained by Tibetan Government pending an answer from Lhasa, already for 32 days. Have to stay in summer tents with scanty food supplies and fodder. Almost no fuel, cold about −30 C...Half our caravan animals already perished. The other half still lingering, being in a pitiful state...The forcible stay bears very hard on all members of the Mission. Madame Roerich has been unwell during the whole trip...I myself nearly died of an acute attack of mountain sickness...The doctor of the Mission himself is suffering from iocardite [sic], Lt. Col. N. Kordashevski, Professor Roerich's private secretary, feels himself so worn out that he does not leave his tent...The presence of women and a child makes the situation very critical."

The Tibetans, it appears, did not deliver the message to Bailey. Instead they again sought his advice on how to reply to the Roerichs' appeals for help. An unnamed British official weighed in with a warning not to abandon the expedition lest "uninformed" American opinion be unfavorably aroused. Presumably at British instigation, on March 4, Tibetan authorities finally allowed the caravan to proceed on a roundabout route to Sikkim, where they were "put across the frontier into India." A telegram from the Roerichs forwarded by Horch to President Calvin Coolidge in May completes the mission's version of the story:

> ...On the Tibetan territory we have been attacked by armed robbers. The superiority of our fire arms prevented bloodshed. In spite of Tibet passports Expedition forcibly stopped by the Tibetan authorities on October sixth, two days north of Nagchu. With inhuman cruelty the Expedition has been detained for five months at altitude of 15,000 feet in summer tents amidst severe cold about forty degrees below Centigrade. The Expedition suffered from want of fuel and fodder. During stay in Tibet five men, Mongols, Buriats and Tibetans died and ninety caravan animals perished. By order of authorities all letters and wires addressed to Lhasa Government, the American Consul at Calcutta, and British authorities have been seized. The members were forbidden to speak to passing caravans. They were forbidden to buy foodstuffs from population. Their money and medicines came to an end. The presence of three women in caravan and medical certificate about heart weakness was not taken into consideration. With great difficulties on March fourth, the Expedition started southwards. All nine European members of the Expedition are safe. Courageously bore hardships of exceptionally severe Winter. Many scientific results after four years of travels.

If the Roerichs divined that Bailey was the author of their difficulties, they kept it to themselves. In George Roerich's *Trails to Innermost Asia* (1931), an account of the expedition (minus the side trip to Moscow), the colonel's name is repeatedly invoked as a well-wishing protector who hospitably received the returning party. In May 1928, they spent "two delightful days" at the Residency in Gangtok. Bailey's account mentions the two camels they presented to Sikkim's maharajah—the first ever seen in Gangtok—and the four large trunks of Helena Roerich's clothes. In his report to the Foreign

Office, Bailey appears to have squeezed every useful drop of information from his guests, particularly about Chapchaev, whom the Roerichs described as "a very dangerous Communist and member of the Comintern." They also passed on to Bailey the news that in Mongolia and Tibet "there were rumors that he [the Panchen Lama] was coming to Tibet with a Chinese army."

In a conversation a year later with a colleague in Washington, preserved in India Office files, Bailey offered his official estimate of the Professor-Mahatma-Guru: "The man is from a literary and scientific point of view a humbug, a bad painter, afflicted with megalomania, but in character rather agreeable in a vague way, and almost certainly not a Bolshevik agent." The political officer was more candid with his mother: "They lived here for some time in Darjeeling and one of the sons stayed here—but they were not Bolshie then but like so many Russians they made peace with the Bolshies and are now working for them. They tried to get into Lhasa but the Tibetans wouldn't let them. Don't mention the above to anyone."

Although the Viceroy invited the Roerichs to lunch at Simla, the professor remained on a "suspects list" of persons not eligible for visas.

As a result of the expedition, the Roerichs turned against the Dalai Lama, blaming him for the alleged decline of Tibetan Buddhism. Their loyalty now rested entirely with the Panchen Lama, whom they viewed as spiritually superior to his corrupt rival in Lhasa. Still, despite their inability to find Shambhala or failing that, extruding the Panchen Lama from his yellow-walled monastery in Mongolia, the Roerich expedition was a remarkable feat. George Roerich's *Trails to Innermost Asia,* and *Altai-Himalaya* by his father, vividly portray a Central Asian world that all but vanished after 1930.

What the Soviets thought of the abortive mission is demonstrated by their treatment of Dr. Ryabinin. On his return to Moscow, the physician was arrested by the secret police and accused of "creating a counter-revolutionary organization which operated under the pretense of studying Buddhism and Masonry" but which served instead the purpose of espionage. When he refused to testify against the Roerichs, he was sentenced to five years' imprisonment. Still trying to learn more about "the American spy Roerich," Soviet authorities tried him again and sentenced him to a further ten years. Released from prison in 1947, Ryabinin died alone, forgotten, and deprived of all his civil rights, in 1953.

A final note on Agvan Dorzhiev. When he fled Tibet with the Thirteenth Dalai Lama, he became persona non grata with the British, who prevented him from returning permanently to Lhasa. After devoting his life to furthering the Buddhist cause in Russia, he was arrested during the Great Terror of 1937 in Trans-Baikalia and indicted for treason and other counter-revolutionary crimes. He allegedly confessed to aiming to overthrow the government he "personally hated for closing the monasteries; also in general for its attack on religion." He died "as a result of cardiac arrest, and general physical weakness due to old age" in a prison hospital in 1938. Buried in secret, he was rehabilitated in 1990 when his case was dismissed "on grounds of lack of evidence and absence of criminal activity." By this time, a chastened Russia had long since given up sending emissaries to the Land of Snows.

CHAPTER NINETEEN

∴

The Guru

Iᴛ ᴡᴀꜱ ᴀʟʟ ᴛʜᴀᴛ H. L. Mᴇɴᴄᴋᴇɴ ᴍɪɢʜᴛ ʜᴀᴠᴇ ᴡɪꜱʜᴇᴅ ᴡʜᴇɴ ʜᴇ
arrived in Philadelphia to cover the launch of the Progressive
Party in July 1948. As he reported with relish for *The Baltimore Sun,*
the convention drew a gaudy assemblage of old New Dealers,
cranks, and Communists, quack professors from one-building "universities," former followers of William Jennings Bryan and Robert
LaFollette and "all the other roaring magicians of recent history,"
plus, he did allow, some reasonably intelligent folk, male and female,
who served as raisins in the cake. These were among the 3,000 delegates who answered Henry Wallace's call for a "Gideon's Army" to
do righteous battle for peace. Mencken, American journalism's
reigning iconoclast, judged their chiefs with a detached eye. ("I am
completely neutral. I'm against them all.") He had been in the same
hall when the Democrats nominated President Harry Truman on a
civil rights platform that provoked a walkout by Southern Democrats, and was present a month earlier when the Republicans chose
Thomas E. Dewey, the dapper Governor of New York. Now it was
the Progressives' turn, and Mencken, typing with two swift fingers,

sought to appraise Henry Agard Wallace of Iowa, standing six-feet-plus, his hair like a sheaf of wheat and a beneficent glow on his friendly face. Mencken dubbed him "the Swami," adding that his more idolatrous delegates would not at all be surprised "if a flock of angels had swarmed down from Heaven to whoop him up, accompanied by the red dragon with seven heads and ten horns described in Revelation 12:3."

Wallace was the wild card in the campaign. Having served as Franklin Roosevelt's Vice President and Secretary of Agriculture, he was a paladin of American liberalism. Though certainly no Communist, he did not reject support of the Party's activists. He became their man from the moment Truman fired him as Secretary of Commerce in 1947 for opposing aid to Greece and Turkey, the move that heralded the Cold War. Wallace barnstormed the country as an apostle of peace, and made it known he was available for the Presidency. Polls in early 1948 gave Wallace seven percent, which on election day could translate into four million votes, most of them at the expense of Harry Truman. Such was the setting on February 11 when Westbrook Pegler, the cantankerous Hearst columnist, published the first of the "Guru letters," which he claimed were written by Wallace. Pegler did not say how he obtained these documents, purportedly sent to Nicholas Roerich, or "Dear Guru"; and to an acolyte, Frances Grant, or "Dear M" [for Modra, her cultist name]; but week in and week out Pegler offered examples, such as:

"I find the W. One [Wavering One, a code name for President Roosevelt] has a very pronounced attitude toward the Rulers as you might guess from the S. One [Sour One, code for Secretary of State Cordell Hull]...He thinks the Monkeys [Great Britain] will be against the Rulers [Japan] two years hence. These are very busy days and openings do not appear...Have you heard from the horoscope? Its analysis will confirm certain of your ideas."

The author spoke of curing his headaches at formal dinners by rubbing his forehead with a Tibetan amulet, and in another letter he ruminated mysteriously: "I have been thinking of you holding the casket—the sacred, most precious casket. And I have thought of the New Country going forth, to meet the seven stars and under the sign of the three stars. And I have thought of the admonition: 'Await the

Stone' [the sign of Shambhala]…We think of the People of Northern Shambhalla and the hastening feet of the successor of Buddha and the Lightning flashes and the breaking of the New Day."

It appears that Roosevelt was the Flaming One, the Russians were the Tigers, Mongolia the Land of the Masters, Churchill the Roaring Lion, and Wallace himself Galahad or Parsifal. The typed letters were signed "HAW," and Pegler challenged their putative author to admit or deny their authenticity. Week in and out, the Iowan refused comment, though it was known he had a past connection with the Russian mystic. Hence the buzz of interest in Philadelphia as Henry Wallace faced four hundred reporters at the convention's opening press conference. Sitting in the pack before him was Mencken, a lion in winter, as much an object of curiosity to younger journalists as Henry Wallace himself.

An unidentified reporter asked straight off, "Mr. Wallace, do you repudiate the 'Guru letters'?" Wallace, face rigid, replied: "I never comment on Westbrook Pegler." Others repeated the question, only to get the same response, with the added barb that Wallace would never discuss anything with Pegler or his stooges. Then, as Pegler himself related in *The New York Journal-American*, "a tall, not handsome chap arose, a man of spiritual mien and prematurely gray, to declare: 'My name is Westbrook Pegler, Mr. Wallace. You twice referred to the subject of letters in your opening remarks and you have reminded us journalists of the important duty of getting available facts. Therefore I ask you to say whether you did or did not write certain letters to Nicholas Roerich.'" Wallace saw before him a big, florid, white-haired man, glowering like a bull, and he answered as if addressing the ceiling, "I will never engage in any discussion with Westbrook Pegler."

Alistair Cooke, then a correspondent for *The Manchester Guardian*, has sketched what followed. Heads craned as H. L. Mencken rose to his feet. "Would you consider *me* a Pegler stooge?" he asked in the softest possible voice. "No, Mr. Mencken," Wallace responded, with a reflexive grin. "I would never consider you anybody's stooge." "Well, then," gently pursued the Sage of Baltimore. "It's a simple question. We've all written love letters in our youth that would bring a blush later. There's no shame in it. This is a question that all of us here would like to have answered, so we can move on to weightier things." Swallowing hard, Wallace would only say he would "handle that in my own time," which he never did. Mencken voiced the general puzzlement: "Wallace's imbecile handling of the Guru matter revealed a stupidity that is hard to fathom. He might have got rid of it once and for all by simply answering yes or no, for no one really cares what foolishness he fell for ten or twelve years ago…He went into the conference with every assumption in his favor. He came out of it tattered and torn." The Swami had stumbled, and the "Guru matter" reinforced doubts about his wooliness, slowing his crusade to a crawl.

This mattered a great deal to President Truman, who trailed Dewey in polls and on all sides was written off as a loser. The gap was so wide that Dr. Gallup stopped conducting polls weeks before the November vote—a monumental blunder. After the election, it was the beaming President who held aloft the famous *Chicago Tribune* headline, "Dewey Defeats Truman." Yet postmortems demonstrated it was a close-run thing. Wallace's million-plus showing cost Truman the electoral votes of New York, Michigan, and Maryland, and a swing of only 30,000 ballots could have lost him California, Ohio, Illinois, and his victory. So close was the outcome that various supporters—unions, farmers, African-Americans, anti-Communist liberals, Catholics, and Jews—could each argue their votes were decisive. By the same logic, Nicholas Roerich could also have claimed a pivotal role in the 1948 election: a feat the more remarkable since he had died in India the year before.

NICHOLAS ROERICH WAS VERY MUCH ALIVE WHEN HENRY WALLACE first met him in 1929, a banner year for the Guru. That March, six months before the Wall Street crash, there gathered on Manhattan's Riverside Drive several hundred distinguished guests, including emissaries of twenty foreign countries, to applaud Louis Horch as he laid the cornerstone, enclosing a bejeweled Rajput casket, for the twenty-nine-story "Master Building." A long and flowery message from Roerich, then residing in India, was read.

When Roerich arrived in New York a few months later for the opening of his new museum, he found himself, thanks to the efforts of Horch and others, momentarily famous. Mayor Jimmy Walker sent the police to escort him from dockside to City Hall where the Mayor greeted him on behalf of seven million New Yorkers. President Herbert Hoover invited him to the White House. That same halcyon year, the Department of International Law at the University of Paris nominated him for the Nobel Peace Prize in recognition of his efforts to secure treaty protection for art treasures in wartime, through what became known as the Roerich Pact.

In connection with the Pact, Roerich designed a distinctive flag known as the Banner of Peace, consisting of three red circles surrounded by another on a white field, denoting religion, art, and science encircled by culture, which the artist described as a universal symbol. The Pact won the support of prominent Theosophists, of socialists like George Bernard Shaw, of futurists like H. G. Wells, and of the Indian poet Rabindranath Tagore. Propitiously, Eleanor Roosevelt and Henry Wallace added their endorsements.

At this point, the Guru decided to settle permanently in India, and with Horch's funds, he acquired an estate at Naggar in the Kulu Valley, "the end of the habitable world," in the Western Himalaya. Called "The Hall" and featuring a "Simla–Surrey style villa," the estate was formerly owned by the Rajah of Mandi. Here, in a gorgeously panoramic setting, Roerich planned a scientific research station. But that required a residency visa for India, which British authorities declined to issue, claiming, in private, that Roerich was "a good deal of a Bolshie, if not an entire one." British objections were summarized in a memorandum prepared by the U.S. Consul in Calcutta for the State Department:

> It may be that he is only a racketeer in art, that his Russian visit was innocent and harmless, and that the Tibetan trek and purchase of land in Kulu were only advertising stunts. On the other hand, these activities may serve to cloak a deeper and more dangerous purpose. The Tibetan Government, which refused to let him come to Lhasa in spite of his urgent solicitations, had grounds for thinking him a Soviet

agent. The Government of India has no evidence that he is, but they are alive to the possibility and they are keeping careful watch on the Roerichs and their associates in India.

In reply, Washington acknowledged that Roerich was controversial, but said it supported "the legal right of an American corporation to acquire real property in British India, while disclaiming all responsibility for the Museum's scientific activities in the Kulu Valley." Protests and appeals poured into India, were seconded in newspaper articles, and as pressure grew, British authorities relented. Urusvati (which means "Light of the Morning Star"), the Himalayan Research Institute, was duly established. Acting on glowing praise by the Tang Dynasty pilgrim Hsüan-tsang for Kulu's medicinal plants, the Institute initiated research into herbs for curing asthma, cancer, and blood diseases, activities "for which it would be much easier to collect a large amount of money than for a botanical or zoological or other purely scientific project." In fact the Roerichs did receive accolades from reputable recipients of their seed and zoological specimens. The New York Botanical Garden received a collection of plant specimens, as did the U.S. Department of Agriculture. However, it was the promise of a cure for tuberculosis, a disease that had afflicted Wallace's family, that first sparked the Secretary's interest in Roerich's research, which was to take the Guru and his son back to Central Asia on the oddest scientific expedition ever sponsored by the United States Government.

AFTER THE GREAT CRASH CAME THE GREAT DEPRESSION, AND IN 1932 a stunned country overwhelmingly elected Franklin Delano Roosevelt. Farmers were among the hardest hit, and to contend with plunging prices and rural poverty, the new President seemed to find a paragon as Secretary of Agriculture. At forty-five, Wallace still looked boyish in his tousled hair; his grandfather had founded *Wallace's Farmer,* an Iowa institution, and his father Henry had served a decade before in the same Cabinet post. Like many Americans, Wallace had deserted the Republicans to support Roosevelt, giving added resonance to his role in FDR's Hundred Days. Still, unlike other New Dealers, Wallace also brought to office (in Arthur M. Schlesinger, Jr.'s phrase) a rhapsodic mysticism. He was the only Cabinet member who dabbled in the occult and who could cast a horoscope.

When Wallace met Roerich in 1929, the Iowan would have already known about Theosophy, a recurrent subject in his correspondence with the Irish poet A.E. (George Russell), an initiate. In a letter to the poet in 1931, Wallace spoke warmly of his first meetings with Roerich, "a great Russian painter who has traveled extensively in Tibet and the Gobi Desert" and who also has "an experimental laboratory in the foothills of the Himalayas."

Wallace was also fascinated, even smitten, with the Roerich Peace Pact. "I believe so profoundly in things for which the Banner of Peace stands," he wrote to the Guru in June 1933, "that I am only too happy to offer you any cooperation in my personal capacity to help make your efforts along this line successful." This Wallace did with a persistence that exasperated the Secretary of State, Cordell Hull, over whose objections Wallace secured White House support for the Pact, which was signed in the presence of Roosevelt and Wallace, by twenty-two diplomats, mostly from Latin America, with much pomp in June 1935.

By this time, too, what can be called Roerichisms seeped into Wallace's prose, doubtless a residual influence of his private correspondence with the Guru. In one letter to the President, the Secretary of Agriculture remarked: "I feel for a short time yet that we must deal with the 'strong ones,' the 'turbulent ones,' the 'fervent ones,' and perhaps even with a temporary resurgence, with the 'flameless ones' who with the last dying gasp will strive to reanimate their dying giant 'Capitalism.' Mr. President, you can be the 'flaming one,' the one with an ever-upsurging spirit to lead into the time when the children of men can sing again."

Roerich's influence was also suspected in another Wallace initiative, the adornment of the one-dollar bill with the verso of the Great Seal, showing a pyramid crowned by an all-seeing eye. Wallace pointed out to an incredulous Treasury Secretary Henry M. Morgenthau, Jr., that underneath the pyramid were the words *Novus*

Ordo Seclorum (*Novus Ordo* can be read as Latin for New Deal), a politically relevant inscription, and the change was approved in 1935. "It was not till later," Morgenthau wrote in his diary, "that I learned that the pyramid . . . had some cabalistic significance for members of a small religious sect."

Wallace's budding friendship with Roerich was not a sudden or surprising aberration. As a youth in Iowa he had drifted from his Episcopal faith and studied Buddhism, Judaism, Confucianism, Islam, Zorastrianism, and Christian Science. His spiritual restlessness combined with an eminently practical interest in agricultural research. So successful were his efforts at developing hardier, higher-yielding corn that he founded a seed company in Des Moines whose profits made him wealthy. It was no doubt Wallace's mental hybridization that led him to believe that Roerich was the right person to scour Central Asia for drought-resistant grasses usable in America's Great Plains to combat the Dust Bowl. This was the genesis of the Roerich expedition through Manchuria, Inner Mongolia, and China, financed and staffed, at the Secretary's suggestion, by the Department of Agriculture.

However, the real motive for the expedition has come to light in overlooked files at the FDR Library in Hyde Park, and through the recent publication in Russia of Sina Lichtmann Fosdick's diary. It appears that the Great Shambhala Project had been reincarnated as "The Plan," as it was called by the "Heart Trust" (the Roerichs, Lichtmanns, and Frances Grant). "The Plan," to be funded by U.S. taxpayers with an additional contribution by Wallace of $4,500, envisioned the founding of a cooperative settlement somewhere in northern Asia under the spiritual leadership of the Panchen Lama. Graham White and John Maze in *Henry A. Wallace: His Search for a New World Order* (1995) describe unsuccessful attempts by Wallace to interest American millionaires of a mystical bent such as Henry Ford and Mary Rumsey, the sister of Averell Harriman, in "The Plan." The records suggest that implementing "The Plan" would also involve the cooperation of the Japanese and U.S. Governments and, as Roerich had prophesied, a future President, Henry Wallace.

The key to "The Plan" was the Panchen Lama. In November 1933 Wallace confided to Frances Grant: "Am talking Wednesday with

[Joseph] Rock,* an American born citizen, who has cooperated with us on occasion who has lived in Yunnan and is now going to Peking and who reports the Panchen Lama nearing Koko Nor [where he would reside at Kumbum monastery]...Am meeting Rock at Ry[erson's] suggestion and will learn from him what I can." Rock had already written to Knowles Ryerson, the director of the U.S. Government's Bureau of Plant Management, outlining the situation on Tibet's eastern border shortly before the Dalai Lama's death in December 1933. Rock reported that the Tibetans were trying to conquer, with British arms and encouragement, territory in Kham, Amdo, and Tatsienlu. British maps, he noted, "always include the entire area of Kokonor and even Tatsienlu into Tibet" even though China "has never relinquished her authority over Tibet." Rock predicted that following the death of the Dalai Lama, the British would annex Tibet, which, if the Tibetans prevailed, would include much of western China. The British would thus gain control over the large wool, tea, fur, and musk trade in that region. China, in turn, was also anxiously awaiting the Dalai Lama's death "to push the Panchen Lama," who was "much better liked" than his rival in Lhasa. When the Dalai Lama died, the pro-Chinese Panchen Lama would "swoop down with Chinese help and take charge of Tibet."

BY 1933, ROERICH HAD ONCE AGAIN BECOME DISENCHANTED WITH the Bolsheviks and decided to throw in his lot with their adversaries— the Japanese and the White Russians living in Manchuria. Moreover, he viewed Roosevelt's recognition of the Soviet Union and the de-

---

*Joseph Rock (1884–1962) was the *National Geographic*'s man in China supplying photographs and articles from remote areas in western China from 1922 to 1935. First and foremost a plantsman, Rock supplied arboretums and botanical gardens throughout the world with Asian plant specimens. After China fell to the Communists, Rock spent his last years in Hawaii working on a Naxi-English dictionary, a compilation of Naxi lore and language published by Harvard.

velopment of trade with "the dark ones" with alarm. He conveyed his qualms to Wallace, who also feared that the rapprochement with Moscow might "activate disintegrating forces" that would interfere with "The Plan." Wallace voiced his gloom frankly: "It seems here at times as though our friend whom you call the m—re one [FDR had been downgraded from the Wavering One to the Mediocre One] is bound to bring about the greatest eventual activity of disintegrating forces. He is lovable and charming but at times does the most appalling things in the most heartless way."

Nonetheless, "The Plan" inched forward. On December 3, Wallace wrote to the President reminding him of *his* suggestion that an expedition might be sent to Mongolia to find drought-resistant grasses. Wallace noted that "the political situation in this part of the world is always rendered especially intriguing by the effect on it of ancient prophecies, traditions and the like."

In 1934, Nicholas Roerich came to America to meet with Wallace and work out details of the mission. The State Department strongly questioned the advisability of sending White Russians to such "political and diplomatic hot spots." In particular, it deplored Roerich's decision to enter Manchuria via Japan. When Wallace delegated Roerich "to lead and protect" the expedition, Ryerson, as director of the Bureau of Plant Management, protested. However, he agreed to send as staff two scientists: Dr. Howard MacMillan, forty-three years old, a plant pathologist; and James Stephens, thirty-one, a specialist in forage grasses and legumes. After a meeting with the botanists, Wallace reported that "Mac" expressed his fear that the Roerichs, "being of the feline race [Russians] might be persona non grata to our friends [the Japanese] on whose graces we are dependent." Because of Chinese sensitivities, "Mac" also warned against using the word "exploration" in connection with the expedition; their mission ought instead be described as a "Study of Plants Useful in Erosion Control." Suspecting the hidden purpose of the expedition, departmental wags gathered around water-coolers joked that the Roerichs would also seek signs of the Second Coming. "I don't dare let a theosophist in to see Henry—he'd give him a job right away," confided Paul Appleby, who was Wallace's Assistant Secretary at the time.

In Central Asia, turmoil and violence were even more prevalent than during Roerich's foray there a decade earlier. Japan had invaded China in 1931, seizing Manchuria and installing Pu-Yi, the deposed Chinese Emperor, as puppet ruler of "Manchukuo." Abandoning their earlier tolerance of Buddhism in Outer Mongolia, the Communists were jailing monks and pillaging monasteries. The Japanese now posed as defenders of Buddhism, threatening to wrench Mongolia from Soviet control while promoting the idea that Shambhala existed in the Land of the Rising Sun. The Panchen Lama visited "Manchukuo," and stories in the Japanese press spoke of plans for a "Great Manchuko-Mongolian Empire" with Pu-Yi as temporal ruler, and the Panchen Lama as its spiritual head.

In China, Chiang Kai-shek had broken violently with his former Communist allies, and his Nationalist regime ruled with diminished authority over a fragmenting country. The Thirteenth Dalai Lama "departed to the Honorable Field" in December 1933, and the intentions of the Panchen Lama were now an urgent concern for the Tibetans. Negotiations for his return to Tibet broke down when the recalcitrant lama insisted he needed a Chinese military escort to safeguard his homecoming.

It was into these cross-currents that Roerich and his Harvard-educated son George sailed in May 1934. They arrived in Tokyo "in a blaze of glory," or so the U.S. Consul initially reported, and the Guru gave the first of many press conferences on the themes of peace and the need for a world "art trust" to replace the "brain trust." Yet it was far from clear who headed the mission, whether it was Roerich, as he and Wallace believed, or Howard MacMillan, as the professionals in the Bureau of Plant Management and the State Department assumed. American diplomats were further surprised when Roerich seemed needlessly to praise the Japanese War Minister after a meeting in which the artist requested introductions to military authorities in Manchuria.

That June, the Roerichs arrived in Japanese-occupied Manchuria, or "Manchukuo," a term Washington always framed in quotation marks. They made a side trip to the capital, Hsinching, for an audience with the puppet emperor, Pu Yi, on whom Professor Roerich conferred the insignia, First Class, of the Roerich Museum and the Banner of Peace, "for resplendent merit in the field of culture." A State Department dispatch stiffly noted that the decoration was presented to the head of a regime "which is not recognized by the Government of the United States."

Meanwhile, the department's two botanists had arrived in Tokyo, but when they attempted to join the Roerichs at Harbin in Manchuria, they were delayed for a month in Dairen. The problem was confusion over travel permits to seemingly distinct American missions, and the suspicious stock of small arms and ammunition they were carrying, at the request of the Roerichs. In Harbin, while waiting for the plant experts, Roerich delivered lectures on Central Asia, visited his brother, Vladimir, gave newspaper interviews, dabbled in émigré politics, and acquired an entourage of Russians outfitted in Cossack uniforms.

Harbin was home to some 70,000 White Russians, thousands of Red Russians, and any number of double or triple agents, all conspiring under the watchful eyes of the Japanese secret police. Newcomers were automatically suspected of being Bolshevik spies. As MacMillian cabled his departmental superiors, the U.S. Consulate "pointed out to me that of all the people in the world to travel with in this part of the world, the last ones to choose are Russian." In a letter home, he enclosed a handbill that had been scattered throughout the city to promote a lecture. It quoted one Hon. George Gordon Battle, identified as "one of America's outstanding statesmen," as declaring that "Nicholas Roerich is unquestionably one of the greatest leaders of history."

"To have these [leaflets] thrown into every door might not be considered presumption on the part of a circus or chain grocery store," expostulated MacMillan, "but it has not helped our case any. I feel that the English language is but a fumbling medium for what the Professor wanted to say; and I am sorry that I was not on hand to suggest a word or two out of some special vocabularies." All this lavish publicity, a U.S. Consular officer wrote, combined with the Roerichs' efforts "to import arms and ammunition, to establish an armed camp in the interior," had roused suspicions and "considerably delayed the expedition in securing permission for its work."

The Roerichs offered their own version of the impasse in a July memorandum to Secretary Wallace. George Roerich explained that the departmental botanists lacked "a clear picture of the organization of the expedition" and that, having disregarded the Roerichs' advice on visas and permits, arrived only after a considerable delay in Harbin, where they kept father and son "in the dark as to their plans and movements." For their part, the two plant experts now complained that they were almost at the end of the seed-collecting seasons and that the professor and his son had complicated matters further by traveling with a Cossack escort. On July 31, a very frustrated MacMillan cabled his bureau director, Knowles Ryerson: "It looks as though I will finally see Papa Roerich tomorrow, and hear what yarns he has to tell, after the lies that have gone before. Papa Roerich rates a Cossack guard at his door at all hours, armed. It makes a great show. What tripe!"

By this time, the expedition had split into two camps, with each party hiring its own personnel and making independent plans to collect seeds. As they headed to Hailar near the Soviet border, although they were booked into the same rail compartment, they were no longer speaking. While the botanists gathered plant specimens near Hailar, the Roerichs visited the Ganjur Buddhist monastery. George copied an old Tibetan medical manuscript while Nicholas posed for a photograph with the lamas and discussed with them the coming "War of Shambhala." When Wallace finally learned of these disputes, he responded by dismissing the two botanists for insubordination, and accused them of spreading "ridiculous" and "extremely malicious" rumors about the Roerichs. Because he supported his subordinates, Ryerson, a noted plant biologist, was demoted and transferred to the Division of Subtropical Horticulture. Wallace then wrote the Roerichs to express his regrets and "complete confidence and approval" of their actions.

Daily attacks on the Guru and his son now appeared in the Japanese-controlled press, and the authorities complained to the U.S. Consul in Harbin that the expedition "had for its object other than agricultural work" and was therefore refused permission to undertake further excavations. Faced with growing hostility in Manchuria, father and son departed for China.

Pausing in Tientsin near the Chinese border, the Roerichs, after a flurry of telegrams to Washington, managed to procure six rifles, four pistols, and ammunition, costing $340.55, from the War Department. These weapons, they insisted, were essential for self-defense. When asked to account for their plans, the Roerichs forwarded to Wallace a report headed "The Desert Shall Bloom Again." In it, father and son claimed to have excavated the "roots of age-old forests" and "bits of woven grasses," indicating that "life once flourished" in arid stretches of Manchuria. The report also described their plan to spend the winter in a monastery translating old Tibetan herbals. The Secretary passed along an excerpt to President Roosevelt, who penciled in response, "I wish I could spend the winter in a Monastery too."

Owing to the growing hostility of the Japanese, the Roerichs' monastery plan was abandoned. They wintered instead in Peking, from whence they embarked in March 1935 for Inner Mongolia, then as now a province of China, accompanied by an armed escort of four bearded White Russians. Before the caravan departed, Roerich dispatched by diplomatic pouch botanical specimens, photographic negatives, a list of Tibetan and Chinese herbal medicines, four volumes of Tibetan medical texts, maps, and botanical drawings.

All this was consistent with "The Plan," as corroborated by the American Minister in Peking, who reported in April that Roerich had visited the camp of a politically prominent Mongolian to announce that "wealthy Americans would be glad to assist the Mongols in building up a thriving business, in this way bringing about a closer relationship between the people of America and the people of Mongolia." However, as the expedition—led by two Russians, escorted by four armed White Russians, relying on Russian Buriats as interpreters, and armed with American weapons—approached the borders of Inner Mongolia, the Soviets assumed, not unreasonably, that Roerich was preparing a Buddhist holy war against Communist rule in Outer Mongolia.

How provocative all this seemed, and indeed was, had begun to register on Henry Wallace. Throughout Asia, newspaper articles recounted the expedition's progress and Professor Roerich's yeastier declarations. With spiteful glee, consular officers gathered the clippings, and relayed them with translations to the State Department. In New York, meanwhile, Roerich's loyal and long-suffering patron, Louis Horch, began to harbor doubts about the professor. In February 1935, as the Roerichs prepared to pursue "The Plan" in Mongolia, Horch acquired legal control of the Roerich Museum, dismissed its employees, and brought suit against the artist to recover upwards of $200,000 in loans. Even so "the Heart Trust" was able in April to push through the signing of the Roerich Peace Plan.

In July, Horch wrote worriedly to Wallace about reports that Roerich was pledging American support for an anti-Communist rebellion in Mongolia, to which the Secretary replied: "I do not know whether there is any foundation whatsoever for the insinuations of political activity on the part of Professor Roerich in Mongolia." This was followed by the Department of Agriculture's directive instructing Roerich to travel to the safer area in the Chinese province of Suiyan, "which is reputedly rich in drought resistant grasses."

What finally caught Wallace's attention was a telegram from Moscow, dated August 20, 1935, from William Bullitt, the American Ambassador. Bullitt's military attaché, it appeared, was informed by a Soviet source that the Roerichs and their White Russian recruits were roaming Mongolia. The cable concluded: "The armed party is now making its way toward the Soviet Union ostensibly as a scientific expedition but actually to rally former White elements and discontented Mongols."

Forthwith Wallace authorized a cable to Roerich terminating the expedition and forbidding public statements of any kind. A Department of Agriculture press release announced that the "two-year grass exploration has ended." An embarrassed Wallace reinstated Knowles Ryerson as chief of his bureau and formally apologized to the two botanists he had dismissed. Off the record, the press was informed that Roerich was "regarded as a spy by certain officials of Manchuko." Writing to Nicholas Roerich's wife Helena in Kulu, the Secretary said he desired "no communication direct or indirect by letter or otherwise between the Roerichs (father, mother, and sons) on their side and myself on the other." Wallace then sent letters to forty-eight ambassadors, to Governor Herbert Lehman of New York and various State Department functionaries, saying he had "decided reservations" about Roerich, who had aggrandized his name rather than his ideals. It would appear that nothing useful came from the thirteen grasses, seven plants, and forage crops that the professor had collected because the trunk remained unopened in storage.

The Roerichs never returned to the United States. Horch now turned against Roerich, and testified against him in an income tax matter. In 1935, while he was in Asia, the Internal Revenue Service audited the Roerich Museum and ruled that its eponymous founder was guilty in absentia "of not filing a tax return for 1926 and 1927 and of tax fraud in failing to report any income at all in 1934," when he was an employee of the Department of Agriculture. The Roerichs lost their appeal against a $50,000 judgment, but by then the family had settled permanently in India. In a parting riposte, Roerich countersued his apostate follower Horch but lost again, and the victorious defendant appropriated the Master Institute, its paintings, and its archives.

NOWADAYS THE CIVIL SERVANTS THAT WALLACE DISMISSED WOULD have taken their story to talk shows or to supermarket tabloids, but Washington in 1935 was a comparatively close-mouthed company town. The Secretary's follies were protected by his staff, his fascination with the occult known only to insiders. So appealing was his public aura that in 1940, FDR overruled party professionals and chose Wallace as his running mate against Wendell Willkie, to whom Republicans had turned. Roosevelt was seeking an unprecedented third term, Hitler's armies were overrunning Europe, and the Presidential campaign was closer than expected. In August 1940, a troubled Harry Hopkins, FDR's closest adviser, telephoned a White House colleague, Sam ("Judge") Rosenman, and asked him to stop by his office. There Hopkins spread photostatic copies of handwritten letters from Henry Wallace. A specimen passage read: "The rumor is the Monkeys [the British] are seeking friendship with the Rulers [Japan] so as to divide the land of the Masters [Mongolia]

between them. The Wandering One [FDR] thinks this is very suspicious of the Monkeys." Hopkins said the originals were in a Wall Street vault, the property of the treasurer of the Republican National Committee. Hopkins had already contacted Wallace, who acknowledged writing the letters ("I guess that's right," were his confirming words, when questioned by his assistant, Paul Appleby). Hopkins asked if it was possible to replace Wallace on the ticket, and overnight Rosenman, having researched the matter, concluded there was no legal way of doing so, even supposing FDR's running mate was willing. At this point copies of the "Guru letters" were provided to *The Pittsburgh Post-Gazette,* and the paper's star reporter, Ray Sprigle, asked Wallace if they were genuine. The indignant nominee replied: "Your publisher must know of the rejection of the material by handwriting experts. He must know the story of the disgruntled discharged employee [Roerich]—a tax evader, who dare not re-enter this land—from which all this stems." Sprigle published the story, along with Wallace's denial, but other papers did not pick it up because the Republicans made nothing of it.

The likely explanation emerged years later in a transcript at the Roosevelt Library in Hyde Park, of a recorded conversation between Franklin Roosevelt and an aide, Lowell Mellett. The White House had learned that Willkie was involved in an adulterous affair with Irita Van Doren, the editor of *The New York Herald Tribune* Sunday book section. As recounted by Ted Morgan in his biography of Roosevelt, the President, having been briefed on Wallace's indiscretions, told Mellett he was prepared to fight back, scandal for scandal, leak for leak: "We can't have any of our principal speakers refer to it, but the people down the line can get it out." The warnings were evidently effective. Nothing was said about "the Guru letters," or about Willkie's affair. Roosevelt won his third term, hands down.

In his Himalayan retreat, meantime, Roerich again tacked with shifting winds. During World War II, he gave his full support to the Soviet Union, and auctioned his paintings for the benefit of Russian war relief. Regrettably, the Roerich Peace Pact was unable to protect cultural treasures from bombs or wartime looting that occurred on an unprecedented scale. His other legacies were more durable. After his death in 1947, the Roerich home in Kulu became a shrine for

Indian nationalists, Prime Minister Nehru among them, and his ashes were interred in a memorial with this inscription:

> The body of the Maharishi Nicholas Roerich, great friend of India, was cremated on this spot on 30 Mahar in the Year 2004 of the Vitram Era, corresponding to 15 December 1947. OM RAM.

Doubtless Roerich oscillated in his feelings about the Soviet Union. Yet he was steadfast in his commitment to the people and religions of Asia, and to his belief that pilgrims there might glimpse a Higher Truth. Was he a spy? His travels to and from the Soviet Union could not have occurred unless he provided information to the Communists. Yet one wonders what Moscow possibly made of his talk of Shambhala, and messages from the Masters. In all, he was a man of the theater as well as a mystic and an artist, and well understood the power of illusion. It is hard to think harshly of this singular figure who befriended and befuddled American millionaires no less than Bolshevik commissars.

Roerich's writings were suppressed in Russia during most of his years abroad, but he was gradually rehabilitated after Stalin's death in 1953. In 1986, Mikhail Gorbachev extolled Roerich as "one of the cultural pillars of Russia," and sent a special plane to India to bring back Svetoslav Roerich's collection of his father's paintings. They are now housed in Moscow's International Roerich Center. George Roerich was invited back to Russia in 1957, and taught at Moscow's Oriental Institute until his death in 1960 in circumstances that are still obscure. But the following year, when Cosmonaut Yuri Gagarin was asked what the earth looked like from space, he said it looked very much like the paintings of Nicholas Roerich. It was an epitaph the old Guru would have appreciated.

∴

CHAPTER TWENTY

The Cousins Discover Tibet

T HE FIRST AMERICANS TO LAY SIEGE TO THE WONDERS OF
Central Asia and Tibet did so in the service of leading art and
natural history museums. Missionaries pointed the way, but their
concern was saving souls. Museums coveted something more tangible: the great wall paintings from the Silk Road, dinosaur eggs from
the Gobi Desert, pelts of the giant panda, or the temple treasures of
Tibet. Going was no longer a low-budget affair, as in the solo expeditions of William Rockhill for the Smithsonian Institution in the
1890's. Sons and friends of Presidents, equipped with Zeiss telescopes and Akeley movie cameras, armed with Springfield and Hoff-
man big game rifles, borne forward by motorcars, riverboats, and
trains of pack-ponies, surrounded by yapping hounds and teams of
shikaries or native hunters, burst with Yankee enthusiasm into the
"world's white rooftree."

The phrase is from Kipling's "The Feet of Young Men," the poem
that inspired TR's sons Kermit and Theodore to journey twice into
Central Asia, first to the High Pamirs in successful pursuit of *Ovis
poli,* the great horned sheep described by Marco Polo, and then to

the Tibetan borderlands. There, in bamboo jungles, they sought and found *Aeluropus melanoleucis,* known locally as *beishung* or white bear, and known to us as the giant panda. Both expeditions were sponsored by the Field Museum of Natural History in Chicago, but romance rather than science was the energizing motive. Ted Roosevelt confessed that he and Kermit could not resist Kipling's challenging lines about "that windy rift where the baffling mountain eddies chop and change" in which the poet demands:

> *Do you know the long day's patience, belly-down on frozen drift,*
> *While the head of heads is feeding out of range?*
> *It is there that I am going, where the boulders and the snow lie,*
> *With a trusty, nimble tracker that I know.*
> *I have sworn an oath, to keep it, on the Horns of Ovis Poli,*
> *For the Red Gods call me out, and I must go.*

The Roosevelts found an ideal companion in a Groton and Harvard schoolmate, C. (for Charles) Suydam Cutting, a wealthy New Yorker and national champion in the ancient and complicated game of court tennis, played in a concrete walled court with windows and a "penthouse" in less than a dozen venues in the eastern United States. He too had an eminent father, Robert Fulton Cutting, "the first citizen of New York City," the scourge of crooked mayors and slumlords, cofounder of the Citizens' Union. City politics did not interest Suydam, nor were his spirits exhilarated by his work as an engineer at the M. W. Kellogg Company. Rather, to escape the ennui of a privileged Brahmin world, Cutting took up exploration and big game hunting. Assam, Upper Burma, Nepal, Ethiopia, the Galápagos, Szechuan and Yunnan in China, the Andaman Islands, the Celebes— these were among the prize notches on his Winchester gunstock. He managed thirteen trips to India, covered 7,200 miles by caravan, collected masses of rare birds and mammals as a trustee of the American Museum of Natural History, and yet his proudest feat was to become the first American invited to Lhasa, where hunting was forbidden.

Cutting's most distinctive features were a prominent nose, and an unusual first name of Dutch origin that strangers often mispronounced (friends called him see-dam, not sigh-dam). It is unlikely he ever uttered an unconventional opinion, yet he confessed to a rare longing to visit the world's least accessible places. The more hard-ships, the better. As he expressed it in *The Fire Ox and Other Years* (1940), being in wild, uncharted lands liberates the mind from "the weight of routines, organized attitudes, conditioned responses." The Red Gods had somehow found a fissure in the keep-your-distance carapace through which Suydam Cutting viewed the less privileged.

His association with the Roosevelts was a lifelong asset. The tradi-tional rulers of Central Asia could not make out the American polit-ical system. When the first Roosevelt expedition reached Yarkand in July 1925, a British consular officer noted in his confidential monthly cable that the "local Begs have been somewhat puzzled as to who the party really are but seem to have decided that they are four sons of the King of America." (The fourth in the party was the naturalist George K. Cherrie.) In China, the Roosevelts showed local officials an official letter of introduction from the Field Mu-seum, on stationery depicting its immense colonnaded edifice—which the Chinese assumed was the Roosevelt palace.

Cutting took practical advantage of the confusion. In 1928 he and the Roosevelts approached Lhasa for permission to cross the Tibetan frontier. At the time the country was closed to foreigners, save for limited access rights gained by the British. Nonetheless the permit was granted. As Cutting later recalled, "the significance of this con-tact was enormous. It was the opening wedge."

In widening that wedge, Cutting became Tibet's unofficial go-between with the United States, its liaison with the Franklin Roo-sevelt Administration, and its unpaid agent for the sale of Tibetan wool. He was responsible in 1948 for bringing a Tibetan trade dele-gation to the United States—reputedly the first Tibetans to reach the New World—and proudly escorted the four delegates to the Newark Museum, whose outstanding Tibetan collection he and his wife Helen helped to create. Gathered there along with sacred art and fine photographs is the extensive correspondence between two Dalai Lamas and "the American Sahib Cutting."

Yet during World War I, Cutting was an intelligence officer in the U.S. Army. He befriended British officials concerned with Tibet, and opened the way during World War II for a top-secret American mis-sion from India to Lhasa. Sifting through his papers, one senses that his

Tibetan forays were to him like court tennis—a rarefied competition whose pleasures were the keener since the audience was select. On his Asian travels, typically, he taught remote tribal peoples the Porcellian song, informing them this was the American anthem, an insider joke likely to baffle future visitors unless they also were "Porkers." (Cutting, Kermit, and Ted all belonged to Harvard's most exclusive social club. Franklin Roosevelt's failure to be elected, he told friends fifteen years later, was "the greatest disappointment of my life.")

CUTTING STALKED TIBET WITH THE SAME PERSEVERANCE, THE same alertness to shifting winds, that accounted for his success as a hunter. Acting on the advice of Colonel F. M. Bailey, the British political officer in Sikkim, Cutting requested and got permission in 1930 to visit Gyantse, about a hundred miles inside Tibet. He then sent a letter in Tibetan to the Thirteenth Dalai Lama, accompanied by a presentation scarf, asking if he might venture further. Gifts were strategically bestowed—Hammacher Schlemmer aluminum ware to border officials, a cuckoo clock to the Governor of Gyantse, and self-winding wristwatches to members of the Kashag, the high council in Lhasa. The Dalai Lama's presents, he later wrote, "naturally, had to be chosen with especial care." He heard that His Holiness loved animals and wanted an ostrich, though Bailey doubted the creature could survive the rigors of the Tibetan plateau. "Hoping to provide something equally amusing," Cutting informs us, "I sent the Dalai Lama a pair of dachshunds. A week went by and then a telegram came from him which showed that some interest was being taken in the animals. He asked what their names were."

This was followed a week later by a message barring a visit to Lhasa but granting Cutting's caravan permission to travel as far as the town of Khampa Dzong. There Cutting was welcomed by the local governor, "the deserving recipient of my last remaining cuckoo clock." More important, the dachshunds initiated an extended correspondence between Tibet's Great Lama and Cutting, involving imaginative gift-giving, novel requests, and a degree of dissembling on the latter's part. "I always made it a point to write to the Dalai Lama every time I could on imposing stationery," Cutting candidly related. "The Dalai Lama knew that the Viceroy of India strongly backed my purpose to visit Lhasa, but the mere fact of my knowing him counted, too. So I was careful to write to Lhasa on the note paper of the Viceroy, also on that of the [Indian] Commander-in-chief, whom fortunately I also knew—never on hotel paper."

Sensing that Cutting might serve as a useful go-between, the Dalai Lama asked if there was an American market for Tibetan wool (there was, for automobile carpets), and whether Cutting as a goodwill gesture might pass along letters to the State Department. Cutting did, sending back a framed photograph of President Hoover and a note on the letterhead of the U.S. Congress. The Dalai Lama also wished to know whether Congress could be induced to buy silver and send it to Tibet in bond, and thereby avoid the Indian export tax (Cutting regrettably concluded the scheme was "decidedly impractical").

All the while the Yankee cornucopia seemed bottomless. Cutting presented the Dalai Lama with a pair of Dalmatians; with books on American architecture and a chair with a folding canopy; with an ornamental glass bowl, a silver-plated polar bear on agate, and more curiously, a long glass cocktail shaker (it would never serve His Holiness in the ordinary manner, Cutting felt, but "would be useful for mixing his buttered tea"). For his part, the Dalai Lama presented Cutting with three pairs of Lhasa Apsos, the hardy mountain dogs known for their intelligence, keen hearing, and long, luxurious coats. In Lhasa, white was the preferred color for the "Bark Lion Sentinel Dog," whose noble owners customarily pierced and threaded one ear. From 1933, the pairs multiplied at the Cutting country home in New Jersey, thus introducing a new breed to the United States. By the 1960's, the American Kennel Club ranked the Apso twenty-fifth out of the 118 breeds on the club's registration list, just ahead of the boxer.

CUTTING'S ATTEMPTS TO WIN GREATER POLITICAL RECOGNITION for Tibet were less successful. By 1933, Franklin Roosevelt, also a friend and schoolmate of Cutting's, became President, the same year that a radiogram from Lhasa informed Cutting that the Thirteenth Dalai Lama had "temporarily passed away." Assuming, prematurely it transpired, that a Fourteenth Dalai Lama had already been identified, Cutting and Kermit Roosevelt jointly wrote to the White House in January 1934 urging that some kind of message be sent. Their letters passed to the State Department, prompting a response from Under Secretary William Phillips, who also erroneously assumed that a new Incarnation had been located:

> I am inclined to think that it would be better not to send a message to the Dalai Lama for the following reasons: The present Dalai Lama is an infant; his government, however, is noted for intrigue and it is hard to tell what use might be made of your personal communication. The Dalai Lama is, theoretically at least, subject to Chinese sovereignty and it is not impossible that your action might be misrepresented and misunderstood in China; the British have a special position in Tibetan affairs; the Soviet Government is full of suspicion in anything going on in Tibet and as for the Japanese, they might claim that such direct communication with a func-tionary over whom the Chinese claim sovereignty is some-what inconsistent with the non-recognition of Pu-yi as sovereign of Manchukuo. And then there is another person, known as Panchen Lama, who we believe is contesting the selection of the present Dalai Lama and he in turn might complain of interference in Tibetan politics. I admit that there are a good many "mights" in my reasoning, but frankly I do not see that anything could be accomplished by a per-sonal letter to this infant in arms.

Phillips prevailed. His note, with its cautious deference to Chinese sensibilities, expressed the State Department's long-standing wariness about Tibet. Yet the Dalai Lama's intuition about Cutting was sound. As a well-connected "Grottie," he did enjoy special access to the President and to an influential brotherhood. Situated thirty miles north of Boston, Groton was meant to reproduce the Tom Brown tone of British public schools, with its mix of robust piety, fiercely contested games, and noblesse oblige. Not only did Groton educate the brighter sons of America's social and business elite, but its remarkable Rector, Endicott Peabody, in a tenure lasting fifty-six years until his retirement in 1940, loomed indelibly in the memories of graduates. It was Peabody's custom to send all Grotonians a handwritten birthday card every year. "If you had not sent me a birthday card I should really have been worried!" the President wrote him in 1936. "Do you know that I have every one of them that you sent me since the earliest days after I graduated?"

"If some Groton boys do not enter political life and do something for our land," Peabody remarked, "it won't be because they have not been urged." The Rector's hopes were personified by Theodore Roosevelt, a favorite chapel speaker. All four of TR's sons entered Groton's red brick buildings, and while President in 1904, Roosevelt took time to exhort a graduating class, "Much has been given you, therefore we have a right to expect much from you." Among the Grotonians in FDR's Administration so motivated were Dean Acheson, Francis Biddle, Sumner Welles, Joseph Grew, and Averell Harriman.

Cutting was part of another influential network. In 1927, he joined with TR's sons and Vincent Astor in establishing an informal roundtable known simply as "The Room," which convened monthly in a Manhattan apartment at 34 East Sixty-second Street. The Room was an unofficial intelligence network, drawing on the knowledge and contacts of its wealthy and well-connected members, nearly all of whom had strong ties to England based on family, schools, and military service.

Astor set the pace. The scion of the American branch of an Anglo-American dynasty, he was not yet twenty-one when he inherited $70 million following his father's death on the *Titanic*. Undeterred by that maritime disaster, Vincent became an avid seaman. His yacht *Nourmahal* was in a class by itself (in Cutting's words) "for efficiency, comfort, and luxury." Astor was linked by ancestral marriages to the Hyde Park Roosevelts, and "Cousin Franklin" was both a periodic passenger and a grateful consumer of strategic intelligence gleaned during *Nourmahal's* voyages (she was equipped with a Radio Direction Finder to pinpoint military stations on far-flung Pacific islands).

Yet "VA" was reclusive, at times taciturn. What lent spontaneous warmth to The Room were the Roosevelt brothers, impulsive, exuberant, and fearless. Kermit was the troubled paragon. He was the second of five children, his mother's favorite, and the closest to Cousin Franklin. While a Harvard undergraduate, Kermit was the photographer on TR's African safari, then joined his father's 1913 Amazonian expedition. After the outbreak of World War I, he enlisted in the British Army, fought in Mesopotamia (winning a Distinguished Service Cross), then joined the U.S. Army as a field artillery captain. He founded with his brother the Roosevelt Shipping Company, from which the two played truant on three Asian expeditions. Kermit was the family linguist, speaking (among others) Swahili, Hindi, and Urdu. In his forties he so outclimbed Chinese bearers in the Tian Shan Mountains that they insisted on an extra day's rest for every day with him. Early in World War II, he rejoined the British Army as a major, was wounded in 1940 at Narvik in Norway, and returned to America with disabling dysentery. Nonetheless, Kermit coaxed a major's commission from FDR. Posted as an intelligence officer in Alaska, he helped clear the Aleutians of a Japanese garrison, then succumbed to depression and drink. In 1943, he ended his life with a revolver. He was fifty-three.

Theodore Roosevelt, the oldest of the siblings, served as did his father as an Assistant Secretary of the Navy, and like him sought election as Governor of New York (he was beaten in 1924 by Al Smith). Twice wounded as an Army captain in World War I, and a founder of the American Legion, he nevertheless broke ranks as a Republican state legislator to oppose expulsion of Socialist assemblymen during the postwar Red Scare. Ted disapproved of FDR's New Deal, but not his interventionist foreign policy. In 1941, he rejoined the army as a brigadier general, fought in Tunisia and Italy, and was the only general in the first wave at Normandy in June 1944. He died a month later of a heart attack while on duty as military governor of Cherbourg. He was fifty-six.

The Room's other members included two future ambassadors to Britain, David Bruce and Winthrop Aldrich; and the English-educated Chicago millionaire, Marshall Field III. Among British "associates" was Sir William Wiseman, a bluff, round-faced baronet, formerly chief-of-station of British intelligence in New York. His tweedy fox-hunting mien cloaked a fine conspiratorial mind, and he helped break in the Canadian-born Royal Flying Corps ace and entrepreneur Sir William Stephenson ("Intrepid"), who took over as American station chief in 1940, with the mission of bringing neutral America into the war.

In those years, the Anglo-American "special relationship" was not an empty platitude. To Americans of Cutting's caste, the sense of a common destiny was real, and had deep roots. It was accepted wisdom that the Anglo-Saxons carried the seeds of democracy from the black forests of Germany to the British isles, and then to America. Suydam Cutting was steeped in this ethos, and was virtually a one-man English-Speaking Union, as well as a fellow of the Royal Geographical Society and the Royal Central Asian Society, member of the Himalayan Cub, and as an Honorary Commander of the Most Excellent Order of the British Empire. Friends recall that the Cuttings on their travels always carried a framed picture of the King and Queen of England, a practice that cannot have hurt as Cutting sought British support for his Tibetan campaign.

THAT CAMPAIGN RESUMED IN 1934, WHEN HE AGAIN JOINED WITH Kermit and Ted Roosevelt in proposing an expedition through Tibet, including a visit to Lhasa, to collect larger mammals, such as bear, sheep, and antelope. Cutting assured the Tibetans that he understood hunting was contrary to their law, but hoped an exception might be made for the sake of science. In Lhasa, the Kashag held firm, and the project was dropped. Cutting now found a new partner, the British hunter Arthur Vernay, who wintered in the Bahamas and was also a trustee of the American Museum of Natural History. They put forward a new proposal: a botanical and ethnographic expedition, sans hunting. The American Government formally endorsed Cutting's appeal—a notch upward—and negotiations were pressed at the frontier post of Kalimpong by none other than David Macdonald, now retired as a British trade agent. Permission was duly granted to visit Shigatse, second in size to Lhasa, Cutting wrote, "but we hoped that once we reached this sacred city we might be allowed to proceed to Lhasa."

Crowds cheered the arrival of Cutting and Vernay in Shigatse, where commodious quarters were provided by the nephew of the Panchen Lama (still living in Chinese exile). A round of official receptions was followed by "truly delightful" outdoor picnics in the parks of the Panchen Lama's summer palace, by a military parade and by an assembly of the 3,500 monks in maroon robes and yellow hats. Nevertheless, the pair waited in vain for permission to continue to Lhasa. Abandoning hope, Cutting and Vernay returned to Calcutta, and there the precious passport materialized.

The exultant explorers prepared an itinerary that would assure their arrival in Lhasa on an auspicious day. Their progress was smoothed by a "red arrow letter" that preceded their caravan by a day or two, giving villagers time to gather provisions. So it was in early October 1935 that Suydam Cutting became the first American to be welcomed in what was still mythologized as the "Forbidden City." Through craft and diplomacy, Cutting wrested the prize that eluded more ardent suitors.

Guides escorted his caravan through broad streets to a small house with a stable set in a walled garden with allées of poplars and willows, near Norbu Lingka, the summer residence of the Dalai Lamas. Here Cutting and Vernay stayed for ten days and met with members of the Kashag, each encounter involving an elaborate preentation of gifts. Cutting reckoned Lhasa's population at 40,000 inhabitants, more than a third of whom were lamas and monks, the dominant force in what he perceived as a "priest-ridden" society.

This was among the few negative words in his 1936 account in the monthly journal of the American Museum of Natural History. Indeed his placid narrative gave no hint of the drama he had witnessed. After the Thirteenth Dalai Lama passed on, Lhasa worriedly let Peking send a condolence mission, the first such high-level visit since the Chinese were driven from Tibet in 1912. The mission was led by a general, Huang Mu-sung, and its real purpose soon became apparent: to restore Tibet to its former vassalage.

Huang's terms were hard: China would cede to Tibet contested territory in the east, but only if Tibet acknowledged it was an integral part of China, put its army under Chinese command, and shunned all "foreign" (meaning British) interference. Tibetans were willing to accept China as a suzerain but refused to surrender the autonomy they had enjoyed for twenty-two years. No agreement was possible, but Huang, a lavish gift-giver who courted clerical opponents of modernization, secured a diplomatic coup. He left behind two "liaison officers" and a wireless transmitter, restoring a permanent Chinese presence for the first time since 1912. Chinese press accounts trumpeted the development, and Huang was rewarded with a new job as director of China's Office of Mongolian and Tibetan Affairs.

All this was noted with dismay by British officials in Delhi, who lamented the indifference in London to these developments. No doubt there were credible reasons for this apathy (as Sir Aubrey Metcalfe, the Indian Foreign Secretary, noted in a minute) given Britain's commercial interests in China proper and British reluctance to incur any suspicion of trying to detach Tibet from China, as Japan had detached Manchuria. In that case, what could be done to enhance British influence in Lhasa, buttress Tibetan autonomy, and keep China from making trouble on the Indian frontier?

The question was put to the political officer in Sikkim, Frederick Williamson, who was currently involved in the frustrating negotiations concerning the return of the Panchen Lama—a major obstacle being His Serenity's wish to come back with an armed Chinese escort. Williamson felt "very strongly" that "we must under all circumstances continue to deal with Tibet as a completely autonomous country" and should not enter into any negotiations with China about Tibet unless Lhasa was a party on equal terms. "The present situation is critical," Williamson wrote in January 1935. "We have for years encouraged Tibet to rely on us, but we cannot give her the one thing she really wants, a guarantee of protection on her Eastern frontier . . . We should, I think, do what little we can. Our intentions are honest enough. We merely want her to be completely independent in substance even if she is merely 'autonomous' in name."

The British Indian Foreign Secretary concurred, as did his energetic deputy and eventual successor, Olaf Caroe, who suspected Russian machinations throughout Asia. In Sinkiang, for example, he viewed the recent restoration of Chinese control as a cloak for the establishment "of a Russian political supremacy not unlike that attained by the Japanese in Manchuria." Still worse, he reported to the Secretary of State for India, the Earl of Ronaldshay, that the Soviets were working with Chinese Communists near the Tibetan border. Therefore, Caroe believed, an autonomous Tibet, "ruled on theocratic lines, is likely to be a stronger guarantee against a Soviet advance to the borders of India than any resumption of effective Chinese control in Tibet."

Caroe's memorandum was dated June 28, 1935, the same month that Williamson and his wife, Margaret, along with a dozen aides and forty servants, arrived on a special mission in Lhasa. Williamson was instructed to encourage Tibetan resistance to Chinese demands, with a big "but" imposed by London—nothing specific was to be promised, and nothing was to be in writing. Adding to his difficulties was the absence from Lhasa of the Regent, the interim chief of state, who was elsewhere searching for the reborn Dalai Lama. The Britons marked time with cinema shows (Charlie Chaplin, King George V's Silver Jubilee, the Hendon Air Display), the usual round of visits, and dining with the Chinese mission (a twenty-eight-course lunch, marred by Mrs. Williamson's suspicion that their hosts were trying to poison her husband "in the most sinister Fu Manchu style").

In October, still waiting for the Regent, the couple entertained Suydam Cutting and Arthur Vernay. Days later, Williamson became violently ill. The cause was not poison but uremia, a chronic kidney condition that had been diagnosed just before his departure for Lhasa. A frantic Mrs. Williamson telegraphed the family physician in Gangtok, who replied he was on his way. When the Royal Air Force offered to fly her husband to Caluctta for treatment, Williamson's deputy located a landing field near Sera Monastery. The Kashag, however, ruled out an air rescue as likely to disturb the spirits or to provoke riots by monks. Moreover, permitting a British landing would make it harder for Lhasa to resist Chinese pressure for air service. On November 17, before his physician arrived, Williamson died. He was interred at Gyantse in a small cemetery near the British mission. It was not an episode that inspired confidence in the theocratic state Caroe believed capable of resisting Russian or Chinese aggression.

NO SOONER HAD CUTTING RETURNED TO AMERICA THAN HE began proposing a second trip to Lhasa, this time with his wife Helen. By this time the wool sales he promoted were Tibet's principal source of hard currency. Monks might scorn air-machines, but others in Lhasa realized Tibet needed foreign help during a vulnerable interregnum. Cutting by now had befriended every British Tibetan hand, notably Francis Younghusband and F. M. Bailey; the great plant hunter F. Kingdon Ward; and Frederick O'Connor, chief interpreter for the Younghusband expedition in 1904–05. On his way back to America in 1935, Cutting paused in London to visit R. A. (Rab) Butler, the Under Secretary at the India Office, with O'Connor as his escort. These contacts may explain his OBE. As a Briton whose family moved in the same stratum remarked to the authors, "We do not throw honors at American cousins for nothing."

Cutting's new status was confirmed when the Kashag not only issued a second invitation for 1937 but more surprisingly, extended it to Helen McMahon Cutting, the first American woman so honored. Hearing the news prompted a letter from President Franklin Roosevelt: "I find a note from Helen on my return telling me of your trip to Tibet. I wish I could go with you! While I cannot properly give you any official letter to the authorities in Tibet, I can at least wish you a most successful trip—and I hope much to hear all about it on your return."

There followed an elaborate pas de trois between the White House, the State Department, and the Cuttings concerning what they might bring to Lhasa. Cutting proposed a signed photograph of the President. The State Department objected that Tibet was "still technically under the suzerainty of China," whose leaders might misconstrue the gesture. FDR compromised by sending a photograph to the Cuttings, inscribed personally to them. A direct letter to the Tibetan Government was "impossible," the President reported a few days later, but a message from Under Secretary of State Sumner Welles, addressed to diplomats posted in Asia, "might be of some use."

However disappointing to Cutting, the compensation was the trip itself. With Helen's personal maid Nakkim (recommended by the Baileys) added to the usual caravan, the Cuttings made their way from Gangtok through jungles infested with leeches and over knife-like passes. He possessed a good eye for floral detail—gigantic hy-drangeas, masses of azaleas, orchids and irises, tiny begonias, large-leafed rhubarbs, a fine welter of pink daphnies, dark asters with brown centers, tall yellow primulas, a pink myosotis, clumps of monkshood, and dazzling white everlastings, "a ravishing *mille fleurs* carpet." In his travel reminiscences, *The Fire Ox and Other Years* (1940), Cutting engagingly notes the virtues of the yak as an equable provider of wool and its defects as a pack-animal: "He can scarcely cover two miles an hour, and nine miles a day is usually his limit. In marching he groans every step of the way, well deserving his latin name of *Bos grunniens.*"

In 1937, the Fire Ox Year, Lhasa basked in a late afternoon calm, untouched by the storms in the world beyond. The holy city had three motorcars—two Austins and a Dodge—but as the Cuttings discovered, they were inoperable. Its garrison of a thousand soldiers drilled smartly for the couple, but the vital mountain guns were ev-idently no longer usable. Yutuk Depön, the army's young comman-der, the scion of a leading noble family, told the Cuttings he was studying French and English and showed them his battered manuals. "Amused, my wife asked how it was possible to study foreign lan-guages without a Tibetan key. Yutuk acknowledged the point with a burst of laughter and changed the subject." The Chinese threat had abated, and the modernizing faction once favored by the Thirteenth Dalai Lama seemed resigned to defeat. The reform-minded Tsarong, no longer a shapé on the Kashag but still an official host to Western visitors, prepared a five-day fête for the Cuttings, with picnics, open-air theatricals, mah-jongg tournaments, and lavishly garbed "chung girls" who plied guests with chung, a thickish beverage resembling beer.

For the Cuttings, Lhasa was a charming curiosity, an escapist paradise akin in spirit to James Hilton's *Lost Horizon*, which had recently made its debut as a Frank Capra film. But Hilton's lamas showed more realism than their Lhasan counterparts. While they took care to conceal their paradise from all prying eyes, they did not shun Western science, and they employed an airplane to bring Hugh Conway to Shangri-La.

THE AMERICA TO WHICH THE CUTTINGS RETURNED IN 1937 WAS caught up in the domestic ferment of the New Deal and unprepared for the looming global crisis. In Asia as in Europe, the initiative seemed to lie with the dictators, brown and red, as democracies experienced a collective loss of nerve. What Auden called the "low dishonest decade" was as baffling to putative leaders as to ordinary people. In search of more light, FDR put together an informal spy service to supplement diplomatic reports and military intelligence, whose limitations he learned as an Assistant Secretary of the Navy during World War I. Among the President's "special agents" were William Bullitt, the first American Ambassador to the Soviet Union and a friend since the Wilson years; and Vincent Astor, his boyhood chum and Dutchess County neighbor. It was scarcely adequate, and Astor, for one, became an early advocate of a national intelligence organization.

The matter became pressing after the outbreak of war in September 1939 and the fall of France the following June. Britain now stood alone against Nazi-occupied Europe. The Room's members all rallied to the British cause. Suydam Cutting headed an American Committee for the Defense of British Homes to supply weapons for civil defense, one of many such groups that sprang up almost overnight. More durable were the ties forged with British intelligence services. The catalyst was the arrival in New York of Sir William Stephenson in May 1940 as station chief for British intelligence with a direct line to Winston Churchill.

Stephenson acquired an entire floor (rent free) in Rockefeller Center as headquarters for British Security Cooordination, or BSC, the hub for all American operations. It was Stephenson who spotted the promise of William J. Donovan, an Irish-American Catholic Republican lawyer, born in Buffalo, the son and grandson of Irish republicans. In World War I, Donovan commanded the Fighting Sixty-ninth, mostly consisting of Irish-Americans, and his valor won him the Congressional Medal of Honor, and the nickname "Wild Bill." Franklin Roosevelt knew and liked him, though Donovan was no admirer of the New Deal. ("Now, Bill, we haven't been that far apart," Roosevelt once said soothingly. "But oh, yes, we have," responded Donovan.)

In a meeting at Hyde Park, arranged by Vincent Astor, Roosevelt heard and liked Stephenson's proposal of sending Donovan on a special mission to see whether Britain was on the verge of defeat—as another wealthy Irish-American, Ambassador Joseph Kennedy, informed all who would listen. On July 14, 1940, Donovan boarded a Pan-American Clipper flight to London. Four days later, he met Sir Stewart Menzies, chief of the Secret Intelligence Service (SIS). Back in America, it was Donovan's turn to tell all who would listen that the British would fight to the end. Together with Stephenson (by now "Big Bill" and "Little Bill"), Donovan helped make the legal and political case for the swap of fifty obsolete U.S. destroyers for ninety-nine-year leases on bases in Canada and the British West Indies.

Donovan's mission was a success in another sense. He and Menzies, known in Whitehall only as "C," found they could trust each other, despite their differences. As Anthony Cave Brown, the biographer of both men, writes, it was an improbable match: "On the one hand there was Stewart Menzies, Eton, Life Guards, GHQ, secret service, White's, Beaufort Hunt, praetorian spymaster, defender of the established order, Protestant, a descendant of the caste held responsible by the Irish for the production of the Celtic twilight." On the other was Donovan, the offspring of Irish revolutionaries, "Silver-haired, silver-tongued, silver-suited, silver-mannered . . . a great example of the American meritocrat of the twenties and thirties, the hired gun of the oil and movie companies."

In July 1941, Donovan left his law practice to direct the Office of the Coordinator of Information, out of which grew the OSS. Fittingly, with the advice of Suydam Cutting, one of the new service's more daring missions would lead to the first direct contact between the American and Tibetan governments.

∴

CHAPTER TWENTY-ONE

Swastikas to Lhasa

NOTHING WAS MORE TEMPTING TO THE SWEDISH EXPLORER
Sven Hedin than the promise of a red carpet. He proved a
ready catch for Adolf Hitler, who baited the way in 1933, his first
year as Chancellor, with a telegram congratulating Hedin on the for-
tieth anniversary of his first expedition to Central Asia. Hedin's sev-
entieth birthday prompted a second telegram, leading to the first of
four meetings with the Führer that Hedin later described in a curious and obscure book, published only in Dublin in 1951, as *Sven
Hedin's German Diary, 1935–1942.* It seemed a natural match. The
explorer was assumed to be Nordic, was known as an ardent Ger-
manophile, and embodied the Nietzschean longing for a heroic master race. But something else made the attraction mutual. Hedin and
the Nazis shared a fascination with Tibet, the supposed cradle of the
soi-disant Aryan race.

A distinguished procession of Germans had taken special interest
in Central Asia, beginning with Alexander von Humboldt, a founder
of modern geographic science and author of *Zentralasien* (1843). He
was followed by the pioneering geographer Carl Ritter; by Hedin's

own teacher, Ferdinand von Richthofen; by Wilhelm Filchner, the Bavarian explorer who headed three expeditions to Tibet (1903–4, 1926–28, 1935–37); and by Karl Haushofer, the geopolitician, whose belief that Germany's destiny lay to the East became a vital ingredient of Hitlerism. But among Nazis like Himmler this fascination was not just strategic and geographic; it was racial.

The idea that the high civilizations of East and West might have a common origin dates back to the first excited Western discovery of Hinduism and its scriptures. The pioneering English authority on Sanskrit, Sir William Jones, divined a connection between the high civilizations of ancient India, Egypt, Greece, and Italy but would not speculate which was the original, which the copy. It was the German scholar, Friedrich Schlegel, who in 1808 proclaimed that Sanskrit was the linguistic godparent of German, Greek, and Latin, and that Aryan tribes had somehow migrated to northern Europe. Such was the seed of a racist doctrine that, when nurtured and fertilized by the moist winds of romantic nationalism, sprang up, like the dragon's teeth sowed by Cadmus, as the armed soldiers that were to devastate Europe.

Schlegel's thesis was given an imperial Oxonian gloss by the German-born Friedrich Max Müller (1823–1900), a Fellow of All Souls and Boden Professor of Comparative Philology. He enthusiastically contended that Anglo-Saxons, Teutons, and Indians all belonged to the same "Aryan race," signifying that British rule in India was a "gathering in," a kind of family reunion. By the time Hitler seized power, these racial theories, by now reinforced by the eccentric French aristocrat, Comte de Gobineau, the Englishman Houston Stewart Chamberlain, and by several generations of Germanic academics, had become a devil's broth. Aryans had once ruled the earth but had lost their position due to the poisoning of their blood and souls by miscegenation with Jews and other "racial inferiors." (*Aryan* is a Sanskrit word connoting *noble*.)

Occultism was also added to this lethal brew. Madame Blavatsky believed that the Aryans were the fifth root race evolved from the subrace of Atlanteans who inhabited the sunken continent, a people whose secrets were in hidden Himalayan monasteries and whose symbol was the swastika, which she used as the seal of the Theosophical Society. Going further, the Austrian engineer, "the German Copernicus," Hans Hörbiger put forward the World Ice Theory (*Welteislehre*), which posited that Nordic ancestors, a race of supermen, had grown powerful in a land of ice and snow. Into this was mixed Edward Bulwer-Lytton's *vril*, a telepathic power held by a super-race, and the antirational *völkisch* philosophy and runic symbols of the Austrian Guido von List. Finally, there was the Thule Society, whose lodge members avowed anti-Semitism, believed in militant action, and maintained close ties with the incipient Nazi party. (Thule, putative cradle of the German race, was supposedly a vanished island, similar to Atlantis but in the extreme north.) Under the Nazis, a great deal of time and money—more, it has been reckoned, than was spent on building the German atomic bomb—was devoted to reconciling these various claims. To the Nazis, these beliefs were not just ethnic chauvinism but scientific facts, consistent with Darwinism and borne out by linguistics and skull measurements, and by the studies of geographers and scholars of international repute. Like Sven Hedin.

In 1936, Hedin returned to Berlin, this time to deliver the opening address at the Nazi Olympics. His "Call to the Youth of the World" delighted the crowd and Hitler, who invited Hedin to his box at the revamped Olympic Stadium. Not surprisingly, Hedin was taken up by Dr. Joseph Goebbels, whom the Swede found interesting and likable, remarking on his "intelligent conversation and the melancholy expression of his lively, keen eyes." Less expected was an invitation, apparently in March 1940, to meet Reichsführer Heinrich Himmler, supreme chief of the SS (Schutzstaffeln).

In his *German Diary*, Hedin describes the Reichsführer's office at Gestapo headquarters on Prinz-Albrecht-Strasse, the most dreaded address in Germany. Its fittings and Himmler's surroundings were "simple and unassuming," striking the visitor as "old-fashioned and makeshift." As for the Reichsführer, his face was "everyday, commonplace, uninteresting." But perhaps, Hedin adds, his outward insignificance was a mask, since women insisted "he was a charmer whom no one could help but love and admire."

Himmler opened the meeting by telling Hedin of a recent trip to Tibet by his protégé, Dr. Ernst Schäfer, of the Ahnenerbe, the SS's "Ancestral Heritage" office. Schäfer was no stranger to Hedin, but the Swede was impressed that the Reichsführer "took such a keen and enlightened interest in the snow-lands north of the Himalayas." Schäfer was the key figure in Nazi overtures to Tibet. This SS officer took part in three expeditions to Tibet, had tried to adopt his Nepalese translator, was once stoned by monks in Lhasa, and had precipitated a diplomatic furor that reached from Berlin to Simla.

At Himmler's orders, the Ahnenerbe was founded in 1935, with all the outward trappings of a scholarly institute, to buttress Hitler's racial ideologies. A number of quacks were associated with it, including some who believed in the Atlantis theory that Tibet was the last refuge of "the Aryan root race" with a priestly caste that ruled an underground realm (even Shambhala was mentioned). But its offices also became a magnet for not a few ambitious young scientists— most of them thirty-year-olds unwilling to wait long years in the wings before being endowed with professorships and institutes.

To his postwar American interrogators, Schäfer volunteered that Himmler "had very strange views. He thought that the Nordic race had come directly from heaven." Of his colleagues in the Ahnenerbe, Schäfer had this to say: "They all believed in the glacial theory of cosmogony. Naturally, this was all completely unscientific. But the gentlemen had not read any other books. It was such a mad business, it's hard to believe. They all tended toward the occult."

Initially, the Ahnenerbe carried out archaeological digs in East Prussia and Bavaria and then extended its work to areas conquered by the Germans, the idea being, according to Bettina Arnold, "to restore real and imagined Germanic cultural relics." (The Steven Spielberg film *Raiders of the Lost Ark* was inspired by these activities.) In its final days, Ahnenerbe "scientists" conducted experiments on Jews and other minorities including, in the case of Schäfer's own staff, Soviet Central Asians, transported from prisoner-of-war camps.

The son of an influential Hamburg industrialist, Schäfer trained as a zoologist at Göttingen. While still in his early twenties, he had twice accompanied the American naturalist Brooke Dolan on Tibetan expeditions sponsored by the Academy of Sciences in Philadelphia (see Chapter 22). He was an avid hunter and exceptional marksman, and his devotion to ornithology did not inhibit his zeal for bagging birds, an inclination that often got him into trouble in Buddhist countries through which he passed. Overweeningly ambitious, he was an eager and early recruit to the SS. He later insisted to the Americans that he joined only at the instigation of Himmler after returning from the United States in 1936, but his captured personnel files confirm that he had applied for membership in 1933, immediately after Hitler came to power. In the India Office's Political and Secret files, Sir Basil Gould, who met Schäfer on his way to Lhasa in 1938, summed him up as "interesting, forceful, volatile, scholarly, vain to the point of childishness, disregardful of social convention or the feelings of others, and first and foremost always a Nazi and a politician . . ." The hysteria which he frequently displayed, Gould charitably added, "was doubtless a result of living for some months at high altitude."

Schäfer had no particular interest in the occult but he was most eager to lead another expedition to Tibet, one that would carry out his own mission of exploring Tibet as a refuge of "syncretic science," which presumed Tibet's environment as a kind of "cradle of mankind," a repository of long-extinct wildlife. According to the German scholar Reinhardt Greve, Schäfer saw himself as not only an SS pioneer and adventurer but also a "prophet of objective science," and "the bearer of the core of German manhood," who must erase the last blank spots from the maps.

Although he financed the expedition himself, raising money from German industrialists and the Nazi Party newspaper—for old times' sake, Brooke Dolan proffered an additional $1,000*—Himmler be-

---

*This is the figure Schäfer quoted to the Americans. He later told Greve that the figure was $4,000.

came his official patron, providing the team with special access to foreign currency and medical supplies. Although Schäfer would allege that the Ahnenerbe had nothing to do with the expedition, one needs only to translate the letterhead—"Ernst Schäfer's German Tibet Expedition in Connection with the Ahnenerbe"—or the photograph taken at dinner in Lhasa showing the Germans and Tibetan nobles under the SS banner, to conclude that this was a wholly SS operation.

In March 1938, Schäfer traveled to London to obtain permission to enter Tibet by way of Assam. He was turned down by the Foreign Office, for reasons of "tribal unrest." Schäfer was told to apply first to Tibetan authorities ("our normal way"), in the secure knowledge that the Tibetans would not assent unless strongly backed by the British. The Tibetan Government's negative reply reached London in May. Meanwhile in April, the British Ambassador in Berlin alerted the Foreign Office to German press reports, written as the team was about to embark from Genoa on the *Gneisenau*, that the expedition was under Himmler's patronage, that all its members were SS men, and that its work "will be carried through entirely on SS principles." Nevertheless, this being the high season of appeasement, a chorus of influential Britons pressed the Viceroy in India, Lord Linlithgow, to let the Germans in. Asian hands Sir Francis Younghusband and Colonel Bailey wrote letters, Lord Astor of Cliveden vouched for Schäfer's bona fides, and Admiral Sir Barry Domvile weighed in from "The Link," Sentinel House, Southampton Row, on May 30 with a letter to Neville Chamberlain explaining that "Herr Himmler, the Head of the German Secret Service," had established an exploration society called the Ahnenerbe that has "no political connections whatsoever and deals only with History, Folklore, Biology, the Ice Age and Natural History." The Admiral enclosed a letter he had gotten from Himmler, and asked the Prime Minister's advice on how to reply. The Reichsführer wrote, as translated:

> You know yourself that up to now my attitude towards every Englishman who has come to Germany has been entirely friendly. For that reason I am the more astonished that the English should treat one of my men in a brusque,

wounding and unfriendly way. I cannot imagine the authorities are so stupid as to see in the scientist Dr. Schäfer, officially dispatched by me, a spy. For the English Secret Service
cannot believe me to be so stupid as to dispatch such a man
officially and under my name if I really was engaged in espionage...You can imagine that this kind of treatment has
upset me personally very much and has given rise to the
thought that apart from personal friendship, such as ours,
there is no point in treating British subjects in Germany in a
comradely way, since on the other side such treatment has
not the slightest echo.

This ominous missive passed quickly from Downing Street to the
Foreign Office, whose Political Intelligence Department pressed for
more information from the India Office, generating a thick and fascinating dossier. The internal lobbying was successful. British Indian
authorities found it "politically advisable" to let the Germans enter
Sikkim, the usual gateway to Tibet, and Schäfer was received by the
Viceroy in Simla. Although the head of the British mission in Lhasa,
Hugh Richardson, opposed admitting Schäfer's team, he was overruled by the Viceroy.

It had become clear that Schäfer intended to negotiate an entry to
Tibet on the spot, a fact, as the India Office records show, that enraged his British hosts. This bold plan nevertheless met with success.
Driving by car to Gangtok, Schäfer arrived on May 18 without
warning and immediately requested permission for his team "to
spend six months in Sikkim for the purpose of scientific observations, collecting birds, and making a film of animal life." Sven Hedin
had promised the British not to go beyond Leh but the Swede had
turned and entered Tibet. His example was not lost on Schäfer, who
now plotted a way around his promises to the Viceroy and to Gould
that he would not cross into Tibet. How was he to reach Lhasa without violating his word? How was the German group to obtain "official permission" that the British had denied him? Suddenly, thanks
to their Nepalese translator, Kaiser Bahadur Thapa, Schäfer's "deus ex
machina" in the form of a Tibetan noble, the minister of the Taring
Rajah, arrived at their camp on the Tibetan border. "Mensch,"

Schäfer said, slapping one of his German comrades on the shoulder: the Tibetan striding into camp was his solution.

While the team's ethnologist, Bruno Beger, kept the dignitary busy by measuring and examining him, Schäfer prepared to meet the visitor in his tent. Orchestrating a theatrical performance, Schäfer surrounded himself with impressive artifacts—movie cameras, field glasses, altimeters, telephoto lenses—and an expedition suitcase that served as a desk. Hot tea and cookies were laid out. Amidst the scattered chairs, he was careful to impress the dignitary by amplifying his own height while seated by using an air-filled rubber mattress. "The preparations are finished, the curtain lifts, the play can begin," in Schäfer's own words.

Presents followed and the final act concluded with a letter dictated from the camp—now called grandly Deutschlandhalle—to the "King" of Taring, as the SS Captain always called the Rajah. He considered himself fortunate, Schäfer's message began, on having already visited the great Tibetan monasteries in the eastern province of Kham. Professing a "great interest in Tibetan culture and the religious life of Tibet," he counted the late Panchen Lama as a valued friend. The letter succeeded, and the "King" of Taring summoned the German, who laid on the charm with a trowel, playing up this historic "meeting of Eastern and Western swastikas." Schäfer later claimed it was his shrewd diplomacy that "won the hearts of his hosts and got him permission to enter Lhasa." The "King," a confidant of the Tibetan Regent, wrote to Lhasa in Schäfer's behalf. It was not long before the expedition received the essential invitation, but only on condition that its members promised "not to harm the Tibetan population" and not "to kill any birds or mammals which would offend the religious feelings of the Tibetans."

Returning to Gangtok for new provisions, the mission hired a large yak caravan and advanced on Lhasa, with Schäfer shooting the evening meals and Beger measuring random Tibetans, spending their nights en route in British rest houses. Himmler's letters when they reached Schäfer were encouraging. In one he wrote, "I am glad to hear that you are getting along so splendidly with your English friends. I am sure that this expedition will do a lot for goodwill and mutual understanding." In another, he noted, "What the English call a gentleman, we call an SS-man." Shortly after they crossed into Tibet during December 1938, their shortwave radio crackled with a broadcast of special Christmas greetings from their patron, who was now visiting the Sudetenland.

The monk Mondo (Mödrong), one of four Tibetan youths Sir Basil Gould had escorted to Rugby in 1913, helpfully smoothed their way in Lhasa. They met Tsarong, no longer a Shapé but whom they still found the "most esteemed and respected man in Lhasa." In *Geheimnis Tibet* (Secret Tibet), Schäfer writes that this "iron man" observed all that went before him with "sharp eyes." However, at every point in their stay, difficulties arose: the SS men quarreled with mule drivers, slaughtered wildlife, and took unauthorized photographs during the Monlam Prayer Festival in Lhasa. Monks stoned the Germans, hitting Schäfer on the head and causing the loss of a camera lens and a pair of binoculars, an incident he used to his advantage to obtain permission to visit Shigatse from apologetic Tibetan officials. Hugh Richardson, then the head of the British mission, was able to report that the SS men had created an unfavorable impression in Lhasa, noting with relish that he was able to monitor all mail sent to the Germans, including a message from Himmler to Schäfer with the inked postscript, "I think of you often."

There was enough ill will between the British mission and the Germans to cause the Tibetan Government to separate them. It began with the frosty "Hello" they had received from Richardson as he passed them on the way to Lhasa. The Germans paid him back by trying to embarrass him whenever possible. Schäfer confessed to a British official at Simla that he had expressed his enthusiasm for Hitler partly "to get a rise" out of Richardson, who had annoyed him on more than one occasion. Their spite was returned by the Scottish mission chief, who subjected them to loud radio broadcasts reporting the German invasion of Czechoslovakia as well as anti-Hitler speeches.

Nevertheless, Schäfer reveled in his success. He reported that invitation after invitation arrived from members of the Government. Tibetan authorities extended the expedition's stay from two weeks to two months—to the intense annoyance of the British. The Germans were permitted to visit a fortress in the Yarlung Valley said to be the oldest building in Tibet, which, so Richardson complained, the British had not been able to visit. Schäfer also persuaded the Reting Regent, who pursued the Thirteenth Dalai Lama's policy of looking everywhere for allies, to initiate a correspondence with Hitler. And as Schäfer boasted, his was the first "scientific" expedition to Lhasa that joined specialists from areas such as biology, ornithology, mammalogy, and botany (Schäfer), geology and geophysics (Karl Wienert), entymology (Ernest Krauss), and ethnography, anthropology, and geography (Beger) even though the science was undermined by the Nazi *Weltanschauung* of the participants. If Dr. Schäfer wanted nothing to do with Himmler's crazy ideas, his colleague Beger was prepared to search for skeletal remains of former Nordic invaders and to examine the natives for the remains of Nordic blood among the aristocrats of inner Asia. Krauss, who doubled as the cameraman, succeeded in bringing back film and slides including some rare footage. Schäfer could claim—later disputed—that he had discovered a new large mammal, the Schapi (*Heitrogus jemlaicus schäferi pohle*). The Schäfer expedition, completed just before the war began, would be the only successful expedition associated with the Ahnenerbe.

RETURNING TO BRITISH INDIA, SCHÄFER ENCOUNTERED SIR BASIL Gould, onetime escort of the Rugby boys and now Political Officer in Sikkim. An Asian youth was on Schäfer's mind, his gifted Nepalese translator, Kaiser Bahadur Thapa, who besides Nepali, spoke Sikkimese, English, Hindustani, and some Tibetan. The German wished to adopt him. This did not play well with Gould, who noted that Schäfer's way with employees was "to pay them well, and beat them often." The SS captain addressed Kaiser in a "loud and blustering tone," inclining Gould to believe that "the gentle Kaiser has some sort of special appeal for the dominant Schäfer."

Gould's doubts prompted three letters from Schäfer in May and June of 1939, saying initially that he wanted to train the talented Kaiser as a taxidermist, and moreover he needed the boy for a talking part in an "evening-filling" motion picture. A second letter was more personal: he wished to adopt Kaiser since "I have lost my wife, I also have nobody." (In an apparent hunting accident, the marksman par excellence had shot and killed his bride of ten months shortly before his departure.) The German went on to explain, "what I like to do is simply following the example set by Sven Hedin," who took his "best boy" to Sweden to make him fit "for more successful work." The SS officer also said he feared that Kaiser might be punished for his help in facilitating an "unauthorized expedition into Tibet." Gould was not persuaded. As the Kaiser affair dragged on, the international climate changed. By this time, the Nazis had occupied Prague, violating the promise given by the Führer at Munich and rudely exposing the illusions of appeasement. Kaiser did not return with Schäfer. When the SS team sought to return by way of Nepal, Richardson succeeded in blocking the request, despite a gift of a Zeiss telescope from Hitler to the Nepalese Maharajah.

In a final report to the Government of India, Gould noted that the Germans made themselves highly unpopular by demanding supplies at less than current rates, and by allowing their Sherpa servants to abuse and beat people. He reported that although the Germans engaged in "genuine scientific work," they were doubtless collecting information of military and political use and "the expedition was a political stunt to boost Germany and Nazism. There are also complaints in regard to anthropometrical measurements."

Schäfer returned to Germany a hero. Himmler honored him with the SS Death's Head Ring bearing a skull and crossbones on the outside, the Reichsführer's signature on the inside, and the Ehrendegen, an honorary sword with the runic double lightning bolt, symbol of the SS. This was heady stuff for someone just turned thirty. The young lion was fêted at parties, accompanied Himmler on his special train, the *Heinrich*, through occupied Poland, visited France on a lecture tour, showed his slides to Hitler, and joined as a junior member the exclusive "Circle of Friends" of Himmler that met for dinner every second Wednesday in Berlin. Back in Munich, Sven Hedin added a final laurel, inviting him to Sweden and suggesting he was his heir—"You are the man who should and must continue my research."

The team had collected a number of artifacts including a Kanjur (now in the collection of the Haus der Natur in Salzburg), as well as a teacup with a decoration of precious jewels and a Lhasa apso dog, a present from the Reting Regent to "the King of Germany," Herr Hitler. Himmler raised Schäfer's rank to major and pored over his protégé's notes and films about Tibet, whose racially "pure" inhabitants were extolled by Schäfer as "brave, sturdy and fit." Through a process of Darwinian selection in the harsh climate in which Tibetans struggled to survive, he found, "weak elements" had been "eradicated." But these hearty warriors had nevertheless been "muzzled by the crippling bonds of their pacifistic, Buddhist-Lamaistic religion." The team's ethnologist, Bruno Beger, was less flattering. Although he wrote admiringly of the Lhasa nobles, he had nothing but contempt for the Tibetans in the borderland Gyantse region, where beggars "were of an especially inharmonious racial type."

Other considerations had entered into Himmler's fascination with Tibet. It had long been reported that fabulous gold riches might be found in the Himalayan kingdom, and Schäfer took this up in his talks with Tibetan authorities, who seemed interested in ties with a potentially helpful European state. Schäfer also returned with maps and charts of military value in the event Tibet became a base for guerrilla operations against British India. According to Louis Lochner, the well-connected Associated Press bureau chief in Berlin, this secret warning was circulated to German editors in November 1940: "The Reich Leader SS requests that there be no further reports on his expedition to Tibet until he himself gives the word. The chief task of the Tibet expedition is of a political and military nature, and has little to do with the solution of scientific questions. Details may not be revealed."

TIBET WAS NOT THE SOLE FOCUS OF GERMAN ATTENTION IN Central Asia. From the moment the Nazis seized power in 1933, Hitler's senior military and foreign policy advisers weighed the classic Great Game option of using Afghanistan as a springboard for fomenting tribal revolts on the North-West Frontier of British India. During World War I, the Germans attempted this very strategy in partnership with Ottoman Turkey in a secret campaign well described in Peter Hopkirk's *Like Hidden Fire* (1994). Under the Third Reich, the plan was revived, indeed by some of the same World War I officials, as related in a hard-to-find book published in Germany by the University of Wisconsin scholar Milan Hauner, *India in Axis Strategy* (1981). But as Hauner found, the plans were undone by bitter intramural feuding in German secret services, and more unexpectedly, by Hitler's admiration for the British Empire.

Both the SS and military intelligence spotted likely partners in either the deposed Afghan ruler Amanullah, a secular-minded modernizer, or an Islamic militant Mirza Ali Khan, known as the Faqir of Ipi, a leader of the fierce Waziris. On its face, the German scheme made sense. In April 1938, according to British figures, there were 472,232 fighting men armed with 233,168 breech-loading rifles on both sides of the Durand Line on the North-West Frontier—potentially the largest reservoir of guerrilla fighters in the world. The problem was how to light the match that might ignite a rebellion in India.

Another, more grandiose, plan for "The Encirclement and Submission of World Enemy England by Germany, Italy, Russia, Iran and Japan" was put forward by a former member of Sven Hedin's Lufthansa Expedition in the 1920's, a certain Major Zimmerman, who urged a concerted attack on the "British Empire's heart, India." He pointed out that in the 1930's continuing raids and rebellions by frontier tribes, the Afridis, Mohmans, and Waziris, severely tested British forces, which increasingly relied on punitive air attacks. And now, with Britain stretched to the limit by a global conflict, and facing in India a Congress-led "Quit India" campaign, the Raj seemed at its most vulnerable. Indeed, a former president of the Indian National Congress, the Bengali militant Chandra Subhas Bose, had turned up in Berlin seeking Hitler's support for establishment of a "Free Indian Government" under Axis auspices.

Yet Hitler gave no encouragement to Bose. Among the Führer's favorite films was *The Lives of a Bengal Lancer*, a 1935 Hollywood "Empire" film glorifying British regiments on the North-West

Frontier, which Hitler, according to his staff at Berchtesgaden, viewed repeatedly. In late 1939, he canceled the Amanullah plan, and in a private meeting with Sven Hedin ten days later explained that preserving the British Empire was in Germany's interest. The very idea of a "Free India" movement, as Bose and his allies discovered, was anathema to Hitler. As he confided at dinner table in 1941, "Let's learn from the English, with 250,000 men in all, including 50,000 soldiers, they govern 400 million Indians. What India was to the British, the territories of Russia will be for us."

Still, Hitler's lieutenants were aware of his impulsiveness and weakness for radical plans ("You should read more Karl May," he exhorted his generals, referring to the German author of Wild West romances). He had hoped to strike a deal with Britain before his attack on Russia, and was angered by Churchill's persistent rebuffs. Taking advantage of the Führer's predilection for vague lines of authority, and his habit of pitting ministries against each other, the SS, the military intelligence agency or Abwehr, the Foreign Ministry, and the Munitions Ministry separately hatched rival "forward policy" projects in neutral Afghanistan. Himmler's men took the most unorthodox initiative, posting an SS officer named Kurt Brinckmann in Kabul under the unlikely cover of opening a dental surgery. Soon Brinckmann was drilling the teeth of the Afghan political elite, including the Prime Minister, Hashim Khan. And soon he was reporting to Berlin that it was "absolutely out of the question" that Khan was pro-British, and indeed would support the return of Amanullah, otherwise his bitter enemy, if he could keep the premiership. Reports from this agent, unknown on the Wilhelmstrasse, caused confusion and bafflement, since the Abwehr was already forging an alliance with the Faqir of Ipi to promote an uprising on the frontier (codenamed TIGER) and had sent its own specialist to train tribal warriors in a demolition and sabotage campaign (codenamed FIREEATER). The Abwehr agents were Professor Manfred Oberdorffer, whose field was tropical medicine, and Dr. Fred Brandt, an entymologist, both posing as "leprosy experts." All these plans misfired, partly because German agents worked at cross-purposes, devoting much of their energy to denouncing each other.

Then, overnight, Afghanistan lost its pivotal position after Hitler attacked Russia in June 1941. Now Britain and the Soviet Union were allies, and as if to underscore what that implied, the two countries partitioned and occupied Iran when Teheran balked at expelling German nationals. Next the British turned to Kabul with the same demand, and—as watchful Afghans noted that Moscow did not fall, and realized that the British now controlled all Afghan imports, including oil—the Kabul Government complied. In October 1941, a total of 204 Axis nationals were given two weeks to depart.

Meanwhile, Abwehr agents Oberdorffer and Brandt (code-named KELL and ARMA) discovered that their chief Waziri contact was an agent provocateur, and the two were captured by an Afghan patrol. Their radio transmitter was confiscated, as were the Survey of India charts essential to their operation, which as it happens, had been copied from Survey maps provided in May 1941 to Major Zimmerman in the Stockholm study of his former expedition leader, Sven Hedin.

In all these botched plans, the Nazi regime displayed the same clumsiness and arrogance that undermined similar Afghan schemes attempted by the Kaiser's agents in World War I. Indeed some of the same officials were involved in both debacles, notably Dr. Werner Otto von Hentig, who in the First War tried to make contact with frontier tribes, and who in 1939 was summoned from retirement to Afghan duty in the Second War. "It was fortunate for the Allied cause," observed Sir Olaf Caroe, the Secretary of State for India, "that the Germans proved so heavy-handed." They used their Asian partners only to serve German purposes, and when totalitarian Germany collapsed, "she dragged down her mercenaries."

As for Tibet, Schäfer, fresh from his exploits, met with Himmler and came up with a bold proposal to send a commando expedition through Soviet-controlled Central Asia in 1940 (during the interlude of the Nazi-Soviet Pact) with arms and gifts for the Tibetans. In the spirit of Lawrence of Arabia, Schäfer's plan was to encourage Tibetans to foment rebellion and disrupt communications in British India—railroads, telegraph cables, mail routes. With Himmler's support, Germany obtained preliminary approval for the scheme from the Soviet Foreign Ministry. The plan, however, became moot when Nazi armies invaded the Soviet Union in June 1941.

During the height of the German offensive that resulted in the capture of the oilfields at Maikop, Himmler gave the Ahnenerbe the order for the "total research" of the Caucasus ("UNTERNEHMEN K"). All those living in occupied areas were to be analyzed "ethnographically" in order to destroy them, deport them, or use them as slaves. Schäfer spent August 1942 planning an expedition that would combine scientific with military objectives. His task would be to win over the mountain peoples in the Caucasus to the German side. The scale of the operation may be surmised by the fact that forty Volkswagens as well as seventeen trucks were requested. Anticipating a quick Nazi victory over the Russians, the institute compiled lists of museums, libraries, and archives in Moscow and Leningrad that possessed ethnological and cultural artifacts, skeletons, or anything of interest that might be removed. However, after the surrender of the German Army at Stalingrad in early 1943, Himmler and Schäfer quietly scaled down these projects.

By 1942, the thirty-two-year-old Schäfer, now a major and a member of Himmler's personal staff, had become the head of his own institute in Munich, the Reich Institute for Central Asian Research. A deputation of scholars, including the rector of Munich University, asked Sven Hedin to bestow his name on the institute and to accept an honorary doctorate. The Swede agreed, later claiming he had been warned "that a refusal on my part would be misunderstood" by the highest authorities, notably Himmler. In January 1943, Hedin was present at the official opening of his namesake institute in Munich. But this was no ordinary academic institution, and the truth about its activities is set forth in captured German documents in Washington.

Hedin had tried to justify his pro-Nazi proclivities in a conversation with Schäfer, who made the difficult trip to Sweden through Denmark in 1942, to interview and enlist the explorer's support for joint efforts with Swedish scientists (which they declined). The SS major found the seventy-eight-year-old chain-smoking explorer still capable of working through the night. In Schäfer's interview, buried deep in the institute's files, the explorer remarks, "One of the most important discoveries of my life, as I have also shown in a book (*Amerika im Kampf der Kontinente*) is that Bolshevism is the most dreaded danger for Europe and for world culture—not least for Finland and Sweden. I myself had not a single doubt: the future of the Nordic lands is closely connected with Germany's."

Yet it is impossible to find any patriotic justification for projects funded by the institute that bore his name. One institute paper titled "Races in the War" recounts a trip to Auschwitz in 1943 by Dr. Beger to measure the bodies and study the physical characteristics of Uzbek, Tajik, and other Central Asian prisoners. As part of his Auschwitz researches, he made casts of the heads of more than a hundred prisoners who were then gassed and their skulls given to Beger for comparison. "Exotics" were also plucked from concentration camps and sent on "vacation passes" to the Institute's Special Command "K" (Sonderkommando "K") experimental racial research facilities at Schloss Mittersill near Salzburg, so that the SS could study the Soviet Union's various racial types. (Schäfer had persuaded Himmler to revamp this burned-out castle whose owner was residing in New York, in order to relocate the institute and escape from the bombing of Munich.) In 1943, after many delays and arguments with his bosses, *Secret Tibet*, the film about the Schäfer expedition, had its premiere. It is still shown (minus provenance, swastikas, and racial theories) as vintage Tibet; his book with the same title was published, lavishly illustrated with color photographs on glossy paper, the war notwithstanding.

The final months of the Thousand-Year Reich brought a shift at the Sven Hedin Institute into less esoteric activities, such as solving the deepening food crisis. Schäfer had returned from Tibet with a thousand samples of grain, including a cold-resistant, fast-growing barley, the staple grain in Tibet. His attempts at growing the hardy barley to feed his hungry countrymen met with success. Less productive were his efforts to develop new breeds of horses. In 1940, Himmler wrote from his special train that he had read in a Nordic fairy tale of a horse with a red mane. Could this horse exist? Could it be bred? After the huge loss of mounts during the Russian campaign, Schäfer was pressed to breed a super steppe horse that would be winter-hardy and stronger than its European counterparts. The putative stud master was now dispatched to Poland to select Asiatic strains of horses. One mare was foaled, but since horses take longer to reproduce than grain, time expired before the project bore fruit. Himmler also sent his researchers delving into archives for information on polyandry and polygamy, both of which the Tibetans practiced. By introducing the practices into the SS, the Reichsführer hoped to compensate for the decrease in population due to the war.

None of this was known in the immediate postwar years, when the German connection with Tibet won more favorable attention with the publication in 1952 of *Seven Years in Tibet*, a worldwide best-seller. Heinrich Harrer, an Austrian mountaineer, described his escape with his companion, Peter Aufschnaiter, to the Himalayan theocracy from a British prison camp in India where both of them were detained when World War II broke out. So compelling was Harrer's affectionate account of Tibet and the young Fourteenth Dalai Lama who befriended him that his book was adapted decades later into a film starring Brad Pitt. Unfortunately for its producers, as the film was nearly finished, an article in Germany's weekly *Stern* exposed Harrer's early membership in the SS, which he joined as a ski instructor, and to which he still belonged when he and Aufschnaiter were arrested in 1939. Hasty emendations were made in the 1997 production, in which Harrer was depicted as regretting his past enthusiasm for martial nationalism, but the exposure was an embarrassment, especially for the current Dalai Lama and his Free Tibet cause.

Harrer acknowledged that he had been in the SS, saying it was the greatest mistake of his life, but insisted he was not a war criminal. This seems to be true, but the Tibetans also seemed ignorant of the Nazi past of Bruno Beger, who was convicted in 1971 and sentenced to three years in prison for complicity in the murder of eighty-six Russian Jews at Auschwitz (the sentence was suspended). Beger was invited to, and photographed at, a festive reunion in Austria with the Dalai Lama, who knew nothing of Beger's conviction. It was a melancholy footnote to an anomalous connection between the genocidal Nazis and a people rightly identified with reverence for life. As for Schäfer, after surrendering to the American military, he was held and questioned at Nuremberg. He was never tried for war crimes, although he managed to implicate several of his colleagues. (His interrogators found him "very helpful in all matters" that did "not involve himself.") Like other Nazis, he made a fresh start in South America, where he worked as a biologist in Venezuela and wrote several more books on his adventures in Tibet.

HEDIN NEVER MARRIED AND ONCE EXPLAINED WHY AT A BANQUET in his honor: "I have been in love many times, but Asia remained my bride. She has held me captive in her cold embrace, and out of jealousy would never let me love any other. And I have been faithful to her, that is certain." After the war, until his death in 1952, he worked on his books in his library, surrounded by the signed photographs of his famous and infamous friends. He expressed no regrets or apologies for his wartime activities, and in his *German Diaries* approvingly quotes a final letter from Hitler seconding Hedin's view that "This war will go down in history as President Roosevelt's war," a sentiment only someone as bitter and politically snowblind as the "Desert Wanderer" might utter.

For all his avowed love of the East, he was faithful only in his fashion. As Milan Hauner observes in *What Is Asia to Us?* (1990), Hedin assisted the German General Staff in its aggressive designs against Central Asia with his advice and maps in two world wars. Knowing the value of those maps, U.S. military intelligence in 1945 diligently searched for them in the rubble of the Third Reich. An army map expert, Martin Schallenberger, located Hedin's Tibetan material in the map files of the German General Staff, hidden in a depot at Saalfeld. He tracked down still more Hedin maps at a publishing house in Gotha, which like Saalfeld was also designated for Soviet occupation. Thus the most detailed available maps of Tibet and its borderlands subsequently went west to the Goddard Space Flight Center of the National Aeronautics and Space Administration (NASA) at Greenbelt, Maryland. With Hedin's cooperation, the Army Map Service incorporated the Swede's findings in its regular series of maps at a scale of one to one million. Subsequent satellite photos taken for NASA confirmed the essential accuracy of Hedin's maps, including his charts of Lop Nor, the brackish "wandering lake" in the Tarim Basin, near China's nuclear testing range.

The story does not end there. Hedin's Himalayan maps were used again in 1962 by the Chinese armies that occupied the barren and disputed Aksai Chin on the frontier between China and India. Very probably Sven Hedin, despite his aversion to Communism, would have taken that as a compliment. In the words of his German biographer, Detlef Brenneke, Hedin "saw the uniform and not the soul, the rank and not the person. He was a cartographer."

CHAPTER TWENTY-TWO

.:.

High Mischief

SOMETHING VERY PECULIAR, IF NOW ALMOST WHOLLY FORGOT-
ten, happened at Peterson Field, six miles east of Colorado
Springs, Colorado, on December 7, 1961. Henry Wood arrived for
work, as he usually did, at 8 a.m. to manage Kensair, a flying school
and aviation company lodged inside a hangar on the field's eastern
fringe. He noticed a C–124 Globemaster parked nearby, but that was
not unusual because since World War II the U.S. Air Force had shared
space at this and other Colorado airfields. All seemed in order as
Wood—"Hank" to everybody but strangers—greeted Bill Watts, his
foreman, and Lynn Boese, a twenty-year-old student who had arrived for her lesson in Kensair's Piper Colt. Watts stepped outside to
take a closer look at the big Air Force transport. Within minutes he
charged back into the company's office crying, "Hank, we're surrounded!"

Wood, sighing skeptically, left the hangar to see what was happening. He was accosted by an agitated soldier in combat fatigues who
thrust a Colt .45 revolver in his face, saying (as Wood later recalled),
"Get back inside." Soon other soldiers stormed around, flourishing

an arsenal of automatic weapons. Wood prudently retreated. At gun-point, all civilians present—Wood, Watts, Miss Boese, two office workers, and a mechanic—were rounded up and shoved into the Kensair office. The telephone lines, however, were not cut, and Wood, striving to sound calm and credible, called the local sheriff, Earl Sullivan, to report that he and five others were surrounded by menacing, gun-waving troops. Unsure what to expect, Sullivan and two deputies made their way by police car to Peterson Field, only to encounter a roadblock. Armed soldiers firmly told them to halt. Meanwhile, through a hangar window, an astonished Hank Wood saw a military bus, its passenger windows all painted black, pull up beside the aircraft. "There were fifteen Orientals [who] got out of the bus and onto the plane," Wood recalled years later. "They were wearing some type of uniform, just like the GI's. Each one of these Orientals had a white tag around his neck. As each man got on the Globemaster, someone at the door checked the tag."

After the plane embarked, an Army officer entered the hangar and lined everyone up in the Kensair office. "We had to hold up our hands and swear we wouldn't talk about it to anyone for six months," under dire threat of federal prosecution, so Wood remem-bered. Nevertheless, reports of bizarre doings at Peterson Field turned up in Colorado newspapers, and the wire services carried a few summary paragraphs. A press agency item that mentioned Chi-nese-looking soldiers caught the eye of a desk editor at the Wash-ington bureau of The New York Times. He asked a reporter to make a routine check. Hardly had the call been placed when a senior aide to Secretary of Defense Robert McNamara phoned the bureau and ap-pealed to the editor to drop the matter. Explaining that the embark-ing troops were not Chinese but Tibetans, he claimed that publication would endanger national security. No story appeared. A day after the incident, General Charles G. Dodge, the Army Chief of Information, called Hank Wood to offer an apology but not an explanation.

There the tale might have ended, as if written in sand and erased by the wind. Yet vague rumors of Tibetans being trained at secret U.S. bases were picked up by David Wise, a longtime correspondent for The New York Herald Tribune. Wise knew a great deal about clandestine operations, having co-authored with Thomas B. Ross *The Espionage Establishment*. On a shrewd hunch, he guessed that Colorado, the state with the highest average altitude, was the likeliest place to train Tibetans, and telephoned the librarian of *The Denver Post*. Within days, Mrs. Rosie Frank sent him a 1961 article about the military harassment of civilians at Peterson Field, but with no mention of Asian soldiers. Wise now had a date and a location. Reeling through microfilm at the Library of Congress, he turned up a story in *The Colorado Springs Gazette Telegraph* on December 8, 1961, that referred to "Oriental soldiers dressed in battle fatigues" and that quoted the student pilot, Lynn Boese. In 1971, Wise pieced together what happened ten years before by telephoning Hank Wood, Miss Boese, and other witnesses. He included the story in his 1973 book, *The Politics of Lying,* but his Tibetan disclosures were lost in the far greater uproar over Vietnam and Watergate.

Even today, few have heard of a CIA operation described in a classified in-house history as "one of the most romantic programs of covert action undertaken by the agency." From 1956 until 1969, the Central Intelligence Agency backed an insurgency by tough Khampa warriors in eastern Tibet, secretly training Tibetan guerrillas at Camp Hale, near Leadville, Colorado, and carrying out at least forty airdrops into China. The CIA was so deeply involved in Tibetan affairs that some claim (mistakenly, the agency insists) that it induced the Nechung Oracle to advise the Dalai Lama to flee Chinese-occupied Tibet in 1959. Operation CIRCUS, launched during the Eisenhower Administration, reflected the activist spirit of the agency's early years. It was a classic "forward school" operation, very much in the frontier tradition. Like so many Great Game ventures, its supposed beneficiaries ended as losers. The details are finally set forth in *Orphans of the Cold War* (1999), the first full account of CIRCUS, by John Kenneth Knaus, once chief of the CIA Tibetan Task Force.

Knaus also restores to memory the daring Office of Strategic Services (OSS) mission to Lhasa that marked the beginning of direct Tibetan contacts with the U.S. Government. The OSS team was led by Major Ilia Tolstoy, a grandson of the novelist, and Captain Brooke Dolan II, an explorer and socialite whom we have already encoun-

tered in Chapter 21. In large measure this initial OSS mission defined the pattern of U.S.-Tibetan relations. For all their affection and
genuine respect for the Land of Snows, Tolstoy and Dolan inspired
hopes of American support that they knew were unrealistic if not
impossible. So it happened in Operation CIRCUS, whose CIA
chiefs found, for example, that Tibetans often did not grasp the difference between "independence" and "autonomy" since their language lacked a word for the latter. Misunderstandings due to the
cultural gulf were a constant problem for CIA managers, Knaus relates, as was the guilty feeling that Tibetans were sacrificial pawns in
the game of Realpolitik. In fact, even political support for the Tibetan cause ended after the Nixon–Kissinger rapprochement with
China. ("There was no role for Tibet in the Kissinger equation,"
Knaus adds in a caustic aside.) The gyrations of American policy
caused considerable anguish even among case-hardened CIA operatives. At Camp Hale, trainers tried to justify their work on the
grounds that the Khampa guerrillas would have fought the Chinese
with or without foreign help, and that most Tibetans tended anyway
to a cynical view of politics. The same guilty doubts attended the
Tolstoy-Dolan mission in 1942–43.

ILIA TOLSTOY AND BROOKE DOLAN WERE A GOOD MATCH FOR A
risky and exacting assignment. Both were proficient on horseback
and with a rifle. They had traveled widely in Asia, spoke many of its
languages, and knew the importance of patience and fair-dealing
with guides and porters. They were in their prime: Tolstoy was
thirty-nine, Dolan thirty-three, when they first met in the War
Room of the Army Air Force Chief of Staff, where Dolan was a
deskbound presentation officer. This was in the bleak spring of 1942,
when Japanese armies, having swept through Asia from Manila and
Jakarta to Singapore and Burma, seemed invincible. Tolstoy had volunteered to lead a mission across Tibet to identify urgently needed
supply routes to China. Permitted a choice of personnel, he asked
only that Dolan join him. "I have never regretted that decision for a

moment," Tolstoy wrote after the war, "and my respect and recognition of Brooke's knowledge, character and ability grew from there on. Besides that, we became fast friends…"

Yet their tempers were very different. Beneath a surface affability, Tolstoy was tautly controlled, a former cavalry officer whose affinity was with horses. Dolan was impulsive, self-punishing, liable to outbursts of violence; his affection was for dogs. Both men bore the intangible baggage of troubled marriages and traumatic pasts.

Ilia's father was Andrei Lvovich Tolstoy (1877–1916), the ninth of the long-suffering Sofia and the great Leo's thirteen children. During the Russo-Japanese War, while his father served at the front, Ilia and his sister Sofia resided in England, and as a youngster he not only read American and English books but corresponded with Jack London and Ernest Seton Thompson, the gifted North American author of animal tales. Tolstoy lived in, and for, the wild. While a teenager fresh from Moscow Agricultural College, he was put in charge of horse breeding in Turkestan and journeyed to Mongolia, Afghanistan, and Northern India in search of stock. In 1916–17, Ilia was a cadet at the Turkestan Cavalry School, and during what he always called the Second (that is, Bolshevik) Russian Revolution, he fought as a cavalry officer with the White Russian Army. For a while, he tried to work with the new regime in organizing a Soviet horse farm at the Tolstoy estate, Yasnaya Polyana, in the province of Tula, his birthplace. During the famine of 1921–22 in the Volga District, he signed as a volunteer with the American Friends Service Committee. He was soon engaged in purchasing and transporting horses from Turkestan and Siberia, some brought by railroad, others overland for 1,200 miles. From these trips he acquired a passion for exploration, which (with Quaker assistance) he carried to America in 1924 on the *President Polk,* entering on a student visa. At Iowa State College, Ilia took courses in animal husbandry and genetics, and worked summers as a farmhand. A meeting with W. Douglas Burden, a trustee of the American Museum of Natural History, propelled Tolstoy into his longed-for career when he was asked to lead an expedition through Northwest Canada into the Arctic to track and film the migration of caribou. The trip yielded a Paramount documentary, *Silent Enemy* (1929). There followed other museum and film expeditions to Mount McKinley, the West Indies,

Central and South America, culminating, with Burden's backing, in a new career in the 1930's as a founder and general manager of Marine Studios, Marineland, near St. Augustine, Florida.

All this Tolstoy set forth in a sketch he prepared in the 1940's for the U.S. Army. Tersely mentioned, without comment, were these items: "Mother: Olga K. Tolstoy, last heard of alive in Moscow, U.S.S.R.; sister, Sophia A. Tolstoy [ditto]; ex-wife, Vera Tolstoy [ditto]; son, Alexander I. Tolstoy [ditto]; daughter, Sophia I. Tolstoy [ditto]." At what must have been immense psychic cost, Tolstoy kept his silence in the Himalaya, saying little or nothing about his Russian family even as German armies trampled through Russia, in a nightmarish reprise of *War and Peace*.

DOLAN'S BACKGROUND WAS MORE CONVENTIONAL, BUT NOT HIS life. While in his mid-twenties, he had already led two expeditions through western China, deep into Tibet. He had covered 10,000 miles on horseback, and contended with river pirates, warlords, and imprisonment. His purpose was to collect specimens, chiefly for the Academy of Natural Sciences in Philadelphia, of which he was a trustee. His harvest was impressive: 3,000 birds and 140 mammals, notably the giant panda and takin groups that are highlights of the academy's habitat displays, along with wild yak, wild ass, MacNeill's deer, muntjac, Lhasa stag, plus a multitude of rare plants, insects, and snails. He was among the few Westerners to explore the headwaters of the Yellow River, the Yangtze, the Brahmaputra, the Mekong, and the Salween.

Brooke possessed the means to realize these goals. His grandfather, Thomas Dolan, was what contemporaries called a utility magnate. He was the first to propose electrifying Philadelphia, and silenced scoffers by illuminating Chestnut Street from river to river at his own expense. He founded Brush Electric, headed United Gas, owned Keystone Knitting Mills, and was many times over a company and bank director, building the fortune that secured his descendants a place in society. His grandson Brooke attended the right schools—St. Paul's, Princeton, Harvard—married the expected debutante, and settled in the appropriate place on the Main Line, Bryn Mawr. Inwardly, he burned with discontent. "You know, Junge," he once remarked to Ernst Schäfer, his German partner on both Asian expeditions, "I hate civilization." This he combined with a mystical bent. On another occasion, he confided, "Actually, Junge, I'm going to Tibet in order to search for the truth. If you help me create in addition some scientific collections, so much the better."

Dolan was all of twenty-one, a year older than Schäfer (hence the "Junge") when the pair met in Hanover in 1930. The German, the future leader of an SS expedition to Tibet, was an aspiring zoologist, and the American had just dropped out of Princeton in his senior year. With family money and Academy sponsorship, Dolan organized a team that included Dr. Hugo Wiegold, a zoologist at Hanover's natural history museum; Otto Gneiser, a German filmmaker; and Gordon Bowles, an ethnologist at the University Museum in Philadelphia. As Dolan often said, it was a "young man's expedition"—all except Weigold were in their early twenties as they embarked eastward by rail from Berlin in January 1931 for Moscow, then across Siberia to Harbin in Manchuria, continued down to Peking, and finally westward from Shanghai and Chungking to Szechuan.

From there, Dolan led a pack train bearing American and German flags toward the eastern Tibetan highlands. The party entered a fascinating patchwork of mini-states, with their warlords, devil dancers, and incarnate abbots, as well as a floral paradise and a habitat for exotic fauna, notably the giant panda. The expedition divided at Tatsien-lu, where Schäfer veered southward into the lamaist Kingdom of Muli, whose existence had only recently been reported by Joseph Rock, the *National Geographic*'s man in Western China. Dolan journeyed east through the Minya Konka range into the country of the Lolos, a non-Chinese people almost as little known as those in Muli. After covering 2,500 miles in close to two years, Dolan and his charges all emerged safely, in either Burma or Haiphong.

Home again, Dolan resumed his studies, this time at Harvard, became engaged, broke his engagement, re-engaged, and then in April 1934 married Emilie Gerhard. The crisis in his courtship occurred in

January, when the Philadelphia papers reported Dolan's arrest on charges of disorderly conduct after purportedly breaking into a friend's Villanova home, allegedly inebriated, and then smashing furniture and a vitrine enclosing Chinese porcelain said to be worth many thousands. One week later, Dolan cabled Schäfer, saying the Academy planned "A quite large Tibet expedition, do you want to come?" The response was prompt and affirmative. When Schäfer learned of the Villanova episode, "Everything was clear to me. Brooky must take a long leave from high society in the wilderness to let grass grow over the thing. What was easier than a new Tibet expedition, particularly when one had a true and tried German friend who would help it succeed?" In short, this second, larger expedition was less the result of careful planning than "the mad caper of a young American who had too much cash." Even so, Schäfer was grateful to have as his friend this "wiry American with the blond tuft and blue eyes."

One guesses that the expedition had less appeal to Emilie, Dolan's bride, who bravely made the best of it, sailing with her husband to Shanghai, from whence they proceeded to Chungchow, her presence never once mentioned in Schäfer's "Boy's Own" accounts of a remarkable adventure.

IT *WAS* REMARKABLE, YET IS SCARCELY KNOWN EVEN TO SPECIALISTS. Dolan kept a private journal, but never published his own account, and Schäfer's half dozen books on Tibet appeared in Germany before, during, and just after World War II; none have been translated. It did not help that soon after Hitler seized power, Schäfer joined the SS, for reasons of ambition no less than conviction. Dolan was well aware of his German colleague's politics, yet the two corresponded as friends until the outbreak of war, and Dolan out of affection contributed money in 1938 to what he may not have known was an expedition under Himmler's patronage. Looking back, Schäfer said he never guessed they would fight in opposing armies, that they would separately reach Lhasa, or that Dolan "should remain faithful to our beloved Tibet until his death."

In 1934 when "Junge" disembarked in Shanghai, "Brooky" was waving his arms on the quay, wearing a smart first-aid corps uniform with a Colt revolver strapped to his belt. ("This he used one night in a hotel bar," Schäfer dryly adds, "where he shot up all the bottles.") The Dolans and Schäfer lingered for two months in the port city acquiring the necessary permits and inland visas, which they did with the help of the expedition's interpreter, Marion H. Duncan, a missionary based in Western China. The German took time to obtain an audience with the Panchen Lama, who chanced to be in nearby Hangchow. The Panchen questioned Schäfer intently about Germany ("Are there wandering nomads?"). The visitor was given what His Serenity described as a "valid passport to all Tibet" (it proved unusable in any territory under Lhasan authority).

Leaving Shanghai and heading inland by riverboat, the young explorers practiced their "Golok cry," like the whinnying of a horse, their distress signal. All the while "our thoughts leaped ahead to the wilderness, where again we would be free" (Schäfer). In Chungking, they encountered further and frustrating delays: proferring the necessary "presents" to a Chinese marshal, and haggling for still more passports and customs permits. Finally, at Chungchow on July 31, writes Dolan, "The dreary crawling travail of our lowland journey is behind us. Tomorrow we climb the first ramp of the mountain ranges that roll westward to the marches of eastern Tibet."

The caravan was armed with fourteen rifles, and carried $5,000 in American cash carefully hidden in boxes of cartridges, all strapped on pack animals tended by a score of porters managed by Lee, an "old boy" from the previous expedition (his pay now $25 a month), and a cook chosen by Duncan ($20 a month). They set out for the Amne Machin range in Amdo. Besides the usual difficulties—foul weather, mud storms, washouts, and avalanches—the start went well, as did the expedition's encounter at Yachow with the first warlord, General Hsiang. "Very pleasant to deal with," Dolan tells us. "He promised us the necessary passports and then, as if getting down to the real business of the day, trotted out a rather startling selection of sporting weapons for our inspection. The prize piece was a single-shot rifle disguised as a walking-stick with the breach and trigger just below the handle, obviously designed as a concealed deadly weapon." So smoothly were things going that Dolan was able to report on August 19 from Waseko to his friend Kermit Roosevelt: "The stag of MacNeill is the real object of the autumn…We will either try Rockhill's road via Derge and Jyekundo or go straight north from Derge across absolutely unexplored country…This is of course the most dangerous Ngolok [Golok] country, but I think by going slowly and perhaps hiring a friendly tribe to supplement our armed Batang contingent we will come out with a fine collection [here he catalogues the possible game]."

It is hard not to be impressed by Dolan's journal, with its unadorned prose and fine drawings of flora and fauna: a good sportsman's notebook, rarely alluding to the abundant perils. Brigands were a recurrent hazard, a precious rifle being the usual price of passage. Also promoting the caravan's safety was Schäfer's marksmanship, which local inhabitants en route respectfully noted. "He is really incredible," Dolan wrote on seeing Junge fell three gorals (a short-horned antelope) at 200 yards, each with a single bullet. "Consistently he shoots as the average hunter shoots once in a lifetime and bears the memory for the remainder."

They were now in Litang country, a contested borderland between Tibet and China. "How the Chinese expect to keep any border in a peaceful state other than that of absolute subjection is a puzzle," Dolan noted in a political aside. "They have supreme contempt for native peoples and a genius for antagonizing them." He was fascinated by Tibetan nomads and (as are today's backpackers) by Litang, "the best concealed city in the world," with its large nearby monastery, hidden in two narrow valleys.

When the caravan reached Batang, its leaders found a sack of mail and dug in for the winter at the mission compound of their evangelical colleague, the interpreter Marion Duncan. Most days Dolan and Schäfer hunted. Hunting was for Dolan *"une grande passion,* half bestial, wholly religious." His supreme moment was felling a takin bull, its pelt rusty gold, its huge body spanning nine feet from its low rump to its massive head and bow-shaped horns, a giant even by takin standards. "So I have come to the end of a long trail, and commingled with my jubilation is more than a trace of regret," Dolan wrote at the time:

Every hunter to whom the chasse means more than simply the trophy will sympathize. Some part of the glamour and mystery of mighty defiles and the hollow roar of tortured glacial streams, of bright and hostile bamboo jungles, and of misty crags is gone forever. The haunting spell of the mist and the secrets hidden in the dripping tunnels of high rhododendron forests are in part explored, in part exorcised by one lucky shot. So much the takin has meant to me and more...I have earned the memory of a long hard trail brought to its climax with an almost poetical finality.

After Batang, the caravan headed in mid-March 1935 for turbulent Koko Nor territory and its administrative outpost at Jyekundo, the trading center of eastern Tibet. Jyekundo was in the unfriendly hands of Governor Ma and Colonel Ma—"Ma" means Muslim in Chinese—who would not let foreigners advance further westward when their purpose was hunting game. After crossing to the eastern side of the Yangtze, the party was surrounded by a "seige army" of Dungan soldiers who, armed with two machine guns, demanded that its leaders return to Jyekundo.

As recounted by Schäfer, Dolan reacted like "a crazy person." He decided to steal out of camp and break for Sining, the provinical capital. There he would seek permission from the local warlord, General Ma Pu Fang, to penetrate further upriver on the Upper Mekong and the Yangtze. "He dismissed all counter arguments with biting mockery," the German remembered. "A few hours later, Dolan, smooth shaven, stood before us disguised as a Mongolian trader." Saying "We'll meet at Tossungnor [a Tibetan lake] or in hell!" the American shook hands and under the cover of darkness, crept on all fours out of the camp, accompanied only by Jimmy, his hunter, and Atring, a courageous local Tibetan. Dolan succeeded in capturing three of the Dungans' best mules, and with only a small pouch of tsamba meal, a lump of rancid yak butter, and three bars of chocolate, he set out for Sining, some 300 miles away. Avoiding the main road, becoming lost in the snow-covered grasslands for nine days, and sick with prostate pain, he subsisted on raw kiang (wild ass), gazelles, and bears that he shot while eluding Golok brigands. Leaving his animals to the wolves, wading through shoulder-high rivers with his last cartridges in his mouth, he arrived, barefoot, ill, and starving with his two companions at Sining. But the mission failed when he was not given an audience with the warlord. Unable to wrest the permission he sought, Dolan made his way to Lanzhou, where eight months later, not in hell but in the local mission, he was reunited with Schäfer. From there they flew to Shanghai, where Emilie Dolan was on hand to greet them. "The journey from Jyekundo was remarkable," commented one of Shanghai's English-language newspapers, "in that it was the first time it had been attempted and successfully completed by a qualified naturalist, and one who traveled without a caravan. Not since General Pereira, the eminent British soldier-explorer, traversed through these territories has it ever been attempted by a foreigner."

AT BEST, HE WAS A HALF-DOMESTICATED DOG, BROOKY ONCE confided to Junge, and back in Philadelphia, where excitement was minimal, Dolan tried his best. He catalogued his copious specimen collection and helped install habitat groups at the Academy of Natural Sciences, for which he paid all expenses. With, or sometimes without, Emmie, he fished and hunted in Norway, Canada, Newfoundland, and Mexico, all the while seeing and corresponding with the select cadre of Americans who knew western China and Tibet, notably Kermit Roosevelt and Suydam Cutting. Dolan was midway in a major study of the migratory patterns of Atlantic salmon when Pearl Harbor was struck. Within months he was a lieutenant in the U.S. Army Air Force, eager for precisely the assignment that grew out of his serendipitous meeting in Washington with Captain Ilia Tolstoy.

The idea for an OSS mission to Lhasa was probably Tolstoy's, but it was the kind of project that appealed to Dolan, and more importantly, to the White House. On July 3, 1942, Roosevelt signed a carefully drafted letter to "His Holiness The Dalai Lama, Supreme Pontiff of the Lama Church, Lhasa." The letter was to be presented personally by Tolstoy and Dolan, but in deference to the State Department's pro-Chinese policies, it referred to Tibet as a "Pontificate," not as a nation. Nation or not, the allure of Tibet was strong as ever. Within days of signing the message, Roosevelt chose the name "Shangri-La" for his new rustic hideaway in Maryland, thereafter more mundanely called Camp David.

The Tibet mission had both tactical and strategic objectives. In July 1940, bowing to Japanese advances, the British closed the Burma Road, the main supply route from India to China. After Pearl Harbor, Japanese armies overwhelmed Singapore, Malaya, Thailand, the Philippines, and the Dutch East Indies. The paramount American aim was to keep a tottering China in the war and tie down Japanese forces at minimum cost in the China-Burma-India Theater, or CBI. An airlift was improvised in June 1942 to carry supplies over "the Hump," a difficult passage in the eastern Himalaya with winds so boisterous they could tear apart lumbering transport planes. To stiffen Chinese resistance, Roosevelt dispatched General Joseph W. Stilwell to command Chiang Kai-shek's armies, a major objective being to open a supply road through northern Burma. In Chungking, the Nationalist capital, "Vinegar Joe" did what he could for Chiang, a leader he came to despise. He believed the Chinese troops were ill-trained and ill-led, the best being held back for a showdown with Mao's guerrillas. Trying (as of 1943) to drive out the Japanese and keep the peace among allies was Lord Mountbatten, Supreme Commander of Southeast Asia, one of three Allied theater commanders (along with Dwight Eisenhower and Douglas MacArthur), who established his headquarters at less-than-central Colombo in Ceylon.

Into this tangle plunged Tolstoy and Dolan, with instructions to gain Tibetan approval for a new overland route linking India to China. However, in the frank phrases of a confidential memorandum to Donovan, the mission was also meant "to move across Tibet and make its way to Chungking, China, observing attitudes of the people of Tibet; to seek allies and discover enemies; locate strategic targets and survey the territory as a possible field for future activity."

Originally, Major Tolstoy and Captain Dolan (as they soon became) planned to proceed from Chungking in Szechuan to Lhasa, but Tibetan authorities categorically rejected any entry from China. The OSS pair had better luck in India. Doors were opened by Major Suydam Cutting, an old Lhasa hand now back in uniform as head of the U.S. Observer Group in New Delhi. In Washington, they had the informed support of Brigadier General John Magruder, Donovan's deputy, who as a military attaché in China toured the Tibetan borderlands in 1921, becoming the first American soldier to visit Tibet.

Yet the decisive boost came from Sir Olaf Caroe, the Foreign Secretary of India, from his Tibetan advisers, Sir Basil Gould, the Resident in Sikkim; and Frank Ludlow, head of the British Mission in Lhasa. Britain was the sole European power represented by a permanent mission in Lhasa, and it had long been British policy to close Tibet's borders and shut out all potential foreign rivals. Now, with Burma and Singapore gone, with India threatened by Japan and beset within by Gandhi's "Quit India" campaign, the British Tibetan cadre saw their cousins in a friendlier light.

In Lhasa, Ludlow was asked if the Indian Government approved the OSS mission. "I said, 'Yes, decidedly so.' I remarked that [this] was no ordinary visit, and emphasized it would be to Tibet's immediate and future advantage to return a courteous answer and a hospitable invitation." After meeting Tolstoy and Dolan en route, Gould informed Caroe that "some good might result" if the Tibetans grasped the opportunity of this first contact "with the President and people of a great nation which champions the rights of small nations. It might also be indicated that Tibet regards itself as independent and is different in race, physical features, religion and language from any other nation." The baton was passing.

THANKS TO THE OPENING OF LONG-CLOSED ARCHIVES, WE CAN look back at the Tolstoy-Dolan mission through contrasting prisms. We have its official report, and the correspondence it generated, in the National Archives, plus Tolstoy's *National Geographic* account and a film, *Inside Tibet,* that he prepared. Extended excerpts from Dolan's fascinating 1942–43 journal appeared in the 1980 edition of *Frontiers,* the annual of the Academy of Natural Sciences in Philadelphia, where his earlier journals are also kept. In 1998, the India Office Library in London declassified Ludlow's diary for the relevant period, having previously released the diplomatic traffic between Whitehall and Delhi. There is also a superb selection of photographs, with a useful text, in *A Portrait of Lost Tibet* (1996), by Rosemary Jones Tung.

Missing is an accessible Tibetan account, save for a brief passage in Tsepon Shakabpa's *Tibet: A Political History* (1967, later updated). This much we know. In Lhasa, a newly established Foreign Affairs Bureau was alarmed in 1942 by credible reports that Nationalist Chinese armies were preparing a full-scale invasion of Tibet. About the world in general, Lhasa was but vaguely informed. News came in telegraphic snippets, in oral accounts from foreigners, or in bulletins on a crackling wireless powered by a generator. Since 1912, while China was otherwise preocccupied, Tibet attained a de facto autonomy that its rulers equated with independence. Yet China never abandoned its claim to Tibet, and no Western power recognized Tibetan sovereignty. For three decades, Britain had provided Lhasa with its link to the West, and the Tibetan leadership evidently assumed that if China invaded, Britain and the world would somehow come to the rescue.

Major Tolstoy and Captain Dolan, with the best of intentions, only enhanced that illusion. Departing from New Delhi in September 1942, they followed the customary route from Calcutta to Gangtok, the capital of Sikkim, where they were "guests in the charming English country house of Sir Basil John Gould" (Tolstoy). They proceeded by caravan to Gyantse in Tibet, with a detour at Samding to meet Dorje Pagmo, "The Diamond Sow," an incarnate abbess, aged six, "an alert-faced, solemn little girl with shorn locks seated on a high throne" (Dolan). By the time they reached Lhasa in mid-December, they were palpably spellbound. Dolan's journal is filled with marveling accounts of the holy city, of its monks and mendicants, of its great prayer wheels and giant fresco of the "Celestial Buddha of the East," of its fluttering votive flags and its wheeling phalanxes of geese and crane. By this time Dolan knew enough of the Tibetan language and the arcane imagery of Buddhism to impress his hosts at the Drepung Monastery, the most important in Tibet, whose four colleges he visited during the Lunar Year festivities (which Tolstoy recorded on film).

Their host for fourteen weeks in Lhasa was Frank Ludlow, a fussy bachelor and former headmaster of the briefly operating British-style school in Gyantse. He helped arrange the important first audience with Tibet's seven-year-old Dalai Lama, to whom the Americans presented a silver-framed photograph of FDR, a Presidential letter in a cylindrical casket, a gold chronograph watch, and a silver ship model, gifts (so Ludlow reported) that some Tibetans deemed miserly for a great power. The Dalai Lama began the conversation by inquiring after the President's health, as he did at every subsequent meeting, and was much taken with Tolstoy; he "positively beamed on him throughout the interview" (Ludlow).

On Christmas Day, 1942, Ludlow arranged a fête at the Residence for the Americans, along with the unofficial greeter of all Western visitors, Tsarong, his wife and son; and a leading noble, Phunkang Se, his wife Kuku, and his sister Kay. On the table was a splendid turkey, very fat and tender. "The evening was very gay," Ludlow writes, "with hunt-the-slipper and all sorts of old-fashioned games. I think Tolstoy and Brooke Dolan were astonished at the cheerfulness—and playfulness—of our little Lhasa lady friends." A round of parties followed, and it appears that Dolan's affection for Kay was reciprocated. Indeed it further appears that months later, when Dolan was on his way to China but still within Tibetan territory, he learned that Kay was with child, and that he was (as Tibetans of that generation believe) the likely father. Half-seriously, he said that if the baby were blond and blue-eyed, he would race back to Lhasa. (In the final weeks of his life, while still in uniform, he indeed returned on his own to the Tibetan borderlands, but he was never able to see Lhasa or Kay again. According to contemporary Tibetan sources, Kay and her daughter drowned near Gyantse a few years later.)

Promoting the Allies' cause, Tolstoy did all he could to make friends in his first weeks there, in order to overcome the Government's reluctance to let them proceed eastward toward a hostile China. He promised that America would provide new wireless equipment (it eventually arrived, but proved inoperable), and offered to help devise a Tibetan typewriter. "He visited the powerful monasteries of Drepung and Sera, and gave them cases of presents," Ludlow reports, "and in a multitude of ways he laid himself out to secure the goodwill of Tibetan officialdom. On the whole he succeeded remarkably well, despite the fact that the presents he bestowed were neither well chosen nor of that costliness and magnificence which Tibetan officials might reasonably have expected."

As the weeks passed, Tolstoy and Dolan, charmed by their hosts, became advocates of the Tibetan national cause. One of Tolstoy's suggestions took on a life of its own. As Ludlow relates: "Tolstoy mentioned one day to the Tibetan Foreign Office that he had recommended to his Government that Tibet should be represented at the Peace Conference at the end of the war. The Foreign Office passed his suggestion to the Kashag [the Tibetan High Cabinet] and Regent. The proposal was immediately approved by the Tibetan Government, who expressed a desire to be informed of the date of the conference." Tolstoy now confessed to Ludlow he wished he had been less enthusiastic, saying he doubted Washington would approve his suggestion since it would anger the Chinese. ("Tolstoy, by the way, promised to give me a copy of his cable, but he never did so," writes Ludlow in one of many prickly asides. "Tolstoy struck me as a man who trusted nobody but himself.")

It was now Ludlow's turn to be pressed, and he informed the Tibetans that, speaking personally, not officially, he favored their attending the peace conference. This did not sit well in New Delhi, where Ludlow was gently reprimanded by Sir Olaf Caroe, and less gently by the Viceroy, Lord Linlithgow, who sent this wintry note to Caroe, his Foreign Secretary:

> I regard with apprehension amateur efforts of two Americans who have recently been in Lhasa. Indications are indeed that they are impressed with Tibetan claims for autonomy, but suggestion…Tibet should be represented at the Peace Conference seems to me strangely inept . . . Nor am I impressed by suggestions recently received from Gould and Richardson [Hugh Richardson, the last British mission chief in Lhasa] that Tibet should be prompted to follow up contact made through these representatives of President of U.S.A. and send letters impressing the American Government on their theory of independence. American enlightenment in matters Tibetan may come in due course, but I

would judge it unsound that we from here should attempt to hasten process.

WHAT THE VICEROY COULD NOT FORESEE IN EARLY 1943 WAS THE impending collapse of China's Nationalist regime and the victory of Mao Tse-tung's Communists. As difficult to conjure was Winston Churchill's defeat at the polls in 1945 by Clement Attlee's Labour Party, presaging the end of British rule in India. After their OSS mission to Tibet, Major Tolstoy and Captain Dolan were themselves caught up in these unexpected crosscurrents.

Their caravan left Lhasa in mid-March 1943, laden with goodwill gifts to FDR ("the King of America"): a letter, scarf, and framed picture from the Dalai Lama; four tapestries of pieced brocade, three gold coins, and Tibetan stamps for the President's collection, all preserved at Hyde Park. The "Lhasa ladies" presented Dolan with a Lhasa Apso, which he named "Miss Tick" and which became his mascot. Tsarong presented him with a fierce, less lovable black mastiff. Their route took them through the Reting Valley, scarcely known to Westerners, with its evocative cloisters, luxuriant junipers, and chattering thrushes, then across Tibet's Great Northern Plain through Koko Nor territory to Jyekundo, the scene of Dolan's ordeal in 1935. This time, he and Tolstoy were welcomed as heroes. The wide main street was hung with flags of the Chinese Republic and Tibetan bunting, and half the population greeted their arriving caravan.

Their feats elicited a congratulatory telegram from Stilwell, warm words from Donovan, and an eventual Legion of Merit for each. In practical terms, the mission was less successful. Tibetans balked at the use of territory they controlled for an overland supply route, unless it were part of a tripartite agreement with India and China, which the latter flatly rejected since it implied recognition of Tibetan sovereignty. The principal military benefit was a voluminous report including detailed maps, photographs, lists of possible sites for airfields, and meteorological and ethnographic notes. Years later, as China again prepared to invade Tibet, Hugh Richardson remarked that aside from the OSS report, "there are no reliable maps and there never has been a comparable geographical survey of Tibet."

More broadly, in Tolstoy and Dolan's words, the Tibetans now realized "that the U.S.A. will have a large share in formulating the future peace and believe that its weight will be thrown toward preserving the integrity and freedom of small countries." It was for that reason, they were granted "a very big favor, unprecedented in twenty-two years, of permitting foreigners to cross Tibet."

Once in China, the two officers were drawn into the CBI's politico-military labyrinth. Tolstoy took on new duties as camp commander of a special operations unit at Shanba, the northern base of the Sino-American Special Technical Cooperation Organization, better known as SACO, pronounced "socko." SACO was the brainchild of an abrasive U.S. Navy Captain, Milton E. Miles, who worked closely with Chiang Kai-shek's secret police chief, Tai Li. This association dogged Tolstoy when Donovan in June 1944 proposed a more congenial assignment—leadership of an OSS mission to Mao Tse-tung's headquarters at Yenan in northern China. The project was instantly opposed by the Army, which was organizing its own Military Observer Group, DIXIE (for China's rebel side, and for the song, "Is It True What They Say About Dixie?"). DIXIE was the brainchild of a State Department civilian, John Paton Davies, a senior aide to Stilwell, who wanted to emphasize the mission's military side and play down its political role.

Tolstoy now proposed a joint Army-OSS mission, which Davies categorically vetoed. Trying hard, and suppressing his annoyance, Tolstoy asked to be included in the observer group. Davies would have none of it, saying that Tolstoy "had been a member of SACO and as such was contaminated by Tai Li," and besides "would be considered a White Russian, which was also not desirable." In an effort to circumvent Davies, Tolstoy befriended a more senior Stilwell aide, Major General Thomas Hearn, the CBI chief of staff, and arranged a showing of his OSS film, *Inside Tibet*. Won over by Tolstoy's charm, Hearn asked why he was not part of DIXIE, which the major interpreted as an invitation from a superior officer. Tolstoy began preparations for Yenan, provoking a War Department complaint that the

OSS was sending an unauthorized mission. The Army prevailed; Tolstoy had overplayed his hand.

It was the end of Tolstoy's "good war." None of his projects won approval. In spring 1945, as the war wound down, the British-born author Robert Payne met Lieutenant Colonel (as he now was) Tolstoy in a vodka factory in southwest China. Owned by a White Russian, the factory was near a U.S. air base and supply depot in Kunming, a gathering place for officers and GI's. Tolstoy was "tall, bronzed, impeccably dressed, and he stood out from all the other officers by a certain refinement of manner." The vodka factory's owner held Tolstoy in great awe, and arranged a splendid party for him— gallons of the best vodka, a suckling pig, and roast pheasant. "It was at this party," writes Payne, "that I learned for the first time that he had been sent on a special mission to Tibet by President Roosevelt. He did not talk about the mission at any length, perhaps because it had been very secret, and he much preferred to talk about his famous grandfather [of whom he said] 'He was always talking about humility, but even though we were children we knew he was terribly proud.'"

After the war, Ilia Tolstoy lectured, worked as a consultant, and settled in New York. As a vice-president of the Tolstoy Foundation, he persuaded its founder, his aunt, Alexandra Tolstoya, to establish a special program for Tibetan refugees fleeing the 1950 Chinese invasion. Yet the high point of his life, literally and figuratively, was his fourteen weeks in Lhasa. He died in 1970.

BROOKE DOLAN CAME OUT OF TIBET WASTED BY MALARIA, AND unsure where he belonged. He returned to America in November 1943 with "Miss Tick" (who died, sadly, in a street accident), and at his request was transferred from the OSS to the Air Force. On his return to China, he represented the Twentieth Bomber Command on the Military Observer Group in Yenan, securing the DIXIE assignment that Tolstoy failed to get. Dolan was among eighteen officers and civilians under the command of Colonel David Barrett, a China specialist. The mission's position was ambiguous, since Mao's Communists were in rebellion against America's Nationalist ally. Dolan's role was also unclear; it was generally assumed that he was still an OSS officer.

So believed the officer to whom he was closest, Major Arnold Dadian, a Japanese-language specialist with an easy Midwestern manner. In their conversations, Dolan said little about Tibet, never mentioned the OSS, and gave almost no indication of his erudition on natural history or his passion for hunting. "We came together because I sensed a fellow non-conformist," recalls Dadian. "He was angry at being denied the rank of major, which he attributed to his allegedly 'messy' appearance. I remember his mysterious manner, and yes, his hard drinking." The drinking was especially disconcerting to Dolan's roommate, Major Charles Dole, because of his habit of playing with a loaded .45 caliber revolver. "Once, I think by accident, he fired the gun," Dole remembers, "and the bullet bounced scarily around the cave in which we were quartered."

What appealed to Dolan at Yenan was its proximity to China's hinterland. Two months after his arrival in August 1944, he was off on a 600-mile trek to a mountainous Communist base at Fou-ping. From there, with a small party of Chinese, he scouted the plains of Hopei Province, then under Japanese occupation. He endured a bitter mountain winter, hiding in caves and tunnels to elude the Japanese, who knew of his presence and were hunting for him. On his return to Fou-ping, he helped rescue a B–29 crew and a fighter pilot who had been forced down near Peking, reaching Yenan in April.

There he took time out to hunt wild goats at Chien-Lu near the Tibetan border, along with a fellow officer, Major David Gascoyne. All this was hinted at in one of his last letters, dated July 2, 1945, in which he apologized for being incommunicado for six months. He had returned from an "arduous, interesting, and at times rather exciting journey," in which he got heartily sick of eating cabbage. He described what was to be his final hunting trip, along the Tibetan borderland, in quest of "Blue Sheep, Takin, Serow, etc." He was escorted ("they would accept no pay") by Jimmy, his former hunter, and Lobsang, a former caravan wallah, who had gotten together "four raw Tibetans." The Red Gods smiled, he reported, and withheld daily rains and mists, and so he was able to fell a takin: "You can imagine how Jimmy and I felt—to have killed another of those magnificent beasts after a lapse of eleven years!... We prepared the skin and skulls as carefully as we prepared a specimen in the old days."

He closed saying he had a new assignment that would take him to a region with superb ducks and geese, and with gazelles and bighorns at no great distance. It was Tibet that beckoned. A month later he was in Chungking, where, not long after the Japanese surrender, he ended his own life on August 19, 1945. How he died was not divulged, but as obituaries asserted at the time, he died on active duty. It was a cruelly unfinished life. Ilia Tolstoy, whom Dolan always called "Bill," was in western China when a telegram was handed to him with news of his companion's death. Standing next to Tolstoy was Colonel David Longacre, who never forgot the moment. "Tolstoy literally turned ashen," recalls Longacre, "he was in total shock, as if he had been struck. But aside from saying that Dolan was dead, he said not a word about what happened."

FOR MOST OF WORLD WAR II, THE CHINA-BURMA-INDIA THEATER was a sideshow, yet it did not seem so to those who served there. For many Americans, it was a time when life seemed at its fullest, when Allied knights-errant challenged real dragons. The exertions of war drew tens of thousands to corners of inner Asia where few Westerners had trod. Seemingly overnight huge airfields were cleared in the jungles of Assam so that lumbering transports could better negotiate the wind-tormented, perilous Hump in the Eastern Himalaya. All who took part in the struggle were affected. Among them was Captain Desmond FitzGerald, an Army liaison officer with a Chinese battalion in the mountainous jungles of Burma. A Boston Brahmin, FitzGerald came to the CBI by way of Harvard; he was then married to Marietta Peabody, daughter of Groton's formidable headmaster (their daughter Frances was to write a reflective book about Vietnam, *Fire in the Lake*). Assigned to a battleground of primal ferocity and discomfort, FitzGerald found a vocation. As Evan Thomas recounts in *The Very Best Men* (1995), FitzGerald enjoyed the exotic life of the bush and learned to eat monkey brains and smoke opium with Burmese chieftains. He developed a particular affection for the mountain tribes of Asia, with their weathered faces and stiff-necked independence. What the Gurkhas were to the British Empire, he once contended, these mountain peoples could be to the Free World's struggle against Chinese Communism. After World War II, FitzGerald brought this conviction to the newly formed Central Intelligence Agency, and in due course became its Far East operations chief.

In the 1950's, FitzGerald's attention was caught by the Khampa warriors of eastern Tibet: tall, long-faced fighters who called themselves *ten dzong ma mi* (soldiers of the fortress of faith). The Khampas were a mountain people with a long tradition of resisting central authority, Chinese or Tibetan. When Mao's armies engulfed Tibet in 1950, overwhelming the Dalai Lama's brave but ill-equipped army, the Chinese did not at first attempt to impose their ideology on "political Tibet," i.e. the great plateau traditionally ruled by Lhasa. Under a nineteen-point agreement signed under duress by a Tibetan delegation in Peking, the new Communist regime promised autonomy to "political" Tibet. But in the borderland Amdo Province, home of the Khampas, Peking sought immediately to impose fiscal and other practices that collided with the traditional mores of culturally Tibetan peoples. Armed resistance promptly developed.

To FitzGerald and his chiefs at CIA headquarters in Langley, Virginia, it seemed just and feasible to help the Khampas wage a secret war that would punish Red China for its 1950 invasion and subsequent occupation of Tibet—a strategy endorsed by the Dalai Lama's brother, Gyalo Thondup, though not by the Buddhist ruler himself. Yet the Dalai Lama did accept CIA assistance in 1959, when he fled the country and sought asylum in India. Before his flight, the CIA had begun dropping weapons into Tibet, an operation planned by FitzGerald and inspired by the example of the Hump. As with other covert operations approved during the Eisenhower years, CIRCUS grew by leaps. In 1958, the Pentagon approved use of Camp Hale near Leadville, Colorado, and there for six years Tibetans received secret training in guerrilla warfare. The political climate changed when

John F. Kennedy became President and especially after the Bay of Pigs debacle in April 1961 when he took a more skeptical view of the CIA's projects. When John Kenneth Galbraith became Kennedy's Ambassador to India, the Harvard economist was disturbed by "one particularly insane enterprise"—C-140 airdrops into China to supply the Khampas were being flown from Bangkok over India to northern Nepal. Galbraith succeeded in aborting those activities in 1962, at least in India, "perhaps my single most useful activity that spring." Nevertheless the agency continued its airdrops from bases in the Mustang region of Nepal until 1969, when the Nixon Administration's overture to China turned CIRCUS into an embarrassment.

Desmond FitzGerald, in Galbraith's view, was "the most sanguinary, imaginative and personable architect of covert operations in CIA history. Also the most irresponsible." As with his senior colleagues at the agency, FitzGerald's honor, sincerity, and patriotism were not in question; his judgment was. CIRCUS necessarily fed hopes that the American goal was the liberation of Tibet from Chinese occupiers. In truth, as Sam Halpern, formerly of the CIA's Far Eastern operations, acknowledged, "Basically Tibet was just a nuisance to the ChiComs. It was fun and games. It didn't have any real effect." Yet this was never made plain to Tibetan trainees at Camp Hale.

Victor Marchetti, an early defector from the CIA, has expressed the essential moral problem succinctly: "Although CIA officers led their Tibetan trainees to believe that they were being readied for the reconquering of their homeland, even within the agency few saw any real chance that this could happen. Some of the covert operators who worked directly with the Tibetans, however, came to believe their own persuasive propaganda. Years later, they would flush with anger and frustration describing how they and their Tibetans had been undone by the bureaucrats back in Washington." Adding to their anguish was an appalling casualty rate; three out of four Khampa guerrillas flown into Tibet were tracked down and killed.

The pattern was established in the Tolstoy-Dolan mission. When President Roosevelt signed a letter to the Dalai Lama, it was understood in Washington that this did not signify American recognition of Tibetan independence; the President was merely addressing the

Dalai Lama in his capacity as a spiritual leader. Yet this interesting distinction, as Melvyn Goldstein points out, was never made clear to the Tibetans, who reasonably assumed the Presidential letter constituted recognition—an impression strengthened after Tolstoy told Tibetans they deserved to be represented at the Peace Conference. Yet, as Knaus bitterly notes, after the Chinese invasion, U.S. support for Tibet at the United Nations was mostly pro forma.

Doubtless Tolstoy and Dolan thought they were helping the Tibetan cause, as did the CIA trainers at Camp Hale. That they loved Tibet cannot be doubted, yet one may justly add they loved not wisely but too well.

The Owl of Minerva

FOR HALF A DECADE, WE HAD SCAVENGED ARCHIVES AND scholarly journals in an effort to look afresh at the modern age's oldest, best-established imperial rivalry, the Anglo-Russian competition for mastery of Central Asia. Out of this duel came spy services, proxy wars, the mystique of maps. Yet the written record has its limitations. We were curious how a flesh-and-blood former combatant might view the contest in hindsight. What now of the centrality of Eurasia or the cult of the frontier? A friend at Oxford suggested that we look up H. V. Hodson, once editor (1950–61) of the London *Sunday Times,* an ex-Fellow of All Souls, and emeritus Provost of the Ditchley Foundation in Oxfordshire. At ninety, Harry Hodson had devoted half his lifetime to serving and interpreting the British Empire. From Balliol and All Souls he moved at twenty-five to the editorship of *The Round Table,* the journal of the influential imperial think-tank of the same name. India became Hodson's special concern when he was appointed an aide to the Viceroy in World War II, and he was to chronicle the demise of the Raj in *The Great Divide: Britain, India, Pakistan* (1969).

A particular item in Hodson's vitae caught our eye. He had been a close friend of Sir Olaf Caroe, the last British Governor of the North-West Frontier, whose life and career Hodson memorialized in a *Times* obituary and in the Dictionary of National Biography. In our own researches we seemed regularly to come across Sir Olaf's tracks. He was among the half-forgotten figures—Sir Halford Mackinder and James Burnham are in the same backstage brigade—whose beliefs formed the link between the old Great Game and our age's Cold War. They mapped the passes that others were to contest, almost literally in Caroe's case.

Sir Olaf was a "forward school" man to his fingertips. While serving in northwest India, he developed an affection verging on adulation for the Pathans, among the most fractious of the "martial races" dear to British frontiersmen. With this he combined a Curzonian suspicion of Russia and all its works. Caroe's views became surer and bolder as he rose through the Indian Civil Service to become the Viceroy's Foreign Secretary for seven years until 1946, when he was named Governor of the North-West Frontier Province (which Curzon established).

Caroe led the way in calling on America to take over Britain's strategic role in the Persian Gulf and on the frontier with Afghanistan. He implored Washington to befriend Pakistan and protect Kuwait and the other Gulf sheikdoms. He set forth these beliefs first in an article for *Round Table* in 1949, then in a book, *Wells of Power: The Oilfields of South-Western Asia* (1951). There he asked Americans not to succumb to schoolboy shibboleths about imperialism in checking the Soviet drive southward. He invoked "the voice of Curzon," citing the Viceroy's vibrant declaration in 1892, that he would regard granting Russia a port on the Persian Gulf ("that dear dream of so many a patriot from the Neva to the Volga") as an international provocation to war.

Not only was the Gulf in peril. We came upon a State Department report of a briefing by Sir Olaf at Peshawar in May 1947, during the run-up to Indian independence. Caroe first expressed the "correct" Foreign Office policy, looking toward a united India. He then spoke more frankly to a visiting U.S. official: "Sir Olaf intimated that the Foreign Office tended too much to look upon India as a peninsular unit like Italy...He felt it did not sufficiently realize the great political importance of the Northwest Frontier Province and Afghanistan, which he described as 'the uncertain vestibule' in future relations between Soviet Russia and India." Caroe regretted that his own Government played down Soviet penetration of frontier areas like Gilgit, Chitral, and Swat, adding "he would not be unfavorable to the establishment of a separate Pakhistan [sic]."

So generally known was Caroe's preference for the Muslim League that supporters of the Congress Party contended that he could not conduct impartially the referendum on the North-West Province's future. Just before that vote, at the Viceroy's initiative, Sir Olaf resigned, nominally for reasons of health. From England, Caroe continued his tutelage of Americans, notably during an extensive speaking tour in 1952 sponsored by the Foreign Office. He became the matchmaker for Washington's partnership with Pakistan, initially within the framework of the Baghdad Pact, modeled on NATO, whose other members were Turkey, Iran, and Iraq. His role was first spotted by a Washington journalist and authority on Asian nationalism, Selig Harrison, to whom Caroe proudly wrote in 1959: "My Pakistan friends regard me as the inventor of the Baghdad Pact! Indeed, I have more than once flattered myself that J. F. Dulles' phrase 'The Northern Tier' and his association of the U.S. with the 'Baghdad' countries in Asia were influenced by the thinking in *Wells of Power*. In that book I called those countries 'The Northern Screen'—the same idea really."

What, we wondered, would Harry Hodson say in retrospect about all this?

OUR MEETING IN LONDON WAS AT THE REFORM CLUB, ONCE THE habitat of both creators and critics of the Victorian Empire. Its colonnaded reception hall, with its busts and pilasters, harbors the determined shades of Palmerston and Gladstone, John Bright and Lord Morley. Faith in reason, progress, and Western superiority—all the suspect creeds of the British Century—still lingers in the interstices of the club's public rooms and its library, where the old John Murray classics of exploration repose in their multi-volume dignity.

Harry Hodson arrived precisely on time, and at table greeted us with curiosity and animation. At ninety, he remained on the *qui vive* for high table gossip from Oxford, spoke with informed gusto about the state (lamentable) of British journalism, and pressed for information about our work-in-progress: "You've told me the subject, but what is your point, your theme, your spin?" Our response was circumspect. It did seem, we averred, that the antagonists in the Great Game were mutually prone to exaggerating each other's capacity for mischief, and that it was hard now to discern what enduring benefit Russia or Britain derived from dominion over so much Asian real estate.

"But of course!" He gripped the table and leaned forward. "Our greatest nightmare, our overriding fear, was that the Russians would occupy Afghanistan, with calamitous results. And what happened? In 1979, they *did* invade—they crossed the Oxus, they rolled their tanks into Kabul on the very highway built by Russian foreign aid, just as many of us said they would." A pause, and with eyebrows mischievously raised: "*And it really didn't matter.*" It obviously did matter to the Soviet Union, he continued, and it mattered all too cruelly to the Afghans. Yet dominion over Kabul did not assure the Kremlin mastery of Iran, Pakistan, or the Persian Gulf. Instead it plunged the Red Army into a ten-year bloodletting that brought on the collapse of the Communist empire.

As to Olaf Caroe, Harry Hodson found it easier to discuss his doctrines than the man. "We were all much surer of what we knew, and more zealous." Sir Olaf was not a person given to self-doubt, Hodson intimated, and like many who served the Raj, he was perhaps too literal-minded, especially about maps. Our talk continued over coffee, and after rising Hodson thanked us for an encounter he found agreeable, a sentiment reinforced by a gracious note the following day. From his ruminative perch, he penned a final thought: "In the light of history, I think the Game really was a game, with scores but no substantive prizes." Hodson died two years later, at ninety-two. We were reminded of an old saying, that the sagacious Owl of Minerva spreads its wings only at dusk.

Harry Hodson's reticence about Sir Olaf Caroe was understandable. He had no wish to speak ill of a deceased colleague, and his allusion to maps implied that he knew what we knew. Acting on his own authority, Caroe attempted by legerdemain to turn cartographic water into wine, his aim being to buttress India's North-East Frontier.

In 1913–14, an earlier Indian Foreign Secretary, Sir Henry McMahon, convened a conference at Simla to resolve the matter of Tibet's disputed frontiers and political status. As related in Chapter 17, China flatly rejected McMahon's territorial proposals, and Tibetans agreed on condition that Britain would secure Peking's assent to the overall Simla bargain, which never happened. McMahon's "strategic frontier" was all but forgotten until 1935, when Olaf Caroe, a middle-level official in New Delhi, "rediscovered" it in old Foreign Department files. Contending that the Tibetan signature gave the McMahon Line arguable legitimacy, Caroe persuaded the governments in New Delhi and London to begin treating it as India's de facto frontier, and to depict it on official maps. He urged doing this discreetly, "with the avoidance of unnecessary publicity!"

There was a problem. McMahon's frontier modification had not been entered in the 1929 edition of C. U. Aitchison's *Collection of Treaties* relating to India, the official repository for such agreements. Caroe arranged for a substitute version of the Aitchison volume to replace all original copies. The altered text in the new version—still dated "1929"—represented the Simla Conference as a success and listed the McMahon Line as one of its agreed achievements. However, two or three copies of the authentic Aitchison escaped Caroe's recall. One was discovered at the Harvard University library in 1963 by a British diplomat and visiting fellow, Sir John Addis. By comparing the original and the doctored version, Addis showed that a key piece of evidence that India was using in its border dispute with China was a forgery.

By then, the Chinese had long since marched into Lhasa, where in 1951 its officials had taken possession of the Tibetan Foreign Bureau. There they found the old Simla documents and consulted with Tibetans involved with border negotiations. Writes the Tibetan historian Tsering Shakya in *The Dragon in the Land of Snows* (1999), "As far as the McMahon line was concerned, the Chinese learned that their views were identical with the Tibetans." Since Lhasa's conditions—Chinese approval of the overall accord—had not been met, the Simla agreements were moot.

In New Delhi, however, the thinking was very different. Under Jawaharlal Nehru, a lifelong opponent of British rule, India adopted a "forward policy" as robust as any advocated by his imperial predecessors. In 1947, when Nehru became India's first Prime Minister, he rejected protests by the Chinese (then still Nationalist) on Indian claims along the country's northern border. Regardless of Chinese maps, Nehru informed Parliament in 1950, "Our maps show that the McMahon Line is our boundary," adding "and we will not let anybody come across our boundary." The following year, to underscore his point, India annexed the Tawang monastery area, which the British had pragmatically left under Tibetan control though it was on the Indian side of the line.

More provocatively, India published new maps in 1954 that also incorporated in India the Aksai Chin, a frozen no-man's land 17,000 feet high abutting Tibet, Ladakh, and China. Although surveyed by the British in the nineteenth century, the Aksai Chin, meaning "desert of white stones," was never formally claimed by the Raj. This was the plateau on which Sven Hedin crossed into Tibet in 1906 after promising the British he would not enter the country from Indian territory. Lord Minto, then the Viceroy, agreed that he kept his word.

China began challenging Nehru's "forward policy" as soon as India established advanced checkpoints. Administering these checkpoints was Nehru's spymaster, N. B. Mullik, director of the Intelligence Bureau, whose zeal often led to conflict with the Foreign Ministry and the Indian Army. There were frequent occasions when Mullik's patrols trespassed into China due to faulty maps. Mullik was always confident, as he tells us in his memoirs, that when an internal dispute "was referred to the Prime Minister, he would decide in our favour, because we were only carrying out the orders specifically given by him to me." Whatever the misgivings within the government, the press and politicians all but unanimously cheered Nehru for resolutely defending what was now deemed hallowed Indian soil.

Alas, the result was a confrontation that humiliated India, broke Nehru's spirit, and hastened his death in 1964. For all his intelligence, Nehru seemingly succumbed to the imperial theses that geography is destiny, that distant frontiers ensure strategic depth, that territories are never to be surrendered, and that dominion over them is in some sense a measure of a nation's vitality and importance.

IN SO SUCCUMBING, JAWAHARAL NEHRU WAS A CHILD OF HIS AGE. Born in 1889 to a wealthy Kashmiri Brahmin father, Nehru was sent to Edwardian England to attend Harrow and Trinity College, Cambridge. There he fell under the spell of Fabian Socialism and its demigods—Beatrice and Sidney Webb, H. G. Wells, and Bernard Shaw—and of Cambridge dons like John Maynard Keynes and Bertrand Russell. Their influence can be sensed in Nehru's sharp and sardonic prose. The British treated India, he remarks in his autobiography, as an enormous country house in which the gentry took the best rooms and consigned the Indians to the servants' hall. As in every proper country estate, "there was a fixed hierarchy in those lower regions—butler, house-keeper, cook, valet, maid, footman, etc.—and strict precedence was observed among them. But, between the upper and lower regions of the house there was, socially and politically, an impassable barrier." What most troubled him was that so many Indians accepted this as a natural arrangement, and too often developed "the mentality of the good country-house servant."

On returning to India in 1912, Nehru sided with the radicals in the Indian National Congress, becoming its president in 1928 and dominating it thereafter. As Gandhi's chief lieutenant, he was frequently in British jails, "the best university in the world." With reservations, he admired the Soviet experiment and echoed the Marxist belief that imperialism was rooted in the capitalist scramble for markets—a view he elaborated in speeches as a leader in the 1920's of the League Against Imperialism.

Nevertheless, when India attained independence in 1947, thereby acquiring the better rooms in the great country house, Nehru was reluctant to abandon the imperial property deeds stowed in the safe. Not only did India contend with Pakistan over title to Nehru's cherished Kashmir, but to the east it inherited an anomalous connection with Tibet. Like the old Raj, India continued to post a diplomat in Lhasa—in fact, a Briton, Hugh Richardson, who for a few years simply stayed on—although like Britain it did not recognize Tibetan independence. In the same spirit Nehru endorsed the McMahon Line, drawn to give India control of the strategic heights facing Tibet. These anomalies became more acute after China's invasion of Tibet in 1950 and its aftermath—harsh Communist repression, an uprising in eastern Tibet that the CIA then assisted, and the Dalai Lama's 1959 flight from Lhasa. India found itself simultaneously conceding that Tibet was part of China, deploring the invasion, and claiming the McMahon Line as India's rightful inheritance. The young Dalai Lama described the basic anomaly after his arrival in India: "If you deny sovereign status to Tibet, you deny the validity of the McMahon Line."

Beginning in 1958, the dispute ceased to be a war of skirmishes. Rebuffed in its efforts to reach a compromise through negotiations, China began to meet force with force. Regular Indian troops had by now replaced Mullik's paramilitary patrols, despite protests by army commanders that they could not repel superior Chinese forces. As detailed in *India's China War* (1970), by Neville Maxwell, who covered the conflict for *The Times* of London, Nehru replaced resisting generals with military courtiers. The conflict became a crisis in summer 1962, when Nehru announced that the Indian Army had been ordered to repel the Chinese from territory claimed by India. The result was a rout. In October 1962, Mao's troops destroyed India's "forward policy" outposts on the Aksai Chin and overwhelmed the Indian brigade deployed across the McMahon Line. Peking then offered a cease-fire and a withdrawal, to be followed by talks. Nehru's response was immediate, and negative, and China launched a second wave of attacks.

Observing all this at close hand was John Kenneth Galbraith, the U.S. Ambassador to India in 1961–63. He had a personal and intellectual affinity with Nehru, with whom he shared a deadpan wit shaped in the Trinity College both had attended at Cambridge University. In public, the ambassador warmly and loyally supported India's territorial claims. Privately, he did all he could to fend off frantic Indian requests for massive military aid. He gambled on the likelihood that the Chinese, having made their point, would withdraw their forces—as they suddenly did, on November 21, 1962, and then offered a cease-fire. "There was no time for instructions from Washington," Galbraith recalled. "I went to see Nehru and urged that he accept it. Tired and worn, he immediately agreed; it was the worst time of his life."

A year later, it was evident to Galbraith that Nehru's life, physical and political, was nearly over. He was visibly depressed. His vision of an India standing above such pointless and cruel conflicts was at an end. And for what? Galbraith judged the Aksai Chin the least edifying non-Arctic landscape anywhere in planet. "Rarely in the long history of human conflict," Galbraith marveled, "have so many been so aroused over such a few acres of questionable terrain." Still, the eminent Harvard economist out of kindness failed to add that his great Indian friend brought much of this on himself. The interesting question is why.

Injured pride was surely a factor. From Nehru's vantage, China had treacherously repaid his support for its admission to the United Nations, his comradely embrace of Chou En-lai at the Afro-Asian Conference at Bandung in 1955, and the festive trip to Peking that followed. For this, his Western critics derided him as a leftist appeaser, while at home the Indian opposition faulted his tepid response to the Chinese invasion of Tibet. Hence his anger and frustration when the Chinese, after lying low for so long, made such quick work of India's forward outposts, exposing Nehru to the most unendurable of reproaches to a world leader—that he had been gullible and weak.

Yet this begs the deeper question. Why from the outset did this dedicated anti-imperialist stake so categorical a claim to disputed territory? A plausible hypothesis is that when Nehru pondered maps of the Himalaya, he saw not just physical features but the figurative lineaments of Mount Slippery Slope, rising above the murky waters of the River Perception. If you yield that Mount, an inner voice warns, the Chinese will next demand the renewed submission of their former vassals, Nepal and Bhutan, as indeed the Indian Ambassador in Peking predicted they might. Besides, when a major power yields up territory, the resulting perception of weakness can only encourage others to join the queue—as happened when the Chinese Empire was stripped of its outlying territories in the nineteenth century.

Certainly the conviction that the British possessions were inalienable was part of the Edwardian ethos during Nehru's school years. William L. Langer's *Diplomacy of Imperialism* (1951) gathers typical quotations on the theme by the giants of British public life, many of whom shared the outlook bluntly expressed by Cecil Rhodes in 1899. "The people of England are finding out that 'trade follows the flag,' and they have all become Imperialists," Rhodes declared. "They are not going to part with any territory...The English people intend to retain every inch of land they have got and perhaps they intend to secure a few more inches"—which with Rhodes's help, and after the Boer War, they did.

Trade does follow the flag, but the cost-benefit arguments about imperialism remain endless. Among the doubters was Professor Galbraith's former Harvard colleague, the economist Joseph Schumpeter, for whom imperialism was atavistic in character, a throwback to feudalism and the warrior state—"the objectless disposition on the part of a state to unlimited forcible expansion." In *Imperialism* (1951), he cites as an example the British acquisition in 1815 of the Ionian Islands, of which Corfu was the most important. One Foreign Secretary after another, he relates, realized Corfu's possession was meaningless, "not in the absolute sense, but simply because no reasonable person in England would have approved of the smallest sacrifice in its behalf." Palmerston fretted over the islands, as did Gladstone and Disraeli, but nobody dared risk the political opprobrium of giving the islands back to Greece until 1864, after the Greeks chose as their king a Danish brother-in-law of the Prince of Wales. Even so, as late as 1900, the legendary Admiral Sir John ("Jackie") Arbuthnot Fisher lamented the loss of Corfu, "a splendid place for the fleet," warning that England's epitaph would be, "What was won by the sword was given up by the pen."

By all odds the most fateful convert to this imperial ethos was Joseph Stalin. Born in the Caucasus, a party worker in the Baku oil-fields, a prisoner for four years in Siberia, and a Marxist specializing in the "nationalities question," Stalin knew more of Russia's non-European peoples than the Westernized rivals he defeated and liqui-dated. He was supremely conscious of what his Tsarist predecessors conquered, and what they coveted. A tough cord of consistency run-ning through Stalin's foreign policy was his patient determination to regain whatever he could of the old Russian Empire: the Baltic states, Poland, choice slices of Finland, the Kuril Islands, Armenia, Georgia, and the rest of the Caucasus, plus dominion over Outer Mongolia and North Korea.

It might be said of Stalin's foreign policy that he sought Tsarist ends with Bolshevik means. Behind all the catchphrases of the Comintern—"Socialism in One Country," "United Front," "Popu-lar Front," "Stop the Imperialist War"—Soviet diplomacy ran not only on ideological but also on Russian imperial tracks. How far this went came as a surprise to the Israeli scholar Gabriel Gorodet-sky, who recently unearthed new documents on Stalin's thinking during the Nazi-Soviet Pact in 1939–41. The archives revealed that during the period that Hitler's troops were massing in Poland's borders, Stalin's eyes were fixed not on northern Europe but on the mouth of the Danube and on Turkey. Stalin sought a Soviet seat on the Danube Commission to reverse the inferior position "imposed on Russia after an unhappy war for her...the Crimean!" (Foreign Minister V. M. Molotov's words, quoted in *Grand Delusion: Stalin and the German Invasion of Russia* [1999]). Similarly, with all the ardor of the old Tsars, Stalin sought mastery of the Dardanelles to redress the setbacks that followed the Russo-Turkish War of 1877–78. Sifting through Stalin's handwritten notes, Gorodetsky found the Russian words for "Great Game" (*Bol'shaia Igra*) approv-ingly scrawled by the General Secretary of the Communist Party of the USSR.

Stalin pored over maps, was obsessed by them. This trait he shared with two former naval persons, Winston Churchill and Franklin D.

Roosevelt, both of whom repaired daily to wartime map rooms, as if to chapel. Out of these maps arose a vision of the world that was simple and compelling, the ultimate cartographic emanation of the Great Game—the belief that mastery of the Eurasian Heartland was the key to dominion. The visionary was Sir Halford Mackinder, and his leading American disciple was James Burnham, the most original theoretician of the Cold War.

THE CLASSIC GREAT GAME, PITTING RUSSIA AGAINST BRITAIN, HAD as its subtext the memory of Genghis Khan. Arising seemingly from nowhere in the Eurasian steppe, there emerged in the thirteenth century the greatest land power the world has known, the Mongol Empire. To the military historian Sir Basil Liddell Hart, the Mongol realm "made the empires of Rome and Alexander appear insignificant." Under Genghis Khan and his successors, the empire stretched from Korea to Hungary, encompassing most of Asia and much of Eastern Europe. Muscovy itself was for centuries a vassal state of the Mongols, and the memory of that servitude hardened into a determination to dominate the empty steppe from which a new Golden Horde might arise.

The steppe was above all the realm of the horse. Mongolian mounted archers could, in today's language, project devastating power over vast distances. Their tireless horses also enabled Genghis Khan to send messengers at a speed of 200 miles a day, using couriers who sounded a horn as they approached a relay station, where they could remount without stopping.

In the nineteenth century, diplomats and generals became aware of an unsettling modern parallel, in the form of railroads and telegraphy. As the Romanov double-eagle moved eastward, rails and cables followed. By the 1870's, the British anxiously pondered the eastward advance of the new technology. In 1888, the first Englishman to secure a seat on Russia's new Trans-Caspian Railroad was Lord Curzon. He described the trip, and the threat he feared it implied, in *Russia in Central Asia and the Anglo-Russian Question.*

When Curzon lectured on the Russian rail advance at a conference in Newcastle, among his spellbound listeners was a former Oxford classmate, Halford J. Mackinder. Impressed and disturbed, Mackinder was struck by the ominous implications for an island kingdom whose imperial reach was based on seapower. In theory, the new mobility made Russia the master of an invincible interior fortress, which Mackinder called the World-Island. As he later put it:

> *Who rules East Europe commands the Heartland*
> *Who rules the Heartland commands the World-Island*
> *Who rules the World-Island commands the World.*

Mackinder was the most influential British geographer of his time. Of Scottish descent and a graduate of Christ Church, Oxford, he later founded Oxford's School of Geography, held a Conservative seat in Parliament from 1910 to 1920, and served as British High Commissioner in South Russia in 1919–20. Yet he is best remembered for a 1904 lecture, "The Geographical Pivot of History," at the Royal Geographical Society, a paper that established the new importance of geopolitics.

As he summarized its central thesis: "A generation ago steam and the Suez Canal appeared to have increased the mobility of sea power, relative to land power. Railways acted chiefly as feeders to ocean-going commerce. But trans-continental railways are now transmuting the conditions of land-power, and nowhere can they have such effects as in the closed heart-land of Euro-Asia, in vast areas in which neither timber nor accessible stone was available for road-making. Railways work wonders in the steppe, because they directly replace horse and camel mobility, the road stage of development having been omitted."

Mackinder elaborated in his distinctive hypnotic style: "As we consider the rapid review of the broader currents of history, does not a certain persistence of geographical relationships become evident? Is not the pivot region of the world's politics that vast area of Euro-Asia which is inaccessible to ships, but in antiquity lay open to the horse-riding nomads, and is today about to be covered with a network of railways? There have been and are here the conditions of

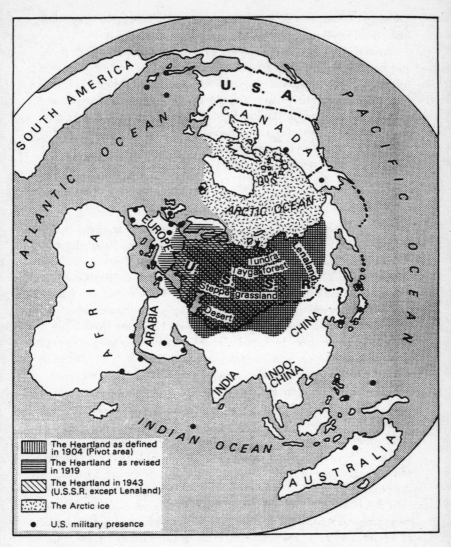

Halford MacKinder's Eurasian Heartland, in its various versions.

mobility of military and economic power of a far-reaching yet limited character. Russia replaces the Mongol Empire."

Russia replaces the Mongol Empire! The thought inspired both dread and fascination, and Mackinder's vision proved as mutable as it was influential. The Bavarian geopolitician Karl Haushofer borrowed from Mackinder to justify a German alliance with Russia, and through his star pupil, Rudolf Hess, influenced Hitler. A more arresting mutation was the work of an American theorist, James Burnham, whose gloomy forebodings and apocalyptic prose passed into the conservative mainstream as the Free World took on the Evil Empire.

Born in Chicago in 1905, the son of British emigrants, James Burnham graduated summa cum laude from Princeton in 1926. He continued his studies at Oxford's Balliol College, began teaching philosophy at New York University, and then less predictably in the 1930's became a Trotskyite, editing *The New International,* the movement's ideological journal. After breaking with Trotsky in 1940, Burnham found a world audience for *The Managerial Revolution,* a book whose admirers included George Orwell and John Kenneth Galbraith. While on wartime service with the OSS, Burnham in 1945 wrote a much-discussed essay, "Lenin's Heir," for *Partisan Review.* Half admiringly, he describes Stalin as a great man in the grand style, whose banquets, with their enormous menus, their flowing liquor and streams of toasts, and the unmoving secret police behind each guest, occur against the background of a starving populace. For Burnham, Stalin inherited the mantle of the most spectacular Tsars, of the great kings of the Medes and Persians, and of the Khanate of the Golden Horde.

In this essay, Burnham embraced Mackinder's thesis, together with his predilection for hypnotic capital letters, in identifying the source of Soviet power in "the magnetic core of the Eurasian Heartland." This core progresses outward through spheres of Absorption, Domination, and Orienting Influence until dissipating beyond Eurasia in zones of "momentary Appeasement and Infiltration (England, the

United States)." In order to take on this Eurasian dragon, Burnham contended, Americans had to assume Britain's global role. (In *The Managerial Revolution,* Burnham was direct and unsentimental: Americans were to be the "receiver" for the disintegrating British Empire.)

Not only Burnham's concepts but his phrases anticipated Winston Churchill's Iron Curtain speech at Fulton, Missouri, in 1946. By co-incidence the following year, Burnham's influential tocsin, *The Struggle for the World,* appeared the same week that President Truman called on Congress to replace the faltering British and provide military aid to Greece and Turkey. The coincidence prompted a twelve-page essay in Henry Luce's *Life.* Focusing on Burnham's provocative thesis that World War III had already begun in Greece, it called on Americans to mobilize the democratic world to challenge the Soviet empire.

Burnham was, to be sure, one voice among many. He himself was of different minds at different times. But his analysis in 1947 was in some respects notably prescient. He anticipated the Marshall Plan and NATO, the Cuban missile crisis, the Berlin Wall, America's plunge into Vietnam, and Soviet interventions in Hungary, Czecho-slovakia, and Afghanistan. He found an important disciple in William F. Buckley, Jr., and the CIA eagerly solicited Burnham's advice. Shorn of their extravagances, many of his ideas became a consensual commonplace. Yet what neither he nor his disciples ever anticipated was the disintegration of the Soviet Union. Indeed few were more surprised by the passing of the Evil Empire than its sworn enemies in the CIA.

WHEN THE BRITISH MILITARY HISTORIAN JOHN KEEGAN VISITED CIA headquarters at Langley, Virginia, in the 1980's, what impressed him was its resemblance to British India's Political and Secret Service in the days of the Raj. "It has assumed the mantle once worn by Kim's masters," he wrote, "as if it were a seamless garment." The resemblance was no accident. The CIA's first civilian director, Allen W. Dulles, did all he could to fix that tone, to create a secret, elitist world, touched with glamour and certain of its lofty mission.

Recruiters went forth to the Ivy League and top law firms in quest of young Americans with the right background. In the early days, Yale and Groton predominated. Yet the results in the long term did not sustain faith in the agency's elitism. As Evan Thomas, author of *The Very Best Men* (1995), was surprised to learn, "Grotties" were in charge of the 1953 coup in Iran that restored the Shah, for the overthrow a year later of an elected leftist leader in Guatemala, for the Bay of Pigs debacle in 1961, and for preparing the poisons that were mixed (but not used) to kill Fidel Castro.

Secrecy breeds its own fantasies. Seeing the political theater from backstage, intelligence operatives commonly pride themselves on their toughness, their realism, their knowledge of how the world *really* works. Often enough, on day-to-day maneuvers, the stage tricks of politicians are thus readily detected. Yet over and again spy agencies, for all their "realism," have misjudged the direction of history. They did not foresee the rise of the mullahs in Iran, the peaceful end of apartheid in South Africa, Communist China's conversion to market economics, or the collapse of the Berlin Wall. Most of all, the intelligence services misjudged the Soviet Union.

Evil as he was, Stalin was supposed to be the supreme realist. One gets the flavor in Henry Kissinger's *Diplomacy* (1994), with its quasi-admiring references to Stalin. The Soviet dictator, he tells us, was a "master practitioner of *Realpolitik*, not a Christian gentleman." He put his ideology in the service of *Realpolitik*, Kissinger says elsewhere, adding: "Richelieu or Bismarck would have had no difficulty understanding his strategy." By contrast, Kissinger suggests, the statesmen leading the democracies truly wore ideological blinkers by rejecting power politics.

Given the disarray in today's Russian Federation, it is perhaps not so surprising that many Russians look wistfully to Stalin and his imagined realism. The chairman of Russia's Communist Party, Gennadi Zyuganov, has published a manifesto, *The Geography of Victory*, which draws on Mackinder. It calls on Eurasians to unite along old Soviet lines to expel the "Atlantic" (i.e. American) influences. Indeed the dream of a new Eurasian Heartland "has become the common focus of Russia's 'red-brown' coalition," reports Charles Clover in a *Foreign Affairs* essay. He begins provocatively, "Few modern ideologies are as whimsically all-encompassing, as romantically obscure, as intellectually sloppy, and as likely to start a third world war as the theory of geopolitics." Concerning Russia, our own researches suggest that Clover, the Kiev correspondent for *Financial Times,* is right.

Writing about James Burnham in 1946, George Orwell found much that was true, original, and interesting in *The Managerial Revolution*, but added that the author, for all his realism, seemed to get everything wrong. Burnham in different editions of the same book had revised his predictions and had successively declared that (1) Nazi Germany was bound to win World War II, (2) that Hitler would not attack Russia until Britain surrendered, but when he did, (3) the Soviet Union was certain to lose. At each point, Burnham predicted a "*continuation of the thing that is happening,*" which Orwell called a major mental disease, rooted partly in power worship, to which intellectuals were especially susceptible.

In Burnham's case, the mental disease persisted. After his rousing *The Struggle for the World* (1947), calling for a collective Western response to Soviet expansion, he seemed not to notice that this indeed duly occurred, starting with the Marshall Plan and NATO. Instead, dazzled by apparent Communist successes in Africa, Asia, and Latin America, he followed up with *Suicide of the West* (1964). He now feared that the democratic world was destined to disappear by the end of the century, the victim of liberalism, the ideology of Western suicide. His criterion for decline was geographic, "effective political control over acreage." When we look at the atlas, he informs us, "The trend, the curve, is unmistakable. Over the past two generations Western civilization has been in a period of very rapid decline"—a dramatic shrinkage—"so obvious and undeniable that it can almost be thought of as self-evident."

To James Burnham, it was axiomatic that global power derived from the control of territory rich in resources, and was expressed in nuclear might and the will to hold whatever a nation possesses. Like many others, he was blinded by the sun of power. Because the Kremlin decreed that socialist gains were irreversible, and evidenced the "will" (a favorite word among realists) to enforce that belief, the Soviet Union was bound to prevail over the liberal West's "inaptitude for power."

An example of where this approach can lead is the contribution to *The Book of Predictions* (1980) submitted by David S. Sullivan, a Soviet foreign policy analyst for the CIA. By 1983, Sullivan predicted, the Soviet Union would achieve "clear-cut, unmistakable strategic nuclear superiority" over America, and a decade later, he grimly pursued, "The U.S. will have ceased to be a great power and will be struggling to hold itself together as a viable nation. The Soviet Union will be approaching hegemony over most of the world." (By contrast, Andrew W. Greeley, a Catholic priest, foresaw in the same volume that by 1990, Soviet Communism would be overthrown internally.)

With this in mind, one can look back at Stalin's "realism," and at the Great Game, from a fresh perspective. Stalin indeed bequeathed a mighty empire to his successors, who, to preserve Soviet hegemony, invaded Hungary, Czechoslovakia, and Afghanistan, and armed leftists across the globe, in Cuba and Nicaragua, Angola and Ethiopia, Iraq and Syria. The Soviet Union itself occupied "the socialist sixth" of the earth's surface, and if you added in the Kremlin's satellites and third-world clients, nearly a fourth of the world was red. Here was Mackinder's nightmare, fully realized, an empire spanning from East Berlin to North Korea, embracing most of the supposed Heartland. In fact, not once but twice in this century Russia commanded a huge Eurasian Empire that its rivals contemplated with dread and suspicion.

And twice in this century, Russia's empire collapsed from within.

The British Empire's disintegration was less dramatic, more graceful, but just as final. Not even the wildest right-wing Conservative would utter the bromidic phrases of a century ago—that the Anglo-Saxons were the world's natural rulers, that everything British was best, and that the Empire was divinely ordained. One can look back with qualified approval at aspects of the Pax Britannica—at its devotion to free speech, the rule of law, and parliamentary elections, and to its promotion of English. For the Empire as a whole, however, the happiest epitaph is Lord Macaulay's wish for India, "Come what may, self-knowledge will lead to self-rule, and that would be the proudest day in British history."

We can look back as well with genuine admiration at the courage, energy, and intelligence of all the competitors in the Great Game, Asian and European, notwithstanding the presumptuous arrogance and careless confusions of imperial politics. Still, it would seem that Harry Hodson had it right. "The Game really was a game, with scores but no substantive prizes."

ACKNOWLEDGMENTS

∴

O UR ABIDING DEBT HAS BEEN TO THE TOLERANCE OF SCHOL-
ars, the generosity of colleagues, and the flexibility of employers. Brashly, we plunged into a dozen specialized realms, and
invariably were aided in our inquiries by scholars who saved us from
egregious blunders, and courteously sought to correct (not always
successfully) careless or premature judgments. Needless to add, none
mentioned are in any way responsible for errors of fact or interpretation that persist, a matter worth underscoring since we realize that
many who helped us will not agree with our own gloss.

Our first steps in India, Pakistan, and Nepal were made possible by
The New York Times, specifically by Jack Rosenthal, then Editor of the
Editorial Page, who allowed time for an extended trip. We were met
by Barbara Crossette, the *Times*'s Bureau Chief in New Delhi. With
her advice, and the essential help of P. J. Anthony in the Delhi Bu-
reau, we were able to visit Lahore, Karachi, Islamabad, Murree, Tax-
ila, Peshawar, and the Khyber Pass in Pakistan; and New Delhi,
Lucknow, Benares, Amritsar, Calcutta, Agra, and the princely states of
Rajasthan. Of special help in New York were Ambassador and Mrs.
Marker of the Pakistan Mission to the United Nations; the Indian
Mission swiftly resolved visa difficulties.

To Jack Rosenthal's successor, Howell Raines, we owe the possibility of an academic year at the Wissenschaftskolleg zu Berlin (the

Institute for Advanced Studies at Berlin), and two terms as research fellows at Oxford University. Of the Editorial Board's too invisible support staff, we are especially obliged to Rosemary Shields, Marion Greene, Sandra Ratkowsky, and Maureen Muenster. In London, Marion Underhill, The *Times* Bureau's Permanent Undersecretary, was there when needed.

Dr. Wolf Lepenies, Rector of the Wissenschaftskolleg zu Berlin, gave us a running start on research in 1994-95. The Kolleg's chief librarian, Frau Bottomley, and her staff somehow spirited books from all Europe. Of the Kolleg's fellows, we were especially indebted for ideas to India's Ramachandra Guha, Germany's Hans Medick and Florian Coulmas, Poland's Wiktor Osiatynski, Morocco's Fatema Mernissi, France's Karine Chemla, Mali's Mamadou Diawara, Russia's Irina Scherbakowa, and Britain's John Onians and Nicholas Boyle—a list that also gives some sense of the Kolleg's diversity.

To Godfrey Hodgson, Director of the Reuter Foundation Program at Oxford, we owe participation in a new fellowship program for journalists, based in Green College. Logistical headaches were resolved by his deputy, Rosemary Allan. For two terms, in 1996 and 1997, we had access to the Bodleian Library and its extensive Indian collection, to the Rhodes House library, and Oxfordshire's excellent public libraries. We benefited from two outstanding courses at All Souls College by the Chichele Professor of the History of War, Dr. Robert O'Neill. We were indebted to the late Dr. Michael Aris of St. Antony's College for providing an invaluable translation of Agvan Dorzhiev's memoirs. Others who generously helped us include Dr. Chandrika Kaul of Nuffield College, Isabel Onians of Wolfson College, and Jonathan and Jennie Power of Boars Hill. Of our press colleagues, two were unstinting in spotting errors in our manuscript: Indrani Bagchi of *The Economic Times*, Calcutta; and Anwar Iqbal, a political journalist, Islamabad. Neville Maxwell, founding director of the Reuter Program, and his wife Evelyn, heard us out in lively discussions at their ambient home. To Anthony Storr of Green College, we owe not only insights on gurus but also a chance to see the Indian memorabilia of Major General Sir Charles MacGregor, a great uncle of Dr. Storr's wife (Catherine Peters). For spiritual succor, finally, we relied on Gwen Robyns and her circle at North Leigh, Oxfordshire.

Special thanks are due to the archives and the industrious archivists who addressed often exotic queries. First in line is John Taylor of the National Archives in Washington, whose unique mastery of OSS documents is among the Capital's scholarly treasures. Keepers of special collections at the Library of Congress, the Smithsonian Institution, and Georgetown University were unfailingly helpful, as were archivists at Harvard's Houghton Library, Yenching Library, Fogg Museum Library, and Botany Library. It was a pleasure to delve at the Franklin D. Roosevelt Library in Hyde Park, New York. Essential information was promptly conveyed by alumni offices at Harvard and Princeton Universities, and St. Paul's School. For rapid response to a complicated request, thanks to Marcie Green, archivist of the Air Force Historical Research Agency at Maxwell Air Force Base, Alabama.

Further thanks are owed to the New York Public Library, which provided both research materials and its calming Frederick Lewis Allen Room. John Lundquist, Chief Librarian of the Public Library's Oriental Division, helped us through the Tibetan maze, as did Valrae Reynolds, Curator of Asian collections at the Newark Museum, Elizabeth Rogers and Rosemary Jones Tung, her predecessor as Director of the Jacques Marchais Museum of Tibetan Art on Staten Island, and Carol Spawn, archivist at the Academy of Natural Sciences in Philadelphia. Rinchen Dharlo and Glen Kelley at the Office of Tibet in New York provided not only published material but also British, German, and American documentary films. Janet Baldwin, the librarian of the Explorers Club, dug out relevant files, as did archivists at the American Museum of Natural History, the Tolstoy Foundation, and the Oral History Library at Columbia University. The New York Society Library, and its British counterpart, the London Library, were an essential source for rare travel books. The Pequot Library, in Southport, Connecticut, its chief librarian, Mary Freedman, and her deputies, David Cappiello and Danielle Carriera, enabled us to secure remote sources via an efficient inter-library loan system.

We followed a well-trod trail to the India Office Library, first to its evocative former quarters on Blackfriars Road, then to its gleaming new home in the British Library, with the help of Frances Wood, Ian Baxter, and Gita Venugopal. As technically impressive is Britain's new

Public Record Office, the source for Foreign Office documents and a model for all such facilities. At the Royal Geographical Society, the Keeper, Dr. Andrew Tatham, did us the courtesy of allowing use of his office when space elsewhere was not available. The library of the School of Oriental and African Studies (SOAS) is unusual in allowing qualified outsiders access to open shelves in one of the great collections of its kind.

We owe thanks to Peter Hopkirk, the ground-breaker in Great Game studies, for advice (and pointing us to the SOAS library); to Helen Wang of the British Museum and her husband Professor Tao Wang of SOAS, for patient counsel on Asia and its Silk Roads; to Geoff Jones, a New York lawyer who knows the whereabouts of all former OSS officers; to two retired CIA officers with great Asian expertise, John Waller and John Kenneth Knaus; to the late Harry Hodson of London; to Selig Harrison of Washington, D.C., among the best-informed of Asian hands; to Thomas Dolan IV of Philadelphia for helpful background; to Arnold Dadian, for his recollections of Operation DIXIE; to Carol McGovern Cerf, who allowed us to see the snuffbox that the Thirteenth Dalai Lama gave to her father; to Elizabeth Errington of the British Museum, for advice on Masson's coins; to Donald Lopez, who obtained for us the hard-to-get "Mythos Tibet" conference records; to Robert Cowley, founding editor of *Military History Quarterly*, for advice on editing chapters on the First Afghan War; to Linda Wrigley, for her editorial labors on the Rockhill chapter for *World Policy Journal;* to Peter Young, editor of *Archaeology,* for shepherding Aurel Stein into print; to Beth Jackson, for smoothing the wrinkles in German translations, likewise to the late Ann Dunnigan for help with the Russian; to Braham Norwick, for sharing his erudition on Tibet; to Roderick Van Engert, for recalling his boyhood memories of Kabul in 1943; to Hugh Richardson, for clarifying important points on the SS expedition; to Previn Patel of Monroe, Connecticut, for Indic illumination; to Madison, Wisconsin's independent scholar Milan Hauner for his monographs on Axis strategy in Asia; to Barbara and Michael Foster of New York, for sharing Tibetan lore; to Thomas L. Hughes of Washington, D.C., for lending the unpublished translation of Werner Otto von Hentig's memoirs; to Gabriel Gorodtetsky of Tel Aviv University; for letting us see his unpublished manuscript of "Grand Delusion"; to Mia Waller, for archival assistance in Washington, D.C.; to Howard and Sally Wriggins, for Asian knowledge; to Carolle J. Carter, for locating veterans of DIXIE. For reading and commenting on portions of our manuscript, very special thanks to David Schimmelpenninck van der Oye, of Brock University, Canada; Dr. Firuz Kazemzadeh, of Alta Loma, California; Nicholas Rizopoulos, New York; Professor Anders Stephanson, of New York; Alastair Lamb, of Lozère, France; Edward and Perdita Burlingame, of Purdys, New York; Carol McGovern Cerf, of Cambridge, Massachusetts; Neville Maxwell, of Oxford; Martin Brauen, of Zurich; Helen and Tao Wang and Susan Whitfield, of London; and Alexandre Andreyev and Vladimir Rosov, both of St. Petersburg.

To the following friends for providing necessary shelter: Robert and Martha Lewis in Washington, D.C.; Michael Horowitz and Gillian Darley; and Ray Bonner and Jane Perlez in London; Henry and Inge Bondi of Princeton, New Jersey, and Lucy Komisar, in Washington, D.C.

Our book, finally, would not exist without the literary midwifery of our agents, Morton Janklow and Tina Bennett, the enthusiasm of our editor Michael Bessie; the advice of Peter Osnos of Public Affairs Press; the copyediting of Norman MacAfee; and the energy and skills of Trish Hoard, John McLeod, and Jack Shoemaker, of Counterpoint.

Shareen Blair Brysac and Karl E. Meyer   August 1999

NOTES AND SOURCES

∴

Authors' Note: This is a selective guide to sources, meant to provide information for both the general reader as well as specialists. References to published sources has been kept to a minimum in earlier chapters. We employ the following abbreviations—OIOC: Oriental and India Office Collection, British Library; LOC: Library of Congress; NARA: National Archives and Records Administration; DNB: Dictionary of National Biography; DAB: Dictionary of American Biography; RGS: Royal Geographical Society.

Chapter One

William Moorcroft was forgotten by all but specialists until his feats were recalled for a wider audience by John Keay in *When Men and Mountains Meet: The Explorers of the Western Himalayas* (London, 1977) and Charles Allen in *A Mountain in Tibet: The Search for Mount Kailas and the Sources of the Great Rivers of India* (London, 1982). These were followed by the first full-length biography, Garry Alder's *Beyond Bokhara: The Life of William Moorcroft, Asian Explorer and Pioneer Veterinary Surgeon* (London, 1985). In attempting a task that defeated two predecessors, Alder, a British academic, retraced Moorcroft's travels, was arrested in India, robbed in Afghanistan (of his notes and manuscript as well as money), buried in snow drifts in Iran, almost murdered in Turkey, and half frozen near the border of Tibet. Not least of his tasks was to decipher Moorcroft's handwriting in voluminous papers at the OIOC in London. The result is a biography worthy of its remarkable subject.

Moorcroft's *Travels in the Himalayan Provinces etc.* (London, 1841), written with George Trebeck and edited (badly) by Horace Wilson, is overdue for revision. A poignant account of "Mr. Moorcroft's death" published in Calcutta is to be found in *The Asiatic Journal*, vol. XXI (1826), 707–15. We came upon the terse reference to Moorcroft's original appointment as stud superintendent in the personnel records of the East India Company (MSS. Eur. 016/3), dated March 8, 1807, in OIOC.

The India that Moorcroft knew is preserved in a number of solid narratives. Sir Penderel Moon's *The British Conquest and Dominion of India* (London, 1989) is notable for its even-handed gravitas; the author served in the Indian Civil Service from 1929 until independence in 1947, continuing under the new Government of India. The entire imperial canvas is rendered, with sympathy and a kick, by Jan Morris in *Heaven's Command: An Imperial Progress* (London, 1973), the first panel in the author's Pax Britannica trilogy. Another ICS veteran, Philip Mason, describes the men who ruled India (and with rare and royal exceptions, they were all men) in two fine volumes, *The Founders* and *The Guardians* (London, 1954), written under the nom de plume Philip Woodruff, and later reshaped into a single volume, *The Men Who Ruled India* (New York, 1985) under his own name. A recent attempt at a balanced reckoning from a British vantage is Lawrence James's *Raj: The Making and Unmaking of British India* (London, 1997). The Raj's most prolific chronicler is Michael Edwardes, and we have used *British India: 1772–1947, A Survey of the Nature and Effects of Alien Rule* (London, 1967), and *Glorious Sahibs: The Romantic as Empire Builder, 1799–1838* (New York, 1969).

Current scholarly work is well represented by C. A. Bayly, joint editor of *The New Cambridge History of India* and author of *Indian Society and the Making of the British Empire* (Cambridge, 1988) and *Imperial Meridian: The British Empire and the World, 1780–1830* (London, 1989). For a consensual Indian perspective on the same period, one may consult Parshotam Mehra, *A Dictionary of Modern Indian History: 1707–1947* (New Delhi, 1985).

The Mughal Empire can be glimpsed through the eyes of marveling Europeans in William Foster, ed., *Early Travels in India 1583–1619* (London, 1921), or through those of Babur, its founder, whose memoirs have been freshly translated by Wheeler M. Thackston in a lavish volume, *The Baburnama: Memoirs of Babur, Prince and Emperor* (New York, 1996). See also popular accounts by Bamber Gascoigne, *The Great Moghuls* (New York, 1971), and Waldemar Hansen, *The Peacock Throne: The Drama of Mogul India* (New York, 1972). Geoffrey Moorhouse's engaging *Calcutta* (London, 1971) can be supplemented by J. P. Losaty, *Calcutta: City of Palaces* (London, 1990), and Jan Morris, *Stones of Empire: The Buildings of British India* (Oxford, 1983). More generally, see Thomas R. Metcalf's *An Imperial Vision: Indian Architecture and Britain's Raj* (Berkeley, 1989).

Lucknow and Oudh are fortunate in their various historians: Rosie Llewellyn-Jones, *A Fatal Friendship: The Nawabs, the British and the City of Lucknow* (New Delhi, 1985); Yogesh Praveen, *Lucknow Monuments* (Lucknow, 1989); Abdul Halim Sharar, *Lucknow: The Last Phase of an Oriental Culture* (New Delhi, 1989); and Michael Edwardes, *The Orchid House: Splendours and Miseries of the Kingdom of Oudh, 1927–1857* (London, 1960).

On the Himalaya, we have found three volumes especially useful: Ian Cameron, *Mountains of the Gods* (London, 1984); Kenneth Mason, *Abode of Snow: A History of Himalayan Exploration* (London, 1955); and John Snelling, *The Sacred Mountain: The Complete Guide to Tibet's Mount Kailas* (London, 1990).

On Central Asian horses, see Morris Rossabi, "All the Khan's Horses," *Natural History,* vol. 103 (October 1994). Jonathan Maslow, *Sacred Horses* (New York, 1994), offers a diverting personal report on the breed's present condition. On the Nepal campaign, see John Premble, *The Invasion of Nepal: John Company at War 1814–16* (Oxford, 1971), and more generally, Byron Farwell's *The Gurkhas* (New York, 1984). On Tibet and its early explorers, the outstanding account is *British India and Tibet 1766–1910* (rev. ed., London, 1986) by Alastair Lamb.

4	The British journalist who was "welcomed to hell" was the London *Daily Telegraph*'s Trevor Fishlock, who describes Bihar in *India File* (London, 1983).
10	Sidney Owen is quoted in Vincent A. Smith, *The Oxford History of India* (Oxford, 1919), 591.
11	Honoria Lawrence is quoted in Llewellyn-Jones, 200–201.
16	John Snelling recently located the manuscript of the journal kept by Hyder Hearsey, and quotes liberally from it in the appendix of *The Sacred Mountain,* 415–25.
17	The broadcloth passage is from Moorcroft and Trebeck, 358 et seq.

Chapter Two

On the discomforts of Indian travel, see Michael Edwardes, *The Sahibs and the Lotus: The British in India* (London, 1988), and "Travel and Transport" in Bruce Palling, *A Literary Companion to India* (London, 1992). On Ranjit Singh and the Sikhs, the noted journalist Khushwant Singh has written a solid two-volume *History of the Sikhs* (Princeton, NJ, 1963 and 1966). Pertinent to Eros and the Orient are Ronald Hyam, *Empire and Sexuality: The British Experience* (Manchester, England, 1990), and David Stacton, *A Ride on the Tiger: The Curious Travels of Victor Jacquemont* (London, 1954).

About Ladakh and its people, see Janet Rizvi, *Ladakh: Crossroads of High Asia* (Delhi, 1983). The Kulu Valley is evoked in Penelope Chetwode, *Kulu: The End of the Habitable World* (London, 1972). Of the many books on the Vale of Kashmir, we commend Brigid Keenan, *Travels in Kashmir* (Delhi, 1989), for its breadth and detail. Mountstuart Elphinstone's classic, *An Account of the Kingdom of Caubul* (two vols.), was reissued in facsimile in Karachi in 1972 by the Oxford University Press with a preface by Sir Olaf Caroe. Harder to find is Brig. Gen. Sir Percy Sykes, *A History of Afghanistan* (London, 1940), in two volumes, of which most were destroyed by a direct hit during the London Blitz.

26–28   Burton's remarks are quoted in Edwardes, op. cit., 104. Burton's
         scandalous Indian years are detailed in Priscilla Napier, *I Have Sind:
         Charles Napier in India 1841–1844* (Salisbury, 1990), and in Fawn
         Brodie, *The Devil Drives: A Life of Sir Richard Burton* (New York,
         1967), from which the passage on the *bibi* is taken (51–52).

39–40   The European response to *Lalla Rookh* and Kashmir shawls is de-
         scribed passim in Keenan, op. cit. See as well John Irwin, *The Kash-
         mir Shawl* (London, 1974), and Caroline Karpinski, "Kashmir to
         Paisley," Metropolitan Museum of Art *Bulletin*, November 1963.

47–48   On Bokhara and its history, consult Wilfrid Blunt, *The Golden Road
         to Samarkand* (New York, 1974). Jenkinson's narrative can be found
         in E. D. Morgan and C. H. Coote, *Early Voyages and Travels in Russia*
         (London, 1886).

49   *"Le jeu vaut bien":* The letter is quoted in the DNB entry on Moor-
         croft.

51   Byron's passage through Afghanistan fills 80 pages in *The Road to
         Oxiana* in a Picador reprint (London, 1981) with an introduction
         by Bruce Chatwin.

Chapter Three

The First Afghan War, the first humbling of a European power by Asian irregulars, prompted a landfill of books. Pride of place belongs to Sir John Kaye,
History of the War in Afghanistan, first published in two volumes in 1851, then
expanded to three volumes in 1874. Many of the same principals also figure in
Kaye's *Lives of Indian Officers,* published in two volumes, also in London, in
1867. Kaye (1814–76) went to India in 1832 as a cadet in the Bengal artillery;
he resigned his commission in 1841 to take up a career as a writer. Returning
in 1845 to Britain, he succeeded John Stuart Mill as secretary of the Political
and Secret Department of the India Office in London. Thus a historian of energy and fluency, familiar with the principal actors and with access to journals
and archives, was able to write an analytic narrative in the tradition of Thucy-
dides. Of the many later books, two can be singled out: John H. Waller, *Beyond
the Khyber Pass* (New York, 1990), by a former Inspector General of the CIA;
and James Alfred Norris, *The First Afghan War* (Cambridge, U.K., 1967), based
on a fresh rereading of primary sources, which depicts Auckland as a sacrificial
scapegoat for Palmerston.

    Kaye's *History* stimulated many first-hand accounts, including that of Mohan
Lal, the first Indian voice as a chronicler of the Raj's battles, *Life of the Amir Dost
Muhammed Khan of Kabul,* (London, two volumes, 1846) and the first memoirs
of India by British women: Emily Eden, *Up the Country* (London, 1866, annotated in 1930 by Edward Thompson and reprinted in 1983 in the Virago Travellers Series); and Lady Florentia Sale's *Journal of the Disasters in Afghanistan*

(London, 1843), reissued in London in 1969 in an edition edited by Patrick Macrory.

Emily Eden also had a talented sister, but not until 1955 did John Murray publish *Golden Interlude: The Edens in India 1836–1842*, bringing together the unpublished journals and drawings of Fanny Eden. Only recently has there been a serious effort to rectify this neglect of British wives, mothers, and daughters. Maud Diver's *The Englishwoman in India* (Edinburgh, 1909) opened the door for such later works as Pat Barr, *The Memsahibs: The Women of Victorian India* (London, 1976); Margaret MacMillan, *Women of the Raj* (London, 1988); and Marian Fowler, *Below the Peacock Fan: First Ladies of the Raj* (New York, 1987), all of which feature Emily Eden.

On Charles Metcalfe, see Kaye, *The Life and Correspondence of Charles, Lord Metcalfe* (two vols., London, 1854), and Edward Thompson, *Life of Charles, Lord Metcalfe* (London, 1937). Hickey's picaresque diaries have appeared in many editions, of which we have used Alfred Spencer, ed., *Memoirs of William Hickey* (New York, 1921), and Peter Quennell, ed., *The Prodigal Rake* (New York, 1962). Macaulay's Indian years are detailed in George Otto Trevelyan, *The Life and Letters of Lord Macaulay* (New York, 1878), and John Clive, *Macaulay: The Shaping of the Historian* (New York, 1973). On the Whig background, relevant authorities include E. L. Woodward, *The Age of Reform, 1815–1870* (Oxford, 1938); Kenneth Bourne, *Palmerston: The Early Years* (New York, 1982); Jasper Ridley, *Lord Palmerston* (New York, 1971); Michael Joyce, *My Friend H: John Cam Hobhouse* (London, 1948); and David Cecil, *Lord M* (New York, 1954), the last being, incidentally, President Kennedy's favorite biography.

The Herat crisis, and its origins, are examined from a British vantage by Brig. Gen. Sir Percy Sykes, *A History of Persia* (London, 1951, two vols.), and J. B. Kelly, *Britain and the Persian Gulf* (Oxford, 1968). A more heterodox view can be found in Edward Ingram, *The Beginning of the Great Game in Asia, 1828–1834* (Oxford, 1979), and *In Defence of British India* (Oxford, 1984). On Pottinger's role, see George Pottinger, *The Afghan Connection: The Extraordinary Adventures of Major Eldred Pottinger* (Edinburgh, 1983). On Burnes, see James Lunt, *Bokhara Burnes* (London, 1969).

Josiah Harlan's curious career is retold in the DAB, in P. E. Caspiani, "The First American in Afghanistan," *Afghanistan*, July–September 1947, and in Frank Ross, ed., *Central Asia: Personal Narrative of General Josiah Harlan, 1832–1841* (London, 1939).

Charles Masson was recovered from obscurity by Sir Thomas Holdich, who mistakenly believed Masson was American, in *The Gates of India* (London, 1910), which drew extensively on Masson's *Narrative of Various Journeys in Balochistan, Afghanistan and the Panjab* (London, 1842, three vols.); and *Narrative of a Journey to Kalat* (London, 1843). Sir Gordon Whitteridge has written a valuable biography, *Charles Masson of Afghanistan* (Earminster, 1986), which helped prompt a new entry in a DNB supplement, *Missing Persons*, written by

Garry Alder. But new Masson material keeps turning up. We came upon an entire neglected file of Masson letters, mostly dealing with his coin collection but also touching on politics, in the papers of Sir Henry Pottinger (Eldred's uncle) at the Public Record Office in London (FO 705/32).

52 On Lady Butler, see Jan Morris, *Heaven's Command: An Imperial Progress* (London, 1973), and her and General Butler's DNB sketches.

57 Metcalfe's dissent can be found in Thompson, op. cit., 282–83.

60 The monsoon is described by Elphinstone in *Kingdom of Caubul,* vol. 1, 67–174.

69–72 Details on the siege of Herat are drawn chiefly from Kaye's *History of the War etc.,* and his sketch of Pottinger in *Lives,* op. cit., and George Pottinger's biography of his kinsman Eldred, op. cit.

Chapter Four

78 "the most splendid fête I had ever beheld": Kaye, *Lives,* II, 10, still the primary source on Burnes, to which the modern supplement is Lunt's biography, cited above.

78 "I was born a Scotsman": Quoted, Linda Colley, *Britons: Forging the Nation 1707–1837* (New Haven, 1992), 127. For a spirited, unabashed recital of Scottish accomplishments, see Duncan A. Bruce, *The Mark of the Scots: Their Astonishing Contributions to History, Science, Democracy, Literature and the Arts* (Secaucus, 1996).

109 "The Afghan war was done by myself": Sources for this archetypal controversy include Norris, *The First Afghan War* (critical of Palmerston), Bourne, *Palmerston* (exculpatory), and *My Friend H* (Hobhouse's behavior was "inexcusable"). The House of Commons debate is eminently quotable and can be found in Hansard's Parliamentary Debates, 3rd Series, vol. CLXII, March–May 1861, 38–95.

Chapter Five

Frederick Jackson Turner's great paper and its sequels are gathered in *Rereading Frederick Jackson Turner* (New York, 1994), with a useful commentary by John Mack Faragher. Ray Allen Billington, Turner's biographer, has also written *The American Frontier Thesis: Attack and Defense* (Washington, DC, 1971). A Texan, Walter Prescott Webb, bravely attempted to recast that thesis in global terms in *The Great Frontier* (New York, 1952), an effort thoughtfully appraised by William H. McNeill, *The Great Frontier: Freedom and Hierarchy in Modern Times* (Princeton, 1983). Owen Lattimore, *Studies in Frontier History: Collected Essays 1928–1958* (London, 1962), applies the thesis to Asia. Also see John Cotton,

Asian Frontier Nationalism: Owen Lattimore and the American Policy Debate (Atlantic Highlands, NJ, 1989).

On Russian expansion: Taras Hunczac, ed., *Russian Imperialism: From Ivan the Great to the Revolution* (New Brunswick, 1974), with a preface by Hans Kohn, is a useful introduction to Hugh Seton-Watson, *The Russian Empire, 1801–1917* (Oxford, 1967); W. Bruce Lincoln, *The Conquest of a Continent: Siberia and the Russians* (New York, 1994); Gerald Morgan, *Anglo-Russian Rivalry in Central Asia* (London, 1981); Seymour Becker, *Russia's Protectorates in Central Asia, 1865–1924* (Cambridge, MA, 1968); Edward Allworth, ed., *Central Asia: 130 Years of Russian Dominance, a Historical Overview* (Durham, 1994); Firuz Kazemzadeh, *Russia and Britain in Persia, 1864–1914* (New Haven, 1968); George Vernadsky, *Political and Diplomatic History of Russia* (Boston, 1936); John A. Harrison, *The Founding of the Russian Empire in Asia and America* (Coral Gables, FL, 1971); Dietrich Geyer, *Russian Imperialism: The Interaction of Domestic and Foreign Policy, 1860–1914* (New Haven, CT, 1987). For works with a strong British bias, see Alexis Krausse, *Russia in Asia: A Record and a Study, 1558–1899* (London, 1899); Charles Marvin, *The Russian Advance Towards India* (London, 1882); and George N. Curzon, *Russia in Central Asia* (London, 1889). For a Soviet interpretation, see N. A. Khalfin, *Russia's Policy in Central Asia, 1857–1868* (London, 1964).

On Russia's California adventure, see Samuel Flagg Bemis, *John Quincy Adams and the Foundation of American Foreign Policy* (New York, 1956); Thomas A. Bailey, *A Diplomatic History of the American People* (New York, 1950); and Hector Chevigny, *Russian America* (Portland, 1965). George Kennan's *The Marquis de Custine and His Russia in 1839* (Princeton, NJ, 1971) is an excellent introduction to the French traveler, whose *Empire of the Czar: A Journey Through Eternal Russia* was reissued in an abridged edition (New York, 1989). Tocqueville's prophecy is examined in an astute essay by Theodore Draper in *Present History* (New York, 1985) and by Paul Dukes, "Two Great Nations: 1815–50," *History Today* (February 1970), 95–106. On Sir Robert Wilson, see Michael Glover, *A Very Slippery Fellow* (Oxford, 1977).

The Stoddart-Conolly affair is memorably retold by Fitzroy Maclean, *A Person from England, and Other Travelers* (London 1958). The basic texts are Joseph Wolff, *Narrative of a Mission to Bokhara on the Years 1843–1845* (New York, 1845), available in an abridged edition published in 1967 with an introduction by Guy Wint; and Sir John Kaye, *The War in Afghanistan* (London, 1851), and *Lives of Indian Officers* (London, 1867).

The Crimean War's great historian was A. W. Kinglake, *The Invasion of the Crimea* (London, nine vols., 1877–88), a favorite of Churchill's and a source of his own prose. Kingsley Martin, *The Triumph of Lord Palmerston: A Study of Public Opinion in England Before the Crimean War* (London, rev. ed., 1963), discusses Tennyson and the boredom factor. Cecil Woodham-Smith, *The Reason Why* (New York, 1954), is the classic study of the Charge. See also Christopher Hibbert, *The Destruction of Lord Raglan* (London, 1961), and Donald Thomas, *Cardigan* (New York, 1975). On Russia after Crimea, and on Miliutin, we have drawn from Forrest A. Miller, *Dmitri Miliutin and the Reform Era in Russia* (Vanderbilt, TN, 1968); Bruce W. Menning, *Bayonets Before Bullets: The Imperial Russian Army 1861–1914* (Bloomington, 1992); and W. E. Mosse, *Alexander II and the Modernization of Russia* (New York, 1962). See also W. Bruce Lincoln, "General Dmitrii Milyutin and the Russian Army," *History Today* (January 1974), 41–47. On Tolstoy and Crimea, see Ernest J. Simmons, *Leo Tolstoy* (London, 1949).

112	He wondered what: *Rereading Frederick Jackson Turner,* 59.
112	Turner's thesis: ibid., 1–2.
115	In Washington: Bailey, op. cit, 182.
116	"The more I see": Quoted, Kennan, op. cit., 83–84.
117	He confided to the empress: Quoted, Draper, op. cit., 378.
117	As Peter Hopkirk: Hopkirk, *The Great Game* (New York, 1992), 62.
120	It lies, in the words: The travel writer is Colin Thubron, *The Lost Heart of Asia* (London, 1994).
122	Entering into a large: Eugene Schuyler, *Turkistan* (New York, 1877), vol. II, 101–2.
123	"To attack or defend": Quoted, Maclean, op. cit., 30.
124	"Here I am": ibid., 31–32.
125	Their exchange: quoted, Allworth, op. cit., 36–37.
126	While in Cawnpore: Kaye, *Lives*, 104.
127	"He is flighty": ibid., 136.
127	"Hip, hip, hoorah": Kaye, *History of the War in Afghanistan,* 1874 ed., vol. II, 71.
128	"in order that His Excellency": Maclean, op. cit., 49.
129	"From our Prison": ibid., 52–53.
130	to Bokhara: ibid, 68.
131	"Tell the Amir": Wolff, op. cit. (1845 ed.), 203.
132	"I have loved you": ibid., 255.
132	"How extraordinary": Maclean, op. cit., 89.
135	"The Negative Aspects": Simmons, *Tolstoy,* 131.
136	"it is not necessary": Kazemzadeh, op. cit., 7.

Chapter Six

Soon after the Great Mutiny, a multitude of personal accounts by Britons (and a scattering by Indians) were shaped into a narrative by Sir John Kaye in *History of the Sepoy War in India, 1857–1858* (London, 1880, three vols.), continued by Colonel G. B. Malleson as *The History of the Indian Mutiny, 1857–1858* (London, 1880, three vols.). Among modern accounts, Christopher Hibbert,

The Great Mutiny, India 1857 (New York, 1978), is notable for its balance and scholarship. On the brothers Lawrence, key works are by Michael Edwardes, *A Season in Hell: The Defence of the Lucknow Residency* (New York, 1973), and *The Necessary Hell: John and Henry Lawrence and the Indian Empire* (London, 1958). R. Bosworth Smith's *Life of Lord Lawrence* (London, 1883, two vols.) is very much the quintessential Victorian memorial. A good appreciation of the Lawrences can be found in Philip Mason, *The Men Who Ruled India: The Founders* (London, 1954). Andrew Ward, *Our Bones Are Scattered* (New York, 1996) brings together what is now known about Cawnpore. The Rani of Jhansi's memory is preserved in Antonia Fraser, *The Warrior Queens* (New York, 1989), which can be supplemented by Kaye and Moon.

To histories of the Russian advance previously cited can be added Januarius MacGahan, *Campaigning on the Oxus and the Fall of Khiva* (New York, 1874), and Eugene Schuyler, *Turkistan: Notes of a Journey in Russian Turkistan* (New York, 1877). Dale L. Walker has written the much-needed *Januarius MacGahan: The Life and Campaigns of an American War Correspondent* (Athens, OH, 1988). Schuyler has yet to find a biographer, but there is a valuable memoir by his daughter, Evelyn Schuyler Schaeffer, in *Eugene Schuyler: Selected Essays* (New York, 1901), which she edited.

Sir Henry Rawlinson's views are robustly set forth in *England and Russia in the East* (London, 1875), republished in 1970 by Praeger (New York and London) with a preface by Denis Sinor. George Rawlinson, Sir Henry's brother, also an authority on the ancient Middle East, has written *A Memoir of Sir Henry Creswicke Rawlinson* (London, 1898); an adequate modern life is overdue. The partisan and readable *Disraeli, Gladstone and the Eastern Question* (New York, 1972, paperback edition) by R. W. Seton-Watson describes the events leading to the Russo-Turkish War from a Liberal viewpoint. Virginia Cowles, *The Russian Dagger: Cold War in the Days of the Czars* (New York, 1969), is a popular account of the Balkan controversies examined in the scholarly classic by Matthew S. Anderson, *The Eastern Question, 1774–1923* (London, 1966).

138	"every European that": P. E. Roberts, *History of British India* (Oxford, 1958), 369.
138	Dalhousie took: Moon, op. cit., 609.
139	Yet his puzzled subjects: ibid., 652.
140	"There is a most": quoted, preface by Christopher Hibbert in Richard Barter, *The Siege of Delhi: Mutiny Memories of an Old Officer* (London, 1984), ix.
143	The massacre: Kaye, *History,* vol. III, 369.
143–144	"She adopted": Fraser, op. cit., 286.
144	"Now every square": Hibbert, *Great Mutiny,* 382.
145	In his own report: Fraser, op. cit., 295.
146	"a kind manner": Mason, op. cit., 335.

146   "There is a judge": ibid., 340.

147   "quite something": Hibbert, op. cit., 316.

147   "render more wide": Edwardes, *Necessary Hell*, 373–374.

148   "We shall offer him": Maud Diver, *Honoria Lawrence: A Fragment of Indian History* (London, 1936), 459.

149   "Time is everything just now": Mason, op cit., 336.

149   "Carefully register": Edwardes, *A Season in Hell*, 63.

150   "how harsh": Roger Hudson, ed., *William Russell: Special Correspondent of The Times* (London, 1995), 159.

150   "a war of religion": ibid., 106.

152   "The position of Russia": Gerald Morgan, *Anglo-Russian Rivalry in Central Asia: 1810–1895* (London, 1981), 120.

153   "each minister has the right": Schuyler, *Turkistan*, 263.

154–155 "the disquieting effect": Rawlinson, *England and Russia*, 279–80.

155   "In the interests": ibid., 285.

156–157 All quotations from the Lawrence Minute, as published in full in Morgan, op. cit., 226–37.

158   "take Khiva": Kazemzadeh, *Russia and Britain*, 25.

160   When he finally reached: *Campaigning on the Oxus*, 155.

160   "He came to": The entire text of Schuyler's official report was published as Appendix B in Fred Burnaby, *A Ride to Khiva* (London, 1877; reprinted in paperback, London, 1983), 391–96.

162–163 "Since my letter": Extensive excerpts of MacGahan's articles on Bulgaria can be found in Louis L. Snyder and Richard B. Morris, eds., *A Treasury of Great Reporting* (New York, 1949), 206–14. Quote at 209–10.

162–163 Among his readers was: Seton-Watson, *Disraeli, Gladstone and the Eastern Question*, 75.

165–166 "I compliment you": Dale Walker, *Januarius MacGahan*, 276–27.

166   "The three men": ibid., 204.

168   "Called from their card tables": ibid., 269.

169   "I hold it as": Hopkirk, *Great Game*, 407.

169   "In Europe we were": F. M. Dostoyevsky, *The Diary of a Writer* (New York, 1949), translated by Boris Brasol, 1051–52.

Chapter Seven

The biography that led to a reappraisal of Bloomsbury, Michael Holroyd's *Lytton Strachey* (New York, 1967, two vols.), in passing details the family's Indian connection. See also Sir John Strachey, *India* (London, 1894). Leonard Woolf recalls his years as a civil servant in Ceylon in *Growing: An Autobiography of the Years 1904 to 1911* (London, 1961). On Virginia Woolf and her imperial antecedents, see Quentin Bell, *Virginia Woolf* (New York, 1972), and Hermione Lee, *Virginia Woolf* (New York, 1996).

Love of letters was a Lytton family trait, and Lord Lytton was well served by his daughter, Lady Betty Balfour, in *Personal and Literary Letters of Robert, First Earl of Lytton* (New York, 1906, two vols.) and her *History of Lord Lytton's Indian Administration* (London, 1899); and by his granddaughter, Mary Luytens, who puts the best possible case for him in *The Lyttons in India* (London, 1979). The more critical prevailing view is expressed in Mark Bence-Jones, *The Viceroys of India* (New York, 1982). On Edith Lytton, see the fine essay by Marian Fowler in *Below the Peacock Fan: First Ladies of the Raj* (New York, 1987).

On Lytton's relations with Disraeli and Salisbury, see W. F. Monypenny and G. E. Buckle, *The Life of Benjamin Disraeli* (rev. ed. in two vols., London, 1929), and Lady Gwendolyn Cecil, *Life of Robert, Marquis of Salisbury* (London, 1922). Robert Blake has written the standard modern biography, *Disraeli* (New York, 1967).

On Afghanistan, important works include Louis Dupree, *Afghanistan* (Princeton, 1980); Sir Percy Sykes, *A History of Afghanistan* (London, 1940, two vols.); W. K. Fraser-Tytler, *Afghanistan: A Study of Political Developments in Central Asia* (Oxford, 1950); and Vartan Gregorian, *The Emergence of Modern Afghanistan: Politics of Reform and Modernization* (Stanford, 1969). Regrettably, we did not find an accessible work by an Afghan on the same period (an autobiography of Abdur Rahman is of disputed authenticity).

The Second Afghan War has not wanted for chroniclers, beginning with Howard Hensman, *The Afghan War of 1879–80* (London, 1881), by a correspondent of *The Pioneer* (Allahabad) and *The Daily News* (London), collecting his day-by-day reports. Colonel Henry Hanna in *The Second Afghan War: Its Causes, Its Conduct and Its Consequences* (London, 1899–1910, three vols.) attempts to do for the conflict what Kaye did the First Afghan War; it is a gentle reproach to say he falls short. The most important modern account is Brian Robson, *The Road to Kabul: The Second Afghan War 1878–1881* (London, 1986), to which a vital additive is the personal diary of Major-General Sir Charles Metcalfe MacGregor, *War in Afghanistan, 1879–80* (Detroit, 1985), as edited by William Trousdale, showing in italics everything that was expurgated in previous editions.

The war is examined from different vantages in Charles Miller, *Khyber: British India's North-West Frontier* (New York, 1977); Victoria Schofield, *Every Rock, Every Hill: The Plain Tales of the North-West Frontier and Afghanistan* (London, 1984); Pierce G. Fredericks, *The Sepoy and the Cossack* (London, 1972); Byron Farwell, *Queen Victoria's Little Wars* (New York, 1972); and Arthur Swinton, *North-West Frontier* (New York, 1967). On General Roberts, we have benefited from his own memoirs, long a standard school-prize book in Britain, *Forty-One Years in India: From Subaltern to Commander-in-Chief* (London, 1897, with many later editions). His military papers from 1876 to 1893 were edited by Brian Robson, *Roberts in India* (Stroud, Gloucestershire, 1993); and for an informed profile, see Bryan Farwell, *Eminent Victorian Soldiers: Seekers of Glory* (New York, 1985).

On Maiwand, Leigh Maxwell, *My God—Maiwand!* (London, 1979), is a minute-by-minute reconstruction based on a survey of the battlefield and its graves. Thaddeus Holt, "You Have Been in Afghanistan, I Perceive," in *MHQ: The Quarterly Journal of Military History,* vol. 6, no. 2 (Winter 1994), performs useful detective work on the battle's celebrated fictional casualty, John H. Watson, MD. The novelist M. M. Kaye's *The Far Pavilions* (New York, 1978) includes a vivid rendition of Cavagnari's fate. (Sir John Gielgud, who depicted an addled Lord Raglan in the 1968 film *The Charge of the Light Brigade,* played Cavagnari in the 1984 television miniseries based on *The Far Pavilions.*)

Cavagnari awaits his biographer. Kally Prosono Dey, *The Life and Career of Major Sir Louis Cavagnari* (first published in 1881, reprinted in Karachi, 1986), tells little of either. It is still hard to determine whether his father was one of Napoleon's generals (as most sources say) or merely a military aide to Jerome Napoleon (as the well-informed Ms. Kaye relates). Wilfred Scawen Blunt's life, by contrast, is candidly related in Elizabeth Longford, *A Pilgrimage of Passion* (New York, 1980), based on the poet's long-sealed papers.

For Gladstone, the great granite monument is John Morley, *The Life of William Ewart Gladstone* (New York, 1903, three vols.), which we have supplemented with *Gladstone* (New York, 1997) by Roy Jenkins, who disappointingly skimps the Second Afghan War. On Gladstone and India, we commend three specialized studies, S. Gopal, *The Viceroyalty of Lord Ripon* (Oxford, 1953); Briton Martin, Jr., *New India 1885* (Berkeley, 1969); and Mary Bennett, *The Iberts in India, 1882–1886* (London, 1995).

173 "who does not know": Lytton Strachey, *Eminent Victorians* (New York, 1920), vi–vii.

176 "The critical state": Disraeli to Lytton, November 23, 1875, see Balfour, *Personal and Literary Letters of Robert, First Earl of Lytton,* vol. 1, 339.

176 "No man was ever": ibid., 339–42.

176 "I have not courted": quoted, Luytens, op. cit., 11.

177 "They had in common": Balfour, *Lord Lytton's Indian Administration,* 28.

177 "This peculiarity": quoted, Gregorian, *The Emergence of Modern Afghanistan,* 111.

178 "I put on paper": quoted, Balfour, *Lord Lytton's Indian Administration,* 45.

178 "We wanted": Disraeli to Salisbury, April 1, 1877, quoted, Seton-Watson, *Disraeli, Gladstone and the Eastern Question,* 539.

178 "I think you listen too much": Salisbury to Lytton, June 15, 1877, see Lady Gwendolyn Cecil, *Life of Robert, Marquis of Salisbury,* vol. II, 153.

178 "With your help": quoted in Bence-Jones, *The Viceroys of India,* 92.

179 "shocked all the proprieties": Lytton to Salisbury, April 25, 1876, see Balfour, *Personal and Literary Letters,* 12–13.

179   "a despotism of office boxes": quoted, Longford, 155. Originally attributed by Blunt to a "Simla wag," but later quoted under Lytton's name in Blunt's *India Under Ripon* (London, 1909).

179   "I have personally": Lytton to the Prince of Wales, August 20, 1976, quoted in Fowler, *Below the Peacock Fan,* 193.

180   "Baboos whom we have": Lytton to Salisbury, May 11, 1876, see Balfour, *Letters,* vol. II, 21.

180   "I can believe": quoted, Fowler, op. cit., 246.

181   "very civil and kind": quoted, Bence-Jones, op. cit., 79.

183   "a perhaps rather rigid": See Fraser-Tytler, *Afghanistan,* 142–43.

183   Less onerous terms: See Henry Kissinger, *Diplomacy* (New York, 1994), 155; and for a different view, A. J. P. Taylor, *The Struggle for Mastery in Europe 1848–1918* (Oxford, 1954), 251–54.

184   "not only as a savage": Lytton to Cranbrook, April 8, 1878; OIOC LP518/3, 226.

184–185 "We were told": Lytton to Cranbrook, August 3, 1878, OIOC, Sir Alfred Lyall Papers, MSS Eur. F 132/21–23.

185   "I have read with some alarm": Disraeli to Cranbrook, September 12, 1878; see Monypenny and Buckle, op. cit., vol. VI, 1252.

186   "the Government was popular": Disraeli to Cranbrook, September 17, 1878; Monypenny and Buckle, op. cit., vol. VI, 1253.

186   "Nothing would have induced me": Disraeli to Cranbrook, September 26, 1878; Monypenny and Buckle, op. cit., vol. VI, 1254.

186   "analyzed the papers before": Disraeli to Queen Victoria, October 26, 1878; Monypenny and Buckle, op. cit., vol. VI, 1258–60.

188   "And yet when I think": quoted, Sykes, *History of Afghanistan,* vol. II, 110.

189   "whatever happens": Disraeli to Lytton, August 14, 1879, Monypenny and Buckle, vol. VI, 1348.

189   "They will all be murdered": quoted, Fredericks, *The Sepoy and the Cossack,* 202.

189   "If my death": ibid., 203.

189   "It may be doubted": Robson, op. cit., 118.

189–190 "to write his report": quoted, Swinson, *North-West Frontier,* 166.

190   "more the man": quoted, Robson, op. cit., 118–19.

190   "I may truly say": quoted, Longford, op. cit., 153.

190   "We came across": Roberts, *Forty-One Years in India,* 381.

191   "treated with every consideration": quoted, Miller, op. cit., 176.

191   "Though all is changed": quoted, Schofield, *Every Rock, Every Hill,* 97.

192   "Never fear": variously quoted: see Robson, op. cit., 120; see also D. S. Richard, *The Savage Frontier: A History of the Anglo-Afghan Wars* (London, 1990), 85.

192   "I have been quite bewildered": Cavagnari to Lytton, August 30, 1979, quoted, Balfour, *Letters,* vol. II, 165–66.

192   "I am afraid": ibid., 177.

193   "I have lost my friend": quoted, Miller, op. cit., 181.

193–194 "This is a terrible day": quoted, Luytens, op. cit., 159.

194   "We now have to weave a fresh web": Lytton to Disraeli, September 6, quoted, Robson, op. cit., 122.

194   "But there was practically": Lytton to Cranbrook, September 14, 1879, OIOC Sir Alfred Lyall Papers, Mss. Eur. F132, 22.

194   "You can tell them": Roberts, op. cit., 386.

195   "he would rather be": ibid., 414.

196   "it is not justice": Lytton to Roberts, September 9, 1879, Robson, ed., *Roberts in India: The Military Papers of Field Marshal Lord Roberts*, 120.

196   "I think Bobs is": William Trousdale, ed., *War in Afghanistan, 1979–80: The Personal Diary of Major General Sir Charles Metcalfe MacGregor*, 111.

196   "Is it according to": quoted, Fredericks, op. cit., 213.

196   "for no other offence": quoted, Jenkins, op. cit., 425.

197   "She will sooner": ibid., 435.

197–198 "Necessary to find": quoted, Fredericks, op. cit., 220.

198   "In other words": ibid.

199   "It may not be very flattering": quoted, Moon, op. cit., 856.

199   "The 'natives', as they call them": quoted, Longford, op. cit., 154.

201   Appositely, the architect: For an astute appraisal of Luytens and New Delhi, see Jan Morris, *Stones of Empire* (London, 1983), passim.

Chapter Eight

A solid history by Derek Waller of Vanderbilt University offers a close-up in *The Pundits: British Exploration of Tibet and Central Asia* (Lexington, KY, 1990). See as well John Noble Wilford, *The Mapmakers* (New York, 1981); Matthew Edney, *Mapping an Empire* (Chicago, 1997); Charles Allen, *A Mountain in Tibet* (London, 1982); Kenneth Mason, *Abode of Snow* (London, 1955); and John Keay, *India Discovered* (Calcutta, 1989). John MacGregor (the nom de plume of the CIA's John Waller), *Tibet: A Chronicle of Exploration* (London, 1970); Sir Thomas Holdich, *Tibet the Mysterious* (New York, 1906); and Peter Hopkirk, *Trespassers on the Roof of the World: The Race for Lhasa* (London, 1983); and Ian Cameron, *Mountains of the Gods* (New York, 1984).

The voices of the trespassers themselves can be heard in Ekai Kawaguchi, *Three Years in Tibet* (Madras, 1909); E. R. Huc, *Travels in Tartary, Thibet and China, 1844–1846* (New York, reprint, 1987); and three books by Sarat Chandra Das: *Narrative of a Journey to Lhasa and Central Tibet* (ed. W. W. Rockhill, London, 1902), *Indian Pandits in the Land of Snow* (New Delhi, 1978), and *Autobiography: Narrative of the Incidents of My Early Life* (Calcutta, 1969); and Sir Clements Markham, ed., *Narratives of the Mission of George Bogle to Tibet and the Journey of*

Thomas Manning to Lhasa (London, 1986). Also useful is Indra Singh Rawat, *Indian Explorers of the Nineteenth Century* (New Delhi, 1973).

For the political context, see Alastair Lamb, *Asian Frontiers* (London, 1968) and *British India and Tibet: 1766–1910* (London, New York, 1986); Firuz Kazemzadeh, *Russia and Britain in Persia, 1864–1914: A Study of Imperialism* (New Haven, 1968); Dorothy Woodman, *Himalayan Frontiers* (New York, 1969); Parshotam Mehra, *The Younghusband Expedition* (London, 1968); and Austine L. Waddell, *Lhasa and Its Mysteries* (London, 1906).

202   "You have been in Afghanistan, I perceive": in Arthur Conan Doyle, *A Study in Scarlet*. For more on Watson and Maiwand, see the article by Thaddeus Holt, op. cit., Chapter 7. According to Conan Doyle, Sherlock Holmes, after his encounter with Professor Moriarty at Reichenbach Falls, journeyed in 1891 to Lhasa, posing as a Norwegian named Sigerson. See *Sherlock Holmes* (New York, 1962) by William S. Baring-Gould; Richard Wincor, *Sherlock Holmes in Tibet* (New York, 1968); and Baring-Gould, ed., *The Annotated Sherlock Holmes* (New York, 1967), vol. II, 320–25.

202   "I'm in love": quoted, Lord Birkenhead, *Rudyard Kipling* (New York, 1978), 63.

203   "the finest novel in the English language": Nirad Chaudhuri's essay in John Gross, ed., *The Age of Kipling* (New York, 1972), 28–35. And see, passim, Peter Hopkirk, *Quest for Kim: In Search of Kipling's Great Game* (London, 1996).

203   "Write for and about boys": Martin Green, *Dreams of Adventure, Dreams of Empire* (New York, 1979), 266.

204   "Imperialism and mapmaking intersect in the most basic manner": Edney, op. cit., 1997, 1ff.

204   eyesores…fixing latitudes, plotting productive lands, and filling notebooks with information on rivers, villages, and terrain: Wilford, op. cit., 161.

204–205   "observe everything on the Road": Surveyor General's report of 1806, quoted, Wilford, op. cit., 162ff.

205   "a mathematical and topographical survey": quoted, ibid., 163.

205   "to an almost unlimited extent in every other direction": Keay, *India Discovered*, 183.

205   "immediately wanted for military purposes": Phillimore, *Historical Records*, vol. II, 238, quoted, Waller, op. cit., 25.

205–206   "a tranquil and exceedingly good-humoured person": DNB, Lambton.

206   the line of triangles: Keay, *India Discovered*, 188.

206   "The old correspondence books": William Donovan, "Clements Robert Markham and the Geographical Dept. of the India Office 1867-77," *Geographical Journal*, vol. 134 (September, 1968), 346.

207   "half savage, nomad populations of Central Asia": quoted, Kazem-zadeh, op. cit., 8.

208   "nothing striking, nothing pleasing, in its appearance": Holdich, op. cit., 122ff.

209   "The ascent of Ahertatopa": Montgomerie's diary quoted, Cameron, op. cit., 119.

209   "When I was in Ladakh": quoted, Hopkirk, *Trespassers,* 23.

210   "the queerest, coolest fish at Rugby": quoted, Allen, op. cit., 125.

210   "both on account of their sound knowledge of the Tibetan language": quoted, ibid., 136.

211   "observations of latitude": quoted, Cameron, op. cit., 120.

212   "over and over" and "a burning desire" and "to train up": Das, *Autobiography,* the source for quotes that follow.

214   "like a dazzling hill of polished gold": Das, *Journal of the Buddhist Text Society,* quoted, Waller, op. cit., 199.

214   "The room was spread": Das, *Autobiography,* 57, also the source for quotes that follow.

217   "There are many other learned men": Das, *Journey to Lhasa and Central Tibet,* 102. Also the source for the Das quotes that follow.

220   Waddell "has done all in his power": Das to Rockhill, December 22, 1902, Rockhill papers, Houghton Library, Harvard University.

221   "small eyes and a scanty beard": Waller, op. cit., 250.

221   "The persistence of foreigners": Bell, *Tibet Past and Present,* 59.

222   "When, in a little while": Kawaguchi, op. cit., 17

222   "The story of the Tibetans": ibid., 224.

Chapter Nine

Despite Przhevalsky's scientific and political importance, surprisingly little about him is available in English. His two travel narratives were translated, but can be found only in the specialized collections: *Mongolia, the Tangut Country and the Solitudes of Northern Tibet* (London, 1876, two vols.) and *From Kulja Across the Tian Shan to Lob Nor* (London, 1879). Of biographies in Russian, the standard work is by an army colleague, N. F. Dubrovin, *N. M. Przhevalsky* (St. Petersburg, 1890).

Donald Rayfield, a professor of Russian literature at the University of London, has written the succinctly readable *The Dream of Lhasa* (London, 1976). But Rayfield arrived at a more stringent view of Przhevalsky's relations with his "favorites" in his more recent *Anton Chekhov: A Life* (New York, 1997). Much valuable light is shed by Daniel Brower, "Imperial Russia and the Orient: The Renown of Nikolai Przhevalsky," *The Russian Review* (vol. 53, July 1994), pp. 367–81; and on the role of the press, see Louisa McReynolds, *The News Under Russia's Old Regime* (Princeton, 1991).

Peter Hopkirk's *Trespassers on the Roof of the World* (London, 1982) fits the Russian into the international competition to reach Lhasa. For a contemporary appraisal by a fellow Great Gamesman, see Eugene Schuyler, "The Russian Traveller Prjevalsky," *Bulletin* of the American Geographical Society (vol. 2, 1889). More generally, on exploration, see Beau Riffenburgh, *The Myth of the Explorer* (Oxford, 1994).

For our purposes, the vital overview was provided by David Schimmelpenninck van der Oye, *Ex Oriente Lux: Ideologies of Empire and Russia's Far East, 1895–1904,* a Yale doctoral dissertation (1997). The author, Dutch-born and a former officer in Canadian intelligence, has scoured Russian archival sources to bring from the shadows a debate commonly ignored in accounts of the period. We have relied on Schimmelpenninck's translations and on his judgments. His work in turn fits into the background drawn by Dietrich Geyer, *Russian Imperialism: The Interaction of Domestic and Foreign Policy, 1860–1914* (New Haven, 1987), and in the underappreciated *What Is Asia to Us?* (Boston, 1990) by Milan Hauner.

On Shambhala, the rich and quirky literature includes Edwin Bernbaum, *The Way to Shambhala* (New York, 1980); Victoria LePage, *Shambhala* (Wheaton, IL, 1996); Peter Bishop, *The Myth of Shangri-La* (Berkeley, 1989); and not least Nicholas Roerich's *Shambhala* (Rochester, VT, 1990)

The St. Petersburg scholar Alexandre Andreyev recently drew on the files of the Imperial Russian Geographical Society for an unpublished article, "The Case of the Secret Dispatch of a Russian Agent to Tibet, 1869–1873: An Unknown Story of the Great Game Era," drawing on Przhevalsky's unpublished diary (Archive of the RGS. F. l3. Op 1. D 68. L 89 ob., 90). For Kozlov, *Lost Empire of the Silk Road*, edited by Mikhail Piotrovsky (Milan, 1993), was indispensable. On Tian-Shansky, see W. Bruce Lincoln, *Petr Petrovich Semenov-Tian-Shansky: The Life of a Russian Geographer* (Newtonville, MA, 1980). Concerning Przhevalsky as possible biological father of Stalin, Edward Radzinsky in his biography *Stalin* (New York, 1996) appraised the rumor, based on the belief that Przhevalsky visited Gori, Stalin's birthplace, approximately nine months before the Soviet dictator was born. The case for the explorer's homosexuality is discussed by Simon Karlinsky, "Gay Life Before the Soviets," *The Advocate*, 1/4/1982, 31–34.

225	"a man of ruthless determination": Rayfield, *The Dream of Lhasa,* xi.
226	"There are about sixty of us": quoted, Rayfield, ibid., 8.
227	"A country has no lasting value": quoted, Agnes Murphy, *The Ideology of French Imperialism* (New York, 1968), 68.
227	"Are you not afraid to go so far?": Kropotkin, *Memoirs of a Revolutionist* (London, 1978), ed. Colin Ward, 126.
228	"as reconnaissance reports": Schimmelpenninck, op. cit., 14.
228	"scientific research will camouflage": ibid., 31.

229 "We have absolutely no supplies left": quoted, Rayfield, op. cit., 77.

229 "would be very glad to receive Russians": quoted, Schimmelpenninck, op. cit., 27.

230 "Unimaginable filth": quoted, Rayfield, op. cit., 52.

230 "The Chinaman here": ibid., 52

230 "we are all very well armed": quoted, Schimmelpenninck, op. cit., 27.

230–231 "Our military conquests in Asia bring": quoted ibid., 12. This bluntly frank passage was in a letter to his superior, Count F. H. Heiden, June 6, 1867.

231 "to teach the Chinese authorities": quoted, Rayfield, op. cit., 89.

231–232 "All that the Sovereign of the Six Cities": quoted, O. Edmund Clubb, *China and Russia: The "Great Game* (New York and London, 1971), 107.

232 "To belong to China": quoted, ibid., 108.

232 "you will be thrashed together": quoted, Rayfield, op. cit., 88.

232 "a carbine in one hand and a whip in the other": quoted, Schimmelpenninck, op. cit., 37.

233 "Nothing more than a political impostor": memo dated 6/6/1877 quoted, ibid., 30.

233 "Yakub Beg is the same shit": quoted in Rayfield, op. cit., 100.

234 "at some future time the followers of this religion will migrate": Przhevalsky, *Mongolia, the Tangut Country,* vol. 1, 250–51.

235 "information about Tibet": quoted, Andreyev, op. cit.

235 "guarantee of safety": quoted, Rayfield, op. cit., 115.

235 "Once this point is occupied": ibid., 123.

236 "took out the maps of Tibet": quoted, Andreyev, op. cit.

237 "Tibet is a country of religion": The text of the Tibetan document is quoted in Rayfield, op. cit, 139.

237 "Search parties were sent for Livingstone, Payer, Nordenscheldt; but no one is even thinking of looking for Przhevalsk": quoted, ibid., 140.

237–238 "A sad, yearning feeling always comes over me as soon as the first bursts of joy on returning home have passed": quoted, ibid., 149.

238 "I was thinking": quoted in ibid., 154.

239 "When I first set eyes": quoted, Mikhail Piotrovsky, ed., *Lost Empire of the Silk Road: Buddhist Art from Khara Khoto* (Milan, 1993), 31.

239 "all yearn to become subjects of the White Tsar": quoted, Schimmelpenninck, op. cit., 42. Przhevalsky's "Essay on the Current Situation in Central Asia" was conveniently omitted from the Soviet reissue of his book in 1948. As Schimmelpenninck points out, when the Soviet director Sergei Iutkevitch arrived in Peking with his crew

to film *Przhevalskii* (1952), the Chinese strongly objected to the project, and it took direct intervention by the Soviet ambassador to permit work to proceed—and this at the peak of Sino-Soviet collaboration. When the epic film opened, in the director's first effort in color, it was gushingly praised in *Pravda* for above all "showing that Przhevalsky's work expresses the progressive role of Russian culture in Asia."

240   "Aside from the scientific results": quoted in Schimmelpenninck, op. cit., 34.

240   The Chekhov obituary is cited *in extenso* in Rayfield, op. cit., 203–4.

Chapter Ten

Madame Blavatsky has never faded from popular memory, and her story has been recently retold in Sylvia Cranston, *HPB: The Extraordinary Life and Influence of Helena Blavatsky* (New York, 1993), and Marion Meade, *Madame Blavatsky: The Woman Behind the Myth* (New York, 1980). Peter Washington's *Madame Blavatsky's Baboon: A History of the Mystics, Mediums, and Misfits Who Brought Spiritualism to America* (New York, 1995) is an astringent corrective to fringe idolators. A two-part essay by Frederick Crews, "The Consolation of Theosophy," *New York Review of Books* (September 19, 1996, and October 3, 1996) is a valuable survey. Two studies by K. Paul Johnson, *The Masters Revealed: Madame Blavatsky and the Myth of the Great White Lodge* (Albany, 1994) and *Initiates of Theosophical Masters* (Albany, 1995), are densely written, fascinating, and controversial (especially among Theosophists). Maria Carlson, *"No Religion Higher Than Truth": A History of the Theosophical Movement in Russia* (Princeton, 1993), draws fruitfully on long-closed archives.

Duleep Singh has been well-served in a thoroughly documented biography, *Queen Victoria's Maharajah: Duleep Singh 1838–1893* (New York, 1980), by Michael Alexander and Sushila Anand, on which we have gratefully relied. A spirited brief for *Duleep Singh: The Maharaja of Punjab and the Raj* (Birmingham, England, 1986) is advanced by Rish Ranjan Chakranarty. Valuable documents concerning British intelligence can be found in Ganda Singh, ed., *Maharaja Duleep Singh Correspondence* (Patiala: Punjab University, 1977). Katkov is the subject of a lively biography, *The Time of the Thunderer: Mikhail Katkov, Russian Nationalist Extremism and the Failure of the Bismarckian System* (Boulder, 1988) by Karel Durman. The wider diplomatic canvas is depicted by George F. Kennan, *The Decline of Bismarck's European Order: Franco-Prussian Relations, 1875–1890* (Princeton, NJ, 1979); and William Langer, *European Alliances and Alignments 1871–1890* (New York, 2d ed., 1950).

On Ukhtomsky, see E. E. Ukhtomsky, *Travels in the East of Nicholas II, Emperor of Russia, When Czarevich 1890–1891* (two vols., London, 1896 and 1905).

241   "How intolerable it is": This and other quoted letters are from Edward J. Bing, ed., *The Secret Letters of the Last Tsar: Being the Confidential Correspondence Between Nicholas II and His Mother Dowager Empress Marie Feodorovna* (New York, 1938), passim.

244   Alexander Hamilton: For a description of how Sanskrit came to Europe, see G. T. Garratt, *The Legacy of India* (Oxford, 1937), 31 et seq.

245   "one of the most interesting": Kipling, *Something of Myself* (Cambridge University Press edition, 1991), 35.

247   "thrilled": Nehru, *Toward Freedom* (New York, 1941), 29.

247   "Your Excellency and my native land": Carlson, op. cit., 216.

248   "some dark forces": Johnson, *The Masters Revealed*, 92.

249   "Another such victory": quoted, Moon, op. cit., 598.

249   "a brat begotten of a *bhishti*": Alexander and Anand, op. cit., 7.

249–250 "all right and title to the sovereignty of the Punjab": Smith, *The Life of Lord Lawrence* (London, 1883), vol. 1, 327–28.

250   "This is the first Indian prince": Alexander and Anand, op. cit., 37.

251   "He is extremely handsome": ibid., 43–44.

251   "It is to me, Ma'am": ibid., 48.

252   In the 1880's: See Johnson, *The Masters Revealed,* 160–61; Alexander and Anand, op. cit., 187–95.

253   "My beloved Countrymen": The full text is in Alexander and Anand, op. cit., 207–8.

254   In India, anxious: ibid., 210–12.

254   "The Queen Empress": ibid., 221.

255   When his appeal: ibid., 225.

255   It was a confusing moment: See Kennan, op. cit., passim; Johnson, *The Masters Revealed,* 226–33. Chakrabarty, *Duleep Singh,* reprints all full texts of the Maharajah's manifestos.

256–257 Katkov's paper was described: Langer, op. cit., 377.

257   He contacted a crony: Alexander and Anand, op. cit., 256.

257   "the humble prayer": Chakrabarty, op. cit., 169–70.

257–258 "I am glad": Durman, op. cit. 297.

258   Moreover, the Tsarina: ibid., 296.

258   "I am ready": Johnson, *The Masters Revealed,* 226–27.

259   "He is quite bald": Alexander and Anand, op. cit., 293.

260   "My mother remembered": Christy Campbell, "A Boy's Own Story," *The Sunday Telegraph Magazine,* October 12, 1997, 18–22.

Chapter Eleven

Dorzhiev's own autobiography is the source for all quotations by him unless otherwise cited. "Dorjiev: Memoirs of a Tibetan Diplomat," translated from the Tibetan by Thubten Norbu and Dan Martin. *Journal of the Institute for the Com-*

prehensive Study of the Lotus Sûtra, Tokyo, 17 (March 1991), 1–105. According to
Andreyev, it was written ca. 1922–23. There are also two Russian texts: "Za-
piska o moei Zhizni—A Note about My Life," belonging to the Archive of the
Ministry of Foreign Affairs (Moscow–AVPRF) written ca. 1900 and an anony-
mous text discovered by Andreyev in the Archive to the Russian Academy of
Sciences in St. Petersburg, ca. 1901-2. Another, Mongolian version of
Dorzhiev's life, apparently written in 1924, is in the archive of the Russian
Academy of Sciences, St. Petersburg. F.208. Op.1. D.146. *Biography of the Senior
Tsanit-Khambo, in the Service of the Dalai Lama, Lharambo Agvan Dorjiev.* It has
been translated by Caroline Humphrey. Another Russian source for the Buriat
is K. Berlin, "Khambo Agvan Dorzhiev in Relation to Tibet's Struggle for In-
dependence," *Novyi Vostok* (*New Orient*) III, 1923.

Alexandre Andreyev is the outstanding authority on Dorzhiev. We have benefited from both his published and his unpublished works. The former include
The Buddhist Shrine of Petrograd (Ulan Ude, 1992), and the latter, "The Case of
the Secret Dispatch of a Russian Agent to Tibet, 1869–1873: An Unknown
Story of the Great Game Era," and his paper "Russian Buddhists in Tibet, end
of the 19th c-1930"; and see "Agvan Dorzhiev's Secret Work in Russia and
Tibet," *Tibetan Review*, vol. 28, no. 9 (September 1993), 11–14. Other impor-
tant sources include Nikolai S. Kuleshov, "Agvan Dorjiev, The Dalai Lama's
Ambassador," *Asian Affairs* (February 1992); "Russia and Tibetan Crisis: Begin-
ning at the 20th Century," *The Tibet Journal*, vol. XXI, no. 3 (Autumn, 1996);
Alastair Lamb, "Some Notes on Russian Intrigue in Tibet" *Royal Central Asian
Journal*, vol. 46 (January 1959); P. L. Mehra, "Tibet and Russian Intrigue," *Royal
Central Asian Journal*, vol. XLV (January 1958); Robert A. Rupen, "The Buriat
Intelligentsia," *Far Eastern Quarterly*, vol. XV, no. 3 (May 1956); and Jeffrey
Somers, "Lama Dorjieff and the Esoteric Tradition, *Theosophical History*, vol. III,
no. 2 (April 1990). Also Premen Addy, *Tibet on the Imperial Chessboard: the Mak-
ing of British Policy towards Lhasa, 1899–1925* (Calcutta, 1984). The biographer
of Dorzhiev is the late John Snelling, whose *Buddhism in Russia: The Story of
Agvan Dorzhiev* (Shaftesbury, 1993) is indispensable.

Regarding Mme. Blavatsky's visit to Ghoom, see Cranston, *H.P.B.: The Extraordinary Life and Influence of Helena Blavatsky*, and K. Paul Johnson, *Initiates of
the Philosophical Masters* (Albany, NY, 1995). Other mentions of theosophical
politics are found in James Webb's *The Harmonious Circle* (London, 1980) and
The Occult Establishment (La Salle, IL, 1976).

For foreign infatuation with Buddhism, see E. Bernbaum, *The Road to Shambhala* (New York, 1980); R. Fields, *How the Swans Came to the Lake* (Boston, 1986);
Albert Grünwedel, *Mythologie du Bouddhisme en Tibet et Mongolie basée sur la collection lamaïque du Prince Ukhtomsky* (Leipzig, 1900).

Adding to our understanding of Ukhtomsky and Badmaev has been David
Schimmelpenninck van der Oye's unpublished dissertation, *Ex Oriente Lux*
(Yale University, 1997), "Tournament of Shadows: Russia's Great Game in

Tibet," *Tibetan Review*, January 1994, and "Tsarist Intelligence and the Younghusband Expedition of 1904" in Michael Handel et al., eds., *Intelligence and International Politics from the Civil War to the Cold War* (forthcoming). We have gratefully relied on his translations. On Tsarist intrigues see Alexander Mikhailovich, *Once a Grand Duke* (New York, 1932); Marc Ferro, *Nicholas II* (New York, 1990); Wilhelm Filchner, *Sturm über Asien* (Berlin, 1924); Patrick French, *Younghusband* (London, 1994); R. Fülöp-Miller, *Rasputin: The Holy Devil* (New York, 1928); Dominic Lieven, *Nicholas II* (New York, 1993); E. E. Ukhtomsky, *Travels in the East of Nicholas II*, ed. by Sir George Birdwood (Westminster, 1900), 135–51; S. Witte, *Memoirs of Count Witte*, Vols. I–III, trans. and ed. Sidney Harcave (Armonk, NY, 1990).

261   "was elevated to the position": French, op. cit., 186

262   "I am myself": F.O. 17, 1745, November 13, 1902, quoted in Alastair Lamb, "Some Notes on Russian Intrigue in Tibet," 60.

262   "cunning enterprise": Andreyev, "The Case of the Secret Dispatch of a Russian Agent to Tibet, 1869–1873."

266   "economical with the truth": Alastair Lamb in conversation with the authors.

267   "His courage and energy were inexhaustible": (jacket copy), Bell, *Portrait of a Dalai Lama* (London, 1987).

270   "luminous realms": Ukhtomsky "Préface," Grünwedel, Albert, *Mythologie du Bouddhisme*, quoted, Schimmelpenninck, *Ex Oriente Lux,* 73.

270   "Trans-Baikalia is the key to the heart of Asia," quoted, Schimmelpenninck, ibid., 74.

270   "this Asiatic wilderness": Ukhtomsky, *Travels*, vol. II, 345.

270   "Properly speaking": ibid., 444.

271   "higher spiritual plane": Snelling, op. cit., 49.

271   "it could depend mainly on benevolence": ibid.

271   "exotic mushroom universities": Ukhtomsky, op. cit, vol. II, 4.

271   "the brighter becomes the name of the White Tsar": ibid., 143.

271   "infusions of asoka flowers": Fülöp-Miller, op. cit., 127.

271   "the effects of which were marvelous": ibid.

271–272   "stood head and shoulders above the crowd of magi and holy fools who clamored around the steps of the throne": Webb, *The Harmonius Circle*, 56.

272   "all so new, strange and fantastic": quoted, Schimmelpenninck, *Ex Oriente Lux*, 53.

272   "From the shores of the Pacific": Seton-Watson, op. cit., 581ff.

274   "the instant the door of his study closed to outsiders": Alexander Mikhailovich, op. cit., 173.

274   "takes counsel from everyone:" Lieven, op. cit., 52.

274   "has a quick mind and learns easily": ibid., 40.

275 "describing in detail the greatness of the Russian people": quoted, Kuleshov, op. cit., 23.

276 "You know how I love Buriats": quoted, Snelling, 66.

277 "broad and well built": quoted, Webb, op. cit., 54.

277–278 "on the ground that it is undesirable": quoted, Snelling, op. cit., 70.

279 "the intercession of Russia for Tibet": quoted, Schimmelpenninck, "Tsarist Intelligence and the Younghusband Expedition of 1904."

279 "cannons of the latest make": quoted, Andreyev, "Agvan Dorzhiev," 19.

279 "gorgeous set of clerical vestments": Hugh Richardson, *A Short History of Tibet* (New York, 1962), 82.

280 "they were met with real Russian cordiality": ibid., 26.

280 "The Buddhist faith of the Tibetan people": quoted, Schimmelpenninck, "Tsarist Intelligence and the Younghusband Expedition of 1904."

280 "about your wish to establish regular connections": Archives of Foreign Policy of Russia, Chin. Dept. f. 1448, p. 103.

281 "Dorzhiev spoke with marked authority and expertise": quoted, Snelling, 84.

281 "I told Witte that our sovereign": quoted, Schimmelpenninck, *Ex Oriente Lux*, 55.

Chapter Twelve

Curzon wrote voluminously and inspired a caravan of biographers. The authorized *Life of Lord Curzon* (London, 1928) by the Earl of Ronaldshay, in three fat volumes, is a better-than-average specimen of the genre, drawing generously on its subject's lively correspondence. Harold Nicolson, *Curzon: The Last Phase* (London, 1934), is salted with insider knowledge about Curzon as Foreign Secretary. See also Nicolson's long and fine entry on Curzon in the DNB. Kenneth Rose, *Superior Person: A Portrait of Curzon and His Circle in Late Victorian England* (New York, 1969), is a portrait of an age as well as "a study in precocity."

David Dilkes, *Curzon in India* (New York, 1969)—in two volumes, "Achievement" and "Frustration"—provides a warehouse of information on Curzon's Viceroyalty. Leonard Mosley, *Curzon: End of an Epoch* (London, 1961), based on papers given by the second Lady Curzon (also an American) to Lord Beaverbrook (Mosley's employer), is unfriendly and not always reliable, and fails to mention Tibet or Younghusband. Nayana Goradia, *Lord Curzon: The Last of the British Moghuls* (New Delhi, 1993), is of interest as a sympathetic but critical study written by a present-day Indian scholar. The latest entry, David Gilmour's *Curzon* (London, 1994), is a reconsideration, especially good on matters unmentioned in the authorized life (e.g., Curzon's friendship with Oscar Wilde).

Lady Curzon has belatedly won her due in Nigel Nicolson, *Mary Curzon* (New York, 1977), and John Bradley, ed., *Lady Curzon's India: Letters of a Vicereine* (London, 1985), but see also the excellent chapter on her in Marian Fowler, *Below the Peacock Fan: First Ladies of the Raj* (New York, 1987). On the famous Durbar, see the relevant essay in David Cannadine, *Aspects of Aristocracy: Grandeur and Decline in Modern Britain* (New Haven, CT, 1994). Of Curzon's own works, especially pertinent are *Russia in Central Asia* (London, 1889); *Persia and the Persian Question* (London, 1892, two vols.); *Tales of Travel* (London, 1923); and *Leaves from Viceroy's Notebook* (London, 1926).

On Oxford, we have benefited from Richard Symonds, *Oxford and Empire: The Last Lost Cause?* (London, 1986), and Jan Morris's *The Oxford Book of Oxford* (Oxford, 1978) and *Oxford* (London, 1965). See also Geoffrey Faber, *Jowett: A Portrait with a Background* (Cambridge, MA, 1957).

Peter Fleming's *Bayonets to Lhasa* (London, 1961), the first book on the Younghusband Mission, reenergized interest in the episode, building on the pioneering research of Alastair Lamb in *Britain and Chinese Central Asia: The Road to Lhasa* (London, 1960), later revised as *British India and Tibet 1766–1910* (London, 1986). Patrick French, *Younghusband: The Last Great Imperial Adventure* (London, 1994), is notable for its zest and research. Parshotam Mehra, *The Younghusband Expedition: An Interpretation* (London, 1968), offers an Indian perspective. Another valuable Indian view can be found in Premen Addy, *Tibet on the Imperial Chessboard* (Calcutta, 1984). For a Tibetan view, consult Chapter 13 of Tsepon W. D. Shakabpa, *Tibet: A Political History* (New Haven, CT, 1957).

Younghusband gives his own account in *India and Tibet* (London, 1910) and describes his earlier explorations in *The Heart of a Continent* (London, 1896). See also his brother's memoirs, *Forty Years a Soldier* (New York, 1923), by Major-General Sir George Younghusband, which reads like a source for the Flashman novels. Of journalistic reportage, the most important are Perceval Landon, *The Opening of Tibet* (New York, 1905; the American edition is dedicated to W. W. Rockhill), and Edmund Candler, *The Unveiling of Lhasa* (London, 1905). For a subaltern's view, see the sparkling *To Lhasa at Last* (London, 1905) by the pseudonymous "Powell Millington," who "occupied a single-fly tent in the back street of the brigade camp." Finally, for a rendering precise as a fine engraving, see "A Late Aggression" in Jan (or James) Morris, *Farewell the Trumpets* (New York, 1978).

284   "writes Harold Nicolson": See Nicolson's entry on Curzon in the DNB. On Miss Paraman, also see Jonathan Gathorne-Hardy, *The Unnatural History of the Nanny* (New York, 1973), 302–9.

284   "Try to suffer": Quoted, Gilmour, op. cit., 161.

284–285   "By his own account": See Rose, op. cit., 199–200.

285   "Everyone remarked": See Winston Churchill, essay on Curzon in *Great Contemporaries* (New York, 1937), 236.

286   "You are a brick": Gilmour, op. cit., 29.

286   "My dear Wilfred": ibid., 103.

286   Subsequently: The text of Curzon's "sin" can be found in Rose, op. cit., 389–90.

286   "The British Empire": Symonds, op. cit., 37.

286   On Jowett, see Morris, *Oxford,* 197–99; *Oxford Book of Oxford,* 272–76.

287   "Jowett once confided": Jowett to Nightingale, December 4, 1873; quoted, Symonds, op. cit., 24.

288   As remarked by: See Philip Woodruff (pseudonym for Philip Mason), *The Men Who Ruled India: The Guardians* (New York, 1954), 76.

288   "There is more great": Quoted, Symonds, op. cit., 27.

289   "Of family": Quoted, Fowler, op. cit., 241.

289   "All these gentlemen": Gilmour, op. cit., 152.

289–290 "Efficiency of": ibid., 153.

290   "It is a proud": quoted, Lamb, *British India and Tibet,* 239–40.

293   Something else important: See French, op. cit., 109.

294   "I have always had": OIOC, Curzon Papers, Younghusband to Curzon, August 16, 1901.

294   In 1902: All details from Cannadine, op. cit., 77–90.

295   At the climactic: See Fowler, op. cit., 290–92.

295   But when Younghusband found himself: French, op. cit., 159.

297   It was in this spirit: Fleming, op. cit., 93.

297   Brodrick's telegram: We have used the text as quoted in ibid., 95.

300   The differences: See Younghusband, *India and Tibet,* 178–81; Fleming, op. cit., 137–52; French, op. cit., 217–27; Shakabpa, op. cit., 210–12.

301   "On political grounds": Fleming, op. cit., 169.

301   "At first, enemies": Shakabpa, op. cit., 218.

301   "If what you desire": "Powell Millington," *To Lhassa at Last* (London, 1905), 41.

301   "The Tibetans as usual": ibid., 172–74.

303   As Brodrick liked to recall: quoted, Goradia, op. cit., 70.

303   "Burning to distinguish": ibid., 354.

304   "We found the city": Candler, op. cit., 250.

304   Smooth and slippery: Landon, op. cit., 339, 345.

305   "The association": quoted, Fleming, op. cit., 215.

306   "All that H.M.G.": Curzon to Younghusband, July 13, 1904; full text in Mehra, op. cit., 394.

306   "Let me beg you": quoted, James Morris, *Farewell the Trumpets,* 128.

306   In Lhasa meanwhile: The full text of the convention is in Younghusband, *India and Tibet,* 439–45. Also in Mehra, op. cit., 381–88.

307   Balfour concurred: Fleming, op. cit., 271–72.
308   Sir Arthur Godley: ibid., 279–80.

Chapter Thirteen

Hedin's own books include *Amerika im Kampf der Kontinente* (Leipzig, 1943); *Central Asia and Tibet* (New York, 1903); *A Conquest of Tibet* (New York, 1941); *Genom Khorastan och Turkestan* (Stockholm, 1893); *German Diary 1935–42* (Dublin, 1951); *Grosse Männer denen ich begegnet* (1951); *History of the Expedition in Asia, 1927–1935* (Stockholm, 1943–45); *Karavan och tarantass* (Stockholm, 1953); *My Life as an Explorer* (New York, 1925); *Trans-Himalaya: Discoveries and Adventures in Tibet* (reprinted, New York, 1968); *Through Asia* (New York and London, 1899); *Ein Volk in Waffen* (Leipzig, 1915); "Journeys in Tibet 1906–1908," *The Geographical Journal*, 33–34 (London, 1909) is the source for Hedin's RGS lecture; *Scientific Results of a Journey in Central Asia, 1899–1902* (Stockholm, 1904–7), contains Hedin's comments on the Younghusband expedition.

The standard biography, not yet in English, is by Eric Wennerholm, *Sven Hedin: en biografi* (Stockholm, 1978). The only biogaphy in English, both admiring and sympathetic, by the geographer George Kish, *To the Heart of Asia: The Life of Sven Hedin* (Ann Arbor, 1987), skimps on geopolitics. Detlef Brennecke has written a brief but useful illustrated biography in German, *Sven Hedin mit Selbstzeugnissen und Bilddokumenten* (Reinbek bei Hamburg, 1991). On Markham and Scott, see Roland Huntford's *Scott and Amundsen* (New York, 1979). Information on the RGS can be found in Hugh Robert Mill, *The Record of the Royal Geographical Society 1830–1930* (London, 1930) and Ian Cameron, *To the Farthest Ends of the Earth: the History of the Royal Geographical Society, 1830-1980*. On women travelers, Dorothy Middleton, *Victorian Lady Travellers* (New York, 1965). Charles Allen, *A Mountain in Tibet* (London, 1994), was essential in leading us to the quarrel Hedin had with the RGS. Petrovsky's condescension toward Macartney was detailed in Jan Myrdal, *The Silk Road: A Journey from the High Pamirs and Ili Through Sinkiang and Kansu* (New York, 1979). Also useful was John Keay, *The Gilgit Game* (Karachi, 1990). One of Hedin's Chinese associates on his last expedition kept a diary, *Huang Wenbi Meng-Xin kaocha riji (1927–30)*, which has been edited by his son Huang Lie (Beijing, 1990). Peter Bishop's *The Myth of Shangri-La* is a postmodern spin on the theme. On Younghusband and Hedin see Patrick French, *Younghusband* (London, 1994); Clarmont Skrine, *Chinese Central Asia* (London, 1926). On Morley, Curzon, and Minto see Stanley Wolpert's *Morley and India 1906–1910* (Berkeley, CA, 1967) and Alastair Lamb, *British India and Tibet* (London, 1986).

Hedin's correspondence with Keltie can be found in the archives of the Royal Geographical Society; his correspondence with Curzon is in the India Office Library (L/P&S/10/186), along with key materials on Sven Hedin's movements in the Morley Papers (MSS Eur. D. 573). The archives of Harvard's Yenching Library contain material relating to the Sino-Swedish Expedition; the issues of the *Geographical Journal* between 1908 and 1909 bear on the dispute between Hedin and the members of the RGS.

310	"incomparable drama": quoted, Fleming, op. cit., 30
311	"more difficult to say goodbye to the dogs than to the men": quoted, *Mountain in Tibet,* 214.
311	"By temperament Hedin was a Nazi": quoted, Allen, op. cit., 12.
312	"Mecca for all true geographers": Mill, op. cit., 94.
314	"Their sex and training render them equally unfitted for exploration": ibid., 110ff.
314	"A lady an explorer": quoted, Middleton, op. cit., 14.
316	"All at once, we noticed a band of running *ferrashs*": Hedin, *My Life,* 27ff.
320	"huge *kibitka* with wooden floors": Hedin, *My Life,* 99.
320	"the most difficult and dangerous achievement": quoted, Keay, *The Gilgit Game,* 180.
321	"overwhelmed with hospitality and goodwill": Hedin, *My Life,* 120.
321	"gold ingots and lumps of silver lay exposed": ibid., 139.
321–322	"The yellow dunes of the Taklamakan," quoted, Hopkirk, *Foreign Devils on the Silk Road* (London, 1980), 11.
322	"They will never come back," Hedin, *My Life,* 143.
322	"For if I was to die and be buried": quoted, Allen, op. cit., 193.
323–324	"it would have been more natural and simple": Hedin, *My Life,* 244.
324	"That is just what I have pointed out all the time": ibid., 244.
324	*"Geographicus nascitur et fit"*: *The Geographical Journal,* vol. II, 1898, 411.
325	"I do not understand what you mean when writing": Hedin to Keltie, April 19, 1899 (RGS).
326	"Let letters be sent with all speed": Another version of this letter appears in *My Life,* 363, in which he replaces "Russians" with "Europeans."
327	"it should be a splendid recommendation for me": Hedin to Keltie, July 20, 1902, (RGS).
327	The description of Curzon appears in Hedin's *Grosse Männer.*
327	"but I think they are more dangerous neighbors": Hedin to Keltie, May 24, 1899 (RGS).
328	"War against Tibet!" Hedin to Keltie, June 7, 1904 (RGS).
328	"The British campaign in Tibet": *Die Woche,* June 18, 1904.
328	"unprovoked aggression by a great power": Kish, op. cit., 72.
328	"as the guardian of India I cannot": quoted, ibid., 72.
329	"For my own part I have never suspected you of being a Russian agent": Curzon to Hedin, November 13, 1904, quoted, Kish, 72.

329   "The Capture of Lhasa": *The Spectator* (London), August 13, 1904, quoted, Bishop, op. cit., 176.

329   "the 'woman's apartment' of the world": ibid.

329   "assisting in drawing aside a purdah": quoted, Bishop, ibid.

329   "the modern Brunhilde asleep on her mountain top": ibid., 150.

329   "The longing that had possessed me": Hedin, *My Life*, 419.

330   "When I see Curzon's immense gifts": Morley to Minto, August 15, 1907, quoted, Wolpert, op. cit., 40.

330   "the affirmation of Superman": quoted, Allen, op. cit., 193.

330   "all in full dress": Hedin, *Trans-Himalaya*, Vol. I, 12.

331   "Here, before the ink on the Chinese settlement": Morley to Minto, June 7, 1906, quoted, Lamb, op. cit., 262.

331   "The Imperial Government has resolved to keep Tibet isolated from India": quoted, Hedin, *My Life*, 378.

331   "fossilized politician": Hedin, *Grosse Männer*, 63.

331–332   "You are wrong in your letter": Hedin to Keltie, June 11, 1906 (RGS).

332   "geographical morals": Sven Hedin, lecture at the Savage Club, London, July 1, 1909.

332   "Sven Hedin put his arms around my neck": quoted, French, op. cit., 265.

333   "My life and my honor": Alma Hedin, *Mein Bruder Sven* (Leipzig, 1925), quoted, Brennecke, op. cit., 62.

333   "Wonderful, never-to-be forgotten Tashi Lama!": Hedin, *Trans-Himalaya*, vol. I, 325.

333   "You have reached the city of my dreams": Heinrich Harrer, *Return to Tibet* (London, 1983), 143.

333   "the finest results": quoted, Allen, op. cit., 219.

333   "the first white man to penetrate to the sources": quoted, Allen, op. cit., 206.

334   "certain people": quoted, Allen, op. cit., 215.

334–335   "faced all difficulties and braved all dangers": Holdich, "Advances in Asia and Imperial Consolidation in India," *Geographical Journal*, vol. 17 (March 1901), 242.

335   "we have learned all there is to know of the general physiography of High Asia": ibid.

335   "I don't want to run Sven Hedin down": Capt. Rawling to Keltie, October 3, 1908 RGS.

336   "I have had hundreds of servants": in Hedin's speech as reported in *Geographical Journal*, vol. 33 (April 1909), 376.

336   "Even light field artillery": ibid., 389.

337   "It occurred to me, while I was listening": ibid., 393.

337   a great service: ibid., 396.

337   "What shall we get from Sven Hedin?": Holdich, "What We Have Learn't from Sven Hedin," *Geographical Journal*, vol. 33 (April, 1909), 438.

338   "useless for scientific purposes": ibid., 431.

338   "I think he did a great deal but it is a pity": Bailey to his parents, May 2, 1909, Bailey Papers, Mss Eur F 157/166, India Office Library.

338–339   "In reality the conditions were such": *Geographical Journal,* vol. 33 (April, 1909), 439.

340   "his lack of modesty in success": Allen, op. cit., 226.

340   "So I am sorry to have to give it up": Hedin to Keltie, August 27, 1910, RGS.

340   "a disagreeable surprise": Hedin to Keltie, January 2, 1911, RGS.

341   "was situated exactly where I found it": Hedin to Keltie, March 17, 1911.

341   "I have tried to find out": Hedin to Keltie, July 9, 1912, RGS.

342   "Sir: At my return from Lemberg yesterday": Hedin, July 15, 1915 (RGS).

342   "the only true ruling personality of our time": quoted, Kish, op. cit., 97.

343   "I am interested": Bell to Hinks, February 3, 1925 (RGS).

344   "The day before yesterday there was a party": Huang Wenbi, *Huang Wenbi Meng-Xin kaocha riji*, 33.

344   "was actually allowed to export, permanently, enormous collections": Owen Lattimore to Langdon Warner, June 25, 1934 (Warner Papers, Harvard Archives).

344   "it isn't the rules that matter, it's all knack": Lattimore to Hicks, June 3, 1930, RGS.

345   "may not have shown any conspicuous": Lattimore to Warner, June 25, 1934 (Warner Papers, Harvard Archives).

Chapters Fourteen and Fifteen

Sir Aurel Stein is among the few fortunate explorers in our book to be blessed not with one but with two fine biographies. Jeannette Mirsky is to be credited with the scholarly spadework, sorting through the voluminous correspondence and archaeological reports from Stein's long life. Her book *Sir Aurel Stein: Archaeological Explorer* (Chicago, 1977) is long out of print. In 1995 Annabel Walker produced an eminently readable update, *Aurel Stein: Pioneer of the Silk Road* (London). These can be supplemented by Peter Hopkirk's lively *Foreign Devils on the Silk Road* (London, 1980).

Stein produced not only scholarly accounts of his expeditions but also popular accounts. For his first expedition see *Ancient Khotan* (Oxford, 1907, 2 vols.)

and *Sand-Buried Ruins of Khotan* (London, 1904); for the second expedition, *Serindia* (Oxford, 1921, 5 vols.) and *Ruins of Desert Cathay* (New York, 1987, 2 vols.). Stein's Lowell lectures, detailing his first three expeditions, form the core of *On Ancient Central-Asian Tracks* (New York, 1964).

Stein's letters, on which we have drawn extensively, are for the most part in Oxford's Bodleian Library (MS Stein); his letters to Keltie are in the files of the RGS, and both the Fogg Museum and the Harvard University Archives have extensive material relating to his fourth expedition, together with the correspondence of Paul Sachs and Langdon Warner (the latter including key letters from Owen Lattimore). We have also consulted the Kashgar Diaries in OIOC for the relevant period. Other Stein material in their archive is listed in L/P&S/10/1218 Travellers: in Chinese Turkestan: Part V; and in the Kashgar Diaries for 1914 L/P&S/10/825.

Other Stein material can be found in the Cornelius Van H. Engert Papers at Georgetown University.

Hsüang-tang was the inspiration for the Ming novel, *The Journey to the West*, which has been translated by Anthony C. Yu (Chicago, 1977–83, 4 vols.). Sally Hovey Wriggins has traced the path of the Buddhist monk in a delightful illustrated account, *Xuanzang* (Boulder, 1996).

The lives of the Macartneys at Kashgar are recounted in Lady Macartney's *An English Lady in Chinese Turkestan* (Oxford, 1983), and in the biography of Sir George by his successor at Kashgar, C. P. Skrine (with Pamela Nightingale), *Macartney at Kashgar* (London, 1973). For Younghusband's views on Macartney, see Patrick French, *Younghusband* (London, 1994).

The adventures of von Le Coq and Grünwedel are detailed in *Along the Ancient Silk Routes—Central Asian Art from the West Berlin State Museums* (New York, 1982) and Albert von Le Coq's *Buried Treasures of Chinese Turkestan* (Oxford, 1987). On Pelliot see Alain Thiote, "Paul Pelliot: A Bridge Between Sinology and China's Scholarship," *Orientations* (January 1995) and *The Arts of Central Asia: The Pelliot Collection in the Musée Guimet,* ed. Jacques Gies (Paris, 1996, 2 vols.).

Langdon Warner recounts his forays to Dunhuang in *The Long Old Road to China* (London, 1927) and in *Langdon Warner Through His Letters* (Bloomington, 1966), ed. by Theodore Bowie.

Kozlov's memoir has not been translated into English, but there is a German version, introduced by Wilhelm Filchner: *Mongolei, Amdo und die tote Stadt Chara-Choto* (Berlin, 1925). We have also drawn on "The Discovery of Khara Khoto" by Kira Fyodorovna Samosyuk in *Lost Empire of the Silk Road: Buddhist Art from Khara Khoto,* ed. Mikhail Piotrovsky (Milan, 1993) and James Bradburne, *Die Schwarze Stadt an der Seidenstrasse* (Milan, 1993). More on the genesis of the Kozlov expedition to Khara Khoto is contained in Alexandre Andreyev's unpublished, "Agwan Dorjiev: the Dalai Lama's Envoy to Russia and his book, *From Baikal to Holy Lhasa* (St. Petersburg, Samara, Prague, 1997).

The Sino-Swedish Expedition led by Sven Hedin published their finds in *History of the Expedition in Asia, 1927–35* (Stockholm, 1943–44). For William Hung, see Susan Egan, *A Latterday Confucius* (Cambridge, MA, 1987).

The British Library, with the support of the Getty Foundation, is engaged in a long-term project for the study, preservation, and publication of the Dunhuang material. Dr. Susan Whitfield edits their lively newsletter (*IDP News*), which may be downloaded from their website (http://idp.bl.uk/). We have made use of their material on Pelliot (no. 4, January 1996), Kozlov (no. 2, January 1995), and Ye Changchi (no. 7, Spring 1997). The recently published (1999) and very useful "Handbook to the Stein Collections in the U.K." is edited by British Museum curator, Helen Wang (British Museum Occasional Paper, Number 129).

348	"I found him a delightful guest": Stein to Allen, June 26, 1922 (Bodleian).
348	"So I have to accept the sad fact": Stein to Engert, December, 1922 (Georgetown).
349	"tamely in the study": Stein to Allen, December 12, 1918 (Bodleian).
349	"a rather strange man": Stein to Rudolf von Roth, November 13, 1884, in Roth papers in the Tübingen University Library, detailed in an unpublished paper by Dr. Gabriele Zeller delivered at ICANAS, 1997, Budapest.
352	"It was sufficient": quoted, Hopkirk, op. cit., 62.
352	"butcher and beat it": quoted, Walker, 58.
353–354	"arranged to send three savants for the exploration of Turfan": quoted, Mirsky, op. cit., 79.
353	"The day before yesterday I had the opportunity to introduce myself personally to Lord C": ibid., 89.
353–354	"were Germany the ruling power in India": ibid., 90.
354	"a tour for ladies": ibid., 88.
355	"a seemingly endless succession of valleys and ranges": ibid., 131.
355	"the most timid unenterprising girl in the world": Macartney, op. cit., 2.
356	"such as every respectable Kashgari loves to own": Stein, *Sand-Buried Ruins of Khotan,* vol. I, 122.
357	"a coward and a fool": quoted, Walker, op. cit., 92.
358	"form and manners which Chinese etiquette considers essential": quoted, Mirsky, op. cit., 139.
359	"Macartney's ever-watchful care": Stein to Allen, March 7, 1914 (Bodleian).
358	"Macartney is a good enough fellow in his way but he is not English": Quoted, French, op. cit., 83.

359   "small personal failings": Stein, *Sand-Buried Ruins*, 116.

359   "ever ready assistance": quoted, Mirsky, op. cit., 147.

359   "rats as big as hedgehogs": ibid., 145.

361   "tame deserts": Stein, *On Ancient Central Asian Tracks*, 5.

361   "a mummy's shroud": Mirsky, op. cit., 113.

361   "of all these old records being carried away to the Far West": *Sand-Buried Ruins*, 470.

362   "they showed types of frescoes": Grünwedel report, October 17, 1899, quoted in Härtel, op. cit., 27.

363–364   "Quite suddenly the sky grows dark":Von le Coq, op. cit., 36.

364   "tormented everyone": ibid., 51.

365   "poaching on his archaeological preserves": Macartney to Stein, January 20, 1905 (Bodleian).

365   "always go hunting in packs": quoted, Walker, op. cit., 209.

365   "V. recognizes strength": April 25, 1902, (Bodleian MS 235).

365   "in any way advise the said Doctor [Stein] to carry out his intentions": quoted, Mirsky, op. cit., 204.

365   "to such a 'deputation' as preeminent": Stein to Keltie, April 17, 1904 (RGS).

366   "apologies about Tibet": Stein to Allen, November 16, 1904 (Bodleian).

366   "It seems a thousand pities": Lockwood Kipling to Stein, September 30, 1904 (Bodleian).

366   "the spectre of Russo-German competition": quoted, Walker, op. cit., p. 127.

366   "Lord Minto understood": ibid., 134.

366   "Rejoice": Arnold to Stein, 1905, quoted, Mirsky, op. cit., 217.

367   "far greater financial resources": Stein to Keltie, April 25, 1900, (RGS).

368   "short cut across the Pamirs": Quoted, ibid., 232.

368   "diplomatically closed an eye": Stein to Macartney, February 6, 1960 (Bodleian).

368   "This concession may be a good omen": Stein to Keltie, April 24, 1906, (RGS).

368   "the only recorded instance of an organized force of comparatively large size": Stein, *On Ancient Central-Asian Tracks*, 39.

368   "to get to the ground earlier than the French expedition": Stein to Keltie, June 9, 1906, (RGS).

368–369   "the archaeological yield of the last three weeks": Stein to Keltie, October 10, 1906, (RGS).

369   "Notwithstanding all antiquarian interests": Stein to Keltie, February 2, 1907, (RGS).

370   "Grünwedel is ill, can't go on horseback": Macartney to Stein, quoted, Walker, op. cit., 131.

371   "He looked a very queer person": quoted, Mirsky, op. cit., 266.

371   "The sight disclosed in the dim light of the priest's little oil lamp made my eyes open wide": Stein, *On Ancient Central-Asian Tracks*, 179.

372   "The whole clearing had to be done in secret": Stein to Keltie, June 18, 1907, (RGS).

373   "passed peacefully, without a single shot being fired": Gies, op. cit., vol. I, 16.

373   "for Western scholarship all those relics of ancient Buddhist literature and art," Stein, *Ruins of Desert Cathay*, 194.

374   "What was my role as imperial envoy?": *IDP News,* no. 7 (Spring 1997).

374   "Sir Aurel Stein, taking advantage of the ignorance and cupidity": Statement from the National Commission for the Preservation of Antiquities, Beijing, China, regarding Sir Aurel Stein's Archaeological Expedition in Chinese Turkestan (Confidential File Sir Aurel Stein, Fogg Art Museum Archives).

374   "The ruined monasteries & temples": quoted, Mirsky, op. cit., 292ff.

376   "My scientific work has always been guided by the conviction": Stein to Keltie April 17, 1904, (RGS).

377   "to publish anything": Stein to Keltie, December 15, 1907, (RGS).

377   "Few more wonderful discoveries have been made by any archaeologist": quoted in Hopkirk, *Foreign Devils*, 165.

377   "an unparalleled archaeological scoop": ibid.

378   "Remember, my dear Pyotr Kuzmich": quoted, Piotrovsky, op. cit., 31.

379   "You will report to me on your research": Kozlov, op. cit., 220.

380   "I shall never forget": quoted, Piotrovsky, op. cit., 39.

380   "resembling lamas, conducting a religious ceremony": ibid., 44.

381   "No city guard turned out to scan my credentials now": Warner, op. cit., 141.

381   "a very Vandal *modus operandi*": Stein to Macartney, June 6, 1914, OIOC Kashgar Diaries for 1914 L/P&S/10/825.

382   "It seems like the irony of Fate": Stein to Macartney, February 18, 1914, ibid.

382   "What this letter means is that you have no right to excavate": Macartney to Stein, March 3, 1915 (Bodleian).

382   "a fresh Chinese attempt at obstruction": Stein to Keltie, July 11, 1915 (RGS).

383–384 "everywhere eyes are gouged out": Warner to Lorraine Roosevelt Warner, quoted in Bowie, op. cit., p. 115.

384   "In twenty years": Bowie, op. cit., 118.

384   "the priest's cupidity": ibid.

385   "entirely Harvard enterprise": Sachs, memo for file, July 16, 1929 (Harvard).

385   "Can you lead Asiatic expedition if Harvard will finance": Keller to Stein, July 16, 1929 (Harvard).

385   "cautiously sidling up and sniffing at each other": Warner to Cabot, July 25, 1929 (Harvard).

385   "Information received by me from friends," Stein to Keller, July 18, 1929 (Harvard).

385   "Chinese *amour propre*": ibid.

386   "devoted to the Fine Arts": Warner to Stein, July 22, 1929 (Harvard).

386   "You are absolutely right about Stein and the British Museum": Jayne to Warner, n.d.[1929] (Harvard).

386   "If Stein is right in thinking that British prestige": Warner to Sachs, August 30, 1929 (Harvard).

386   "naturally hoped to receive a characteristic and representative selection": Sir Frederich G. Kenyon to Stein, February 11, 1930 (Harvard).

387   "As a matter of fact": Engert to Stein, Van Engert papers, Box 7, Folder 27 (Georgetown).

387   "great *lacuna*, the want of all geological training": Stein to Keltie, June 18, 1907 (RGS).

387   "Mr Hung, you are young": quoted, Egan, op. cit., 122.

388   "to avert Young China agitation": Memo of conversation between Stuart and Sachs, March 21, 1920 (Harvard).

388   "some colloquial knowledge of Hindustani": Stein to Bramlette, March 22, 1930 (Harvard).

388   "entirely to ignore": Lampson Memo, May 22, 1930, OIOC.

389   "would be likely to bring about that publicity": Stein to Sachs, May 4, 1930 (Harvard).

389   "to refrain from pressing for more specific facilities": Lampson to Stein, May 9, 1930, OIOC.

389   "to avoid whatever embarrassment *soi-disant"*: Stein to Forbes, January 11, 1930 (Fogg).

389   "the personal goodwill of the Mandarins of the old scholarly type": Stein to Keller, June 21, 1929 (Harvard).

390   "carried away without permission": Dispatch from Sir M. Lampson (Peking via Siberia), June 12, 1930, to India and sent to F.O. OIOC.

390   "under distinct obligations": Stein to Warner, October 18, 1930 (Harvard).

390   "a steady and thoroughly useful helper": Stein to Sachs, August 1, 1930 (Harvard).

390   "easy to admit that a young man cannot stand up to conditions": Bramlette to Sachs, November 10, 1930 (Harvard).

391   "I only know Old China": *Peking and Tiensin Times*, December 29, 1930.

391 "my nostrils twitch whenever they pick up the scent of Hung & Co. on the trail of Stein": Lattimore to Warner, June 25, 1934 (Langdon Warner Papers, Harvard).

391 "scientific archaeology": Statement from the National Commission for the Preservation of Antiquities, Pejing, China regarding Sir Aurel Stein's Archaeological Expedition in Chinese Turkestan (Fogg).

392 "wholly unwarranted allegations": *The Times,* July 16, 1931.

392 "expenditure incurred": Stein to Sachs, March 14, 1931 (Harvard).

392 "Times have changed": Lampson to Stein, July 19, 1931 (OIOC).

393 "antiquarian exploration, not merely a rapid visit to Kabul": quoted in Mirsky, op. cit., 542.

393 "I am fully aware that the winter months": Stein to Engert, April 20, 1943 (Bodleian).

393 "apparently in good health and spirits": Engert to Secretary of State, November 2, 1943, Box 8, Folder 54 (Georgetown).

393 "I have had a wonderful life": ibid.

393 "the most prodigious combination of scholar, explorer, archaeologist and geographer of his generation": quoted, Hopkirk, *Foreign Devils*, 68.

Chapter Sixteen

The only readily accessible source for the life and work of William Woodville Rockhill is his short entry in the *Dictionary of American Biography*. Books by and about him are hard to find except in bigger libraries. Rockhill's papers, including his Peking diaries and family correspondence, are preserved at Harvard's Houghton Library. His expedition reports, photographs, and letters from China are scattered in several archives at the Smithsonian Institution. Paul A. Varg's *Open Door Diplomat: The Life of W. W. Rockhill* (Urbana, IL, 1952) is an admirable first take. See also his own key works, *Land of the Lamas* (New York, 1891); *Diary of a Journey Through Mongolia and Tibet in 1891 and 1892* (Washington, DC, 1894); and *The Dalai Lamas and Their Relations with the Manchu Emperors of China, 1644–1908* (Leiden, 1910).

Rockhill's era is readably introduced by Howard K. Beale, *Theodore Roosevelt and the Rise of America to World Power* (Baltimore, 1956), to which can be added Patricia O'Toole, *The Five of Hearts* (New York, 1990). A standard account, Thomas A. Bailey, *A Diplomatic History of the American People* (New York, 1950), can be supplemented by George Kennan, *American Diplomacy, 1900–1950* (Chicago, 1951); John Paton Davies, *Dragon by the Tail: American, British, Japanese and American Encounters with China and Each Other* (New York, 1972); and O. Edmund Clubb, *China and Russia: The "Great Game"* (New York, 1971).

Besides the standard histories of China by John K. Fairbanks and Jonathan D. Spence, we have benefited from *The Ageless Chinese* (New York, 1965) by Professor Dun J. Li. On special topics, we have used Alain Peyrefitte, *The Im-*

mobile Empire (New York, 1992), on the Macartney mission; Marina Warner, *The Dragon Empress* (New York, 1972), on the Dowager Empress; Peter Ward Fay, *The Opium War* (Chapel Hill, 1975); and Peter Fleming, *The Siege at Peking* (New York, 1959), on the Boxers.

On the British Resident in Sikkim who became the Thirteenth Dalai Lama's friend, Alex McKay, *Tibet and the British Raj: The Frontier Cadre 1904–1947* (Richmond, Surrey, 1997), breaks interesting new ground. On the Younghusband Mission, see Peter Fleming, *Bayonets to Lhasa* (London, 1961), and Sir Francis's own account, *India and Tibet* (London, 1910). For an Indian view, see Parshotam Mehta, *Tibetan Policy: 1904–1937* (Wiesbaden, 1976).

398   One of the country's two ablest diplomats: The other diplomat was Robert White, an adviser to Presidents from Cleveland to Wilson; see DAB sketch on Rockhill.

398   "I feel quite a new spring": quoted, Varg, *Open Door Diplomat,* 1.

398   "Let me say": *Congressional Record*, June 14, 1898, quoted, Varg, op. cit., 27.

399   "Our mighty republic": Address at Mechanics Pavilion, San Francisco, May 13, 1903; quoted by Beale, op. cit., 172–73.

400   "We stood in holy terror": Nelson Johnson, Oral History, Columbia University, vol. 1, p. 80.

402   "Army discipline had made of him": quoted, Varg, op. cit., 9–10.

403   The British led the way: On Warren Delano, see Geoffrey Ward, *Before the Trumpet: Young Franklin Roosevelt 1882–1905* (New York, 1985), 67–80 passim.

404   "much rivalry and disorder": quoted, Peyrefitte, op. cit., 465.

405   "very impressive": Rockhill Diary, November 21, 1908; Rockhill Papers, Houghton Library, Harvard University.

406   "My outfit was simple": Rockhill, *Land of the Lamas,* 288.

409   "How to travel": "Explorations in Mongolia and Tibet," *Annual Report,* Board of Regents, Smithsonian Insitution, 1892, 659.

410   "Living in Sinico-Mongolo-Tibetan": ibid., 671.

410–411 "I am ten days from": Rockhill, *Journey Through Mongolia and Tibet,* 238.

411   "The method I followed": Rockhill, "Explorations," 667.

411–412 "I had traveled": quoted, Graham Sandberg, *The Exploration of Tibet* (New Delhi, 1973), 201.

412   The ranking military authority: See Thomas Holdich, *Tibet, the Mysterious* (London, 1908), 174–89; Hamilton Bower, *Diary of a Journey Across Tibet* (London, 1894).

412   "Had it not been": Das to Rockhill, September 9, 1989; Rockhill Papers, Houghton Library.

413   "Where his intolerance antagonized": quoted, Varg, op. cit., 23.

413   "Now about Rockhill": Roosevelt to Charles McCauley, USMC, March 9, 1899; Rockhill Papers.

414   It was, as George Kennan pungently: See Kennan, *American Diplomacy*, Chapter 3, and for an even dimmer revisionist view, William Appleman Williams, *The Roots of the American Empire* (New York, 1969).

415   "Your open door is already": quoted, O'Toole, *The Five of Hearts* (New York, 1992), p. 318.

415   "I feel as if a load": Roosevelt to Rockhill, July 21, 1900, Rockhill Papers.

417   "from the dangers that threaten": quoted, Snelling, 120.

418   "He seemed deeply impressed": Rockhill, *The Dalai Lamas of Lhasa*, 90–92.

418   To be seated familiarly: Rockhill to Roosevelt, June 30, 1908, Rockhill Papers.

418   "I think that this is": Roosevelt to Rockhill, August 1, 1908, Rockhill Papers.

419   "You must always remember": quoted, John Paton Davies, *Dragon by the Tail*, 90.

419   "behind the Chair": *China Daily News*, October 5, 1908; Rockhill Papers.

419   Rockhill found Dorzhiev: Snelling, op. cit., 133.

420   Rockhill consulted the archives: Rockhill, *The Dalai Lamas*, 18.

420   An Imperial edict in November: quoted, Mehta, op. cit., 20.

421   "I fear he will not": Rockhill to Roosevelt, November 8, 1908; Rockhill Papers.

421   Bryce recalled: quoted, Mehta, op. cit., 21.

422   "We are greatly pleased": Letter from Dalai Lama to Rockhill, Rockhill Papers, 49M-284(85).

423   "The world would hear little more": quoted, Lamb, *The McMahon Line*, 221–22.

Chapter Seventeen

For all who journeyed to Lhasa from the 1904 until the Communist takeover in 1950, producing a book was obligatory. Out of these materials Alex McKay has fashioned a work, *Tibet and the British Raj 1904–1947,* which unscrolls like a tapestry and to which he has added a pendant, "Tibet 1924: A Very British Coup Attempt," *Journal of the Royal Asiatic Society*, Series 3 (1997), 411–24. Two figures predominate, Bell and Bailey. Lieutenant-Colonel F. M. Bailey has a biographer, Arthur Swinson, but the pages of *Beyond the Frontiers* (London, 1971, with a preface by Sir Fitzroy Maclean) read as if redacted by a vigilant widow and the Secret Service; no surprises here. Bell has no biographer, but C. J.

Christie has written a thoughtful memoir, "Sir Charles Bell," in *Asian Affairs,* vol. 64 (1977), 48–63. For a distinctly sour view of Bailey, see Mark Crocker, *Loneliness and Time: The Story of British Travel Writing* (New York, 1992).

Bailey's classic *Mission to Tashkent* was reissued handsomely by London's Folio Society in 1999, and doubtless similar honors will be accorded his *No Passport to Tibet* (London, 1957). And Bell's four important books on Tibet have been reprinted: *The People of Tibet* (New Delhi, 1998); *Tibet Past and Present* (New Delhi, 1996); *The Religion of Tibet* (New Delhi, 1994); and *Portrait of a Dalai Lama* (London,1987).

Against this backdrop, with McKay as a scout, one can better tackle the archival maze at the Oriental and India Office Collections (IOC) at the British Library, drawing on Alastair Lamb's two-volume *The McMahon Line* (London, 1966); Amur Kaur Jasbir Singh's *The Himalayan Triangle* (London, 1988); and Melvyn Goldstein's *History of Modern Tibet 1913–1951* (Berkeley, 1989). It then becomes clearer why William McGovern, the first American to reach Lhasa, caused such an uproar on the frontier with *To Lhasa in Disguise* (London and New York, 1924).

426　　"He moved as if he had no bones": All references to Ranji and cricket are from John Lord, *The Maharajahs* (New York, 1971) and Geoffrey Moorhouse, *Calcutta* (London, 1971), with input from Ramachandra Guha, an Indian social scientist and cricket columnist, author of "The Empire Plays Back," *Jahrbuch 1994–1995* of the Wissenschaftskolleg zu Berlin.

427　　"They all have the traits so characteristic of Clifton": French, op. cit., 9–10.

427　　"I look upon the war": quoted, Byron Farwell, *The Great Anglo-Boer War* (New York, 1976), 54. For the full flavor of his anti-imperial passion, see Wilfred Scawen Blunt, *My Diaries 1888–1914* (New York, 1921), passim.

428　　"gradually clouded by disillusion": Nicolson, *Curzon, The Last Phase,* 4.

430　　"An excellent fellow": quoted, McKay, *Tibet and the British Raj,* 30.

431　　"Thur. 18. Went to Drepung [Monastery] with White and Wilton": quoted, French, op. cit., 245.

431　　"He would stand there covered": Bailey, *No Passport to Tibet,* 55.

432　　"as if to make sure that nobody was wanting to take a shot at him": B. J. Gould, *The Jewel in the Lotus* (London, 1957), 74.

433　　"the only time on record when His Majesty's mails": Jan Morris, *Farewell the Trumpets: An Imperial Retreat* (New York, 1978), 416.

434　　"was not increased when his wife undertook, with considerable success": Alastair Lamb, *The McMahon Line,* II, 600. From the appendix, entitled "Tom Browns from Central Asia," which can be read alongside Gould's blander account in *Jewel in the Lotus.*

435   "Makes it very difficult to get things done...No one feels capable of taking any responsibility": Bailey papers, OIOC, MSS Eur F 157/245.

436   "extremely mad scheme": Quoted, McKay, *Tibet and the British Raj*, 36.

436   "In the world of imperial *Realpolitik*": ibid., 35.

440   "He was the first European we had ever seen": Rinchen Dolma Taring, *Daughter of Tibet* (London, 1986), 67–68.

441   "I hope Sir Charles Bell does not stay with you": Bailey to his mother, November 11, 1924; OIOC, Mss EUR F/157/291.

441   "he went about in a dandy": ibid.

441   "queer crowd" who "clearly show the cloven hoof": McKay, *Tibet and the British Raj*, 106.

442   "immediately stopped and asked me who and what I was": McGovern, op. cit., 323–24.

443   "Sir Charles Bell aimed": ibid., 39.

444   "every native is absolutely under his thumb": McGovern, British edition of *To Lhasa in Disguise*, 23.

445   "absolutely necessary to send a military advisor to Tsarong": quoted, McKay, "Tibet 1924," 418.

446   "tom foolery on the part of Laden La": McKay, *Tibet and the British Raj*, 117.

446   "It is amazing to me how Laden La": quoted, ibid.

Chapters Eighteen and Nineteen

The literature on Roerich is enormous. Since the fall of the Soviet Union, a cottage industry has added considerably to the shelf—alas, none of it translated. A recent biography by Jacqueline Decter is *Nicholas Roerich: The Life of a Russian Master* (New York, 1989). However, she is almost entirely concerned with Roerich as an artist and writer, and mentions but does not address such Roerich critics as Robert Williams in *Russian Art and American Money* (Cambridge, 1980), the first scholar to attempt sorting out conflicting accounts in the archives. Indispensable for understanding the fin de siècle context of Roerich's work is Maria Carlson, *No Religion Higher Than Truth: A History of the Theosophical Movement in Russia, 1875–1922* (Princeton, 1993).

Nicholas Roerich speaks for himself in three characteristic books, *Altai Himalaya* (New York, 1929); *Heart of Asia* (New York, 1930); and *Shambhala* (Rochester, VT, 1990). George Roerich's account of the Central Asian expedition is in *Trails to Innermost Asia* (New Haven, CT, 1931). Two books recently published in Russia that are particularly illuminating on the Central Asian expedition are Sina Lichtmann Fosdick's diary, *My Teachers: The Diary Leaves 1922–1934* (Moscow, 1998), and the diary of Konstantine Ryabinin, *Tibet Debunked: The True Diaries of N. K. Roerich's Expedition* (Moscow, 1996).

On the setting, see A. W. Forbes, *Warlords and Muslims in Chinese Central Asia: A Political History of Republican Sinkiang 1911–1949* (Cambridge, 1986), and for the rivalry between the Dalai and Panchen Lamas, see Parshotam Meha, *Tibetan Polity, 1904–37* (Wiesbaden, 1976). John Snelling, *Buddhism in Russia* and A. I. Andreev [*sic*], *The Buddhist Shrine of Petrograd* (Ulan Ude, 1992), deal with the influence of Dorzhiev on Roerich. For background on the Diaghilev Ballet, see Lynn Garafolo, *Diaghilev's Ballets Russes* (New York, Oxford, 1989); Richard Buckle, *Diaghilev* (New York, 1979); Simon Volkov, *St. Petersburg* (New York, 1995); Suzanne Massie, *The Land of the Firebird* (New York, 1980); Alexandre Benois, *Memoirs* (London, 1960); and Peter Lieven, *The Birth of Ballets-Russes* (Boston and New York, 1936).

Sources on the 1948 campaign include Curtis D. MacDougall, *Gideon's Army* (New York, 1968), a three-volume compendium by a professor of journalism at Northwestern University and a sympathetic participant; and Irwin Ross, *The Loneliest Campaign: The Truman Victory of 1948* (New York, 1968), still the basic overall work. H. L. Mencken's *Baltimore Sun* dispatches have been compiled and introduced by Joseph C. Goulden, *Mencken's Last Campaign* (Washington, 1976). Alistair Cooke's reminiscences are in his profile of Mencken in *Six Men* (New York, 1977). On Henry Wallace's mysticism, see Arthur M. Schlesinger, Jr., *The Coming of the New Deal* (Boston, 1959), and Graham White and John Maze, *Henry A. Wallace: His Search for a New World Order* (Chapel Hill, NC, 1995). See also Dwight Macdonald's stylish polemic, *Henry Wallace: The Man and the Myth* (New York, 1948). On Roerich and the 1940 campaign, see Charles Michelson, *The Ghost Talks* (New York, 1944), and Ted Morgan, *F.D.R.: A Biography* (New York, 1985). We have also consulted J. S. Walker, *Henry A. Wallace and American Foreign Policy* (Westport, CT, 1976); J. M. Blum, ed. *The Price of Vision: The Diary of Henry A. Wallace 1942–1946* (Boston, 1973); and N. D. Markowitz, *The Rise and Fall of the People's Century: Henry A. Wallace and American Liberalism 1941–1948* (New York, 1973).

Articles we found useful include Alexander Andreyev, "Soviet Russia and Tibet: A Debacle of Secret Diplomacy," *Tibet Journal*, vol. XXI, no. 3, Autumn 1996, 4–33; Robert A. Rupen, "Mongolia, Tibet and Buddhism or, a Tale of Two Roerichs," *Canada-Mongolia Review*, vol. 5, no. 1, April 1979; Oleg Shiskin, "In the Embrace of the Impertinent Monster," *Segodnya*, October 29, November 19, December 10, 1994. Konstantin Ryabin's "Deposition" when he was arrested by the OGPU, July 23, 24, 1930, is contained *Ariavarta*, no. 1, 1997, 172–79.

The Wallace papers are available on microfilm from the University of Iowa.

In NARA, relevant files are in the State Department General Records (RG 59 031.R62) and State Department Office of Consular Records (U–2 000–2457); on the Manchurian Expedition, under RG 54 170/27/8/2, there are three boxes, "Records relating to the Roerich Expedition, 1934–37." More MacMillan-Stephens Material is in RG 59, State Dept. General Records 102.7302.

The Franklin D. Roosevelt Library at Hyde Park has a collection of "Guru" letters and letters written by Helena Roerich to FDR as well as the Rosenman papers pertaining to the 1940 campaign. Under the Freedom of Information Act, we obtained Roerich's FBI files, much expunged. The Roerich files in OIOC are L/P&S/10/1145 and 1146. The Bailey papers are also in the OIOC MSS Eur F 157.

448	"in an unusually powerful mystical movement": quoted, Carlson, *No Religion Higher Than Truth,* 4.
449	"Admirers of Theosophy": quoted, ibid.
449	"idolatrous pagoda": quoted, Andreyev, *Buddhist Shrine of Petrograd*, 95.
449	"power of Darkness and the times of Anti-Christ": ibid.
449	"the Buddhists should feel themselves under the wing of the mighty eagle," ibid., 88.
450	"as though he ought to have been a mystic or spy": Robert Craft, *Conversations with Stravinsky* (New York, 1959), 105ff.
451	"the Russians have come not with ships and sailors to conquer our territory": quoted, Garofolo, op. cit., 275.
451	"was ready to stand up": quoted, ibid., 34.
451	"were all the nations of the Russian Empire come to pay homage": quoted, ibid., 13.
452	"In the surpassing fury and magnificence of the Russian ballet": ibid, 22.
454	"a New Age of peace, brotherhood and enlightenment": Snelling, op. cit., 138.
455	"Vulgarity and bigotry, betrayal and promiscuity": quoted, Shishkin, *Segodnya,* October 29, 1994.
457	"to fuse the teachings of Buddha and Lenin": Williams, op. cit., 116.
458	"No doubt that we will be greatly watched": Nicholas Roerich, November 10, 1923 (FDR Library, Hyde Park).
458	"obtain concessions for mining businesses in the Altai and for agricultural development": Fosdick Diary, October 24, 1924.
459	"to paint panoramas": Stephen Gaselee Confidential Memo, Sept. 1930 (OIOC L/P&S/10/1146).
460	"organized mob": telegram, Aug. 8, 1924 (OIOC L/P&S/10/1146).
460	"extremely foolish": letter from Kashmir Resident, August 10, 1924 (OIOC L/P&S/10/1046).
460	"to collect objets d'art": British Consul, Kashgar, November 19, 1925 (OIOC L/P&S/10/1046).
462	"an anti-revolutionary ex-Russian subject": Gaselee memo (OIOC L/P&S/10/1046).
462	"a passport issued by the Provisional (1917) Government": ibid.

462–463   "Today Roerich, his wife, and son have visited me": Bistrov Diary, April 19, 1926, Archive of the President of the Russian Federation.

463   "strongly and openly criticized": ibid.

463   "half-Buddhist, half Communist": Williams, op. cit., 126.

464   "where the names of Maitreya and Shambhala were pronounced," Fosdick Diary, August 1, 1926.

464   "the whole idea of the Soviet government": quoted, Rupen, op. cit. 7. The entire English version in X. J. Eudin and R. C. North, *Soviet Russia and the East* (Stanford, 1957), 199.

466   "unmask English machinations": Andreyev, "Soviet Russia and Tibet," 13.

466   "could not understand": Bailey diary (OIOC MSS Eur F 157).

467   "to return to Tibet": Nikiforov to Karakhan, March 1926, Russian State Military Archives, quoted in Schishkim, *Segodnya,* October 29, 1994.

468   "Did you notice the direction this sphere moved": Roerich, *Shambhala*, 7.

469   "I think you will admit that it is not a pleasant story": Stephen Gaselee, July 8, 1927, (OIOC L/P&S/10/1146).

470   "Americans named Mr. and Mrs. Rigden": Tsarong to Bailey, May 11, 1927, (OIOC L/P&S/10/1046. MSS Eur F 157/291).

470   "The Mission is detained by Tibetan Government": Letter from George Roerich to Bailey, November 10, 1927 (OIOC L/P&S/10/1145).

471   "On the Tibetan territory": Roerich, *Altai Himalaya*, vii ff.

472   "a very dangerous Communist and member of the Comintern": Memo from Bailey to the Foreign Secretary for India, June 6, 1928, (OIOC L/P&S/10/1045).

472   "The man is from a literary and scientific": Bailey (OIOC L/P&S/10/1046).

472   "They lived here for some time in Darjeeling," Bailey to his mother, May 15, 1928. (OIOC MSS Eur F 157/214).

472   "creating a counter-revolutionary organization": Ryabinin Deposition.

473   "personally hated for closing the monasteries": ibid.

473   "as a result of cardiac arrest": quoted, Snelling, op.cit, 249.

Chapter Nineteen

474   "all the other roaring magicians of recent history": Mencken's reports can be found in Goulden, op. cit., 73–90.

474   "I am completely neutral": Goulden, op. cit., quoted on dust jacket.

475   "I find the W. One": Westbrook Pegler column, *New York Journal American*, March 11, 1948.

475–476 "I have been thinking of you holding the casket": Pegler, March 10, 1948.

476 "Mr. Wallace, do you repudiate": Cooke, op cit., 104–9.

476 "Would you consider *me* a Pegler stooge": ibid.

477 "Wallace's imbecile handling": Goulden, op. cit., 87–88.

478 "a good deal of a Bolshie": letter to Robert Kelley, Division of Eastern European Affairs, State Department from B.A.B, State Department (NARA).

478 "It may be that he is only a racketeer": Memo from Consul General Robert Jarvis, June 28, 1932, State Department, (NARA).

479 "the legal right": Mr. Bannerman to Mr. Castle, July 22, 1930, State Department, (NARA).

479 "for which it would be much easier": Memorandum of conversation with Walter Koelz (circa 1930) State Department, (NARA).

480 "a great Russian painter": quoted, Williams, op. cit., 136.

480 "I believe so profoundly": ibid., 136ff.

480 "I feel for a short time": Henry Wallace to NR, December 20, 1930 (Hyde Park).

481–482 "Am talking Wednesday with [Joseph] Rock": Henry Wallace to Frances Grant, November 13, 1933 (Hyde Park).

482 "always include the entire area of Kokonor and even Tatsienlu into Tibet": Joseph Rock to Ryerson, May 13, 1933 (Hyde Park).

483 "activate disintegrating forces": White and Maze, op. cit, p. 73.

483 "It seems here at times": ibid., fn. 49, 75.

483 "the political situation": ibid., 83.

483 "to lead and protect": Wallace to Roerich, March 16, 1934 (Iowa, microfilm reel 19).

483 "being of the feline [Russians]race": Wallace to NR, April 17, 1934 (Hyde Park).

483 "exploration": MacMillan memo, March 21, 1934 (Iowa, reel 19).

484 "in a blaze of glory": MacMillan to Ryerson, June 9, 1934 (NARA).

485 "pointed out to me": ibid.

485 "one of America's outstanding statesmen": Handbill sent by MacMillan to Ryerson, July 20, 1934.

485 "To have these [leaflets] thrown": ibid.

485 "to import arms and ammunition": Report on Roerich Expedition, U.S. Consul General, Harbin, September 27, 1934, (NARA).

486 "a clear picture of the organization": "Georges de Roerich" July 20, 1934 (Iowa, reel 19).

486 "It looks as though I will finally see": MacMillan to Ryerson, July 31, 1934 (NARA).

486 "ridiculous" and "extremely malicious": quoted, Williams, op. cit., 139.

486   "complete confidence and approval": Wallace to Roerich, September 27, 1934.

486   "had for its object other than agricultural work": Report on Roerich Expedition, U.S. Consul General, Harbin, September 27, 1934 (NARA).

487   "The Desert Shall Bloom Again": Harbin, September 24, 1934 (NARA).

487   "I wish I could spend the winter in a Monastery": Roosevelt to Wallace, December 10, 1934 (NARA).

487   "wealthy Americans would be glad": fn. 16, White and Maze, op. cit., 93.

488   "I do not know whether": Horch to Wallace, July 3, 1935.

488   "regarded as a spy by certain officials of Manchuko": Daniel A. Doran to Wallace, July 9, 1936, State Department, NARA.

489   "decided reservations": Wallace to various ambassadors, October 23, 1935 (Iowa, Reel 20).

489–490   "The rumor is the Monkeys": The silence on the 1940 affair was first broken on this episode by a Democratic speechwriter, Charles Mickelson, in *The Ghost Talks* (New York, 1944), p. 197. The fullest subsequent treatment is in Morgan, *FDR*, 531 et seq., which draws on Roosevelt's indiscreet taped discussions with Lowell Mellett. But see also Macdonald, op. cit., 115–24.

490   "I guess that's right": This and further quotations all from Morgan.

Chapter Twenty

Suydam Cutting left few footprints, as one might expect from a big-game hunter and sometime intelligence officer. Besides his *Who's Who* entry and a self-sketch in the fiftieth anniversary report of the Harvard Class of 1912, there is a *New York Times* obituary (August 25, 1972). See also the useful note in *Tibet: The Sacred Realm* (New York, 1983), an album of photographs from 1880 to 1950, and the Newark Museum guide *Tibetan Collection: Introduction* (1983), by Valrae Reynolds and Amy Heller. Cutting's *The Fire Ox and Other Years* (New York, 1940) is a sumptuous production written in Basic Travelese. His account in *Natural History* (February 1936), "In Lhasa—The Forbidden," is more valuable. His father, Robert Fulton Cutting, has a good entry in the DAB, and one can consult a curiosity, the verbatim record of a *Banquet to R. Fulton Cutting and Elgin R. L. Gould: Given by Their Friends* (New York, 1902), complete with a menu and seating chart of the Waldorf-Astoria fête.

Cutting's correspondence with two Dalai Lamas and FDR in re Tibet are in the Newark Museum Archives; there are however no diaries and but a few Cutting letters. The American Museum of Natural History files on Cutting contain only a bureaucratic miscellany. The Franklin Roosevelt Library at

Hyde Park has a slim sheaf of letters and memoranda relating to Cutting and Tibet.

In re Theodore and Kermit Roosevelt, see Sylvia Jukes Morris's biography of their mother, *Edith Kermit Roosevelt: Portrait of a First Lady* (New York, 1980), and the reminiscences of Mrs. Theodore Roosevelt, Jr., *Day Before Yesterday* (New York, 1959). Kermit Roosevelt wrote *War in the Garden of Eden* (New York, 1919) about the Mesopotamia campaign, and co-authored with Ted accounts of their Asian expeditions, *East of the Sun and West of the Moon* (New York, 1926) and *Trailing the Giant Panda* (New York, 1929). On Groton and the Roosevelts, see Geoffrey C. Ward, *Before the Trumpet* (New York, 1985); Ted Morgan, *F.D.R.* (New York, 1985); Arthur M. Schlesinger, Jr., *The Coming of the New Deal* (Boston, 1959); and James MacGregor Burns, *Roosevelt: The Lion and the Fox* (New York, 1956).

A full study of The Room awaits its author. Opening the way is Jeffery M. Dorwart, "The Roosevelt-Astor Espionage Ring," *New York History* (July 1981), drawing on Kermit Roosevelt's papers at the Library of Congress. See also Ernest Furgurson, "Back Channels," *Washingtonian* (July 1996). On the rise of Donovan, and the attendant controversy, see Anthony Cave Brown, *The Last Hero* (New York, 1982) and *"C": The Secret Life of Sir Stewart Menzies, Spymaster to Winston Churchill* (New York, 1987); Thomas Troy, *Wild Bill and Intrepid: Donovan, Stephenson and the Origin of the CIA* (New Haven, 1996); R. Jeffreys-Jones, *The CIA and American Democracy* (New Haven, 1989). See also G.J.A. O'Toole, *Honorable Treachery* (New York, 1991); John H. Waller, *The Unseen War in Europe* (New York, 1996); Thomas E. Mahl, *Desperate Deception: British Covert Operations in the United States* (Washington, DC, 1998); and Nicholas John Cull, *Selling War: The British Propaganda Campaign Against "Neutrality" in World War II* (Oxford, 1995).

Sir William Wiseman makes an appearance in David Fromkin, *In the Time of the Americans* (New York, 1995); Burton Hersh, *The Old Boys: The American Elite and the Origins of the CIA* (New York, 1992), and W. B. Fowler, *British-American Relations 1917–1918: The Role of Sir William Wiseman* (Princeton, NJ, 1969).

On Lhasa in the 1930's, the standard sources are Melvyn C. Goldstein, *A History of Modern Tibet* (Berkeley, 1989); Tsepon W. D. Shakabpa, *Tibet: A Political History* (New York, 1984); H. E. Richardson, *A Short History of Tibet* (New York, 1962); Alex McKay, *Tibet and the British Raj* (London, 1997); and Alastair Lamb, *Tibet, China and India 1914–1950* (London, 1999). These can be supplemented by Margaret D. Williamson, *Memoirs of a Political Officer's Wife in Tibet, Sikkim and Bhutan* (London, 1987), and F. Spencer Chapman, *Lhasa, the Holy City* (London, 1940).

494   "the significance of this contact was enormous": Cutting, "In Lhasa—The Forbidden," *Natural History* (February 1936), 103.

495   "the greatest disappointment of my life": See Geoffrey C. Ward, *Before the Trumpet* (New York, 1985), 236.

495   "naturally, had to be chosen with especial care": Cutting, op. cit., as are all the subsequent references to gifts.

497   "I am inclined to think": William Phillips to FDR, January 25, 1934; NARA, 893.00 Tibet/16. Also see in same file Kermit Roosevelt to FDR, January 18, 1934.

498   "If some Groton boys do not enter political life": This and other references to Groton are drawn from Ward, op. cit., Morgan, op. cit., and Schlesinger, op. cit.

501   "but we hoped that once we reached this sacred city": Cutting, op. cit., 105; this and other references to his trip are from the same article.

502   "The present situation is critical": The details of the Williamson Mission are drawn from Lamb, *Tibet, China & India 1914–1950;* McKay, *Tibet and the British Cadre;* Goldstein, *History of Modern Tibet;* and Margaret D. Williamson, *Memoirs of a Political Officer's Wife in Tibet, Sikkim and Bhutan* (London, 1987).

504   "I find a note from Helen": FDR to Suydam Cutting, May 17, 1937. This and other letters that follow can be found in the Franklin D. Roosevelt Library at Hyde Park.

504   "Still technically under the suzerainty of China": Letter to Missy Le Hand, Aprtil 27, 1937, from Sumner Welles.

505   "a ravishing *mille fleurs* carpet": This and other descriptions of Cutting's second trip to Lhasa are from *Fire Ox and Other Years,* 173–246.

507   "Silver-haired, silver-tongued, silver-suited, silver-mannered": The rise of Donovan is taken from sources listed in the headnote above; this passage is from Cave Brown, *"C,"* 265.

Chapter Twenty-One

We are fortunately not wholly reliant on Ernst Schäfer's self-serving interrogations at Nuremberg, summed up in Final Interrogation Report (RG 338 OI-FIR No. 32, dated February 12, 1946) and separately filed at NARA. In these he is careful to mention in asides that he once had a half-Jewish secretary and "saved different people from concentration camps." None of these good deeds appear in the captured files of the Ahnenerbe on microfilm in NARA (RG 242 T 81 Roll 128). His SS records (RG 242 SS 138803) are also at NARA on microfilm. The Archives also possess a letter from Tibet's Reting Regent to Hitler, as well as photographs. There is only a brief mention of the Tibet expedition in the State Department files, also in NARA.

    The photographic and ethnographic materials the SS expedition brought back are today in the Haus der Natur, Salzburg. What appears to be part of the original manuscript of *Geheimnis Tibet* is wrongly catalogued in the Library of

Congress (Ms. Division German captured Documents) as the diary of the first Schäfer-Dolan Expedition. The OIOC records on the Schäfer expedition can be found in L/P&S 12/4343.

Michael Kater is the preeminent authority on the Ahnenerbe. Unfortunately his *Das "Ahnenerbe" der SS 1935–1945* (Munich, 1997) is not available in English. Nor are Reinhard Greve's articles, "Tibetforschung im SS-Ahnenerbe," in Thomas Hauschild, ed., *Lebenslust und Fremdenfurcht* (Suhrkamp, 1995), and "Das Tibet-Bild der Nationalsozialisten," Thierry Dodin and Heinz Raether, eds., *Mythos Tibet* (Cologne, 1997).

Schäfer's own contemporary accounts of the expedition are contained in *Geheimnis Tibet* (Munich, 1943), from which our quotations on the mission to Lhasa were taken. In later years he continued to write about Tibet experiences, but from afar. See *Fest der weissen Schleier* (Braunschweig, 1949) and *Über den Himalaja ins Land der Götter* (Braunschweig, 1950).

On Nazi strategy in Afghanistan, the essential source is Milan Hauner, *India in Axis Strategy: Germany, Japan and Indian Nationalists in the Second World War* (Stuttgart, 1981), and his monograph, "One Man Against the Empire: The Faqir of Ipi and the British in Central Asia," *Journal of Contemporary History,* vol. I (1981).

Very little has appeared in English on the SS expedition, the exceptions being Alastair Lamb's *Tibet, China & India 1914–1950,* Alex McKay's *Tibet and the British Raj,* and an article by Ed Douglas in the London *Observer* (November 2, 1997). By contrast, fringe literature on the Nazis and the occult proliferates on the Internet, most of it running the gamut from bizarre to loopy. Among books on the subject, Nicholas Goodrick Clarke, *The Occult Roots of Nazism* (New York, 1992), is a scholarly antidote. There is no evidence for the wild claim that in the ruins of Berlin in 1945 Russian soldiers found a thousand Tibetan corpses in Wehrmacht uniforms. Similarly, although the geopolitician General Karl Haushofer may have introduced Hitler to the concept of *Lebensraum* for Germans, based on the professor's readings of the "heartland" theory of Sir Halford Mackinder, it is extremely doubtful that he traveled to Tibet, persuaded the Nazis to adopt the swastika, or was a member of the Thule Society, as some have insisted.

We have drawn gratefully from Bettina Arnold's article on archaeology during the Third Reich, "The Past as Propaganda" in *Archaeology,* July/August, 1942. Walter Sullivan's article on Hedin's maps, "Hedin's Data on Tibet Revised by Satellite Photos," appeared on February 13, 1969, in *The New York Times.*

511	"intelligent conversation and the melancholy expression of his lively, keen eyes": Hedin, *German Diary 1935–42,* p. 121.
511	"simple and unassuming": ibid., 122.
511	"everyday, commonplace, uninteresting": ibid., 121.

512   "took such a keen and enlightened interest": ibid.,122.

512   "had very strange views. He thought that the Nordic race had come directly from heaven": Schäfer Interrogation 1018—April 2, 1947, (NARA).

512   "They all believed in the glacial theory of cosmogony. Naturally, this was all completely unscientific": Schäfer Interrogation 1018—April 2, 1947, (NARA).

513   "interesting, forceful, volatile, scholarly": Gould contained in H.A.F. Rumbold, India Office, to G. E. Hubbard, Political Intelligence Dept., FO (Foreign Office), Whitehall, January 13, 1943, OIOC L/P&S 12/4343.

513   "syncretic science": Greve, "Das Tibet-Bild", 105.

514   "will be carried through entirely on SS principles": Henderson telegram, 19 April, 1938, OIOC, L/P&S 12/4343.

514   "Herr Himmler, the Head of the German Secret Service": Barry Domvile to Neville Chamberlain, May 30, 1938, OIOC L/P&S 12/4343.

515   "to spend six months in Sikkim for the purpose of scientific observations, collecting birds, and making a film of animal life": Gould contained in H.A.F. Rumbold, India Office, to G. E. Hubbard, Political Intelligence Dept. FO, Whitehall, January 13, 1943, OIOC L/P&S 12/4343.

515   "deus ex machina": the whole account that follows is taken from Schäfer's *Geheimnis Tibet*, Chapters 4–5, passim.

517   "I think of you often": quoted in McKay, op. cit., 176.

518   "to pay them well, and beat them often": Gould to Savidge, June 26, 1939, OIOC L/P&S 12/4343.

519   "I have lost my wife, I also have nobody": Schäfer to Gould, OIOC June 30, 1939, L/P&S 12/4343.

519   "the expedition was a political stunt to boost Germany and Nazism": Gould in file from H.A.F. Rumbold of the India Office to G. E. Hubbard, Political Intelligence Dept., FO, Whitehall, January 13, 1943, OIOC L/P&S 12/4343.

519   "You are the man who should and must continue my research": Schäfer interrogation. NARA.

520   "muzzled by the crippling bonds of the their pacifistic, Buddhist-Lamaistic religion": Greve, "Das Tibet-Bild," 108.

520   "were of an especially inharmonious racial type": Beger

520   "The Reich Leader SS requests that there be no further": quoted in OIOC L/P&S 12/4343.

522   "Let's learn from the English, with 250,000 men in all": *Hitler's Table Talk* (Oxford, 1988), 15.

522   "You should read more Karl May": quoted, Hauner, *India in Axis Strategy*, 166.

525   "One of the most important discoveries of my life": Schäfer's interview with Hedin, (T81 Roll 131 165430).

527   "I have been in love many times": quoted, Kish, op. cit., 109.

527   "This war will go down in history as President Roosevelt's war": Hedin, *German Diaries*, 252.

528   "saw the uniform and not the soul, the rank and not the person. He was a cartographer": Brennecke, op. cit., 121.

Chapter Twenty-Two

Relatively little has been published on Washington's covert operations in Tibet, starting with the Tolstoy-Dolan OSS Mission in World War II and continuing with the CIA's Operation CIRCUS during the Cold War. The journalist David Wise described the agency's training camps in Colorado in *The Politics of Lying* (New York, 1973), and the peculiar events at Peterson Field on Pearl Harbor Day, 1961, but little was made of it. What might be called a remaining white spot on the American national security map has been tardily and partly filled with *Orphans of the Cold War: America and the Tibetan Struggle for Survival* (New York, 1999), by John Kenneth Knaus, a retired CIA operations officer. Otherwise, those curious about CIRCUS have had to glean from snippets in diplomatic memoirs, censored references by disgruntled former CIA operatives, and a scattering of short references and articles, the latter including a detailed account of CIA airdrops by William M. Leary, "Secret Mission to Tibet," *Air & Space/Smithsonian,* January 1998.

Nor has much been written about the Tolstoy-Dolan Mission. Rosemary Jones Tung, in *A Portrait of Lost Tibet* (New York, 1980; reissued in paperback at Berkeley, CA, 1996), brings together a selection of Tolstoy's 2,000 photographs with a description of their mission. We also have Brooke Dolan's "Across Tibet: Excerpts from the Journals of Captain Brooke Dolan 1942–43" in *Frontiers,* Annual of the Academy of Natural Sciences of Philadelphia, vol. II, 1980; and Ilia Tolstoy's "Across Tibet from India to China," *National Geographic*, August, 1946. On Dolan's expeditions in the 1930s, see Marion H. Duncan, *The Yangtze and the Yak: Adventurous Trails in and out of Tibet* (Alexandria, VA, 1952); and Ernst Schäfer's accounts in German, *Berge, Buddhas und Bären: Forschung und Jagd in geheimnisvollem Tibet* (Berlin, 1933); *Auf einsamen Wechseln und Wegen: Jagd und Forschung in drei Erdteilen* (Hamburg, 1961); *Dach der Erde: durch das Wunderland Hochtibet* (Berlin, 1938); *Unbekanntes Tibet: durch die wildnisse Osttibets zum Dach der Erde* (Berlin, 1937–38, two vols.); and *Unter Raubern in Tibet: Gefahren und Freuden eines Forscherlebens* (Braunschweig, 1952). The IOLC's file on the Tolstoy-Dolan Mission is L/P&S/12/4313.

On DIXIE, the OSS Mission to Yenan, two recent books bring forth a wealth of information: Cariolle J. Carter, *Mission to Yenan* (Lexington, KY, 1997), and Moachun Yu, *OSS in China: Prelude to Cold War* (New Haven, 1997). Carter's book has valuable photographs.

Three thick paperbacks provide a wide perspective on the "Tibet Question": Hugh Richardson, *High Peaks, Pure Earth* (London, 1998), gathers the essays and fascinating, once classified "Tibetan Precis" (1945) by the last of the British diplomats serving in Lhasa; Tsering Shakya, *The Dragon in the Land of Snows* (1999), takes the story from the Chinese invasion and the Cultural Revolution, from which the author and his family fled in 1967; and Warren Smith, Jr., *Tibetan Nation* (Boulder, 1996), by an independent American scholar, attempts a balanced account of Sino-Tibetan relations. Melvyn C. Goldstein has added *The Snow Lion and the Dragon: China, Tibet and the Dalai Lama* (Berkeley, 1997) as a supplement to his history. See also A. Tom Grunfeld, *The Making of Modern Tibet* (Armonk, 1996).

Finally, we turned up pieces of the puzzle in the India Office Library, the Explorers Club, and the alumni offices at Princeton, Harvard, and St. Paul's School.

529   "Hank, we're surrounded": This and other details of the Peterson Field episode are from Wise, "The Case of the Colorado Tibetans," in *The Politics of Lying.*

532   "There was no role for Tibet in the Kissinger equation," Knaus, *Orphans,* 309.

532–533   "I have never regretted that decision for a moment": Memorial article on Brooke Dolan in John B. Edmonds, *St. Paul's School in the Second World War* (1950), 178.

534   "Mother: Olga K. Tolstoy": Autobiographical sketch prepared for the U.S. Army (NARA RG165/E79/Box 1993).

535   "You know, Junge": Schäfer, *Unter Räubern* (1952), 13–20, is devoted to Dolan.

535–536   Villanova episode: See "Arrest Explorer in Dinner Rumpus," *Philadelphia Ledger,* January 11, 1934.

536   "A quite large Tibet expedition, do you want to come?": Schäfer, *Unbekanntes Tibet,* 1.

536   "should remain faithful to our beloved Tibet until his death": *Auf einsamen Wechseln,* 9.

537   "This he used one night in a hotel bar": Schäfer, *Unter Räubern,* 13ff.

537   "The dreary crawling travail of our lowland journey": ibid.

537   "Very pleasant to deal with": Dolan Diary, Academy of Sciences Archives, vol. I, 95 (August 5–6, 1934).

538   "The stag of MacNeill is the real object of the autumn": letter to Kermit Roosevelt, ibid., 147 (August 19, 1934).

538   "He is really incredible": ibid., 51 (September 5, 1934).

538   "How the Chinese expect to keep any border": ibid., 55 (September 6, 1934).

538   "The best concealed city in the world": ibid., 85 (September, 1934).

538   *"une grande passion,* half bestial, wholly religious": Letter to C.S., signed "Johann Jäger," ibid., vol. III, 17.

538–539   "So I have come to the end": ibid., vol. I, 21 (August 1934).

539   "a crazy person": Schäfer, *Unter Räubern,* 82ff.

539   "He dismissed all counter arguments": ibid.

540   "The journey from Jyekundo was remarkable": undated clipping, from Shanghai newspaper, Academy of Sciences Archives.

541   "to move across Tibet and make its way to Chungking": OSS Report, September 30, 1943, NARA RG 226, E 092, box 200.

542   "I said 'Yes, decidedly so'": Frank Ludlow's weekly letter from Lhasa, August 24, 1942; OIOC L/P&S/12/1401.

543   "guests in the charming": Tolstoy, "Across Tibet," *National Geographic,* August 1946.

543   "The Diamond Sow": Dolan, "Across Tibet: Excerpts from the Journals of Captain Brooke Dolan, 1942–43," *Frontiers,* vol. II, 1980, 6.

544   "positively beamed": Frank Ludlow Diary, December 20, 1942, OIOC MSS Eur D979/1.

544   "He visited the powerful monasteries of Drepung and Sera": This and Ludlow's other remarks are from his diary.

544   I think Tolstoy and Brooke Dolan were astonished by the cheerfulness—and playfulness—of our little Lhasa lady friends: Ludlow, December 25. By January 5, at a dinner for the Chinese representative, Dolan "made some very foolish remarks about Tibetan independence."

545–546   "I regard with apprehension": OIOC L/PS/12/4229/ dated May 3, 1943; quoted in Goldstein, *History of Modern Tibet,* 396. In his final diary entry, April 13, Ludlow writes: "Called on Foreign and found Caroe very peeved because I had agreed (quite privately and unofficial) with Tolstoy that it would be a good thing if Tibet were represented at the coming Peace Conference. Apparently I should have kept my mouth shut . . . Well, well, we all make mistakes . . ."

547   "had been a member of SACO": Tolstoy's attempts to reach Yenan are detailed in *OSS in China,* 159–63.

548   "tall, bronzed, impeccably dressed": Taken from Payne's preface to Rosemary Jones Tung, op. cit.

549   "We came together": Interview, Arnold Dadian, 1998, Washington, DC.

549   "Once, I think by accident, he fired the gun": Telephone interview, Charles Dole, 1998. See also Carter, *Mission to Yenan,* 45, the first published reference to Dolan's suicide.

550   "Tolstoy literally turned ashen": Telephone interview, 1998, David Longacre.

552   "perhaps my single most useful activity that spring": John Kenneth
           Galbraith, *A Life in Our Times* (Boston, 1981), 397.
552   "the most sanguinary, imaginative": ibid., 436.
552   "Basically Tibet was just a nuisance to the ChiComs": Quoted, Evan
           Thomas, *The Very Best Men* (New York), 278.

Epilogue

On the making of books about imperialism, there will be no end. It needs only
to be added that we have benefited from the works of a connoisseur, A. P.
Thornton, who has taught variously in such outposts as Canada, the West Indies, and Scotland. See his *The Imperial Idea and Its Enemies* (London, 1959) and
various other titles, including *Imperialism in the Twentieth Century* (Minneapolis,
1977). Among many British authorities, we liked Ronald Hyam, *Britain's Imperial Century: A Study of Empire and Expansion* (London, 1993); Lawrence James,
The Rise and Fall of the British Empire (London, 1994); Denis Judd, *Empire* (New
York, 1996); Michael W. Doyle, *Empires* (Ithaca, NY, and London, 1986); Eric
Hobsbawm, *The Age of Empire 1875–1914* (New York, 1987); and a critical
view from one of Britain's Indian subjects, Romesh Dutt, *The Economic History
of India in the Victorian Age* (London, 1903, two vols.). A selection of basic texts
can be found in Harrison M. Wright, *The "New Imperialism"* (Lexington, MA,
1976).

Aside from memorial notices, Caroe has no biographer. See his own works:
The Wells of Power (London, 1951); *The Pathans* (London, 1958); *Soviet Empire*
(London, 1954); and his interview in the oral history collection at OIOC,
where his papers can be found. For the first assessment of his influence, see Selig
Harrison, "India and Pakistan: Case History of a Mistake," *New Republic*, August
10, 24, September 7, 1959; and *The Widening Gulf: Asian Nationalism and American Policy* (New York, 1965).

On Caroe and the McMahon Line, besides works already cited, see "The
Further Development of the Disputed Frontier," in Michael Aris, ed., *Tibetan
Studies in Honour of Hugh Richardson* (Warminster, U.K., 1980). For the current
views of Neville Maxwell, whose *India's China War* (New York, 1970) reopened
the debate on the "line," see "China's 'Aggression in 1962' and the 'Hindu
Bomb,'" *World Policy Journal* (Fall 1999). For an Indian view, see Parhshotam
Mehra, *The North-Eastern Frontier* (New Delhi, 1979–80, two vols.). On Nehru
and "the line," we have drawn on two biographies, M. J. Akbar, *Nehru: The Making of India* (New York, 1988), and Marie Seton, *Panditji: A Portrait of Jawaharlal
Nehru* (London, 1967). Even more, we have relied on John Kenneth Galbraith's
triad, *Ambassador's Journal* (Boston, 1969); *A Life in Our Times* (Boston, 1981);
and *Name-Dropping* (Boston, 1999).

On Mackinder, his basic geopolitical texts are gathered in Halford J.
Mackinder, *Democratic Ideals and Realities* (New York, 1962), and he is the sub-

ject of two competent biographies, W. H. Parker, *Mackinder* (Oxford, 1982), and Brian W. Blouet, *Halford Mackinder* (College Station, TX, 1987). The works of James Burnham are worth picking up at library sales as Cold War mementoes, especially *The Struggle for the World* (New York, 1947), and *Suicide of the West* (New York, 1964).

556   "the voice of Curzon": Caroe, *The Wells of Power,* 64–65.

556–557   "Sir Olaf intimated that the Foreign Office": National Archives, State Department Papers, LM 160 – Roll 8, Memorandum of a Conversation with Sir Olaf Caroe, Governor of the North-West Frontier Province, May 26, 1947.

557   "My Pakistan friends": Letter from Caroe, published in Selig Harrison, "Case History of a Mistake," *The New Republic,* August 10, 1959, also in Harrison, *The Widening Gulf,* 264.

560   "Our maps show that the McMahon Line": Quoted, M. J. Akbar, *Nehru,* 541.

560   "was referred to the Prime Minister": B. N. Mullik, *My Years with Nehru: The Chinese Betrayal* (New Delhi, 1971), 80.

561   "there was a fixed hierarchy in those lower regions": Jawaharlal Nehru, *Toward Freedom* (New York, 1942), 264.

562   "If you deny sovereign status to Tibet": Quoted, Maxwell, *India's China War,* 99.

563   "Rarely in the long history of human conflict": J. K. Galbraith, *A Life in Our Times* (Boston, 1981), 426.

564   "the objectless disposition": Joseph Schumpeter, *Imperialism* (New York, 1955), 6.

565   "What was won by the sword": Quoted, George Woodcock, *Who Killed the British Empire?* (New York, 1974), 50.

567   "A generation ago": Mackinder, *Democratic Ideals and Reality,* op. cit., contains the full text of his address, 240–64.

570   "It has assumed the mantle": John Keegan, *Warpaths: Tales of a Military Historian in North America* (London, 1995).

572   "continuation of the thing that is happening": George Orwell, *Collected Essays, Journalism and Letters* (London, 1968), IV, 160–81. On Burnham, also see Christopher Hitchens, *Blood, Class, and Nostalgia: Anglo-American Ironies* (New York, 1990).

573   "clear-cut, unmistakable strategic nuclear superiority": David Wallechinsky, Amy Wallace, Irving Wallace, eds., *The Book of Predictions* (New York, 1980), 103–5.

INDEX

.:.

*This index does not cover
acknowledgments, notes, and sources.*

PHOTO CREDITS AND PERMISSIONS

∴

Unless otherwise noted the illustrations are from the authors' collection: